The Disruption of

American Democracy

ROY FRANKLIN NICHOLS

The Disruption
of American
Democracy

THE FREE PRESS, *New York*
COLLIER-MACMILLAN LIMITED, *London*

To

The Memory

of

WILLIAM A. DUNNING

Preface

"AMERICAN DEMOCRACY" is an ambiguous term characteristic of the intellectual chaos that prevailed during the period in which it was coined. The years just prior to the Civil War were confused by romantic sentimentalizing, erratic emotion, and careless thought, manifestations, perhaps, of the explosive forces generated by the nation's phenomenal growth processes. It was a period when people were naïve or careless about the use of terms. Since Americans were not certain even of the nature of their own political creation it is not surprising that they were vague as to the meaning of the oft-spoken shibboleth, "American Democracy."

When the Greeks invented the word from which "democracy" was derived, it meant the self-government achieved by their city states. When twentieth century Americans use "democracy" they generally intend to refer to their own complex system of government and the nature of their own social relationships and opportunities. In the 1850's the word as commonly used in the United States had neither significance.

When the Republic was founded the fathers saw no need to use the term in the official language describing their handiwork. As the nation grew, the United States, usually then a plural word, "were" referred to as a federal system, a confederacy, or a republic, but not as a democracy. At the same time there was frequent reference to "Democratic-Republicans," "American Democracy," the "Democratic party," and "Democrats"; but these phrases were merely party labels. Then in the 1850's new meaning came to the name. Spokesmen from the more populous states, irked because of the frustrating control of the federal system by southern representatives, demanded that the majority rule, that there be democracy in the nation. Southern leaders of the Democratic party, or the "American Democracy" as it was officially renamed, began to resist this "dangerous" demand for "mob rule," and thus there developed a paradox. Members of the American Democracy were fighting democracy.

A party could hardly keep its unity and power amidst such confusion. Yet it was vital that it should, for the operation of popular government in the United States depended then as it does now upon party machinery. If that machinery is not reasonably efficient the processes of self-government are correspondingly hampered. So swift has been the growth of the nation that the party mechanism has had to be adjusted constantly to perform more complex operations. In the 1850's the party engineers failed, the master unit of the machinery broke down, and civil war followed.

The most successful and adequate political machine created in the early days of the Republic was the Democratic party, officially known as the "American Democracy." This organization ruled the federal government, with only slight interruption, from 1829 to 1861. But its control, so long exercised, was dominated by policies which grew increasingly unpopular as they frustrated and antagonized ever larger groups in the population.

The following pages describe the disruption of this great power aggregate during the years 1856-1861. Because the confusion of these crisis years was so great, and the innumerable factors which affected, deflected, and obscured the onrush of events were so various, it has been necessary to place the situation under the microscope. This must be done, in some scores of states, because the disruption of the American Democracy cannot be explained accurately by any concise formula of nation-wide application. The party, like the nation, was a federal system; it was not so much a national organization as a federation of state machines. It can be understood only by a microscopic examination of the particular relations of the three elements which were its most important constituents—the voters, the machines, and the leaders—both in their national and in their state relations.

As this is the history of a political party, not of the whole people, the detail of social, cultural, and economic development can only be suggested. But a background has been sketched in so that the politicos do not strut on an empty stage. Population movement, economic panic, religious ferment, romantic trends of thought and hyperemotionalism were dynamic forces; they were as potent to affect the behavior of the politicians as the latter were unconscious of their real nature.

The relation between political behavior and social and economic forces is not as clear and simple as is sometimes represented. The classic tradition is that parties represent interests or groups which can be neatly isolated and ticketed. They do not. They represent attitudes conditioned by prevailing prejudices, passions, idealisms, and loyalties. They often are made up of people of the most diverse interests who for various reasons find satisfaction in a common name.

The contemporary influences which surround these parties are so confused that no definite measure of their relative strength can be estimated. Truth concerning them can be more nearly approximated by suggestion than by any attempt at dogmatic statement. But it is important to remember that a party develops a complex behavior which is more than a reflection of influences surrounding it. This pattern of behavior is made up of customs and habits which are self-perpetuating and dominating. They are not weakly dependent upon economic or cultural influences; in fact they become cultural influences themselves which at times determine social and economic behavior.

This analysis not only sheds what light it may on the intricacies of partisan behavior and its relation to the American Civil War but gives food for thought regarding a problem of even greater moment. Popular government has certain weaknesses and limitations—fewer perhaps than those of other forms, but nevertheless indubitable. In these changing times when American political institutions are in process of alteration, it is well to be conscious of the limitations of our historic system, so that ignorance of them may never again contribute to the calamities of social disruption. Furthermore since the United Nations, including the United States, are now committed to a kind of world federation, mankind, if it is to succeed in this experiment, must become expert in the operation of federalism. The founding fathers of this new order must seek skill in counteracting divisive attitudes, so that they may not nourish the fears and frustrations which breed secession and war. They may well heed today the uncomprehended danger signals which in the 1850's lined the road leading to the disruption of the American Democracy.

May 31, 1947

Acknowledgments

WHEN THE MAKING of a book takes its author into twenty-six states and the District of Columbia in search of material, he necessarily meets many custodians who place him greatly in their debt. Considerations of space permit mention of but a few; my gratitude is no less sincere to the many whose names do not here appear.

Keepers of the record who made me particularly welcome were Kirk Mechem, Lela Barnes, Louise Barry, Martha Caldwell, Nyle Miller and Marion Wolfe of the Kansas State Historical Society; Mary M. Smelser of the University of Kansas; the late Max Farrand of the Huntington Library; Herbert E. Bolton of the Bancroft Library; Edgar E. Robinson and Jeannette M. Hitchcock of Stanford University; Nellie B. Pipes of the Oregon Historical Society; Dan E. Clark and Mrs. Mabel McClain of the University of Oregon; Paul M. Angle then of the Illinois State Historical Library; Herbert A. Kellar of the McCormick Historical Association; the late Christopher B. Coleman and Caroline Dunn of the Indiana Historical Society Library; J. G. de R. Hamilton and his staff at the University of North Carolina; Ruth K. Nuermberger and Nannie M. Tilly of Duke University; C. C. Crittenden of the North Carolina Archives; Sylvester Vigilante and his staff in Room 300, Robert W. Hill and W. L. Leech of the Manuscripts Division, New York Public Library; the late A. J. Wall, R. W. G. Vail, Dorothy C. Barck, and their staff of the New York Historical Society; Mother Buck, her superiors and associates at the Manhattanville College of the Sacred Heart; R. D. W. Connor, Solon J. Buck, Philip M. Hamer, Mrs. Natalia Summers, and Miss Josephine Cobb of the National Archives; Miss Craven of the Navy Department Library; Arthur V. Sullivan of the Treasury Department; Luther H. Evans, St. George L. Sioussat, and the staffs of the Manuscript Division, the Reading Rooms and the Periodical Division of the Library of Congress; R. Norris Williams, 2nd, and Julian P. Boyd, present and former directors of the Historical Society of Pennsylvania, and Mary Townsend, Catherine Miller, George H. Fairchild, and J. Harcourt Givens of their staff; Charles W. David and C. Seymour Thompson, present and former librarians at the University of Pennsylvania and

11

their associates, Edith Hartwell, Lilian Guthrie, Delphine O. Richardson, Elisabeth L. Gordon, Anita Moldonado, Edith W. Holbrook, Arthur T. Hamlin, Elliott Morse, and Hans Burkhard.

I am grateful to those owning or controlling family letters for their kind permission to read them. These include David Rankin Barbee, S. L. M. Barlow, Norris S. Barratt, Jr., C. Frederick Beach, Thomas Ewing, Reginald B. Henry, Mrs. Florence Bayard Hilles, Elisha Kent Kane, Francis Fisher Kane, George Fort Milton, James L. Patton, Mrs. Julia Kennedy Taylor, and particularly Miss Mary Lamar Erwin whose generosity was unusual and therefore the more appreciated.

I am indebted to academic colleagues for favors, particularly to Philip G. Auchampaugh, E. Merton Coulter, John A. Krout, William E. Lingelbach, Robert L. Meriwether, Frank Monaghan, Allan Nevins, James C. Olson, Richard H. Shryock, Stanley P. Shugert, Mulford Stough, Charles C. Tansill, Louis Warren, David B. Wenrich, Arthur P. Whitaker, and Edwin B. Wilson.

I have enjoyed the cooperation of graduate students at Pennsylvania and Columbia in consultation, classroom, and seminar, particularly of Mrs. Jane E. Bishop, George Bauerlein, S. W. Higginbotham, Austin E. Hutcheson, William A. Itter, Philip S. Klein, Reinhard Luthin, Richard P. McCormick, John Munroe, Theodore Thayer, Joseph G. Tregle, Jr., and Rudolph von Abele.

I am indebted for much secretarial aid to Miss Sarah E. Calhoun and Miss Maria Peredo, who must know a great deal of this book by heart.

It is my pleasant duty to here express my appreciation of substantial financial assistance from the Research Committee of the University of Pennsylvania.

When the work came to its conclusion Pendleton Herring and James C. Malin read and improved parts of it. I have had the inestimable privilege of a careful and illuminating criticism of the whole by Charles A. Beard. My sincerest thanks go to these three.

My greatest obligation is to Jeannette P. Nichols; it cannot be described but only here inadequately acknowledged.

Contents

Preface   7

Acknowledgments   11

I. *Leadership Made to Order*
1. Conservatives to the Rescue   17
2. A Bewildering Task   33
3. Victory by a Narrow Margin   54

II. *The Leadership Fails*
4. Reorganizing the High Command   65
5. Re-forming the Party Ranks   86
6. Territorial Nightmares   104
7. The Lecompton Fiasco   125
8. Shadows Over Congress   139
9. The Majority Crumbles   156
10. The Power of Money   182

III. *Demoralization and Defeat*
11. Repudiation at the Polls   205
12. A Runaway Session   226
13. State Machines to the Rescue   246

IV. *The Cost of Faction*
14. Rehearsing for Charleston   271
15. The Disruption of the Democracy   288

16. Everybody's Plans Go Awry   305

17. Congressional Stalemate   321

18. A Campaign Like None Other   332

19. Mounting the Blue Cockade   348

V. *The Union Falls with the Party*

20. The Peril of Dissolution   367

21. The Weakness of Divided Counsels   388

22. Reorganizing the Administration   410

23. Peace Hangs by a Thread   433

24. A Republic Made to Order   453

25. Stalemate in Washington   466

26. The Last Stand   483

27. Clues   502

Appendix: The Slavery Pronouncement of the American
    Democracy, Cincinnati, 1856   507

Notes   509

Bibliography   563

Index   589

PART I

LEADERSHIP MADE TO ORDER

Chapter 1

Conservatives to the Resue

WASHINGTON IN THE SPRING of 1856 was a city of magnificent distances and unfulfilled hopes. It was a city of contrasts: mud and marble, fragrant magnolias and the odoriferous Tiber, fine mansions and hovels, beaver hats and filthy boots. It had been so long in building; the Treasury, the Patent Office, the aqueduct, and, above all, the Capitol itself remained in various stages of congressional indecision. Indeed the Capitol seemed to be a symbol of the unfinished state of the Republic.

That spring the Palladium of the people's liberties stood in all its peculiar artistic splendor; its imposing plan and certain of its ridiculous details presented as much contrast as the city which it dominated. Its east pediment was adorned by John Quincy Adams's strange conception of art, as near as Persico could translate it into sculpture, and on the porch beneath in various uneasy postures were grouped stiff representations in stone of Mars and Ceres, of Columbus and an Indian maiden, of a savage red man and a rugged pioneer. Across the plaza, in lonely, half-naked grandeur, marble Washington sat in a curule chair, viewing the nation's incomplete handiwork. All around were piles of stone, sheds, tools, and the debris of building. The two great new Capitol wings were fairly complete externally; but internally they were in the chaos of finishing. The old kettle-shaped dome was off, but the new one was hardly at a stage where anyone unfamiliar with Thomas Walter's plan could predict what it would be like.

Congress within was grinding out statutes under difficulties. The House had a grand colonnaded hall, but its acoustics were weird. The Senate chamber was a little architectural gem, but it was cursed by deplorable ventilation. The lack of oxygen was wearing down senatorial health, temper, and efficiency. In summer the Senators worked in suffocating heat; in winter they labored in cold so intense that they must hug the fireplaces at the chamber's rim or wear their greatcoats and mufflers. At all seasons their hall had a mephitic atmosphere scarcely conducive to clear thinking.

The Senate and the House legislated in noise and confusion. Both chambers had to serve as workrooms as well as debating halls. Since office buildings for the members then were non-existent and committee rooms were few, curious visitors could see Senators and Representatives bent over their closely crowded desks, in session and out, occasionally even with their hats on, toiling away at their correspondence. As a grateful nation provided free snuff for the solons, the air could be rent by sounds which on occasion might suggest a hay-fever convention.

In the spring of 1856 the "deliberations" of the lawmakers were excited and interrupted by unusual violence. Charles Sumner, whose oratory though classic was not always chaste, had recently indulged himself in a philippic against slavery, in which he deliberately referred to fellow Senators in terms suggestive of the brothel and of the stench of noxious little animals. Congressman Brooks, enraged kinsman of one of the Senators under attack, armed with a gutta-percha cane, strode into the chamber where the unsuspecting Sumner was writing at his desk, and gave him a severe beating. Down the Avenue another Congressman, angered by the characteristic inefficiency and impertinence of Washington's hotel dining-room service, shot and killed an Irish waiter. Out in Kansas, according to the newspapers, a sheriff was "murdered" and a town "sacked."

These outbreaks could scarcely be quieting to the denizens of this Capitol. They already were suffering from the worries which affected most of them quadrennially on the eve of presidential contests; for, uncomfortable as the Capitol might be, few wanted to leave it; and those seeking reelection were further harassed because their own fate and that of their party were intertwined with the livelihood of the horde of civil servants holding office largely on the nomination of the lawmakers. Surely the times were more than ever out of joint.

In the midst of the turmoil, four Senators made a fateful decision. They would go to Cincinnati, to the Democratic National Convention there about to assemble. They would seek to direct its deliberations and thereby save what they feared might be a tottering government. To them the success of their party in the coming election seemed essential to the unity and continuance of the Republic.[1]

II

These four Senators were men of varied and lengthy experience, men who prized success and efficiency. John Slidell, from Louisiana, was an adventurous political opportunist. Born in

New York, he had excellent business and family connections, by kinship allied with the Perrys of naval fame and August Belmont, the Rothschilds' American agent. He had left New York in the early Jackson epoch—it was charged because of the fruits of an irregular youth—and had gone to New Orleans. This cosmopolitan center proved a challenging field for his political and business talents. His ruthless nature well fitted him to cope with its confusion and corrupt political gangsterism and with the rural infelicity of the sprawling upriver parishes. His tactics, particularly in the election of 1844, had brought political sharp practice into national notice. He was now elderly, white-haired, red-faced, with a haughty and supercilious expression, hard-boiled, domineering and none too scrupulous. He was engaged in a bitter feud with President Pierce, because the administration had prosecuted one of his henchmen for malfeasance in office. He felt that Pierce had made him lose face, and he would not forgive.

Slidell's colleague from Louisiana, Judah P. Benjamin, a Sephardic Jew, was smooth and urbane, his countenance suffused with a perpetual smile. He possessed a superior intelligence, but he was just as opportunistic and just as lustful for power and place. His Creole wife preferred to keep the Atlantic between them and dwelt in Paris, confining her connubial responsibilities to whatever favors she would grant him during his occasional summer visits to the French capital.

Jesse D. Bright, a paunchy and ungrammatical speculator and political manipulator, hailed from southern Indiana and had started his career as a rough-and-tumble athlete and bully. He, like the other two, was dominated by ambition for power and uncontrolled hates; he would brook no opposition among retainers or associates. He was the friend of speculators and adventurers and represented the exploiting forces of the West. He had the confidence of the Washington banker, W. W. Corcoran, and his daughter was married to the son of Riggs, Corcoran's partner. His residence within sight of the South in a community on the Ohio River largely southern in origin and sympathy, and his political shrewdness, made it easy for him to work with southerners. So he well earned the title "doughface," which those opposed to southern dominance conferred upon their northern associates who did not share their antagonism.

James A. Bayard was a talented man of excellent family and came from Delaware. This political bailiwick was small and compact, habitually giving allegiance to a few families among whom the Bayards were chief. He was a man of culture and wide experience who could be practical. He added a touch of aristocracy and social prestige which the other three could less readily supply. The members of this curiously diverse quartet were alike, however, in their lack of illusions. Together they might be said to be well endowed with the talents necessary for winning and holding power in politics.[2]

These men were past masters in the operation of political machinery. For many years they had been working at it early and late, because in the United States the recurrence of elections is relentless. By constitutional prescription political contests must take place at stated intervals, regardless of the condition of public affairs. The calendar rather than the need of the moment summons voters to the polls.

The incessant procession of artificially ordered electoral conflicts frequently meant nothing more than the routine return of pleasurable electioneering excitement; but in the 1850's it had become dangerous. The campaigns of that critical decade focused public attention too sharply upon conflicting attitudes, exaggerated them to perilous proportions, and generated dangerous power-conflicts in the course of the political maneuvering. They aroused passion to such a pitch that only bloodletting, occasional or wholesale, could relieve the tension. Election campaigns thus became the catalytic agents which fatally hastened the processes that brought on secession and civil war.

The perilous politics of the decade were the more fraught with danger because of the loose and unwieldy construction of party machinery in that day. That machinery rattled, creaked, and groaned partly because it was patterned after the federal system of thirty-one state governments under which the nation lived and worked. The gears were not well meshed. Coherent central direction had not yet been achieved; and without it the most effective organization could not be created. The national parties then, much more than now, were but loose federations of state machines. As there were at least two parties in each of the thirty-one states in 1856, and three in sixteen of them, there were seventy-eight practically independent state organizations, uniting into three national aggregations only for presidential campaign purposes. Thirty-one of these state parties, plus some more or less fluid groups in the territories, acknowledged the name Democrat, and in national conventions styled themselves the "American Democracy." Yet each represented a separate state with its individual social organization, personal antagonisms, economic interests, and political issues. Each was subject to local attitudes and prejudices, to internal rivalries and struggles for leadership.

The state political organizations maintained election calendars which made contests much more frequent, and therefore potentially more disturbing, than they are today. In the fifties, the first Tuesday after the first Monday in November, now so universally an electoral climax, was general only for the choice of presidential electors every four years. Some few states used it as a local election day, but they were exceptions rather than the rule. Each state had its own appointed times and seasons. In fact there were elections, somewhere, in every month of every year, save January, February, June, and July.

This federal as distinguished from national electoral procedure had certain chaotic implications. It meant that campaigning was going on in the United States almost all the time; political agitation seldom quieted. Efforts were constantly being exerted to arouse enthusiasm or distrust, to point with pride or, with even more vehemence, to view with alarm. This was the more unfortunate because the rapid growth of the country was ever raising the stakes of elections higher and creating a new and dangerous power politics. As new territories approached statehood they presented new interests and new, or revamped, personalities to be fitted into the congressional and party convention circles.

There was a rising appreciation of the profit which might be realized from government policies favorable to rapid development. There were insistent demands for appropriations, land grants, and protective tariff policies, all of which went counter to the Democracy's pet principles of "laissez faire," of refusal to vote subsidies from the public treasury. In these years the lobby became an institution; agents were everywhere. The nature of Congress was almost as much political as it was legislative. Whenever national campaigns approached, political interests dominated purely legislative concerns. Similar pressures affected the executive branch and even sought to operate on the judiciary.

Success at elections was the more intensively sought as the rewards of power became greater. Campaign methods therefore grew more ruthless, and corruption more frequent. The temptation grew, to seek advantage by arousing passions. It was harder for the statesmen at the capital city to calm the emotions stirred in these countless local contests when their representatives brought them to Washington. They had to spend much time formulating compromises to subdue the wrath so heedlessly roused. As the fifties advanced, these adjustments were harder to negotiate, and fewer legislative leaders were either sufficiently interested, or able, to write formulas of peace.

The extreme danger in these frequent elections arose partly from the skill with which campaigners and candidates could exploit prevailing conflicts of interests, conditioned by geography and custom and by the traditions, needs, and hopes of a mobile and expanding population. These antagonisms, it is true, were occasionally sponsored by statesmen or party leaders but usually dictated to them. Politicos prospered or failed in the degree to which they consciously or unconsciously recognized, understood, and utilized the opportunities which these enthusiasms and prejudices afforded. The peculiar and ofttimes conflicting qualities of popular attitudes made their constant exaggeration dangerous, never more so than in 1856.

III

The four Senators—Slidell, Bright, Benjamin, and Bayard—were going to Cincinnati to operate the political machinery of the American Democracy, now grown old in experience and power. With its stormy history they were quite familiar. Their party had gained its name almost by accident as the result of a curious evolution. The partisan use of the word "democracy," as Beard has shown, has an English origin dating from the Puritan Revolution, when the conservatives characterized their radical opponents as "democratical," for advocating rule by the "lower orders."[3] In the formative days of American politics, opponents of the Jeffersonians referred to them in this sense as "Democratic-Republicans," and President Washington denounced the political clubs or "Democratic Societies" as subversive. Jefferson's followers showed no consistency, sometimes calling themselves Republicans, sometimes Democrats, and sometimes Democratic-Republicans. Jefferson himself usually favored the term "Republican." After the Federalists disappeared in name, if not in nature, all participants in *national* politics seemed to be Democratic-Republicans.

This amorphous, all-inclusive "party" was shattered, about 1828, by the rise of the Jacksonians. The wing opposing Jackson generally was called "National Republican," while the followers of Old Hickory whenever they bothered to discuss the matter, in their early days at least, claimed they were good Jeffersonians, entitled to the name "Democratic-Republicans."

During the eight years of Jackson's presidency some of his closest associates—such as Van Buren, Francis P. Blair, and William B. Lewis—saw the need to transform his personal, almost caudillolike following, into a more formal and lasting party organization. A number of very independent state parties united to form a "holding company" to capitalize the fame of Old Hickory, and they were commonly nicknamed "Democrats." This name was not displeasing to the Jacksonians, who used it to advertise their sympathy for the common man, particularly in towns and cities where corporations and other "privileged" interests might be unpopular. Without too much difficulty they elected Van Buren as Jackson's successor.

As the National Republicans saw the Jacksonians thus digging in, they denounced their power as the personal tyranny of "King Andrew" and changed their own name to Whigs in 1834, inspired by their revolutionary forebears of that label who fought a similar tyrant, George III. Seizing upon the unrest following the panic of 1837, these Whigs staged in 1840 a singing, drinking campaign for "two dollars a day and roast beef," and elected the "Hero of Tippecanoe," William Henry Harrison, as President.

The Whig victory shocked the Democrats into a new concern for organization, and in 1844 they provided themselves with better equipment, including an official name. Their platform of that year proclaimed them the American Democracy and placed their trust in "the intelligence, patriotism and the discriminating justice of the American people." Reflecting the glory of Jackson, and employing superior organization, they cleverly capitalized the Whigs' political ineptitude and the voters' love of glory and territorial expansion, and brought themselves back into power in 1844.

Unluckily for the Democrats, the Polk administration had to face problems which overtaxed party unity. Parties then—as now—would not stay unified for long. So, revolting Democratic factions in New York and other northern states, seeking local control, echoed Whig criticisms of Polk's expansionist policies in slave areas. It went so far that seceding New York Democrats (known as Van Burenites or Barnburners) revolted against the nomination of General Cass for President by the Hunker (conservative) wing of the party, and nominated Van Buren on a third-party ticket. They were joined by enough free-soil sympathizers to cause the defeat of Cass and the return of the Whigs to power. Again the day of Whig sway was brief; this second victory, like their first, brought control more apparent than real. Within a few short months they lost most of it; they had no popular appeal, little or nothing to attract voters, and so a superior Democratic organization elected Pierce President in 1852. His administration was uniformly unlucky and, as 1856 approached, the Democracy—dominant most of the time since 1828—faced special hazards, of which its leaders were but dimly aware.

In politics, popular interest is subject to fluctuations. There are years of calm, of political relaxation; then periodically interest quickens, the electorate becomes more highly emotional, and tension develops. Such fluctuation recurs with singular regularity in the United States, and a political "new deal" of one sort or another comes about every twenty years.

Other forms of behavior move in somewhat similar patterns. Both business panics and religious revivals recur at more or less regular intervals, accompanied by emotional instability which is unsettling. When a political crisis and a business collapse occur almost simultaneously, as has happened several times in American history, society feels no slight shock. Further, when these two are followed by an outburst of religious enthusiasm and revival, the nation's nerves are shattered and popular behavior becomes hyperemotional. Such a conjunction of tensions occurs rarely, but woe betide the Republic when it does.

Such a time was the period of the middle fifties in America. Then political frictions were mounting; then the nation was strangely moved by economic and emotional upheavals. The triple conjunction of tensions in politics, business, and religion was gathering in all its force, making perilous this period of political reshuffling.

In politics, it seemed that a new game was to be called with new rules. The major parties had been wont to avoid dangerous issues in their platforms, and the Whigs in fact had won national campaigns only when they made no program at all. But the Whig party was played out and ready to change its spots. Signs pointed to a new type of party, exploiting differences and thriving on controversy. Such a party had begun to form in 1854, when popular indignation in the North was hot over the Kansas-Nebraska Act with its repeal of the Missouri Compromise. This measure, because it enlarged the area open to slavery, had roused antisouthern prejudices as they never had been roused before. Was not the act part of "an atrocious plot"? Did it not prove that the Democrats were serfs of southern slave drivers? Furthermore the "friends of freedom"—unlike the Democracy—preached federal largesse, which attracted to their banner people eager for national subsidy in railroading, manufacturing, education, and other fields.

The new allies met in convention in 1856 and took to themselves the old Jeffersonian name "Republicans," which they declared the Democrats had forfeited by subservience to the slave power. According to the Republican platform, slave territory could be enlarged no further; they would forge an iron ring around the fifteen slave states, hold them an ever smaller minority in the expanding nation, keep the southern power from further growth. Here was a new party with appeal to all who shared this antipathy. Its advent marked the beginning of a political new deal.

The Democracy, old and faction-scarred, institutionalized, and no longer spurred by pristine enthusiasm, was not in shape to meet the demands of 1856. This the Senators starting for Cincinnati knew only too well. The party was lacking in the most vital essential of power; namely, responsible, continuing leadership. Modern organization technique had not yet been created. To be sure there was what passed for a national party committee; but it functioned only once in four years and then only to make arrangements for the national convention and to conduct the ensuing campaign. Neither the committee nor its chairman in 1856, Benjamin F. Hallett of Massachusetts, would assume any responsibility for plans to strengthen the party position prior to the meeting of the convention.

Where could the Democracy find leadership? Not in the President, thought the four Senators, for Franklin Pierce was no leader. This convivial, good-natured, weak official had won nomination not by himself, but by an alliance of state leaders bent on preventing the palm from going to Lewis Cass by default. Pierce had proved neither successful nor popular as Chief Magistrate, and bore the onus of the hated Kansas-Nebraska Act—a gift invaluable to Republican organizers in free-labor states. Nor did the four want Stephen A. Douglas, Pierce's floor manager in the Senate, to assume leadership; he probably wished to, and had the capacity, but he was branded with actual authorship of the Kansas-Nebraska policy. This swarthy, young Illinoisan—the "Little Giant" of short stature, large head, rotund torso, and dynamic personality—had refused to stay on the back bench assigned him by dominant, southern Democrats. He had made himself a chieftain with a following and insisted on preaching that the people of a territory, not Congress, should determine whether slavery was to abide among them. Southern Senators would have none of Douglas.

There seemed to be one other possibility—one which united the four in their western trip. They might find a leader in James Buchanan of Pennsylvania. His advantages were impressive. Now aged sixty-five, he was as ripe as Pierce had been green. Public office had been his almost continuously through forty-two years: as Representative, Senator, Jackson's Minister to Russia, Polk's Secretary of State, and Pierce's Minister to Great Britain. The last had kept him blessedly free from all Kansas-Nebraska taint. The old functionary had gained place by a crafty, plodding, uninspired, but effective intelligence. He was canny and took "sound," conservative ground, which commended him to the solid German constituency of his home, Lancaster County. Backed locally by this substantial community, he tirelessly cultivated support outside, writing countless letters. The Commonwealth of Pennsylvania had diverse social and economic elements which placed a premium on the craft and industry of a man like Buchanan; he represented a common denominator too ordinary to arouse either envy or a sense of inferiority. Indeed, the dull level of Pennsylvania politics in this era was not one to inspire the rise of men of outstanding talent or striking personality.

Furthermore, Buchanan had built up a powerful machine, in the course of seeking the presidential nomination in 1844, 1848, and 1852. The last was a near-miss; his bloc of southern supporters—among whom Henry A. Wise of Virginia, Howell Cobb of Georgia, and particularly John Slidell of Louisiana were most effective—had stuck with the Pennsylvanians until they saw their plan blocked. Now that cleverer leadership than Pierce could supply was obviously essential to defeat the Republicans, these Democrats turned again to Buchanan. He, Pierce, and Douglas had their separate adherents among the warring state factions busily building candidates.

The four Democratic emissaries to Cincinnati were further animated by fear that a deadlock would bring nomination of another dark horse. Some weak, compromise candidate might slip in, if Douglas and Pierce pooled their strength against Buchanan. How strong were they? Douglas could command Illinois, Missouri, and Iowa with some support in Ohio, Kentucky, and Wisconsin. Pierce, though he had probably lost Louisiana, Virginia, Pennsylvania, and some New England states, still could count on a substantial section of his 1856 bloc. He had warm friends in the South, principally from the lower tier, with some allies in North Carolina, Arkansas, parts of Kentucky, and possibly Tennessee. This bloc was swayed by a romantic sense of loyalty to Pierce as a symbol. He had stood firm for southern rights, had tried to administer Kansas in defiance of New England tactics, and had used his veto to kill subsidies; he was opposed to the hated protective tariff. His loyal southern supporters were not going to be driven by threats to desert him and nominate some other northern man; such tactics would give advantage to the opposition in their section, who could then claim that the Democrats were taking dictation from the enemies of the South. This phalanx was to remain firm behind a ticket of Pierce and General John A. Quitman, a filibustering Mississippi Mexican War veteran whom it hoped to nominate for Vice President.[4]

The Senators' trip had a personal animus, as well—the bitter hatred of Bright for Douglas. Bright was contesting with Douglas for control of the Northwest, and had dreamed of a ticket of Hunter and Bright, since Senator Robert M. T. Hunter of Virginia had a wide following among southern leaders. However, Pierce and Douglas managers, seeking to gain Virginia, had projected a Pierce-Hunter ticket which completely ignored Bright. The discarded Senator translated his several resentments into a burning determination to nominate Buchanan.

The final shock necessary to galvanize the Senators to action was word of the tactics of their opponents. The Pierce-Douglas forces seemed to be concluding effective arrangements for controlling the Cincinnati convention, with the help of some of the same New Englanders who had labored so adroitly for Pierce in 1852; their convention set-up included Representative William A. Richardson of Illinois, an astute parliamentarian, as floor manager. Buchanan's convention plans evidently had been left to the Pennsylvania Representative J. Glancy Jones and the exuberant, alcoholic John W. Forney of the state machine, with such tatterdemalions as the Kentucky speculator George N. Sanders, who had left Douglas for Buchanan. Worried observers wrote Slidell that this was dangerous; a more responsible and convincing convention management was necessary.

As Slidell now found that Bright was with him in supporting Buchanan to stop Douglas, the two operators decided to organize their senatorial cabal to direct Buchanan's support at the convention probably with the blessing of the banker Corcoran. They enlisted Benjamin and Bayard, the latter also an official delegate from his "family's state," and set out to cross the Alleghenies a little ahead of time. Their efforts were to have unforeseen consequences.

IV

Cincinnati, the Queen City of the West, was hostess to the convening Democrats, an unprecedented event in the history of the party, in fact in the history of American politics. Never before had a national party convention met beyond the mountains. However, the defeat in 1852 of Cass and Douglas had called for some concession to the constituencies of the West, and so the Democratic managers had decided to leave Baltimore, their traditional place of meeting.

Cincinnati, throbbing center of western life, was situated on the north bank of the Ohio. Its fast-growing population, which had increased some 90 per cent in the preceding decade and now was approaching two hundred thousand, was distributed six miles along the mighty river. Most of the people were foreign in origin; more than half were German, and a large contingent Irish. The city was strategically located as a railroad center enjoying a substantial river trade and had become a hive of manufacturing and commerce. The citizens had cultural pretensions, too. They were proud of their school system with its two fine high schools. They likewise boasted of a college, a law school, and six medical "colleges," and supported well their institutions for the care of the sick and the unfortunate. Seven daily papers—three printed in German—brought the news of the world; and if there were those interested in things beyond the range of terrestrial news-gathering, the observatory with its up-to-date astronomical apparatus might bring them at least into mathematical and visual touch with other worlds.

The convening politicians congregated mostly at Cincinnati's great hotel, the Burnet House. This hostelry, the "finest in the United States," stood on the Third Street terrace, several blocks from the water front, some fifty feet above the river, and rose to a height of five stories. It was entered by a grand flight of steps through a colonnaded porch, and its two hundred forty rooms were crowned by a great round dome. Its verandas and windows afforded a commanding view of the Ohio River and Kentucky.

The four Senators did not make this hotel their headquarters. Their friend S. L. M. Barlow, who had been one of the most insistent in urging them to come, had invited them to use his home. He was a New Yorker, temporarily established in the West to push the Ohio and the Mississippi Railroad to completion. He was also an ardent supporter of Buchanan. In his large house, across the street from the Burnet, the four took quarters. With them were George Butler of the New York *Journal of Commerce,* a conservative metropolitan organ, and Daniel E. Sickles, recently Buchanan's secretary of legation in London.

The Senators unpacked their bags at Barlow's and went to work, encouraged by the fact that no one of the three leading competitors had the two-thirds necessary to secure a nomination. They found it advantageous to quiet some factions and encourage others. In the Northwest factionalism could be used to cripple Douglas's chances of united sectional support. New York quarrels might be manipulated to destroy Pierce's hopes.

Bright and Cass were using their influence to keep Indiana and Michigan from the Little Giant. In Ohio, a local fight right at the convention doors helped Buchanan. Washington McLean of the Cincinnati *Enquirer* was for the Pierce and Douglas combination, and McLean's enemies were contrary-minded. To discredit McLean and to advertise their strength, his foes organized a series of committees to visit each state delegation with a demand for Buchanan. Whether or not they conjured up these tactics without aid from others, the operation made a lot of noise, and Bright and Slidell welcomed the racket.

The decisive blow was struck by Bright, when it developed that Douglas's hold on various states was not too firm. Besides his loss of Michigan through Cass, who laid his failure of renomination in 1852 to Douglas, he had suffered defection in Wisconsin. California was actually hostile, Iowa was shaky, and Ohio opposed him, though united on nobody else. Stressing this weakness, Bright cleverly persuaded the Indiana delegation to vote for Buchanan. Thus in his own section Douglas was sure of only Illinois and Missouri.

Elated by the Indiana coup, the Buchanan manipulators began to work on the remaining Douglas supporters. They used the telling argument of age. If young, forty-three-year-old Douglas now gracefully stepped aside for the elder statesman and prevented a long deadlock and the final nomination of some outsider, he might expect wholehearted support in

1860, when Buchanan would not seek a second term. Douglas must also be doubtful whether a Pierce ticket could be elected. Such arguments when spoken, and such thoughts when pondered, impressed Douglas's managers, who were playing their own game. Besides, Slidell had just received a mysterious letter from Buchanan which he showed with effect. The odds in favor of the Pennsylvanian seemed to be mounting, despite factionalism in such important states as his own and Virginia.

New York remained the worst hazard, for its brawling politicians kept their evil genius for wrecking the peace of each administration as it came up. There the wounds of 1846-1848 were still festering. Instead of the old Barnburner and Hunker factions, there were now the Softs and the Hards. The Pierce administration had sought by treating all factions alike to cement the reunion arranged in 1852, which had returned the state to the Democratic column. Unfortunately the Hunkers had split over the recognition of the less conservative Barnburners as Democrats in good standing. One group, the Soft Shell Hunkers, were willing to cooperate with them again; but the other, the Hard Shell Hunkers, rebelled. Then Pierce tried to discipline the Hards, but failed, and the result was a new factionalism. The Soft Shell Hunkers and the Barnburners united to support Pierce and were generally called Softs. Their leaders were the Secretary of State, William L. Marcy, and Governor Horatio Seymour; they controlled the patronage.

Certain Hard Shell Hunkers and many who disapproved of Pierce or were disgruntled over the patronage were now called Hards. The Softs and Hards had held separate state conventions and sent separate delegations to Cincinnati. Just as in 1848, the national body in 1856 must decide between the two New York factions. As the Softs were for Pierce, the Hards sought to make capital for themselves by supporting Buchanan. If the convention seated the Soft delegation, Pierce and Douglas might control the nomination. Could the Buchanan cabal, strengthened by their victory over Douglas in the Northwest, deprive Pierce of New York?

The schemers transferred their operations, June 2, from Barlow's and the Burnet House to Smith and Nixon's Concert Hall. This building had been leased for the formal convention and was peculiar for its lack of certain usual facilities. It had no street frontage, being located in the center of a block and completely surrounded by lesser buildings. Delegates entered through a passageway from the sidewalk. More inconvenient, it had no near-by saloons, which somewhat surprised a *Herald* reporter.

No sooner were the opening formalities over than the effects of Pierce's lack of a convention majority became apparent. The Buchaneers won their first triumph by electing John E. Ward of Georgia as permanent chairman; they got control of the committees also, and saw to it that the credentials committee split the Empire State vote by giving each faction one-half. Would Douglas withdraw if they made it easy for him? They adopted the platform before voting on nominations, and it tactfully included a version of Douglas's squatter sovereignty dogma.

With these outworks carried, the Buchaneers began the main assault on the afternoon of June 5. Fourteen ballots were cast without a decision; none had even a majority.[5] That night the Pierce men conferring with the Douglas managers agreed to withdraw the President's name. They would vote for Douglas next day and expected him to hold on, until either he was nominated or a dark horse was chosen: Buchanan must be stopped. Next morning their votes went for Douglas but did not add up to two-thirds. Then the Buchanan propaganda worked. To the anger of the Pierce men, Floor Manager Richardson withdrew Douglas's name and Buchanan was nominated forthwith.

At its final session the convention endorsed a Pacific railroad, paid belated tribute to the Pierce administration, and proceeded to nominate a vice presidential candidate. Here again southern supporters of Pierce were disappointed. Their man, General Quitman, was passed over, and Slidell accepted Richardson's proposal that John C. Breckinridge of Kentucky, the candidate of the Douglas bloc, be the party nominee. Thus the deed was done; and the irony of it was not revealed until 1860, when Breckinridge stopped Douglas.

These arrangements left heartburnings. The Pierce men, particularly those from New England, charged bad faith. They said they had switched to Douglas on condition he stay in the contest until he was nominated or Buchanan defeated. They felt he had deprived them of an opportunity to bargain for a compromise candidate more friendly to them than Buchanan was likely to be. Of greater significance was the disappointment of the more radical southern delegates. They had lost both Pierce and Quitman and had to accept a Douglas platform. Buchanan was decidedly not their candidate, and they took him grudgingly. They wanted no cautious compromiser, even if he were known to have southern sympathies. The possibility of Republican victory and the certainty that their Whig-American opponents would charge them with disloyalty to the South prescribed, they thought, a more belligerent ticket to impress constituents, nervous over the future.[6]

Within a fortnight the new Republican party convened at Philadelphia and nominated John C. Frémont, "the Pathfinder." Their platform was strong for free soil and demanded a Pacific railroad and federal appropriations for internal improvements. The American party (which was anti-Catholic and antiforeign) split, and the northern branch, which had seceded from the party convention when southerners won control of it, accepted Frémont. This marshaled behind him most of the opponents of the Democrats in the free states. The southern branch of the American party nominated Millard Fillmore of New York, who was endorsed also by a poorly attended Whig convention; this ticket was to be formidable only in the South. Thus the lines were formed.

Chapter 2

A Bewildering Task

BUCHANAN HAD BEEN NOMINATED. Next the Democracy must gird itself to inspire at least a million and three-quarters voters to rally to the standard. Thirty-one state machines must gear themselves to deliver the vote. It was no easy task, for the party confronted a most bewildering opposition. As in 1848, when it faced both Whigs and Free-Soilers, it again had two opponents; then it had been defeated.

Besides the Republican party, which by now was organized on a national basis and was vigorously at work in northern states, there was the American (Know-Nothing) group—more mysterious and frightening, in some respects, than the Republicans. The coming of large groups of immigrants, particularly from Ireland in the late forties, had greatly strengthened both the Catholic Church and the Democratic party. This reenforcement revived Protestant antipathy, which was as old as the Reformation, and many opponents of the Democrats seized upon it as a weapon with which to defeat them. Throngs of Whigs, North and South, joined the secret political organization, the Order of the Star Spangled Banner, commonly called the Know-Nothings, which campaigned in local and national elections as the American party. Its platform was 100 per cent Protestant Americanism, and its spokesmen demanded that Catholics and foreigners be kept from politics and public office. "Americans must rule America."

At first the fact that there would be two opposition groups had seemed to be an advantage to the Democrats; but they had not expected the American party to split over slavery. When this occurred early in 1856 and most of the northern wing of the Know-Nothings went over to the Republicans, the Americans became almost wholly a southern party with no northern contingent to conciliate. The result was that this new party could go all out for southern power and interests to an extent which the Democracy, with its northern wing, could not match. Likewise the Republican party with no southern support at all could concentrate on promoting northern interests. The Democracy therefore must fight two campaigns against two enemies. How could it meet both? If it stressed southern views, it would be doomed in the North, and vice versa. It could not win the election without support North and South. The Democrats planned to meet this situation by nominating a safe candidate and formulating their Cincinnati platform.

II

Vastly more complex than the struggle against two regionalized opponents was the basic political situation faced by the managers in this campaign. Their problem was more involved than any of them realized. They were well aware that they were operating the political mechanism of a federal republic composed of thirty-one states; but they scarcely comprehended that the most powerful conditioner of voting behavior was not political but "cultural" federalism. It harbored a greater threat to the success of the Democratic party and to the permanence of the United States government than did the sectional rivalries inherent in political federalism. In truth cultural federalism is a primary fact in American history, too little appreciated and therefore clamoring for understanding.

As the federation of the states composing the United States has constituted a political federalism, the association of people and communities exhibiting various attitudes has constituted a cultural federalism. Each attitude contributes its quota to the national complex of feeling, thought, and behavior. But attitudes are never wholly confined to one group, state, or region. Different attitudes may exist side by side in a given community, on the same street, or within a single family. The task of the political leaders therefore was more subtle than keeping slave and free states in a political union; it was the task of finding ways and means to hold citizens dominated by a variety of attitudes in one body politic. The elements of conflict bred by these attitudes must be eliminated or restrained. Politicians must forever be busy composing formulas, organizing through legislation, patronage, and power, political combinations strong enough to insure continued cooperation in the federal Union.

Of the countless attitudes composing this cultural federalism, ten were most influential in conditioning political behavior at this time. They are here classified first according to their origin and type of influence; then they will be explained individually. Two of them may be classed as pervasive, five as divisive, and three as cohesive. The pervasive group—attitudes which vitally affected the behavior of most people—were dominated by ideas and modes of thought traditional and

common in occidental civilization, with few or no native roots.
They were American only in so far as they were sharpened by
certain local circumstances. These attitudes were Protestantism and romanticism. The divisive group—attitudes foment-
ing antagonism—were for the most part indigenous, the products of American conditions, but were also intensified by
Protestantism and romanticism. This group embraced metropolitanism, territorialism, southernism, New Englandism, and
antislaveryism. Finally, the cohesive group—attitudes tending
to unite—were less well defined and were only partly developed; but if they spread more widely they might prove
sufficiently attractive to offset the divisive second group.
These soothing cohesive ideas were nationalism, regionalism,
and democracy. Many people who realized the danger in the
divisive attitudes were striving to promote this cohesive group,
so that common adoption of one or more of them might overcome the perilously accumulating antagonisms.

The pervasive attitudes, Protestantism and romanticism,
fundamentally influenced emotion and action within the Republic. They stood in the way of realistic consideration of
troublesome questions at issue. Protestantism had supplied a
dominant motive from the earliest days of colonial experience,
and though many people had fallen away from its strict code
of behavior and no longer admitted its religious implications,
still its impress was felt in most communities. The great
majority of the people yielded active or passive allegiance to
some Protestant denomination, having been brought up in a
Protestant atmosphere of moral and religious ideas.

The most significant characteristic of the Protestant attitude
was a consciousness of the evil nature of sin. Protestant ex-
pounders made a simple and clear-cut distinction between
right and wrong. Man was either saved or damned. Righteous-
ness would be rewarded, sin punished. Sin must be fought.
If it existed in the community it was because the righteous had
not been sufficiently diligent in driving it forth. Moreover the
prevailing belief that God ruled the universe gave promise
of divine aid in the crusade against evil. It was the duty of
the righteous to wage constant warfare against Satan's hosts.

This sense of duty, this sensitiveness to the promptings of
conscience, had been the main precept in the education of a
large proportion of those who in the fifties were at years of
maturity. In childhood they had been taught that only by
doing right, by heeding the commands of conscience when
duty called, could they secure happiness on earth or the hope

of heaven. Evil influences always brought degradation and destruction, for the punishment of transgressors was part of the divine plan. So impressive was this early influence that, though many abandoned its dogmas, they were never without the possibility of experiencing sharp twinges of conscience.

The growth of Catholicism in the years just preceding had intensified this attitude in two ways. In the first place it had stirred up Protestant-Catholic rivalry, which had characterized Northern Europe since the Reformation, even though the Catholics numbered a very small proportion of the population of the United States before the Civil War. Secondly, the growth of Catholicism further intensified Protestantism because, despite their antipathy, earnest believers in the two groups had similar or identical basic concepts of religious interpretation, moral principle, and zeal for a faith. Their similarity frequently meant like reactions on public questions involving integrity, duty, and morality. Yet, because the Protestants were so numerically predominant, the attitude is best described as Protestantism.

Religious influence was the more pervasive because of ill health and early mortality in that day. So uncertain was the prevailing state of health that suffering and death were constantly near; life expectancy then was not above forty years. Lack of sanitation and refrigeration, insufficient medical knowledge and skill, and ignorance of hygiene took heavy toll. The plagues of tuberculosis, yellow fever, cholera, and malaria were murderous. Less spectacular but no less disastrous were dyspepsia, childbirth fatalities, and social diseases. Invalids were common. Young women were often "delicate"; subject to early withering, they might enter a "decline." Mothers constantly struggled with sickness, mourning over the loss of beloved children.

Relief from the frequent sorrow was found in the "fellowship of suffering" wherein Christians sought to comfort one another with the hope of meeting in eternity and with admonitions to submit with resignation to the will of God. The frequency of mourning stimulated sentimentality. Human sympathies were often aroused, tears came easily. Many professed willingness to suffer if it were God's will and to endure hardship and sacrifice if thereby the kingdom of God might be extended on this earth. Emotions leading to active, even violent campaigns against evil, were easily aroused. The call of duty was strong and might awake men and women to fanatic zeal. If political exhorters could invoke the moral law they could count on a sentimental response capable of intense opposition to reputed evil.

Romanticism was closely akin to Protestantism. It was an attitude common throughout western culture of the time, for this was the so-called "Romantic Age." The American, like the European of the day, was hospitable to romantic concepts. He gloried in the melodramatic and utopian. Life was thronged with heroes and villains; virtue was ever triumphant, and vice inevitably punished. Education was dominated by classic lore, rhetoric, logic, and moral philosophy. Contrariwise there was slight training in science. Sex was not discussed, nor biological reproduction mentioned, except by elaborate Victorian circumlocutions. Even the most learned had little real knowledge of human physiology and psychology. Though they might be freethinkers in matters of dogma they usually were satisfied with the current religious explanations of human behavior.

Such romantic concepts could not supply rational correctives to the emotional impulses of the time. The American mind often viewed its problems unrealistically. The people easily espoused causes and went forth on crusades instead of giving constructive thought to grave social questions. They were willing to accept simple explanations for complex social problems, easy "cures" for pervasive ills. Political behavior was much affected by this romanticism, for voters could be swept along by impassioned oratory playing upon fears and hates and could rush heedlessly into the chaos of civil war.

III

The pervasive Protestantism and romanticism made all the more formidable the five divisive attitudes which were ready at hand to lend themselves to strife. Schooled in Protestantism and romanticism, the American people tended to follow stubbornly the "path of duty," without the realism which would have opened their eyes to the consequences of sharpening antagonisms. The divisive attitudes—metropolitanism, territorialism, southernism, New Englandism, and antislaveryism—were a dangerous array.

Metropolitanism* is so called because its exponents

* The term "metropolitanism" is used rather than "urbanism" because the attitude described is dominated by the desire of the few commercial and financial centers to exploit the opportunities of the great national hinterland, i.e., the dominance of the metropolis. "Urbanism" does not seem to the writer to express that implication so well.

stemmed from the growing centers of business, especially New York, Philadelphia, Baltimore, and Boston in the Atlantic region and Cincinnati beyond the mountains. These centers dominated the phenomenal business growth of the nation. The attitude was conditioned by the great potential wealth of the Republic coupled with its incomplete development, and the spirit of enterprise. It was easily exaggerated into the lust to exploit, exhibited by a great variety of economic interests. The many corporations and businessmen utilizing American resources were in constant competition and often disagreed vigorously on projects and policies. Yet in their fundamental optimism and faith in the future they were remarkably homogeneous and thus subject to political mobilization.

The most active group among the exponents of this attitude looked westward. They thought in terms of real estate development, railroad and canal building. They depended on loose banking and cheap money and on the rose-colored dreams of citizens, native and foreign, forever seeking new Edens.

There were others who thought in terms of trade more than land. They would manufacture and sell, planting factories in towns and tenements around them. Stores were multiplying, peddlers abounded. There was more demand for commodities, domestic and foreign. Importers and shipping operators were extremely busy seeking crops and securities to export, in payment of the adverse trade balances which were long to rule. Steamship operators and clipper-ship owners were charting routes on the seven seas and entering into rivalries with nationals of other countries to carry the trade, passengers, and mails of the world.

While capitalists were creating business they were also assembling battalions of workmen and voters. Labor organization so far had met with indifferent success. A promising move in that direction had been blasted by the panic of 1837, and since then the employers had been seeking to control workmen, as a political auxiliary, by supervising their voting—not difficult before the day of the secret ballot. The labor vote was often more an adjunct of the employers' power than an independent force.

In and out of these interests, bankers threaded their way. Compared with the financial powers of today, their numbers were small and their resources puny. America had only three millionaires in 1861. Bankers were unorganized, untrained, uncontrolled, competitive, and chaotic in their operations. Banks, particularly in the West, generally issued their own notes to the limit of public credulity, with scarcely any effective government control or even supervision, save in one or two eastern states. As hard money was scarce and the government issued no paper currency, this rag money served as an indifferent and fluctuating medium of exchange for an optimistic people.

Politics became a growing obsession with the exponents of metropolitanism. Government, if properly advised, could contribute to them so much of largesse and sympathetic policy. Their wants were so numerous and on occasion so conflicting that they further confused politics already very chaotic. Those who looked westward wanted the region organized as territories and states; they wished grants of land for settlers and railroads, and appropriations for public improvements. The manufacturers and their labor battalions wished protective tariffs. Importers, cotton factors, and their planter clients wanted free trade. Shippers and steamboat operators asked for mail contracts and cash subsidies to aid them in their struggle against foreign competition.

Here were sources of conflict, for the manufacturers might oppose western development because it drained off their cheap labor and increased their costs. Importers and planters would oppose protection as a matter of interest. Most bankers would oppose any form of government supervision of finance. These interests often fought among themselves and made legislative halls and political campaigns scenes of corruption and debauchery. They subsidized lobbies and pressed favors upon such legislators and administrators as might be tempted. They contributed to campaign funds, and sought control of urban policy and mass voting. They expected profitable returns from their political investments. Impatient of delay, they were often amoral or unscrupulous in pushing their plans.

All this welter of business and promotional activity, which served and conditioned metropolitanism, was sectionally distributed. It was not widespread in the South. Here were but four of the eighteen sizable cities which the United States then boasted, and these included St. Louis, which was as much western as southern. The relative absence of metropolitanism from the South on the one hand, and the growing concentration of its leading exponents in New York City, even then fast outstripping its rivals, were bound to stir up antagonism between rural and urban politicians, breeding the resentment against Wall Street which was to function increasingly as a divisive attitude in the operation of American politics.

Territorialism, the second divisive attitude, in many respects was metropolitanism in a different locale, for both stemmed from promotional enterprise. This attitude, as its name implies, was dominant in the newer portions of the country, where institutions, customs, and individual fortunes and reputations were on the make. It was displayed by people who were restless and speculative, insecure and quarrelsome, ambitious and impatient, hurrying to fulfill the promise of virgin lands. Amid their more solid citizenry floated the flotsam and jetsam of humanity, those who never succeeded anywhere but were always hoping for a change of fortune. Also the criminal and the leech sought to fatten on the frontiers.

Foremost exponents of territorialism were those who had gone West for political advancement. Politics was played in the territories from the start, and it was profitable politics. The legislatures there had valuable franchises to grant; they could vote lands and charters. Also the courts had many important property suits to hear and decide. These newer communities were constantly seeking to promote their own development by negotiations with the federal government and were not loath to join in schemes with metropolitan representatives. Persons dominated by territorialism were eager for advance and none too scrupulous as to means.

These two attitudes—metropolitanism and territorialism— were dynamic, ever in motion. They surged hither and yon with that impulsive eagerness for growth in wealth and power which was characteristic of the young Republic in general. Had they been shared equally by all sections of the nation, or had they not been obstructed in expansion, they would not have proved so divisive. However, they were concentrated predominantly in the free-state regions and, in certain areas, met inertia which blocked their dynamic onrush.

The 26,000,000 people, or 84 per cent of the inhabitants of the United States, who lived in rural environments, were divided about equally into two contrasting groups. Half lived in the non-slaveholding states, dominated or overshadowed by metropolitan or territorial attitudes which they frequently shared, opposing them and the enterprises of their exponents only when they thought them too potent in local government. By and large, they had no deep-seated hatred of the noisy tide of metropolitan and territorial advance.

This was not so with the other, the southern half of the rural population, whose social experience shaped a different attitude, southernism. It became violently antagonistic to

metropolitanism and territorialism, and was mainly concentrated in a single area of contiguous states. It reigned supreme
in thirteen of the fifteen which permitted Negro slavery, being
less dominant in Maryland and Delaware, and was found in
a number of outposts in distant regions such as the southern
parts of Ohio, Indiana, and Illinois, and in California, Oregon,
New Mexico, and Kansas, whither southerners had migrated,
carrying with them the behavior patterns bred in the region
of their birth. Southernism was conditioned by a peculiar
dichotomy. It had certain characteristics of dominance and
leadership while on the other hand it was burdened by colonial
insufficiency and dependence. This dichotomy resulted from
the failure of the South to emerge from its almost purely
agricultural status.

Until well after independence the South had experienced a
normal social evolution. Like certain other raw regions with
similar physiographic conditions it had undertaken to live by
planting, with slave labor in use on the larger farms, a characteristic of "colonial" economy. Then, just at a time when it
normally would have diversified its interests and substituted
white for slave labor, the upswing of the English Industrial
Revolution and the invention of the cotton gin encouraged
enterprising large planters to invest heavily in land and slaves
and induced the multitude of small farmers who owned few
or no slaves to raise cotton almost exclusively in order to take
advantage of the insistent demand for the crop.

While these circumstances were keeping the South in its
colonial economy, its economic dependence on other regions,
the section was dominating the politics of the Union. It kept
its unified political power in part because of this very same
colonialism. Elsewhere the greater variety of interests, the
freer movement of population and the swifter growth of communities had carried many able citizens into nonpolitical pre-
occupations, while southern leaders kept government as their
principal interest. Also the greater inertia of southern communities meant that their representatives in government held
longer terms and gained rights of seniority very effective in
enabling them to direct congressional politics and legislation.
Furthermore the South had an almost feudal respect for leaders and gave greater adulation and support to them than was
accorded elsewhere.

The fact that the South was dominant in the federal government at a time when its interests were diverging from those
of the rest of the nation enabled the section so to use its power

as to endanger the unity of the Republic. The growth of the nation had brought home to the South certain economic and social disadvantages rising from its continued colonial status. When southerners sought to participate in the westward advance, to carry their institutions, their attitudes, and their property into the more southern territorial regions, there to establish their own pattern, they found competition severe. Obsessed with their large-parcel landownership, they often undertook to transplant their slave plantation economy and found it an expensive, slow task. The footloose Yankee could pack a mere wagonful of household goods or even travel with but a carpetbag; he need buy on credit only as much land as he could clear and till, and could set himself up quickly and cheaply. There were thus a score of Yankees to one southerner who could or would move. The South therefore could not compete on even terms in the rush of expansion.

The almost exclusively agricultural nature of the South's social and economic patterns and its failure to hold its own in territorial competition were reflected in its views on federal policy. It was not to southern advantage to promote rapid development of other and diverse interests which would build up communities North and West unsympathetic to southernism and bound in time to break its power. The planters wanted a large export trade and cheap imports; the protective tariff of the factory towns was anathema. This later antipathy could be shared generally by rich and poor in that region, for southern publicists industriously reiterated that protection enriched the free states at southern expense. Also realizing their disadvantage in the competition for western lands and territorial control, they were loath to see federal aid used to speed western growth. They urged their representatives at Washington to block subsidies, grants, generous appropriations for improvements, as well as protective tariffs; their demands were heeded. The veto of "progress" by southernism was bitterly resented by representatives of the other attitudes.

The South was accordingly under constant attack. Had all these assaults been launched against the economic policies which it imposed upon the federal government, the consequences would not have been so dangerous; but the opposition was directed also against southern institutions and morals and was made possible by the persistence of slavery. Southernism though dominant was therefore on the defensive, fearful of loss of power and sensitive to the charge of wicked and cruel exploitation of human beings. As the southerners shared the prevailing Protestant and romantic attitudes, these charges roused the resentment natural to confused thinking and troubled conscience.

The danger of conflict was heightened by a fourth attitude in this divisive group, which can be called New Englandism. The region which gave it this name was originally as important as any other and had furnished much of the initial talent that promoted the creation of the Republic; but other types of growth had left it behind politically. It was the area of the most widely diffused culture and refinement. Here were great wealth and the sense of achievement brought by economic success. Yet the section grew less and less significant in federal politics until it could exercise little effective power at the national capital. No longer were many from that section in high places in the central government. Therefore numerous New Englanders developed a political self-consciousness born of frustration; it manifested itself in a particular type of tactics well adapted to the Protestant attitude.

This peculiar political behavior was dominated by ways of thought inherited directly from the Puritans. The unhappiness and frustration from which New England suffered must be due to sin and, urged on by conscience, the dissatisfied soon found that the sin was the sin of slavery. This cancer of society should be cut out, and stern duty called upon the foes of sin to remove it. This attitude was of course not universal. Many New England men of prominence were tolerant of the South and denounced its detractors. William Lloyd Garrison had been mobbed by Boston merchants, and abolitionist lecturers were rotten-egged by New Hampshire countryfolk. Yet there was less of this tolerance of the South in the fifties than in the thirties, and too many New Englanders hated southerners and their institution to permit bright prospects for good feeling. These intense foes of the South were going to do everything possible to destroy slavery. They found their duty all the more compelling as the sin was largely in the body politic of the South, and attack upon it must weaken those who held power. Thus hate of the South in large part stemmed from hate of its power but took the guise of a bitter attack on its institutions.

In the region beyond the Alleghenies had developed a fifth attitude peculiarly divisive in character. This may be termed antislaveryism or antisouthernism; it was distinct from New Englandism in that it arose out of a direct contact with southernism such as New England never had. In the states of the "Old Northwest" were large numbers of people who had come from the South and had seen slavery at first hand. Many of them heartily sympathized with slavery; and they made southern Indiana and southern Illinois proslavery. But there were others, frequently people of religious bent, dominated by the prevailing Protestantism, who thought otherwise. They hated the personal demoralization sometimes manifested by such slave owners as could not maintain their moral integrity under the strain of owning human beings. These westerners opposed the spread of slavery as they would leprosy. Others had left the South because they could not prosper in competition with slave labor. They did not or would not own slaves and could not compete with those who did.

Another factor sharpening antislaveryism was the political, economic, and social competition which marked the development of each of the Ohio valley states. Here migrants from New England, from the middle states, and from the South met to vie with one another for leadership and wealth in the new communities. Their differences in background and attitude upon occasion stimulated antagonism. Here New Englandism made its divisive contribution, and those who had fled the South to escape slavery and competition with its supporters added their antislaveryism. The middle western sum of the two was in many cases more intense and fanatical than any eastern emotion; it was tragically divisive, bound to be destructive of national cohesion. Especially in Ohio and in Kansas, people swayed by these attitudes displayed a sense of aloofness, of moral inflexibility, of superiority, and of hatred of the sin of slavery which became more powerful political factors there than in the older regions. When such settlers met southern immigrants and struggled with them over the control of the government and the institutions of the western regions, blood would flow.

IV

The danger in the conflict between these varying attitudes lay in the fact that metropolitanism, territorialism, New Englandism, and antislaveryism were in the process of becoming united in a general hatred of southernism. The South was constantly aware of this convergence of opposition and reacted in a fashion also threatening to the future of the Union. The danger arose from certain peculiarities of southern life. Conditions among those of southern residence or origin were such as to make them resent opposition belligerently. Paradoxically, the South became tenacious of its attitude partly on account of an internal division. Of the 8,000,000 white people in the section but 1,500,000 had any direct property interest in the 3,500,000 slaves. Less than 20 per cent of the population were of the slaveholding group. Also, there were wide variations in environment and culture. Nearly every one of the southern states was divided by geography into sections. Along the Atlantic were tidewater, piedmont, and back-country groups. Along the Gulf, there were the rich black belts and the upcountry. The interior slave states were also sectionalized, and all had the accompanying social cleavages. Migrants from the older states tended to settle together or at least to act in sympathy. Alabama had her northern region settled by people from the South Carolina piedmont, while her southern area showed a preponderance of Georgians. Ancient rivalries persisted in the newer states and raised the heat of politics. Finally there was a division between the older states of colonial origin and those of the "New South" in the lower Mississippi and Gulf regions, a certain subtle jealousy between them which made them compete to see which region was the more "southern." As a result of all these factors sectional rivalry and local jealousy were particularly rife within the South.

Yet out of this variety, and in large part because of it, arose a defensive homogeneity not visible elsewhere, generated and fostered by politics. In the frequent elections which agitated the South, faction capitalized southern fears. Each rival sought to show that the danger was great, that his opponents were incompetent to meet it, and that he alone could preserve, protect, and defend the Southland. The partisan leaders encouraged an intense determination to enforce the adoption of southern rules, such as the slave-code idea of protection of slave property in the territories. In their pertinacity it is easy to see the influence of Protestantism among them, in their insistence on the acceptance of creeds and statements of religious principles. Under such constant stimulus, apprehension mounted with each electoral season and instilled throughout that section a unifying sense of common danger.

This fear was the easier to arouse because of the extensive absorption in cotton raising. It was the great source of income, and the fortunes of the planters depended on whether or not the year was "good" in terms of bales and prices. As the section had no control over either the weather or the grades of the crop, there was an annual period of anxiety followed either by easy prosperity or by the melancholy discontent with disappointment and debt. Because of this complex situation the southern states developed a sentiment akin to a separate local nationalism; it was antagonistic to the over-all nationalism and boded ill for the perpetuity of the Union.

A second sectional pecularity which made constant agitation so dangerous was the isolated situation of southern voters. Most of them lived in rural environments and had few contacts with the outside world and little change. Towns were few, transportation meager. The railroads had not spread a comprehensive network over the South, and only among those who lived near a river upon which steamers plied was there much travel except by horse and mule transportation. This way of living commonly meant isolation. There was relatively little reading matter available to the general public, and so the mass of southerners mainly depended for their information about the outside world upon what they heard, which could not in most cases be extensive or accurate. Also this was before the day of cheap illustration; scarcely any illustrated magazines and no movies existed to give everybody pictures of the world at large. In the fifties, particularly in the South, there was a poverty of visual imagery which made it easy to acquire distorted notions of other places and peoples, expressed by word of mouth. Never having seen a Yankee, many a southerner had no difficulty in picturing him as a nasal-toned, penny-grabbing, pious hypocrite whom it was easy to despise.

Isolation in the South placed a premium upon means to break its tedium and to satisfy the common craving for human association. Three such opportunities were most available: political rallies, court days, and church services. In all three the great delight was listening to speeches. The South specialized in oratory—political, court, and pulpit. Its politicians, lawyers, and ministers became past masters in the art of pouring out emotional rhetoric. The average southerner would stand for hours in the heat to hear the impassioned flow of speech. The result was sharp rivalry among candidates for command over crowd emotions.

Political orators pressed by these demands developed the themes most certain to rouse and engross their hearers. As interests were narrow they must stick to certain well worn channels. The great glory of the Republic and its superiority

formed one of them. Another was even more effective because it had the power both to arouse pride and self-satisfac-
tion and to stir up indignation and hate. This theme harked
back to the familiar heroic tradition of the Revolution, when
sacred rights had been attacked by the British tyrant and the
land invaded by a hireling foe. When orators now spoke of
states' rights and southern rights, as endangered by Yankee
tyrants, the emotions of the crowds surged upwards in tor-
rents. Speakers skillfully hunted for this sure response, as
the contending parties and candidates vied with one another
in their efforts to arouse the greatest resentment against assaults from without. From these oratorical effusions southerners got a spiced version of abolitionist propaganda with its
colorful denunciation of the South as sinful and as harboring
a cancerous institution. Many a listener undoubtedly jumped
to the conclusion that all Yankees were abolitionists, and that
the non-slave states were solidly in league to destroy the
South.

In such circumstances southern orators cleverly aroused
or augmented fears for personal and social safety. Indeed the
dangers in the situation of the South were very apparent. If
the 3,500,000 slaves were freed or stirred up to rise, there
would be a social revolution. The rich and well-to-do would
lose a large share of their property, and the poverty-stricken
whites would be thrown into competition with the liberated
Negroes. Another, though lesser, source of uneasiness was
the fact that several million southerners—poor whites—were
not directly attached to the plantation system. If they learned
the disadvantages they suffered from slavery, if they became
attracted to some other form of economy, or if they were
marshaled behind some leader unfriendly to the plantation
way of life who might play in with the forces of mechanical
progress, what would happen to their system?

Southern monetary disability added further to the ease
with which political orators could capitalize the Yankee peril.
Like most people in a colonial economy, rural southerners
failed to understand the full significance of money. The
wealth of the South was in lands, in crops, and in slaves.
The people, whether poor or rich, saw relatively little cash,
and they were not accustomed to thinking in terms of its
use or value. There were few cities, few banks, few stores.
Crops were sent away, the proceeds deposited in distant banks,
often in the North, supplies were ordered from afar and paid
for by drafts and bills. Surplus money usually meant buying

more land and slaves. In other words they were in much the same state of mind as feudal landholders in the days before the rise of capitalism. Also they usually lacked the bargaining and competitive sense of the capitalist, and they had all the dislike or contempt which one who knows he is deficient in bargaining power has for those who can outdo him in the trading arts.

Southerners could easily think of northerners as money-mad, corrupt speculators who were attempting to cheat the South. They naturally massed their opposition against over-large appropriations and taxes adopted by Congress. They charged that the Yankees wanted to develop the rest of the country at the expense of the South. A protective tariff was but a device to rob the South and to build out of the proceeds a stronger group of interests antagonistic to the section and determined to ruin it. The few Yankees seen in the cotton country were generally traveling salesmen and peddlers who might be, and sometimes were, abolition agents in disguise seeking to spread ideas of freedom among the salves.

The bitter resentment welling up in the South was intensified by the fact that its people shared the prevailing Protestantism. The preacher was often as much a factor in passion rousing as the political orator. Evangelism flourished. Church meetings were eagerly attended by isolated farmers. The Methodists, Baptists, and Presbyterians particularly set much store by preaching, and they stressed the Protestant tenets earlier described, emphasizing morals, conscience, and the hatred of sin. Stung to anger by attacks upon their institutions and by slurs upon their moral integrity, their pulpits became rostrums of defense. Thus southern clergymen fought northern ministers in the same Protestant vocabulary, but their themes differed. Southern divines became increasingly satisfied that slavery was ordained of God and justified in the Bible. God would condemn those who bore false witness against the South—the northern hypocrites who attacked the South as morally delinquent. Did not the North enslave its laborers in a horrid wage slavery? Did not its people worship the golden calf of money and serve Mammon instead of God? They were Pharisees who kept clean the outside of the cup and the platter but like whited sepulchers were inwardly filled with all uncleanness.

Feudalism was yet another southern characteristic which with democracy encouraged the section's solidarity and was equally paradoxical. Certain feudal remnants survived because of the identity of southern polite society with the land. The rural population in the plantation regions looked up to the great landowners, in part because of their wealth and power which made them natural objects of respect, also partly because their houses were sometimes beautiful, their way of life magnificent, their manners imperious. Yet the South was in a way as democratic as it was feudal. Classes were fluid, and many a poor man admired and supported the plantation system because he hoped that he or his children might by industry, thrift, and luck rise to that class. It was done often enough to keep the fires of ambition alight. Hence desire to own slaves was one paradoxical aspect of the democratic optimism which marked America. Thus huge areas of the South remained in a common mold despite the curious differences.

Publicists and average citizens outside the section accepted its homogeneity, often without discrimination, and were blind to its diversity. They easily adopted as true the pattern which Harriet Beecher Stowe supplied in 1852. *Uncle Tom's Cabin* became the "Baedeker" for the non-traveling north. What abolitionist agitators, what Garrison and the *Liberator* had never succeeded in doing was accomplished by Mrs. Stowe. She gave non-southerners a distorted but convincing picture of life in the South. The southerners had resented the abolitionist propaganda, they had excluded the *Liberator* from the mails; but this resentment was nothing compared to the anger aroused by this Stowe tract in novel form. It hurt them deeply. They found compensation in intensifying their efforts to justify their institutions as ordained of God. All classes alike united in a defense of their society, because it was under attack. The attempt to paint the section as the home of degraded and degrading institutions made southerners all the more insistent that theirs was a civilization with higher standards than anything their neighbors had produced.

Under this pressure the South clung to a colonial state of mind while the remainder of the country was set to a different tempo. Rapidly industry, transportation, and business developed elsewhere, accelerated by periods of extravagantly optimistic speculation producing a more mature and diversified society. Not so in the South. Their attitude toward the rest of the United States became increasingly colonial, like that of the thirteen colonies toward the British government in the late eighteenth century. The South had a sense of being exploited, of being discriminated against, not so much at any one time as in the future. Subjugation had not happened, but it always might, particularly if southerners were not able to maintain control of the federal government to protect themselves.

It was this control of federal government which was at stake; northerners dominated by the metropolitan, the territorial, the New England, and the antislavery attitudes were tireless in their efforts to deprive the South of control, and they had the decennial census with them. The speculative and industrial centers grew more and more impatient with the obstructive tactics of southern politicians in matters financial and economic. So often had their schemes been blocked by southern committeemen in Congress or by southern men in the executive offices. This constant frustration was generating a power of attack that was likely to blast away the existing controls and set up new devices. The conflict between all these divisive attitudes boded ill for the permanence of the Union.

V

Those who wished to heal the breaches in social and political cooperation cut by the divisive attitudes cultivated three types of cohesive sentiment which they hoped might prevent the threatening clashes. Some appealed to the rising nationalism which was becoming more closely associated with the concepts of the Union and the power of the central government. In the earlier years of the Republic this feeling of national identity had been largely taken for granted; but there followed the growth of the population, the addition of new states, and the consequent expansion of the federal system. These developments emphasized anew the existence of two powers, state and national; two complex loyalties resulted, inducing the emotional conflicts inherent in these dual ties. In many people this dilemma stimulated attitudes in which local pride predominated, but among others it produced a clearer definition of the new over-all loyalty. They had somewhat transcendental gleams of understanding that the whole, the nation, was greater than the sum of its parts, and that union created a strength that mere federation never could produce. This gave nationalism a new value and a strength which evoked passionate loyalty, something akin to, though much more inclusive than, southernism. Employing the inspired words of Webster in his reply to Hayne, nationalists mobilized their efforts to intrench his ideas in the thought of the people, calling upon Americans to submerge local attachments in the greater and more satisfying and profitable patriotism.

While nationalism was the attitude of many who wished to forget antagonisms, to quiet discord, and to realize peacefully the potentialities of American opportunities, the idea was otherwise useful. Nationalism became a political tool. Aggressive activists demanded their land grants and subsidies in the name of greater glory and power for the young Republic. Also those who tried to quiet fears and allay apprehensions by compromise preached of the advantages of union; they sought to prove that only by cherishing and preserving nationalism could its benefits be enjoyed and its security maintained.

But many political and economic implications of nationalism made it plain to certain leaders of thought and action that it could not be a formula consonant with their interest. This was particularly true in the South, where the appeal to nationalism seemed but a device to cover with fair words the frustration and suppression of that region. Calhoun and his disciples sought to dignify another long-standing attitude; namely, regionalism. He wished to capitalize the old states' rights philosophy, join it with the growing solidarity of southern interests, and create a new formula which would fortify the dignity and autonomy of the South. Means must be found to secure some sort of veto for the South in the federal system whereby that section could curb national legislation against its interests. A new doctrine of minority or regional rights was formulated, and various designs were suggested to give the South certain autonomous powers which she might use for her protection. While spokesmen for this idea generally used the language of states' rights they were talking in terms of regional autonomy. Their meaning was quite clear. The powers of the central government must be curtailed in general, though they must be augmented or implemented enough to insure the protection of southern property interests (i.e., slavery) in the territories and the return of fugitive slaves who fled northward.

Spokesmen of the South were all the more insistent upon this regionalism because of the growing prominence of another attitude which its exponents hoped would prove cohesive. The idea of democracy in another sense than a party label had enjoyed some currency even though the American government was not in those days so described. Tom Paine and others in the eighteenth century had grasped the fact that the American experience was making possible a new type of democracy, not the government of city states, but a system suitable for larger areas, representative democracy. A federal government composed of representatives of the states whose governments were increasingly democratic had demonstrated the practicability of this larger concept. The French visitor, De Tocqueville, observed the achievement in the early 1830's and described it in his monumental work, *Democracy in America*. Yet in these early decades, when the onward march of universal manhood suffrage was popularizing the idea of majority rule, democracy had still been considered as something pertaining to the states, as a form of suffrage which each might adopt or not as it saw fit; the Constitution even left to the states the power to declare who should vote for members of the lower house of Congress and for presidential electors.

In the 1850's the sectional quarrel over the organization of new territories produced the disputed formula of popular or squatter sovereignty, which in its most extreme meaning was democracy in the form of congressional authorization to the early settlers to decide the question of the institutional patterns of the embryo states by mere majority votes. Finally in the midst of this prolonged territorial sovereignty debate appeared a more startling concept: questions of broad national policy should be decided by the will of the popular majority in the nation at large, without regard to the equality of the states.

The opponents of the Democrats were beginning to make this appeal. Pleas were heard for the acceptance of the democratic principle as the means of substituting fair play for the fractious negativism of minorities; there was no more equitable rule than the will of the majority. Such sporting words, however, did not make southerners forget the warning of the census. If the voice of the majority became the will of the Republic, they might well be at the mercy of their free-state neighbors. They feared the tyranny of numbers. Plainly the effort by northern spokesmen to make democracy a cohesive formula would have only slightly more chance of success than the labor of their southern antagonists to secure the acceptance of regionalism and the recognition of the right of minority veto.

Thus the three general concepts, nationalism, regionalism, and democracy, which some people hoped would overcome the divisive strains, were themselves accentuating conflict. The very efforts to avert strife, in vital respects stimulated it. Protagonists of nationalism and democracy could not, even by appealing to the grandeur or force of their ideas, divert the attention of the advocates of regionalism from their concern with minority rights and the need of regional veto power.

The leaders of the Democracy and the rank and file of their followers were hardly equipped to understand the subtle implications of the cultural federalism with which they had to cope. They were in reality going blindly into the maze of opinion and attitudes which were its constitutents. Their blindness was not their fault but their lack of culpability made their blunders none the less dangerous.[1]

Chapter 3

Victory by a Narrow Margin

THE CAMPAIGN OF 1856 was fought while the nation was riding the crest of a wave of prosperity. Business was very active, for money was "easy." Speculation was rife, people were pouring into the territories carrying the infection in their blood. Big projects filled the air. Many dreamed of expanding commerce and national interest into the Caribbean and the Pacific. The transcontinental railroad, to which Pierce, Buchanan, and the platforms of all parties were committed, was held up by the fight between northern and southern Congressmen as to routes, and most subsidy bills were beaten by the Democrats. But the success of the Republicans in gaining control of the House committees at this session relaxed restraint on appropriations. Congress loosed the purse strings and overrode some of Pierce's internal improvement vetoes, thanks to the aid of obliging Democratic brethren in the Senate.

The speculative buoyancy ruled out, at least in the free states, such a campaign emphasis as subsidy versus laissez faire. Rather, popular enthusiasm focused there on the idea of a political new deal. A new generation of enthusiasts, many of them young and idealistic, saw an opportunity to unhorse the Democratic party, so long in power. They rallied round the Republican banners of liberty and free soil, to break the hold of the Democracy and its southern leaders. As in 1840 there was much singing, parading, and enthusiasm for a new cause. This fitted well the Protestant, romantic, antislavery, and New England attitudes, and also presented gainful possibilities to many with metropolitan and territorial interests. In the South, the Americans used southernism to attack Buchanan. They asked, Could a northern candidate on a squatter sovereignty platform, interested in a Pacific railroad, be trusted to regard the rights of the South? Such was the opposition the Democrats must face.

Their candidate had been well chosen for the part. This experienced politico should succeed where Pierce had failed. He should appeal to the conservative Union-loving, nationalistic type and to quite a number of like-minded Whigs. Also he should keep a number of metropolitans from joining the

Republicans because of his safe conservatism and his interest in a Pacific railroad. His endorsement of popular sovereignty should prevent the territorialist wing of the Democratic party under Douglas from aligning with the Republicans. Buchanan's well known sympathy for southern rights, and the belief that he alone could defeat Frémont, should provide the necessary strength in the South.

The campaign by today's standards was simple. Buchanan was to stay at home in Lancaster, Pennsylvania, receiving visitors and answering mail with the help of a clerk, William V. McKean, sent up by Forney. The national committee organized an executive committee of seven to collect a campaign fund of $20,000 by seeking $100 from each congressional district, and a resident committee of eight in Washington to get out the pamphlets and organize a speakers bureau. More important was a group of congressional managers with no official designation: Slidell, Bright, Cobb, and Glancy Jones, together with a party angel, the banker Corcoran. They did what was needful. Important as were these efforts, the bulk of the work was to be done by the state organizations.

The main problem was publicity. The principal party editor, Bennett of the *New York Herald,* caused consternation by refusing to support Buchanan. He was disgruntled because he thought the candidate had deceived him when denying a wish to run. Worse, the official organ, the *Washington Union,* had no regular, satisfactory editor, so that Slidell and Cobb had to assume direction of it. Under their vigorous policy the paper published campaign material equal to ten octavo volumes of seven hundred pages each and contributed $10,000 worth of documents to the party without charge. What the party lacked in newspaper power it must compensate for by pamphlets.

The resident committee worked particularly hard at preparing such material, for people still set great store by this reading matter. Voters in the country and the small villages prized the pamphlets received by mail as their special contact with the outside world. Avidly they read and passed them around. Various writers were enlisted to prepare such literature, and John W. Forney, Amos Kendall, Judge Jeremiah S. Black of the Pennsylvania Supreme Court, and William B. Reed, lawyer and lecturer in American history at the University of Pennsylvania, took up their pens. Many speeches made in Congress were printed in quantity and despatched broadcast. The committee corresponded with the county chairmen all over the nation, asking for statistics and lists of voters. They encouraged the organization of Keystone clubs, named after Buchanan's home state. Pamphlets were sent directly to those on the lists, generally under congressional frank, and packages of them were mailed to the local chairmen and to the clubs for circulation. Some clubs opened reading rooms where this hortatory literature might be consulted and discussed. By August 1 the clerks of the committee were mailing out forty thousand pieces a day.

Writers and orators did not have much inspiration. They concentrated on showing how safe and conservative Buchanan was, how radical and dangerous were Frémont and the Black Republicans. They had to show the free-state voters that Buchanan was not a serf of the South, and the Southern voters that he was friendly to their interests. They wooed the Germans and other foreign voters by showing that the Republicans were Know-Nothings. They went after the labor vote by portraying Buchanan as a friend to workmen and judicious protection. To Whig voters they displayed impressive endorsements from former Whigs, like Rufus Choate of Massachusetts and the Maryland Senators, Pratt and Pearce.

The gravest danger to the Democrats came from the way the Republicans used "Bleeding Kansas." In order to quiet the slavery issue, President Pierce sent an experienced governor, John W. Geary, to Kansas; the congressional leaders devised the unsuccessful Toombs bill to provide for a speedy admission of Kansas following an orderly vote on the slavery issue. Free-state men in Kansas and Republicans in Congress, however, kept the issue very much alive.[1]

II

The campaign proceeded without event until the barometric election in Maine in September. The Democrats had had no real hope in this state, but the resident committee had sent up speakers and $2,500 to keep the Republican majority as small as possible. Then came disaster. The Republicans rolled up a huge vote and freely predicted victory in November.

The smashing Maine defeat aroused various Democrats to intensified effort, for one state might decide the election. Buchanan, determined to overlook nothing, took thought of distant California, whose four votes might be needed. After the Maine election he sent thither a letter reiterating his endorsement of federal aid to a Pacific railroad, deriving the authority from "the Constitutional power 'to declare war'

and the Congressional duty 'to repel invasion.' " This letter
would arrive in time to be useful in California but too late
to be reported back East where it might cause trouble among
the more strict laissez-faire Democrats.

Southern Democrats received news of the Maine debacle
with consternation. To some it spelled the certainty of Frémont's election and the need for preparation for such a
calamity. Governor Wise of Virginia, perhaps further alarmed
by rumors of slave insurrection plots, went immediately into
action. He wrote his fellow Democratic governors of the
South, September 15, of the threat and invited them to an
emergency conference at Raleigh, North Carolina, "to ad-
monish ourselves by joint counsel, of the extraordinary duties
which may devolve upon us from the dangers which so palpably threaten our common peace and safety." Next day he
ordered his militia commanders to get their forces in readiness
and wrote a kinsman: "If Frémont is elected there will be a
revolution." A few days later Senator Mason of Virginia
wrote to a committee in South Carolina that, "in the event
of Frémont's election, the South should not pause but proceed at once to 'immediate, absolute and eternal separation.' "
To a friend he commented: "So I am a candidate for the first
halter."

Just what Wise intended is not too clear. He was a restless,
ambitious man with hopes of the presidency. At any rate,
he did not impress his fellow executives. Some of them, in
fact, feared his move might create hostility and harm Buchanan's chances. So only one, Governor Adams of South
Carolina, bothered to come to Raleigh, and he and Wise
found their North Carolina host, Governor Bragg, very chilly
to the conference. Seemingly Wise had had his trouble for
his pains; yet he had unloosed a devastating idea—southern
secession if the Republican party should ever triumph in a
national election.[2]

In New York City a group of prominent Democrats read
these signs and quaked in their boots—agitation which added
much-needed reenforcement of both the party's finances and
its management. A debt of $20,000 had been piling up, for
only $4,000 was contributed during the first month of the
campaign and it had come from only three sources: Forney
had collected half in Pennsylvania, and Douglas and Corcoran had each given $1,000. The ineffective efforts of the
executive committee headed by Ward had moved Slidell,
Cobb, and Jones to reorganize the high command, with the

aid of a caucus of congressional Democrats. This new group combined the executive and resident committees and constituted Slidell and Ward a subcommittee on finance. Slidell had many business connections in New York, and he with Jones and Faulkner went to Wall Street for $50,000. They had the support of local Hard leaders, like the wealthy Augustus Schell, and enjoyed the energetic aid of that effervescent lawyer, Daniel E. Sickles. They stressed the financial efforts of the Republicans, who were raising money industriously.[8]

The capitalists whom they approached were jittery after an uneasy summer. Many of them favored Fillmore, but it was apparent that he lacked the strength to secure election. Many feared Buchanan because of his Ostend manifesto, which was popularly interpreted as a plan to seize Cuba by force. If he were working for foreign war would he not disrupt the exchanges and trade? On top of this anxiety came the Frémont victory in Maine and Wise's threat of southern revolt—both of which gave the Democratic collection committee a handle to pump. They warned the capitalists that Buchanan was the only means of defeating Frémont, that Pennsylvania's October election must be saved to reverse the trend, that salvation there would cost many thousands of dollars, and that Indiana, also, had an October election.

Time pressed; purses opened slowly. Slidell and his associates of the national committee got numerous influential men, including Schell, S. L. M. Barlow, Royal Phelps, Reuben Withers, James T. Soutter and Watts Sherman, to sign a call for a private conference. September 25 a group of merchants met in Room 1 of the old New York Hotel, organized what came to be called the New York Hotel Committee and pledged themselves to seek $50,000 to win the key states of Pennsylvania and Indiana.[4]

The committee had to confront rival political harvesters in the Wall Street vineyard, for the Republicans proposed to sell Frémont's election as a profitable undertaking. At the very moment when the New York Hotel Committee was organizing, Speaker Banks was addressing an interested throng from the porch of the Merchants' Exchange. Banks was shouting that the South was destroying opportunity for progress and business promotion, and that the filibustering foreign policy of the Democrats was frightening foreign trade.

Banks was so effective that counterattack was imperative. The canny speculator, Robert J. Walker, was engaged by the Democrats to prepare campaign material. The porch of the

Merchants' Exchange was preempted by twelve hundred Democratic merchants, sponsoring an address by ex-Governor John B. Floyd of Virginia, who had New York connections through Robert W. Latham and John C. Mather. Floyd told this throng that New York's strength depended upon the maintenance of the Union, and that southern cotton sales were vital to the exchange on which New York based her business transactions and capital movements.[5]

During the "Wall Street War" frantic pleas reached the New York collectors from Pennsylvania. There the state committee was active despite such delicate obstacles as unfriendliness among Forney and Jones and Ward. The rivals were as one in their importunity, for Pennsylvania's need was indeed great. The New York Hotel Committee managed to send $18,500 over to the Pennsylvania treasurer, George Plitt. That gentleman received also $1,000 from Corcoran and proved himself a man with wide resources, exploiting contacts made with him as a close friend of Buchanan; besides, his wife was an intimate of Harriet Lane, the nominee's niece. For example, Plitt had met at Newport a New England whaler and speculator, W. C. N. Swift, whose wife was related to Mrs. Plitt, and the treasurer agreed to help Swift get contracts at the Navy Department, of course for a percentage, and persuaded Swift, who was an old Whig, to turn Democrat, to give money himself, and to collect contributions from some old Whig associates. Thus, funds came from outside into Pennsylvania for her rescue. Within the state, the officers were assessed three days' pay. The combined total from all sources reached $70,000.

This sum gave scope to Forney's talents; he sent a document into every single home in Philadelphia, which boasted with reason that it was a "city of homes." He incurred heavy bills for printing and organization. Hundreds of foreigners were naturalized, with the help, rumor charged, of naturalization papers issued in blank. A flood of oratory was turned into the state; from Georgia in the person of Howell Cobb, from New England through such spellbinders as Charles Levi Woodbury and Benjamin F. Hallett, from Kentucky through James B. Clay.[6] From the farther Middle West Douglas sent money obtained by selling some of his real estate. He had not visited Buchanan, but they indulged in a gracious exchange of notes, marred only slightly perhaps by the fact that the nominee addressed the Little Giant as "Hon. Samuel A. Douglas." At the same time the Middle West's doubtful state of Indiana was receiving the active attention of Senator Bright.[7]

In October came the great reward. Pennsylvania and Indiana went Democratic, accurately foretelling Buchanan's election three weeks later. The Democrats had won by appealing to the nationalistic and metropolitan attitudes, in which conservatism, order, and opportunity were the treasured concepts. They had likewise spent money, Indiana probably costing half as much as Pennsylvania. Not only had they naturalized the foreign-born liberally, but it was charged that they had colonized voters where most needed, particularly in Pennsylvania, Indiana and Illinois. Buchanan and his sponsors pledged themselves to use all their talents to keep the Democratic party effectively organized, as insurance against the disunion seemingly implicit in a Republican triumph.[8]

III

This first campaign in the new political cycle was marked by portentous new omens. A threat loomed behind the Democratic victory, taking shape in the statistics of the election. Buchanan had carried nineteen of the thirty-one states and 59 per cent of the electors; but he had polled only 45 per cent of the popular vote, Frémont securing 30 and Fillmore 25 per cent. Furthermore, although Fillmore had carried but one state, Maryland, Frémont won eleven with 114 electoral votes, including all the non-slave states save five. In other words, the Republican party had lacked but thirty-five electoral votes of victory. The five states lost in the North were Pennsylvania with twenty-seven votes, New Jersey with seven, Indiana and Illinois with thirteen and eleven respectively, and California with four. If the Republicans could gain but two more states, Pennsylvania and either Indiana or Illinois, the doom of Democratic power was sealed, at least for four years. It mattered naught that the Republicans had no southern wing, there were votes enough in the East and West. And if the Democrats were beaten, what of the future of both party and Union?

Nor were these statistics the only threatening signs. The effort of Governor Wise to organize a southern secession in the event of Republican victory was ominous. If a large section of the nation were to assume the attitude that defeat at an election would destroy the Republic, self-government was in a perilous situation. Furthermore, there are indications that the narrow margin of Buchanan's victory was obtained by fraud in several close states. The use of so much money to carry an election alarmed persons not directly involved who knew of it. Did this new usage mean the inevitable growth of corruption? Was self-government to be manipulated by bribery and graft? Such rottenness boded ill for the future of the great experiment.

Equally significant was the destruction of negation as the safety device of politics, a device which had been painfully adopted during twoscore years of experiment. Those who built the political machinery which ran the national parties had learned that in a country as large as the United States and constantly growing, success could be most surely obtained on a negative platform. So varied were the attitudes that positive attention to any major interest would draw down the opposition of the others and court defeat. The Democrats had been the first to learn this, and when they came to write their platforms in the thirties they chose two ideas admirably suited to this purpose, laissez faire regarding controversial domestic issues and a spread-eagle foreign policy attractive to most interests. Also they had abandoned obvious leadership in the executive. After Jackson's retirement, they had suffered no leader to become President.

Their opponents had not learned quite so easily. Under Clay's guidance the National Republicans and the Whigs had tried a positive program, an American system, only to meet defeat. Their accidental and short-lived successes had been won with hand-picked "heroes" like Harrison and Taylor, who in no sense led the party, and who were given no platform at all. Thus both Democrats and Whigs had abandoned positive programs.

However, in 1856 it was apparent that political wheels had been turning furiously and had carried partisanship into strange and more dangerous paths. A new aggregation, the Republican party, had emerged with a new type of platform. It had abandoned any attempt at compromise or the use of phrases of universal acceptance. It deliberately sought to capitalize the divisive attitudes, to organize the antisouthern sentiment in platoons to follow the banners of free soil and destruction of southern power. Its direct approach forced the Democratic party into destructive ambiguity.

The Democratic platform made at Cincinnati contained a formula over which the chairman, Benjamin F. Hallett, had struggled as hard as he had four years before over the language accepting the Compromise of 1850. The new plank pledged the party to popular sovereignty but not until the statehood stage. "We recognize the right of the people of all the territories, including Kansas and Nebraska, acting through the legally and fairly expressed will of a majority of actual residents, and whenever the number of their inhabitants justifies it, to form a Constitution, with or without domestic slavery, and be admitted into the Union upon terms of perfect equality with the other states." [9]

Three times during the campaign Buchanan had expressed his whole-hearted approval of the Democratic platform. But he had interpreted the territorial plank in two different ways. In June he had told the notification committee that the people of the territories were "perfectly free to form and regulate their domestic institutions in their own way." He not only endorsed the platform but quoted Douglas's own language from the Kansas-Nebraska bill. In October, however, when a throng gathered at Wheatland to celebrate the Indiana and Pennsylvania victories, he retreated to Hallett's position: that the party pledged popular sovereignty only at the statehood stage. Buchanan's phrase was, "when about to enter the Union as a State." He followed with a rhetorical question: "Who contest the principle that the will of the majority shall govern? What genuine republican of any party can deny this?" [10] Unfortunately there were those of the South who could and would.

The formula of popular sovereignty was ambiguous, and in 1856 it officially meant what Buchanan said it meant in his last utterance. But in northern states Democratic orators had been busy showing that it was a safeguard of freedom. Under it, said they, migrants from the free states, who could always move in greater numbers, would go to the territories and invariably make them free. Slave states could no more be admitted under this doctrine than they could under the Republican free-soil dogmas. News of this form of double talk filtered into the South, raising many a question there. Was the idea of the will of the majority, "the original and pure fountain of political power," to be used to deprive the South of rights of property in the territories? Was it not just as dangerous to their future power and safety as the "sentence of outlawry" contained in the Republican platform? Could the South have faith in the Democratic party? Was Buchanan to be trusted? If southerners had known how much money the victory cost they would have raised yet more suspicious queries. As it was they were none too sure that the election of Buchanan was the right answer.

PART II

THE LEADERSHIP FAILS

Chapter 4

Reorganizing the High Command

THE DEMOCRATIC victory of 1856 settled nothing. A four-year truce had been established only to form the lines for a greater conflict, that of 1860. The Republicans had shown phenomenal energy before the decision; now they had even greater reason for exertion. The Democrats knew their margin was slight, the loss of two more states would mean disaster four years hence. The new administration must prevent their opponents from gaining any further advantage.

Buchanan must re-form the ranks of a divided party. He had been nominated because he represented the conservative attitudes; but he had been elected only because certain divisive groups, like the radical exponents of southernism, had supported him. His was the task of keeping intact a party in danger of splitting into two opposing factions.

Buchanan's known conservative tendencies caused the spokesmen of the radical southern element to lose no time after the election in serving notice upon him that they must be recognized generously. They came forward with their demands immediately. Through their press they started an educational campaign which was widely noticed by other editors. The *Charleston Mercury,* the organ of the South Carolina radicals edited by Robert Barnwell Rhett, and the *New Orleans Delta,* reputed to be the mouthpiece of Jefferson Davis, took the lead. The South would neither agree to any policies, nor accept any party leadership, that failed to emphasize full protection for southern rights. The only way to preserve the Union was to leave the South in a position to prevent an antisouthern triumph.[1] The *Mercury* even went so far as to suggest a new federal constitution with guarantees for southern safety. Rhett's alternative was secession and the formation of a southern confederacy. The South would not accept minority status.[2]

The radical organs took the lead in demanding aggressive attempts to secure more slave states and acquire more slave territory so that the balance between the slave and free states might be restored. Various schemes were afoot for increasing southern power. The proslavery group in Kansas was arranging to draft a proslavery constitution for the new state they hoped to create. Buchanan was urged not to interpose any insistence that their work be submitted to the voters.[3] Others realized that the preponderance of free-state people in Kansas made that scheme hopeless and began to plan for acquisition of Nicaragua, Cuba, and northern Mexico. General Quitman was reported to be seeking recruits, particularly from the discouraged fire-eaters in Kansas, to join him in a filibustering expedition to Nicaragua. Also to spread its system, the South needed more and cheaper slaves, and in his annual message that November the governor of South Carolina called for the reopening of the slave trade. In December this was debated at a southern commercial convention in Savannah, and a committee was appointed to report on it at the next gathering.[4]

These editorial writers and political spokesmen were none too confident of Buchanan and the northern wing. They knew how the free-state Democrats had interpreted squatter sovereignty. They had heard that Buchanan had told summer visitors he was not in favor of the extension of slavery and he believed Kansas was destined to be free.[5] Some of them, including even the President elect's friend Wise, had not liked the letter the candidate had written to California, endorsing the Pacific railroad project. Wise chid him for encouraging a "corrupt Yazoo speculation," and vowed to block Corcoran's great financial schemes.[6] Southern apprehension was further increased by bad news from Kansas. Trouble had broken out there again, and Pierce had removed Chief Justice Lecompte, a southerner, at Governor Geary's insistence; this move was violently denounced.

Southern radicals were watching Buchanan's every step, but he realized this was no time to satisfy them; to adopt the program of Rhett and the radicals would lose the party that small margin of votes in the key northern states needed to remain in power. Buchanan saw his duty plainly. He must build an administration that would conserve the party strength and stop the Republican advance. He must seek conservative, national, Union-loving men, who had public confidence. He must encourage national attitudes and simple, harmless formulas which would mark the Democratic party as the party of "safety." As he wrote to Justice Grier,[7] he must "destroy the dangerous slavery agitation . . . strengthen the Democratic Party . . . and thus restore peace to our distracted country." He was confident that he had the situation well in hand, and when the Franklin and Marshall College faculty and students trudged the mile out from Lancaster to congratulate him on his victory, he told them that the object of his administration "would be to destroy any sectional party —North or South—to harmonize all sections of the Union under a national and conservative government, as it was fifty years ago." [8] He would turn back the clock.

II

The immediate scene of Buchanan's labors was his pleasant mansion, Wheatland, just outside Lancaster. To this Mecca hundreds flocked to see him, to advise him, and to ask place of him. It was sixty-eight miles, i.e., three hours, west of Philadelphia as the trains steamed. The pleasant little county seat was surrounded by prosperous farms of numerous comfortable Pennsylvania Germans; the land was fat. Its main thoroughfare, Queen Street, ran through a public square flanked by a courthouse decorated in the Corinthian order. The visitors found numerous hotels, and discovered that it was a region noted for its gastronomic delights. Here were The Grapes, Bear's House, Trout's Tavern and—to Buchanan's taste finest of all—Michael's, where he declared could be had the "nicest dinner in the world." His visitors found him either at Wheatland or at Michael's. Many of them he invited to his table, which was a mighty one, for he was a valiant trencherman. Nor was he loath to lead the way to the sideboard where decanters and bottles of varying potencies stood in bold array. He relished their contents and was never affected thereby, so hard a head had he. Occasionally those who knew him best were bidden for the night. But with this gracious hospitality they must be content; for his confidence he would not share with them. He could keep his own counsel better than most men, and he exulted in this unusual power. It gave him keen pleasure to keep the political world guessing.

Though he gave his thought to none he sought to learn from many. While he had few close friends he had a multitude of acquaintances and numerous hangers-on. Two were particularly close to him in these months of planning. Needing a confidential secretary and agent to assist on patronage and other pressing business, he summoned John Appleton of Maine, a forty-four-year-old editor and Congressman, who had been his chief clerk in the State Department and his secretary in London. Buchanan trusted him implicitly and believed that everyone who knew Appleton loved him.[9] Appleton arrived in Wheatland within a fortnight after the election, and remained constantly at Buchanan's right hand in the busy weeks that followed.

The other intimate was his old-time henchman, John W. Forney, now thirty-nine. This unstable, energetic, voluble, and versatile newspaperman had adopted Buchanan twenty years before, and had made the political advance of the elder statesman his religion. In season and out, Forney had managed to push his patron's advantage (and his own), and in the year 1856 no one had been more active than he. He assumed leadership in that great drive which saved Pennsylvania to the Democracy and insured Buchanan's election. He was in and out of Lancaster continually and liked to be considered as the President elect's confidant, although he knew less of his patron's purposes than the world at large gave him credit for. Buchanan found him both useful and trying, for Forney would drink and talk, and always had much advice to give.

Two other Pennsylvanians were much at Wheatland. One more trusted than Forney was Jehu Glancy Jones, the middle-aged Berks County Congressman who did confidential errands for the President elect in Washington. Jones had been an Episcopal clergyman with a parish in the South before entering politics, and enjoyed the confidence of southerners as few northerners could. The third Pennsylvanian in the group was Senator William Bigler, from the center of the state. He was a plain, plodding politician who in certain characteristics, such as dullness, ponderosity, and dogged industry, resembled Buchanan. The latter did not hold him in high regard; in fact for years they had been on bad terms. Bigler, however, had a shrewd sense of possibilities and early in 1856 had sought reconciliation. That fall Buchanan found it convenient, in fact essential, to use him without trusting him much, because the President elect had no relations whatever with the other Pennsylvania Senator, Richard Brodhead. Indeed Buchanan was hoping that Brodhead might be succeeded by Judge Jeremiah S. Black, a long-time friend from Somerset County.

Buchanan depended a good deal upon a few friends from other states. Senators Slidell and Bright were in constant touch with him, particularly the former. These men were realists who had few romantic notions about politics. They supported Buchanan because they thought he would organize a conservative administration. Less hard-boiled was Governor Wise of Virginia, who was a friend in need at this time when so many of the southern radicals were aloof and critical; but he was also erratic and hard to handle. These men, with Appleton and the Pennsylvanians, were to keep their ears to the ground, to circulate among their fellow politicos, and to bring back information and advice. Both were sorely needed, for the situation was full of conflict and confusion. As will soon be seen, Buchanan must choose from among many hard choices.

The President elect was looking for a cabinet representative of all sections but not all attitudes, for he knew full well how Pierce had suffered from dividing patronage among all shades of opinion. Buchanan would invite only conservatives, and his determination soon passed along the grapevine. The burning question became, *which* conservatives to choose from each section.

Selection of cabinet members representing the South proved extremely difficult. When Congress assembled in Washington, December 1, rumor said the first place—the State Department —would go to a southern Union man, probably Congressman Howell Cobb of Georgia. Cobb had been very effective in the recent campaign, because he was one of the relatively few southerners who would come North and talk eloquently, and convincingly, in a manner indicating that love of Union still existed in the South. In Pennsylvania and Indiana, during those crucial October days, he had spoken very effectively, even holding forth for an hour and a half in a northern Pennsylvania snowstorm. No sooner had he arrived in Washington from Georgia than he was approached by both Forney and Jones to learn whether he would accept a cabinet post. Not particularly anxious to leave Congress, he replied that he would consider only the State Department.[10]

The probability of Cobb's appointment became one of those fixed facts that unauthorized rumor so firmly establishes, and it immediately aroused the more radical southerners. In their newly acquired, exaggerated assertiveness they scorned to accept the Unionist, Cobb, in a major position, or a minor place as their own allotment. Their candidate for first place was Robert J. Walker, Secretary of the Treasury in Polk's administration, expansionist and prince of speculators; as Secretary of State he would seek the new territory which southern interests demanded. Numerous southern senators— including Jefferson Davis, Clay and Fitzpatrick of Alabama, and Iverson of Georgia pushed him; and Douglas soon joined them. Also he was urged by such New York City operators as Daniel E. Sickles and John A. Dix; "Young America," in the person of George N. Sanders, untiringly advocated Walker, arranging convivial dinners where he could meet men like Toombs, who enjoyed hilarity.[11]

Cautious Buchanan naturally could not warm to the speculating Walker, despite his intersectional backing. Searching elsewhere, the President elect invited first Governor Wise and then Senator Slidell; both preferred to keep the jobs they had and both recommended other persons. Wise, and the Virginia members of the electoral college, proposed one of their own number, John B. Floyd, who was perhaps less addicted to southernism than Wise.[12]

To Slidell's recommendations Buchanan listened most earnestly, threading with him the labyrinthine maze of antebellum politics, as they sat closeted together at McKibben's Merchants Hotel in Philadelphia that December. Without the door to their chamber strutted Forney as doorkeeper and "fixer" who summoned or turned away the favored and the unfortunate. Among the many they considered was Aaron V. Brown, Polk's former law partner, who was urged by the Tennessee electors. Another was Jacob Thompson of Mississippi, a former Washington messmate of Buchanan and a friend to some of Slidell's New Orleans interests. A third was Judah P. Benjamin, Slidell's colleague in the Senate, who was important as symbolizing Whig support in the recent Buchanan victory.

Cabinet choices from the Northwest and New England were no less difficult. In the Northwest the Bright-Douglas feud spelled caution. Bright, up for reelection to the Senate in January, wished a cabinet office if he were defeated. Douglas wanted recognition given his lieutenant, William A. Richardson, recently defeated for governor of Illinois, and also his Missouri henchman, Judge Samuel Treat of the anti-Benton faction. To choose between these meant trouble. There was, however, a path to safety. If Buchanan took General Lewis Cass, who was about to be turned out of the Senate by Michigan Republicans, Douglas would acquiesce in relief that Bright was out, and Bright himself would be satisfied. The rub was that Buchanan and Cass never had "got along"; Cass was aged, inefficient and was a British-baiter. How could Buchanan settle British difficulties with this obese, almost senile, Anglophobe in his cabinet? For the New England appointment the President elect was considering former as-

sociates in Polk's cabinet, Nathan Clifford of Maine and
Isaac Toucey of Connecticut; the latter was pressed by the
Pierce men as their best hope for recognition in the new
regime.[13]

III

Making a cabinet was but one of Buchanan's responsibilities. He and the party leaders had also to rewrite the policies
and propaganda of the party in the light of changed conditions. The old, faction-rent Democracy must meet the challenge of the young, vigorous Republicans, and of a radical
southern press, at one and the same time. It must revise its
propaganda to appeal to all who feared radicalism, whether
southern or Republican. Buchanan must write an inaugural
and look to the press.

While pondering his inaugural Buchanan sought to repair
his press fences, for, while the Republicans had a very able
and aggressive press led by Greeley and the *Tribune,* Democratic journalism was in a sad state of confusion. The largest
and most influential party paper, Bennett's *New York Herald,*
had bolted Buchanan for Frémont. The most vigorous southern papers, the *Mercury,* the *Delta,* and even Wise's *Richmond Enquirer,* were very much involved in the southern
revolt. Worse, the *Washington Union,* the so-called official
"organ," was without effective editorial management; the campaign arrangement, whereby prominent Democrats like Slidell
and Cobb had helped edit it, could only be temporary.

Buchanan's first task was to get Bennett back into the fold.
Knowing that this editorial prima donna was not noted for
supporting lost causes, Buchanan wrote some conciliatory
letters—by way of lowering the steps to the bandwagon—
and Bennett promptly climbed aboard.[14]

Finding a new editor for the *Washington Union* was not
going to be so easy, for it had been a party headache for ten
years, ever since Polk had driven Frank Blair from its sanctum. The trouble was that this so-called organ was not self-
supporting and had been financed by the profits from two
separate businesses—the official printing of the House and
Senate. As long as the editor and owner of the paper, and the
official printers, were one and the same person or several
persons in on a deal, the paper and printers could be nicely
supported by the excess from the extravagant profits charged
for the official printing.

But Buchanan faced a weird combination. The Democratic henchmen elected as printers by House and Senate had sublet their perquisites to an amazing politician-printer, Cornelius Wendell, an ex-Whig lately turned Republican. He had come down from Albany some ten years previously to employ his talents at arrangements in printing, money-making, and bipartisan alliance and had amassed a fortune thereby. Some of it he had invested in a superb printing plant, in which he was wont to do official printing as subcontractor when not elected printer. Some he used to purchase half-ownership of the *Union*. Owner of the other half was Alfred O. P. Nicholson of Tennessee, the Democratic printer of the Senate. The bipartisan Wendell and Nicholson agreed to accept any editor whom Buchanan should name and appointed J. Glancy Jones, the President's close friend, to act for them in making a contract.

Buchanan was embarrassed because Forney, whose half-interest in the *Union* Wendell had bought, wanted to be editor again. His powerful enemies, the Virginia Senators and Bennett, protested so vigorously that Buchanan dared not gratify Forney and chose his campaign aide, John Appleton. He was to be editor, and Wendell, who was scheduled to buy out Nicholson's share of the paper, was to pay him the munificent salary of $6,000, the salary of a justice of the Supreme Court. In return Appleton, when elected printer of both houses, was to sublet the work to Wendell on a percentage. Both would be enriched. At this time Wendell seemed to be a party convenience, but the leaders were to rue the confidence they so unwisely placed in this Republican marplot.[15]

While reorganizing the machinery of party publicity, Buchanan had to consider what doctrines should be publicized. The main party tenet, popular sovereignty, remained as ambiguous as during the campaign, when Buchanan himself had juggled it. Northern Democrats had proclaimed that the first settlers in a territory, through their first legislature, could exclude slavery. Southern Democrats vociferously denied this; only when the territory was ready for statehood and came to make its state constitution could it take such action. Both factions were painfully aware of this swearing on both sides and wanted clarification. The northern partisans were so hard pressed that they felt it a life-and-death issue, while the southern branch knew that a northern interpretation would give potent weapons to the Americans. Both sides were demanding a pronouncement from Buchanan in his inaugural.

He was inclined to adopt the southern version; the issue was explosive.

So certain prominent Democrats in Washington sought means to free Buchanan from the necessity of handling this stick of political dynamite, and a new idea emerged. Alexander H. Stephens of Georgia, who had been Democratic leader in the House and undoubtedly would continue in that post, believed that the Supreme Court might well remove the controversy from the political arena. He was not alone in this opinion. Bigler had talked with Douglas and found he agreed that the ambiguity was a judicial question. The opportunity for such disposal seemed providentially at hand, for a case was before the Supreme Court, brought by the Republicans, which the Democrats might turn to account. They suggested to Buchanan that under the circumstances he might omit the planned insertion from his inaugural, and leave the question to the highest tribunal. He immediately saw the value of such an evasion. He knew that Stephens was exerting "all the influences [he] could bring to bear" to get the Supreme Court to decide "the case on the Missouri restriction." Stephens undoubtedly could confer with his fellow Georgian, James M. Wayne, associate justice on that bench.

The litigation in question was the Dred Scott case, soon to become famous. Dred Scott was a Missouri slave who, strangely enough, while ostensibly the property of John F. A. Sanford, at that time really belonged to Buchanan's friend Barlow. Under Republican auspices he was suing for his freedom, on the ground that a one-time residence in Iowa Territory, where slavery was prohibited by the Missouri Compromise, had emancipated him. His suit involved the constitutionality of the Missouri Compromise, if the court chose to cover all its ramifications, and the Compromise might involve squatter sovereignty. Consequently, if the tribunal should pass on the Compromise, it might also rule on the question whether Congress, or territorial legislatures, had the right to interfere with slavery in the territories. The Democratic leaders then were sufficiently naïve to believe that if the court adopted the southern interpretation of the question the rest of the nation would accept it and quietly cease agitation. As the court of nine justices included seven Democrats, five of them southern, the probability of a southern interpretation was high.[16] But would the court speak in time to relieve Buchanan of the responsibility? That remained to be seen.

IV

While the badgered President elect struggled with publicity and propaganda, with his inaugural in the back of his mind, he continued to grapple with cabinet and patronage. These questions were complicated by his decision regarding the *Washington Union,* on which Forney was so bitter that he was about to upset the applecart in Pennsylvania. Buchanan realized he must do something, and Forney had a second choice; if he could not be the journalistic spokesman, he would like to be Buchanan's mouthpiece in the Senate. Therefore he asked for Senator Brodhead's seat, which the legislature was about to fill.

Buchanan had planned to support his friend Black for this position but recognized the force of Forney's claim and after some hesitation agreed to it. Unluckily, he proved clumsy at this type of interference. He wrote a letter to one legislator, he sent word to others by messenger and talked to those who came to see him. Some said he used promises of patronage, especially to get rivals of Forney to withdraw. Unfortunately a small bloc of Democrats from the western part of the commonwealth refused to take Forney and thus gave an arch manipulator his chance. Simon Cameron, once a Democratic Senator from Pennsylvania, now a member of the "Opposition party," was quick to seize an opportunity. He still had a small personal following among the Democratic legislators, and three of them in January joined the Opposition members to elect Cameron over Forney. This defeat, after he had interfered, made Buchanan feel that he had lost face.[17]

This blow to his prestige came at a time when he was having particular trouble with his cabinet making. After Appleton went to Washington to close the *Union* deal he had reported much southern sentiment favoring the inclusion of J. Glancy Jones in the cabinet. Also he and Forney had persuaded Cobb to reconsider his refusal to accept anything but the State Department; Cobb had agreed that Cass had prior claims and he would give place to him, but to him only. Buchanan therefore thought to give Cobb the second post as Secretary of the Treasury and another to Jones as pleasing to the South.[18] He also expected to follow the endorsement of the Virginia electors and take Floyd.

These prospective decisions raised a row with the Hunter faction in Virginia and with Forney. The Hunter men did not relish this Wise-Floyd alliance with a direct line into the White House. Senator Hunter had ambitions for 1860, so his friends now put him forward for the State Department, hoping to win Wise's approval by proposing him for the Senate. Forney was stung almost to frenzy by his own senatorial defeat and by the possibility of cabinet appointments for his old enemies, Jones and Hunter. He went off on a violent rampage of cabinet making. He wanted a place there himself; if he couldn't be editor or senator he wanted a department. If he could not go into the Administration Jones must not. Nor must Hunter; against him, Forney rushed to support Robert J. Walker. Poor pregnant Mrs. Forney wrote Buchanan a pitiful appeal, asking the Post Office Department for her now generally inebriated spouse who, she wrote, could neither eat nor sleep.[19]

Buchanan, suffering from Forney's defeat, at last decided that he had better go to Washington himself. He could not let people there believe that Forney's rages were representations of his will. For a few days he was delayed by a tremendous blizzard which isolated Lancaster, but when traffic was opened January 26 he proceeded to the capital, where he registered at the National Hotel run by his old Lancaster friend, John Guy. He was entertained at dinner by President Pierce, attended a reception at the White House, and talked with many. He made inquiries about General Cass's health. He saw Cobb and Douglas and heard the latter's tirade against Bright and his insistence that Walker was the man to head the cabinet. Douglas concluded from this interview that Buchanan had consulted him only as a formal courtesy, and that his wishes were not to be considered. In fact Buchanan was not impressed. He had definite ideas about seniority and its privileges, born in his own obsequious youth. Douglas must not presume too much, even though he had just married a Washington belle and was preparing to cut a social swath. He later heard from Slidell that Douglas was morbid and resentful, ready to "run amuck" because he was left out of Buchanan's counsels. Here may be marked the beginning of a most fateful antagonism.[20]

A second disastrous result of this visit was physical rather than political. The capital had been gripped by a terrific cold wave accompanying the blizzard, and the weather had wrought havoc. Guy's National Hotel had suffered from the unusual cold. The plumbing had frozen, and the sewage system had been stopped up. The result was that the waste backed up and contaminated kitchen and pantry. Soon the kitchen help were either sick or active carriers of disease, and many of the guests became ill from infected food. The most prominent symptom of these illnesses was a persistent and debilitating diarrhea which would not yield to the unskilled treatment of the day. The cause, as well as the cure, was quite beyond the medicos, who divided over whether miasmic vapors from the bad sewage or arsenic poison was laying everyone low. Some thought it was a poison plot of discharged servants or of abolitionists who wanted to wipe out the Democratic leadership. This "National Hotel disease" attacked no less a one than James Buchanan, and it was long before he could rid himself of the plague which troubled him constantly in the trying months that followed. Dysentery was hardly an advantage when organizing an administration in the midst of troublous times.[21]

V

Buchanan had used his unhappy Washington visit for still another purpose which helped to bring catastrophe upon him. He had discussed his pronouncement on popular sovereignty, becoming more impressed by the possibility of the Supreme Court taking the responsibility. He talked it over with at least one member of the court, his long-time friend, Judge Catron of Tennessee. On his return home he wrote Catron, February 3, a letter which may have been agreed upon in Washington, one which the justice might show his colleagues. It contained a simple inquiry whether the Dred Scott case was to be decided before March 4. Catron replied promptly that nothing had as yet been done. Taney had not brought it up, partly at least because a tragedy in Judge Daniel's family had interrupted the court's deliberations; Mrs. Daniel's gown had caught fire as she dressed for a party and she had burned to death. Catron felt, however, that Buchanan should know "whether and when" the matter was to be adjudicated, and wrote again February 10. He revealed that the case would be decided the 14th, but without canvassing the question of the rights of slave property in the territories. This was cold comfort to Buchanan.

Within the next week politics broke out in the Supreme Court and changed the situation, moving Catron to write Buchanan again, February 19, relating a strange story. As the judge had anticipated, the court had taken up the Dred Scott case in conference and a majority had decided to dispose of it with a mere statement that the court would not assume jurisdiction, thus leaving Scott in slavery as the Missouri courts had ruled. But this was not the final disposition of the case. The two minority judges, Curtis and McLean, determined to file elaborate dissenting opinions justifying the Republican contention that Congress had full power to control slavery in territories. This platform writing aroused Judge Wayne of Georgia, who may well have been talking to Stephens. He argued that such partisanship must be met; if the minority were going to discuss congressional power, the majority should counter their arguments, not avoid the issue.

Wayne's proposal found the majority in an embarrassing position. Six of the seven believed that the Missouri Compromise was unconstitutional; but to say so would involve several of them in inconsistency with former reasoning, and Wayne and Campbell would have to reverse themselves. Also they were not all agreed as to the grounds of unconstitutionality and the northern Democratic members—Grier and Nelson— were particularly anxious to avoid anything that looked like politics, especially to southern advantage. Despite these obstacles, Catron reported that the "political" attitude of Curtis and McLean had won over Campbell, Daniel, and Taney to Wayne's proposal that the majority incorporate, in their opinion upholding the Missouri court, a dictum that Congress did not have power over slavery in the territories and that the Missouri Compromise was unconstitutional. Catron would join them on the latter premise. He believed that the Compromise was void because the Louisiana Purchase treaty guaranteed slavery in that region; but he held that Congress did have power over slavery in the other territories. Thus a bare majority of five would agree to half of Wayne's proposition— that the Compromise was unconstitutional; but only a minority of four judges (all southerners) would accept Wayne's other half—that Congress did not have power over slavery in the territories—as an attempt to undermine the Republican contention.

Catron's letter to Buchanan summed up the unhappy situation by stating that the five, "forced up to this point by two dissentients," would declare the Compromise unconstitutional; but the case would be much stronger if either Grier of Pennsylvania or Nelson of New York would join them. Here he thought Buchanan might help: "Will you drop Grier a line, saying how necessary it is—and how good the opportunity is, to settle the agitation by an affirmative decision of the Supreme Court, the one way or the other?" Buchanan hastened to seek this way out; Grier was a fellow Pennsylvanian who owed his place on the bench to Buchanan's refusal to accept it when Polk had offered to appoint him. He wrote Grier explaining what an opportunity this was to settle the slavery agitation. He did not reveal his knowledge of the inside situation in the Court.

Grier was impressed. He seemingly had been ignorant of much of the politics going on around him and went to Wayne and Taney with Buchanan's letter. He was now convinced, he said, that the peace of the country demanded a nonsectional decision, and therefore he was ready to concur with them and would endeavor to persuade Daniel, Campbell, and Catron to do likewise, not knowing that they needed no persuasion. He reported this to Buchanan, giving him much of the history of the court's difficulties and assuring him of at least six "who will decide the compromise law of 1820 to be of non-effect." He concluded, "We have thought it due to you to state to you in candor and confidence the real state of the matter."

Buchanan's, therefore, may well have been the deciding voice that determined the fateful Dred Scott decision. Had he not written to Grier, the latter might not have concurred; and had he not concurred, the five southern judges not in agreement on fundamentals might have finally refused to issue the dictum. Buchanan always had desired to be a member of the Supreme Court; in this instance he practically participated in their deliberations and influenced their judgment. As a result he could now dodge the issue in his inaugural; yet, as Taney's health would prevent a pronouncement by the court before March 4, he was embarrassed as to just what to say. For the time being he left the decision unmade.[22]

VI

While Buchanan was corresponding on the Dred Scott case the advance of the days was a continual prod to him to finish his cabinet work; as his illness still hung on, his constitutional indecision was aggravated. But the way began to open, for Bright came to see him, reelected to the Senate and now quite out of the cabinet race. They discussed the northwestern situation. Bright defended himself against Douglas's complaints and urged the appointment of Cass who, as anticipated, had just been defeated. Probably this visit was what Buchanan needed to make up his mind.[23]

Through J. Glancy Jones he told Cass's friend, Nicholson, that Cass could be premier, if he accepted humiliating conditions. He could not have his son-in-law, Ledyard, upon whom

he depended, as his assistant. Buchanan would appoint John
Appleton to that position to guide the ancient politico's feeble
hand. Also Cass must surrender his anti-British prejudices.
In other words he would have the honor but must consent to
constant supervision. These conditions Buchanan embodied in
a letter which Slidell and Bright took to Cass. When the terms
were read to him he seemed overjoyed and accepted hungrily.
He would not now have to return to Detroit under the cloud
of defeat. His agreement to the stipulations was duly sent to
Buchanan, and the empty honor became his.[24]

This decision freed the President elect to dispose of the
South. He settled on Cobb for the Treasury, despite determined and continuous opposition from southern radicals who
had espoused Francis W. Pickens of South Carolina after
Walker became hopeless. They could not move Buchanan;
Cobb was to have it. Floyd, as Virginia's choice, got the War
Department. Buchanan sent letters to all these appointees
February 21.[25] Buchanan proceeded to attempt to placate
southerners further with the Post Office and Interior Departments, since they had complained loudly when Pierce gave
these posts to northerners. They had been particularly dissatisfied at the way James Campbell had run the Post Office,
cutting off many of their rural routes because they did not
pay. Southerners also feared lest speculation might influence
the head of the Interior Department to push swift development of western regions into free states; Pierce's secretary had
not yielded to these influences but some other northern man
might. So Aaron V. Brown of Tennessee and Jacob Thompson
of Mississippi were allotted the Post Office and Interior.
Brown was openhanded and generous; he would not shut off
poorly paying routes. Thompson was dour and closefisted; he
would not yield an acre to speculators. Both were firm adherents of southernism, but they were not of the fire-eating
school.

The invitations to Cass and the four southerners left but
two places remaining, the Navy Secretaryship and the Attorney Generalship. But there were three interests which Buchanan yearned to favor: the old Whigs, the Middle States,
and New England. In view of the preponderance of southern
representation already accepted, Buchanan reluctantly gave up
appointing the former Whig, Senator Benjamin of Louisiana.
He proposed to take Jones of Pennsylvania and Clifford of
Maine.

This stirred several hornets' nests. Forney vetoed Jones, and

the Pierce Administration insisted upon Toucey instead of
Clifford. So effectively did Forney marshal Jones's Pennsylvania enemies that Buchanan yielded to them. He next inclined
to substitute Black for Jones, as Attorney General; but he must
first get from Jones a release from a promise given him that
no Pennsylvanian should enter the cabinet if he did not. Jones,
suffering from the National Hotel disease, finally released
Buchanan, but would not be comforted with the Mission to
Berlin. Further, his southern friends said that if he were
dropped their other friend, Toucey of Connecticut, must be
taken instead of Clifford, for the Navy Department. These
arguments raged so long that the Navy and the Attorney Generalship, like the inaugural, were still unsettled when Buchanan
left for Washington March 2.[26]

At Washington Buchanan would find a situation which
boded ill for him and his party. The atmosphere in the capital
city was foul with suspicion and distrust. The fire-eater Edmund Ruffin dined at one of the southern headquarters there
on February 17, as a guest of the famous mess where Senators
Hunter, Mason, and Butler and Congressmen Goode and
Garnett dwelt. Their talk was pessimistic, and he recorded in
his diary that enough was said to make him think that Buchanan had "very little of the respect or the confidence of
the men from the South by whose support alone he was
sustained and elected. I anticipate for him a reign that will
bring him but little of either pleasure or honor. The victory
in the election . . . such as it was, was gained by the southern
states and the democratic party, as I inferred, only because
Buchanan was a Pennsylvanian and had the vote of his state
because of favor and not because of their approval . . . it was
repeated today, that enormous sums of money were sent
from the city of New York and a good deal also from the
democrats of New England to buy votes in Pennsylvania, and
which turned the vote in that state. The victory over Frémont
and abolitionism if thus gained by bribery, is worth less than
I had before estimated."[27] Ruffin two days later heard an
investigating committee ask the House of Representatives to
expel four Republican members, for corruption. The
Republican-controlled House had had to set up the committee
because of charges published by the *New York Times;* and its
two Democratic members had shown no lack of zeal.

Testimony under oath indicated that some of the Congressmen accepted money and land for their votes, with a regular
scale of charges according to types of influence. With them

lobbyists were allied, in pushing or retarding bills or specific items of appropriations. Their joint racket was to spread the idea that legislation required bribery, and to introduce "nuisance" bills, or oppose legitimate bills, in order to be paid for killing or for not opposing them. Their racket enriched the lobbyists—who were hired as "experts" to put the cash into the right pockets—no less than the legislators. Three accused Congressmen resigned—one of these being also expelled—and on the fourth the House voted the evidence inconclusive.[28]

The Georgia member of the committee told his colleague, Cobb: "I had no idea that I was in such a den of damned thieves." The future Secretary of the Treasury rejoiced that "so far no democrat or southern man has been implicated" and hoped that none would be.[29] The Democrats claimed that the Republicans had brought corruption to Washington, conveniently forgetting that graft seldom is absent from government. Could the Democrats drive it out? Or were they a bit tainted themselves? Buchanan had the misfortune to assume control of the national government when both he and Congress lacked public confidence and lay under somewhat heavy clouds of suspicion.

VII

The morning of March 2 dawned cold and cheerless at Lancaster. It had been snowing most of the night, and now a bitter wind was blowing. At six, the church bells began to peal, for it was to be a great day for the town and the people must be up betimes. James Buchanan was at length to bid farewell to his fellow citizens, and they wanted to do him honor. By seven the rosetted and bescarfed marshals began to appear on horseback and directed the Lancaster Fencibles and the motley citizenry to form a procession. Out on West King Street they marched at quickstep to overcome the cold, preceded by the band in a wagon. Music seemed to be a good livener; but it soon ceased, for it was too cold to play and a number of bandsmen preferred walking to freezing. At the head of West King Street the populace had expected to meet the President elect; but he was not there, and rather than stand in the icy breeze they set forth on the Marietta Pike to Wheatland. There they discovered that Buchanan was still engaged in last-minute details. He hastily greeted the throng and returned to the business of departure, or was it to finish his breakfast?

At last the family carriage came around from the barn; the

crowd pressed close, almost too close for the coachman's comfort. As the house door opened for the last time Buchanan, his niece, the charming Harriet Lane, his nephew, efficient and self-sufficient J. Buchanan Henry, and his housekeeper, Miss Hetty Parker, entered the carriage. They were off, to the relief of the shivering crowd, and before long they had passed through the town to the railroad station where the special train provided by Buchanan's friend, Joseph Baker, superintendent of the State road, waited. A private car had been specially prepared, decorated with stained-glass windows picturing Wheatland and Lancaster scenes. A great cheer, much hand-shaking and at last the train was off, but not until several pickpockets had done their work.

At Baltimore, another reception was in readiness; but his dysentery made Buchanan decline the sumptuous—and lengthy—banquet. He pushed on to Washington on the three o'clock train and arrived before he was expected. As the party drove from the depot, the horses became frightened and started to bolt. Only the presence of mind of a young man on the box with the coachman, who jumped on the back of one of the horses and pulled him up, prevented what might have been a fatal accident. Shortly after this mishap Buchanan alighted at Guy's National Hotel, to stay for two days and nights. Slidell and Bigler had tried to place him elsewhere, but he stubbornly refused to desert his fellow Lancastrian; besides, he didn't see how he could be any worse. Guy ran up the flag so that Washington might know the President elect was a guest—at his hotel.[30]

Down the Avenue the Thirty-fourth Congress was in its final hours, revising the tariff and passing the large appropria-tion bills. The prospective cabinet members, senators, and others hastened to Guy's to talk inaugural and appointments; far into the night and all the long next day they conferred and counseled. Buchanan could not make up his mind on his cabinet vacancies and left them unfilled. But on the refer-ence to the Dred Scott case in the inaugural he reached a decision. He would say that the territorial question was now, "happily, a matter of but little practical importance," because the Supreme Court would "speedily and finally" decide it. "To their decision, in common with all good citizens I shall cheerfully submit, whatever this may be." A safe promise for Buchanan with his foreknowledge.

Cunningly or stupidly enough, Buchanan could not now forego including his own views, for southern consumption. So he added, "It has ever been my individual opinion that under the true construction of the Nebraska-Kansas Act" the question of slavery in the territories could only be decided when the number of residents in the territory should be sufficient to justify the formation of a state constitution. This opinion he inserted himself in what his secretary already had copied.[31]

Inauguration day was balmy, the crowd was immense. But Buchanan was unhappy; his cabinet was unsettled and the "National Hotel disease" gripped him. Dr. Foltz must stand near to hand astringents. Off to Willard's they drove to meet the retiring executive—and confronted a distraught General Cass. He was in a dither over Buchanan's proposed definition of the "true construction" of the Nebraska law even though it was only the President's individual opinion and declined to enter the cabinet. After a long argument Buchanan crossed out the offending words, Cass was mollified, and the address was sent to the printer. Then the President elect must ask Surgeon Foltz for brandy, and as a last straw Pierce was late. The managers in fact had forgotten to send for the retiring President. Finally he appeared in his own carriage, and he and Buchanan lost no time in entering the open barouche. "Hail to the Chief"—the procession was off.

When Buchanan at length appeared on the stand on the east portico, after the installation of Vice President Breckinridge in the Senate chamber, he held a whispered conversation with Chief Justice Taney about procedure. Little did he imagine that it would later be charged that at that instant Taney told him how the Supreme Court would decide the Dred Scott case. None but the court itself suspected that Judge Grier had done this in writing some days before.

The inaugural, as Buchanan delivered it, was not particularly striking. He was no orator, nor had he talent with words. He began by stating his determination not to seek another term—a promise which weakened his influence from that instant—and then went on to lay down guides for domestic and foreign policy. A new era of internal peace was dawning, exulted Buchanan; everything was working to destroy any excuse for dangerous regional parties such as the Republicans. The will of the majority was the great safeguard; at this point he made his reference to the Supreme Court and extolled his interpretation of the Kansas-Nebraska Act. He himself would do everything possible to allay sectional strife and secure the perpetuity of the Union.

He went on to warn against corruptionists with their

schemes to plunder the full treasury (a last-minute insertion). Legitimate expenditures would include paying the debt and enlarging the navy. Also the public domain should be protected by building a military "road" to California to transport soldiers and supplies to the Pacific. He was careful not to say "railroad," and his road reference was less emphatic than in an earlier draft. Finally, came a few words about foreign policy. The United States desired peace, commerce, and friendship with all the world. But if the Republic sought new territory none of the powers had the right to object, nor any nation cause to fear; for this government would proceed honorably in its expansion. His address ended, Buchanan took the oath and became fifteenth President of the United States.[32]

It took two more days to complete the cabinet. No Whig could be included, but one of them, James B. Clay of Kentucky, was offered the Berlin mission refused by Jones. Toucey became Secretary of the Navy and Black, Attorney General.[33] The Senate duly confirmed the slate, and the new high command could assume its responsibilities. Their chief had committed them to hold a middle ground, to maintain a balance. They must keep internal peace, fight corruption, and promote a vigorous, expansive foreign policy. Such a program was designed to quiet divisive attitudes and to ensure domestic tranquility—and the ascendancy of the Democratic party.

Postscript

On the day Buchanan's cabinet appointments reached the Senate, the Supreme Court held its usual daily session below stairs in the Capitol basement. Chief Justice Taney proceeded to read an opinion in a voice so low as to be scarcely audible. It was the long-waited decision in Dred Scott v. San[d]ford, of which Buchanan had been so fully advised. The Court denied Scott's plea, holding that he was a slave and as such had no right to sue in a federal court as a citizen of one state against a citizen of another. Taney went on to pronounce on the partisan issue, as Buchanan had desired; he declared the Missouri Compromise unconstitutional, on the ground that Congress could not interfere in the territories with property or other vested rights enjoyed in the states. Such rights, Taney said, were protected by the Fifth Amendment.

The next day Justices Daniel and Wayne echoed Taney's logic and Grier acquiesced in it. Justice Campbell agreed that the Compromise was unconstitutional by denying what he had previously accepted; namely, the power of Congress to make rules and regulations in the territories. Catron concurred in the unconstitutionality, but on the ground that the Compromise violated the guarantees of the Louisiana Purchase treaty; he believed Congress did have power over slavery in the territories in general. Justice Nelson of New York avoided any opinion on the Compromise or congressional power. The two Republican justices filed the vigorous dissents expected of them.[34]

Thus a bare majority of the court, four southerners and one free-state judge, all Democrats, denied the constitutionality of the chief plank in the Republican platform. Congress could not make territories free soil, in their opinion. What this court might do to squatter sovereignty if the question of the power of a territorial legislature to abolish or exclude slave property ever came before it was anybody's guess; but there seemed to be a fairly clear indication that such power would be denied. Buchanan hoped fervently that the South could now have sufficient confidence in the sympathy of the Supreme Court, to leave to it the question of the status of slavery in the territories, and not to inject the embarrassing question into congressional debates or political campaigns.

Chapter 5

Re-forming the Party Ranks

THE NATION WAS STANDING on the brink of disaster. Civil War raged in the territories; international complications were piling up; the economic bubble was inflated nearly to the breaking point. Yet in the face of these grave dangers, members of the new administration immersed themselves in the peculiar needs of their party, which to them seemed paramount.

Their most immediate concern was the re-forming of the Democratic ranks. Discipline was lax; in some quarters, whole platoons were out of step, and confusion and insubordination were dispersing the battalions. The phenomenal rise of the Republicans had lowered party morale, and a further danger lay in the pending quadrennial resurvey of the civil service. Most federal appointees served four-year terms, and each new administration must decide whom to retain and whom to replace. Frequently party loyalty and political effectiveness were the tests applied. For the nonce, therefore, Buchanan and his advisers must act as patronage brokers. They must summon all their skill for this exacting task, if party defeat in 1860 were to be averted.

They had none of the modern conveniences available. Today every national party has a permanent, salaried, professional organization to bear the responsibility of maintaining and promoting party strength, working under the direction of the chairman of its national committee. In the fifties there was no such staff. Those on the public pay roll, from the President down, must spare time from their state duties to maintain party discipline and morale. The executive officers, members of Congress, and federal officeholders in Washington and in the states bore a heavy burden of party leadership, shared only in part with state leaders. The efficiency of the chain of command depended largely upon the skill with which collectors of the ports, postmasters, navy agents, storekeepers, and foremen, district attorneys, and marshals were chosen. If they proved efficient, resourceful party workers, all would be well. If they were not, or if they did not practice the requisite political arts, the party in their bailiwick might be weak and distracted.

The job-filling preoccupation plaguing Buchanan and his advisers was aggravated by an unprecedented situation, unlike any since the patronage system had flowered during the Jackson regime. One Democratic administration was succeeding another. To be sure Jackson had been followed by Van Buren; but this was by Jacksonian fiat, with little break in policy. Between the Pierce and Buchanan administrations, on the other hand, yawned a gap of aversion, if not hostility. The Buchaneers had taken the nomination from the partisans of Pierce, and during the campaign had charged the latter with apathy. Their triumph made them psychologically like a new party, for though they bore the same label as their predecessors, they were as eager for spoils as though they were driving out opponents.

Unfortunately the new administration, although made up of men of wide political experience, was hardly prepared for so unprecedented a test. The President himself had the initial weakness of overconfidence. He felt that his long public service—almost continuous through forty-two of his sixty-five years—had taught him all the answers. However, he had come of political age in the Jacksonian epoch, and his most intimate political experience had been as part of the successful Polk regime. Now he was outdated, his behavior adjusted to the ways of an older, fast-disappearing society. The Democratic party of the fifties was not the successful organization of the thirties and forties.

The President knew his rural Pennsylvania constituency and was familiar with foreign affairs. Yet he had never come to understand city politics, territorial conditions, or the rapacity of speculative interests. Neither did he comprehend the intensity of southernism; he thought it could be placated by concessions, such as he had made in constructing his cabinet and in formulating his inaugural statement of policy.

Besides lack of understanding, Buchanan had weaknesses of body and spirit to handicap him. These were not at first visible. He appeared ruddy, hearty, and heavy. He had the advantage of six feet of height crowned with a high mass of white hair. Newspapers commented that he had no need to shave. His eyes, however, were not an asset. They were of different color, one blue and one hazel; and as his vision was myopic he had a peculiar method of focusing his gaze which attracted attention. His squint induced him to hold his head to the left, at an angle accentuated by scars from a severe operation which drew his neck further awry. These blemishes he attempted to cover by a large collar and expansive neckcloth, both of frigid whiteness. In dress he was careful, if somewhat out of date, and could generally be seen in an old-fashioned dress coat which gave him an austere and clerical appearance.

Despite his weight and his years he was active and light on his feet. He was particularly vain of his small pedal extremities and generally shod them neatly in patent leather. He maintained a springy gait by constant walking, and during most of his administration few days passed when he did not take a brisk turn through the Washington streets. A contemporary suggested that this elasticity might be due to his bachelor status, quoting an Irishman as saying that "he had not the fatigues of a wife."

Underneath this imposing façade were psychological and physical weaknesses that time was to reveal more clearly. Emotionally he had never been perfectly adjusted. His only effort at matrimony had been thwarted by the young lady's father and brothers, who were certain that he was not a fit husband for her. She had vaguely sensed his inability to return affection adequately, and had yielded to her father's command, but she died shortly "of a broken heart." Her father refused to let Buchanan join the mourners, and this public rebuke had been the last straw. The young man sought to shield himself from the truth of his loss of face by abandoning any further attempt at marriage and by building up a romantic legend which he shared with others. He instinctively desired the world to sympathize with him as he loyally cherished the tender memory of a cruelly blighted love. Ever after, he had the ill equipped bachelor's eagerness for feminine attention to hide his peculiar lack, and he quite shone in the drawing room.

Among men he had few intimates; even at college, he had not found the society of his fellows congenial. He had clumsily engaged in their pranks, trying to prove he was one of them, only to be caught and suspended, leaving Dickinson College in a bitter frame of mind which he never completely forgot. In his public life he elicited little warmth of friendship. One looks almost in vain among his legion of correspondents for any who used informal address. Vice President William R. King, who died in 1853, was almost the last of the few who wrote him as "Dear Buchanan."

He endeavored to compensate for his lacks by seeking political power and by cultivating an exaggerated sense of propriety. He assumed an extremely dignified deportment, ever fearful lest he be charged with any breach of decorum. He permitted little familiarity; even his niece was required to address him as "Mr. Buchanan" whenever anyone was present. He naturally trusted few, in this state of mind, and insisted upon overseeing all the details of matters under his charge. As President, he was to spend countless hours of unremitting toil pouring over the multitude of papers which he required to pass over his desk. He would work far into the night in an ancient dressing gown and slippers, chewing a frayed cigar as he read and read. His cabinet, meanwhile, were to be held at a distance, except the irrepressible Cobb; the President wished them to realize they were subordinates. Behind his back they called him "the Squire," in half-jocular recognition of his success in imposing this inferiority upon them.

Another internal conflict which he had never resolved was religious. He had been unable to enjoy any convincing "experience of salvation," and it troubled him. He tried to seek grace by constant church attendance and private devotion, but as yet he had received no manifestation. It was just another phase of himself that he somehow could not understand, and his mounting years and presidential disasters were to make his complexes more troublesome.

Finally he was plagued by bad health. He had been ill, off and on, for a decade. He had suffered from glandular difficulty in his neck and from polypus growths in the nasal passages, from which he had sought relief by submitting to the crude operative techniques of the day. He was also bothered by heart trouble which recent arduous diplomatic experiences in London had not helped. Now he was weakened by the National Hotel disease from which he recovered slowly. These physical handicaps accentuated his natural tendency to be indecisive and even timid. Also he became more stubborn, and his cabinet learned he could be neither coaxed nor driven. When crossed he was mean and petulant, and he sulked when he could not have his own way.

Yet now on the threshold of the White House most of these weaknesses were not apparent. He seemed to be the vigorous, experienced leader, the expert who would avoid and repair the mistakes of his inexperienced predecessor. That is undoubtedly the picture he had of himself.[1] Likewise he had surrounded himself with a cabinet of veterans. All save Floyd and Black were habitués of Washington; and, of these two, the former had been governor of Virginia and the latter a justice of the Pennsylvania supreme court. They might all be presumed to know their way around in politics. Unfortunately time was to show that they were no better able than their chief to meet conditions of rapid change.

Buchanan's premier was worse than useless. At seventy-four senility was creeping up on the obese, indolent Lewis Cass. He was liable to attacks of vertigo and was unable to do effective, concentrated work. Whatever wisdom he had gained from his long political experience had not sufficed to save his Michigan constituency for him.[2] Now, he was a constant trial as an adviser, because he could not make up his mind and was glad to be made the mouthpiece of others. Almost his sole use was as a way out for Buchanan in the Douglas-Bright rivalry over the cabinet. However, Cass did not interfere much and seemed content with the title of Secretary of State while Buchanan and Appleton directed diplomacy.

The Postmaster General and the Secretary of the Navy, like Buchanan, were political veterans in their sixties. Aaron V. Brown, however, had been scarcely more than a local politician with some experience as a Congressman. He had spent most of his life in Tennessee with little opportunity to understand any but the southern attitude. An expansive individual, he wished to administer his department for the satisfaction of as many as possible, and to eradicate the bad taste left by the strait-laced and economical Campbell. He had married a rich widow with a charming daughter and was going to put lavish hospitality to political use.[3]

Isaac Toucey, once Tousy or Tousey, who had changed the pronunciation as well as the spelling of his name, was a perfect example of the cautious Yankee. He was a self-made Connecticut citizen who had come in from the country to Hartford to practice law and marry into a leading family. Very happy in the circle of his wife's distinguished relatives and very conscious of his good fortune, he gratefully accepted patronage. Careful always to be noncommittal, he had risen in Connecticut politics by a strictly middle course and by several rapid shifts with the tide. Never once did he differ from Buchanan, and he administered the Navy carefully and according to precedent. He interfered neither with the officers nor with the contractors.[4]

John Buchanan Floyd, Secretary of War, was much younger, only fifty. A states' rights Virginian, he came of excellent family, his father having been governor before him and Vice President Breckinridge (but not Buchanan) being known as kin to him. He was remarkable in nothing else. He was not particularly intelligent, energetic, efficient, or interested. He was expansive and easy-going and was a poor administrator. He could be persuaded to participate in questionable practices, though not to his own advantage. He was accompanied by his business manager, Robert W. Latham. Through him he gave unfortunate confidence to so-called friends, particularly some New York speculators and army contractors; in fact "careless" is the word that describes him. Buchanan was to have many anxious moments because of Floyd's unfitness for his position. As the observant Edmund Ruffin confided to his diary at this time, "In Ex-Gov. Floyd's integrity, public or private, I have no confidence."[5]

The last three members of the cabinet were in their forties, and the President came nearer to friendship with them than with their elders. Thompson, Black, and Cobb formed a pleasant social group. Mrs. Thompson and Mrs. Cobb were intimate, and Buchanan enjoyed their society, particularly Mrs. Thompson's. Jacob Thompson was a matter-of-fact, humorless, relentless, and ambitious self-made man who lived by careful calculation. He could be vindictive to the point of embracing questionable means of retaliation. He had been an unattractive, unhappy boy at home in North Carolina. After an early break with his father he had set out on his own in the young and growing state of Mississippi, where he amassed political power and a fortune. He had chosen his wife when she was a very young girl, and after their marriage had sent her off to be educated before their union was consummated. They made a striking administration couple; she was vivacious and socially clever; he managed the Interior Department efficiently, shrewdly calculating how southern the state of Mississippi was, and then adopting that attitude.[6]

Jeremiah S. Black, like Thompson, was forty-seven. He was an emotional and sharp Scotch-Irish son of thunder from Pennsylvania's mountainous Somerset. He was fluent and witty, loved literary quotations, and could write and speak most effectively. Also he had been associated with Buchanan in Pennsylvania politics and would do his bidding, with rare instances of independence. As Attorney General and patronage arbiter in some difficult disputes he could be a useful go-between and spokesman. He was the only one of the group who by temperament or independence could be said not to be under the sway of southernism.[7]

The junior member of the cabinet was Howell Cobb, an attractive, jolly Georgian of forty-one. He had an easy-going sense of humor and was to lighten many a tedious discussion by his sallies and practical jokes. Though in charge of the Treasury he was without any particular financial genius. The prevailing policy of laissez faire gave him little to do outside routine administration, save in political matters. Here he was engulfed with woe for, next to the Post Office, his department was the great source of patronage. As a southern Union man he was the object of constant sniping from the radical group. On the other hand the President probably was as near to being fond of him as of any man. Therefore when the incidents of childbearing kept Mrs. Cobb from Washington twice during the administration, Buchanan had Cobb practically board at the White House for long periods. His humor and good-fellowship made him a diverting companion.[8]

All told, it was a "solid" administration, conservative in sympathy. The President and four of his advisers were well-to-do for those days. Cass, Thompson, and Brown were reputed very rich, and Buchanan and Cobb had fortunes of about $200,000 each. Cass and Thompson had made their money by hard work and fortunate speculation. Brown and Cobb had married well, and Cobb had the additional advantage of good management of his wife's fortune by her relatives. Secure in their wealth, their years of activity, and their high position, they settled down behind cautious conservatism and glibly reiterated superficial formulas as abracadabras of magic potency. In spite of their experience, none of these men had sufficient breadth of view to understand the intensity of the volcanic and divisive attitudes now coming to eruption. What the nation needed was understanding and statesmanship, not backward-looking politicos.

The new administration made the initial mistake of underestimating the difficulty of its task. Buchanan had rashly assumed that the patronage would be no problem. When an admirer remarked shortly after his election that he would be overrun with office seekers, the executive-to-be replied, "I'll be damned if I will."[9] He soon found he was damned. He and his advisers were immediately put on the patronage rack. They were determined to have strong and unified party backing to make it possible for their administration to function, and this strength could be commanded more by skillful patronage manipulation than by larger statesmanship. So, they neglected the pressing problems that endangered the stability of the nation, to devote most of their energy to apportionment of the spoils.

In their first confident hours as administrators, they devised a formula to be announced as the rationale of their actions. All officeholders against whom no charges were pending might serve out their four-year terms. Then the principle of rotation in office would go into effect, and the Buchanan men would garner the fruits of their labors. But it soon became apparent that the situation was too complex to be comprehended in a formula.[10]

The federal character of the party prevented any such uniform administration. The President and his cabinet were dealing with thirty-one state organizations, each with different plans, problems, and personnel. State leaders and congressional representatives had their own ideas, and so did the constituents. Countless petitions and letters of recommendation were showered upon the dispensers. More pressing were the personal interviews of individuals and delegations. The new administrators must seek to extract the truth from a maze of conflicting testimony regarding local rivalries which had little or no connection with national issues and policies.

Buchanan had to learn that the patronage was but a reflection of the complex society in which it operated, and that it represented the prevailing attitudes of this vibrant period. Office holding was not alike in urban, rural, territorial, and southern regions and required special handling in each. Urban patronage involved city machines and business interests; rural patronage, the small concerns of scattered farmers. Territorial patronage was the goal of the speculator and the political ne'er-do-well. Southern patronage was more stable, more of an honor, more of an opportunity for public service.

While these intricacies were laboriously studied, the operations of government were stalled for weeks. Local squabbles were sifted and debated in cabinet meetings which seemed endless. The nation's real business was conducted at night or at such odd hours as the cabinet members could snatch from office seekers.

II

The difficulties involved in dispensing the patronage varied with the complexity of the locality where the officeholder was to serve and its diversity of interests and attitudes. The largest and most complex of the states was New York, and its patronage had for years been the most difficult. Its factions reflected social cleavages, clashing interests, and conflicting ambitions of various leaders within the Empire State. The most obvious conditioning factor was the conflict in interests between New

York City and upstate, rural New York. The metropolis was America's greatest port, and its customhouse and post office handled huge quantities of goods and mail, vital to the commercial, maritime, and financial interests, not only of the city but of the nation. Albany was a railroad center, the headquarters of the growing New York Central system. Buffalo and the towns along the Erie Canal represented another transportation interest, and political machines flourished in each. Likewise manufactures were growing, and their wage workers, as well as the transportation employees, were on the poll lists. The rural vote was large and frequently suspicious of the growing urban strength; rural legislators had learned the dangers of being gold-bricked by city slickers. There was a natural and inevitable antagonism.

The growing cities and towns at the mouth of the Hudson and upstate made city machines necessary. The great numbers of voters encouraged invention of new methods of control so that party propaganda and more direct influence might affect large aggregates of citizens. Hordes of interested party workers were essential, and the practice of supporting them on the public pay roll had been increasing. Certain federal services offered fine opportunities for this.

In New York City and Brooklyn were the customhouse, two post offices, and the navy yard. The size of the port required many employees at the customhouse; and its system of bonded warehouses meant that numerous carters and freight handlers, ostensibly in private operation or employ, were susceptible to political influence. The post offices handled tremendous quantities of foreign and domestic mail; therefore their clerks were almost legion. Also their revenues were immense, and the postmaster upon occasion might loan some of them for party purposes between quarterly accounting periods.

The navy yard had fifteen hundred civilian employees under a dozen or so master workmen. Each of the city Congressmen was allotted some of these foremen, who in turn employed laborers capable of showing some political enthusiasm. At election times employees were excused for party duties, and additional men were taken on as a reward for loyalty or as an inducement to political labor. Supplies were purchased from generous campaign contributors, and this item at the Brooklyn Navy Yard was tremendous. Wherever such possibilities were present they were exploited, and often they were the controlling element in the politics of the growing cities.

The handling of these regiments and platoons of workers

by the distributors of the patronage long had been a most difficult task. The growing complexity of life in New York and Brooklyn, to say nothing of Albany, Buffalo, Syracuse, Rochester, and the score of municipal striplings in the Empire State, had become the curse of the federal administrators. Polk and Pierce had suffered from it. It had contributed much to wrecking the Democracy in the disastrous schism of 1848, when the Whigs put Taylor into the White House. Buchanan could hardly expect to escape it. So complicated a situation cannot be thoroughly examined within the limits of this book; therefore a sampling will be made by a display of New York City's rather soiled patronage linen.

Internecine warfare of a peculiarly vicious type was resounding through the political purlieus of Gotham. In the previous administration there had been the three factions—Hards, Softs, and Barnburners. Now these were proliferating. A new figure had come on the scene during the past few years in the person of an adventurous youth from Philadelphia, who had crossed New Jersey destined to show the experienced Tammany boys a few new tricks. Fernando Wood had been elected mayor in 1854 as a reformer and apostle of good government. Safely in office, he had advanced quickly to a point where he was teaching corruption to corruptionists. He had produced an organization capable of dealing with barroom loafers, Hell's Kitchen thugs, panderers to vice, and anyone tough enough to bully votes. Backed by his city patronage he was ambitious to control the state party organization. Originally he had been a Soft, but he now had an organization of his own that had been as hostile to Pierce's Soft state machine as any Hard.

The Soft men were divided into two groups. One division was fighting against Wood in New York City. They were led by the Pierce officeholders and the city Congressmen, and, because Wood had driven them from Tammany Hall, they made their headquarters at the New York Hotel. Here some of the "silk-stockings" had formed a club or "ranche" where they maintained a well stocked cellar and a French chef. Associated with them were many of the ocean steamship, importing, and banking men, including August Belmont, agent of the Rothschilds. The other Softs were upstate, with headquarters at Albany, and were led by Dean Richmond and Erastus Corning of the New York Central Railroad, and Peter Cagger, a prominent Catholic layman. These men dominated the Democratic state committee and had associated with them John Van

Buren, son of the former President, and the old Barnburner faction.

The only real difference between the Softs and the Hards was that the leaders of the former were more generally in office and in positions of party responsibility. The Hards were of late the "outs," but they had leaders of wealth and experience. In New York City their spokesman was Augustus Schell, the national committeeman for the state; while "upstate," former Senator Daniel S. Dickinson, or "Scrip Dick," was the leader. The chief asset of the Hards was their early support of Buchanan in the prenomination days. These factions had united on the state and national tickets in 1856; but at the boundary of Manhattan harmony ended. The party had lost the state to the Republicans and was at the moment a seething mass of crimination and recrimination.

The New York City situation was an open and bleeding wound which threatened once more to cause the death of the party. In the municipal election of 1856, Wood's enemies had made a desperate attempt to crowd him into his political grave. His foes, mostly Hards, split the party trying to defeat him but failed, despite the Republican victory throughout the state. Wood's triumph gave him the idea that he should control the federal patronage in New York City. The Softs and Hards now united to prevent this, and the feud in the city disrupted the local party completely.

Buchanan and his cabinet were now in the middle of this war. Each faction had a candidate for every office, and they all descended upon the administration with their slates. As one humorist put it, March, 1857, was the one time to hold honest primaries in New York City because all the professionals were away. The division of pressure gave the President pretty much of a free hand. He used it to take the customhouse from the Softs who had opposed him and give it to his wealthy friend, Augustus Schell, the Hard. Each faction got something though none was satisfied, least of all Wood. However, he proceeded to make the best of it and work with Schell. The war, however, had only begun. The magnitude of the patronage problem, in that one state alone, can only be glimpsed in this New York City sample.[11]

Pennsylvania, like New York, was *sui generis*, with a congeries of many interests. The Keystone State was definitely divided into eastern, central, and western sections. It had its distinct social groups such as the Quakers, Pennsylvania Germans and Scotch-Irish. Also it had three important economic

groups. Agriculture was strong; no finer farms nor more prosperous farmers were to be found anywhere. Transportation
interests, notably the growing Pennsylvania Railroad, were
increasingly influential, with Philadelphia the second port in
importance in the nation. Manufacturing, though mainly
centered in Philadelphia, was in fact advancing throughout
the state and flourishing in Pittsburgh; vast coal and iron
interests were powerful. The wage-earning vote was large and
was something to be reckoned with. As the manufacturers
grew more insistent on a return to a protective tariff, Pennsylvania Democrats realized that if this interest were mobilized
against them effectively they would lose the Commonwealth.

Pennsylvania factions were not as complex as those of
New York, but Buchanan's long association with the politics
of his home state and his personal machine gave the tangle an
extra twist. Through many years he had built up a great following by tireless correspondence. He had written to almost
countless men, giving them the feeling that they were his
close associates, so that he had gained their votes. It was not
surprising that all too many now expected offices and were
eager and importunate in their clamor.

Here again only a sample can be examined; and, as the
greatest perplexities arose over the Philadelphia scramble, that
is the exhibit chosen. This metropolis, like its more northerly
sister, had great prizes—the customhouse, the post office, and
the navy yard; and it had the mint as well. Buchanan's relation
to the great city was peculiar. He had never been popular
there, for Philadelphians with characteristic detachment had
looked upon him as a country politician and a rival of their
own distinguished George Mifflin Dallas. Worse, the difficult
Forney was at large in the City of Brotherly Love to Mr.
Buchanan's embarrassment.

In dealing with Philadelphia patronage the President felt
he must first settle with Forney. After he failed to secure the
Senatorship for that gentleman he offered the choice of the
Liverpool consulate, to which was to be added the perquisite
of well paid letter-writing to administration newspapers, or
the naval office at Philadelphia. The former Forney refused
because his political interests could be maintained only if he
stayed home to watch them. The naval office be declined, as
he said, because he had promised to back someone else. It is
nearer the truth probably to say that he considered this office,
inferior to the collectorship or the post office, as beneath his
dignity.[12] He was thoroughly disillusioned. "Mr. Buchanan

was to me for half my life," he wrote, "an Idol—not a man; a God—not a fellow being. I am now utterly disenchanted— . . . and I am punished for my romantic, devoted and single-hearted zeal."[13]

Buchanan washed his hands of Forney for the time being and turned to making the Philadelphia slate according to his own views. His knowledge of his own unpopularity in Philadelphia plus the Forney embroglio undoubtedly led him to decide to give some of the Philadelphia spoil to the politicos of the interior. This was eagerly urged upon him by non-Philadelphians, particularly by a long-time supporter, Hendrick B. Wright of Wilkes-Barré; and J. Glancy Jones of Reading was not opposed to it. Therefore Buchanan gave the big plum, the Philadelphia customhouse, to his old Lancaster friend, Joseph B. Baker, a railroad operator and Harriet Lane's brother-in-law. The naval office which Forney had declined, the surveyorship, and the marshal's post went to friends of Jones. Friends of Forney got the district attorneyship (a reappointment) and the navy (purchasing) agency. The postmaster was acceptable to both Jones and Forney.[14] No one was very well satisfied, but there was general acquiescence. Jones was to be busy as chairman of the House ways and means committee in Washington, and Forney planned to take over the *Daily Pennsylvanian* and run it on the profits from the printing of the Post Office Department blanks, which he expected to receive from Buchanan. The President, however, was in no hurry to make this printing assignment, and the Pennsylvania combustibles might explode at any moment.[15] They were in fact dynamite.

III

The patronage situation in the Northwest at first blush seemed much less complex and dangerous than that in the eastern communities; but it proved eventually to be even more disastrous. In most of these states also there was factionalism. Here as elsewhere the Democrats were faced with rising opposition. The antislavery, territorial, and metropolitan attitudes were vigorously expressed, and, although their exponents found no sympathy among the Democratic machine leaders, so great was their appeal that they fostered discontent in the Democratic ranks and resentment against southern domination and continued laissez faire. Also the younger men resented the more conservative elders clinging to office and called them "Hunkers," after their New York prototypes, because they hankered after jobs. Factionalism was bound to flourish on such substance.

In Ohio, the Democracy had two groups. The Sawbucks or Hunkers, under William Allen and other followers of Cass, were still willing to applaud the time-honored national policies of the party. They were opposed by the Miamis, including Sam Medary, Clement L. Vallandigham and others like-minded who resented the neglect of the West.[16] In Wisconsin, the old machine led by federal officeholders who had been built up by Senator Henry Dodge, was plagued by a speculating faction known as Monks Hall.[17] In Michigan, Cass's organization was not appreciated by Senator Charles Stuart, whose followers laid the party's defeat there to Hunker doctrines dictated by southern leadership and Cass's ambition for the presidency. In these states the discontented generally thought of Douglas as the man to save the party from the sprouting opposition. Their feeling was bound to grow when they found how generally Buchanan would favor Hunkers.

Indiana likewise was faction-ridden, with Senator Bright and Governor Wright the principal leaders. The Senator hailed from the southern section, whose many citizens from slave states had pronounced southern sympathies. His connections were also speculative and metropolitan, although there was little of the metropolis as yet in Indiana. Wright was from the center of the state, an agrarian, who opposed speculative schemes, Treasury raids, and southernism; his faction fought for laissez faire and was friendly to Douglas. These rivals had just been through a fight over the recharter of a state bank; the Governor had tried to break the institution in true Jacksonian style, but the charter had been voted by the legislature—through bribery, it was charged.

As Wright's gubernatorial term expired in January 1857, he sought to go to the Senate, for Indiana had a long- and a short-term seat to fill. Bright and his friend, Dr. Graham N. Fitch, were working for them; but Wright wanted to forestall Fitch. Bright and Fitch had been able to prevent a fight in caucus over this question only by persuading Wright to accept a foreign mission instead, and Buchanan obligingly offered Berlin. Then Bright and Fitch were elected to the Senate, but by irregular procedure, which was to be used by the Republicans as the basis of a contest against seating these two solons during the next winter. Buchanan's sympathies were all with Bright and Fitch and so the Hunker faction got the patronage. The new Governor, Ashbel P. Willard, was taken care of; he was a poor man, and Indiana paid her governors only $1,300 a year. So he was permitted to select a rich man to be post-master at Indianapolis with the understanding that the new appointee would keep the governor in funds. Thus provided for, Willard settled down to his steady occupation of drinking himself to death, which was now and then arrested by brief periods of reform. Wright's organization, left out in the cold, would be more earnest than ever in its support of Douglas.[18]

The remaining state in the Northwest was the Little Giant's bailiwick of Illinois. Internally the party was in fine shape, for Douglas had developed a relatively compact and harmonious organization. There was only one possible danger. Would the new administration play ball with him on the federal patron-age? How was rotation in office going to work? Douglas soon learned that it would be rigorously applied. The Senator who had recommended most of the present incumbents must ac-quiesce in their retirement at the end of their terms. However, as he and his congressional associates would name their suc-cessors, the game to a large extent was still in his own hands. In one instance, the rule should be made to work to the ad-vantage of his organization.

Douglas set out to get rid of his Chicago postmaster. He originally had recommended Ike Cook, liquor dealer, specu-lator, and political manipulator; but Cook had proved a poor administrator, and thievery had developed in that important mail center. Pierce had been on the point of firing him. The Senator now recommended William Price, a wealthy contrac-tor, who was willing to give financial support to James W. Sheahan, editor of Douglas's organ, the *Chicago Times*. Price was named, but Cook was to have his revenge.

Douglas's Illinois organization was disappointed in most of its patronage ambitions outside the state. Not only were its hopes of a cabinet position blasted, but its concerted effort to have John McClernand appointed to a foreign post was frustrated; the assignment of Wright to Berlin was all that the Northwest seemed entitled to in diplomacy. The best office Illinoisans secured was the governorship of the territory of Nebraska, which went to Richardson. The straw pointing straightest in the direction of the wind was the elevation of Colonel R. B. Carpenter. He had applied for the Chicago postmastership, but Douglas refused to recommend him. Then without the Senator's knowledge he was made disbursing officer for the new Chicago post office and customhouse build-ing then under construction. These indications were not im-

portant enough to make a major issue, but they were galling
to Douglas's pride and made him increasingly suspicious that
the administration was coldly indifferent to his success, if not
hostile to it.[19]

Far to the westward another winter of senatorial discontent
was being made more frosty by a storm over patronage. On
the Pacific shore, California had a politics all her own in
which the local Democracy had been riding high, wide, and
handsome. The gold rush had invited all sorts and conditions
of men, and they had poured into the treasure valleys in a
great flood. This tide of humanity carried on its current many
who were as ambitious for political strikes as they were for
treasure trove. A number of Democratic politicos hurried out
there, ex-Congressmen, Tammany henchmen, rural and city
operators. They found themselves in a social maelstrom, in
an environment different from their previous experience. The
feuds were man-sized, involving not only the bravado and
bluster well recognized as inevitable in more settled and older
regions, but also violence and murder. Out in this beautiful
but rapacious land, even death might befall political contenders.

The California Democracy was plagued by its own complex
internal factionalism. All the current attitudes were projected
on this great stage. Many persons were of southern origin—
so many in fact that the new region was sometimes called
Virginia's poorhouse; and they seized early leadership. The
first legislature, in 1849, named a Tennessean, who had been
a Congressman from Mississippi, to be one of the United
States Senators; Dr. William M. Gwin went to Washington
and, with his southern connections, became a prominent
figure in the select circle of the Senate. When Pierce came into
the White House he was the principal adviser on California
patronage. At home he marshaled a group in collaboration
with an ex-Congressman from Ohio, John B. Weller, who had
no antislavery taint. This group, commonly known as the
Chivalry, sent Weller to the Senate to join Gwin, and for the
first year or so of Pierce's regime they were in control. But
their dominance was constantly challenged by other adventurers, some of whom found it profitable to emphasize antisouthernism. One of the most resourceful of these was an
ex-Tammany ward boy, fireman, and saloon keeper, David C.
Broderick. He and his following challenged Gwin, with such
success that they blocked Gwin's reelection in 1855 and the
seat was vacant for two years.

Finally, on the eve of Buchanan's inauguration, Broderick forced Gwin into a humiliating bargain. Weller's term had now expired, and there were thus two vacancies to be filled. Gwin could have his old seat now if he would agree to Broderick as a colleague and turn over the patronage to him. He had to sign an agreement to that effect. Thus Gwin had returned to the Senate in February, 1857, and Broderick was sworn in on Buchanan's inauguration day. Then the new Senator found how much the agreement was worth. 'Twas true Gwin made no formal recommendations. These were all to come from Broderick, but he was required to submit them in writing. When Buchanan and his cabinet considered California patronage they called in Gwin, and it was soon apparent that his informal advice was the guiding influence. A mighty wrath was beginning to smolder in Broderick's bosom, one day to burst forth.[20]

The perplexities which these varied factions in the northern state parties were forcing on the patronage brokers were made more galling by the inadequacy of their formula of rotation in office. Each week they were driven into ever more apparent inconsistency. In the South, particularly, their principle just could not be applied uniformly. Southern politics was not like anything else in the United States, nor would its patronage fit into a general pattern. Most southern voters lived in stable environments where persons and opinions were well known, and candidates made intensive personal canvasses. Their constituencies did not fluctuate much, and there was less stimulus to change. Senators and Congressmen from that region remained longer in office, and, as many of them had stood sponsor for the incumbent officeholders, they now could see no reason to change just because Buchanan was President. He comprehended this situation. He could not risk giving any cause for turning the indifference or dislike, which was too prevalent in the South toward him, into more positive opposition. So it soon was obvious that rotation would not be applied in that section; nor was it politically expedient to pretend to apply it.

Observers were not slow in noting that there was to be one rule for the South and another elsewhere.[21] This discrimination did not soothe the sectional troubles afflicting the nation nor make political antagonisms less bitter. It did not improve Douglas's temper to know that his ranks must be re-formed while southern organizations remained undisturbed.

IV

During this hectic distribution of the patronage Buchanan had to look after the press spoils. He had not settled the *Washington Union*, for the appointment of Appleton as Assistant Secretary of State had destroyed the plan to have him run the paper. Negotiations of various kinds ensued whereby J. Glancy Jones and Wendell reached a new agreement. A former Virginia Congressman, William A. Harris, who had migrated to Missouri, was to come to Washington and "buy" the *Union*. That is, he was to give Wendell notes for $25,000 and take title to the paper. He would be the candidate for congressional printing in both houses, and when elected would turn it over to Wendell the Republican. In the meantime Wendell was to hire two editorial writers—S. M. Johnson, a friend of Buchanan's, and R. W. Hughes, a relative of Floyd's —to do the editorial writing for the *Union*. This arrangement was concluded April 2; two days later Appleton's appointment to the State Department was announced, and within a fortnight Harris's name was at the head of the *Union* as "sole editor and proprietor." He consulted Buchanan from time to time and duly prepared for his election as congressional printer.[22] He was to advocate national attitudes, healing alike to the party and the Union.

In this fashion the party ranks had been re-formed, in so far as that difficult task could be accomplished by reordering the patronage and tuning the publicity organs. But it had not been done effectively or skillfully, because those in charge looked upon their task too naïvely. The publishing of a rotation formula impossible to follow, and their instinctive sympathy for conservative or Hunker factions had been noted by political observers and had roused much resentment. Since this came generally from the more unstable and the disappointed elements, they might be written off as soreheads. To the wise, however, there were evidences of lack of understanding which boded ill for the future. With the nation poised on the brink of disaster, no administration could afford to be so completely engrossed in party expedients.

Chapter 6

Territorial Nightmares

THE FATE of the Democratic party was being spun out in the scattered settlements of far-off territories. Kansas, Minnesota, Oregon, and Utah, distant as they were, became the sources of both embarrassment and hope. The strange behavior of the settlers in Kansas and Utah had furnished the Republicans explosives almost powerful enough to blow up the Democracy in 1856. Would the ammunition be completely effective in 1860? Also Minnesota and Oregon as well as Kansas were practically ready for statehood. Their electors in 1860 might decide the contest. Every effort must be made to see to it that the Democratic organization should command in each of the new state governments. The administration found a heavy responsibility in territorial affairs.

Many interests were converging on frontier settlements as population constantly pressed farther west. Minnesota was the seat of much real estate, railroad, and lumber speculation. Kansas and Utah were on the direct line of westward march; the California road ran through both of them, and the Santa Fe trail passed through Kansas also. Here was one of the possible routes for a Pacific railroad. It took no great imagination to show any one that these regions held unusual possibilities of money-making in lands, roads, ferries, bridges, townsites, banks and other corporations—particularly railroads. Speculators were constantly scheming to gain by political influence.[1]

Much of the difficulty in Kansas had arisen from the union of the speculator and the politician. While the proslavery legislature had been passing laws to protect slave property, it had been granting charters and franchises. Most of the prominent territorial politicians who led the dominant proslavery faction, including the federal officeholders, were involved in these speculations, as incorporators and stockholders. Part of the territorial bitterness arose out of the fact that the free-soil emigrants hated to see all these opportunities monopolized by their opponents.[2] Also there was keen rivalry over land ownership, the location of townsites, improvements, and utilities. Furthermore, Indian title had not been extinguished in certain areas and though consequently these regions were not open to settlement squatters had gone in and taken-up claims.[3] As government surveys had been slow, settlers had guessed at section markings in staking claims.[4] When Indian claims were extinguished, surveys made, and lands at long last opened for public sale there were bound to be much dispute, violence, and bloodshed. If, as it often happened, rival claimants were proslavery and free-soil in sympathy, that made the flow of blood the greater.

The territories were also swarming grounds for political speculators. Those who were cut into the first territorial governments had excellent chances to become governing forces in the new states, to reap substantial rewards in financial opportunities and to go to Washington as Senators or Representatives. So, much of the territorial turmoil was due to the constant jockeying of politicos for position and favorable national recognition. Federal officials had political as well as administrative responsibilities. The governors, assisted by their staffs and by appointees in the land and Indian agencies, were expected to organize new units of their own party. So far Kansas governors had had no time for this duty. They were so beset by the paralyzing anarchy that they had attempted little and accomplished nothing in the way of party mobilization. The proslavery men had not wanted a Democratic standard because that would have split off the Whigs and Americans from them. So Kansas was almost ready for statehood and the Democracy had no machine ready to take over.

Buchanan and his cabinet found it difficult to understand the tangled situation which they sought to straighten out; the territories were far away, and none of them had traveled there. Since the beginning, news had been distorted by partisan reporting and administration politicians had come to discount tales of bleeding Kansas which they called "Republican propaganda." Their imperfect knowledge did not prevent these men from assuming to know the answer to the problem. They thought that what was needed was the organization of the conservative peace-loving men, both southern and northern, into a national Democratic party, led by responsible and competent federal officials. Such a party would command respect, quiet disturbance, and make Democratic strength for 1860.

Buchanan and the cabinet advised with the titular territorial authority, Stephen A. Douglas, chairman of the Senate committee on territories, in searching for competent officials, particularly in Kansas. They realized, as the Pierce administration had not done, that Kansas called for something better that the usual type of territorial official. They gave Kansas immediate priority and decided that Governor Geary should be displaced by a man of greater prestige.[5]

Buchanan turned to his old associate in the Polk cabinet, Robert J. Walker, erstwhile Secretary of the Treasury. Since his retirement from office in 1849, Walker had been devoting himself to promotion and speculation, particularly in railroads. He had the ear of capitalists and was looked upon as an organizing genius. He still had political ambitions, and the President thought that the idea of coming back to Washington, either as a Senator from the new state of Kansas or even as successor to Buchanan himself, might tempt him. Buchanan may have thought that it was just as well for Douglas to have a rival for the succession. Besides, Walker's strong fight for the post of Secretary of State made it almost imperative for Buchanan to give him some place of prestige. Douglas, too, was favorable to Walker; and his northern birth, his long experience in the South, his knowledge of the West, his political shrewdness, and his administrative experience, all made him an excellent selection.

The choice of Walker gave the President a new experience. Usually he was the one importuned, the one sought after, the one urged and pleaded with. Now he must turn beggar. Walker did not want to go to Kansas, particularly because he would have to abandon some of his promotion schemes. Then there were family complications. Mrs. Walker, who was a Bache and was connected with the Dallases, objected. Her interposition seems to have been more real than the usual political excuse that "my wife's health" won't permit. Walker evidently prized his wife's comfort highly, and she depended upon him. Four years before, he had actually agreed to take the Chinese mission and had even drawn the "outfit" money, when her distress prevailed upon him to give up the post. Now again her objections were vigorous, so Walker declined verbally and in writing.

But Buchanan was persistent. He sent various Senators to Walker's house, including Douglas, and himself called frequently. When Walker told him of his wife's objections Buchanan took a new line. He set about charming Mrs. Walker into acquiescence. He used his arts well and at length

convinced her; at least so the story goes. The press claimed
that Walker was holding out for patronage concessions to
the Softs in New York; he did not want to go out West without leaving a friendly organization well intrenched in the
East. This would be essential if he were planning to return
as Senator from the new state and run for president in 1860.
He finally allowed himself to be persuaded.[6]

Some of the terms of his acceptance he set forth in a letter
of March 26 to Buchanan which was forthwith published
widely: "I understand that you and all your cabinet cordially
concur in the opinion expressed by me, that the actual bona
fide residents of the territory of Kansas, by a fair and regular
vote, unaffected by fraud or violence, must be permitted, in
adopting their state constitution, to decide for themselves
what shall be their social institutions."[7] In other words,
Kansas was near enough to statehood for popular sovereignty
to apply. He planned likewise to set forth his views in an
inaugural address, which the administration must approve
beforehand. He was going to have them committed to a
popular referendum on the constitution. He would not be
left holding the bag.

He and the President took special pains to see that he
would have adequate support. Much more than usual attention was paid to the appointment of the secretary of the
territory, who was really a vice governor who acted for his
chief during his absence. Frederick P. Stanton was chosen.
He was a native of the District of Columbia who had served
ten years, 1845–1855, as a Congressman from Tennessee and
was now a busy lawyer at the capital with a lucrative legal
and lobby business. Walker had confidence in his prestige and
his strength of character. He was difficult to persuade, but at
length terms were made. Reverdy Johnson would take over
his law practice, and it seems Stanton was to receive the
profitable Central Indian superintendency at St. Louis in
January, 1858, when it was expected Kansas would be well
on the road to statehood and his task ended.[8]

Walker and Stanton were to have full military support.
Fifteen hundred troops were in the territory, and new orders
were issued placing them at the Governor's disposal. General
William S. Harney, a vigorous fighter, was ordered from
Florida to take active command.[9] Walker's political way was
to be made easier by a decision to permit Chief Justice Lecompte to serve out his term. This would please the proslavery men and their backers in the Senate. Buchanan and

his advisers thus laid careful plans to keep Kansas from being of further use to the Republicans. Could they bring the territory into the Union as a Democratic state in time for 1860?

II

The situation in Utah was equally embarrassing, for that territory was "out of this world." When the Mormon Zion was organized in 1850, President Fillmore adopted the policy of appointing both Mormon and Gentile federal officials. He made the head of the church, Brigham Young, Governor and superintendent of Indian affairs, and the remaining offices were divided between the two groups. President Pierce, however, attempted to appoint a Democrat in Young's place, only to have his candidate decline and join in recommending that Young continue, which Pierce permitted him to do. Thus, when Buchanan was inaugurated there had been no change in the governorship since the beginning.

The great distance which separated the territory from any center of federal control, the lack of any efficient communication, and particularly the character of the inhabitants had produced a peculiarly independent community. The Mormons were people of intense and fixed purpose, thrifty, hard-working, and enterprising. Their religious concept of themselves as a chosen people and their belief in implicit obedience to their prophet, Brigham Young, led them to have little regard for federal authority except as he represented it. He was really in sovereign control of his own flock and of the Indians in this vast region. A Mormon militia maintained order, and local courts had been assigned jurisdiction by the territorial legislature, which practically stripped the federal courts of their functions. The Mormon excuse for this was the disreputable character of certain of the federal judges sent to them. In this, one may well sympathize with the Mormons.

The whole history of the Mormons and their federal relations was affected by an accident. The discovery of gold in California had altered their situation completely. Instead of remaining hidden in distant mountain isolation they found themselves on the highroad to the coast. Instead of remaining remote from Gentile association they saw thousands of Gentiles passing through their Zion. Although they were dismayed at this unexpected turn of affairs they were not unaware of some of its advantages and proceeded to use them. The Mormons were shrewd traders. Their supplies were scarce and

difficult to replenish, because of high transportation costs, and
they undoubtedly sought to monopolize any profits that might
be made in Utah from the migrants passing through their
settlements. When easterners, used to another scale of prices,
sought to buy food and equipment they found trading difficult and prices high. Their reports luridly described out-
rageous charges and "swindling" methods.

When the question of a transcontinental railroad began to
be discussed, the territory gained a still greater speculative
interest. Utah lay on the central route, and the railroad
promoters who had their eyes on Kansas became interested
in the region beyond. Robert J. Walker and his associates
were definitely uniting the two regions in their plans. Other
speculators and jobbers were likewise intrigued. The mail
contracts were a source of controversy. They had been in
the hands of a firm of Missouri stage-line operators, Hockaday and Magraw, but during the Pierce administration Young
decided to get the contract and establish an express company
which would create a sort of freight monopoly and put control of the supply traffic in his hands. So a Mormon underbid
Hockaday and Magraw in 1856 and began a new service.
Thus Young had shown himself equally effective in maintaining absolute political and economic control of his strategic
location. Certainly the way of speculators and contractors
would be much easier if the Mormon monopoly could be
broken. It would be very convenient if the federal government undertook this formidable task.

Shortly after Buchanan was inaugurated the patronage
possibilities stimulated a controversy which burgeoned into
war. Democratic contractors and speculators thought it high
time to get rid of Young, as both governor and Indian superintendent. The Mormons were equally determined to get rid
of disreputable Gentile judges, and sent the Delegate from
Utah, Dr. Bernhisel, to the White House with a slate of
officials desired by the hierarchy and a memorial voicing a
vigorous demand for removal of Gentile appointees. The
chief desire of course was continuance of Young as Governor. Buchanan asked if there were not some other man as
acceptable; it would be difficult if not impossible to secure
Senate confirmation for the prophet. Bernhisel admitted this
difficulty but maintained there was no living person except
Young who would satisfy the people of Utah. The President
need only allow him to remain in office as Pierce had done,
there was no need of an appointment.

The administration had been hearing lurid tales of federal officials flouted, of court records burned, and of the murder of an army surveying party. These appeared in many newspapers in March. Also the Republicans had been using Utah as leverage on Kansas. In 1856 they had declared themselves opposed to the "twin relics of barbarism," slavery and polygamy, and urged intervention. This embarrassed the Democracy because of their commitment to nonintervention in the territories. The Republicans hoped to force the Democrats to intervene in Utah so that they would convict themselves of inconsistency and be pushed into abandoning the doctrine of nonintervention in Kansas. Also certain southern Democrats were not averse to using force in Utah as a precedent for employing it in Kansas or elsewhere—to protect slavery.[10]

Buchanan and his advisers soon decided on intervention in Utah. The President was a stickler for obedience and regularity. He and his cabinet resented the cavalier disregard of federal authority by the Mormons. A show of force and a successful reduction of Mormon power, coupled with Walker's hoped-for success in Kansas, would be a double feather in the administration's cap. So decision soon was made to supersede Young, send out a new governor, and despatch an army with him to enforce the law. While Buchanan was searching for a Utah executive, orders were issued on May 28, 1857, mobilizing an expedition of some fifteen hundred men to assemble at Fort Leavenworth and to proceed thence under the command of General Harney.[11]

The task of finding a suitable governor was difficult. Able leadership was necessary, and great diplomatic talent imperative, for the Mormons were powerful and resolute. Just as difficult would be the social strain of living among a polygamous people. The President first sought Major Ben McCulloch of Texas, an officer of much frontier experience. He refused. Finally Buchanan took the advice of an old Philadelphia friend, Thomas L. Kane. This adventurous romantic enthusiast for "oppressed" peoples had been interested in the Mormons ever since 1846, before they went to Utah, when he had visited them and had become a firm friend of the leaders. He never embraced their faith, for he did not believe in religion, but he became their defender. He had lectured about them to many eastern audiences, and he had always acted as a sort of unofficial liaison officer between the hierarchy and Washington.[12] He had advised the several

Presidents about appointments and had been one of those who urged Fillmore to appoint Young.

Young had offered to make Kane Utah's delegate to Congress with a handsome fee in addition to the salary paid by the government. Kane had refused but had done much unofficially to serve the Mormons, and, just as soon as the news notices of March, 1857, appeared, Bernhisel probably had communicated with him. Kane endeavored to secure evidence refuting the charges and discrediting the accusers. When he found Buchanan determined to remove Young he urged the appointment of Alfred Cumming of Georgia, Indian Superintendent at St. Louis. After McCulloch declined, Buchanan accepted Kane's advice. Interestingly enough, John M. Hockaday of the mail-carrying firm was named district attorney, and W. M. F. Magraw, now superintendent of the construction of military wagon roads, was operating where he could keep in touch with developments.[13] Another Magraw, Robert, was a close friend of Buchanan's and was reported to be courting Miss Lane at the White House.

At all hazards, the Utah military expedition was belatedly despatched, and the newly appointed civil officers eventually caught up with it. The outfit reached Utah in time for winter weather and a warlike reception from the Mormons, who would not sell any provisions and ran off the cattle of the troops. The necessary food had to be contracted (without prior congressional authorization) from the plains carriers, Russell, Majors, and Waddell. They charged heavily, for the task was huge and they would have to wait on Congress for payment.[14] It would be a cold December, holding the nation in the grip of a financial panic, when Secretary of War Floyd would be asking Congress to make good a $6,700,000 deficiency, incurred in violating the Democracy's time-honored principle of nonintervention in the territories.

III

The first act of the political tragedy in the territories was staged on the plains of Kansas with Robert J. Walker attempting to direct the show. He was writing some inspiring lines proposing to inaugurate an elaborate politico-economic program for the development of Kansas. He went over them in part or in whole with Buchanan, Douglas, Stanton, and undoubtedly others in the administration. His plan was typical of the reasoning about territorialism current among those dominated by metropolitan and nationalistic attitudes. He would join popular sovereignty with a gigantic speculative scheme, in a combination so attractive to the tatterdemalion tyros of the territory that they would help insure the quick organization of Kansas as a Democratic state.

The core of his program was a huge grant of federal land. It had become the custom, when a territory applied for statehood, to send Congress a land ordinance with the draft constitution. The ordinance fixed the proportion of the federal land within the borders of the would-be state which it would receive as compensation for an agreement not'to tax the rest of the national tracts. This amount had become practically stereotyped. Also Congress since 1850 had been making additional grants of land to certain of the states to permit them to subsidize railroad building within their boundaries. Walker's plan provided a much more pretentious scheme. Kansas would ask for double the usual amount of land, both for general purposes and for large railroad grants. Such largesse would give the new state the power to offer subsidies and promote development on a scale such as no other had ever possessed. Kansas would become a promoter's paradise, and most frontier politicians could see themselves getting rich on the bonanza.

These plans, unfortunately, were perfected with strange inattention to the irrational emotionalism of territorial behavior. The promoters naïvely overrated the power of self-interest. Furthermore they assumed that there would be little difficulty in building up a national Democratic party under the command of Walker and Stanton supported by the federal officeholders and their recruits. They anticipated obstruction only from the rabid free-soilers, abolitionists, and Republicans, little dreaming of trouble rising in their own camp. Lulled by these misapprehensions, the administration agreed that only Stanton should go to Kansas immediately. Walker was to delay in the East, ostensibly to wind up some business affairs. It may be suspected that he was also lining up capital for development projects in land and railroads. There is some indication that at first it was thought that Walker would remain most of his time in the East working on Kansas promotion, leaving to Stanton the actual task of governing.[15] So the secretary took the oath at Washington on April 2 and proceeded to Kansas as acting governor. Two weeks later he was in Lecompton.

Stanton soon learned that the plans concocted in Washing-

ton did not fit. Walker and he had expected to organize a
Democratic party themselves and arrange for a constitutional
convention. Now Stanton found that John Calhoun, the federal surveyor general and would-be boss of the territory, had
already done these things, arranging a June election to choose
constitutional convention delegates. Loyal party workers were
already busy making up a census upon which the voting lists
would be based. However, few free-state men would cooperate with these "border-ruffian" henchmen; and they refused
to allow a census in their settlements, partly because they
were not going to provide any data for proslavery tax-
gatherers. The convention would probably be exclusively proslavery. Also the Republicans were reviving their free-state
government, under direction from Boston with funds from
all over the North, and bloodshed was breaking out.[16]

The situation was further complicated by incoming hordes
indifferent to slavery but wild over money-making, for in
Kansas as elsewhere in the nation the speculative bubble was
near the breaking point. Real estate speculation was working up to fever pitch. Great tracts of Indian lands were to be
thrown on the market in 1857 at a series of public sales. The
settlers were organizing to control the bidding as against the
government. The riffraff also would be at these sales because
all transactions were in cash and hundreds of thousands of
dollars would be within reach! A hullabaloo of sprees and
brawls would cover up thievery and even murder. No one
will ever know how much of the political uproar was due to
gangsters and racketeers.[17]

Railroad promoters were also active. The rails had crossed
Missouri and now awaited Kansas connections. Intense rivalry had developed among the river towns, each wishing to
be the eastern terminus of the Pacific Railroad. In fact
charters had been granted to some fifteen companies by the
session of the legislature just closed—charters to proslavery
men for proslavery towns; none other might apply to that
legislature. But free-state Topeka and Lawrence were likewise
ambitious, and their "Governor" Robinson, Jim Lane, and
Cyrus K. Holliday wanted to be railroad promoters. Lobbyists from both camps were working in Washington for congressional subsidies;[18] as the Kansas delegate wrote, "every
town either wants a land office or a grant of land for a railroad."[19] However, they found Congress wary, because of
fraud detected in the process of passing the recent Minnesota
railroad land grant act. Walker and many of the promoters

believed that the only hope for a Kansas subsidy lay in the land ordinance planned as a companion piece to the constitution.

IV

Acting Governor Stanton plunged into the midst of these confusing and alarming conflicts. He set about proclaiming vigorously the new policy of forgetting the past and looking to a glorious future. He tried his best to divert attention from the old feud. First of all, he issued an address in which he announced:

"The government especially recognizes the territorial act which provides for assembling a convention to form a constitution . . . the act must be allowed to have provided for a full and fair expression of the will of the people through the delegates who may be chosen to represent them in the constitutional convention. I do not doubt, however, that, in order to avoid all pretext for resistance to the peaceful operation of this law, the convention itself will in some form, provide for submitting the great distracting question regarding their social institution . . . to a fair vote of all the actual bona fide residents. . . . If the constitution be thus framed, and the question of difference thus submitted to the decision of the people, I believe Kansas will be admitted by Congress without delay."[20]

This utterance was not very explicit about what was to be submitted, or in what fashion; but in a less formal statement, made at Leavenworth, he said something extremely significant in the light of future developments: "It is my opinion that the convention ought to adopt all the necessary provisions usually found in state constitutions and which are not subject to controversy in Kansas. Thus there would be a constitution adopted and a state organized, ready for admission into the Union. Then I think the convention ought to prepare a separate article on the subject of slavery, either for or against it . . . [and] submit this to the people."[21] This statement invites close scrutiny in the light of later charges of "swindling." Stanton, be it remembered, was fresh from Washington.

Rumors and verified reports of Stanton's difficulties came East and changed Walker's program. Evidently he must go to Kansas as soon as possible. He wound up his affairs speedily and wrote to Stanton cautioning him not to use troops.[22] By the middle of May he set out, glowing from the banquet which prominent politicians and capitalists had given him in New York as a send-off.[23] He bore with him an uncompleted inaugural address, some of which had been studied by leading party administrators. Parts of it had been many times rewritten, and in some cases Buchanan himself had substituted his own phrases.[24] Walker stopped in Chicago to give Douglas a final sight of the document.[25]

Meanwhile, the road between Kansas and Washington was carrying traffic in both directions. The proslavery land-office ring had come East that spring laying plans to organize the new state. Surveyor General Calhoun, his chief clerk, L. A. Maclean, and A. J. Isacks, recently district attorney and now land speculator, had journeyed to the capital in March. Resolutely determined to control the new state, they wanted to see to it that the Washington authorities were posted and would not interfere with their schemes for distributing offices and subsidies. Also they wanted to size up the new governor.

These promoters discussed Kansas with Secretary Thompson, Senator Douglas, and others. They discovered two determinations on slavery and the constitution. In the first place, slave property in the territory must be protected, whatever the future action of the state. Administration leaders were agreed that this could best be done by making the constitution silent on slavery. The doctrines of the Supreme Court as revealed by the Dred Scott case would secure the institution as long as federal authority existed in Kansas. Thereafter it would be a matter of states' rights. An alternative plan was that which Stanton had mentioned, of submitting the slavery article separately when the constitution was voted on.

The second discovery made by the land-office ring was that the constitution must be submitted to the people. The Buchanan chiefs would tolerate no other plan. The South might object, but the safety of the Democracy in non-slave states was believed to depend upon it. In the light of these imperatives Isacks drew up a program for a constitution which has not survived. Presumably its land ordinance was the one adopted by the convention, but its scheme for slavery submission, we are assured by sworn testimony, was different.

During the course of their stay these men called on Walker, to find out whether he would support the proslavery program. He received them cordially enough, and when they suggested whisky he served them wine and brandy; but he would not take sides. He was to be governor, he told them, of the whole people. His alcohol did not cheer them, and they left him in stern mood. They looked at one another and then agreed, "He won't do." Evidently they must discipline another governor. Calhoun and Maclean then hurried to Kansas ahead of their chief magistrate, ready to make it warm for him if he made any concessions to free-soilers.[26]

V

Blissfully ignorant of the hostility of his disgruntled visitors, Walker set out for Kansas with a most unusual staff. He had chosen Charles McIlvaine, nephew of Bishop Charles P. McIlvaine of Ohio, as his private secretary and Patrick H. Carey, late of the *New York Times,* as his stenographer and publicity man. Carey was to send out the news from headquarters for the use of the party press throughout the nation and try to counteract the efforts of Greeley's *Tribune* reporters. Two military aides, Captain William S. Walker, his nephew, and Lieutenant Eugene A. Carr, were part of his suite, and their duties were to be onerous as well as ornamental. An unusual member of the Governor's retinue was a liaison man from the American party. The Know-Nothings were particularly numerous in the territory, and it would be politically handy to have a way into their lodges. So Stanton's brother-in-law, Edwin O. Perrin of Brooklyn, formerly of Tennessee, came along for this purpose. He was a spread-eagle orator, reputed to be humorous, who was always ready to oblige a crowd with a thrilling harangue. Walker was alive to all sorts of contingencies.[27]

Thus surrounded and equipped, the Governor disembarked from a steamboat upon the soil of Kansas at Leavenworth on May 24. Next day there was open house and hilarity. Walker ordered champagne and brandy for all who would drink—and they were many. He, however, must press on. He sought to settle his bill at the end of the day only to be assured that he was the guest of the town. When the city fathers came to the item of $210.00 for liquor, they were shocked—or was there politics in it? At any rate they declined to "open the city treasury for the encouragement of intemperance, the mother of crime." Just who, if any one, finally paid the bill, history does not relate. In the meantime the Governor proceeded to Lawrence with the Republican United States Senator, Henry Wilson of Massachusetts, who had been a fellow passenger on the Missouri River boat. Walker spent the night of the 26th at the free-state metropolis and then reached his journey's end at Lecompton, five miles farther on.[28]

This little capital on the banks of the Kaw was a straggling one-street village. It boasted a wooden office building containing rooms suitable for meetings of the legislature, a hotel, a few stores and dwellings, and a very obvious collection of drinking and gambling outfits. It was on an elevation above the river, and a road stretched down to a boat landing some distance from the settlement. Plans had been made for the building of a stone capitol, and some property owners foresaw a great future for the town. However, the Missouri River port of Leavenworth, and the free-state settlement of Lawrence to the eastward, also on the Kaw, were the natural centers of enterprise. Lecompton was a boozy, speculative, slatternly town, dominated by the federal officeholders.

Here at the territorial capital Walker finally gave utterance to his much conned inaugural. The world could now share with him the long-kept secret of this rambling document. Equal care had not been expended on all its sections. The first portion was the political statement which had been worked over by Buchanan, Douglas, and perhaps the cabinet. Here Walker carefully stated that the Governor had no power to dictate to the convention. Nevertheless he ventured his own conviction that unless the constitution was submitted to the people the document "will and ought to be rejected by Congress."

The second portion of his remarks contained his economic policies—policies that predicted so rosy a future for Kansas. The territory would receive a great grant from the federal government. This would make possible the building of railroads and the development of the land, which in turn would bring population and wealth. A needless quarrel over slavery should not be permitted to hinder or destroy the chance of this happy fortune. He declared that the climate, not politics, would decide the issue and tried to reconcile the proslavery people to its decrees. Though an "isothermal" line, determined by the thermometer, had made Kansas unsuitable for slavery, nevertheless its development as free territory would aid the South. For beyond Kansas to the southwest was the Indian territory, which would become a slave state the sooner Kansas was developed. Therefore it was folly to resist a vote on the constitution, and he closed with an even more forceful warning "that in no contingency will Congress admit Kansas as a slave state or free state, unless a majority of the

people shall first have fairly and freely decided this question
for themselves by a direct vote on the adoption of the Constitution, excluding all fraud or violence."[29]

The ceremonies were to continue with a banquet and a ball
in the whisky-drenched atmosphere of the sprawling capital
village. The chief tavern had put on its frowzy best for the
occasion. The feast was laid in its dingy dining room on a
series of small tables. At one of them sat the new Governor.
Here he was, a one-time Congressman, Senator, Secretary of
the Treasury, a man of speculators' uncertain wealth, married into the distinguished Dallas and Bache families. But in
a frontier gathering these honors and achievements were not
apparent. He was just an undersized little man, almost bald,
with a fringe of iron-gray hair, whose countenance seemed
lost in a high standing collar that half hid his profile from
the men on his right and left.

Flanking him were John Calhoun and his clerk Maclean;
they personified the frontier. Calhoun, whose name was
originally Cahoun, was the son of an Irish Protestant immi-
grant father and an American mother. He was born in
Boston but had migrated to Illinois, where he became a surveyor, a political henchman of Douglas, and an employer of
a young man named Abraham Lincoln. When Kansas was
organized Douglas had secured Calhoun's appointment to
the most lucrative job in the territory, the surveyor generalship, which controlled the bulk of the patronage. He had
trimmed his sails to the proslavery tornado and had fellow-
shipped with the invading Missourians. Frontier hardships,
the hazards of homicidal living, and too liberal potations of
the "rot-gut" so freely available had told on him. Once a
handsome figure of a man, he now looked dissipated, had a
red face and hair prematurely white at fifty. When called
upon for a toast after the banquet he spoke urbanely, and
the Governor beamed.

At length Maclean's turn came. He was a tall young Scots-
man with decided southern sympathies. He was also a tough
and reckless frontier exploiter who was not going to yield
power easily. He was bound by no convention of after-dinner
amenity. He derided Walker to his face as "the pigmy" sent
to govern them. They had broken governors before, and they
would do it again if he proved troublesome. Walker could
send this notice back to Buchanan—they cared little for Presidents. This tirade broke up the dinner, and the ball was a

sorry affair. Walker began to have some idea of what he was up against.[30]

For the moment he was not daunted and proceeded to his task. Ignoring the opposition in his own party, he concentrated on winning the free-soilers. In this first fortnight of his residence in the territory the new governor mingled freely with the free-soil citizens and learned much. He was trying to offset the impending menace of the Topeka legislature scheduled to meet on June 10 and a political convention which was going to assemble at the same time. The free-state leaders were considering the passage of a code of laws which their people would obey in preference to the "bogus laws" of the territorial legislature. Such a code would create a conflict of laws which would give new license for civil disobedience, resistance to officers, violence, and bloodshed.

Faced with this danger, Walker concentrated on persuading the free-state men to abandon their plan. He attended church at Lawrence. He presented $1,000 in local railroad stock to aid a projected young ladies' seminary. All told, he spent a week at the meeting of the free-state legislature and convention at Topeka, laboring with the various delegates in public and in private.[31] The climax of his effort was his so-called Topeka speech, which was quoted from one end of the country to the other.

In planning this speech Walker tried to be realistic. He had learned that it was useless to urge the Republicans to participate in the delegate election for the administration's constitutional convention; even had they been willing, few of them had been enumerated in the territorial census, and most therefore were ineligible. Instead, he would try to persuade them to enter the contest for the third territorial legislature, which was to be chosen in October; the right to vote in this poll was not dependent upon the census rolls. He also hoped they might be deterred from enacting their own code of laws. Most important, he would attempt to induce them to take part in the referendum on the constitution, which he was determined the convention yet to be chosen should order. If he failed in this, his mission had been in vain.

So Walker put into his Topeka speech everything he had. He pledged the free-state "assembly" that, if the constitutional convention did not submit slavery as a separate question, "I will join you, fellow citizens, in lawful opposition to their course. And I cannot doubt, gentlemen, that one much

higher than I, the chief magistrate of the Union, will join
you in opposition."[32] This pledge and the Governor's other
efforts were effective, at the moment. The Topeka legislators
disbanded without enacting their own law code, and without
committing themselves against Walker's other propositions;
also they seemed more inclined to participate in the fall balloting. But they kept their separate political identity; they
applied the money sent by their eastern friends to maintaining their militia and to taking a census for their own future
"free-state" elections. They were not disarmed by any manner
of means.[33]

VI

Walker worked hard all summer. He attended land sales
and various public gatherings including the territorial Democratic convention in July. Here he won an endorsement for
himself although he was unable to secure the nomination of
his candidate for delegate to Congress. He sought some military glory as well. When the free-state city of Lawrence
wrote its charter, in "defiance" of the proslavery legislature,
he led a detachment thither, riding to the fray in a mule-
drawn ambulance without, however, winning much glory
from this show of force. When Cheyennes were reported on
the rampage he telegraphed to Washington that he was leading all available forces; however, no Cheyennes were found.
Also Walker made some progress in press relations. He established a newspaper at Lecompton, the *National Union* edited
by S. W. Driggs. He persuaded Dr. George W. Brown, editor
of the *Herald of Freedom* of free-soil fame, to support his
policy of national parties and peace. For this and other purposes he used money, and in ways best known to himself he
spent $1,930 from secret service funds for information from
the free-soil ranks relayed by his agents.[34]

He likewise sought to find out what the delegates to the
constitutional convention chosen in June might do. As few
free-state men had taken any part in the election, those
chosen were practically all of the proslavery stripe. Of fifty-
three listed, seven were still Whigs or Know-Nothings, and
thirteen others had been. Nine had been born in free states,
but only six of these had come directly from such an environment to Kansas.[35] Of the delegates, only John Calhoun and
ex-Judge Rush Elmore had any standing, political or otherwise. He saw they were a difficult lot and probably would
resent much suggestion. He reported to Washington that they

would not write a constitution silent on slavery as had been
hoped; rather they would probably prepare one "very similar
to that of some of the southern states, securing the right to
slaves now in the territory, . . . but prohibiting the introduction of any more slaves, excluding all free negroes."[36]
Douglas's headquarters in Chicago seem also to have had
similar reports, perhaps from Calhoun, for the *Chicago Times*
asserted: "We have no doubt but Kansas will have a constitution prohibiting the introduction of slaves and with that
constitution will be admitted. She will not owe her freedom
to the Abolitionists but to the National Democracy, northern
and southern."[37]

VII

Walker's 1857 summer was watched all over the Union,
because congressional campaigns were in progress, particularly in the South. In those days members of Congress were
not selected on the first Tuesday after the first Monday in
the November of even years, with the total result known in
less than a week thereafter. In the ante-bellum days each
state had its own election customs; relatively few Congressmen were voted for on the regular presidential election day.
Many were not selected until the odd year, after the new
executive had been sworn in. When Buchanan was inaugurated, it was still uncertain whether the Democrats had regained the House. Thirteen states, three from New England
and ten from the South, had still to elect eighty-two Congressmen. Within these states the Democrats must increase
their numbers from forty-seven to fifty-four, if they were to
control the House. They were none too sure of getting the
necessary seven and were hoping, particularly in the South,
that no distracting questions would arise to supply their
Whig-American opponents with ammunition. Any Kansas
development might be of major importance.[38]

Stormy winds fanned the flame of revolt among the
southern Democrats, many of whom were still suspicious of
Buchanan and Cobb. Their emotions were made more uncertain by the indefinable tension which is present on the eve
of a financial panic. Worse, was a growing fear of northern
invasion, a premonition of John Brown. The South learned
from the press that Eli Thayer, who had been the principal
organizer of the New England Emigrant Aid Company for
Kansas, was now proposing a free-labor migration to the
South, to refurbish and reform its somewhat shabby and

decayed economy. Thayer was particularly interested in securing men with industrial skills who would go into the worn agricultural areas of Virginia and Maryland. Many southerners believed that this would repeat Kansas experiences. They feared that if Kansas were "lost" Missouri might become free soil, and if Thayer's scheme prospered the whole upper South might be detached from the slave-labor states. They took Walker's "isothermal" utterance at Lecompton to mean that he would acquiesce in such a plan. Tormented by such fears, they bitterly resented Walker's inaugural,[39] and denounced him in order to further factional fights among themselves which had nothing to do with Walker or Kansas.

In Virginia Governor Wise continued to challenge the leadership of Senator Hunter, whose term was about to expire; the knowing ones said that Wise and perhaps Floyd might not be averse to his defeat for reelection. Rival newspapers kept things hot. The leading ones were edited in Richmond, where the *Enquirer* was Wise's organ, the *Examiner* was Floyd's, and the *Whig* was the spokesman for that party. Hunter's faction felt the need of a more sympathetic mouthpiece and subsidized Roger A. Pryor of the fire-eating school, to establish a new paper, *The South*. This sheet immediately took its place with the *Charleston Mercury* and the *New Orleans Delta* in the ranks of bitter-enders and began to feature the Kansas issue. Pryor took exception to Walker's terms of acceptance, particularly to his stipulation that the Kansas constitution be submitted to the bona fide residents of the territory. He declared that the constitutional convention was the sole judge of procedure and, if it saw fit to send its work directly to Congress, it was only following a long accepted precedent.[40]

Similar factional difficulties troubled Democrats in other states. In Georgia the party had been split for years. In all parts of the state there were states' rights Democrats and Union men, while North Georgia Democrats had long been battling with their tidewater rivals in a continuous struggle for offices and power. Cobb's appointment gave advantage to the Union Democrats and roused the fire-eaters. They used Walker's utterances against Cobb and secured a resolution in the state convention calling for the governor's removal.[41]

In Mississippi, Walker's state of residence, his speeches likewise became campaign material. Secretary Thompson continued to be his enemy. Jefferson Davis, brought from the

Pierce cabinet back to the Senate by the narrowest of majorities, was unfriendly; he found Walker's words a help in his attempt to lead the states' rights wing and defeat his senatorial colleague, Albert G. Brown. The state convention voted "unqualified condemnation" of Walker's efforts to secure submission of the constitution to the people.[42]

These hostile gestures awakened Buchanan to the need of counter propaganda. Visitors to Kansas were bringing back good reports of Walker's administration, and the President had Attorney General Black write an approving article which appeared in the *Union* of July 7. Five days later Buchanan wrote Walker a private letter commending his course, a letter which three years later took on great political significance.[43]

The President also seized a chance opportunity. A group of clergymen, Yale professors, and citizens of Connecticut had become alarmed at the large armament in Kansas marshaled against the free-state city of Lawrence, and wrote him a letter protesting against the use of troops "to force the people of Kansas to obey laws not their own, nor of the United States." Buchanan made his reply in effect a message to the South. In this epistle, much more lengthy than a reply called for, he affirmed his faith in the principles of the Dred Scott decision, protecting slave property in the territories. He also expressed his confidence in the approaching constitutional convention, which he took for granted would submit its work to the people. He would use these troops to protect the voters in the free expression of their views. His supporting editors gave his letter extensive circulation.[44]

By this time the effort to make Walker an issue in the southern state and congressional elections of that summer apparently had failed. The Know-Nothings, or Americans, had not proved formidable. In Alabama they ran no candidate for governor and made a real campaign in only one congressional district. In Mississippi their gubernatorial nominee failed to arouse any interest, and anti-administration Democrats faded away. Senator Albert G. Brown conducted his campaign there in general harmony with the administration, and when Jefferson Davis started a speech-making round against him he found so little response that he soon quit.

In Georgia there seemed for a time to be a real threat. The Americans nominated a talented orator, Benjamin H. Hill, who proceeded to make a vigorous fight, but the Democrats quickly rallied their forces against him. Also Joseph E. Brown

made his peace with Cobb and the administration officeholders, and the convention resolutions condemning Walker
were for all intents and purposes abandoned. Only in Missouri was there real danger.[45] The Democratic candidate for
governor was hard pressed by an "emancipationist" backed
by the St. Louis Republicans, the Americans, and a number
of ·Benton's followers. It seemed to be anybody's race.

The tension was relaxed by the August returns. In that
month five states voted, and the Democrats made a net gain
of ten seats in Congress and carried Missouri by the narrowest of margins. Kentucky, Vice President Breckinridge's state,
made the best showing, increasing her Democratic Congressmen by four. The party was now sure to control the House.
The long uncertainty was over.

The Democrats had need of comfortable control because
it was clear to some of them with their ears to the ground
that the Kansas question might yet have to be brought to
Washington. The Washington *Star,* on the eve of the September meeting of the Kansas constitutional convention, gave its
opinion in a vein that was prophetic: "Our idea was that
[Kansas] Northern Democrats would sustain Gov. Walker's
policy to the end. That is, the adoption of an old-fashioned
Democratic State Constitution, it matters not by whom
formed, provided matters were so arranged as that the slavery
question would be submitted as a separate and distinct issue,
to be voted on by itself. We no longer think so, and we are
consequently prepared to see the final settlement of the
question of the admission of Kansas indefinitely postponed,
to be contested over in Congress with redoubled acrimony."

The animadversion of the *Star's* editor is worthy of note,
not only because of its prophecy of doom—all too accurate,
it turned out—but also because of the method of submission
which he described. In April Stanton, fresh from Washington,
had spoken of detaching the slavery question and presenting
that by itself to the voters. In July Senator Bigler had written
to Buchanan and Black that there was danger that the Republicans could make a successful effort to reject the entire work
of the convention. He believed therefore that "the Constitution and the slavery question will evidently be submitted as
distinct propositions." Now the *Star* referred to the same
procedure. Evidently this idea had some currency and was
not as startling as it was made to appear at a later time.[46]

Chapter 7

The Lecompton Fiasco

THE MEETING OF THE constitutional convention scheduled at Lecompton on September 7 was destined to bring unanticipated woe to the Democracy, territorial and national. Governor Walker's efforts to control its organization were not very fruitful. Only forty-four of the prescribed sixty delegates appeared, and they proved recalcitrant. First they defeated Walker's slate. They chose John Calhoun president over ex-Judge Rush Elmore and voted down Driggs, Walker's newspaper editor, for printer, choosing John Henderson of the *Leavenworth Journal* for the place. Then they turned on Calhoun. He knew as well as Walker that Washington demanded submission of the constitution. Yet many southern newspapers were urging the convention not to do it, but to send their work direct to Congress.

The majority of the convention were disposed to take the southern advice, and, to Calhoun's dismay, a caucus decided not to submit. Calhoun, perhaps with Walker's help, then took refuge in delay. Since the territorial legislature was to be elected in October, and the free-state men had decided to participate in this contest and had nominated candidates, the voting would be a test of strength. The convention should recess until after the election. Calhoun probably hoped the election would go Democratic, which might then persuade the members of the convention that it would be wise and safe to submit their handiwork to the people. Also delay would mean he could obtain outside aid and influence. His arguments told. After four days the motley convention dispersed until October 19.[1]

II

The October election was to be another chapter in the peculiar history of Kansas politics. On the face of it, there might seem to be little significance to the contest. If everything went off according to schedule Kansas would become a state early in the winter, and those chosen at this "last" territorial election would hardly have time to qualify before they would be superseded. Yet it presented two unusual features. It was the first election there in which the Democratic party appeared as such, and it was the first in which free-state and proslavery candidates were going to face each other. There was some division of opinion among the leaders of the former group about participating, for hate and fear of the "border ruffians" was very lively. But the northern men had a strong organization, they had Jim Lane's militia and a flock of "marshals" paid from eastern funds. They were evidently well able to protect the ballot boxes from any Missouri invasion. So Democrats and free-soilers locked horns for the first time in an electoral contest in Kansas.

The situation was made more explosive by real estate quarrels which flared up during the summer. A land sale began July 23 at Osawkee, which was in a free-state region. The usual influx of gangsters took place, attracted by the $400,000 in cash involved in the sale, and Governor Walker used some of his troops to maintain order. These disputes over property were made more acute by the various acts of the irresponsible territorial judiciary. Chief Justice Lecompte had been embittered by the attempt to get rid of him, and his associate, Judge Cato, was reported as seldom sober; on one occasion at least he was picked up out of the gutter, and on another he was so drunk in the hotel dining room that he knew not where he was. Both of these justices issued writs and warrants against free-state men and ordered arrests which stirred them to a new sense of persecution.[2]

The most alarming exhibition of judicial power was directed to the election itself. Judge Cato appeared in a role which gave the free-state people new cause to doubt the good faith of their opponents. The original territorial election law had provided a taxpaying qualification for voters, a provision not included in the law governing the October election yet not expressly repealed. Now the proslavery leaders bethought themselves to get an opinion from Cato stating that only taxpayers could vote, and he responded as desired. As no free-state people had ever paid any taxes, the purport of this opinion was to prevent any votes from that party.[3]

Walker felt the tenseness of this situation, and he took steps to relieve it. Again he secured a delay in removing the troops, once more required for the Utah expedition. He made it plain to Buchanan that with Jim Lane's militia in the territory he must have federal troops, at least until after the October election. Also he reported Judge Cato's opinion to Attorney General Black and asked that it be speedily overruled.[4]

Black replied in short order as requested,[5] and Walker immediately issued a proclamation, September 16. This document informed the citizens that all bona fide male residents could vote, regardless of taxpaying. The Governor also ordered the free-state militia in effect to stay away from the polls and condemned the persistence of the citizens of Lawrence in continuing to operate their "revolutionary" town government. These latter items were included to make his interest seem impartial. In the meantime he was doing his best to help Epaphroditus Ransom, running for delegate, and the Democratic legislative ticket.[6]

Election day itself passed off without event. The soldiers kept the peace at polls where danger was expected, and it was reported that the troops at Fort Leavenworth had the Governor's permission to vote. The returns came in slowly and with mixed results. However, it was quickly apparent that the Republican candidate, Marcus J. Parrott, recently a national Democrat, had defeated Ransom for delegate to Congress, while on the other hand it seemed that the legislature might be Democratic. Walker reported to Cass and Buchanan, October 10, that, in his opinion, a Republican delegate and a Democratic legislature had been elected. He reiterated his view that the reassembling convention would submit the constitution to the voters. Probably he was more disquieted by news from the East. Financial panic was abroad which might ruin him. He asked for a leave of absence.[7]

Having made his report and his request, he began to canvass the returns, and learned to his dismay that another Kansas electoral absurdity had been perpetrated. He received a written protest against the certificate from Oxford precinct on the Missouri border just south of Kansas City. Its return purported to record 1,628 votes, mostly Democratic. Every one knew that there were not more than 100 people in the vicinity; but to be doubly sure Walker drove over in his now famous mule-drawn ambulance and carefully inspected the region; no such population was there. Although Cass had warned him that he had no authority to judge returns and although these votes were necessary if the Democrats were to control the legislature, this fraud was too brazen. Walker knew too well what the reaction of northern public opinion toward him would be if he allowed that larceny. He was incensed that a border ruffian crowd could think they could get away with this.

As he drove back to Lecompton in his ambulance he fell sick of fever and Stanton took him to his great new house built at Benicia, on a slope outside the town overlooking the river, later to be known as "Rebel Hill." Here on his sickbed, Walker took counsel with Stanton and George W. Brown and decided he would not go behind the returns; he would declare that from this precinct there were no returns, for those which were sent in were palpably spurious. On October 19, therefore, he issued a proclamation to that effect. This document Jim Lane encountered while he was leading a crowd over from Lawrence to protest against the Oxford robbery. Despite the proclamation Lane made a fiery speech in a mass meeting on the Lecompton main street; ex-Sheriff Jones called him a liar and in the ensuing scuffle Lane barely escaped with his life. Only the efforts of "Captain" Samuel Young, probably an agent in Walker's pay, saved the melee from becoming a murderous riot.

The wrath of the proslavery gang was now turned on the Governor. Their weapon was a writ from the bibulous Cato. He was persuaded to sign a mandamus ordering Walker to give certificates to those "elected" by the Oxford poll. This writ was served on Walker at his bedside, and the upholders of "law and order" went off to take part in their own mass meeting, which passed resolutions denouncing Walker's "usurpation."

Walker and his supporters fought back. Brindle and Moore of the land office got up a third mass meeting to endorse the Governor's courage in standing for clean government and honest elections. He and Stanton prepared an elaborate answer to Cato's mandamus, refusing to obey it, and then fired another broadside. Returns had since come in from McGee precinct in the extreme southeastern corner of the territory, a region still Indian property in which at most there could be no more than fifty voters. McGee reported 1,200 votes, nearly all Democratic. On October 22 Walker issued a second proclamation refusing to accept these fictitious statistics.[8]

III

The peculiarities of this election were to have national repercussions. The Governor's actions enraged the delegates to the constitutional convention, who were returning to resume their sessions. There was indeed some fear that the riotous tendencies of the daily mass meetings might prevent the deliberations of the convention, and Walker brought in troops to preserve order. This frontier lawmaking body had the fate of the national Democratic party in its hands, and observers with any discernment might well tremble.

The Lecompton Constitutional Convention, as it was to be called, was not a body to reassure the fearful. Even with allowance for prejudiced free-soil reporting, it was composed of poor material. Its members were largely ignorant, unstable, frontier adventurers, too often drunk. Though the convention officially numbered sixty, a large part were irregular in attendance and inattentive when present. Any Democrat was permitted to sit with them, and the manner of conducting business was slovenly in the extreme. There had been some initial difficulty in finding anyone who could keep minutes, and that problem was solved only by the choice of Walker's private secretary, McIlvaine. The actual work of shaping the constitution was in the hands of Calhoun, Hugh Moore of Georgia (president pro tempore of the convention), former Territorial Judge Rush Elmore, and Editor John D. Henderson, with Walker and Stanton in the background.

The managers of the convention were hampered by certain facts. The convention members, being proslavery, were against the submission of any constitution. The recent recess to allow time for the territorial election had not changed their minds on this point; they knew, as did almost everybody in the territory, that a majority of the voters would reject any document which bore any mention of slavery. Yet Calhoun and Walker and the federal officeholders knew that as loyal Democrats they were bound to submit some constitution somehow. Walker, taking his cue from Washington conferences, had been suggesting that, if no mention of slavery were made in the constitution, the doctrines of the Dred Scott case would insure property rights in slaves and thus a document could be drawn which the voters might accept. But the convention was so bitter against Walker for his rejection of the late election returns that his influence was at a low point.

The Governor realized this and decided that things might go better if he were away. As soon as he could get out of bed he was driven, once more in his ambulance, to George Sanders's place near Leavenworth. He left Stanton to watch the convention and probably did not return to Lecompton more than once, if then, during the proceedings. His absence was not unwelcome to Calhoun. He and the Governor had never seen eye to eye, and now they had split over the Oxford and McGee returns. This schism had divided the land-office officials. William Brindle and Ely Moore, the receiver and register, had followed Walker and Stanton while Calhoun and his rabid southern chief clerk, Maclean, were in opposition.

It seemed to be Calhoun's task, almost singlehanded, to find some means of securing submission. The obstacles in his way were difficult. So much influence was being exerted to persuade this motley convention to send its work directly to Congress. The southern press was clamoring for such action. A sackful of private letters appeared, some with impressive signatures. No less a statesman than Senator Hunter of Virginia wrote two widely published pronouncements giving his high authority for such action. Yet Calhoun knew he must find some way of making his associates submit the document to the voters. Much depended upon it: his job, the fortunes of his patron, Douglas, and any last chance there might be of making Kansas a Democratic state and securing for himself and his party associates the rewards of office and the distribution of the railroad lands. He was hoping to hear from Douglas, to whom he had written for advice. In the meantime other aid was at hand.

The two ambitious southern members of the cabinet had become much concerned over Walker's misfortunes. His course had embarrassed them at times, and his failure would lower the prestige of the administration. Under these circumstances Thompson, who was a man of action, and Cobb determined to take a hand. Various charges had been filed in the Interior Department against the land officers in Kansas, and Thompson decided to send out an investigator, Colonel Henry L. Martin of Mississippi, a clerk in the general land office. While he was investigating the land records, which were located in the basement of the building where the Lecompton convention was being held, Martin might well look in on its deliberations. He was to impress upon this body that the constitution must be submitted; the fate of the administration and the party depended upon that. Cobb undertook to write to his Georgia friend, Hugh Moore, to the same effect.

Calhoun found Martin a great help, and they put their heads together to discover a way out. The answer seemed to be a variant of the scheme mentioned by Stanton in April, by Bigler in July, and by the *Star* in September. Why not submit simply the question of slavery? This would have the great advantage of insuring that, whether slavery were voted in or out, the constitution would still be ready to send to Congress and the Democrats might be able to elect the first legislature and state officers. Calhoun was able to take advantage of a situation which chance had arranged for him. He had written to Douglas for advice but had received no reply. Curiously enough, no correspondence between the two during this summer seems to have survived. Lacking instructions, Calhoun turned to the Douglas organ, the *Chicago Times* of October 14, where there appeared a pointed editorial which advised that "if any members of the Convention desire . . . to have a regular, direct vote upon Slave State and Free State, let a Free State Constitution . . . and a Slave State Constitution be prepared. Let them both be submitted to the people . . . and have the long controversy settled finally. . . . In the six months after the admission of Kansas Black Republicanism will be no more." Thus in either case there would be a constitution and immediate admission. Kansas would be out of politics.

Calhoun believed that this was the word of Douglas. So he went to work. He had some old correspondence from Douglas about submission to the voters, and with this and the editorial he went to certain of the Senator's friends and persuaded them that a compromise drafted by Martin was what the Little Giant would want. Under this compromise a constitution which protected slave property already in the territory would be submitted to the voters, December 21, in two versions; one would permit the future admission of more slaves, one would forbid it. But in either case the constitution would be adopted with its clauses protecting the owners of slaves already there. Calhoun thought he had succeeded when in the last week of the convention's schedule the appropriate committee, headed by Cobb's friend, Hugh Moore, reported the compromise favorably. The more radical committee members had to be content with a minority report recommending direct despatch of the document to Congress.

The crucial vote was scheduled for Friday November 6, on the eve of adjournment. Then to Calhoun's dismay the minority report was adopted by three votes. He immediately adjourned the convention and summoned a caucus. Here he used everything he had; some charged that money from federal funds played a part. He may also at this time have again produced the early Douglas letter and the *Times* editorial. Certainly there was much of the cup that cheers, and one of the delegates, the Wyandotte chief also named Walker, lost his sense of direction and wandered away. He had been voting against Calhoun, but just as the caucus decision was being ticked off on roll-call the surveyor's henchmen discovered him in the streets and brought him back. When his name was called a Calhoun man said, "Say 'Yea,' " and he all uncomprehending said, "Yea (hic)." The Calhoun-Martin plan was carried in caucus by twenty-seven votes to twenty-five, and, we are asked to believe, by the involuntary aid of the tipsy chief. Next day three of the most ultra members withdrew in disgust, others excused themselves, and the plan was ratified. In the end but forty-five delegates signed the engrossed document.

The Lecompton constitution thus created seemed to carry most of the original plan. Slave property then in Kansas was protected; though the future of slavery was to be submitted to the voters. The Know-Nothing interest of some of the delegates was reflected in provisions that governors must have been citizens for twenty years before election, and that suffrage was confined to male citizens. Their agrarian predilections were illustrated by the provision that the legislature might incorporate only one bank, with not more than two branches, and this only with popular approval. No free Negroes were to be permitted. The document by peculiar wording gave many the impression it could not be amended before 1864. The extraordinary land grant, the real object of the constitution, had been included. It provided that each alternate section for twelve miles on both sides of the track be granted for two railroad lines, one crossing the state from north to south and the other from east to west, numbering in all seven million acres. Furthermore this land ordinance provided that four instead of two sections in every township be set aside for the support of the common schools, totaling nine and a half million acres. In other words, instead of asking for four and three-quarters million acres, this convention demanded more than sixteen and a half million acres of land, approximately one-fifth of the territory.

Calhoun and Martin had succeeded. Governor Walker at the last minute had been more or less cast aside. In fact Calhoun in his triumph had rubbed salt on the Governor's wounds and at the same time had feathered his own nest. He knew that Walker was leaving for the East immediately; perhaps he knew that Stanton was scheduled to take over the central Indian superintendency at St. Louis shortly. More probably Calhoun and his friends wanted to make sure that neither Walker nor Stanton could throw out more election returns. At any rate they took all connection with voting out of the Governor's hands; Calhoun, as president of the convention, was by the Lecompton constitution made canvassing officer. He was to canvass the returns of the election of December 21 at which the constitution was to be submitted. He was to canvass the returns of the first election for state officers set for the first week in January. He was to issue election certificates and to call the first state legislaure. In all this Walker and Stanton were ignored. Thus Calhoun had finished the task. In his own estimation he had saved the administration, Douglas, and himself. He did not know that this latest manifestation of territorialism was pushing the nation over the precipice into disunion.[9]

IV

National repercussions were already manifest. Governor Walker had had another bout of illness at George Sanders's, but he was now starting for the East, November 17. He had hoped to go three weeks sooner, but Buchanan had insisted that he remain until the convention was through; and then the second attack had delayed him further. He was going in no pleasant frame of mind. Not only his finances were suffering, but his political fortunes were endangered by Kansas. He had been unable to secure Democratic control of the territory. In working to persuade the free-state people to vote and to recognize the authority of his government, he had roused southern opposition against himself. When he had thrown out the election returns he had increased the opposition to a point where it was likely to cause southern Senators to vote against his confirmation.

Just where did he stand? Like Reeder and Geary before him, he was going to Washington to find out. His fate was precarious, for old charges long slumbering were being revived against his personal honesty, and his enemy, Jacob Thompson, always had the ear of the President. Would the Senate confirm him? Finally, whether he realized it or not, he, like his predecessors, was fleeing from the frightening behavior of the territorials. He had been forced to live through nerve-racking experiences. Twice he had been in the midst of civil war. He had been defied and threatened. Calhoun had triumphed over him. In so much he had failed.

In Washington President Buchanan had been anxiously waiting the outcome. Reassured by Walker's letters of October 10, he had written a friendly and congratulatory reply shortly after their receipt, October 22.[10] Also he had granted Walker's

leave of absence, probably without realizing the hardship
which his order for delay had occasioned. He was busy at his
annual message and was sharing with much of the nation the
dismay created by the panic of 1857, which was then at its
worst. He hoped that good news from Kansas might aid in
restoring public confidence. Within a week unpleasant despatches once more began to come in from the troublesome
territory. The President learned how Walker had "tampered"
with election returns and had thereby handed the legislature
over to the Republicans. All this he had done despite explicit
orders from the administration that he had no authority to
sit in judgment on election returns.

The flow of denunciation from the South welled up again
as southern editorial guns roared against Walker. No longer
was there any doubt the Governor was a traitor to the interests of the South. He was a renegade who had sold out to
the Black Republicans. Political leaders began to speak out
likewise. Buchanan was now attacked without polite evasion.
He had harbored the viper too long. Walker must be removed.
The legislature of Mississippi, Walker's home state, denounced
him.[11] Prominent Senators like Toombs declared that, if the
President had the temerity to ask his confirmation, the Senate
would reject him.[12] On the other hand, Walker's action in
throwing out the returns had been popular in the North.
His New York friends had used his efforts in their state campaign and had sought to protect him. When rumor had it that
Buchanan might remove him for his acts, Sickles demanded
of the President a denial of such intent. On the eve of the
election the executive had complied by telegraph. He did not
intend to remove the Governor for throwing out the returns.[13]

For the time being it seemed to the President that the fat
was in the fire. Only one ray of hope gleamed; perhaps the
Lecompton convention would save the situation. Within a
fortnight the word had come. The action of the convention
was known in the East between November 15 and 17. It
seemed certain that the convention had submitted the slavery
question and had also taken action ensuring the adoption of a
constitution, no matter what the vote on the slavery clause.
This was a great relief. Buchanan's worst fears had been
groundless, the pledges of 1856 were to be redeemed; the
question was to be decided by the people of Kansas. The
Union of November 17 and days following voiced the administration's rejoicing.

Leading Democrats did not all share the President's relief.

The action of the Lecompton convention brought no such emotion to the troubled mind of Senator Douglas. He had even more at stake in Kansas than Buchanan. He was the author and chief advocate of the scheme being worked out in Kansas; as chairman of the Senate committee on territories, he was the leading exponent of territorial policy. He had labored with Buchanan and Walker to bring about final submission.

Douglas was oppressed by the necessity of reelection to the Senate; only if reelected could he hope for presidential success in 1860. He needed every vote in the legislature, yet in Chicago his party now was divided and weakened to a dangerous degree. He must do something to draw the discordant wings together. It was reported that a fusion might be achieved if he would oppose Lecompton. He began to give utterance in typical fashion. He told friends that the Lecompton plan was a scheme by some members of the cabinet to ruin him. He was all injured innocence. He had been unfairly accused by the Republicans of originating this trick.[14]

The Illinois Senator recognized the political weaknesses of the Lecompton device, apparently getting the details from Walker, and proceeded to exploit them. First of all was the damning fact that despite the submission of the question of future slave introduction to the voters, slave property already in the territory was guaranteed. Also the wording of the amending procedure made it seem likely that no change in the constitution could be made before 1864. Worst of all was the unrepresentative character of the convention; fifteen of the thirty-four counties had not been represented therein, and equally bad was the disreputable character of the delegates. Those who knew the Kansas situation could not help realizing that this body was in no sense the choice of Kansas voters, but an accidental body with little popular support.

Douglas therefore concluded that his original plan to disregard it and start anew ought to be followed. Congress should immediately pass the enabling act which he had been advocating since 1855 and hold a fair election under some plan similar to the Toombs bill which he had fought for in 1856. Despite the utterances of the *Washington Union*, he probably thought that the administration might be brought around. His organ, the *Chicago Times*, began to pour buckshot into Lecompton.[15] He prepared to go to Washington to discuss this strategy with the President and his colleagues.

More intimate personal matters were intruding to make him

irritable and pugnacious. Neither he nor Mrs. Douglas was well. Also he had lost heavily in the panic, and his debts were oppressive.[16] He and his wife had just planned a heavy and expensive social season in Washington. He had built a fine new house at New Jersey Avenue and I Street, in Minnesota Row with Vice President Breckinridge and Senator elect Rice of Minnesota as neighbors.[17] He had even changed his appearance, now sporting a full beard. He probably realized that his approaching senatorial campaign was going to drain his pocket and his strength.

Most trying was Douglas's grievance against Buchanan. No important patronage plums had come to Illinois. In fact this situation had been shown to the public by the publication of an unpleasant correspondence between Douglas and Buchanan. The President had appointed the Senator's father-in-law, J. Madison Cutts, to a Treasury position. Douglas did not want it thought that he was seeking places for his own family at the expense of his Illinois supporters, so he wrote to Buchanan asking a statement to this effect and alluding to the neglect of Illinois. To this Buchanan replied in a tart letter, expressing executive displeasure over this question and assuring him that Mr. Cutts owed his position to his own qualifications and not to any relationship to Douglas.[18] Douglas, like Walker, therefore, was angered over grievances and was not in a frame of mind to accept further affronts. He was in a mood to demand rather than to acquiesce. He announced: "I will show you that I will do what I promised. By God, sir, I made Mr. James Buchanan and by God, sir, I will unmake him."[19]

According to newspaper report Walker and Douglas met in Chicago as the Governor traveled eastward and each strengthened the other in opposition. Walker arrived in Washington first, on November 25, and saw Buchanan the next day. His attitude was not pleasing to the President. Here came the Governor to urge him to abandon his hopes of an immediate settlement. Walker wanted him to scrap the Lecompton scheme and begin all over again, to defy the South and bring their abuse again upon his head. The President would not do it. The Lecompton plan was the legal will of the people of Kansas; it must be carried through. After at least two interviews Walker was convinced that Buchanan had succumbed to the influence of Thompson and others in the Cabinet who, he believed, were determined to ruin him. He hurried to New

York to look to his panic-shattered fortunes; perhaps he wanted to see Douglas, who had been spending a few days there before he came to Washington. They may have met in Philadelphia with Forney on December 1 or the day after.[20]

The Illinois Senator reached the capital city late on December 2 and presented himself at the White House the next day. Here he learned what Walker had discovered. Buchanan had committed himself to Lecompton, had written his message, and had telegraphed it to Kansas without consulting Douglas, the senatorial authority on the territories who must bear the brunt of the fight over Kansas which was bound to arise. This arbitrary disregard of Douglas was high-handed and insulting, but Buchanan was determined to push Lecompton through, despite what he had been told by Walker and the Chicago press.

As both President and Senator were in dictatorial moods, there could only be a clash. Buchanan insisted that the admission of Kansas would remove the territory from politics, deprive the Republicans of a potent weapon, and permit the Kansans to settle their own affairs. Douglas countered with the emphatic assertion that such a fraud, instead of depriving the Republicans of a weapon, would place in their hands explosives that might blast the party of Jackson out of Washington. Finding argument vain, Buchanan asserted his authority as party leader. This was a party measure made so by the administration and the national convention; Douglas must fall in line. The President reminded the Senator of some history, of how Jackson had dealt with such insubordinate Senators as Tallmadge and Rives, and had broken them. Since Jackson's day, no Senator had bolted the party and survived. Douglas snorted at this and hurled back the unpardonable insult: "Mr. President, Andrew Jackson is dead."

They parted in anger, both surprised and anxious,[21] and thus on the eve of the meeting of Congress the fine springtime plans of Buchanan, Walker, and Douglas to develop Kansas into a Democratic bailiwick were in a sad muddle. The territorials had paid scant heed to the blueprints and had once more demonstrated their insubordination. No one knew just what the situation was. There was a free-state territorial legislature ready to convene if called and a delegate elect of that party on his way to Washington. The Lecompton constitution was to be voted on within three weeks. Then would come a state election at which the newly organized Democratic party might have an opportunity once more to try its strength. Would the free-state men participate in the voting? Would the Democratic majorities in both houses accept the Lecompton constitution and make Kansas a state? Over this issue the three principal party leaders were precipitating a quarrel destined to strike the party majority in Congress with unprecedented violence.

Chapter 8

Shadows Over Congress

THE THIRTY-FIFTH CONGRESS was assembling amidst these territorial alarums and excursions. The explosive situation which surrounded the convening lawmakers this December, 1857, was unprecedented. An unheralded conjunction of tensions was to confuse and complicate the labors of Congress and to draw its bewildered members into a whirling vortex.

Three behavior patterns were affected by mounting tensions almost simultaneously, producing a phenomenon previously unknown in the nation's history. The successful organization of the new Republican party underlined the possibility of a new deal in political power. The panic of 1857 was marking the violent end of a period of economic expansion. The first signs had recently heralded the coming of a revival in religion, which would mark a climax in the emotional life of the nation. Much of the confusion and chaotic clash which were to destroy the capacity for statesmanship and plunge the nation into civil war arose from this unusual, simultaneous mounting of tensions, political, economic, and religious.

The panic had been in the making all summer and finally shattered public confidence at the approach of fall. World conditions, overbuying abroad, overproduction at home, overbuilding of railroads, too wide freezing of money in unproductive real estate speculation, and an unregulated and chaotic banking structure, which had leaned too heavily upon inflated collateral, were responsible. A house of cards falls easily. The Crimean War had upset world economy, taking Russian wheat off the market and increasing the sale of American grain. With the war over, this extra demand stopped, curtailing the income of American farmers and exporters. There was thus less American exchange in Europe to meet balances due European creditors. Then the heavy financial drain upon French and English banking institutions had produced a situation which made the English interest rate very high. Numerous British investors sought to take advantage of this and began selling American securities. This produced new demands for the export of gold. Likewise English purchases of American stocks and bonds were largely curtailed so that the proceeds of such sales were no longer available to meet balances.

European selling sent down the price of stocks, customary collateral for too many loans, and began to drain away gold. The falling stock market made all businessmen fearful of credit and purchasing power. Mills with overflowing inventories stopped operating, and their workers were without wages. Purchases were reduced because of this unemployment. Savings were withdrawn from banks, bankers called their loans and curtailed their new advances.[1]

Cracks in the business structure began to yawn. On August 21 there was a decided fall in stock prices, and within the next two days failures were reported; but real apprehension was not aroused until the 24th, when the New York office of the Ohio Life Insurance and Trust Company went under. This middle western company was an active and extensive agent in placing eastern loans in western ventures, and its failure meant that many New York firms were dragged down, for they could not get their money out to meet maturing liabilities. Failures and suspensions were contagious, and things went from bad to worse.[2]

A number of banks and business houses managed to hold on because the September shipment of California gold was about due. Days passed; the ship did not appear. On September 18 came the bitter truth. The steamship *Central America* was reported as lost at sea with $1,600,000 in specie and 500 crew and passengers. This was a hard blow, for gold production already had fallen $5,000,000 below normal since January.[3] Failures immediately followed and September 25 was a black Friday indeed. The Philadelphia and Baltimore banks suspended; only by a miracle, it seemed, was New York holding out.[4]

At this point the government attempted to stem the tide. The administration took counsel, and Cobb entered the money market with federal gold. There was a balance in the Treasury of substantial proportions, and the Secretary announced he would endeavor to put it at the disposal of business by a simple device. He offered to redeem various classes of the public debt in gold at a premium if bonds were submitted immediately. He urged instant action and enforced his urgings by stressing the very temporary character of his offer. This policy he had announced on Wednesday September 23.[5] He also ordered the New York Assay office to send a large amount of its bullion to the Philadelphia mint to be coined and made ready to relieve the shortage of specie. Wherever he could, he moved supplies of coin into active markets. The Secretary further made use of authority to pay out gold in purchase of foreign silver no longer acceptable in the United States as coin. He spent a good deal of money for this in New Orleans, thus easing the specie shortage there. The Secretary of the Interior joined the effort by investing nearly a million dollars of Indian trust funds in state stocks, thereby throwing that much more cash into circulation.

These aids unfortunately had their limits. During the last week of September the Treasury received only $660,000 and paid out $1,666,000. This could not go on very long. Cobb was further disturbed because he must make up his estimates for the coming year, and he had no idea what the revenue would be in these troubled times. He wrote to the collectors to get statistics and received a welter of them. For example, Schell, the collector at New York, got each merchant to estimate on the probable foreign imports for the next year and a half. Cobb now began to come back to the Treasury Department after the usual late afternoon dinner, between three and four, and labor far into the night.[6]

The first of October provided some encouragement. The 3rd, on which much commercial paper was due, passed safely. Also the October shipment of gold arrived on the to-be-famous *Star of the West*. But this relief was only temporary. The balance in the Treasury continued to fall, and at the end of the first fortnight in October Cobb had to stop redemptions and disbursements. On October 13 eighteen New York banks suspended, and that night the rest agreed not to open on the morrow. Boston followed, and the panic was on. Railroads, manufacturers, merchants, banks, and brokers collapsed. Thousands lost their jobs. The daily transactions of the New York clearing house fell from $28,000,000 to $8,000,000.[7]

II

The tensions and uncertainties caused by the political and economic turmoil were tightened and heightened by the third climax as the emotional cycle came to fullness. Religious climaxes are much rarer than those in politics or business. These periods of cumulating emotion are longer, more irregular in length, and their completion therefore less predictable. The signs of fullness are religious revivals which sweep through communities and whole regions like a tornado and produce the deepest stirrings of the emotions of men and women in all walks of life. No such general "awakening" had occurred since the second decade of the century, after the War of 1812, and an emotional stirring was overdue.

The early days of the panic of 1857 brought signs of a new interest in matters of faith. Late in September special daily prayer meetings were started in New York City in the Fulton Street Church. This interest gathered momentum during the fall, and the winter promised to be one of intense religious fervor. Disaster and insecurity were drawing men and women to seek the peace of God. Countless clergymen zealously preached to receptive crowds. Conversions and ecstasies were frequent as the oppressed found release. The sorrowing discovered joy; the fearful, courage. Prayer meetings for children were held in the schoolroom. Workingmen flocked to churches, halls, and even theaters during their noon hour to hear the word of life. In the business districts daily prayer meetings attracted crowds at midday. Church attendance increased impressively, and clergymen had appreciative audiences to stir them to new flights of emotional appeal. At prayer meetings many who in normal times would never have dreamed of public utterance were upon their feet testifying to the wonders of regeneration.

Of the potent themes discussed in this great period of expression, the most general was repentance for sin. Only by atonement was salvation possible. If the sin were cast out and forgiven, then would come newness of life. The prevalence of individual repentance and self-searching, so characteristic of the Protestant attitude, naturally intensified and quickened the functioning of public conscience, leading to mass crusading zeal against sin. Theaters were closed, gambling and vice diminished in a revulsion against moral laxity, and an outcry rose against corruption in government. A surge of hatred of slavery flared up in a new burst of oratory bound to have political repercussions.

This revival was widespread in the South as well as in the non-slave regions. Here, too, such a deep emotional upheaval could not fail to affect political behavior. But in this slaveholding area the revival took the form of raising doubts about mammon. The Yankee speculators, corrupt and money-mad, had brought the nation to the verge of prostration. It was the duty of southerners who had developed the perfect Christian society, which had saved thousands of heathen from darkest Africa and brought them into the light of Christian salvation, to save the nation from corruption and dishonesty. Further, they must protect themselves from such polluting touch and, if all else failed, must withdraw from the debauched Union before the corruption contaminated them.[8]

The force of this revival was gathering as the Congressmen left home, and was to reach a high pitch during the winter. It was to make strange, unexpected, and frequently unrecognized appearances in the halls of Congress and in the hotels and parlors of the capital.

III

Congressmen returning to Washington were to reap the results of these economic and religious upheavals. They had left their districts, in many instances, in the throes of despair and they arrived in the capital to be met by numerous insistent demands for remedial aid—or just aid. Everywhere there was importunity. Many of the nation's most daring speculators were on hand. Plungers stripped of their resources by the crash were now pressing various schemes for the United States Treasury to refund their losses. They were preparing the stage for some of the greatest lobby efforts in legislative history.

The public lands were the perennial source of hope, and plans for their appropriation were legion. In the foreground were bills to subsidize a transcontinental railroad. Hardly less sweeping was the homestead proposal to give a farm to any one who asked. The land ordinance attached to the Kansas constitution was quite in keeping with this spirit of subsidy. Further proposals were made to negotiate with the Indians for the release of portions of their great enclaves. Another ambitious schedule was a land grant to each state to support agricultural colleges. Besides, there were innumerable smaller schemes for grants to individual states for railroad purposes.

The feverish activities of railroad lobbyists, particularly those for the Pacific railroad, stirred up opposition. The steamship interests were looking to their guns, for they had much at stake. The lucrative contracts for carrying the mail by steamer to California would expire in 1858–1859 unless renewed. If a railroad were built there would no longer be any need for such ocean mail transport, and renewal would be impossible. So the New York steamship lobby was out to get the railroad schemes pigeonholed. It was aided by certain southern, interests anxious to divert trade to southern ports and to establish steamship runs to facilitate this trade. The Pacific railroad, they thought, would stimulate the growth of free states and further concentrate trade there. The steamship people were fertile in their own schemes. They wanted, besides renewal of the Pacific mail contracts, higher rates and extra subsidies. "Strikers," as lobbyists were then called, were pushing new lines to Europe, to Brazil and the western coast of South America.

A less spectacular source of hope was a multitude of construction projects for which appropriations of money were demanded almost in the twentieth century manner. If Congress would authorize expenditure to widen rivers, deepen harbors, remove obstructions to navigation, provide lighthouses, and to build such things as docks, new customhouses, post offices, marine hospitals, barracks, and subtreasuries, this money would help alleviate the distress of business collapse in the locality of these projects. The fortune of such construction was always uncertain when the Democrats were in power, during this era. A large "pork-barrel" bill for river and harbor improvements had been vetoed by Pierce during the Thirty-third Congress. When the Opposition gained control of the House of the Thirty-fourth Congress, it had sufficient power and enthusiasm to drive through a number of individual improvement bills in spite of Pierce's veto. Now the pressure for these "pump-priming" expenditures was bound to be redoubled.

Lobby activity for congressional largesse was nowhere more active than in the patent field. Holders of lucrative patents had much at stake as their expiration dates approached. Renewal of their monopolies would give them an advantage worth a hard fight to obtain. Samuel Colt was seeking a renewal of the patent for his revolver, Cyrus McCormick for his reaper, and Edwin M. Chaffee for his rubber process. These men were prepared to spend small fortunes to lobby their propositions through Congress.

Among the "strikers" the patent lobbies were best equipped for operation. They set up headquarters in hotel rooms or, sometimes, in rented houses. Here various types of hospitality were dispensed at open parties or more private interviews. Wine flowed plentifully, food was often served, and presents were distributed, at least in the case of Colt, whose products could be easily passed around and appreciated. He had a number of beautifully decorated revolvers made up for the purpose.

If the tactics of the Chaffee rubber people are any indication, the campaigns were elaborate. Horace H. Day, the director of the Chaffee interest, came to Washington from his

Rhode Island home and hired Alexander Hay of Pennsylvania, the representative of other interests, to manage his campaign. They paid letter writers resident in Washington either to write occasional puffs of the measure for local papers or, in some cases, not to write uncomplimentary notices. Such possibilities made some of these activities a species of blackmail. There were lobbyists who were paid only on a contingent basis—so much money if the bill passed. Women were considered expert in these matters and sometimes received handsome fees. Mr. Day retained the services of two spiritualists, a Mrs. Gould and Mrs. Sarah H. Whitman of Providence, described as "an authoress of some celebrity." A Mrs. Stone, wife of one of Day's clerks, also was active "moving with members." A witness later testified, when asked if Mrs. Stone were a spiritualist, "I think not—I think she was more material." The patent agents were a host to be reckoned with.

Most numerous of all the agents were those interested in claims against the government. Some agents made a business of persuading people that they had claims and collecting on these—usually for a percentage, say half, of the proceeds. The lobbyists generally knew one another and often made combinations, exchanging help on their separate projects. It was complicated, confusing, and demoralizing. Hundreds of wishful people, each intent on gaining some object, thronged the lobbies of the hotels and the corridors of the Capitol. They operated seemingly without rest, and Senators and Congressmen were never surprised when a stranger followed his greeting in the next breath with some demand.

All this was surprisingly nonpartisan. It is difficult to realize, after reading reports of the fierce partisan debates and the press controversies of the day, that in so many matters partisanship was a sham. With regard to a multitude of money projects involving subsidy bills and appropriation items, Democrats and Republicans worked together in closest cooperation. Weed and Seward, hated "Black Republicans," were close friends of eastern Democratic city bosses and western Democratic Congressmen. Southern Senators had such confidence in Seward that he was called in to reconcile their quarrels, and seemingly hopeless deadlocks over legislation might be worked out if Seward were on the conference committee and used his champagne as a lubricant.[9]

Despite the increased pressure the panic and the bipartisan interests brought on Congress, these claims were to have hard going. This was due in part to a feeling which John Bigelow described to William Cullen Bryant: "There is an unusual dullness and inactivity in all departments of business, arising from the general distrust, as Emerson used to call it. But I use the word in a somewhat more comprehensive sense than he did. There is a limited degree of the same want of confidence in the men who conduct enterprises requiring capital in this country now, that you found in Spain and that exists in Mexico, in China and in all half-civilized countries. The character of our Presidents of late years is but a reflection of the national morals. Buchanan is a far better representative of the American people today I fear than Washington would be. The financial storm . . . has made every man suspicious of his neighbors and the consequence is that no one who has money knows where to put it to be safe. It is as plenty in New York as paving stones and yet no one can find a decent security to invest it in. No reliance whatever is placed upon the integrity of Railroad, Bank or Insurance officers. It is taken for granted apparently that none of them however unexceptionable their previous standing, are beyond the reach of temptation to use the property entrusted to them for their own benefit, without respect to the interest of their employers. I am in hopes that the inconvenience that will result from the general faithlessness . . . may raise integrity and fidelity to a premium."[10]

Suspicion of promoters was due in part also to the religious revival which had aroused the moral sense of many, particularly those cherishing the Protestant attitude. Therefore Congress proved to be more sensitive to attack and more interested in punishment. Charges of corruption became more numerous than usual and aroused an interest in exploring them not known before. Thus as the pressure for jobbery and subsidy was mounting, the will to resist it was strengthened.

IV

The darkest shadow over Congress was not the unusual cloud of political pressure; it was the city of Washington and its peculiar ways. Most trying of these was weather. Washington winters have always been a series of gamblers' chances. Dazzling sunshine on occasion fails to make up for the devastating periods of rain and dampness. Humidity covers the pocket of the Potomac valley with an oppressive blanket that encourages respiratory enemies, such as viruses and germs, to make sinuses, bronchial tubes, larynxes and lungs places of death-dealing irritants. Every year in December Senators and

Congressmen assembled in the badly heated and worse venti-
lated Capitol, fairly well prepared for political strife but almost unarmed against the various forms of grippe, influenza,
and pneumonia which just as surely would beset them.

To make it worse, those who had been there during the
summer, as well as the executive officers of the departments,
bureau chiefs, and clerks, were just recovering from the prevailing malaria which subjected so many of the summer population to the tortures of the damned. A large proportion of
the countless tensions which marred the smoothness of
American democratic procedure was due to the hazards of
health in the capital city. What the history of the Republic
might have been had the Capitol been located in a healthful
region will ever be a matter of speculation.

This capricious meteorological vortex on the banks of the
Potomac was distinctly lacking in home comforts for the lawmakers. Few except some of the more important and wealthy
Senators brought their families to leased or purchased homes.
Most lived in hotels and boarding houses, and many, particularly in the House, did not bring their wives. Some of the
members clubbed together to live in the same dwelling and
eat at the same table, as messmates. One Senator paid $200
a month for such accommodation. Even the best of the boarding houses and hotels were dreary places badly kept. A Congressman described the dining room of one of the better estab-
lishments in summer in the following terms: "The only activity
is amongst the flies. The table is literally black with them
and no one pretends to brush them off." Mrs. Senator Clement
C. Clay once talked so much about the deficiencies of the
Ebbitt House that her husband and the proprietor had a
fight.[11] In accommodations so decidedly uncomfortable their
occupants were often irritated and lonely or "under the
weather," and diversion was at a premium. Such conditions
of temporary residence were important factors in any political situation.

The available diversions were by no means tame. Washington was a highly developed center of commercial vice. Sumptuous gambling "hells" were well known, and the political
patronage of these parlors was notorious. Their operators
were often concerned with legislative moves, using their power
for or against pending measures. A fluctuating number of
Congressmen were in debt to the managers, who could and
did force votes on the floors of both houses by threatening

exposure or by demanding payment. An unfortunate member might see a stack of IOU's disappear in the flames if he voted right.

Less easy to describe was the feminine power. This ranged all the way from the subtle and genteel influence exercised in the drawing rooms of the wealthy and fashionable to the more direct and commanding efforts put forth in the "houses" in the alleys by the "madames" and their "chicks." A number of stylish and seductive women of all shades of respectability or lack of it were in Washington to gain influence and information, which by various blackmailing devices might and did secure votes and support for the measures before the national legislature. Congressmen could be "framed" or might more frequently find themselves caught in the toils of their own indiscretions.[12]

The capital city was indeed a lawless place, to put the case baldly. Its police force was weak, and crimes of violence were frequent. At the June municipal elections gangsters had come over from Baltimore, and Buchanan had been compelled to call out the marines. Order was restored only after rioting had been quelled with bloodshed. Congressmen went armed, some probably because of the growing sectional bitterness and of the floor fights in which everything from epithets to cuspidors was hurled. Yet it may be claimed that much of this weapon carrying was due to the fact that Washington was not a safe place for pedestrians after dark.[13]

V

These dark shadows were not unrelieved. An unusually gay social season was planned by the political elite. The administration was responsible for a social leadership which could on occasion be put to political use. The President and his advisers could make Washington a brilliant place of entertainment. Here Buchanan was prepared to inaugurate a change. Pierce had been in no sense able to organize socially. His wife was ill, melancholy, and inclined to be a recluse. Mrs. Marcy and Mrs. Davis had been in mourning part of the term, and the other cabinet families had shown no particular social interest. Now all was different. President Buchanan liked to entertain, and his handsome niece, Miss Harriet Lane, was planning a full season.

In this giddy whirl Buchanan and most of his cabinet families were eager to play prominent roles; some of them in a big way. Secretary of State Cass was wealthy and had two experienced daughters. They had lived with him in Paris when he was Minister to France and were prepared now to entertain on a grand scale. Cass had taken Marcy's house on Vermont Avenue and had also rented George W. Riggs's residence next door and thrown the two into one. His daughters, Mrs. Ledyard and Miss Belle Cass, had furnished it elaborately. The settees and chairs were covered with blue and white damasked silk, and there was a profusion of marble medallions, statuary, and paintings, valued at $400,000. Medallions of St. Peter and St. Paul had once graced the church built by Constantine on the spot where St. Peter was crucified. Marble medallions, highly enameled, of Innocent XI and Leo X had been brought from a monastery, and a group of twelve others, including likenesses of Jesus, the Virgin, and some of the Apostles, had come, it was said, from the first Christian church built in Rome. A crucifix of Cardinal Antonelli adorned the walls in company with paintings such as Giulio Romano's St. Agnes and the Lamb, and Carlo Dolci's Madonna. Against the background of this Italian "splendor" Cass's hostesses were planning certain social innovations such as refreshments at morning receptions, which caused the other cabinet ladies some concern.[14]

Secretary Cobb had rented Captain Montgomery's house on Fifteenth and I streets within sight of Cass's and opposite St. Matthew's Catholic Church. He and his brother-in-law furnished it from A. T. Stewart's in New York, and Mrs. Cobb came up in August to prepare for her season. She was regaining strength from her recent accouchement and was not particularly enthusiastic over the program of entertainment required by her position. But she was conscientious, and with the help of her dear friend, the sprightly army widow, Mrs. Elizabeth Craig, she was going to play her role.

Secretary Thompson's charming wife and her niece, Miss Wiley, were to preside over the mansion once occupied by Edward Everett, at Eighteenth and G, which her husband's wealth commanded. As hostess and guest she was an indefatigable participant in the round of social events, and her servants and her horses were continually busy.

The greatest splurge was made by Postmaster General Brown. He had married a rich widow, and she and her daughter, Miss Narcissa Saunders, were prepared to exhibit dash and daring even more extravagantly than Secretary Cass's hostesses. They rented William Wirt's former mansion on G street near 19th, west of the White House and Thompson's, and prepared to break precedents. Mrs. Brown, bedecked with diamonds, paid no attention to social protocol. She announced she had not known any in Tennessee and she would not be burdened by it in Washington. Instead of taking her place in the series of cabinet dinners according to her husband's rank, she barged into line after Mrs. Cobb. When her guests assembled she disturbed the English and French ministers by mixing her seating according to her taste rather than by protocol. She had music at her dinners and, all told, became an Emily Post of her own creation.

Mrs. Toucey was ill much of the time. The Blacks were neither rich nor fashionable, and the Floyds showed no style sufficiently startling to provoke comment from press or private correspondents. These three families were to be a less notable group, though ever present when the occasion required and health permitted. The administration was thus organized for the social duties which upon occasion could have much influence upon politics.

The social whirl was continuous. Many of the Congressmen and some of the Senators were men of little or no social background, and their introduction to the White House and the mansions of cabinet members, Senators, and others who entertained politically, impressed them. Some were awed and not quite sure of themselves in such new and glamorous surroundings. These unaccustomed uncertainties might make them more amenable to suggestion than they were ordinarily, and if their wives were with them the possible avenues of influence multiplied. Some great lady might accomplish much by adroit attention to the wife of an obscure Congressman.

The White House was the center. The President received every Saturday at one o'clock and alternate Tuesday evenings at eight. Miss Lane gave morning receptions enlivened by startling innovations on her part, such as wearing a bonnet while greeting the public. Mr. Buchanan and his niece gave a series of elaborate, formal dinners during the season, and introduced new fashions of service sometimes a little disconcerting to people who were used only to dining "family style."

As one lady reported it, the President's servants handed the various dishes around. "I was perplexed when a dish with two large boiled fish was handed me first—as I went in with the President. A spoon and fork were lying upon them and I had to make the first dive into it. I did it awkwardly . . . and got for my pains only a small piece of fish but I minced at it until the plates were changed. Roast beef was carved at a side-table, then came a course of mutton chops, corn (baked) and tomatoes and then birds and egg-plant. I got on bravely with all these until the pyramid of ice cream came in and I thought veritably I should tumble the whole on the President or myself before I secured a small slice, not as much as I wanted. . . . These dinners are all humbugs . . . I never eat enough to satisfy a small mouse."[15] Mice must have been larger in those days.

Secretary of State Cass was to open the official season with a dinner. This the President attended, letting it be known that he would come to no other. His associates therefore were instructed not to send him any formal invitations though he would occasionally welcome an informal bid to a family dinner at the cabinet houses. Secretary Cass likewise accepted no invitations as he was too old and frail to go out of an evening. With these two exceptions there was a remarkable repetition of guests and even menus from house to house. A prominent caterer, frequently Gautier, served most of these meals, and his food could be easily recognized.

There was magnificence at some of the tables. General Cass's board was decorated with three gilt vases filled with artificial flowers—one in the center and one at either end of the table. There were two tall gilt candelabra, one at each end between the line of vases; fruit and spun candy were heaped on tall gilt stands and others of lower stature. Nearly every dish on the table sat on a gilt or silver stand. The dessert plates were of Sèvres china—ordered from France.[16]

Such a program of receptions and dinners was augmented by "at homes" and calling. Mrs. Thompson was not used to the morning receptions with refreshments that Miss Cass was prescribing, and so she decided to attend one given by Mrs. Justice Campbell to see how it was done. She found no refreshments there, but nevertheless she felt she must do something: she decided to "have some cake and wine or coffee set on a table and let those that want go help themselves. I keep a servant standing to wait on the table and endeavor to appear not to know it is there and give it as little attention as possible."[17]

The trials of this round are indicated by an intimate account of two weeks in the life of a cabinet lady:

It is hard to find here a leisure moment that the corporeal part is in a condition to second the wishes and dictates of the "inner man." Unless you are here you can form no idea of the hurry, worry and confusion of everything pertaining to Society. And when a rest day comes it is enjoyed, *physically* complete lassitude unites us to the lounge or rocking chair and all mental exercise is a bore. This is the blessed Sabbath which we denizens of Washington hail with greater earnestness than I conceive it can be elsewhere. We appreciate it as a wise and glorious institution granting to all nations a time for rest and resuscitation. As life advances with me I understand and appreciate more fully the wisdom of God in decreeing one day of rest. But never before now have I entered fully into all its privileges and advantages with as great wish and thankfulness.

We were too late for church—therefore I have the morning to devote to you while Mr. Cobb is in his office—busily engaged preparing "a piece of writing" which he says *must be ready* by 12 o'clock. The nature of it I did not ask, for we wives learn betimes at Washington that there are many things pertaining to government business that it is not safe to commit to women—and I at least have learned to ask no questions and studiously avoid making myself acquainted with politics lest in an unguarded moment something slip from my lips that evil minded listeners can seize upon and make capital of for the newspapers.

The children have dispersed themselves about the house —and I am left sole occupant of the sitting room. Sarah came in a few minutes ago—asking for candy—holding in her hand an empty cornucopia that St. Claus brought Christmas morning filled with candy. The children missed the numerous presents that "Santa Claus" brought them at Macon last Christmas. Mary Ann thought it was no Christmas at all. I asked her what St. Nick brought? With a sad air she replied "nothing but an apple, an orange, and some candy—I wanted toys." I had no time to think of preparing for them. My visiting list keeps me on go—when I am not resting for a dinner or evening party.

I wish to give you some idea of the whirl I am kept in. I write the doings of last week and the engagements of this week. On Monday and Tuesday I superintended getting the whole house, silver, china, glass, etc. in order for *our first dinner,* which came off at 6 o'clock on Friday, the 22nd etc. including the entire Cabinet (excepting Gen. and Miss Cass who had a dinner engagement at home) and Mrs. Floyd (unable to come from a fall down stairs the week previous). Also Mr. and Mrs. John Appleton, Asst. Sec. of State, Mr.

and Mrs. Clayton, and Mr. J. Buchanan Henry, nephew and secretary to the President . . . I said the rest of the Cabinet should "be thankful for small favors" from the White House inasmuch as we were permitted the honor of having the presence of the private secretary and nephew of the President. . . . On Wednesday I visited from 12 o'clock till near 4 o'clock leaving our cards for Senators and their ladies, it being the duty of the Cabinet to make the first call upon the Senate. The Cabinet ranks lower than the Supreme Court, the Senate and Diplomatic Corps. The only privilege it enjoys is to be called upon by the Representatives of the House and "*the people.*"

On Wednesday night we went to Gov. A. V. Brown's to dinner—a grand, magnificent, mellifluous, poetic entertainment. A *band* of *music* playing during dinner—an unheard-of innovation! Lady Napier styled it "regal," a sumptuous dinner. Three vases on high stands of gilt filled with the most exquisite collection of wax and glass plants— bouquets of natural flowers before each lady's plate in vases of red Bohemian glass. . . . Judge Catron handed me to the table—and as he looked around the table he remarked that as long as he had been coming to Washington (a long while) he had never seen such a variety of people thrown together at one table.

On Thursday 24th I had my third morning reception and such an influx of company as I have not had previously. Senators, Representatives, Foreigners, Residents, and Strangers. At night Mrs. Clayton sent for me to come down and bring my cards and envelopes and she would help me to get them ready to send out for my first evening reception the 6th January. Friday was Christmas day—I spent the morning recording in my book the names of my visitors of the previous week—and at 2 o'clock we had a company of Georgians dine with us. At night Howell called off the names and residences of my previous day's visitors—while I recorded them. Saturday we had a snow storm and I spent the entire day in writing cards of invitation, that is inserting the day of the week, day, month, 6th January and 3rd February, expecting to go to dinner at Mr. W. W. Corcoran's at 6 o'clock—but about 2 o'clock a note with mourning paper was brought me which informed us that a death in the family would prevent W. W. Corcoran meeting his friends at dinner. His nephew died on Friday. Today I am writing to you.

Monday evening Mr. Cobb, Lamar and I are engaged to attend a party at Judge Jno. A. Campbell's given by his daughter Kate. Tuesday we go to a Grand Ball at Mrs. Gov. Brown's, 15 hundred invitations—report says. Wednesday Mrs. Thompson gives Lamar a party. Thursday is my reception morning. Lady Napier has issued her cards for a dancing party, it being customary with the English to dance out the old year, and dance in the New Year. Friday is New [Year's] Day—when our doors will be open and the whole city will be in motion running in a track to and from the President's and around to the Cabinet Houses. Don't you think I will be *glad* twice when Sunday comes, again. On Tuesday the 5th Jan. Miss Cass has her first evening reception and my first follows the next evening—the 6th Jan.[16]

Outside the administration circles there were various political drawing rooms of greater or lesser splendor. Mrs. Senator Douglas had her fine new mansion on English Hill, where she undoubtedly had her husband's political future in mind as she planned her entertainments and made up his invitation lists. Mrs. Senator Gwin undertook to illustrate the fabulous California Golconda by magnificence which was reputed to cost her husband $75,000 annually. In April she gave a costume ball which was still talked about fifty years later. Lesser hostesses were busy in various ways, including Mrs. Douglas's aunt, Mrs. Rose Greenhow, who was very southern and was politically opposed to her niece. She had a way with northern senators, even Republicans, which was disconcerting at times to their orthodoxy, more particularly with reference to appropriations than to principles.

It was all very thrilling, for as the ladies clattered in out of the mud in their treble-thick-soled boots, to dance the lancers, some of the southern belles invited flirtations in a fashion which amazed, upset, and probably at length delighted certain of the political males from more severe climes.[19] It was reported, too, that matrimonial ties were none too tight in some quarters. Even foreign ministers and Senators were keeping trysts with vivacious ladies, not always widows. The climax came a year later when Congressman Sickles felt obliged to kill the district attorney of the District of Columbia for regularly meeting his wife in a secluded little house on a back street. Sickles received a good deal of sympathy and was freed by a local jury. Many of the ladies seemed indignant only when he took his erring wife back to his bosom.[20] Moral laxity was evidently not confined to the gambling "hells" and alley houses. No wonder the pulpits resounded with lamentations and prophecies of doom that hectic winter.

VI

Such were the lights and shadows which formed the background of Congress. Each of the two houses was a conglomerate group of factions representing the various, often conflicting, attitudes. The tide of danger was rising not only from pressure of rival sectional interests but particularly from the conflict of attitudes shaped by great internal changes A restless and mobile population, some parts of it expanding and other parts concentrating in growing urban centers, was confused by the triple coincidence of tensions—by the political reorganization, financial panic, and religious revival. The new habits and new wants rising from a multitude of social adjustments unsettled people just when they needed most to keep their balance.

The danger of crisis was made acute by the representative system which brought together in close and uncomfortable proximity, in this peculiarly unfavorable environment, the spokesmen of these conflicting attitudes and pressures. The inevitable antagonisms, feuds, and hatreds, so exaggerated by rasped nerves, bad health, discomfort, and dissipation, generated disruptive forces which were beating with increasing intensity against the constitutional system of 1787. Could it adjust itself with sufficient speed to the new strains?

Thus Congress had to deliberate under conditions which at best were difficult and nerve-racking but, under stress of these converging forces, were demoralizing to the point of crisis. Could the Democratic party dominate so perilous a situation, maintain its power, restore the stability of a bewildered nation, and successfully cope with public issues that called for statesmanship of the highest order?

Chapter 9

The Majority Crumbles

AT NOON on December 7, 1857, Rev. Stephen P. Hill appeared on the Senate rostrum and opened the deliberations of the new session with "an impressive prayer." The House assembled at the same time without benefit of clergy. The Democratic leaders seemed to be in full control, but those of them who were mindful of history could not help being somewhat apprehensive. They were meeting in the midst of a panic. Twenty years before, a similar upheaval had disrupted and defeated their organization. Would 1860 be as bad as 1840, or worse? Few of the Democrats had any real sense of security; on every hand there were too many signs of disaster. Yet none of them realized that they were about to enter the most complicated legislative tangle of the antebellum period. This is perhaps an understatement.

The group most vitally concerned with the immediate prospects of the Democracy were the party members from the free states. Most of them would have to stand for re-election sometime in 1858, in contrast to their southern brethren who had just come through their trials. From Douglas down they were all aware that there must be no mistaken policies which might further antagonize the northern voters. The southern Democrats and the administration must see that northern defeat in 1858 would mean party rout in 1860. The northerners were determined to shape policy to protect themselves. Control of the legislative machinery therefore was more than ever important.

Maneuvering for position had been going on all summer over organization of the House. Although the Democrats seemed in comfortable control with a membership of 128 as opposed to 92 Republicans and 14 Americans, this majority was sharply divided; the 75 southern Democrats were not sure of their 53 northern colleagues. The focal office was the Speakership. The chief contender for this post, James L. Orr of South Carolina, was backed by those who were to be the administration bloc, the veteran conservatives from southern and non-slaveholding states. Their chief objective was to hold the fire-eaters in check. Orr was their choice because he was an outstanding exponent of their tactics in the South. He had been organizing the Democratic party in South Carolina, bringing a respectable group to believe in the wisdom of national party affiliation, despite the radical impulses of his state. Also he had visited Kansas and had supported Walker's Kansas policy when Buchanan was under the strain of southern criticism. He was thus high in presidential favor. Not the least of his accomplishments was his skillful hospitality. His Washington rooms had a "little convenience" always at the command of the thirsty.

Orr had to overcome some opposition. His defense of Walker had aroused sufficient apprehension among the southern revolters to cause some of them to start a move for Alexander H. Stephens of Georgia, the most skillful parliamentarian in the House. He would have none of it, however, and suggested John Letcher of Virginia. From the southwest some claim was made for another House veteran, John S. Phelps of Missouri. Symptomatic of developments to come, Douglas's Illinois delegation was trying to line up votes among northern Democrats for their House leader, Thomas L. Harris. They were strong enough to negotiate a deal, whereby the caucus nominated Orr for speaker and James C. Allen of Illinois, a Douglas man, for clerk. The combination thus defeated the southern anti-Walker group.[1]

Caucus action on the printing was more difficult. Cornelius Wendell, although he had been the printer of the Republican House just past, aspired to be retained by the Democrats. He felt he merited it, because he really had done the printing for the Democratic Congress from 1853 to 1855 and now he was maintaining the Democratic *Union*. His candidacy touched off an explosion when a Virginian charged that Wendell was trying to bribe members. The caucus cast two ballots without giving any one a majority, and then adjourned.

This bribery charge and the adjournment gave Wendell's opponents their chance. An Ohio and Virginia combination had been conspiring against him all summer. Alexander Walker and Washington McLean, editor and owner of the *Cincinnati Enquirer,* promoted the fortunes of James B. Steedman, a supporter of Douglas, on the understanding that Steedman, if successful, would share the proceeds with them. They expected that their candidate would attract a sufficient bloc from the northern and southwestern Democrats to insure success. When they discovered that they needed more southern support, they associated with them a Virginia editor of Petersburg, A. D. Banks, who was likewise to share the proceeds. This alliance made the most of the charges against Wendell, and they were effective in spite of his denials.

At the adjourned meeting of the caucus on Monday evening, Steedman was nominated over Wendell, 60–31; and the will of the caucus was duly ratified by the House. But the new printer, like his senatorial colleague, Harris, now made a bargain with Wendell to do the work just as he had in the previous congresses. Steedman agreed to pay Wendell 64 per cent of the receipts, and the remaining 36 per cent was to be divided among Steedman, Banks, McLean, and Walker. Harris took out a lump sum rather than a percentage. These terms were later to be featured in the headlines of that day.[2]

Though the administration bloc had shared the elected House offices with the Douglas cohorts on a numerically even basis, it had retained the appointing advantage. Speaker Orr controlled the committee appointments, and there the Douglas men were ill favored. The important committees were ten: ways and means (by far the most powerful), commerce, public lands, post offices and post roads, judiciary, Indian affairs, foreign affairs, territories, patents, and claims. Of these ten, six—public lands, judiciary, Indian affairs, foreign affairs, territories, and patents—had southern chairmen friendly to Buchanan. Ways and means was headed by J. Glancy Jones, the Pennsylvania friend whom President Buchanan had supported for the post after his cabinet disappointment.[3] Commerce was presided over by John Cochrane of New York.

The western Democrats had only claims, and post offices and post roads, chaired by Marshall of Illinois and English of Indiana; and only Marshall was friendly to Douglas. The Douglas men had a particular grievance in that they were given charge of none of the committees which handled their sectional interests. It was particularly galling, in view of the expected Kansas difficulty, to note that the committee on territories had been carefully chosen so as to exclude any real friend of Douglas and squatter sovereignty. On the other hand, as far as the House was concerned, the fire-eaters had been suppressed.

In the Senate the administration had comfortable control. The 37 Democrats had an overwhelming majority as against the 20 Republicans and 5 Americans. The 25 southern Democrats controlled the party caucus and could count on 7 "doughfaces" from their northern brethren, Bright and Fitch of Indiana, Gwin of California, G. W. Jones of Iowa, Bigler of Pennsylvania and Thomson and Wright of New Jersey. Benjamin Fitzpatrick of Alabama was chosen President *pro tem,* and William A. Harris of the *Union,* Senate printer.

While the formalities of organization were in process, Buchanan's message was received. In the Senate on December 8, the secretary, Asbury Dickins, a notoriously poor reader, droned indistinctly through the lengthy document, which embraced so many topics. One stood forth as the center of all attention, and that was Kansas. The President related at length the history of the Lecompton convention; "every citizen," he wrote, would have an opportunity December 21 to vote on slavery, "and thus this exciting question may be peacefully settled in the very mode required by the organic law." He was careful to make no recommendation as to whether Congress should accept the decision of the Kansans. Douglas, when he rose to move that an extra quantity be printed, professed not to have heard the message clearly. He thought that he was in accord with most of it, except what he believed Buchanan had said about Kansas. He would speak more at length next day.

This message surprised the radical southerners, who had expected to fight Buchanan over Walker. Now the President's failure to endorse Walker and his implied acceptance of Lecompton, which reputedly had been written solely by southerners in Kansas, left them seemingly without need of arms. They only feared lest Douglas might break loose before December 21, the date of the Kansas voting on Lecompton.

Their fears were justified; despite some attempts to persuade him to delay, he spoke December 9, bitterly, sneering at this "fake" popular sovereignty which left the voters no chance to rid the area of slaves already in it, or to pass judgment on the constitution itself. One of his colleagues noted about him "an air, of having taken a decisive and irrevocable step." He demanded that a new convention be called and introduced a new enabling act for this purpose.[4]

Even as he spoke the wires brought word that Acting Governor Stanton was calling a special session of the recently chosen territorial legislature. As this body was free-soil, it would probably try to destroy the Lecompton plan. Buchanan instantly removed Stanton for thus playing into the hands of the Republicans, and on December 10 appointed James W.

Denver, Commissioner of Indian Affairs en route to Kansas, as acting governor. Denver was appointed governor early in January and confirmed six weeks later without a roll call. But the damage already had been done; the territorial legislature met and ordered a real referendum, for or against the Lecompton Constitution as such, to be held early in January.[5]

Where did all this leave Walker? He had been in New York since December 2. The day after Denver's appointment he returned to the capital and had his final interview with Buchanan. He was now probably aware that the southern senators would block his confirmation; also he and his backers were perhaps so crippled financially by the panic that there was no hope of putting his grand Kansas plans into operation. At any rate he resigned December 15 in protest against the administration's determination to back Lecompton, a scheme hateful to a large proportion of the territorial population. In spite of much historical writing to the contrary, Walker seems to have been getting out from under an impossible situation, taking refuge in the usually profitable role of martyr.

Buchanan accepted Walker's resignation over Cass's sprawling signature, as the State Department had technical supervision over the territories in those days. The letter sent to Walker contained a curious interpretation of events, claiming consistency for the President in his stand favoring Lecompton. The letter coolly asserted that Buchanan "never entertained or expressed the opinion that the convention were bound to submit any portion of the constitution to the people except the question of slavery." Considering his previous expressions regarding the submission of the constitution to the people, and the probability that he had never seriously thought of the Lecompton method of referendum until the preceding spring, this statement could not fail to strike informed citizens as untrue.[6]

II

While waiting for the results of the December voting in Kansas, Congress turned to other matters. The House proceeded to business in new quarters. The old hall had been uncomfortable and badly constructed for its purposes; its acoustics were abominable, for at certain spots no one could hear what was going on. New chambers—north and south, for Senate and House—had been under construction since 1850, and now the southern wing was ready. On December

16, Speaker Orr led the Representatives into their new glory, and here the House deliberated on the nation's problems. But they were not much better satisfied; the members complained that the ventilation was bad, the heating system inadequate, and their rooms damp.[7]

Meanwhile Kansas continued to produce her peculiar brand of political statistics. On December 21 occurred the referendum arranged by the proslavery constitutional convention, which had met at Lecompton in September; 6,143 votes were tallied for the Lecompton constitution "with slavery," 569 "without." On January 4 occurred the referendum arranged by the special session of the free-state legislature, which had been elected in October and had met in December; 10,266 votes were tallied against the Lecompton constitution as such, 162 for it. Apparently at least 4,000 more persons had voted against Lecompton in January, than for it in December. Vociferous cries of "Fraud" against the December poll, and sworn testimony that 2,655 of the "with slavery" votes were fraudulent, did not deter Calhoun from certifying to Washington that the Lecompton constitution had been approved "with slavery." However, the January poll for state officers (to be inducted if Congress accepted Lecompton) was so irregular that even Calhoun dared not certify to their election; he contented himself with a mere announcement that the proslavery ticket had won.[8]

What would Buchanan do? Would he stand on Lecompton as the legal will of Kansas and ask her admission as a slave state, or would he conclude from the election of January 4 that the majority of the voters opposed this? Naturally the southern radicals wanted the first while the incipient Douglas bloc demanded the second. The cabinet discussed a compromise, by which Kansas should be admitted under Lecompton, with the condition that the first legislature submit the constitution to the people once more. Buchanan, Cass, and Toucey were described as favorable, Black not reported, and Cobb, Floyd, Brown, and Thompson opposed.[9]

The trouble with the compromise plan was not so much the southern opposition to it, as the fact which was becoming plainer every day, that Douglas would have none of it. The riddle was, how far would the northern Democrats in the House follow Douglas, how many could Buchanan command? The whole issue was complicated by the dominating reality of the situation: most of the fifty-three northern Democrats must stand for reelection that fall, and the Republicans were all geared to take advantage of another Kansas embroglio. Douglas was laboring among the fifty-three to see how many could be lined up against Lecompton. If even a dozen followed him the Democratic majority would be lost. It was a splendid opportunity for a small minority to gain the balance of power, and a perfect bargaining position.

An anti-Lecompton bloc in the House took definite form in late January as the confused story of the Kansas election returns became more confused. The five Illinois Democrats were joined by six each from Ohio and Pennsylvania, three from Indiana, two from New York, and one each from New Jersey and California. This group of twenty-four held caucuses to plan their strategy. Occasionally Niblack of Indiana and Pendleton of Ohio voted with them, though they avoided the caucuses. These twenty-six, however, were one short of a majority of the fifty-three northern Democrats.

Most of the northern Democratic delegations split; only Illinois and Connecticut Democrats were united, the former against Lecompton, the latter for it. In the East the schism leaned toward Buchanan. Of the twelve New Yorkers only two joined the anti-Lecomptonites, Haskin of Westchester and Horace F. Clark, Vanderbilt's son-in-law from New York City. If Clark were following his father-in-law's tactics he was angling for advantages in his fight for steamboat subsidies; at times the administration thought he was with them. Of the three Jersey-men, two supported Buchanan; of the fifteen Pennsylvanians, nine were steadfast to him. In the West the schism turned from Buchanan. Only one of Ohio's eight Democratic Representatives and two of Indiana's five remained strictly loyal to the administration fiat. The California delegation of two was equally divided. This northern split was based as much upon factional and sectional differences within the states, disagreements over patronage and the like, as upon antagonism over principles.

The anti-administration bloc proceeded to organize. They chose Thomas L. Harris of Illinois and John B. Haskin of New York as chairman and secretary. They advised with Douglas and had the aid of R. J. Walker and Stanton, who were attempting to arouse public sentiment against the "fraud." They secured some southern support. Governor Wise of Virginia, possibly with an eye to northern aid for the Presidency in 1860, wrote a letter to Tammany denouncing Lecompton; and Henry Clay's son James, now a Democratic member from Kentucky, sometimes fraternized with the bloc.[10]

When General Clarkson arrived with the official copy of the Lecompton constitution January 30, the anti-Lecompton bloc moved into action. At a meeting attended by James B. Clay they appointed a committee of Clay, Haskin, and S. S. Cox to wait upon the President and urge him to refuse to endorse the document. The committee went to the White House on a fruitless errand. They reported public opinion rising against this travesty and told Buchanan plainly that he could not command enough votes to pass it. Would not the President heed the handwriting on the wall? He would not. He replied to the committee that he was committed. The Lecompton constitution with slavery was the *legal* will of the people of Kansas, and he would urge Congress to accept it. He had decided to drive Lecompton "naked" through Congress in thirty days, and thus destroy Kansas as a political weapon in plenty of time before the elections. He would carry Lecompton or die.[11]

The President had made this decision despite confidential word from Kansas of which his opponents were presumably ignorant. Ex-Judge Rush Elmore, the largest slaveholder in Kansas, who was brother-in-law of Senator Fitzpatrick and was otherwise well connected, had just arrived with a private message from Governor Denver. The new Governor strongly advised against accepting the Lecompton constitution. Bloody civil war alone would result, for there was an oath-bound organization determined to kill any man who tried to take office under this constitution. Denver recommended that Congress pass an enabling act (much after the Douglas plan) and thus provide for a new start. Then a Democratic party could be organized, just as Walker had hoped, composed of those opposed to the extremists of both types, and the state saved for the Democracy.

Buchanan lacked the intelligence to heed this sound advice. He had promised southern leaders to support Lecompton, and he feared the effects if he changed his mind. He needed their support for his foreign policy and his legislative program.[12] He had carefully measured his forces. He needed 118 votes, and he was sure of 102. Even if most of the hostile bloc held out, he thought he had other resources. Fourteen Americans were from the South and, on a close vote, might be counted upon to support their sectional interests. Also the

President was confident that his authority and his patronage could eventually bring over several of the less determined antis when he cracked the whip. So he wrote a message to Congress, which he first showed to Alexander H. Stephens, submitting the Lecompton constitution as the will of the people of Kansas regularly approved at a legal election. Under the terms of the Kansas-Nebraska Act, he recommended that Kansas be admitted to the Union.[13]

III

It was 3:30 in the afternoon of February 2 when this message reached Congress. Both sides had their plans laid. An administration poll of the House had indicated that it would be impossible to pass Stephens's usual motion to refer the message to the territorial committee, which was "safe"; and so the Buchanan side planned to divide the northern Democrats by having Hughes of Indiana move reference to a select committee without instructions to investigate, to which committee the Speaker would appoint the "right" men. The foes of Lecompton planned that their man Harris, of Illinois, should move a select committee *with* powers to investigate. Buchanan knew that such a move would mean delay and the manufacture of campaign material for the Republicans, according to the precedent set by the Kansas committee of the previous Congress. On the test votes of the first day the administration was defeated, 109–105.[14]

Here the matter rested for three days until Friday afternoon, when Harris acted unexpectedly. Dinner parties were scheduled that evening by the President, the Speaker, and Secretary Toucey; and many of the administration forces left early to get ready because formal dinners began at six. Suddenly, at 3:30, Harris moved the previous question on his resolution for a committee to investigate. If this prevailed, debate would automatically be prevented and a vote must be taken immediately. Stephens, the administration floor leader, saw at a glance that a vote would be fatal; so he began a filibuster by demanding roll call after roll call on successive motions to adjourn. These began at four o'clock and continued all night. Harris and his new majority would not yield, despite the lack of a quorum. They ordered the sergeant-at-arms to go out and summon the absent, and the various dinner parties were interrupted from time to time by officers of the House. At the risk of being judged in contempt, a number of administration men refused to return.

At two A.M., much to everybody's surprise, proceedings were thrown into riotous tumult. Grow, who had things in charge for the Republicans, was objecting to various administration maneuvers and was over on the Democratic side of the House, conferring with some anti-Lecomptonites, when Quitman offered another proposition. Again Grow objected. Near by, Laurence Keitt of South Carolina, half asleep, lay stretched out on two seats with one shoe off. He immediately roused and ordered Grow to go over on his side to do his objecting. Grow replied truculently that it was a free House and he moved where he pleased. Keitt was furious and yelled: "Wait till I put on my shoe and I'll see." Grow, nothing daunted, waited. The Carolina fire-eater put on his shoe and then jumped for Grow's throat, saying: "I will choke you for that." Grow hotly told him he "need not think to come from your slave plantation and expect to apply the lash to me," whereupon Keitt grabbed for his throat again. Grow struck at him but missed, and the fight was on in earnest.

In the melee Henry Clay's son, despite his liquid state or maybe because of it, jumped up on one of the desks and shrieked that members should stop fighting. Washburne of Illinois knocked off Barksdale's wig. The Mississippian was angry, because few knew he wore one, and now not only was his baldness exposed, but his precious scalp was trampled under the scufflers' feet. He managed to retrieve it, but in his haste donned it wrong side out. Laughter drowned out fury, and the rumpus died out. Night was a long time dying, and the contest continued until 6:25 A.M. when an agreement was reached to adjourn until Monday and then take a vote. The administration had gained the week end in which to work.[15]

It was not idle. Buchanan did not hold his usual Saturday reception but devoted his time to seeing individual Congressmen and urging them to come to Lecompton's support. His task was all the more difficult because tuberculosis was detaining Congressman Caruthers in Cuba at a time when the vote of this Missouri Democrat seemed to be much needed. Furthermore Buchanan saw John Calhoun, who had just arrived with the Kansas returns. He discussed with the surveyor general the various dispatches, letters, and news items which had been accumulating. The President learned definitely that frauds as notorious as those of Oxford and McGee precinct probably had occurred elsewhere, and that the territorial legislature was investigating the returns from Delaware Crossing, Kickapoo, and Shawnee. Whatever result Calhoun might declare was bound to be challenged. Buchanan saw too plainly the advantage the Republicans would take, and he argued with his northern Democratic visitors to vote Lecompton in and deprive the enemy of their field day. But Buchanan did not have to face free-state voters that fall, and these Congressmen did.

The social possibilities of exerting pressure were not neglected. The "season" in Washington was in full swing and was exceptionally brilliant. Many a night was danced and feasted away, with many a Senator and Congressman appearing in his place next morning somewhat the worse for wear. While southern ladies were adept at influencing votes their northern sisters were not without resources. The northern Democrats found themselves the center of social attention, particularly the Ohio delegation. That Saturday night the Whig ex-Congressman Samuel F. Vinton of Ohio and his sister Mrs. Goddard gave a little party to which the Buckeye Democrats were invited. They paid particular attention to Groesbeck, whose vote on Monday would be needed against the administration. No doubt there were others. It was a busy week end made more exciting because the *Union* in its Sunday edition undertook to read Harris and the anti-Lecomptonites out of the party.[16]

Monday morning came, the House assembled. The members straggled to their seats. Some of the cabinet were there, particularly Cobb and Thompson, cajoling, persuading, arguing, and cracking the patronage whip. The House printer, Steedman of Ohio, was laboring with his recalcitrant delegation. The Speaker called the session to order, and, as agreed, without further parliamentary ado, Stephens's motion to refer the President's message to the committee on territories was put. Various roll calls were ticked off as the result hung in the balance. Groesbeck voted nay—Mrs. Goddard's party had not been in vain—and Pendleton likewise. These two Ohioans were offset by Burns of Ohio and Niblack of Indiana who remained with the administration. The clerk announced the result: the administration's motion was lost, 114–113. Ten minutes too late, another Buchanan Democrat wandered in.

Next Harris's motion, for a select committee with power to investigate, was put and carried, 114–11; Niblack had come over to the antis but Pendleton had fallen away. The average anti-Lecompton vote from the Democrats was twenty-two, but in the series of votes Pendleton and Niblack showed themselves uncertain, while Burns seemed to have deserted to Lecompton. This uncertainty and the fact that three from their ranks were absent led the administration to believe that eventually they would win. In 1854 Stephens and his aides had broken down an adverse majority of twenty-one in the great Nebraska struggle. History might repeat itself. Even in its victory the anti-Lecompton bloc was disappointed; it had expected a margin in its favor of six or seven. Then it would have voted to take the appointment of the special committee out of the Speaker's hands. Its margin, however, was so narrow that it feared to try this move.[17]

When on the same day the President's Lecompton message was referred to Douglas's Senate committee on territories, it seemed as if he and Harris were now in a position to investigate freely and make as much political capital as possible out of the situation. But the ruthless administration leaders in Congress would yield no such advantage to Douglas. The Senate committee set the pace. Its majority—consisting of Green of Missouri, Sebastian, Fitzpatrick, and, most unkindest cut, Jones of Iowa—snatched control of the Kansas question away from its chairman, Douglas, and gave it to Green. He was to prepare a bill and a report as soon as possible. In the House the tactics were even more offensive to the anti-Lecompton forces. Speaker Orr made Harris chairman of the select committee, but he packed it with a pro-Lecompton majority. Such procedure was denounced as a cheat. The anti-Lecompton men had control of the House on this issue, and they held they were entitled to a majority of the membership. Orr denied this; the President's message was at issue, and therefore the administration was entitled to control. The majority of the committee proceeded under the leadership of Alexander H. Stephens to vote down Harris's attempts to start an investigation. When Stephens got around to it, he would write a report upholding Lecompton; in the meantime, the committee would wait for the Senate to proceed.[18]

Across the rotunda Green was endeavoring to hurry a decision on Kansas. He and his colleagues of the majority decided on a simple bill admitting Kansas under Lecompton, but with only the customary land grant. He prepared a report to accompany this bill and was ready within a week. Douglas, of course, would write a minority view which probably would be the rallying point of the opposition, but he was in the midst of domestic calamity. Mrs. Douglas had nearly died in childbirth and the baby had lived only a few hours. He was up night after night in this fortnight in February, watching in the sickroom.

When on February 15 the Senate committee met to consider its final report, Douglas asked for another week; he was exhausted and had not been able to finish his minority views. The majority agreed reluctantly, half suspecting him of delay. Next day the administration pressed them to hurry and persuaded Green to bring in the bill on Thursday the 18th. He was not sure of his committee strength, for Senator Fitzpatrick was ill, and so the latter was excused and his colleague from Alabama, C. C. Clay, Jr., was given the berth to maintain the majority. Then Green wrote Douglas to be ready in two days. Douglas was taken by surprise but sat up two nights with his clerks and by Thursday, perhaps to the astonishment of his colleagues, he handed in his views, first telegraphing his work to the *New York Tribune*. On February 18, therefore, Green reported his bill.[19]

The task of the party leaders was made increasingly difficult by the news from Kansas. Calhoun in Washington was the center of some attention because in his hands, as president of the constitutional convention, lay the decision as to the political complexion of the state officers and legislature. Since he had arrived, various news despatches had come eastward. The most important consisted of affidavits in Kansas papers swearing that the rumored frauds were facts. Douglas took these items to Calhoun and asked him whether he would grant certificates based on fake ballots. Secretary Thompson also told Calhoun that Governor Denver had advised him that the election was a sham. Calhoun, in a quandary, finally said that if crooked voting were proved he would throw out the returns. By the end of February the investigating committee of the Kansas antislavery legislature concluded taking testimony and reported startling evidence. Certain federal officials, it was proved, had sought to hide proofs of tampering with election returns in a candle box buried under a woodpile in the dead of night. Authenticated copies of this evidence were brought to Washington by one of the investigating committee on March 2. Seemingly nothing regular or honest in the way of an election could be held in Kansas.

Much pressure was exerted upon Calhoun to disregard this

evidence or to make an arbitrary decision in the nature of a compromise. He might accept proofs of fraud at Delaware Crossing, Shawnee, Oxford, and Kickapoo and thereby recognize the choice of a Republican "state" legislature. On the other hand charges of irregularities in certain Republican areas might justify him in rejecting enough votes there to elect the Democratic "state" officers. He refused to make up his mind for weeks. Finally on March 19 he announced that he would certify to the election of the legislature with a Republican majority. He said nothing about the state officers; but he planned to leave to the legislators, if they ever met, the task of deciding who had been chosen to the state posts. In some quarters it was believed that this decision might aid in getting the votes of northern members of Congress for Lecompton. It was claimed on the floor of the Senate that this step was taken on the advice of prominent southern leaders.[20]

This action of Calhoun's was but one of several efforts afoot to promote some form of compromise. Ever since the House votes in early February, the most acute observers had thought it impossible to push Lecompton through, and as these unsavory details of the Kansas election came east it seemed even less desirable to do so. Might not some new formula be found, acceptable to the Douglasites, which would reunite the party and permit the majority to go on to other legislation?

IV

The month of March was spent in searching for a compromise formula. At one time the Senate managers thought of uniting the admission of Kansas and Minnesota in one bill, one to be perhaps slave and the other free. Senator Crittenden proposed to resubmit the Lecompton document to the Kansas voters. In the House there was much jockeying for position, made difficult for the administration by the unstable habits of a score or so of their bibulous adherents who at crucial roll calls might hardly be made to hiccough "Aye" or "No" as the case demanded. The anti-Lecompton coalition retained its strength. When the Senate finally passed a bill, March 23, it was the original measure admitting Kansas under the Lecompton Constitution with specific guarantees of the right of immediate amendment.[21] The compromise plan to admit Minnesota and Kansas together, one free and the other slave, had been dropped. The Crittenden plan had been defeated.

The only change in the Lecompton scheme was the elimination of the exorbitant land grant.

This measure came to a hostile House where the chief danger was that the anti-Lecompton Democrats might join with the Republicans and some Americans to accept the Crittenden plan. Congressman Montgomery from Pennsylvania, of the anti-Lecompton bloc, seemed willing to lead such a move in the House. The administration therefore doubled its efforts to reduce the anti-Lecompton bloc. The President called many of them to the White House and commanded, argued, and even pleaded with them. He attempted to show them that the fate of the nation hung in the balance. He pointed out that the legislatures of Alabama and Georgia were threatening secession if Kansas were kept out of the Union. In fact Georgia's Governor, Joe Brown, believed that because of the Georgia platform of 1850 he was expected to call a convention in that event. The Texas legislature declared itself ready to send delegates to such a convention. In the face of these dangers to the Union, patriotism demanded the immediate admission of the new state. At the same time loyal Democrats would destroy the Republicans' most important ammunition dump.[22]

The patronage had been brought into play. The head of three prominent Douglas postmasters at Chicago, Columbus, and Cleveland were chopped off as a warning. The administration went so far as to approach Trumbull, the Republican Senator from Illinois; Slidell intimated that if he would not oppose their new appointees in Illinois he might have some hand in making them. Douglas fought against the confirmation of the new nominees but was defeated. Isaac Cook, the new postmaster of Chicago, was to organize an anti-Douglas wing in Illinois and try to gain control of the state Democratic convention. Similar efforts were made in Ohio, and in Indiana where the district attorney was removed and Douglas postmasters were not reappointed. Also the President let it be known he would send in no other important appointments, none of the New York, Philadelphia, or other city slates, until Lecompton was disposed of.[23]

Buchanan may have felt it beneath his dignity to make patronage promises directly to Congressmen, but others had no such scruples. Cobb and Thompson, with the immense patronage of the Treasury and the Interior, Brown with the Post Office battalions, Floyd with contracts for feeding and equipping the army and commissions in the new regiments,

Toucey with contracts for new naval vessels, Cass with consulates: all these could speak and did. Officeholders were called to Washington to work on Congressmen. The number of Buckeyes who were brought on from Ohio appeared to be legion. The angel of the party, Cornelius Wendell, seems to have supplied much of the money for this. He also contributed or secured funds to revive or establish Lecompton newspapers in doubtful districts. He paid certain lobbyists to work on Ohio Congressmen and was later declared by a witness under oath to have offered one bright young Ohioan $5,000 a Congressman if he changed any votes.[24]

Besides laboring to win over those holding the balance of power, the administration leaders had the difficult problem of keeping their own followers in line. Douglas and his associates were likewise trying to make converts. Many elements in northern constituencies were vocal in their efforts to compel Democratic Congressmen to defeat this scheme of the "slave power." Mass meetings and press campaigns were outspoken. More difficult to combat was the carelessness of a number of the Democratic members loyal to the administration. They disliked to sit in the House, were often absent, and several were habitually drunk. Thus while the Republican and anti-Lecompton Democrats were stubbornly in their seats, always ready to muster full strength on a vote, the adminstration ranks were often thinned; and Stephens upon occasion found himself betrayed by his own followers.

Early in the struggle the House Democrats in caucus appointed an executive committee to discipline the ranks. Stephens was chairman, and his associates were Hatch of New York, Phillips of Pennsylvania, Phelps of Missouri, and William H. English of Indiana. They were to do what they could to see that the full strength of the administration was available and, at need, were to summon other caucus meetings. Theirs was a difficult task. At times they must keep intoxicated members off the floor, but near enough at hand to be brought in and made to utter a thick monosyllable when their names were called. On one call of the House an absent Kentucky member was found on the street. He seemed all right, but suddenly he screamed, "Oh God, I am drunk, drunk, drunk!" He was on the verge of delirium tremens and fell sprawling into a grocery cellar. Holding the majority in line was not inspiring work.[25]

The sum of the difficulties emphasized the common legislative fact that only compromise could avert defeat. The discovery of some such formula became ever more imperative. The introduction of a resubmission plan by the anti-Lecompton Democrat, Montgomery of Pennsylvania, not unlike that of Senator Crittenden, suggested the possibility that these two factions might unite on some such scheme. Representatives of the groups met, agreed on joint action and, further, decided to propose to the Republicans that they lend their aid and force the administration to defeat. The Republicans were reluctant to assent because they had fought squatter sovereignty so bitterly. Resubmission seemed an admission, theoretically at least, that Kansas might be slave. However, they were confident that they were in a majority in Kansas and could not lose, so they sent three representatives to join with three Americans and three antis. This conference of nine reached an understanding that at least twenty antis, and enough Americans to insure a majority, would join with the Republicans, stick to a slightly altered Crittenden plan, and accept nothing else. A written agreement was signed by the committee, the anti-Lecompton members of which were presumably Harris, Davis of Indiana, and Adrain of New Jersey.[26]

The administration realized the formidable character of this combination and stepped up its efforts to find another formula. Alexander H. Stephens and the House leaders had been keeping close check upon the members, particularly on the anti-Lecompton group. They knew that English, an ambitious young member, was willing to compromise. He was a protégé of Jesse D. Bright and probably amenable to flattery and encouragement; furthermore the Republicans seemed intent on running candidates in opposition to him and some other anti-Lecompton men in the 1858 elections, and he resented it. His district was anti-Lecompton, but he valued his administration friends too much to be willing to affront them. He from the first had considered compromise, writing to political friends in Indiana about it. Some of his supporters had advised against it because it would seem like "backing down." Nevertheless English gave Bright to understand that he would support a compromise and made a speech in the House to that effect.[27]

English was the man to split the anti-Lecompton bloc, and the administration began to court and advise him. Stephens was his chief mentor. The first plan was to make him chairman of a House caucus committee and have a compromise emerge from this group which would be inserted in the Senate bill under the spur of the administration caucus whip.[28]

This idea ran on the rocks because it appeared that some southern fire-eaters would have none of compromise. When the possibility was first tried out in the Senate caucuses early in March, a conference of thirty-five southern members of both houses had agreed to oppose adjustments which might weaken the slavery safeguards in the Lecompton instrument, particularly the scheme to permit immediate amendment of the Lecompton constitution by the Kansas voters. Senator Iverson of Georgia, who had tried to read Douglas out of the Senate caucus, now refused to attend himself and protested against concession just before the last vote in the Senate on the bill. Secretary Cobb was more disturbed by southern defection than he was by the Douglas vote.[29]

The strength of this opposition prevented House caucus agreement on any compromise suggested by the English committee, and so the administration leaders determined upon a desperate expedient which they held in reserve. Failing caucus unanimity, the House would now undoubtedly amend the Senate bill by inserting the Montgomery-Crittenden proviso, resubmitting the Lecompton constitution to the Kansas voters. The Senate would refuse this amendent, and then the administration blocs would vote a conference committee of both houses. English would be a member from the House, and the bill would be rewritten in the conference committee.

Stephens and his colaborers now adroitly led English to "invent" this strategy. The Hoosier Congressman reported it to Buchanan as something new, writing him just how it could be done and advising him to trust to a committee of conference between the two houses. "I am sincerely desirous of doing all that I can honorably do under the circumstances which surround me to carry out your wishes." Buchanan sent this letter immediately, and in strict confidence, to Howell Cobb who was managing the administration's relations with the House. "Mr. English's name must not be used or communicated to any one." Cobb got it just in time, for the legislative battle was coming off next day, All Fools' Day.[30]

On April 1 the plan began to work. The House as expected amended the Senate bill, by substituting the Montgomery-Crittenden bill to resubmit Lecompton, 120–112. Only Reilly and Dewart of Pennsylvania and Burns of Ohio failed the anti-Lecomptonites. Even Pendleton voted with them, though Niblack went with the administration.[31] Harris, dying of consumption, was carried in to vote.

The Senate, of course, rejected the Montgomery-Crittenden substitute. The last hope of the administration now seemed to be its expected majority in a conference committee of six. Could it rewrite the bill in acceptable form?

It was not immediately to get a chance, for Senator Slidell ruthlessly engaged in high-handed procedure. He persuaded or, perhaps more accurately, ordered the secretary of the Senate not to send the bill back right away. Important elections in Connecticut, Rhode Island, and Cincinnati were scheduled the first week in April. He thought they might favor the Democrats and therefore impress the antis, if the House could be prevented from voting until their results were in. But the returns were no comfort; they went against the administration. The bill could be sent back to the House; there was no longer any point in holding it, and it was that much worse off. Worse still, the wires bore the news that in Kansas a new constitution had been completed by a Leavenworth convention and would be submitted to the voters within a month. The House insisted on its amendment and returned the bill to the Senate.[32]

The Senate again rejected the amendment, asking this time for a conference, and attention was riveted on the House. Would it consent to confer? It would not—if the agreement made among the Republicans, Americans, and anti-Lecomptonites were stuck to. The administration had to go to work again, to win at least four more. English of course was amenable, leaving only three. Executive suasion was used; patronage was held up. None of the important New York appointees had yet been nominated to the Senate, and they and their friends were on hand in force to work on Clark and Haskin. A vigorous drive again was made on the Ohio sector. It was proposed to accept two regiments of Ohio volunteers into the Utah expeditionary force; their prospective officers, eager for commissions, bore down on Cox, Hall, Lawrence, and Pendleton. Wendell still was operating with his bushel of gold.

The heat now turned on the anti-Lecomptonites was sizzling. Administration whips promised them that the conference would accept a version of the Montgomery-Crittenden compromise and therefore they would surrender no principle in voting for a conference. All loyal Democrats, surely, had the duty to stand by the party and save the President from humiliating defeat. Craftily it was insinuated that in the event of favorable action southern votes might be had for certain favorite measures desired by western Congressmen and long pigeonholed. How much the anti-Lecomptonites knew of English's negotiation with the administration is not revealed. They were, naturally, suspicious of any choice of conferees made by Speaker Orr and the Senate managers. Yet the administration succeeded in bringing about their first split. At their last caucus six of their twenty voted for conference.

Time seemed to side with the administration. Pendleton had been voting with it since the House on April 14 received the Senate's request for conference. Caruthers of Missouri returned to the scene of battle. If two more antis would join English a tie was possible, which Orr would break the right way. Hall of Ohio made one (it was later testified that Wendell had paid Hall's roommate $5,000 a few days before); and Owen Jones of Pennsylvania made the other. Thus came the tie, 108–108. Orr duly broke it. The conference was assured.[33]

The committee met two days later; Senators Green and Hunter, and Representatives Stephens and English were the Democratic majority. Senator Seward and Representative Howard of Michigan were the Republican minority. It was plain that Stephens and English would have to do the work without much help from Green and Hunter; the Senators in fact were very discouraging in a talk they had with Buchanan on the day the conference was voted. Hunter was in a mood to accept only the Senate bill, and although Green had no such stiffness he could not see any formula acceptable to both the Senate leaders and the House anti-Lecomptonites. Furthermore, Stephens was sick; the committee convened twice only to adjourn because of his absence. However, he was very active mentally, in search of the formula.

To his sickroom, to hear his formula, went the Democratic committee members on Sunday April 18. He had been over it with Toombs, who had done some canvassing and thought it would carry. The new plan would focus on the exorbitant land grant, which the Senate had refused to allow and the House had reduced to normal size. The conferees now proposed to make this gigantic proposal the cloak for compromise. They would couple admission not with slavery, but with reducing the grant. If Kansas would agree by a popular referendum to accept merely the normal grant of land, she would be admitted; but if she refused she would have to wait until her population was great enough to entitle her to a representative under the current federal ratio. In effect, this resubmitted Lecompton to the people; and English therefore felt it would satisfy enough anti-Lecompton Democrats to obtain passage.

On the evening of the 19th English had perfected this plan, and he took it to his Republican associate, Howard, so that he would be able to discuss the matter in full committee next morning. At ten of the morrow Seward and Howard came to the committee room and found Stephens on the sofa. English kept them waiting an hour. When he arrived the plan was read aloud, and Stephens from his sofa declared it would do. Howard tried to amend it so that the Leavenworth constitution might be submitted at the same election; this was refused. Then Seward urged that the matter be postponed until he could confer with Crittenden, who was more concerned even than he. The majority were in a hurry, however, and said that it must be concluded at two o'clock that afternoon. The committee then recessed, while Seward and Howard hurried away to confer and to formulate their dissent.

The Republicans returned promptly at the time set, but their colleagues, despite their hurry, were not there. After waiting nearly an hour Seward went to look for Green and finally discovered him. Green seemed depressed. He answered Seward's inquiry by saying the majority had decided not to report that day and did not know when they would. Seward and Howard would be notified. What had happened?[34] The Democratic conferees had suffered a shock. Hunter, Green, and Stephens, on showing the formula to some of their colleagues, met a flat refusal to support it. Southerners, even of the less violent type, like Hammond of South Carolina, objected emphatically; they were not willing to resubmit under any circumstances. For this reason the conferees did not dare report on the 20th as they had planned.

The administration took a hand; Jacob Thompson doctored the proposal with altered phraseology. On his advice, the committee changed the voting formula. The ballot which would have read "For the proposition and admission" and "Against the proposition and admission" was now to read "Proposition accepted" and "Proposition rejected." This change, it was hoped, would satisfy some southern scruples against resubmitting the question of admission under the Lecompton instrument. Stephens took this statement to the more important southern Senators, even invading Davis's sickroom, and secured their consent. Thus fortified, the conference report was submitted April 23. Then to his chagrin, Stephens found the revolt was by no means stifled.

A Georgia American, "Josh" Hill, hurled a monkey wrench into the House machinery by moving the postponement of the whole subject until the second Monday in May. On a test vote the administration "majority" was worsted, 108–105. Quitman of Mississippi, Bonham of South Carolina, Shorter and Stallworth of Alabama, and Hill and Trippe, Georgia Americans, voted to delay. Newspaper gossip had it that some southern Congressmen merely wanted to go home for spring race meetings. At any rate, it caused great excitement. After Trippe had explained his vote, Josh Hill wished to do likewise; but his Democratic Georgia colleague, Gartrell, objected. "Who objects?" demanded Hill. "I object," rejoined Gartrell. "Where is your graveyard?" yelled Hill, rushing at him "with great fury." Members intervened. Gartrell replied: "We will talk of graveyards elsewhere." The Speaker sent the sergeant-at-arms with the mace to take Hill back to his seat.

However, the Hill postponement was prevented from immediate passage. It hung fire over Sunday, while the administration spent another strenuous week end of whip cracking and suasion to prevent further delay. Cobb, Thompson, and other men who could influence the recalcitrant southerners worked indefatigably. They succeeded; on Monday Hill was absent without pairing, and Trippe of Georgia, with Cox and Lawrence of Ohio and Chapman of Pennsylvania, changed their positions. Thus immediate consideration was voted. Cobb on the House floor openly rejoiced with Stephens, while English hurried over to the Senate to tell the news. Floor debate on the conference report was to begin Wednesday.[35]

V

The ensuing days saw the final efforts, for the last roll calls were at hand. The administration hoped that the English compromise would win all the anti-Lecomptonites and thus restore the fiction of a united front for the Democracy. For a time it seemed that this might be possible. Robert J. Walker, for reasons unknown, agreed to accept it and undertook the task of bringing Douglas in. On Saturday evening Walker, Douglas, Stanton, and Forney had a long conference.

The erstwhile Governor of Kansas talked long and eloquently to the Little Giant in a very moving fashion.

It had been a very unhappy winter for the Illinois Senator. He had been plagued by ill health and domestic affliction. The uncertainty of his political position on the eve of a hot reelection campaign in Illinois wore upon him. He had sought to offset administration opposition by negotiating with the Republicans in the hope that they would not oppose him for the Senate. Cameron and Seward at Douglas's dinner table had agreed to persuade the Illinois Republicans not to contest his reelection. Certain other national leaders of the party, like Horace Greeley, were agreeable to that idea; but the Illinois Republicans, with victory on their doorstep, were not going to pass up such a chance. They were going to put up their strongest candidate.

Could Douglas in such a situation accept the compromise? It practically submitted Lecompton. He needed united party support if he were to succeed in 1860 in his quest for the Presidency. But there was Illinois. He had found the Illinois voters enthusiastic over his defiance of the southern bloc. The state Democratic convention had recently met and endorsed his stand. He had been renominated for the Senate. He knew his Republican opponent would be the skillful vote getter, Abraham Lincoln. Could he afford to lose the advantage in his home state accruing from his opposition to the bill? If he were defeated in 1858 he must leave the Senate, and then where would he be in 1860? No wonder, as Walker talked to him, he walked the room with large drops of sweat springing from his forehead; "they were almost drops of blood." At length Walker convinced him. He even agreed to put up $100 to pay for nation-wide telegraphic announcement of his decision.

But Douglas had yet to tell his anti-Lecompton colleagues. On Sunday he met Broderick, Montgomery, McKibbin, and others at the rooms of the California Senator to acquaint them with his change of heart. No sooner had he announced his new purpose than Broderick turned on him, his face livid with anger. "Sir, I cannot understand, you will be crushed between the Democracy and the Republicans. I shall denounce you, sir. You had better, sir, go into the street and blow your damn brains out." Douglas quailed before him and stayed with the opposition. He dared not do otherwise in the pinch.[36]

Nor was this such bad strategy from the administration

standpoint. They would have been embarrassed if Douglas had accepted the English formula. The bolting House members from the South would then have been placed in an impossible position. They had sworn never to resubmit. If Douglas had accepted the bill all the world would have been convinced it was resubmission, and the southerners would not have come back. Douglas's opposition served to bolster the idea that the bill was not resubmission. Douglas's tactics therefore may have been the secret of the bill's passage. If Douglas hoped for peace with the administration, he may have been shrewd enough to see this.

While Douglas was in this state of uncertainty the final drive by the administration was made on the two fronts, on Ohio and on the radical southern lines. In Ohio, Cox and Lawrence were the key men and Walker worked on them, even writing a letter which was published, in which he stated his belief that the conference plan did resubmit the constitution for popular approval. Cobb and Thompson redoubled their efforts upon Bonham, Quitman, Stallworth, Shorter, Trippe, and Hill. Cobb no longer went to the Treasury, and when he appeared at Cabinet meetings, Buchanan urged him to go to the House, where his influence was potent. The Treasury business was attended to by the tired Secretary, after the House adjourned, far into the night. Senate leaders added their pressure by holding back a deficiency appropriation bill in which House members were much interested. Latham, Floyd's business manager, moved about with Wendell, and they were accused of talking in terms of financial rewards for changed votes.

Until the last moment S. S. Cox of the Columbus, Ohio, district with his colleague Lawrence continued to be centers of attention. Cox particularly was in a dilemma. Everybody seemed after him, and he was pulled and hauled one way and then another strenuously. Cox, moreover, had heard from home that he was receiving no promises of aid from the Republicans in his reelection fight; quite the contrary, in fact. His Democratic supporters were divided, and a strong opponent was on the horizon. He feared defeat if he could not get administration backing; so he caved in. On Thursday he and Lawrence announced they would vote for the conference report. This threw consternation into the tri-party coalition; their mutual agreement had been broken by these anti-Lecompton Democracts. The American leader, Humphery Marshall, denounced the measure. John Sherman, Republican floor leader, charged bad faith; Joshua Giddings fell down in a fit.

So the battle was won. Stallworth, Shorter, and Trippe, southerners, came back. Thirteen anti-Lecompton Democrats —the seven from Ohio, Owen Jones, Dewart, and Reilly from Pennsylvania, and English, Niblack, and Foley from Indiana —voted with the administration forces. The House adopted the conference report, 112–103. The Senate did likewise, 31–22, with Douglas, Broderick, and Stuart still in the minority.[37]

The administration had won a victory of a sort. It had carried a Kansas bill and had, it believed, removed the troublesome issue from national party councils. But at what a cost! The leaders had rallied the conservatives to compromise, but the Douglasites and the southern radicals were more than ever disappointed. The compromise was definitely ambiguous and politically dangerous. Northern Democrats declared they had won because there was to be another vote. The southern wing denied that Lecompton was being resubmitted. The Republicans, led by Henry Wilson and the *Tribune*, were denouncing the whole scheme as a bribe. Curiously enough they succeeded in spreading a false impression of the act, which was to persist for many years; namely, that Congress had offered the Kansans a large land grant as a bribe to accept the Lecompton constitution.[38]

The House majority had been shattered. The Democratic party would go into the elections of 1858 with its divisions emphasized and dangerously operative. Worse still, the view was more than ever prevalent in the non-slave states that the Democracy was the instrument by which the southern attitude dominated the nation. If some sort of political restorative could not be found, the elections of 1858 might be disastrous.

Epilogue

In the last days of the session, just two days before adjournment, a political pay-off was made. The Indiana Senators, Bright and Fitch, had been challenged at the beginning of the session, and their right to their seats questioned. The judiciary committee had been ostensibly considering the case for months, but it did not see fit to speak until May 24. Then Hunter kept the vote on seating of the Senators out of the way of the appropriations bills despite Bright's insistence, until June 11, three days before adjournment. The brutal facts at length came out in an afternoon debate. Indiana, it was revealed, required election of Senators by a joint session of both houses of the legislature. In 1855, when the Republicans had a majority on joint ballot, the Democratic minority in the Senate had prevented a joint session and caused a vacancy. The Republicans remembered this and in 1857, when the Democrats had a majority on joint ballot, the Republican majority in the Senate refused to go into joint session, probably hoping for a deal whereby they would be accorded the Senator who had been denied them two years before. The Democrats had refused to trade, and the Senate minority led by the Democratic lieutenant-governor joined the house in an irregular joint session which elected Bright and Fitch by a clear majority of both houses.

By this series of sharp plays the Democrats had secured the reelection of Bright, to which they were entitled, and were attempting to sneak in Fitch for the rest of the other term, 1857–1861. The latter was plain larceny. In the United States Senate most of the Democrats ignored the details and took the high ground that a Republican minority was trying to steal the rights of a Democratic majority. The party, with the aid of the Maryland Whig, Kennedy, on June 12 seated the two Hoosiers, 30–23. Broderick, Douglas, Houston, Mason, and Pearce of the Democrats refused to concur. Bright and Fitch were thus rewarded for their southern sympathies and their "loyalty" on Kansas.[39]

Chapter 10

The Power of Money

THE CONFUSION THAT confounded the Democratic majority in the Thirty-fifth Congress was more clearly demonstrated, if that could be possible, when the lawmakers were struggling with appropriations. Here the rivalry of the representatives of the various conflicting attitudes completely broke down party lines and produced further demoralizing political chaos. The Democratic leadership, exhausted from the tense struggle to whip through Lecompton, had little strength left to cope with what approached party disintegration.

The effects of the prevailing panic oppressed representatives of all attitudes, particularly those most concerned with metropolitan and territorial interests. The dangerous condition of the Treasury, which Buchanan and Cobb had duly reported, seemed to place insuperable obstacles in the way of large appropriations and subsidies; yet the financial stringency made such projects all the more desired, and generated pressures even stronger than usual. During the Kansas struggle lobbyists for these schemes were steadily at work and utilized that conflict and probably intensified it for their own purposes. The real drama of the session was the little publicized contest for money going on behind the screen of the Kansas smoke.

The official position of the Democratic leadership was "economy." Both the President and the Secretary of the Treasury in their official utterances were positive that Congress could do little to remedy the sad state of affairs except retrench. Government spending, they said, was no way out of a depression.[1] The Democratic House leadership entered heartily into the move for economy. They were particularly interested because the Republican majority preceding had been extravagant and the Senate had not even tried to check it. Worse, if they did not practice economy they must raise the tariff—the last thing they wanted to do. But it was one thing for the administration to preach economy and another thing to practice it. Numerous interests and individuals were scheming to recoup their fortunes with government appropriations. They were sufficiently desperate to make the struggle sharp.

The fight began as soon as J. Glancy Jones had organized the ways and means committee in the House and R. M. T. Hunter the finance committee in the Senate. The appropriation bills which soon began to appear on the Speaker's table proved that the committee had been reasonably economical in paring down departmental estimates. So far, so good. But the waters ahead were dark and stormy.

The Democratic leadership was much embarrassed by the huge cost of the Utah expedition. Floyd had to ask Congress for a $6,700,000 deficiency appropriation and money for five new regiments. Also he faced the vigorous opposition of Brigham Young, who was going to oppose the government expedition with his own Utah militia and was mobilizing political support in the East. Young had sent Samuel W. Richards and George G. Snyder from Utah, and they and the congressional delegate, Dr. Bernhisel, had been working with Kane. This lobby proposed that Buchanan send commissioners to investigate Utah—*without the army*. The President would not agree, but he let Kane hurry out via Panama ahead of the army, to negotiate with Brigham Young on means of avoiding blows. Kane, traveling under the name of Dr. Osborne, went West while Bernhisel devoted himself to spreading the idea that everything could be settled bloodlessly and without further expense. This scarcely helped Floyd's appropriations.[2]

The battle over money to finance the new regiments began in the Senate when Jefferson Davis, recently Secretary of War and now chairman of the military affairs committee, rewrote Floyd's proposals. He did not believe in new regiments but wanted more and larger companies in existing regiments. This immediately aroused political dogs. Floyd's plan called for high-salaried colonels and majors, and a number had been in the making with political backing. Davis would dash their hopes, for under his proposal new officers would be in the modest ranks of captains and lieutenants. Then, too, the foes of militarism were alarmed. Hale of New Hampshire denounced the increase as a step toward military despotism; he and the other Republicans rather thought the troops might be used in Kansas, as well as Utah, to the discomfiture of free-state men.

The Democrats did not like it any too well, either. Toombs feared that if the Republicans were successful in 1860 they might use the army to "enforce the law" in southern states. For various reasons Douglas, Broderick, Pugh, Toombs, Sam Houston, and Andrew Johnson joined the Republicans to defeat the bill on February 25. A similar measure was beaten in the House, and the administration had to be content with a law permitting the acceptance of volunteers for the emergency.

The deficiency appropriation bill evoked an equally embarrassing debate. The expedition was called a "contractor's" job. It was known that army supply contracts, made during recent Indian difficulties in Florida, were running out and the contractors wanted to switch their profits to Utah. Also the prices paid Russell, Majors, and Waddell, who were supplying the plains column, were under fire. They were high; but the cost of transportation was prohibitive, and the government slow in paying. Despite their defense, Congress delayed endlessly. In despair almost, Buchanan finally took the plan of Kane and the Mormons and sent out commissioners to overtake the army, and go ahead of it, offering pardon in return for peaceful acknowledgment of federal authority.[3] Floyd on his part adopted his own expedients. The contractors were desperate for money in the midst of the panic, and they told him they were about through. So the Secretary in April started a practice which one day was to ruin him. He endorsed the bills of Russell, Majors, and Waddell for services to be paid out of deficiency appropriations and informed banks it would be safe to loan money on paper upon which he inscribed, "Accepted, John B. Floyd."[4]

The House played much politics with this deficiency bill, at one time defeating it with the help of twenty-nine Democrats, mostly southern though including seven anti-Lecomptonites. However, it was reconsidered and at length sent to the Senate. There was a disagreement, and a conference committee which in turn could not agree. Whether by coincidence or by design, this disagreement was reported only to the Senate; and as soon as the Senate knew that the House accepted the English report it withdrew its opposition to the House appropriations, on motion of Senator Hunter, and the House learned on that eventful April 30 it had won. Buchanan signed the Lecompton bill and the deficiency appropriation on the same day, May 4. That there was a tenuous financial connection between this Kansas Act and the money bill is certain; unfortunately the actual relationship is not clear.[5] The volunteers were never accepted, because on June 9 a report from the Gentile governor, Cumming, reached Washington. He and "Dr. Osborne" had succeeded before the official commissioners arrived, and

Brigham Young had agreed to acknowledge Cumming's authority.[6] With the danger of war averted, the appropriation bill for new regiments now could be dropped. However, the Utah debate left the impression in some quarters that the administration was not too much addicted to economy when it came to certain contractors.

II

The Utah expedition was not the only warlike move to spike economy. That spring, conflict with Great Britain threatened over the slave trade. The demand for slaves in Cuba and Brazil kept the nefarious traffic in vigorous operation. The United States and Great Britain were agreed to stop it; but as the American government would not let British naval vessels interfere with ships flying the Star Spangled Banner, and as most of the slavers were so adorned, it fell to the United States Navy to act. However, that arm of the service was neither large enough nor interested enough to be very effective.

Lord Palmerston, the British Prime Minister, had been in a heated paper controversy with Buchanan over responsibility and grew tired of talk. He turned to action. The British navy would attack this traffic in the Caribbean. Some young naval officers that spring went to work in earnest. When suspected slavers refused to heave to they were fired upon, and American headlines roared. The hotheaded demanded retaliation. Buchanan sputtered but did nothing.[7]

Congress, particularly the House, was more ready to talk war than to spend money on one. In fulfillment of Democratic economy ambitions, the ways and means committee had reduced a special fortifications bill from $2,000,000 to $350,000, which was considered quite an improvement over the $4,000,-000 extravagance of the preceding Congress. The House summarily rejected even this small sum, but the Senate proved more mindful of national security. It tacked $1,200,000 upon an army appropriation bill that came along conveniently, and the House finally consented to a compromise allotting $562,-000 for work on forts. Curiously enough, one fort thus neglected was Fort Sumter. If they had continued work on this fort in Charleston Harbor it would have been much nearer completion in December, 1860. Who knows how it then might have altered the course of events? The victory for economy was what seemed important in 1858.

On naval appropriations, however, economy fought a hopeless battle with the war scare. The House naval affairs committee—less economy-minded—had initially planned expansion in navy yards and shipbuilding, and now added to its own bill a sum for construction of ten sloops of war. Its amendment was ruled out of order by Speaker Orr because no law had been passed authorizing these sloops, and he held that without such authorization no appropriations could be made. Likewise navy-yard extensions, particularly in New York and Georgia, were thrown out. The Senate was not hampered by Orr's scruples and allowed funds for five sloops. Alarmed by war clouds rising late in May, the House about-faced and doubled the number to ten, which the conference reduced to seven. Thus Congress added $1,200,000 more to the appropriations.

III

The Post Office bills invited another battle in the economy war. The department always ran an annual deficit, recently averaging about $3,500,000. The friends of economy demanded that it be placed on a paying basis, that non-paying routes be discontinued, that postage rates be raised, and that the franking privilege be abolished. Also, there was the question of ocean-mail contracts and subsidies which involved rival operators and their lobbies.

The steamship men were a political force in those days. Edward K. Collins, A. G. Sloo, Marshall O. Roberts, William H. Aspinwall, William H. Davidge, George Law, Edwin Croswell, Prosper M. Wetmore, Mortimer Livingston, and Cornelius Vanderbilt were the best known; most of them were shrewd and ruthless men and knew how to play politics for contracts. The prizes were ocean-mail subsidies. The most important group was a combination of two steamship companies and a Panama railroad which operated from New York to San Francisco.

The United States Mail Steamship Co., often spoken of as the Sloo line, ran from New York to Aspinwall (Colon) and Chagres; this was the Atlantic lap of the California mail line. It had been established by Albert G. Sloo of Cincinnati, who had come into the limelight at the time of the Mexican War. He had then obtained the first contract to ,carry the mail to the Isthmus of Panama on the initial lap of the journey to California. Because of financial difficulties his mail contract had been long in litigation, and his steamship interests were managed by trustees. The original trustees had included George Law, also of steamship fame; but he had withdrawn, and Marshall O. Roberts, Ellwood Fisher, and, strangely enough, Vanderbilt's Congressman son-in-law, Horace F. Clark, now composed the group. These men managed the United States Mail Steamship Co., and Fisher looked after Sloo's other steamship properties not connected with this line.

The Pacific lap of the contract for California mail had been secured by Arnold Harris, a political speculator, who had turned it over to the Pacific Mail Steamship Co., controlled by William H. Aspinwall and William H. Davidge. This company had secured some British capital to augment its own and had built the Panama Railroad to carry passengers and mail across the Isthmus. The railroad and the two steamship companies worked together and earned the title "The Monopoly." Their mail contract, obtained in 1847, would expire in 1859. It made the Monopoly the object of a series of attacks by a wily rival.

The redoubtable "Commodore" Cornelius Vanderbilt was an antagonist to be dreaded, and the Monopoly had no illusions about him or his methods. Nearly ten years before, shortly after the original trans-Isthmian mail contracts had been let, Vanderbilt had entered the field. He and Joseph L. White had organized the American Atlantic and Pacific Ship Canal Company to build a canal across Nicaragua. Failing to enlist English capital in so costly a plan, he created the Accessory Transit Company and in 1851 opened a boat and stage service across Nicaragua. The Commodore operated this competitor of the Monopoly for five years. Then his Pacific agents, Charles Morgan and Cornelius K. Garrison, sought to freeze him out. Through their instigation William Walker, who had filibustered his way into control of Nicaragua, deprived him of his concession. The Commodore then had begun a warfare against Morgan and Garrison in which no holds were barred, and his intrigues in Nicaraguan politics and Walker's stormy career had effectively blocked transit across that republic for a time. Recently he had regained sufficient influence to propose to reopen his line. The Monopoly so feared his power that it paid him a monthly sum not to try, while in fact he was busy seeking to destroy its mail subsidy by political intrigue.

A second steamship "war" was being fought over the Atlantic mails to Europe. Subsidies had been granted to lines which ran to Liverpool, to Le Havre and to Bremen.

The first of these had been secured by E. K. Collins of New York City, who was competing with the Cunard line. The second was in the hands of Mortimer Livingston's New York and Havre line, while the third was enjoyed by the Ocean Steam Navigation Line, partly German-owned. Commodore Vanderbilt wanted to enter this business, too, and he had started after Collins's Liverpool subsidy in the previous administration, offering to perform the service for half the cost. Pierce had put the finishing touches on Collins by vetoing the renewal of his subsidy—to expire in 1860—while Vanderbilt waited to pounce on it. The Havre and Bremen contracts had expired in 1857. Brown had no authority to renew the subsidies, so he offered contracts based solely on the postage fees. This the Havre people agreed to take; but the Bremen company declined. Thereupon Vanderbilt stepped into the Bremen mail-carrying, on the same terms as the Havre company. The Commodore was now in the transatlantic service, to Bremen, eager for more. Congress was going to feel the impact of the steamship war.

E. K. Collins still had many friends in Congress, some of whom remembered the generous entertainments of his more prosperous days. They now secured an amendment by the Senate to the mail steamer bill, which would give him the advantage of a shorter route, from New York to Southampton, over the route to Liverpool of his dying contract. Because this concession would also give him an advantage over Vanderbilt and the Havre operator who put in at Southampton, their friends, no doubt encouraged by Congressman Clark, Vanderbilt's son-in-law, blocked concurrence by the House, and the Collins provision was lost in conference. In the meantime, possible compensation to Vanderbilt and the Havre line was materially reduced by another Senate amendment. The Commodore seems to have tried to defeat the whole bill, hoping perhaps the sooner to break the Monopoly and Collins, and to improve his chances of more mail-carrying business. In this he failed, and the bill as passed prohibited the Postmaster General from contracting to pay ocean carriers of foreign mail any more than the amount of the postage on the mail they carried—there were to be no more subsidies. Nor could contracts be longer than two years. Gone were ten-year contracts such as the Monopoly had been enjoying since the Mexican War. The steamship lobbyists would return next session.[8]

A second mail controversy, indicative of the growing tension, was fought over the overland mail. The Thirty-fourth Congress had authorized Postmaster General Brown to make a six-year contract for overland service from the Mississippi to San Francisco, to compete with the steamship monopoly. He advertised for bids and received eight, for various routes north, central, and south. He let a contract for a semi-weekly stagecoach mail, but neither to the lowest bidder nor over the most direct route.

John Butterfield and associates were to be paid $600,000 annually to run stages from both St. Louis and Memphis, Tennessee (Brown's home state), to Preston, Texas, on the Red River; there they were to unite, proceeding to El Paso and across what later became Arizona to Fort Yuma on the Colorado, thence into California and up that long state to San Francisco. Most people considered this an extremely long way around, dictated by Tennessee and southern interests. Brown justified it on the ground that it would not be obstructed by weather and mountain difficulties. Also when he made the contract the Mormon trouble had placed the direct central route in a most uncertain status. Brown then had immediate need of mail service to Utah so that the government could keep in touch with the troops. On April 1 he had contracted with Hockaday and Liggett for a weekly mail from St. Joseph, Missouri, to Salt Lake City and beyond to Placerville, California; for this central route the contractor was allowed thirty-eight days and paid $310,000 annually.

No sooner was the news of the peaceable ending of the Mormon difficulty at hand than the proponents of the central route sought advantage. In June they moved immediately to expedite their service. If the mail were to go through in competition with the twenty-five-day service from Memphis to Fort Yuma, their time must be reduced far below the thirty-eight days. This would take more stock and equipment, and the contractors wanted extra compensation. Brown could have paid it had he wished; but he was reluctant, it was charged, because of his Memphis pet route. So the Missouri and California politicos decided to force his hand. Craig of Missouri got the rules suspended by a combination of southwestern, western, and Republican votes, and the House on June 10 passed a joint resolution for the expedited service, over the opposition of the administration leaders.

In the Senate Gwin and Broderick of California, Polk and Green of Missouri immediately got it up. Hunter and Toombs tried to stop it, but the traffic lights were set against them.

Green reported that Brown had told him that he was in favor of this proposition but wished the weight of a congressional mandate before he moved. A brief debate on the 12th sufficed; it was voted 29–17. The southwestern and western Democrats, joined by the radical Georgian, Iverson, the Tennessee Whig, Bell, and the Republicans, thought they had a winning combination. But Buchanan foiled them. The joint resolution was passed on the next to the last day of the session; thus Buchanan could neatly pocket-veto it, and he did so. Perhaps Brown was not so much in favor of it as he had told Green. Again a western interest had been frustrated.[9]

Other significant controversies grew out of attempts made by the Senate to insert in the Post Office appropriation bill clauses to increase the postage rates and to abolish franking. The Senators did not value franks as much as the House members, because they were generally richer men. In making their gesture toward economy they were safe enough, for no House would ever agree; but their action produced a tension between the houses which had most unfortunate consequences. The Senate did not get through with the bill until the last hours of the session. The House hastily refused to accept these provisions, and twice the bill went to conference, where it was stymied. Next the House hurriedly passed a new measure omitting the objectionable features, and in the last moments of the session the Senate yielded. This piece of history was to repeat itself within a few months in fateful fashion. In the meantime no appreciable economies were discovered in postal matters.

IV

More discouraging tests of the validity of the desire for economy were made on another major appropriation bill which was considered late in the session. Then under the pressure of time and early-summer heat Congressmen fought through long days and tedious nights. Each member always hoped for some slices of the appropriations to be used in his district. There were various building projects, ranging from customhouses to forts; also there were river and harbor improvements of numerous kinds. These appropriations brought people representing all attitudes into conflict. Innumerable rivalries among legislators of various localities and opposing interests complicated the picture. In recent Congresses sectional trading had succeeded in getting several such projects started. These, as usual, cost more than the original appropriations, and now the sponsors were actively seeking more money "to finish the work" or "to preserve that which had been started," so the projects would not "deteriorate through neglect."

The funds for the projects were generally included in the sundry civil appropriation bill; and its progress through the houses, if economy was enforced, was bound to be stormy. It provided funds for the coast survey, public-land surveying, lighthouse service, public buildings in Washington and elsewhere, and a variety of purposes. These segments of government activity offered many possibilities for construction projects and for profit in the building trades. The Secretary of the Treasury had supplied the annual estimates, and the chairman of the ways and means committee had gone over them with him. The committee studied them carefully, and its final decision was to cut off $240,000 and report a bill containing authorization to spend $3,800,000. It had decided not to complete certain customhouses and hospitals and the Treasury Department building itself.

The fun began in the House, where politics was played in most curious ways as when Sherman of Ohio attacked the practice of paying for the President's coal and Buchanan's fuel bill was saved by only two votes. Also the House ungraciously refused to finish the Capitol. It was in its new quarters, and what mattered it if the Senate still operated in its old and cramped apartments. The Representatives actually succeeded in cutting off $1,000,000 from the bill as submitted to them. The Senate was not complaisant, and put back almost everything and added more, returning the bill to the House heavier by millions. The conference committee was in generous mood, and its draft finally provided for $2,000,000 more than the original ways and means committee bill. The battle for economy was a dismal failure.

V

While economy was so disastrously worsted in the appropriations fights, money's corrupting hand was outstretched over government, in ways increasingly embarrassing to the American Democracy. Charges of fraud and dishonesty were becoming too common, and Congress during this turgid session was maneuvered into giving them much publicity.

Most noxious was the printing mess. The accusation of graft hurled at the Republican, Wendell, in the Democratic caucus started a series of moves for investigation, retrenchment, and reform. A special House committee was appointed to examine the printing laws. As the preceding Congress had ordered some $2,000,000 worth of printing without adequate appropriation, the ways and means committee had now to present an $800,000 deficiency bill. Half of it was for work already done, half for work authorized but not yet started. The obvious sympathy of the committee for Wendell was probably not lessened by the fact that its chairman was his attorney and by his helpful outlays on Lecompton. The trouble was, the struggle over the election of the official printers had revealed so much that this deficiency appropriation for the real printer was bound to reveal more.

Debate was stormy from the outset. Burnett of Kentucky, a Democrat, led off with the significant statement: "It is charged that it is a source of corruption through which the public Treasury is robbed, that gentlemen who hold the office of Public Printer acquire in a short time princely fortunes, and that extensive combinations are formed at the commencement of each Congress by which the printing is to be obtained and controlled."[10] While Burnett neither preferred nor affirmed these charges, he declared it high time they were aired. He was certain that Congress knew too little of the printing situation, and was too careless with it. Certain works, once started, were kept going indefinitely. A glaring example was the publication, authorized four years earlier, of Lieutenant Gillis's report on a naval astronomical expedition to Chile. Three volumes had been printed, a fourth was in process, but the other three were untouched. Perry's report on the Japanese expedition, Emory's survey of the Mexican boundary, the explorations of routes for the Pacific railroads, the annual reports on commercial relations and the coast survey were piling up volumes literally by the score. Most of these works were of large size and included a variety of expensive engravings, diagrams, and maps.

The cost of printing for the Thirty-second Congress had amounted to only $950,000; but for the Thirty-fourth, in which the Republicans controlled the House, it had jumped to $2,300,000. Now was the time for economy. Letcher and others joined Burnett in demanding it. The friends of the outlay relied upon the argument that the work had been authorized and in part completed, so that the only honorable thing to do was to fulfill the contract. This argument seemingly was not enough, for economy won, 135–67, on February 2, just as Buchanan's Lecompton message was laid on the clerk's desk. The hostile majority included 57 Democrats from all parts of the Union.

The ways and means committee cut the appropriation to $340,000, to be used solely for work completed on which money was due. This figure was accepted, and it seemed that economy still was taken seriously. A little later, however, $316,000 was tucked into the sundry civil appropriation bill which went into the printers' pockets. Wendell was presumed to have made $800,000 profit on the printing of the last Congress alone.

In the course of this conflict plans for reform emerged from the special House investigating committee and from the regular joint committee on printing, including a daring proposal for the government to do its own printing and save 40 per cent. The solons, however, did not hanker after reform enough to adopt any general scheme. Clauses were inserted in one of the appropriation bills to remove a few of the worst abuses, but the printing remained to haunt and curse the Democracy.

The chain of investigation, once started, lengthened rapidly. The Democratic leaders had not been too unhappy when suspicions against the clerk and the doorkeeper of the last House, an American and a Republican respectively, had become so certain that investigating committees had been called for. These inquiries, however, implicated their own doorkeeper, uncovering a "racket" in which Democrats were profiting. The office of the current House doorkeeper emerged as a patronage bureau, with that factotum appointing numerous clerks and pages. Lately Mr. Hackney had been doing this in defiance of the committee on accounts, to which he was responsible, and which probably wanted to pass on his choices. Also doorkeepers habitually enriched themselves by selling many of the sumptuous books published by Congress which the members did not take. The committee on accounts raised such a fuss about his insubordination that the House removed him from office.[11]

Removal of House members, themselves, for bribery and other dishonesty, came up again with the return to Congress of the reelected, but more recently expelled, Orasmus Matteson. Although he was a Republican and a New Yorker at that, a Democratic investigating committee and a House majority decided that his previous expulsion was punishment enough. He kept his seat.

When congressional corruption was rudely bared by events

outside Washington it was not so easily disposed of. A Massachusetts woolen manufactory had gone bankrupt, and a state investigating committee examining its affairs disclosed that $87,000 had been spent by the firm to lobby through the tariff of 1857. This outside report compelled Congress to set up its own, additional "select committee." It discovered that W. W. Stone of this firm had gone to Washington to seek advice on how to get the duty on raw wool lowered, and Matteson had told him money would be needed to influence Congressmen.

The firm then had hired a lobbyist, John W. Wolcott, who had retained Thurlow Weed and D. M. Stone of the *Journal of Commerce* to "collect statistics" for $5,000 and $3,500 respectively. Also on Wolcott's pay roll was A. R. Corbin, clerk of the committee on claims, already well started on a career of swindling, and later to be General U. S. Grant's brother-in-law and marplot of the infamous gold corner. Corbin had impressed Wolcott with his influence and received $1,000 for it. Then, mysteriously, Wolcott had appropriated all the rest of the $87,000 for his own use. The committee could not make Wolcott testify, for he preferred to go to jail. The result was that the committee could not find that any money had been paid to Congressmen; its investigations simply showed what influences surrounded Congress.[12]

The taint of corruption was not confined to Congress. Its dark stain was found marking at least one of the cabinet, as proved by investigations pressed by a Douglas Democrat and an anti-Lecomptonite. Secretary Floyd, they showed, was extremely accommodating to a New York speculating group—to their great profit though seemingly not to his. Easy-going, careless, Floyd could be used by friends. He let a few of the New York Hards, John C. Mather, Augustus Schell, the collector of the port, and his brother Richard operate on the inside of deals as widely separated as New York and Minnesota.

These gentlemen had succeeded in persuading the War Department to pay $200,000 for a site for fortifications in New York Harbor, a plot which recently had been offered for $130,000 and turned down by army engineers as too high at that. Other property just as suitable could be had at half the cost. Another combination of Mather and the Schells who cut-in some of Floyd's Virginia friends was permitted to buy the seven-thousand-acre Fort Snelling reservation in Minnesota for $90,000, when it could have brought much more. The deal finally fell through because the panic broke the speculators temporarily. Yet the telltale evidence remained. Floyd had let friends dictate a sale to them of government property which recently had been declared essential, and had obligingly arranged it as an inside job on the quiet.[18]

The sum total of this unprecedented series of investigations was to implant a general belief that the federal government was dishonest. Washington seemed to the uninitiated who read these lurid details to be a sink of graft and a den of shame. Was not the federal system, the Union, a source of corruption which should be destroyed? Such thoughts could stir emotions that politicians were to find useful.

These struggles over the unusual demands for money and the disastrous disclosures of corruption served to demonstrate more clearly than ever the wide divergence of interests which the various attitudes represented. The question of money was destroying the unity of the Democratic party as it was straining the ethics of the nation. In many southern communities and in the thinking of numerous southerners, money did not play such a large part. Many persons activated by southernism did not value it so much nor seek so diligently to secure it. Also they had stricter views regarding its proper functions. They were less tolerant of its use in politics, and they more and more mistrusted the "money-grabbing" qualities which they often sneered at in their northern neighbors.

On the other hand the possibilities of money were bulking large in the minds of representatives of other attitudes such as metropolitanism, territorialism, and nationalism. Money was such a source of power, such a means of overcoming frustration. Zeal for its possession was stimulating a careless ethics which was erasing the distinction between right and wrong. Clever corruption was smart business. "Do unto others as they would do to you, only do it first." The growing ethical divergence was no small cause of the troubles yet to come. Within the Democratic party early Jeffersonian moral austerity was weakening.

VI

The financial chronicle of this unhappy Congress was not all extravagance and graft. The champions of laissez faire and the foes of corruption did win some skirmishes. They defeated various efforts made to revive river and harbor appropriations, accomplishing it only after an acrimonious series of exchanges truly ominous of the future. The panic had increased the demand and a great flood of petitions was referred to the House committee on commerce headed by John Cochrane of New York. His committee had set up an old-fashioned pork barrel, such as Polk and Pierce had vetoed, and brought it to the House April 15. Washburne of Illinois likewise introduced one of Republican manufacture. No such procedure was followed by the Senate commerce committee, dominated by C. C. Clay of Alabama and Robert Toombs, both of whom were bitter opponents of such expenditures. In fact Clay was on a rampage against all subsidies; he even made a futile attack on the small but time-honored bounties paid to the New England fishermen.

Despite the hostility of their commerce committee, a bloc of Republican and "otherwise minded" Democratic Senators were fighting vigorously for internal improvements. Zack Chandler, Michigan Republican, took this matter up just as soon as Kansas was disposed of, and on May 3 he and Benjamin of Louisiana, an attorney for speculators, secured approval of a resolution prodding the commerce committee. Clay responded a fortnight later, not with one bill but with twenty-three separate ones, each with a single item. In this he followed a procedure suggested by Pierce to keep out jokers. Two of these bills, caring for Chicago harbor and Milwaukee, were passed. Then one for Sheboygan was taken up, whereupon Pugh, an Ohio Democrat, moved to put them all together. In the midst of debate, this proposition had to be laid aside for essential appropriation bills, and as the end of the session was near at hand, appropriations for internal improvements seemed unlikely.

Yet efforts continued right up to the end with Chandler and Pugh persistently trying to tie favorite items to the sundry civil appropriation bill. Representative Andrews, a New York Republican, tried to get a bill calling for $1,100,000 in these projects attached to the last-minute loan bill; on the next to the last day of the session he failed. So bitter was the hostility to internal improvements that even the usual lighthouse appropriation bill was lost. This modest measure, calling for only $330,000, was killed by Clay and Toombs when it reached the Senate on the last day.

The friends of laissez faire and economy could boast also of rebuffs to many other schemes for government aid. Both the Pacific railroad and the homestead bills were postponed by the Senate until the short session. The agricultural college land-grant bill, though it passed the House, slept peacefully in the Senate. Patent renewals sought by Colt for his revolver, by the Chaffee people for vulcanizing rubber and by McCormick for his reaper failed, despite much personal attention from the principals and their lobbies. Bills to increase the pensions of the veterans of the War of 1812, to pay the war debt of Florida and Oregon, the damages of the Indian wars in Washington territory and to satisfy the ancient French spoliation claims all failed. The bitterness of the rival attitudes was such that every scheme was blocked by some suspicious opponent. Yet the sum total of the appropriations shook the Treasury. Although the House ways and means committee had earnestly tried to economize, it had brought in bills which exceeded the estimates by $6,000,000; and the House and particularly the Senate had added a further excess of $4,000,000. Totals of over $81,000,000 were $10,000,000 more than the falling revenues could stand. Secretary Cobb therefore at the end of the session was forced to take an action that raised the lid of another Pandora's box. He had to come before Congress on May 19 and admit that the declining receipts of the government could not meet these appropriations. He did not want the tariff or other tax questions opened, for they would provide the Republicans with new weapons. So he asked for more borrowing power, to increase the national debt by $15,000,000 to be obtained by ten-year bonds at an interest rate not higher than 6 per cent.

The Senate finance committee reported a bill in short order, and its proposals consumed most of the Senate's time, May 24–26. The situation was slightly eased by news that peace had been arranged in Utah, and that the $5,000,000 anticipated for the volunteers would not be needed. Nevertheless a debate was precipitated which boded ill for sectional peace. The Republicans came forward immediately with a demand that the necessary revenue be obtained by increasing the tariff, thereby protecting industry and rescuing American labor from starvation, they said.

The tariff had been injected into debate ever since the question was first raised in December, when Cobb asked for the Treasury notes. Crittenden of Kentucky, Simmons of Rhode Island and Cameron of Pennsylvania had introduced resolutions, attempted to add amendments to bills and presented petitions. All this was of course mere gesture because the Democratic majorities were determined to keep the tariff of 1857. Now the tariff moves were repeated, and Simmons tried to advance a small step forward. He introduced an amendment which would have levied duties on the "home valuation" of imports, rather than on the "foreign valuation," thus increasing revenue, eliminating fraud, and providing a little protection. He was defeated, 25–17, but he was not discouraged. He tried again with no better success a few days later, when he offered the proposal as an amendment to the sundry civil appropriation bill. The House in the meantime held back Cobb's loan bill until the final amounts of the appropriations could be learned. Then the authorization was changed to provide a loan of $20,000,000 at 5 per cent and passed. The Republicans had wheeled their guns into position and fired the opening volley in a new tariff fight.

Thus ended the battle for economy. The Democratic leaders had won some notable successes, but the Utah expedition and the threat of foreign war had caused the appropriation of $9,000,000 more than the preceding session of Congress had voted. The panic and the Utah trouble had increased the public debt by $16,000,000 during the fiscal year, July 1, 1857, to June 30, 1858, and forced the prospect of borrowing some $20,000,000 in the fiscal period about to commence. The bitter struggle for money had widened the political divisions and intensified the rival attitudes which encouraged them.

VII

Congress had made its record, and the pages were not encouraging reading. Sectional controversy, quarreling over money, fraud, and corruption gave little heart to patriots troubled over the inefficiency of republican government. More disquieting, however, were the free and frequent expressions of lack of confidence, disillusionment, and despair of the future. Even doubts of the success of the American experiment were recorded.

John Bell, old-line Whig Senator from Tennessee, uttered a solemn warning. He was sure that at no period in the last thirty years had so many circumstances conspired to awaken apprehension about the future. The chief threat, he believed, was "the extreme and anomalous party action to which the Government has been subjected by the prevalence of party spirit stimulated to excess by the magnitude of the prize of victory," in presidential elections. He particularly feared the potent weapon so often used in these contests, the fostering of sectional jealousies and resentments. This vague but very general sense of impending crisis he believed to be similar to one felt all over Europe.

Charges of bad faith were exchanged. William O. Goode of Virginia declared that other sections always cheated the South. Northern urge to open western lands only lowered land values in the old states and depleted their labor supply. W. P. Miles of South Carolina charged long weary years of unjust and unequal legislation. Nine-tenths of the federal expenditures had inured to the benefit of the North. Tyranny and injustice, he said, were worse than revolutions; they were part of a slow undermining process by which the high spirits of a free people were sapped, their strength destroyed, their faith in themselves crushed out. On the other hand Henry Wilson of Massachusetts was bitter about the business ethics of the South. That section carried on, he charged, by not paying its debts. It owed to the free states more than the value of the cotton crop of that year. The South forced its neighbors to sell to it on long credit often renewed. During the panic the southern debtors refused to satisfy their debts, and numerous northern merchants failed because they could not collect.

Bitter grievances were expressed by westerners, Democrats and Republicans alike. Democratic Senator Pugh of Ohio demanded to know "whether the people of the Northwest are entitled to any benefit from this Union, or whether they are merely conquered provinces, to be taxed for the benefit of the Atlantic coast." His Republican colleague, Wade, declared "it is time for Senators from the West to insist upon their rights." He urged his colleagues "to get that justice which belongs to us of the West" and "be not over nice" about it. When the West came into power there would be a day of reckoning. In this respect there were some southerners who thought that the antisubsidy policies of the leaders from their section were dangerous. Seward of Georgia complained that progress was being blocked by "a set of extreme southern men who belong to the do-nothing school, men who refuse to become the recipients of the blessings of the General Government." He pleaded for peace so that the sections "will generously vie with each other in improving the whole country."

Disturbing references were made to a new and dangerous symptom. There was talk now of class conflict, of the loss of faith in the equalitarian idea. Blair of Missouri charged that the privileged classes of the South, a party of oligarchs, were trying to deprive the free white men of the nation of landownership in the territories. He uttered the agrarian cry, calling upon white labor in the South to revolt; the masses must smite the power of the few. John P. Hale of New Hampshire likewise lauded agrarians, those who would distribute land to the poor, and recalled the exploits of the Gracchi, slain by men of property. Henry Wilson of Massachusetts declared that the South wished to tax the people for the benefit of property, to tax the poor and laboring masses for the relief of the wealthy. Cameron of Pennsylvania, a century ahead of his time, predicted that labor would control the policies of the nation and urged it to send men to Congress who were familiar with its needs.

Others saw the demoralization of the original experiment in freedom. Hale saw it transformed into a military despotism. James M. Mason deplored the "improvident waste of money" which was promoting "the unsettling, the loosening, the destroying of the fabric of the Government itself"; wasteful subsidies "would debauch the morals of this people beyond recovery," eventually "breaking down the Confederate government, or converting it into one of entire consolidation." Toombs denounced appropriations for public improvements as "plunder of the agriculturist and laboring man" both in New York and in Georgia. "We have acted on the idea that the freemen of the country are capable of maintaining the law, of maintaining peace, of maintaining order. If that is wrong, if that is not true, if we have been mistaken, then our Government is a failure. While I am not able to express the confidence that was felt twenty years ago, and which I then felt . . . I am at least not yet prepared to give it up."

Most alarming of all was the questioning of the majority principle of the democratic experiment. Mallory of Florida asked: "Who are the people of Kansas? The honorable Senator from New York . . . said the people meant the majority. I deny any such doctrine in this country . . . whoever a state chooses to confer her political authority upon, are the people." C. C. Clay was most revealing in his utterances. "Our governments are republics, not democracies. The people exercise their sovereignty not in person, at the ballot-box, but through agents, delegates or representatives. . . . It is unwise and inexpedient for the people themselves to assemble and adopt laws. . . . An absolute majority . . . is the most cruel, rapacious, intolerant and intolerable of all tyrants. . . . This is sheer radicalism. It is the Red Republicanism of revolutionary

France . . . not the American Republicanism of our fathers. Their Republicanism was stable and conservative . . . it afforded a shield for the minority. . . . When [the Black Republicans] get control of the Federal Government . . . the Southern States must elect between independence out of the Union or subordination within it."

Or, as Linton Stephens wrote to his brother: "A pure democracy, in a small State of homogeneous interest, is tolerable, but in a State divided into two permanent antagonisms, with a large numerical majority on one side, is the most despotic of all governments. A mob, when unrestrained by interest, is terrific in its utter irresponsibility. If Kansas is rejected, our government becomes a pure Democracy; the only law is that of superior numbers; the only power is that of an irresponsible mob, and that mob is hostile to us. We have got to fight it, or deter it, or succumb to it. I am for the first, whenever it is necessary, for the second if it can avail, but for the last, *never, never!*"[14]

The concurrence of the political, economic, and emotional tensions during the winter of 1857–1858, had brought new and ominous hostility among the representatives of the various attitudes. The Democratic party had shown itself demoralized thereby. Its only real measure had been passed at a dreadful expense of reputation, for the English bill on Kansas was labeled the most dangerous and dishonest compromise yet. The economy program had been hamstrung. The integrity of prominent Democratic officials had been shown to be faulty. Foreign policy had been ineffectual and the plaything of financial interests. Small comfort was it that none of the subsidy schemes had been passed. While this failure may have saved the Treasury, it had sent the enemies of the Democracy home with a quiverful of arrows which they knew well how to use. That there was handwriting on the wall was plain to see; but far too many failed to grasp its meaning.

PART III

DEMORALIZATION AND DEFEAT

Chapter 11

Repudiation at the Polls

THE STATE ELECTIONS in the even years midway between presidential contests gave excellent opportunities, in the antebellum days, for barometric readings of popular opinion in the northern states. A pivotal bloc of states, north of the Mason-Dixon line and the Ohio River, then chose state administrations and reviewed the work of their Congressmen. These polls were bound to be dominated by local issues, and Congressmen felt less a part of their national organization than during presidential battles. They were often caught between the devil of national legislative bargains and the deep sea of state politics. So it was in 1858.

Northern Congressmen had to go home to face what purported to be "the music" but was really a horrid cacophony. Their seats in the Thirty-fifth Congress were bound to be striven for desperately. Not only were these prizes in themselves, but the results would point more clearly the road to 1860. During the remaining months of 1858 a series of battles would be fought in the non-slaveholding states. In October and November crucial contests would be decided in a pivotal phalanx of five states; and the victors in the majority of these contests would almost certainly determine who was to control the next House of Representatives. Democratic defeat in 1854 in New York, Pennsylvania, Ohio, Indiana, and Illinois had been the first indication of Republican strength. In 1856 the trend had been reversed there, and the Democrats had proved finally victorious, winning forty-seven seats in these states. Now two years later the returns would be avidly scanned.

The task of winning was a fearful one because of the unusual instability of the voters. Northern Democrats were hampered by the ambiguities in which that confused epoch abounded. Not only was their principal tenet, popular sovereignty, capable of double meaning, but their party name, the *American Democracy,* seemed hardly suitable for one which included powerful undemocratic elements. The Democrats were, supposedly, disciples of Jefferson and Jackson, presumed to be earnest in their championship of the com-

mon man, believers in liberty and equality. Yet among them
were slaveholders who demanded that slavery be given a
chance to spread and be protected wherever it might go.
Northern Democrats opposed to slavery found it hard to take
Republican denunciation of that institution.

Another troublesome contradiction grew out of the industrialization of some northern cities, where large groups
of laborers were mobilized with the gap between them and
their employers ever widening. Signs had been multiplying,
through thirty years, that labor could play a part in politics;
in 1858 southerners sought political advantage by stirring-up
labor discontent on the heels of the panic. Senator Hammond of South Carolina, speaking for himself and his associates who were weary of constant northern denunciation of
slavery, turned the tables. Abolitionists had no right to
assume tones of superior morality; southern pride had a good
conscience. On the floor of the Senate, Hammond exposed
the exploitation of white labor by northern employers. These
unfortunate "mud-sills" of society, he charged, were worse
off than the Negro slaves; and their pious, hypocritical ex-
ploiters were morally more reprehensible than southern
slaveholders.

Hammond was not alone. He and his associates had been
imbibing the spirit of the poet Grayson, who recently had
published *The Hireling and the Slave,* and of George Fitzhugh's books, *Sociology for the South* and *Cannibals All.*
Such writers defended Negro slavery, and denounced the
white slavery in the mills. Fitzhugh wrote bitter diatribes
against democracy; democracy and liberty, he believed, were
antagonistic.

A few northerners had been using this same propaganda,
with some newspaper editors even defending Negro slavery.
In Lowell, Massachusetts, I. Doolittle began printing a little
sheet, *The Spindle City Idea,* which called on the workingmen to free themselves from a blacker slavery than ever
existed in the South. The opponents of the Democrats, particularly in Pennsylvania, had been quick to see an advantage and brought forward the protective tariff as the solution
to the wage workers' problems. They had made a clean
sweep of the Keystone state, giving the Democratic leaders
much to worry about. The panic had caused a good deal of
unemployment, with food riots and bread lines; and many
people were feeling the pinch of misery. If they took this
propaganda seriously, what might happen? They had votes.

This attempt by southern sympathizers to stir up northern labor was another count in the indictment against the slave power, another sharp stimulant to northern determination to destroy that power before it became too adept in the use of its new weapon.[1]

This same industrialization was but one aspect of the great national growth, which was attracting immigrants from Europe with the idea that the streets of America were paved with gold. Thousands of them were soon to be welcomed into the ranks of voters, and the Democracy was anxious to have them. But could a party which stood for laissez faire, for limited powers to the federal government, and for states' rights, which opposed tariffs, subsidies, and free homesteads —and in effect condoned slavery—gain the support of the incoming hordes?

In this day of romantic optimism, which saw the wealth and power of the nation growing fabulously, particularly if helped by the federal government, could such a party attract people of enterprise? Also, in the face of the prevailing Protestantism and revivalism, how could a party win which seemed to approve of liquor selling, polygamy, and slavery, and which seemed to welcome Catholics to its ranks? If a party proclaiming itself the friend of the common man refused to raise the tariff—which, it was said, was needed to keep him on his job—how could such a party hold an electoral majority? The Democratic Congressmen in the North were in a dilemma. Would any leadership arise to think them out of it and enable them to win, faced by their host of enemies?

The Republicans were formidable indeed. They had the impetus of projected victory to buoy them up; they looked into the future with the great expectancy of the zealous and the young. The tenseness and uncertainty of the panic period were upsetting many a political loyalty and lifelong habits of thought and action. The high tide of religious revival was awakening dormant consciences to thoughts of freedom and the destruction of corruption.

The increasing prevalence of such attitudes placed the ancient Democracy on a hot griddle. How could this hoary party, tinged with corruption and plagued with feuds, stand against youth, enthusiasm, and idealism? The continuous signs of disintegration, which had been too plainly manifested in the session of Congress just adjourned, were not encouraging; nor were the schisms so common in the state organizations. During the summer of 1858 the congressional campaigns were to demonstrate these weaknesses all too plainly, especially in the five key states, New York, Pennsylvania, Ohio, Indiana, and Illinois.

II

The largest bloc of seats at stake was made up of the fifteen which the Democrats held in the President's own Pennsylvania. These constituencies, three-fifths of the state's twenty-five, were scattered through all portions of the Commonwealth, more in the east, south, and center than in the west and north. Philadelphia and the coal and iron counties were still Democratic, as were many of the agricultural districts in the center and south. The headquarters of the opposition was in the Pittsburgh region and in the northern counties. Two situations were particularly dangerous. First, ancient schisms were still unhealed despite Buchanan's elevation; rather they were more painful because of the heart-burnings over the patronage. Second, the panic had paralyzed Pennsylvania's industries, leaving many of her workmen unemployed; they were potential recruits for clever promoters of a protective tariff.

The party had been united in supporting Buchanan in 1856. and many came forward thereafter to receive rewards for their loyalty. Although Buchanan had appointed Pennsylvanians with such frequency that their number became a joke in Senate executive sessions, he had left legions forlorn. The same ill fortune that made so difficult the selection of a member of his cabinet from Pennsylvania followed him into the lower ranges of the patronage.

A place for Forney remained the most trying puzzle. Buchanan and Black labored hard to find some reward acceptable to him. As no office was available that he would take, they turned to journalism and considered helping him to reestablish himself in Philadelphia. There William Rice, editor of the *Pennsylvanian,* the party organ, was a millstone around the neck of the Democracy; a more vital spokesman was essential to restore dwindling confidence and arouse new enthusiasm. Why not let Forney taken over the *Pennsylvanian,* giving him the contract for printing post-office blanks so that he could buy this paper and finance it? However, Rice wanted too much, and so Forney started a paper of his own, the *Press,* still expecting the post-office blanks. Then Lecompton arose, and Forney and his friend Governor William F. Packer realized the Pennsylvania voters would not stomach Buchanan's position. Therefore the *Press* condemned Lecompton and upheld Walker. This "insubordination" cost Forney the blanks contract and any further favors from Buchanan. A feud developed between the federal machine of officeholders, and the Packer-Forney combination, which embraced the holders of the state patronage. A bad sign in the spring of 1858 was the defeat of Buchanan's friend, Mayor Vaux of Philadelphia, by a candidate, Alexander Henry, who would have been called a Republican in other states.[2]

There was further cause for concern as the effects of the panic became more widespread, particularly in the coal and iron regions which generally had been Democratic. The local capitalists had supported the party in 1856, and the miners themselves had voted for it. Before the panic the iron manufacturers had devoted their political talents to urging the government to use more iron and to use only American iron. In the months following the financial collapse, many iron plants had closed down, leaving employers and employees uncertain of the future and frequently in distress.

The opposition seized the opportunity to revive the tariff issue; protection would save Pennsylvania's interests and give the laborer's job back to him. They hoped that many Democrats, who did not relish Lecompton, might be the more ready to seek the benefits of a new tariff policy. In June it was announced that the "United American Republican and Peoples Committee of Superintendence" had called a state convention to meet at Harrisburg in July and make nominations and plans for the campaign.[3]

Collector Baker of Philadelphia, titular leader of the administration forces in the congressional campaign, was thus beset by unusual difficulties. While the opposition was revivified and reenforced, his own ranks were wavering. He was not sure of the Governor and the Harrisburg influence, and he could hardly count on Forney and the *Press.* He had no editorial support which could worst Forney. The collector tried to strengthen Rice's feeble hands by assigning his brother, George W. Baker, to act as assistant editor of the *Pennsylvanian,* maintaining him meanwhile on the customhouse pay roll. Rice grew more and more querulous as his sense of his own inadequacy became more apparent. He was dissatisfied with his subsidy and was trying to sell his paper. Forney, in the meantime, maintained a high degree of independence. He chose to support some congressional candidates, generally those who had opposed Lecompton, and denounced others. Nor were these all of Baker's disadvantages. As a personal appointee of the President brought down from Lancaster, he was resented by some of the old-time federal officeholders, notably the district attorney, James C. Van Dyke; there was less harmony than was needed. Surely Baker's lot was not a happy one.[4]

Money was more than ever necessary for such a campaign and, because of the panic and the party factionalism, was harder to get. The ambitious Baker schemed to split the anti-Democratic vote; he would finance American party candidates to run in the Philadelphia districts, so that all his opponents would not flock to the opposition or People's party. Such tactics, he calculated, would take $10,000 extra. The usual assessments of the federal employees would not be sufficient, though he pursued them energetically enough, particularly in the customhouse and the navy yard. Surely government contractors, such as the builders of the recently authorized sloops of war, should make contributions. He suggested to the President that these contracts be used for the benefit of the party. Also he thought a local man might contribute if a marble contract was given him. As the campaign advanced, funds were not forthcoming. Baker's efforts to organize the Americans were not very successful, and things were going at sixes and sevens.[5]

Help was needed from the outside, and it was at hand. The government printing profits were again the answer. Wendell had bought out the Senate and House printers for about $75,000 and was piling up profits averaging 33⅓ per cent. Besides the congressional printing gains he had the lucrative printing and binding contracts for the executive departments and the binding work for the House. Under an agreement with Gales and Seaton, publishers of the Whig *National Intelligencer,* who had been awarded a contract for editing and printing the new series of *American State Papers,* Wendell would print these volumes for $20,000 of the $50,-000 which they would receive. Only the most "ultra" prices for government printing could have supported such split-ups. Nor did Wendell overlook other means of "turning an honest penny," as later investigations showed.

As before, much of Wendell's profit was siphoned off to deserving Democrats. He financed the *Union* at a cost of about $19,000 a year and supported other party papers. He split his Post Office printing profits, first with Rice of the *Pennsylvanian,* and later with Thomas Florence, Congressman from one of the Philadelphia districts and owner of the Philadelphia *Argus.* Its assistant editor, Theophilus Fisk, was carried on the customhouse pay roll; and according to Florence its editor-in-chief, Severns, merited some of the post-office-blank money. Wendell considered this demand something of a shakedown; but, at the administration's behest, he cut down Rice's share somewhat and made payments to Severns.

Wendell's large profits made him fair game to other democrats than newspapermen. Why should he not contribute to 1858 campaign funds? The Pennsylvanians became particularly insistent. Wendell found himself getting short of funds, and decided that since Congressmen had votes for printing appropriations they should be the ones to get the pap. Accordingly he informed Buchanan that he was going to stop payments to Rice and Severns, as a waste of money from the party standpoint. He would pipe the money into congressional campaign funds. His political contributions, he told the President, were running up to $25,000 or $30,000 yearly, in addition to the expense of the *Union* and the payments to Harris and Steedman.[6]

Party needs called for more angels than Wendell, and the heads of bureaus in the Interior and other departments authorized solicitation of their clerks for contributions to carry Pennsylvania. The commissioner of the general land office headed a subscription paper with $10.00, and the clerks were expected to subscribe 2 per cent of their salaries. Also the state societies of officeholders in Washington, those from Indiana for instance, contributed to aid Pennsylvania.

Despite this outside aid things were in confusion in the party's Keystone ranks. Nothing went right. American candidates were dividing the opposition in only two districts, and they not very effectively, while the Douglas-Forney Democrats were splitting the Democracy in three districts by running their own candidates. Workers in the coal and iron counties were disaffected. Worse, the Catholic vote in Philadelphia was developing sympathies for Douglas because, it was reported, of his wife's religion and his own generous contributions to her church in Washington.[7] Forney was in great form. He even went to help the anti-Lecompton Congressman Haskin of New York State, who was being purged. At Tarrytown he made a telling speech against Buchanan which was widely printed. Could the party in Pennsylvania be worse demoralized?

III

Hardly second to Pennsylvania in importance was New York State, where the Democrats had twelve of the thirty-three Congressmen. Most of them came from the cities, New York and Brooklyn and their suburbs, Albany and Buffalo. Only one Democrat represented a predominantly rural district, while eight were definitely connected with New York City. Metropolitan politics was the crux of the unhappy situation. New York City was more and more apart from the rest of the state, and the predicament of its machine was taking it out of the national Democracy in everything but name.

The city machine continued to be torn by rivalries of individuals and factions in which the erstwhile mayor, Fernando Wood, and his organization figured disastrously. Wood's alliance with the collector, Augustus Schell, made at the time of the federal appointments in 1857, had not impressed the party generally. Postmaster Fowler with George N. Sanders, District Attorney McKeon and two of the city Congressmen, Sickles and Cochrane, had taken control of the Tammany organization and sought to reorganize the city Democracy. This had produced a split in the party which in the mayoralty election of 1857 caused the defeat of Wood. The ex-Mayor then broke with Tammany Hall and organized his own headquarters at Mozart Hall. He was planning to raid the districts of the city Congressmen who had opposed him, and defeat them in 1858.[8]

Many efforts were made to get Washington to take sides. Would Schell, the chief federal officeholder, and Wood dominate there, or would Sickles, Cochrane, and the rest of the New York City Congressmen? When the House battle over Lecompton started, Clark and Haskin bolted, while Sickles and Cochrane remained loyal to the administration. For this the latter expected a good share of the local patronage. Schell, however, had no interest in their Kansas votes, and he continued to be unfriendly to their pretensions. He was trying to reform the customhouse and did not want it cluttered with their "heelers." His attitude was embarrassing to Buchanan and Cobb, who labored with him during the summer of 1858, trying to persuade him to take the recommendation of the city Congressmen. Schell thus importuned yielded something, but he never granted anything more than he had to.[9]

Such schism in Gotham endangered the eight New York City seats. If they were lost, the Democrats could expect a delegation approaching zero. Regardless, they gave themselves over to factionalism with wholehearted abandon. Representatives Clark and Haskin found the administration determined to punish their bolt on Lecompton and setting up candidates against them; in self-preservation, they accepted Republican support. In Taylor's Brooklyn district, also, two Democrats slugged it out, and in Jack Kelly's Manhattan bailiwick there were no fewer than three. Both Tammany and Mozart Hall set up tickets in the municipal election, thus making victory likely for Mayor Tiemann's slate of Republican and American councilmen and city officers.

Ex-Mayor Wood followed his own devious path. In the state committee he introduced resolutions supporting Douglas and Wise in their opposition to Lecompton. After his delegation was refused admission to the state convention, he offered to sell out to Buchanan, for appointment as governor of the territory of Nebraska. The President, whose attitude toward Wood is still obscure, would not agree; whereupon Fernando solaced himself by financing Douglas's senatorial campaign whilst professing great loyalty to the President.[10] As Wood relaxed none of his efforts, Sickles particularly became nervous. He asked Buchanan to buy off his competitor, Williamson, with an office for a relative, and permit soldiers from Governors Island to come over to Manhattan and vote. Buchanan would do neither; he simply urged Schell to be fair with the patronage and Wood to remember that he wanted Sickles reelected. Schell, at least, prepared to subsidize some of the precinct workers, with places on the customhouse pay roll at election time and with ten-dollar fees for services certainly not rendered on the docks. Two facts became obvious: that no one was in command of the New York situation, and that the prospects of the Democratic delegation were extremely dubious.[11]

IV

Across the mountains in Ohio a third large bloc of seats was at stake. The Democracy held nine of the state's twenty-one. Six of these were in districts opposite Kentucky and Virginia, where Cincinnati was the Democratic headquarters. Two were in the center of the state, including the capital,

Columbus. Only one lay in the northern, Cleveland, region. Party fortunes late in 1857 had seemed bright, with the Republican state treasurer proved a defaulter and with Henry B. Payne, friend of Douglas, coming within fifteen hundred votes of defeating Republican Governor Chase for reelection. Also the legislature had gone Democratic.

The party itself was led by a combination of newspaper editors and federal officeholders, with Senator Pugh of Cincinnati as titular chief. At Cincinnati, McLean's *Enquirer* was edited by James J. Faran. At Columbus Samuel Medary was proprietor of the official organ, the *Ohio Statesman,* until Buchanan made him governor of Minnesota; then he sold the paper to James Smith, who was financed by Thomas Miller, the postmaster. At Cleveland, Payne's home town, J. W. Gray edited the *Plain Dealer* and held the commission as postmaster; he and Smith managed the appointments of postmasters in their regions.

The congressional session of 1857–1858 wrecked this promising set-up, because the Lecompton struggle split the leadership, from Cincinnati north. Faran supported Lecompton but Smith, Miller, Payne, and Gray followed Douglas. Buchanan retaliated. He made Faran postmaster at Cincinnati. At Columbus he removed Miller, putting Medary in his place since Minnesota had become a state; but he could not take the party organ from Smith and Miller, because they were district henchmen of Congressman S. S. Cox, who had supported the English bill. Miller even got the post office back, when Buchanan decided he must have Medary as governor of Kansas. At Cleveland Gray lost the post office and his successor removed thirty-six postmasters in that northern area where Douglas was strongest. Also Buchanan appointed a new marshal up there, Matthew Johnson, who with Faran and Medary managed to control the July state convention and get resolutions endorsing Buchanan.

Such were the tortuous intricacies of Lecompton patronage, in all its futility. Ohio sympathy for Douglas grew as his Illinois campaign progressed, in spite of patronage. The deposed Gray edited the *Plain Dealer* effectively, countering Buchanan's efforts to control the party. All this was relished by the Republicans, who made great progress in their battle for congressional seats.[12]

In Indiana a similar division boded ill for Democratic success that fall. The war between Bright, backed by Buchanan, and the friends of Douglas was waged unceasingly. The

Bright faction nominated a Lecompton Democrat to run against Congressman Davis, who had opposed the bill and had Republican endorsement. Former District Attorney Hovey, whose removal probably was due to Bright's engineering of the intraparty feud, rather than to Lecompton factors, nevertheless was proclaimed a Douglas martyr. He was nominated by the Republicans to run against Congressman Niblack, who had voted for Lecompton; in this crazy quilt of politics it made no difference that Niblack had protested Hovey's removal.[13]

V

The most spectacular of all the campaigns in this pivotal phalanx was that in Illinois. Here the contests for the seats in the House of Representatives were overshadowed by the struggle for the Senatorship. This fight not only involved Douglas's continued congressional career but might determine the fate of the Democratic party in 1860. Therefore the election was really national in implication and attracted national interest.

The voters had not been very favorable to the Illinois Democracy in recent years. The state had a Republican governor, and Douglas a Republican colleague in the Senate. The five Democrats in the House were a scant majority of the delegation of nine. They came from the southern part of the state, from the counties east of Missouri, and were favored by an apportionment made in the days of Democratic ascendancy. Buchanan had indeed succeeded in carrying the state in 1856, but by a very narrow margin, with a vote smaller than the Frémont-Filmore total combined. If the trend were not arrested Douglas might be brought home by a Republican legislature; and such a defeat would probably destroy his chances for 1860. Douglas had powerful enemies in his own party who would even aid in his downfall. When he broke with Buchanan he risked his political life. Whether he anticipated it is not recorded.

In January, 1858, the Democratic organization belonged to Douglas. Most of the federal officeholders had been appointed on his recommendation. When he broke with Buchanan on Lecompton, reprisals were not long in following. The administration determined to organize a squad to undermine Douglas within his own organization and, if unsuccessful in this, to marshal a battalion of bolters into a suicide column. Secretary Cobb directed this campaign. He was hostile to Douglas—some said, because the Illinois Senator seemed to block his presidential ambitions—and entered the contest with the aid of Postmaster General Brown. Cobb and Brown knew that Chicago was Douglas's weak point politically because of a local vendetta, and they sought out Ike Cook. This was the notorious, defaulting "ex" Ike Cook—the ex Douglas man, ex postmaster, ex financial backer of Douglas's *Chicago Times*.

The vengeful Cook was conjuring up grievances to compensate him for past misdeeds and was probably about to commit more. Cobb and Brown knew that he had a large city following, particularly among the Irish; and when Postmaster Price was removed as a punishment of Douglas, they helped establish Cook in his place. There was a little matter of a default in his accounts to be cleared up before reappointment. He had earlier offered to reimburse the government by turning over a Chicago lot, but as his title to the land was not clear Cobb had refused it. Now Cobb with Attorney General Black to counsel him, saw the matter in a new light; the lot was accepted, the accounts declared settled, and Ike again was postmaster.

His first task was to secure control of the state convention scheduled for April. His chief aide was Dr. Charles Leib, sometimes doctor, lawyer, liquor dealer, Mormon, and Kansas adventurer of free-state tinge, who had edited a campaign paper in Chicago for the Democrats in 1856, and served as city sealer of weights and measures. He was made a mail agent and as such had a pass on the railroads and could round up the postmasters. Colonel R. B. Carpenter, government disburser in the building of the new Chicago post office and courthouse then under construction, was another local lieutenant. In the southern part of the state ex-Governor John Reynolds, commonly known as the "Old Ranger," took the lead, assisted by John Dougherty. The efforts of this gang were not such as to compel the Democratic state convention to follow their lead. The party enthusiastically endorsed Douglas and adjourned, leaving Cook and his tattered remnant to meet by themselves. The rump organized their own state central committee headed by Cook and set June 9 for their own convention. Their chief interest was in drawing up recommendations, to be forwarded to Washington, for the decapitation of some of their enemies.[14] When finally they held their convention it was so thinly attended, and their ticket was so unimpressive, that Douglas did not hesitate to denounce Cook and Leib on the floor of the Senate. Others saw the futility of Cook's efforts, and it began to be whispered that if Douglas were cautious and would occasionally speak well of the administration all might be forgiven and Cook's ticket forgotten.

Meanwhile, no more Douglas men of importance were beheaded except Fry, collector of the port at Chicago, and the district attorney of northern Illinois. The latter was a particularly nasty move, as Buchanan appointed in his place a son of Senator Fitch of Indiana, Douglas's mortal enemy. Douglas's marshal for northern Illinois, whose removal had been urged and confidently predicted, was reappointed.[15]

For a time after the English bill had passed and during the British war scare, the feuding died down. Douglas was working with Mason and Slidell to secure for Buchanan sufficient powers to meet aggression. Numerous friends were laboring to heal the breach, and in June it seemed that they might succeeed. The cabinet was divided, with Floyd rather interested in harmony. Indeed, Douglas had more southern support than has been generally recognized, for the English bill was not popular in that section and Douglas's opposition to it was applauded. To the realistic, of course, schism on the eve of national campaign was always to be deplored. Just before the session closed Douglas made a speech designed to show his willingness to cooperate with the administration, and the Washington *Union* chimed in on the same note. Douglas left Washington late in June with the knowledge that friends were working to eliminate the Cook ticket, and he confided to them that if Buchanan would support his reelection the feud was over.

That was Douglas's thought in Washington; but events in Illinois were moving faster than he had anticipated. The prairie Republicans had held a state convention at Springfield, June 16, the day after Douglas's olive-branch speech in the Senate. After nominating a state ticket they did an unheard-of thing. Ignoring the prerogative of the party caucus of the legislature—to make any nominations for the Senate—they adopted a resolution naming Abraham Lincoln as their candidate for Douglas's seat. The Illinois Republicans were experimental, and Lincoln's friends wanted to head off another candidate. Lincoln accepted immediately, in one of the great speeches of his career. He charged a plot by Douglas, Buchanan, Pierce, and Taney to create new slave states; he warned: "A house divided against itself cannot stand." Douglas thus was to have as his competitor one of the ablest debaters in the Northwest.

The Little Giant made a leisurely trip homeward, preparing for the coming ordeal. His first concern was money. He had been hard hit in the panic, and this campaign was going to cost a great deal. He stopped in New York to seek a loan, offering his Chicago real estate as security, and obtained $40,000 from Fernando Wood. Proceeding westward, he received encouragement everywhere. He was surprised to find how unpopular Buchanan and Lecompton were, and how rapidly Republican strength was growing. If the Republicans were as strong in Illinois as they appeared to be in Ohio and Indiana, surely his condition was precarious. Was Buchanan worth placating? Or would concessions to the administration only invite defeat?[16]

The Republicans were keenly alive to their advantage and eagerly pressed it. They were willing to give some sort of left-handed help to Cook. Buchanan's man Dougherty was reported in conference with Lincoln, whose partner, Herndon, gave extravagant expression to the hopes of the Republicans. "The Illinois State Journal and each and every Republican is trying to create the split [in the Democratic party] . . . we want to make it wider and deeper, hotter and more impassable. Political hatred, deep-seated opposition is what is so much desired, and if we can do this between the worshippers of Buchanan and Douglas we will effect it . . . I am this day ready to go further than I have ever gone, if the nigger drivers force Kansas on this free People. I am ready to go *any length for self defense,* though that length should *end in war* bloody and to the hilt. This is a matured opinion not hastily expressed. . . . I hate power and I hate and dread the nigger power."[17] This was what Douglas was facing.

Back in Washington his friends were busy negotiating with the administration to arrange the hoped-for truce. The *Washington Union* was conciliatory. Wendell sought to make friends with the *Chicago Times.* George N. Sanders, his own father-in-law Cutts, Governor Wise of Virginia, and Senator Gwin of California were working upon Buchanan and his cabinet. They at length succeeded in arranging a compromise to which even Slidell agreed. Douglas's bête noire, the mail agent, Leib, would be removed; both Democratic conventions would reassemble, nominate Douglas, endorse Buchanan, and acquiesce in the English bill. The Cook ticket would be withdrawn, and Bright would come over and stump for Douglas. Telegrams to this effect from Sanders and Cutts were dispatched to Chicago; but they arrived too late.

When Douglas reached home in Chicago he had concluded that Buchanan's hatred was too valuable to lose and any concessions would gain him more enemies than friends. So he appeared on July 9 before a great Chicago rally and made a speech revealing that his conciliatory mood had vanished. He denounced Lecompton as a fraud and boasted that he and his friends had forced its abandonment and the submission of Lecompton to the people. Had the telegrams been received before this speech, would he have uttered it? Probably, for Lincoln was too dangerous an opponent. Douglas's defiance flashed across the wires—a scornful refusal of conciliation.

After the full text of his speech arrived in Washington, Buchanan and his advisers were through with compromise and peacemaking; Douglas must be defeated.[18] The *Washington Union* turned its none too vigorous batteries, now fired by William B. Gulick as well as Johnson and Hughes, on the Illinois Senator.[19] More of Douglas's officeholders were removed. Senator Slidell, as if to purge himself for having considered conciliation, went to Chicago to strengthen Cook's hands. Candidates were nominated in opposition to Douglas Democrats wherever possible.

The campaign now took on a character which attracted nation-wide attention. Long before the day of the radio, it was to be broadcast as widely as type and telegraph could carry it. Lincoln maneuvered Douglas into a joint debate, and the press all over the nation prepared to publish it. Douglas found many friends in the party despite the administration's hostility. Vice President Breckinridge, Speaker Orr, Governor Wise, Alexander H. Stephens, James B. Clay, and Senator Crittenden published declarations of support. Stephens visited Chicago during a vacation tour of the Northwest and may have given aid and comfort. Some Republicans were none too keen for Lincoln, and no less an authority than Horace Greeley of the *New York Tribune* thought it a mistake to oppose Douglas. On the other hand Cook, Reynolds, and Dougherty continued their efforts. Postmaster's heads began to fall into the basket. Douglas's marshal of northern Illinois was finally removed in September, making a pretty clean sweep of the Senator's important officeholders. The contest waxed more exciting as joint debate followed joint debate on the hot and dusty prairies.[20]

VI

Elsewhere than in the pivotal phalanx, significant development in party tactics pointed to the campaign of 1860. New methods and combinations were being tried out in the hope that the already discernible currents might be accelerated or deflected. The Democrats had always been weak in national organization. Their state machines were too autonomous. The Republicans were born with the secret of management. In 1856 their national committee had worked harder than that of the Democrats; they had created a more centralized party and were operating on a centralized basis in this congressional year of 1858. They had set up the National Republican Association in Washington, which was busily engaged in preparing documents to be distributed through the northern districts at 75 cents a hundred.[21]

This procedure also demonstrated their weakness. Though they called themselves national they had no following in the South. They were relying on the fact that the northern states, if solidly marshaled, could control the Electoral College despite combined southern opposition. This situation had encouraged men like Forney and Greeley to try to get Douglas to join the Republicans in return for refraining from opposing him in Illinois in 1858. They failed because Douglas still thought he could get the Democratic nomination in 1860, and the larger part of the Republican leadership wanted none of him. They wanted victory for themselves.[22]

The schisms in the ranks of the Democracy and the sectional character of the Republicans gave certain nationalists the hope that a non-sectional combination might be arranged. Many of the Old Whigs and Americans, who had still numbered 22 per cent of the voters in 1856, were hoping to reorganize around the standard of nationalism, with the slogan "Save the Union." Crittenden had essayed to give leadership to such a bloc in Congress with his Kansas compromise. After the Kansas question was disposed of some of the northern associates of Fillmore and some "South Americans" in Washington thought they saw an opportunity.

The Democrats were split; the Republicans no longer had an issue. Here was where the conservative nationalists might come in. A circular issued from Buffalo by certain Fillmore Whigs called for a new combination. Nathan Sargent and some southern American Congressmen followed this call with a platform for a Peoples Party of the Union. Their program featured protection of popular rights and elimination of sectional differences. The franchise must be protected from foreigners, the federal government should finance a judicious system of internal improvements, and Congress should devise a procedure whereby citizens of territories could frame their state constitutions more effectively. This platform undoubtedly had a Whig tinge, and the promotion of Crittenden's candidacy for the Presidency was probably behind it; but no outstanding Whig statesman or editor would acknowledge any part in it, nor would the cautious *National Intelligencer,* the Whig party's Washington organ, even print the program. No important response was given to this move at the time; but it wakened Democratic fears, particularly in the South.[23] There, opposition to the English bill, if ever organized and consolidated, might be dangerous.

In the face of this threat, the southern Democracy had need of all the unity it could command. Party ranks not only were badly shattered in the free states, but seemed to be in danger in the South. There radical southernism was reviving in a more menacing form. William L. Yancey of Alabama, whose ambition for the senatorship had been blocked by the state organization headed by Senators Fitzpatrick and Clay, was trying desperate expedients to rally the discontented. During this summer he set about organizing a "League of United Southerners," which he hoped would spread outside Alabama. The League would not nominate candidates but would seek to purge the major parties of leaders who were not sufficiently alive to southern interests. The compromises of the national parties only brought loss to the South.[24] When the Kansas voters refused the English project in August and showed definitely their determination to come in only as a free state, Yancey's words had more weight. His challenge was "A Southern Republic is our only safety"— pregnant words.

The influence of the Kansas vote was as nothing, in rousing radical southernism, compared to a flash from the Lincoln-Douglas debates. On the dusty square at Freeport, the two candidates faced each other, August 27. Lincoln maneuvered Douglas into a categorical statement, which was eventually given wider circulation than any other he ever uttered. "It matters not what way the Supreme Court may . . . decide as to the abstract question whether slavery may or may not go into a Territory . . . the people have the lawful means to introduce it or exclude it as they please." He had said it earlier, but never before such a nation-wide audience. Yancey was right; the South could not trust national compromise legislation.[25]

The discontent of southerners who resented the English bill and who sought compensation in threats of radical action, called forth counter attempts to allay fear and restore calm. Senator Hammond of South Carolina reminded them of their powers; "An overwhelming majority of the South would ... decidedly prefer to remain in the Union rather than . . . set up a separate government" if the Constitution were properly adhered to. The South could protect herself in the Union and control it. "Our history proves that no man and no measure has yet been strong enough to stand against the South when united. I believe none ever will." The South could continue to rule if it would only keep its head.[26]

But it was harder than ever to keep calm in the face of northern utterance. Douglas had spoken. Lincoln had proclaimed, "A house divided against itself cannot stand." A climax came October 25, when Seward made a speech at Rochester which seemed to bury hope of an amicable understanding. He declared that the South was determined to revive the slave trade and spread slavery. The Democratic party always surrendered to this power. "It is an irrepressible conflict between opposing and enduring forces, and it means that the United States must and will, sooner or later, become either entirely a slave-holding nation or entirely a free-labor nation."

To be sure this prophecy was only a local political device of Seward's. As he described it: "I saw a reserve Republican power of 70,000 or 80,000 in [New York] state in the rural districts who had slept two years since the last Presidential Campaign, betraying the state to the Democratic party last year, needing to be roused with a battle cry that they could respond to. I saw the invidious efforts of the Ultras undoing the confidence of this mass in the Republican party . . . local divines threatening to disgust the people and to result in such a diminution of zeal as would lose our ticket here in the country where alone it could be saved." Hence the "irrepressible conflict."

But Seward's phrase traveled far beyond New York's "rural districts." Not the irresponsible Yancey but the distinguished Senator from Mississippi, Jefferson Davis, took it up. Speaking to the Mississippi legislature November 11, he proclaimed Seward a master mind, dangerously powerful. If an abolitionist were elected President, the result would be revolutionary—the purposes of government would be destroyed. "In that event," he warned, "I should deem it your duty to provide for your safety outside of the Union."[27]

VII

Even before Seward spoke and Davis replied, most of the returns of 1858 had been cast up. This was truly the most significant congressional election in the history of the Democratic party. Some signs of its outcome began to appear as early as August. In Missouri the Democrats won the state offices and all the Congressmen, even defeating the radical opposition member from St. Louis, Frank Blair, Jr.; but throughout the state their opponents showed unexpected strength.[28] In September Maine and Vermont voted Republican, which was hardly a surprise. So far the results were mixed. October would be the month of decision.

The long awaited second week of that fateful tenth month finally passed into history, leaving its statistics to tell the story of the Democratic debacle. In Indiana, though the state ticket was victorious by a slight majority, the party lost the legislature and three of its six Congressmen. Niblack and English survived and were joined by a new recruit in the fourth district. Davis was to return with them, but as a Republican. In Ohio also there was a net loss of three seats; Pendleton, Vallandigham, and Cox survived for later deeds. The Republicans got Burns, Hall, and Groesbeck, and Lawrence avoided defeat only by not running. Lecompton again had taken its toll.

The climax of that dolorous October Tuesday was discovered to be in Pennsylvania. Here the state ticket and eleven of the party's fifteen Congressmen were engulfed. Of the four that survived, Florence had triumphed in Philadelphia with the aid of the navy yard despite the candidacy of an anti-Lecompton Democrat supported by Forney. Dimmick from the northeastern district, and Montgomery from the southwestern, survived two-party contests. The fourth to triumph was Hickman, who, with Forney's help, beat both the opposition and the administration Democrat. In the coal country Dewart had been defeated by the nomination of an anti-Lecompton candidate. The greatest blow was the loss of J. Glancy Jones, chairman of the House committee on ways and means and administration floor leader. His district had been held to be the "Gibraltar of Democracy." Unless this tide were arrested in November, the party control of Congress would be gone.[29]

November brought no comfort, with its cross-purposed Illinois result. Here the congressional delegation—in which five of the nine members were Douglas men—remained intact notwithstanding Cook's efforts. The Douglas state slate was defeated by the Republicans—and Cook; but the gerrymandered legislature was still pro-Douglas, thanks to the holdovers; and so the "Little Giant" would return to the Senate. He had defeated the administration and the Republicans, but at a cost which he had not begun to reckon.

The issue was finally decided in New York. Although the Republicans and Americans had failed to unite, the Democrats lost the state. Four New York City members of Congress and the three upstate representatives were gone. Clark and Haskin had defeated the administration candidates set up against them, and with Reynolds of Albany were coming to Washington, elected by the full Republican strength of their districts. Cochrane and Sickles had survived, the latter without benefit of soldier votes from Governors Island. In the Manhattan city election Tammany and Mozart halls failed to unite, and the Republicans won. State, city, and congressional delegations were overwhelmingly Republican.

The national leadership of the Democratic party thus was defeated. Its net loss of eighteen seats in Congress probably meant that its control of the House of Representatives had vanished. This loss in the North was too great to be offset by any gain that might be made in the southern elections of 1859. Even harder to take, for some of the administration, was the fact that Douglas and his anti-Lecompton associates had generally been successful. Thus there were at least ten nominal Democrats in the House who probably would give little heed to efforts of the party leadership to marshal them, and who might hold the balance of power in the next Congress.[30]

The emotional chaos of the time was reflected in the psychological reactions of men high in authority. A note of despair was creeping into public utterance, replacing the usual boastful optimism. Direful forebodings were voiced even by the President of the United States. He saw a greater evil at work than disunion, which he warned the nation against in a published letter. "In the last age, although our fathers, like ourselves, were divided into political parties which often had severe conflicts with each other, yet we never heard, until within a recent period, of the employment of money to carry elections. Should this practice increase until the voters and their Representatives in the State and National Legislatures shall become infected, the fountain of free government will then be poisoned at its source, and we must end, as history proves, in a military despotism. A Democratic Republic, all agree, cannot long survive unless sustained by public virtue. When this is corrupted and the people become venal, there is a canker at the root of the tree of Liberty, which must cause it to wither and die."[31] Such philosophy was not inspiring, and it is not to be wondered at that some of the younger Democrats cursed this direful prophecy.

Chapter 12

A Runaway Session

CONGRESS is frequently as much of a political convention as it is a law-making body. Its members often are more concerned with party fortunes than with legislation. The periodic congregation of party representatives from all over the country at public expense provides an unsurpassed opportunity for political conferences and maneuvering. In hotels, boarding houses, drawing rooms, committee rooms, saloons, restaurants, gambling hells, red-light houses and churches, political events can be conceived and incubated.

These men in the 1850's were isolated in Washington for at least three months each year. They were away from their familiar environments and might be completely out of touch with home, except by means of unsatisfactory mail service and the telegraph. There were no Gallup polls, airplanes, telephones, or radios to bring accurate or immediate bulletins of home feeling. The influence of this periodic congregation and isolation is impossible to define very accurately, but its importance ought not to be underestimated.

The political character of Congress used to be most pronounced in the short sessions that opened in December of even years (eliminated in 1933 with the adoption of the Twentieth Amendment). These three months offered a last chance for members of Congress who were retiring or had been defeated to finish whatever they might wish done. The fixed terminal date, March 4, made that short session a profitable period to play politics. The rules of both houses were so framed that, if time were an object, small groups could dominate procedure. In the Senate, any member who had the endurance could talk indefinitely on any subject of legislation. In each house rules could be suspended only by a two-thirds vote, and thus a third of the members present could often block consideration of important matters in the last days of the session, if so disposed. Under such circumstances trading of votes and log rolling were profitable, and legislation which had little chance in long sessions might slide through in short ones.

The defeated Democrats came back to Washington in December, 1858, in an uneasy frame of mind, ready to play politics for all it was worth. Some were bitter, others discouraged; and all were apprehensive of the party future. Democrats from the South were under the shadow of their elections impending in 1859. They feared lest their old opponents, the Whigs, might revive as an opposition party with Senator Crittenden as presidential candidate. He was a moderate, and it was far from certain that most southerners were fire-eaters. If the Crittenden movement grew it would threaten Democratic control of the South. Northern Democrats also were jittery; defeat rested heavily upon them, and not a few were there for whatever they might get out of the session, including revenge. Many of them felt they had been let down by the administration and their southern associates.

With these apprehensions and resentments disturbing both wings of the Democracy, the administration leaders had a disastrous experience in attempting to marshal their defeated party. It became more evident than ever that the House majority was fictitious. The greatest blow suffered by the administration had been the defeat of J. Glancy Jones, chairman of ways and means, and House floor leader. Buchanan made it worse by depriving himself and the party of Jones's services through the short session. Conscience-stricken because he had broken his earlier promise to put Jones in the cabinet, and anxious to save him the embarrassment of returning to Congress under the stigma of defeat, Buchanan hastened to make him Minister to Austria. His very important House responsibilities fell to John S. Phelps of Missouri, who lacked his ability and his influence and was not in particularly close and confidential relations with Buchanan or his advisers.[1]

The President and the cabinet were to figure in this session in secondary roles. Whatever prestige, power, and patronage they once had possessed had been dissipated by the devastating Kansas fight. Buchanan's sole legislative triumph remained the English bill. Like Pierce before him with the Kansas-Nebraska Act, he had exhausted his strength on one measure. These laws were both empty victories; it would have been better for the party and the nation had neither of them been won.

Democratic leadership was in no position to make capital out of a legislative program, for both program and prestige were lacking. No widely popular proposition was trumpeted in the annual message of December, 1858, as a clarion call to party unity; the chief proposals—tariff revision through specific duties, and construction of a Pacific railroad—were unpopular with southern Democrats. Also, in that wing of the party, presidential prestige was ebbing over a slave cargo captured on the high seas by the Navy and brought into Charleston. The law required that the Negroes be shipped out of the country. Buchanan contracted with the Colonization Society of Liberia to receive and care for them, and to educate the children. This act of civilized concern for human welfare brought southern wrath down upon his head, for trafficking with "abolitionists" and for using government money to educate "niggers."

The American Democracy was in imminent danger of bankruptcy, South and North. Revolt was even more menacing this session than before, because of the peculiar state of the presidential prospects. A Gallup poll probably would have shown that the voters expected the Republican candidate to be Seward and the Democratic to be Douglas. To many southern Democrats, however, either possibility seemed calamitous. Their hatred of Seward had been intensified by his announcement of the "irrepressible conflict"; but hatred of Douglas was even deeper, because he jeopardized southern control of the party and of the government.

Among southern Congressmen, Douglas's great sin was not so much the Freeport doctrine as his defiance of the party line on Kansas. Both had been so well advertised by the Lincoln-Douglas debates that if he were nominated a number of Democrats—how many could not be estimated reliably—would refuse to support the ticket. For whom would they vote? The old Whigs and southern Americans thought they had the answer. During this session they revived Whiggery and moved to organize a national compromise ticket to be led by Crittenden, Clay's heir and assign, to compete with the Democrats for the southern vote.

The force of all these circumstances drove the more radical of the southern Democrats to one conclusion: Douglas must be stopped. No sooner had Congress assembled on December 2 than they began efforts to block him. Slidell, and other friends of the administration in hearty accord with this objective, joined in an unprecedented move to discipline him. It was perhaps easier because he was away. The Illinois Senator had decided to keep out of sight politically until the legislature had reelected him. His margin was slim, and

Cook was trying with federal help to break it. If he resumed his place in Washington he might be drawn into debate and say things which could be used against him in Illinois. He therefore went on a cruise down the Mississippi and to Cuba.

His senatorial enemies undertook to punish him in his absence. Slidell and Gwin, who was chairman of the Democratic caucus committee on committees, proposed to the caucus that Douglas be deprived of the chairmanship of the committee on territories. No action could have been more drastic, for it was this post which had been the center of his interest and in which he had made his fame—and his enemies. The correspondent of the *Baltimore Sun* reported that there was much opposition to the proposal. Such martyrdom might aid rather than injure Douglas. He wrote that it passed finally, 17–7; Bigler of Pennsylvania, Thomson of New Jersey, Shields of Minnesota, and four southern Senators—A. G. Brown, Clingman, Green, and Hunter—voted "No." Broderick was not invited to attend. Thus Douglas was disciplined and Green designated to preside over his committee. It was not a very astute move as time was to prove. Douglas at any rate was reelected early in January and appeared in his seat on the 10th of that month.[2]

The Little Giant found his colleagues in new quarters. At long last the Senate wing of the Capitol had been finished, and on January 4 Jefferson Davis reported that arrangements were complete for moving. Senator Crittenden, in making the motion to leave the old cramped quarters where so much history had been made, indulged in a short speech. He recalled the significant events of the past and the great names of Clay and Webster, Calhoun and Benton. This hall seemed to him "a local habitation for their names." He hoped that the future of the Senate would not "be dishonored by any comparison to be made with the past." Breckinridge then delivered an historical address and led his colleagues to their new scene of action. Rev. Dr. Gurley made a prayer of dedication, calling upon Almighty God in any hour of peril to be there to guide the nation's councilors "to hold fast that which is good." Thus began the use of the new stage, a more pretentious one upon which tragedy was to be enacted so soon.

Here was struck the next blow at Douglas or, perhaps more accurately, here the "radicals" took the first step to rally the South behind a new position chosen by themselves. They intended to challenge all presidential aspirants to accept their type of platform if those candidates hoped for southern support. Their first moves were not coordinated, for they had no recognized leader—no Calhoun; but they had one emotion in common, burning political ambition. They, and indeed practically all of the southern Senators, according to Senator Hammond of South Carolina, hoped that presidential lightning might strike them.

Early in the session several of these radicals had begun to seek the spotlight by continuing the attacks upon Douglas. They aimed to blow him up with his doctrines. The first to fire had been Senator Iverson of Georgia. A man of no particular fame whose term was about to expire, he was uncertain of reelection. Cobb and his friends were opposed to him and his radical views; in fact Cobb was looking to his seat in case he himself failed to gain the presidential nomination in 1860. So Iverson carefully prepared a speech, which he read to the Senate on January 6. The Pacific railroad was under debate and gave him his text: unjust taxation of the South and unequal distribution of federal favors. There must be equality betwixt the sections. Otherwise he believed that "the time will come when the slave States will be compelled . . . to . . . erect an independent Confederacy."

Iverson's chief purpose was to serve notice on persons looking to 1860 that three men were anathema to those who felt as he did. Seward, Hammond, and Douglas were arraigned for their utterances of 1858. Their doctrines, Iverson declared, were ruinous to the South; and he was particularly caustic with Douglas. The victory of the Illinoisan was a victory over the South and its constitutional rights. Squatter sovereignty was worse than the Wilmot Proviso, for the latter was "open, manly and decisive," while the former was a cheat. All this led up to an arresting climax. The election of a northern President, such as Seward, "will be considered cause enough to justify secession. . . . There are more than one of the southern states that would take immediate steps toward separation."

Slidell and his associates realized the danger from this sort of thing; it spelled the break-up of the Democratic party and the destruction of the Union which they loved to rule. They were perfectly willing, yea eager, to kill off Douglas, but they did not want to destroy their party and their power. So administration and senatorial leaders turned to an expedient once found useful.

II

The Democrats for many years had sought to offset the negative qualities of their laissez faire, do-nothing views on domestic issues with a swashbuckling spread-eagle foreign policy. Polk had been successful with his annexation of Mexican territory, but Pierce had failed in efforts to acquire Cuba. When Buchanan came to the White House he believed he could succeed. His wide experience in foreign affairs, his European contacts, and his own craft made him supremely confident. He had tried to settle differences with Great Britain, to work out transisthmian diplomatic problems, and to acquire new territory. Here he showed vision, stubbornly resisting British pretensions. So far he had been uniformly unsuccessful; but now, in desperation, the party chieftain was going to try for one grand coup.

Slidell and his associates on the foreign relations committee —aided by Douglas despite his disciplining—now sought to implement a plan for securing Cuba, which the President had been secretly pursuing, ever since his days in the State Department under Polk. He had learned in the Pierce days from August Belmont that financial intrigue might secure what open diplomacy could never obtain. Spain's proud refusal to sell her rich island might be overcome by secret temptation to Spanish financial necessity and avarice. The prospect of United States payment of $100,000,000 or more into the Spanish Treasury might move at least three important groups to aid the transfer. Powerful influence could come from the Spanish Queen mother, because the sale would raise the value of her extensive holdings in Cuba. The clergy should be interested in payments likely to stop bankrupt Spain's present practice of selling church lands. European bankers well might aid, to recover the principal and interest on large blocks of Spanish bonds now in default.

Buchanan had gone over this with Pierce and Marcy, and the Ostend conference had been arranged to aid the scheme. However, ineptitude of the conferees and ill timed publicity had ruined the plan, abroad and at home. Spain would not sell, and Republican orators seized upon the project as further proof of Democratic desire to expand the slave area. Yet Buchanan did not despair; immediately after inauguration he went to work. He called Christopher Fallon, Philadelphia agent of the Spanish Queen mother, in secret conference. Fallon, born in Spain of Irish parents, had settled in Philadelphia with his brother John while another brother, Henry, located in Havana. They developed business connections in the very inner circle of European finance with August Belmont of the Rothschilds, Frederick Huth and Company of London, the Barings, James McHenry of Liverpool, who handled Spanish railroad bonds, and Léon Lillo of Léon Lillo et Cie. of Paris. Through Léon Lillo, Christopher had been agent for the Spanish Queen mother since Polk's time, investing much of her money in Pennsylvania lands. Fallon told the President that, if the interest of three certain persons were secured, they could control the press and form public opinion; but to get their interest would be difficult because the sale of Cuba seemed to the Spanish an unforgivable sacrifice of honor and prestige. He was confident, however, that he could arrange it, and Buchanan authorized him to try. With a letter from the President expressing his desire for Cuba in rather general terms, Fallon departed for Europe.

Fallon's efforts took him to Paris, Rome, and Madrid. In Paris he conferred with certain politicians who "happened" to be there. In Rome he saw the Queen mother. In Madrid he perfected a plan. The banking influence, he concluded, would be useless because the politicians could see that such operators were only working to get repayment of their loans. What would it profit the political leaders if the bankers secured all the proceeds? Arrangements must be made to assure a generous share for Spanish politicians of the two principal parties. Then the party in power would negotiate the sale and be driven out of office by indignant public opinion. The "opposition," coming in, would find Spain committed to the sale, and "reluctantly" fulfill the contract; and each side subsequently would collect its "commissions."

Fallon reported in April, 1858, that this scheme had been on the verge of success when certain American legislators and publicists began agitation for purchase. Their clamorous publicity had scared off the Spanish politicos, or so Fallon claimed. He next recommended that Buchanan send a new minister to Spain, with no written instructions and no ostensible interest in Cuba, but with a plentiful supply of money for under-cover use. If the sum were large enough, Fallon said, the scheme should work.

Before Congress assembled for the short session, Buchanan sought a new minister. Failing to interest Senators Mallory and Benjamin, or Vice President Breckinridge, he persuaded

William Preston of Kentucky to go. He took with him no word of Cuba in his written instructions, but conferences with Fallon preceded his sailing. Back in the Senate, January 10, Slidell was introducing a resolution for an appropriation of $30,000,000 to facilitate negotiations.

This bill, reported out favorably by the foreign relations committee a fortnight later, proved the signal for a series of Republican attacks on the Democratic party and its southern leaders. Seward led off, and before the debate was over fifty-three of the sixty-five Senators had entered the lists. If the Republicans missed any opportunity to denounce the slave power, and if the southern members neglected any means of resenting it, they went unrecorded. The measure was talked to death and had to be abandoned.[3]

The Democratic party thus had fared badly in its hope of securing prestige from the handling of foreign relations. The experienced President had tried to make some grand plays, but relations between Congress and the Executive were so tangled by schism in the party that the results were negligible. Worse was the fact that finance was interfering at every turn. Conflicting interests, rival concessionaries, bondholders' committees were represented by agents ranging from the merest adventurers to United States Senators. They were ever at the elbows of the President and his cabinet, they threaded their way dexterously through the social maze, they peered through the keyholes of committee rooms and private offices. Some of them wore diplomatic garb. Well might the purists conjure up fears of increasing corruption in high places. Even the President was involved in financial intrigues to acquire Cuba.

III

The neglected appropriation bills, when they were at length taken up late in February, offered the Republicans more opportunities to blast at other sections of the Democratic bastions. An angry session was fought through on Washington's birthday when the legislative, executive, and judicial appropriation bill was up. Chandler of Michigan moved to discontinue appropriations for the mints at Charlotte, North Carolina, and Dahlonega, Georgia. These ancient institutions, now no longer particularly busy, had sizable pay rolls, and at a time when economy was imperative it seemed reasonable to curtail them. Many prominent Senators from the South acquiesced, and the move succeeded, 34–15. Then Trumbull of Illinois moved to repeal the laws establishing these mints, which also carried. Finally as a climax of this Democratic baiting, Hale submitted an amendment to the appropriation bill that would have removed the restriction keeping Kansas out of the Union until its population equaled a unit in the federal congressional ratio.

This threefold assault in one day plus the failure of the Senate leadership to make any capital out of foreign affairs, roused the radical southern Senators to try their hand again on the day following. This time it was Brown of Mississippi, who like Iverson was never accepted into the inner circle. He served notice on the Democratic leadership that he and those whom he represented would demand a platform which promised federal laws to safeguard slave property in the territories. If such laws could not be obtained, it would be an admission that the Constitution was a failure and the Union a despotism. Brown was then "prepared to retire from the concern." When questioned he replied he had not promised to dissolve the Union, he had stated that "we *ought* to retire from the Union."[4]

Douglas hitherto had said little; but he felt that this was a challenge to him. He could not let it be assumed that he had abandoned squatter sovereignty and nonintervention, cowed by Senate discipline. He reiterated his doctrines and yielded not an inch. Furthermore he declared that no candidate could carry a single state in the North on any such platform as Brown proposed. The platform of 1856, reaffirmed, was the party's only hope. Other Democrats followed for six hours, and then the Republicans kept on until midnight. February 23 had been a long and bitter day; the dangerous schism in the Democratic ranks was clearly exposed once more.

The conflicting propositions made in these debates laid bare the dilemma of the Democratic party. If the manifesto of the fire-eaters were accepted by the southern Democrats, if they were prepared to demand that slave property must be protected in the territories by federal law and were to refuse any other platform, Douglas would be ruled out. Was there any one who could carry northern states on their platform? And, if not, how could there be a Democratic victory? The talk of secession, in the event of election of a Republican, might be written off as preelection bluff for the time being; but it was ominous. Wiser counsels, moderate Democrats hoped, would prevail; but now the bit was in the teeth of the southern radical Senators, who were endeavoring to stampede the more responsible into accepting their new definition of southern demands.

Party solidarity was threatened further by a new series of frustrations, as the bill of complaint of the western wing of the party mounted. One by one the measures most needed by western Democrats had been counted out. Gwin's Pacific railroad subsidy bill was amended again and again until nothing survived but a denatured substitute concocted by John Bell, Whig Senator from Tennessee. It merely authorized the Secretary of the Interior to advertise for bids for building a road over the northern, central, and southern routes. Bidders were required to know the unknowable. Every bid must contain an estimate not only of cost, but of how large a subsidy from the government in land or money would be required by the bidder, and the price for which he would carry the mails. Bids were to be reported to Congress for action. This pale excuse for a railroad bill passed, 31–20. Gwin was in a rage and snarled that no such farce had ever before been enacted by the Senate. The House ignored it. The transcontinental railroad was dead for another session.

On river and harbor appropriations, also, the westerners were frustrated. The low state of the Treasury could be used effectively by opponents of these measures, and the general bill carried over from the previous session was not even considered. Senator Chandler of Michigan did succeed in getting through the Senate a measure for dredging the channel over St. Clair flats, but it was not acted on by the House until the last day; and Buchanan pocket-vetoed it.[5]

The westerners had more hope of land donation measures, and several of these were pushed vigorously. Senator Andrew Johnson of Tennessee and Congressman Galusha A. Grow of Pennsylvania, Democrat and Republican, worked at such a project unceasingly. Grow saw a homestead bill pass the House on February 1 by a vote of 120 to 76. Thirty-seven northern Democrats made it possible. In the Senate, test votes showed that it would pass unless some absentees came back. The administration hastily summoned them, and a vote to postpone produced a tie. Vice President Breckinridge then killed the bill by his casting vote. Whether this was arranged to help him in his presidential ambitions is not recorded. Two westerners, Gwin of California and Lane of Oregon, were really responsible for this defeat. Both were tinged with southernism and ambition and usually followed the senatorial high command.[6] Oregon had just been admitted, and Lane had taken his seat in the Senate barely in time to show his gratitude for the southern votes which had brought his bailiwick into the Union.

The promotion project which most nearly reached success was a land donation bill to encourage establishment of agricultural colleges in the several states. This had passed the House in the preceding session, and Senator Stuart of Michigan was anxious to bring it to a vote. His efforts were aided by an "Agricultural Congress" which met in Washington at the Interior Department under the auspices of the Patent Office. The project raised objections from southern Senators in language understandable today. This, they charged, was the work of a farm bloc demanding that government do something for agriculture. The federal Treasury was to be made a "source of alms"; soon there would be a Department of Agriculture, and "in a very short time the whole agricultural interests of the country will be taken out of the hands of the States and subjected to the action of Congress." The real, evil object of the measure was that "the States may be bribed by federal power to conform their domestic policy to federal will." The bill passed when Allen of Rhode Island, Gwin and Broderick of California, and Thomson of New Jersey voted with the Republicans and Whigs. However, President Buchanan vetoed it, unwilling to encourage what he called land jobbery.

Once again western Democrats had to go home empty-handed. Once more they must confess to their constituents their inability to get anything from an administration of their own party. Cavanaugh of Minnesota accused his southern colleagues of turning northern states Republican, as "they to a man almost, vote against the free, independent labor of the North and West." The position of these unhappy western Democrats would make them cling more desperately than ever to Douglas as their only hope for continued power in 1860.

IV

Southern radical demands and western discontent were threatening party security, but even more demoralizing was a flame of revolt which suddenly sprang up among the usually complacent eastern members of the Democratic House majority. The Pennsylvania delegation had come back to Washington humiliated by defeat. Ten of the fourteen were not to appear in the next Congress. The voters of their commonwealth were leaving the Democracy to follow the prophets of protection. If the party were to survive in Pennsylvania some concessions must be made to tariff sentiment there. The Keystone Congressmen felt that the southern members of the party must be forced to take some interest in the general welfare of the organization. The fourteen might in this short session hold the balance of power, and they were determined to use their advantage.

The estimated deficit in federal revenue played into their hands. More money must be raised, and a revision of the tariff might be forced, particularly as the party leadership was at loggerheads. The President recommended tariff revision, with ad valorem duties abandoned in favor of a system of specific duties, to the surprise of Senators Hunter and Bigler who had not expected such a proposal. Secretary Cobb disagreed publicly, recommending in his annual report the retention of the ad valorem system with an increase in the percentages in certain of the schedules. This was only a friendly difference which did not disturb the close relationship between the President and the Secretary of the Treasury, but it was heralded abroad as evidence of party disorganization. It was generally understood that most of the cabinet was with Cobb, and he was quoted far and wide as saying that "Old Buck is opposing the Administration!"

The Pennsylvanians began their fight on the opening day, that December of 1858. Dewart, the defeated member from one of the coal districts, moved to suspend the rules so as to instruct the ways and means committee to report a bill increasing the duties on coal and iron. This motion failed because it lacked the required two-thirds vote; but it commanded a majority made up of Republicans, Americans, and Democrats, including ten of the Pennsylvania group. Various tariff bills were immediately introduced by Republicans and Democrats in both houses. On New Year's the ironmasters of Pennsylvania met in Philadelphia to organize a pressure group and were addressed by ex-Senator Cooper in "secret convention." Soon Congress began to feel their influence.[7]

While occasional references were made to the question in debate in both houses, the committee on ways and means wrestled with the problem behind closed doors. Before it were a bill which its chairman, Phelps of Missouri, had written in consultation with Cobb, a second bill sponsored by

Phillips of Pennsylvania which had the support of all the
Democratic members from that state, and a third by Justin S.
Morrill of Vermont, the ranking Republican on the committee, destined to write many such bills in the future. Phelps's
bill was an increase in the tariff of 1857, Phillips's was a
return to something similar to the rates of 1846, including
a large list of specific duties, notably on iron. Morrill's proposal was a regular protectionist document, prophetic of many
to come. By the end of January it was apparent that the
committee was hopelessly divided; yet revenue was still short,
and the end of the session was approaching. The Pennsylvania tariff men were tired of inaction and, believing they
held the balance of power, certain of them threatened to
oppose all appropriation bills until some tariff legislation was
forthcoming. As Phelps could not get his committee to agree
on anything, the question was turned over to party caucuses.

The Senate Democrats met first, January 29. Bigler of
Pennsylvania introduced a resolution to raise the tariff, but his
colleagues would have none of it. They refused to bind the
party and voted that it was inexpedient to alter the tariff at
this time. The anti-tariff Democrats in the House sought to
endorse this move and held a caucus on February 1; but
hardly any from free-labor states attended. Since this body
could not agree on any alternative, it appointed a committee
to study economy and voted to hold a caucus of all the
House Democrats. The Pennsylvanians refused to attend this
next meeting but gathered by themselves and restated their
position.

The general meeting February 5 heard an optimistic report
from their economy committee. These political students of
finance had concluded that Cobb's estimates of revenue were
too low, and with certain economies in printing, in public construction, and in army and navy appropriations the available
revenue would do. Crawford of the ways and means committee offered a plan to cut $10,000,000 from the appropria-
tions and to reissue $12,000,000 of the Treasury notes. Dis-
cussion grew so warm that the caucus had to adjourn; when
it reconvened four nights later, it agreed to a new resolution
presented by Phelps, which also recommended a Treasury
note issue and reduced appropriations. Its decision only aggravated the tariff Democrats and seemed to endanger the
supply bills.[8]

The struggle continued on the floor of each house. Bigler

started debate in the Senate by introducing his defeated caucus resolution for raising the tariff. In the House Phelps hoped for some light from Cobb and put through a resolution requesting recommendations from the Secretary. When Cobb merely repeated his annual report, Phelps swore; but that did not supply funds. Finally in desperation Chairman Phelps brought in a bill February 14, merely authorizing the reissue of Treasury notes, and moved suspension of the rules so that it might be considered immediately. The tariff men promptly ganged up on him and defeated his motion. Next they attempted to get action on a resolution forcing Phelps's committee to report on the tariff; but Speaker Orr ruled their spokesman off the floor.

Nothing daunted, the tariff men had just begun to fight. A few moments later the Indian appropriation bill was up and Phillips, in committee of the whole, attacked Cobb's estimates. Hunter's kinsman, Garnett of Virginia, rushed to his defense with the same arguments Hunter had used in the Senate. At the close of the debate Phillips tried to get permission to introduce his tariff bill. Objections and the absence of a quorum blocked him.

The tariff Democrats next moved with the Republicans. Morrill, together with Howard of Michigan and H. Winter Davis of Maryland, had prepared a protective measure. Phillips and his Pennsylvania colleagues now offered to support that bill. Here again their tactics failed because the coalition could not muster a two-thirds vote. When Montgomery tried to get an amendment providing specific duties for iron tacked on to the Post Office bill, he was ruled off the floor. Positively the friends of the tariff had gotten nowhere, but negatively their influence was becoming more formidable.

The days were passing rapidly, the long-delayed appropriation bills found going heavy. Every day that passed without action made the tariff group stronger, as the Pennsylvania Democrats cast their embarrassing votes. Finally on February 26 the ways and means committee yielded, to the extent of agreeing to report out all the tariff bills before it. When Phelps brought them in, the foes of the tariff, though in a minority, still could prevent the two-thirds vote necessary to receive the bills. By this time it had been demonstrated that no tariff measure could reach the floor of the House. The administration forces could prevent that. But they could not prevent the reprisals that were about to be made by the vengeful Pennsylvanians.

V

The long delay caused by these political and regional interests made the fate of the appropriation bills uncertain, as
the shortness of time played into the hands of the tariff advocates. The Senate did not begin on the important appropriation bills sent over from the House until February 16 and
passed its first major one only on the 21st. At the close of
this day the House had completed but three. Only nine days
were left, and the House had still to work up the Post Office,
the Navy, the sundry civil, and mail-steamer bills.

On Thursday, February 24, with only seven more legislative
days remaining, the appropriations crisis came to a head; a
revolt rejected the general Post Office appropriation bill in
the House, 119–86. This hostile majority contained nine
Pennsylvania Democrats and certain radical southerners who
ostensibly wanted the Post Office Department to pay for itself.
The same day in the Senate, the effort to reform the postal
service was renewed. Yulee of Florida, chairman of the
Senate post-office committee, submitted with the usual House
bill for postal routes an amendment to abolish franking and
increase the postage from three cents to five, reforms which
he believed would wipe out the postal deficit. Such a measure
was a favorite of the Senate, which had tried to get it through
in the preceding session, and now sent it again to the House.
The Representatives paid no attention to it whatever, but did
reconsider their rejection of the general Post Office appropriation bill; and on Saturday February 26, two of the Pennsylvania Democrats and an Alabama colleague changed their
votes and allowed this bill to pass the House, 108–104.

On Monday, with only four days to go, the Senators took
up Post Office matters once more, when the general postal
appropriation bill came before them from the House. After
prolonged debate Yulee succeeded in getting the reform
clauses, abolishing franking and raising the postage, added to
it by one vote. The majority had been made up of the solid
southern phalanx, plus their satellites Bright and Fitch, Gwin,
Lane and Jones of Iowa, whom Crittenden joined. Their enthusiasm was caused by a real desire to raise revenue and
economize, coupled with a wish to cut off a valued aid to
Republican propaganda. Letter writing and document franking were much more useful in the free states than they were
in the South. Northern business, too, would be penalized by
the increased postage rates more than any southern interest.
After hours of argument over California mail routes the ap-

propriation-plus-reform bill was passed late on March 1, but did not get back to the House until the 2nd, after the Representatives had been in session some hours.

The Republicans were now sure of their power to block appropriations, because the tariff Democrats and occasional southern radicals could be counted on to join in most maneuvers against the House managers. It was alleged that the Republican leaders wanted to kill one or two vital supply bills to force Buchanan to call an extra session. Their victories in the election of 1858 meant that they could organize the new House, if it were called into extra session before all the southern states had held elections. Then the Republicans could write the supply and tariff bills of the next Congress. Furthermore the Republicans were eager to serve notice on the Senate control that they were now a force to reckon with. Elated with their new sense of power, Grow, Sherman, Covode, and several of their associates enacted a last-minute drama.

When the Post Office appropriation-plus-reform bill returned to the House on the night of the 2nd, Grow objected to removing it from the Speaker's table. His plan was to introduce a resolution sending it back to the Senators as unconstitutional legislation, because by increasing the postage rates they had originated a revenue measure, thus usurping a prerogative of the House. Phelps refused to admit Grow's resolution, and adjournment was had without action. Grow then went to Phelps and warned him that, if he did not permit a vote on his resolution, his following would kill the vital appropriation bills still uncompleted. Phelps was forced to consent. On the morning of the 3rd, the last day, the plan was carried out. The House returned the Post Office bill to the Senate with a rebuke; Grow carried this easily, 106–80 and 117–76. The House likewise passed a new post routes bill, shorn of the Senate reforms, and rejected the mail-steamer appropriations bill. Thus they had put the Senate in its place.

Meanwhile, House behavior had been watched by the Senate with much misgiving. The Senate leaders were pretty sure now that the House was out of the hands of its leaders; important appropriations were in danger unless the Senate could force measures through as riders, on bills which might be assured passage for other reasons. Jefferson Davis already had used this device the preceding Saturday; when the House failed to act on the fortifications bill, he had attached appropriations for them to the army bill.

The sundry civil bill was being used similarly by R. M. T. Hunter, after the House tariff bloc refused to heed the pleas of Buchanan and Cobb, for an extension of the power to issue Treasury notes needed to obtain loans. Hunter and the finance committee tacked such a provision on the sundry civil bill, although to accomplish this they had to suffer the Republicans to debate protection and use up precious time in manufacturing party propaganda. Yulee now tacked to the same bill the mail-steamer appropriations and the abolition of franking, which the House had trampled. Thus loaded, the sundry civil bill got back to the House on the 3rd, the last day of the session.

When the Representatives received from the Senate the sundry civil bill with its load of Treasury loan provisions, mail-steamer appropriations, and postal reforms, Sherman of Ohio stepped into Grow's role. He refused to permit its receipt on the ground that this was a revenue bill concocted in the Senate. Phelps tried to overcome this by a message from Buchanan warning the Congress that without the loan extension the Treasury could not operate, and by bringing out his Treasury note bill as an alternative. His moves accomplished nothing, and the new coalition reasserted its power, refusing by a vote of 107–77 to consider the sundry civil bill.

The Senators in the meantime had received the House rebuke on the postal increases while they were still at work on the civil bill. Officially they paid no attention to it, other than to adopt Yulee's amendment, while the bill was under consideration. However, the veterans had been busy behind the scenes, and after the appropriation bill was finished, they brought out their handiwork. Senator Crittenden, as usual the conciliator, presented a resolution declaring both houses "equally competent, each to judge of the propriety and constitutionality of its own action," and sending the Post Office bill back. In the meantime Yulee, fearing that the civil bill might fail to pass, took steps to salvage some of the mail-steamship service. A small Indian appropriation bill was brought up, and an amendment inserted providing enough money to pay for the isthmus mail until the contracts expired in September.

When the Senate's resolution returning the Post Office bill arrived in the House, evening had fallen. In spite of the fact that but few hours remained, the House was adamant. Let the Post Office bill fail; the House would not permit the overweening Senate to usurp its functions. Phelps in desperation brought in a new Post Office bill, really the old one without the Senate amendments; this the House passed without debate. It was now midnight, and the civil bill with its loan provisions lay still inert on the Speaker's table; in this coffin lay the Treasury's hope for fiscal solvency.

The administration had not been idle during these tense hours. Since first signs of revolt during the early days of the tariff maneuvers, both Cobb and Postmaster General Brown had feared for their financial lives. Brown had worked unusually hard. He had used the hospitality of his great house lavishly. He had given "stag parties," trying to get the disaffected tariff men back into the fold. When the Post Office bill first got into difficulties he was suffering from a heavy cold, but he kept at it until pneumonia felled him. Marron, the Third Assistant Postmaster General, was likewise dangerously ill, and the Post Office lobby was thus weakened. While Brown was trying to direct the fight from his bed, Cobb was indefatigable on the floor of the House. He spent this fateful night trying to prevail upon some of the revolters to save the national finances by taking up the civil bill.

At three A.M. the Treasury gods were appeased, and the Representatives heeded Cobb's pleas. The members wasted time in strategic roll calls designed to block action, but finally after four o'clock settled down to consider the Senate amendments to the sundry civil bill. They were quite ruthless with most of them; they refused to concur in the mailsteamer provision or the Post Office reform. They made the most fuss over the loan feature, at first discarding it by one vote. Then a series of roll calls and divisions, with Cobb strenuously at work, finally reversed the result. Florence, Gillis, and Ahl of Pennsylvania, among the revolting tariff Democrats, changed their votes, and seven other opponents refrained from voting; thus the bill passed. Dawn had broken, and the day was well along when the civil bill was sent back to the Senate.

The upper chamber in the meantime had been wrestling with the Post Office problem. When shortly after midnight the new bill had come from the House, Stuart of Michigan, Douglas Democrat, led a fight to save it. The Michigan Senator wanted a committee of conference appointed to adjust the matter. The punctilious declared there was no basis for it. The Senate had sent a bill back to the House, the House had refused to act, there was no basis for a conference. The new bill the Senate refused to consider, and so there was nothing to confer on in that quarter. Conciliation finally triumphed in the small hours of the morning, when the Senate asked a conference to consult with the House despite the fact that the House had "departed from the proper parliamentary usages and method of transacting business."

About seven A.M. on March 4 the House consented to conference; and it adjourned for breakfast shortly after, to resume at nine. At eleven o'clock the conferees came back with a recommendation that the original House bill be accepted, neither House waiving "any constitutional right which they may respectively consider to belong to them." This the House accepted, and the word was hurried to the Senate; there were only forty-five minutes of the session left.

The Senate had been dawdling through the night waiting for the House to act on the civil bill and the Post Office conference proposal. It recessed at four-thirty until five o'clock, at five subject to call, at six until six-thirty, and then at six-thirty until nine. Shortly after they resumed at nine o'clock the civil bill was checked and back. Hunter was so relieved that the loan provision had been accepted and so apprehensive that, if the Senate refused to concur in the House treatment of the many amendments, the House would refuse conference and the bill be lost, that he urged the Senate to accept the bad medicine for the sake of the loan. After much debate and many roll calls for the record, the Senate concurred, and the civil bill was passed just in time for final engrossment. The Treasury was saved.[9]

More dallying and routine filled up the Senate's morning until eleven-twenty, when the news of the House acceptance of the Post Office conference report arrived. The Senate then learned that its conferees had accepted the House bill without the Senate amendments in return of a proviso that neither house waived any rights. The wrath of certain Senators overflowed. Toombs of Georgia denounced this surrender and was followed by the milder-mannered Bayard. They talked the bill to death, and in so doing spoke words which should have roused apprehension. They declared that the Senate was the stronghold of the South; if the House representing the population of the nation and thus favoring the faster-growing sections ever got the power to dictate to the upper body, it would destroy the ability of the South to protect itself. As Bayard put it "the form of this Government [is] a mixed republic, not a pure democracy; . . . our fathers never would have constituted a mere democracy to be governed by the will of the great mass of the people, because they would have known that it was an unpracticable government." To the accompaniment of this dirge the bill died, leaving the Post Office no legacy of funds or reform. The Postmaster General in his delirium was calling, "The Bill, the Bill!"[10]

By these unusual means and the cost of party demoralization, economy had been achieved and the Treasury kept solvent. Appropriations had been literally cut in half. The preceding session had appropriated $81,800,000, this session $41,367,000. Nearly half of this saving, $18,000,000 for the Post Office was involuntary and fictitious, for of course most of it would have to be spent to keep up the mail service. Nevertheless real economies had been effected. Army and navy appropriations had been reduced $14,000,000, and sundry civil costs $2,500,000. Even printing had been reduced to only $500,000, and reforms inaugurated which were to save more.

The Democratic party had been shattered. The southern radicals were out for Douglas's scalp and were using dangerous ideas to rally the South. Men like Slidell, Hunter, Mason, Benjamin, with cool heads and love of power, were losing control. Northern Democrats were growing desperate. The tariff fight of the Pennsylvania men had accomplished nothing except to defeat the Post Office bill and destroy party control of the House. Douglas had probably had his eyes opened by the treatment accorded him. Outwardly he had not resented it, but a new determination began to appear in his bearing. He was usually an easy compromiser, but these southern radical attacks were driving some iron into his soul. Association with Broderick had helped.

The radical southerners, with their eyes on the coming congressional elections and the possible revival of the Whigs, had carried things as far as they could with a high hand and had made practically no concessions. They were particularly angered at the ruthlessness of the new Republican leadership.[11] Southern refusal to concede was a sign which should have been more frightening than it was. All this spelled an alarming obsession with local party control and an indifference to the fortunes of the Democratic party, nationally speaking. If such tendencies could not be arrested the outlook for success in 1860 was dark indeed.

Chapter 13

. State Machines to the Rescue

THE DEMOCRATIC members of the Thirty-fifth Congress returned home with their spirits draped in mourning. Not only was the Post Office appropriation bill dead, but the dark angel had visited the Department itself twice in a week. In the last hours of the session John Marron, Third Assistant Postmaster General, had died almost coincidently with the appropriation bill. Four days later, his chief gave up the struggle. Word of the defeat of the bill had reached Brown's bedside, aggravating his pneumonia. President Buchanan must seek a new Postmaster General.

The Post Office Department was such a vital part of the Democratic machine that demoralization, through death and the failure of appropriations so near a national campaign, was nothing short of a catastrophe. Unless remedies could be found speedily, party morale would be severely tried. The postmasters were the key men in countless communities, and if they were weakened, by lack of direction or embarrassment for funds, their effectiveness would be curtailed just when their efforts were most needed. A new Postmaster General must be found immediately.

The Democratic party needed every available agency working at top efficiency. The elections of 1858 had shown the party defeated in the free states. If 1859 brought similar disasters through the South, the party would have little prospect for 1860. The congressional and state elections in that section were at hand in most of the important states, and 1859 was to decide. The issue was doubtful with the new opposition rising out of the ashes of Whiggery and Know-Nothingism. In the northern states the active canvass for delegates to the national convention of 1860 was intensifying. Here Douglas, victorious in Illinois and martyred by southern Senators, was making new moves for delegates. The high command in Washington had need of every resource to crush the opposition in the South and to prevent the choice of Douglas delegations in the free states.

Buchanan and his cabinet, particularly its southern members, Cobb and Thompson, watched the uncertainties of 1859 with great concern. Much depended upon executive leadership if the party were to be re-united. The problem confronting the President and the department heads was manifold. In the midst of difficult administrative problems they must direct the party along safer lines than those demanded by southern radicals or by Douglas's manifestoes; neither of these could keep the party intact. They must refute charges, hurled at them especially in the South, of extravagance and corruption, favoritism to contractors, and inefficiency. Finally they must strive to create a new formula, a new party shibboleth, to enable the various factions to work together through 1860. They labored under difficulties, for Congress had thrown more than one monkey wrench into the party wheels, especially those of the Post Office.

II

The first task was to select a suitable Postmaster General. The expansive Brown had piled up a deficit larger than usual. Someone must be found who could say "No" to persistent supplicants. Secretary Thompson and Senator Yulee had such a man in the person of Joseph Holt, at present Commissioner of Patents under Thompson. He had practiced law successfully in Kentucky and Mississippi. His marriage into the prominent political family of "Duke" Wickliffe, sometime governor of Kentucky and Postmaster General, had made Holt brother-in-law to Governor Robert Wickliffe of Louisiana, as well as to Yulee. He had made an efficient Commissioner of Patents, besides helping Buchanan to solve some ticklish questions in setting up a retirement system for naval officers. Surely this was the hardheaded, stern administrator needed as Postmaster General. Holt was appointed on the day of Brown's funeral.[1]

This choice did not solve the problem of vanishing appropriations. Where would money come from? Should a special session of the new Congress be called to provide the funds? This was politically dangerous. The important southern states and the Pacific states had not held their elections and thus would be unrepresented in the House. Therefore the Republicans could organize the new body and appoint the committees. It was charged that this was the reason they had engineered the defeat of the appropriation. Buchanan would not take such a chance. He decided to administer the department by economy and on credit, trusting to Congress to ratify his acts. To a man who dreaded responsibility not required by law, this was a fearful step; but, in the interest of the Democratic party, Buchanan was willing to take it.[2]

Expedients were adopted. The individual postmasters would not have to make their first quarterly returns until after Congress met in December; they might use the money they took in and replace it when the deficiency bill was passed. Contractors would be given special certificates showing that the government owed them money, which the banks would discount for cash.[3] With these expedients the department would manage. Holt also thought that this would be a good opportunity to discontinue unprofitable services. Despite this shrewd program there was no doubt that the political usefulness of the Post Office had been diminished at a time of danger.

Holt set to work vigorously. Not only did he begin investigations to promote economy and to stamp out fraud but, more significantly, he tried to follow these investigations to their logical conclusions. He found that the Philadelphia post office harbored thieves, and so he dismissed the postmaster, personal appointee of Buchanan's though he was. Also he tackled the unsavory Chicago situation, where Ike Cook was loosely managing an office in which even registered mail was pilfered. This corruption had been condoned by the administration because of its hatred of Douglas, and Holt found his efforts here constantly frustrated. Nevertheless he persisted. Unfortunately, reforms such as these were not appreciated by the party workers, and their results only soured many of the "ward boys" and gave them grievances which Buchanan's foes found useful.[4]

III

Buchanan had scarcely settled the Post Office difficulties when he must perforce start tuning the party organ. Wendell was again proving an embarrassment. During the last session a House committee had uncovered a mass of printing extravagance and corruption. The superintendent of public printing, A. G. Seaman, appointed by Pierce because of his connection with Anson Herrick, proprietor of the *New York Atlas,* had been reaping a harvest before his term expired in December, 1857. Under the law he was required to keep watch of the political printers and protect the government. Seaman had been otherwise interested. He had made an alliance with Wendell. They had "shaken" down the contractors who sold paper to the government, or did binding or supplied engraving and lithographing; and it is hard to see how their profits could have been less than a million dollars. Likewise they operated through a series of agents to whom would-be contractors must pay gratuities. They were also linked to certain local Washington capitalists like the auctioneer, J. C. McGuire. The ramifications were bewildering, and as a result of the testimony Seaman was indicted and convicted.[5]

This publicity was bad for Wendell and had aroused the Thirty-fifth Congress to end two gross abuses. Heretofore, when the House and Senate produced identical documents for their members, using one typesetting for the two jobs, they had paid as if the documents had been set up twice. This double profit to Wendell was now stopped. Furthermore, Congress forbade its ostensible printers to sell out their contracts to practical jobbers. Never again could a Cornelius Wendell collect $2,000,000 in six years.[6]

Buchanan, too, shut down on Wendell somewhat. He had replaced Seaman with his old friend, General George W. Bowman, journeyman printer in Jackson's day for Duff Green of the Washington *Telegraph* and for the last twenty-five years proprietor of a paper in Bedford, Pennsylvania. The General tightened up immediately. He awarded contracts to low bidders, rather than to those who paid "commissions." He watched the official printers and Wendell. That prize money-maker found his affluence on the wane. The profits from the post-office blanks were taken away from him, and the new law showed him that unless he could be elected printer to Congress his day was done. Even then the profits would be much smaller.

As his gains shrank, Wendell repented his generosity to Democratic presses and party funds. He had served notice upon Buchanan during the last session that he was not going to carry the *Union* any longer. The administration did not regret this, for Wendell was a liability; but it must find another angel. Those most immediately available were too friendly to Douglas, or too much influenced by metropolitan, speculating, racketeering capital. Buchanan and his cabinet wanted an experienced editor of a country paper, someone who understood the habits and opinions of people who did "not live so fast as in the city."

After a futile effort to persuade John Appleton to accept the dubious task, Buchanan determined to put the heat on Bowman to buy the *Union*. He balked, reluctant to give up his salaried position as superintendent of the printing—at which he had proved a success—to take over a paper losing $20,000 a year. Elaborate and tortuous negotiations began.

Buchanan tried to hold himself aloof. It was finally left to
Black to arrange the terms of a contract remarkably like
earlier Wendell instruments. They agreed that Bowman would
take the *Union* and Wendell continue to do the executive
printing and binding, regaining the post-office blanks. Bowman presumably would be elected printer to the Senate, come
December, and would let Wendell do the Senate work in his
plant, and would not compete with him for the executive
printing. Wendell was to give $10,000 a year to Bowman
to run the *Union,* and smaller sums to the Philadelphia editors
of the *Pennsylvanian* and the *Argus.* Rice had been relieved
of the *Pennsylvanian,* and Dr. Morwitz was in his place.
Details of this complicated arrangement were not revealed
until an evil day in the future; on March 29, 1859, it was
merely announced that Bowman had "bought" the *Union.*
He secured William M. Browne, an Englishman by birth,
sometime resident of Ireland and a writer for the *New York
Journal of Commerce,* to serve as his "writing man." On
April 13 the paper appeared with a fresh name, *The Constitution,* and began its career anew. Bowman's recent work
as superintendent of printing would meanwhile be emulated
worthily by John Heart of the *Charleston Mercury,* likewise
chosen by Buchanan as a man divorced from metropolitanism
and speculation.[7]

No sooner had Buchanan completed the transfer of the
organ to Bowman than he undertook to direct its retuning.
In the midst of the intellectual confusion of the day, the
President sought to confound Hammond, Douglas, and
Seward by producing a magic formula which should bring
order out of chaos and, more important, build a platform
for 1860 upon which all Democrats could stand. The position
of the advocates of federal protection of slavery in the
territories and of popular sovereignty seemed now quite
irreconcilable. What compromise formula could bring them
under one banner? Buchanan put all his statesmanship to
work at solving this problem, for he knew the future of the
party and the nation depended upon it. Determined to use
the columns of the chief party organ for the purpose, the
President called in "Constitution Browne," as the new editor
was nicknamed. He, with a good deal of help from Cobb,
Black, and Thompson, began an editorial campaign to
redirect Democratic thought and emotion.

Economy and reform were emphasized to offset charges of

extravagance and corruption. Popular rights were to be protected against special privilege; favoritism to contractors and speculators was denounced. The crux of the program was naturally the slavery discussion. This issue, the *Constitution* in all seriousness maintained, was dead and must not be revived. The Cincinnati platform and the Dred Scott decision had settled it by denying the extreme claims. The Republican contention that Congress could meddle with slavery was wrong; the Dred Scott decision declared this form of property could be held in the common territories by virtue of the Fifth Amendment. Congressional legislation to protect it there was unnecessary; and it was dangerous to seek, because of the controversy it would raise.

The remedy was not a new law but recourse to the federal courts. If any man found his property rights in danger in the territories, all he need do was to apply to the federal courts for protection. These courts, appointed by the Democratic authorities in Washington, would be backed up if necessary by federal troops in enforcing decrees and writs. Therefore why agitate, why raise issues when judicial protection was available? Thus to the South the administration offered the protection of the federal courts. The free states were reminded that the people of the territories could prohibit slavery in most of them when the time for admission arrived. This doctrine Buchanan sought to spread among the officeholders by threats of removal.[8]

In this fashion, by act and thought, the high command had sought to discharge its political, as well as its administrative stewardship. Was its effort sufficiently astute to arrest the trend of popular discontent and fear? The elections of 1859 would give some answers.

The reorganized Post Office and the retuned organ (with some ineffective efforts at capitalizing foreign relations) were all that the administration could contribute to redeploying the party battalions in preparation for the encounters of 1869 and the great battle of 1860. It was all too little. The real work must be done by the state organizations.

IV

The burden of campaigning which fell upon the state workers, under the federalized system of party organization, was heavier than ever in 1859. Could the state leadership, south of the Mason and Dixon line, bring in the necessary victories? Could it carry the load of the administration's un-popularity and stem the flood of opposition to the Democracy fast rising in the South?

This opposition was taking shape in formidable fashion. The Whigs, who had never completely passed from the picture, now saw an opportunity for revival as a conservative party. Many could not bring themselves to fellowship with their old Jacksonian enemies, the Democrats; nor would they tolerate the idea of joining the Black Republicans. Such men as John Bell of Tennessee, John J. Crittenden of Kentucky, Edward Everett of Massachusetts, ex-President Fillmore and Washington Hunt of New York still clung to the idea of a conservative party opposed alike to northern and southern radicals. The capture of the Democracy in 1856 by the friends of Buchanan, in the name of conservatism, had robbed these leaders of their appeal for a time, and Fillmore had made a very poor showing on the Whig-American ticket of that year.

Since then, however, the conservative element of the Democratic party had proved unable to control policy; the southern radicals had forced Buchanan to fight the Douglas wing. Could not this schism be capitalized? Now seemed the opportune time for conservative Union men to attempt to revive the Whig party. It formerly had been chiefly a miscellaneous assortment of enemies of the Democracy. Could it now, at last, espouse a principle with general appeal? Some of the leaders felt that they might even attract factions of the new Republican party, which in spite of its youth was none too congruous or united. They would use the southern elections of 1859 for trial mobilizations, with the hope that they could develop sufficient strength to make possible a national, conservative, Union-saving ticket in 1860.

There were to be elections in Louisiana, Georgia, North Carolina, Tennessee, Kentucky—five states the Whigs had carried in their heyday—and in Virginia, Alabama, and Mississippi. The Americans had almost won Virginia in 1855. What had once been done, might be done again. During the short session of Congress the effort at a Whig revival, begun in the spring of 1858, had been pressed forward by the same persistent though insignificant Washington coterie. Their plan seemed to be to build up Senator Crittenden. He had been feted in New York City by prominent Whigs before Congress met, and when the Presidency was mentioned to him he had not seemed too surprised or resentful.

Before Congress convened, Nathan Sargent, a Washington

newspaperman, began corresponding with Whig leaders about a conference arranged for December 15 in Washington. Senators Crittenden and Bell, Alexander H. H. Stuart and C. M. Conrad, who were former cabinet members, and a few others attended. They were asked by some one-time Whigs, now Republicans, like Senator Simmons of Rhode Island, to join forces with the new party on the tariff issue. This the old Whigs refused, knowing that it would kill their hopes in the South. There they would organize vigorous state campaigns in 1859, to test whether a Union party in 1860 might well profit by Democratic schism. They adjourned without giving out any plans or statements.[9]

The Whig-opposition groups started out vigorously in the upper South. In Virginia, Kentucky, and Tennessee, they held state conventions early in the year and began active campaigning. Maryland Americans sought to unite all opposed to the Democrats. They invited a union state convention and suggested a national convention of all who loved the Constitution and the Union to make a ticket for 1860. In the lower South the opposition showed less vigor. In Georgia there seemed to be some chance that they might be effective; but not so in Louisiana, Mississippi, or Alabama.[10]

The Democrats found themselves the butt of bewildering tactics, since some of their opponents emphasized the Union and others southernism. On the one hand they were pilloried for betraying the national Union and on the other for destroying southern states' rights. In several campaigns the opposition ignored the fact that Buchanan was fighting Douglas and hammered on the Little Giant and his Freeport heresy as traitorous to the South. When Buchanan's administration was noticed it was attacked as weak and corrupt.

The Democrats were further weakened in the South by internal feuds. The Democracy in Virginia, Georgia, Louisiana, Alabama, Mississippi, Kentucky, Tennessee, and Texas was rent by bitter factional struggles. Some of these fights grew from social unrest. The poorer whites, those who owned few or no slaves, found their advocates in Senators Andrew Johnson of Tennessee and Albert G. Brown of Mississippi and Governors Joseph E. Brown of Georgia and Henry A. Wise of Virginia. Johnson and the Browns had themselves risen from humble circumstances to public place by warring against the aristocracy. Johnson had marshaled the yeomanry and mountain people of the eastern end of Tennessee against the more prosperous planters and town residents to the west. In

Georgia "Joe" Brown was disputing for control with the Cobb organization and the more radical southern group. In Mississippi there was less open hostility, but tension worked between the representative of the plain people, Albert G. Brown, and the wealthy Davis and Thompson, particularly as they all had presidential ambitions.[11]

Elsewhere feuds were more personal. In Virginia Wise was still waging war against Hunter's ambitions. He wished to secure his seat, or Mason's, in the Senate, and beyond that he wished to be President. He was doing what he could to spoil Hunter's chances for the nomination in 1860. In Louisiana ex-Senator Soulé was trying to break Slidell's control of the party by appealing to the small farmers and the Creoles. He was calculating upon an alliance with Douglas. In Alabama the two Senators, Clay and Fitzpatrick, represented different sections and intensities of southern loyalty. They were united in opposing Yancey's violent southernism. John Forsyth had just returned from Mexico, furious with Buchanan for interference and lack of support before his recall as minister from that Republic. He was resuming control of his paper, the *Mobile Register,* and was about to espouse the cause of Douglas. In Texas the organization was rent by the efforts of Sam Houston to control the party and beat down the radical southern-rights men who thirsted for his retirement.[12]

In general the reputation of the administration was the focal point in these several struggles for party dominance. One faction, generally that to which the principal federal officeholders belonged, would seek endorsement of the President's policy, while their foes would feature the weakness and disloyalty of the Executive. In the Virginia Democratic convention, the only substantial victory the Wise forces won was an endorsement of Buchanan. In Kentucky the Breckinridge forces did likewise, and Postmaster General Brown's organization was successful with the same program in Tennessee. In the lower South it was more difficult. After a hectic fight Slidell forced an endorsement of the President's policies through the Louisiana convention by three votes. Cobb's henchmen in Georgia could secure only the weakest kind of resolution. In Mississippi, no effort was made to get one. In the North Carolina congressional district conventions, Buchanan was endorsed where the opposition was weak; where it was strong, all mention of the President was prudently omitted.

The southern Democracy was embarrassed by some inept pronouncements of Cass which offended immigrants and gave the American party an opening. When the Austro-Franco-Italian war broke out in 1859 some men who had come to America were wanted for military service by their countries of origin, and Cass seemed disinclined to acknowledge the duty of the United States to protect them. His press releases caused the opposition to ridicule the impotence of Buchanan's administration.

Yet more embarrassing was the conscientious effort Buchanan was making under British goading to stamp out the slave trade. Attempts to punish the owners and operators of two notorious slavers, the *Echo* and the *Wanderer*, had shown that southern juries would not convict these traders even in federal courts, and that the administration was only losing face by attempting the impossible.

Some audacious southerners tried to make political capital out of the slave trade. They saw the poor whites becoming more and more conscious of the difficulty of competing with slave labor. Would they not be reconciled if the price of slaves were brought down by importations so that many more farmers might afford them? No less a man than Alexander H. Stephens, though he carefully refrained from advocating the reopening of the trade, pointed out in a summer speech that probably no further slave states could be created without the importation of more slaves. There were not enough to break new planting acres. Therefore it became with some politicians a mark of southern loyalty to advocate such a policy. The strength of the importation move was indicated when the Southern Commercial Convention, meeting in Vicksburg in May, 1859, recommended the repeal of state and federal laws prohibiting the traffic.

The planting interest itself, and the humanitarians, were divided on this issue. Any increase in numbers would lower the price and thus depreciate the value of slave property generally. Also, new acres meant a larger crop and the danger of a lower price for cotton. This was not desirable. The years 1858 and 1859 were good ones for the wealthy, and they did not want values deflated. Besides, importations were dangerous; many would be savage, hard to handle, and likely to spread discontent among those longer in bondage. Even some of the poor whites feared that new supplies of slave labor might make it even more difficult for them to compete. Humanitarians argued both ways. Those who were in favor descanted on the privilege of the Christian religion which would now be bestowed on the heathen Africans. Those opposed argued against the horrors of the traffic and the terror of the middle passage from the Gold Coast to America. The Democracy remained badly split on the question, and despite the various efforts made no real political capital out of it.[13]

An issue which gained the southern Democracy much more advantage was the irresistible conclusion which the leaders were reaching, that they must stake their future on demonstrations of loyalty to the South; nationalism, even of Buchanan's denatured brand, for the time being must be soft-pedaled. They were preparing the formula for their own rescue. They were going to unite on a demand for federal protection of slave property in the territories. This meant a reversal for many, because the time-honored stand formulated by Calhoun had been non-intervention in the territories; but the prominent were willing to risk it. If the Democratic national convention would not recognize this right of protection, then the southern Democratic parties would leave the organization; that was the threat of at least a few.

Even darker of portent were signs of more drastic counsel. A South Carolina Congressman, W. W. Boyce, and a Mississippi county convention, declared that if the Republicans won the South should secede. Congressman Curry of Alabama wrote to Secretary Thompson: "I have been amazed to find the growth of the disunion sentiment among our people. Many absolutely desire such an event, many would not resist it, while nearly all seem to regard it as but a question of time. Douglas's disaffection has demoralized us and we cannot persuade the South to confide in any Northern Democrat." The Mobile *Mercury* was advocating a Gulf confederacy.[14] Such doctrines were pressed to stir up enthusiasm for one or another of the candidates, cliques, or factions. There were still few secessionist *per se,* but events seemed to be bent on enlarging their ranks. This series of state and congressional campaigns was, to say the least, not quieting.

Late in May the returns from Virginia were scanned even more eagerly than they had been four years previously. The result was so close that it was in doubt for several days. Finally the moderate Democrat, Letcher, was found to have won by only 5,000 over the opposition, fire-eating Goggin, as compared with Wise's plurality of double that figure in 1855. However, statisticians showed that the Democratic margin had fallen only from 53 to 52 per cent of the vote, as the number voting had declined considerably. It was disconcerting, nevertheless, for the state Democracy to realize that the victory had been won only because the western Virginians, none too sympathetic with southernism, had turned out loyally to support a candidate from their section.[15]

The second round of the battle was not concluded until August, when Alabama, Kentucky, Tennessee, North Carolina, and Texas went to the polls. Kentucky and Tennessee came out almost alike, in the battle between radicalism and conservatism. The opposition gained four Congressmen in Tennessee and three in Kentucky, although in both it failed to capture the state governments; in North Carolina the opposition gained two Congressmen, but there was no state-wide contest to give further indications. In Alabama, the opposition failed to organize, but a fire-eating Democrat, William F. Samford, ran against Governor Moore, charging that he was weak and careless of southern interests in failing to call a state convention when Congress refused to admit Kansas under the Lecompton constitution. Samford advocated reopening the slave trade and vigorous defense of southern rights, but Moore had no difficulty in securing reelection. On the other hand in Texas, Sam Houston beat the regularly nominated candidate, Governor H. R. Runnels, who had defeated him in 1857 and had been renominated this year. Houston ran independently as a conservative, protesting against Runnels's fire-eating and his advocacy of the slave trade. As far as the August elections could be interpreted, they indicated that conservatism had the advantage.[16]

The October and November results were less striking. In Georgia, Mississippi, and Louisiana, opposition tickets were formed somewhat belatedly but failed to challenge the Democracy seriously. Most significant was the course of the Mississippi Democratic candidates. They abandoned the mild and indefinite plank in their platform, which probably had been drawn up and inserted under the moderate influence of Jefferson Davis, and turned to fire eating. The election of a Republican President, they were agreed, should be the signal for secession.

These elections of 1859 reset the stage in the South. The opposition was reawakened and was studying new points of attack. Following an invitation which the Maryland Know-Nothings had issued for a national convention to meet in Baltimore the next spring to nominate candidates for President and Vice President, a self-constituted opposition committee in midsummer issued a "secret circular" for the same purpose. They were going to capitalize their gains in preparation for the 1860 campaign.[17] The southern situation was dangerously paradoxical. There was a bumper cotton crop, and a planter group reasonably contented and conservative. On the other hand, there were stirrings among the yeomanry, the poor whites, and the relatively few city wage earners; these were not so sure of the benevolence of slavery, and were increasingly aware of their disadvantage in competing with it. Some few of them may have been reading a book, reputedly by one of them, Helper's *Impending Crisis*. If agitators could rouse them, what might not happen? Or if the conservatives became frightened?

V

While the heavy campaigning in the South held the political spotlight, some interesting skirmishing took place in the comparatively quiet northern sectors. Though there were no elections of particular importance in that quarter, certain maneuvers were to be of greatest consequence when 1860 arrived. The condition of the Democratic party in Pennsylvania and New York was becoming a menace to unity.

In organizing the March state convention the administration wing, led by Collector of Customs Baker, decided to crack down on Governor Packer, who was at odds with the federal officeholders; their platform commended Buchanan but ignored the Governor. Forney thereupon raised the standard of revolt and engineered an April convention which was largely attended by the Packer, anti-Lecompton forces. They did not nominate their own state ticket, but they endorsed Packer and went home to work for the opposition, or People's ticket as it was called, for Pennsylvania had no regular Republican party as yet.

Baker and his officeholders found it hard to secure a united delegation when they had as yet no presidential candidate, their interests being mostly negative, anti-Douglas. Attorney General Black appeared upon the scene occasionally; but he was ill a good deal of the time, and little help came from Washington. While Buchanan was taking his annual summer cure at Bedford Springs, one obscure editor tried to rally state pride around a second term for him by hoisting the name of the Commonwealth's only President at the head of his columns. Buchanan thought he had made it crystal-clear that he would not run again, and now had Cobb and Thompson draft a vigorous disavowal; but he named no heir, around whom his friends might rally. Thus the Keystone Democracy limped toward 1860 in a state of nervous apprehension.[18]

The New York Democracy was in a volcanic state, destined to crack the national party nominating convention wide open at Charleston in 1860. Therefore its boiling politics must be analyzed, with all its poisonous mixtures. The clash of fighting factions in the Empire State was never ending. No battle was ever won, because no leader or faction ever accepted defeat. Now Fernando Wood was staging a comeback in what promised to be a big way. He was planning to run for mayor again and did not consider himself beneath the Presidency; looking to the latter, he was corresponding with southern politicos, hoping to make connections with Wise and others that would be useful in case of a convention deadlock. At home he and Schell were still trying to secure for New York City the influence in the party which they thought the metropolitan politicians deserved. With Mozart Hall they were fighting against the Albany Regency of Dean Richmond and Peter Cagger, who were operating in alliance with Tammany and with most of the New York City Congressmen and officeholders, except in the customhouse, where Schell ruled.

For its part, the Regency was on the alert, demanding help from Washington. As Wood was not an officeholder and therefore not subject to presidential discipline, they bent their efforts to persuading the President to remove Collector Schell. For a time they thought they had succeeded, but in the end Representative Cochrane and Sheriff Kelly decided to support him. However, Wood was not to be encouraged too much by this. Buchanan assembled fourteen of these leaders—including Schell, Fowler, Kelly, Cochrane, Cooper, Connelly, and Wilson Small—in his office, where they signed a solemn treaty December 17, 1858, by which they all agreed that the federal patronage in New York City should "be exclusively employed to sustain the organization at Tammany Hall." Officeholders who did not cooperate would be dismissed; however, Schell kept his job.

Wood was busy organizing, despite this setback; in fact he was a genius at it. His primary objective was to prevent the Regency from controlling the New York State delegation to Charleston, and this involved capturing the September, 1859, state convention at Syracuse. Ordinarily the state convention preceding a national convention chose the delegates to it— carefully along Regency lines. Wood planned to force this convention to confine itself to naming the delegates at large, leaving the district delegates to be chosen at local conferences. At Astor House meetings, friends of Wood from thirty counties ratified his plan and authorized him to negotiate with Richmond and Cagger for the adjustment. Wood expected Buchanan and Cobb to help because the Regency was favorable to Douglas.

Curiously enough, the wishes of Wood and Schell fitted nicely into Cobb's plans for economy. He had decided that further savings could be effected in customhouse methods. The collectors had been maintaining storehouses where goods were kept in bond until their owners withdrew them and paid the duty. This permitted employment of numerous ward heelers, mostly on Tammany's recommendation. If the bonded warehouse business were turned over to contractors the Treasury could save $80,000 a year. Early in September, 1859, just before the state convention was to meet, Cobb contracted with Mather, Craig, McIntyre & Bixby to take over the business. Incidentally the senior partner of this firm was a partner of John Cochrane, the city Congressman, was a business associate of the Schells, and had profited in several deals with Floyd, two of which had been aired in the last Congress. As the new firm had its own facilities, the leases on the government stores were canceled, and two hundred seventy men, mostly Tammany henchmen, were turned off. This weakening of Tammany advantaged Wood, who almost at once announced he would run again for mayor.

In the meantime Richmond and Cagger had been moving their steam roller into position, to prevent Wood from attending or influencing the Charleston convention. They saw to it that the state committee pigeonholed Wood's demand that delegates be chosen by districts. Although they were Softs— in the old-time "war of the Shells"—they wooed the erstwhile leader of the Hards, Daniel S. Dickinson, with promises of support for the Presidency, an office he always had wanted; this alliance was calculated to prevent him from being pushed by his hatred of Douglas into support of Wood, to whom his kinsman, Birdsall, had turned. Also they published correspondence of Wise in proof that he was anti-Douglas, and that Wood was wooing the South.

The meeting at Syracuse was reminiscent of the virile days of the Hunker and Barnburner bloodlettings. As usual, the state convention had been preceded by two sets of primaries in New York City, with Tammany and Mozart Hall each sending up its delegates. This time Wood thought he could seat his contestants. He mobilized a force of bruisers led by the "Benicia Boy," then hero of the ring, arriving at the meeting hall very early. His delegates proceeded to organize the convention before the regulars arrived. When other delegates had appeared Peter Cagger mounted the platform for the state committee, and declared John Stryker temporary chairman. In the melee that ensued, Stryker was pushed off the platform. Cochrane then moved that the convention adjourn until one o'clock. The regular delegates marched out to settle it in various bars, while the Mozart boys, having declared themselves the organization, moved to adjourn until seven and joined their opponents in search of liquid refreshment.

The regulars came back in the afternoon, heard an address by Dickinson, nominated a state ticket and selected a complete set of delegates, choosing a combination of Hards and Softs. The Hards, followers of Dickinson, had between twelve and fifteen of the thirty-five Charleston delegates, and their hope, and certainly Dickinson's, was that the lightning might strike him at the convention. The other twenty or twenty-three of the Regency were for Douglas, and under the unit rule all thirty-five votes must be cast as the majority willed. The narrow margin of Richmond's control over the delegation finally proved to be one of the causes of the Charleston debacle.

Dickinson's alliance with Richmond, Cochrane, and Cagger split the Hard strength so that Wood could secure only a part of it. His convention in the evening nominated the same state ticket but refused to take the Charleston delegates, claiming that the afternoon convention had no right to select the whole group. They planned to choose the district delegates in local primaries and come back in February to another state convention, there to name the delegates at large. The Richmond-Cagger slate, standing behind Douglas, certainly enjoyed the advantages of early choice by the regular organization. The Wood devices ensured two New York delegations to Charleston, and another display of New York's dirty linen before a Democratic convention.[19]

VI

While the Pennsylvania and New York parties waged their lusty wars, President-making was also forward in other portions of the Union. Foremost was the candidacy of Douglas, who from the adjournment of Congress devoted his whole time to it. First of all, he went South to discover whether

262 / The Disruption of American Democracy

he could rally his friends and supporters to take advantage of developments in the local campaigns therein boiling. He was particularly hopeful of mobilizing those Democrats who feared the increasing demands of the radical wing. John Forsyth was one of his most prominent allies, and Pierre Soulé of Louisiana, another. He saw many others and, when he left, his cause seemed to be prospering. Many an unknown sat down to write that Douglas had friends in most parts of the South, but that their difficulty was their lack of men of standing who could mobilize them against the state machines.

This trip set rumors afloat that efforts were being made to reconcile Douglas and Buchanan, and that Senator Green of Missouri was an active peacemaker. The White House issued flat denials, but the rumor persisted that Douglas might be compromising. The Senator realized that if northern supporters believed he would abandon his fight they would drop him. Since it was up to him to make a statement to quell these apprehensions, he addressed a letter to J. B. Dorr of Iowa, June 22, 1859. Dorr had asked whether Douglas would permit his name to be used before the Charleston Convention. He replied that it could be done only if the Cincinnati platform were used. He would not accept a nomination on a platform approving the revival of the slave trade, providing for a congressional slave code for the territories, or endorsing "the doctrine that the Constitution of the United States either establishes or prohibits slavery in the Territories, beyond the power of the people legally to control it as other property."[20]

Having thus reassured his northern supporters, Douglas turned to another task which involved him with Attorney General Black. He felt that his position was weakened by the constant interpretation of the Dred Scott opinion as outlawing squatter sovereignty, and that he must establish his principle by a resort to history. He consulted George Bancroft and read widely that summer to gain material. The result was an historical exposition, in the worst modern dissertation style, in which he tried to demonstrate that the colonies had exercised sovereignty over slavery, and therefore the territories could do so, in strict American tradition. This article was published the first week of September in *Harper's Magazine* and immediately attracted wide attention.

It must be answered, and Black sat down to reply. He spared no words, but the gist of his argument was trenchant: the Supreme Court had decided that a territory did not have the power which Douglas claimed for it. This reply inaugurated a pamphlet debate. Douglas replied, Black rebutted, Reverdy Johnson made his contribution, and in the end no minds were changed. Nobody had ever been able to get behind Douglas's realistic statement of the fact that the people in any locality did do as they pleased; but men could and did brand him as a rebel against law and order, as an opponent of the Supreme Court, just like the Republicans.[21]

Douglas was really making some progress toward his goal. Conventions in Vermont, Maine, and Massachusetts had yielded a few delegates. In New York the split in the party was at the moment not so important as the fact that his friends were to control the delegation. Yet he had telling disadvantages. His position was too well known, and his enemies could work under the cover of favorite sons. Misfortune was beginning to stalk his steps. His wife came dangerously near to death again in childbirth and survived only to lose the little girl in a few short weeks. Thus twice in two years they had suffered this most devastating tragedy.[22] Less personal, but of great political significance, was another disaster on the distant Pacific shore.

VI

A new element in American politics and particularly in the Democratic party was now coming into prominence, as the rising communities of California, Oregon, and Washington played their peculiar brand of politics. In California the Gwin-Broderick feud had been growing in intensity. Broderick's alliance with Douglas in the Lecompton battle had brought all the administration guns to bear upon him and certainly Gwin's Chivalry would have all the aid Buchanan could give them. As soon as Congress adjourned, Broderick went home to fight the battle of his career, to crush the Chivalry, drive Gwin from the Senate, and organize the state for Douglas in 1860. He had secured aid from the East. With the help of the Republican, Senator Seward, he had obtained funds for the battle.[23]

The contest in California this summer was as deadly as that turbulent environment could provide. No holds were barred. The Chivalry in desperation would stop at nothing, nor did Broderick give them any quarter. At the height of the campaign a fiery southerner, Judge Terry, challenged Broderick to a duel and killed him, September 16, 1859. This was a body blow to Douglas as well; bitterness flowed afresh. When Senator Gwin took ship to attend the coming session of Congress he had to pass under a likeness of Broderick, around which were written these words, "The will of the people of California is that the murderer of D. C. Broderick will never return to the State."[24].The friends of Douglas in other sections of the country were to make much of the "murder" of Broderick. In the Senate, Douglas would be sadly handicapped without him. He supplied essential iron which Douglas, who was getting flabby, lacked.

In Oregon, the other western outpost on the Pacific, politics was breeding a formidable candidate against Douglas. When that territory was organized in 1848, Polk chose General Joseph Lane, the "Marion of the Mexican War," to be its first governor. Lane, of North Carolina origin, had been active in Indiana politics before going to Oregon to make a career. He undertook to govern the territory, quell the Indian menace, and organize the Democratic party. In the latter effort he was associated with a newspaperman of Jewish origin, Asahel Bush. When President Taylor sent out a Whig governor, Lane was elected delegate to Congress, where he piloted an act making two territories out of the vast region by creating Washington, north of the Columbia. Pierce four years later sent Lane back as Governor of Oregon, accompanied by Colonel I. I. Stevens (who had surveyed a Pacific railroad route) as Governor of Washington. Lane served only long enough to put out his Whig predecessor and then resigned to seek a second term as delegate. He had ambitions to be President which could be promoted better in Washington, D. C., than in Salem, Oregon.

Democratic machines were erected in these territories. In Oregon, Bush and a varying group of associates, known as the Salem Clique, ruled the party with an iron hand. Lane generally worked with them; but they dictated to him on federal patronage, and he was irked by their tight rein. At the beginning of the Buchanan administration there was a growing coolness. North of the Columbia, Governor Stevens organized a Democratic machine and in 1857 chose to join Lane, his close friend, as delegate from Washington Territory in Congress.

Since 1857 a bitter feud had developed in the Oregon Democracy, and rebellion against Bush and the Clique had grown. After the statehood bill was passed and Lane elected the first Senator, Bush broke with him, and Lane joined the rebels against the Clique. Bush with his cohorts now decided to thwart Lane's presidential ambitions, using the name of Douglas as a rallying cry for protection from the results of the Clique's despotism in local matters.

The efforts of Bush and the Clique to control choice of the delegation to Charleston, and to retain hold of the party, split the Oregon Democracy in the legislative session of 1859. This prevented election of a Senator to act with Lane and nearly defeated the party ticket in the state canvass.

The final round was fought in the state convention which met in November to choose the Charleston delegates. Here the Clique, in the name of Douglas, fought Lane's supporters with all they had. The Lane Nationals fought back with the sharp weapons which are available to those who control a state committee. They did as the Clique had done and juggled the apportionment of delegates to favor themselves. The result was a Lane-controlled convention. Lane's son-in-law cleverly concocted a resolution endorsing the candidate, which could be voted for by some of the delegates instructed for others. A group of Lane's opponents then withdrew while those that remained adopted the resolutions unanimously and chose Lane and six friends as delegates and alternates. The Douglas-Clique men from seven counties, who had seceded, held a protest convention, but decided not to choose a contesting delegation; in fact they pledged support of the Charleston nominee. Yet the party was shattered in Oregon as it was in California. On the face of things, however, Lane had control of his constituency and could dream of the Presidency as of yore.[25]

VIII

While the stars of Douglas and Lane were describing their uneven orbits, northern Democrats had been going to the polls as well as to conventions. The returns were not encouraging. The September elections showed increased majorities for the Republicans in Vermont and Maine. In October, Ohio Republicans had won the governor and legislature with increased pluralities. In Indiana, what little voting there was showed Republican gains. In Pennsylvania, though the lead of the "opposition" for the state ticket was slightly reduced, it finally captured for the first time both houses of the legislature. In the New York campaigns, which would not climax until November and December, the situation remained complicated. The American party, instead of nominating an independent ticket, had decided to endorse four Democrats and five Republicans. They thus annexed the title, "Balance of Power" party. This move gave the Democrats some hope of partial success for their state ticket.[26]

In the midst of these mixed political signs, news flashed over the wires that set the nerves of the nation on edge. About eleven o'clock Monday morning, October 17, a message came to President Buchanan. President Garrett of the Baltimore & Ohio Railroad telegraphed a report from one of his conductors that Harpers Ferry with its arsenal was in the hands of insurrectionaries, white and Negro. Buchanan immediately called Floyd and the acting Attorney General (Black was not available), and despatched artillery from Fortress Monroe and marines from the Navy Yard. He summoned Colonel Robert E. Lee and Lieutenant J. E. B. Stuart to join in council, and the group drew up plans for putting the section under martial law if required. Lee and Stuart set off armed with the necessary papers, and they and the marines, whom they overtook, arrived at Harpers Ferry about midnight. They discovered then that local militia and townsmen had cornered in an engine house all that were left of the twenty-two raiders. At dawn Lee summoned the beleaguered to surrender and, when they refused, battered down the door and captured them.

That day Governor Wise and Senator Mason arrived and cross-examined the leader. They learned details which the press broadcast on the 19th. The nation then discovered that old John Brown of Kansas, who had figured in killings, slave and horse stealing, and antislavery activity in the territory, had attempted to set up a center for freeing the slaves of Virginia with the arms at Harpers Ferry. Furthermore, from papers captured it appeared that he was backed by philanthropists and Republican politicians. Governor Wise secured this prisoner from the federal authorities, and it was decided to charge him with treason and murder in the Virginia courts. As the local tribunal was about to sit at Charlestown he was tried there almost immediately and found guilty on October 31. His execution was set for December 2.

As Brown's comet crossed the political skies in the last weeks before the November elections, it was immediately put to campaign use. New York, New Jersey, Maryland, and Massachusetts were in the midst of exciting contests. Here was quite an opportunity for the Democratic press to smear Seward, and they availed themselves of it. The *New York Herald* led off with an effort to show that the foray was part of a Republican plot, the legitimate fruits of Seward's irrepressible conflict. No conclusive proof of Republican political complicity was ever provided, and as Senator Seward was in Europe he could not make a reply. In general the Republicans ignored the charges. On the other hand they did not show much indignation at this assault, and their indifference enraged certain southern publicists.

Governor Wise found Brown ready-made to help his hopes of the nomination, which had been somewhat dimmed by his letter-writing proclivities. He was accused of exploiting Brown for his own benefit; that, however, was not necessary. The events themselves were spectacular and provided natural publicity.[27]

Wise was bombarded with letters telling of conspiracies to rescue Brown, and at one time the threats were so definite that he took a militia contingent to protect the jail. It was a false alarm, but rumor persisted that places in Maryland, Ohio, and Pennsylvania had been occupied by desperadoes planning to invade Virginia on the eve of the execution. Wise wrote of this to the governors of these states and to the President, whom he asked to take steps "to preserve peace between the states." Evidently he thought Republicans from Ohio and Pennsylvania were coming over with at least the tacit approval of their governments.

Buchanan replied he was sending two companies of artillery to Harpers Ferry. He could take no steps "to preserve peace between the states" because he had no authority to enter Ohio and Pennsylvania and could only call out armed forces in case of invasion "from any foreign nation or Indian tribe." Nothing happened, and John Brown went to his death as scheduled. However, Buchanan's reply to Wise was to prove highly significant in the crisis to come.[28]

John Brown's raid of October 16 was timed for the worst possible psychological effect. It raised the specter of revolution while preparations were afoot for state conventions to select delegations to Charleston, while some elections were being held, and while the new Thirty-sixth Congress was approaching its first session. Northern response was mixed; there was a struggle between hatred of violence and zeal for the antislavery cause. Out of it came a rationalization that John Brown was a martyr for freedom, slain by the barbarous slaveholders when he struck for liberty.

The response was much stronger below the Potomac than in the free-labor regions. To the South it seemed that the Republicans were hiring gangsters to foment slave uprisings. Now many southerners believed they had evidence that they would not be safe if the Republicans were in power. This experience capped the climax of nerves which had shown itself in the political reshuffling, the business panic, and the religious revivals of the preceding years. The attitudes and actions of many people were now conditioned almost entirely by emotion; the strength of reason had been broken.

Political behavior was affected only slightly at the moment. The Democrats did show some gains. In New York the Republicans lost three of the state officers whom the Americans had refused to endorse, but they gained the other six and kept the legislature. In New Jersey the Democrats won the legislature, though they could not capture the governorship. In Maryland they regained the legislature, but lost the state ticket; the Americans elected Governor Hicks. In Massachusetts Ben Butler cut down Bank's lead somewhat, and the old Whig ticket gained; but the Republicans were safely in control. Thus the trend slightly favored the Democrats, perhaps because of reaction to the rumored complicity of Republicans with John Brown.[29]

The final political straw showing the direction of the winds for 1860 came from New York City. There the city elections were held in December some five weeks after the general election. The Republicans nominated George F. Opdyke, and the Whigs and a People's party each put up a candidate. The Democracy split. Since Wood had decided to stage a comeback, Mozart Hall had nominated him. Tammany, the Softs, and some discontented Mozartians put up a reputable Democrat, William F. Havemeyer. This schism was due in part to a rising feeling that there should be some respectability in New York City Democratic politics. Wealthy and socially prominent Democrats, including Royal Phelps, a friend of Buchanan, Judge James Roosevelt, August Belmont, and John A. Dix, with the support of the *Herald,* were trying to stamp out rowdyism and give to the Democracy the respectability it needed in order to defeat Seward. Fernando Wood's "b'hoys" just laughed at these "silk stockings"; with the party widely split they brought Wood into office, though cumbered with a hostile board of aldermen and council. But he was mayor again and went ahead with the creation of his delegation to Charleston.[30]

With returns completed from all sections, political eyes, albeit somewhat bloodshot and congested by the nervous strain of the Harpers Ferry incident, could be turned to the assembling Congress. Here was to be more woe, for no party was in control of the House, and a nation-shaking battle over the speakership was at hand.

PART IV

THE COST OF FACTION

Chapter 14

Rehearsing for Charleston

THE CONGRESS ASSEMBLING in December, 1859, was in reality as much a presidential nominating convention as it was a legislative body. The Democratic party was in a difficult position and was desperately hoping that some advantage might be snatched from the deliberations to make the prospects of success in 1860 a little brighter.

The signs at the opening were forbidding because no party had control of the House. Twice before, in 1849 and 1855, such a situation had produced a long deadlock over the election of a Speaker and an extended period of legislative chaos. The uncertainty and confusion in the party situation had been increased by the John Brown Raid. This foray presented an arsenal of weapons which would be seized eagerly by the various candidates and factions. The pronunciamentos of the *New York Herald* were but forewarnings of what was to come. The raid was going to play its part in the struggle for the Speakership.

Much depended upon the Speaker, for in those days he appointed the committees. Their control was deemed particularly important in this Congress because they might be used to affect the presidential contest. Three questions would involve committee study and action, from a distinctly political angle. The Republicans would continue to look for fraud in Democratic administration. They hoped, by securing the right committees, to blow the lid off the printing racket and expose the patronage practices of their opponents; they had already shown up the Navy abuses in the preceding Congress. Then there was the struggle for a protective tariff, which was bound to be renewed; a sympathetic ways and means committee could do much for the Republicans.

Most significant of all was the question of contested seats, for they might determine the Presidency. Observers were predicting that at least four candidates would run for President, and that probably no one of them could obtain an electoral majority. The election, therefore, would be thrown into the House, where each state would have one vote, determined by whatever party held the majority in that state's delegation. The successful candidate must receive the votes of seventeen states. But how could these be obtained? The Republicans controlled fifteen, the Democrats fourteen, the Americans one, while three—Kentucky, Maryland, and North Carolina—were tied. Election contests were filed which might give the control of Kentucky and Maryland to either the Democrats or the Americans, and might change Oregon from Democratic to Republican. Therefore the make-up of the House committee on elections, considering these contests, might be decisive in the presidential struggle.

The Democrats were not without hope despite dubious odds. It would take 119 votes to organize the House. Technically they had 101; but as 13 of these would be cast by anti-Lecomptonites, who at various times had been "read out of the party," there were really only 88. However, the Republicans were in a minority also. They had only 109 members, 10 short of a majority. The rest of the members were variously listed as Americans or Whigs and numbered 27. Of these 23 were southern American-Whigs and 4 came from New York and New Jersey. During the summer, negotiations had been going on between the Republicans, the anti-Lecomptonites, and the 4 northern American-Whigs. It was predicted that a majority had been secured for a ticket comprising John Sherman for Speaker and John W. Forney for clerk.

The administration leaders must prevent consummation of that coalition. They could count on only 86 votes, for one of their men, Brown of Kentucky, was under age and could not qualify, and another, Stallworth of Alabama, was at home ill. Mathematically, however, there were possibilities. If some issue could be raised which would unite with them the 13 anti-Lecompton Democrats and the 23 southern American-Whigs, a Speaker could be elected. Had John Brown's raid raised such an issue? The leaders of the 86 thought it had.[1]

Fate had forged a useful weapon which Brown's foray made formidable. Two years before, a North Carolinian of humble birth, Helper by name, had published a book, *The Impending Crisis of the South,* possibly aided by a group of Republicans. It was addressed to the submerged white classes in the South. This volume was an indictment bristling with statistics designed to arouse his fellow southerners to the burdens which slavery imposed upon them. Revolution was preached in no uncertain terms. Thousands of copies were sold, and so effective a document was it that the Republicans decided to use it for campaign purposes. They planned to supervise the preparation of a compendium, somewhat shorter and easier to read. Just at the close of the short session in March, the leading Republican Congressmen had signed an endorsement of a plea for funds from Republican subscribers to print this compendium. Their endorsement had been sent out in circular form. Now the Democrats seized it.

Democratic editorial batteries had already blazed forth the charge that John Brown's Raid was the direct result of revolutionary doctrines, such as were preached in Helper's *Impending Crisis*. The nation would not be safe if those who preached such incendiary dogma were in power. All peace-loving men must fight such dangerous irresponsibles. The hope was that once again a conservative coalition might be rallied; the anti-Lecompton men might be dissuaded from traffic with the Republicans; and the southern American-Whigs might be prevailed upon to join the southern Democrats in a union to prevent Republican control of the House.

Two grave difficulties stood in the way. Recent successes in the 1859 elections had raised the hopes of the Americans and accentuated their natural distaste for fraternizing with their ancient enemies. Furthermore, the administration had been so bitter in its warfare upon the anti-Lecomptonites that most of them, particularly the eight outside Illinois, owed their return to Congress to the Republicans and were therefore under obligations. Had not the Sherman-Forney negotiations gone too far to permit the election of a non-Republican speaker? Such was the perplexing situation as Congress assembled, one which made much trading inevitable.[2]

On the Saturday preceding the opening session the party caucuses were held, and sectionalism marred them all. The Democrats found as they anticipated that they could not muster full party strength. Eight of the thirteen anti-Lecompton men—Clark, Haskin, and Reynolds from New York, Hickman and Schwartz from Pennsylvania, Adrain and Riggs from New Jersey and John G. Davis from Indiana—would not caucus though Douglas had urged it; neither would the fire eater, Pugh of Alabama. On the other hand, Douglas's five Congressmen from Illinois were there, willing to forget the past and play ball. The caucus proceeded to nominate for Speaker a Virginian of long experience in Congress, Thomas S. Bocock; and they adopted the unusual procedure of appointing a steering committee of five, under the chairmanship of Winslow of North Carolina. His associates included John McClernand of Illinois, evidence that Douglas men were back in regular standing. Could the other eight, not present at the caucus, be wooed into fellowship?[3]

The Republicans, too, were troubled by factions, young as they were. Their eastern and western wings could not agree on a candidate, largely because the one cared chiefly for protective tariffs and the other stressed antislavery. Since they could not fix on a caucus nominee they decided that the Republican getting the highest vote on the first House ballot Monday should be their man; it would be either Sherman of Ohio or Galusha A. Grow of Pennsylvania. The Whig-Americans were also divided, North and South. The southern Americans could not help elect a Democratic Speaker on the one hand, for fear of harming their hopes for 1860 in their section. On the other hand, if they hoped for a bargain with the Republicans they dared not enter such a combination after John Brown's Raid. The four northern Whig-Americans were close-mouthed and kept to themselves.[4]

II

At noon on Monday December 5, the clerk from the previous Congress called the House to order, and the Reverend Dr. Phineas Gurley invoked much-needed Divine guidance. Balloting began immediately, and Sherman was highest, becoming the Republican nominee; but he failed of a majority that afternoon, and at least three stubborn votes stood between him and the Speakership through many weeks thereafter. Three of the anti-Lecompton men voted for him, but the other five would not; nor would enough northern and border-state Whig-Americans. In fact it was his failure to secure border-state support which defeated him; and those votes were kept from him by the clever and timely exposure by the Democrats of Sherman's endorsement of Helper's *Impending Crisis*. No southerners of any party dared aid a man who had put his name to a plea to southern poor whites to revolt against slavery.

Nor could the Democrats obtain a majority for Bocock or any other of their party. They would not pledge a protective tariff as the price of Pennsylvania support. They could not command the eight anti-Lecomptonites even when Buchanan's organ, the *Constitution*, lashed them in stinging editorials as "the Black Republican Reserve."[5] Moreover, whenever the Democrats appeared to be on the point of winning the southern Americans to unite on a candidate with them—a union Douglas strove vigorously to promote—the

Alabama fire eater who had refused to caucus with them was joined by eight others from Alabama and South Carolina in declining to support the candidate. They effectually prevented an anti-Republican coalition.

As December dragged on, tempers frayed. The more radical southern Democrats contemplated walking out if Sherman were elected, and found support at home for that revolutionary procedure. The delay was the more trying because it was expensive. As Congress was not organized it could not appropriate any money. No one had been paid. A number of the members would have been in financial straits had not the sergeant at arms of the previous House, Adam J. Glossbrenner, borrowed money and loaned it to them in advance of their salaries. This pocketbook stringency did not ease things.[6]

While the Republicans sat quietly and waited, the exasperated Democrats and Americans hurled charges of bad faith backwards and forwards. Christmas brought no surcease. The Republicans sat tight and refused to recess. Monday December 26 found the House in session although most Washingtonians were celebrating it as a holiday. Some Congressmen carried an air of conviviality into the House by bringing in eggnog, and "Extra-Billy" Smith of Virginia flourished a cup while speaking to the great question.

Pressure was brought by mail contractors, as the delay in appropriations postponed payment of the Post Office deficit, now up in the millions. They descended on Washington in force, to try to make Congress organize—or at least elect a temporary Speaker—so that the Post Office deficiency bill might get through. All to no avail. President Buchanan sent his annual message to the Senate on December 27, as if that commonplace document could do any good.[7]

After the thirty-fourth ballot, on January 11, showed no result, voting was abandoned for a fortnight to concentrate efforts upon negotiation. Undercover deals had been attempted from the outset, some of them by Congressman Clark of New York, who proved that he was not Vanderbilt's son-in-law for nothing. When such efforts leaked into the press, they did not prove unifying. For example, a *New York Herald* revelation almost precipitated a riot in the House.[8] Haskin of New York had a difference of opinion with Clark in the course of which Haskin was accused of drawing a pistol. He claimed that it fell out of his pocket, and that he had it with him only because he had been out late the preceding night. He lived on the outskirts of the capital near English Hill, where thugs operated. The two weeks passed slowly, made tedious by the constant flow of speech from opponents of the Republicans, who sat silent, always present in force, never caught napping. The Democrats were no match for the Republicans at sitting.

At the end of the fortnight the House decided to spend the next two weeks in doing nothing but voting, which recommenced January 25. Five days later, Sherman withdrew in favor of Pennington, a New Jersey Whig who had tried to help him by working to substitute a plurality for a majority vote. A deal had been made for a coalition ticket: Pennington, Whig-Republican, for Speaker; John W. Forney of Philadelphia, anti-Lecompton Democrat, for clerk; Henry W. Hoffman of Maryland, southern American, for sergeant at arms; Thomas H. Ford of Ohio, American-Republican, for printer. The coalition put through the Speaker at noon, February 1, by 117 votes, the exact number necessary on that day. Election of the rest of the slate was completed after a prolonged and scandalous struggle over the printer.[9]

The House was organized at last. Through nearly two months of conflict the nation had been threatened with legislative demoralization, because of the possibility that no Speaker would be chosen. Political demoralization had become an accomplished fact, with the corrupt use of printing profits shamelessly flaunted during the struggle and with the "reforming" Republicans proved to be stooping to some of the same unsavory practices.[10] Douglas, at least, might take some satisfaction in the fact that the contest ended with his man, McClernand, the official Democratic nominee and with most of his followers in good and regular party standing. Thus the notorious Speakership fight of 1859 was ended; but the hatreds of the fight survived. Nine radical Southerners had preferred destroying their party's chance of victory to voting for a Douglas man. This spirit foreshadowed the fate of the Charleston convention.

III

During the long weeks of confusion in the unorganized House, the coming party conventions were ever in the minds of the dickering members. The Democratic National Committee had set April 23 as the date for the Charleston meeting of their party. As the customary time for conventions was June, this early date meant that the campaign would be longer and the period of preparation for it shorter than usual. When the committee met at the opening of Congress its members found new responsibilities driving them to unprecedented action.

They must give heed to organization and publicity. Such heed was demanded by the superior publicity techniques of their opponents. The Republicans had been particularly efficient in directing the content of Associated Press despatches, a new agency in political strategy. The Democratic National Committee sought means to combat this efficiency, and it set up a committee to be resident in Washington. Seven Representatives and Senator Bigler made up this body. They were instructed "to take into consideration the telegraphic misrepresentations affecting the interests of the Democratic party forwarded to the Associated Press and to provide, if possible, a remedy therefor." They engaged rooms on Four and a Half Street and employed M. W. Cluskey as their secretary. He began to prepare and place various kinds of news releases and editorial matter. After this unusual activity the members of the committee dispersed to do what each could in the remaining state conventions.[11]

Senator Douglas to date was out in front of all the Democratic aspirants. He and his allies had secured a string of delegates, but unfortunately for him they were all in free-labor states. He had won the Vermont and Maine contingents and thought he had that of Massachusetts. During the next few weeks he obtained Rhode Island, New Hampshire, and that part of Connecticut's choice which Toucey could not keep from him. January and February also brought a series of victories which made the Northwest fairly solid. His own Illinois led off on January 4, and by Washington's Birthday he had won majorities in Ohio, Indiana, Minnesota, Iowa, Michigan, and Wisconsin.

This northwestern triumph did not come without a struggle, for administration forces and his senatorial enemies had tried hard to frustrate him. Bright and Fitch of Indiana and his erstwhile partner, Rice of Minnesota, had succeeded in securing minorities in the delegations of their states; but these minorities were presumably helpless because the Douglas-controlled conventions had ordered the delegations to vote as a unit. In Illinois Buchanan had followed political expediency at the cost of honest administration, keeping Ike Cook as postmaster despite Holt's proof of mail pilfering. Cook reciprocated by organizing a Danite (the Illinois term for administration men) convention after the regular one, placing himself at the head of a contesting delegation to Charleston.[12]

In the Far West, the Pacific outposts were figuring more prominently this year, as Lane's candidacy already had proved. The spring of 1859 had brought some breath-taking politics in the schismatic California Democracy. The Gwin-Broderick factions were fighting harder than ever over the filling of the slain Broderick's Senate seat. Collector of the Port Milton S. Latham, born in Ohio but more recently from Alabama, had made hay under the burning sun of California's politics. Elected governor with the aid of Gwin and the Chivalry, he entered a deadlocked legislature only five days after his inauguration, and snatched the Senate seat from the Chivalry's candidate. After his departure for Washington, Latham's henchmen in the state convention contrived to get seven of the state's eight delegates to Charleston. These men were like Latham, opportunists out to feather their own nests, and ready to vote for the man most likely to win. Their defeat of Gwin heartened the Douglasites, since Gwin had headed the caucus committee which took Douglas's chairmanship from him; but the convention was to show there was slight cause for rejoicing.[13]

In the South the picture was blurred. Cobb wanted to inherit the Presidency, but Buchanan seemed not in a bequeathing mood. Editor Browne of the *Constitution* gave the Secretary friendly publicity, and he could utilize his Treasury employees. But his efforts to stamp out the slave trade and his attempts at customs reform made him extremely unpopular with radicals in the South and spoilsmen everywhere. This Union Democrat, who had gained fame and power by his defeats of the fire eaters might now be eaten by the fire. At least his erstwhile allies, Stephens and Toombs, now were no help to him. Cobb's henchmen, determined he should have the indispensable endorsement of his own state, tried to clinch it by rushing things. When the Georgia legislature met in November, 1859, they secured signatures for a call for a state convention in December. As the state committee already had made arrangements for a March date, Cobb's enemies shouted, "It's a Tammany trick!" The December convention, carefully engineered, duly endorsed the Secretary and chose a delegation of his friends.

Despite this, the state committee refused to be flouted and held its scheduled convention in March. The Cobb managers sought to have this assembly merely ratify the December

action but found they could not control its will. The delegates refused to vote a formal ratification of Cobb's endorsement; and while they did designate his twenty delegates, they
added another twenty to them and instructed the forty to
vote as a unit. As a matter of fact a majority of this enlarged
delegation was actually for Cobb, but he had lost face by
the incident. Pondering the matter, he thought best ostensibly
to retire, and published an open letter of withdrawal. Nevertheless he did have the Georgia vote and was still to be
reckoned with.[14]

Outside Georgia Cobb had no other apparent strength, for
each southern state tended to push its own favorite son. In
Virginia Senator Hunter had been hotly challenged by the
Wise men; but his friends were able to secure an uninstructed
delegation who would be faithful to him, and he had wider
southern support than Cobb.[15] In Mississippi the party convention had nominated Jefferson Davis.[16] Tennessee had endorsed Andrew Johnson,[17] and Louisiana, John Slidell.[18]
From Kentucky came the news that James Guthrie, Pierce's
Secretary of the Treasury, had been presented.[19]

Douglas himself was by no means without support in the
South. He had not been idle, and his friends were trying to
make alliances. In the hope of securing votes they experi-
mented with various men as vice presidential possibilities on
his ticket. He himself seems to have favored Alexander H.
Stephens, although his friends made several people believe
that they were preferred. No one seemed sure how much
southern strength Douglas had; many an obscure Democrat
was for him, but he lacked influential henchmen. Certainly
his friends did not figure prominently in the state delegations
that were being chosen.[20]

The most significant signs coming from the southern party
conventions were not the candidates nor the delegates but
the truculent tone of their official and unofficial utterances.
Most of the local conventions passed resolutions opposing
Douglas's doctrines and making it plain they would have none
of his squatter sovereignty. Southern rights in the territories
must be recognized and protected.

Alabama made a highly significant move in its January
Democratic convention. The legislature had met shortly after
John Brown's Raid, had armed the state and authorized the
governor to call a state convention if a Republican President
should be elected in November, 1860. The Democratic state
conclave was of the same mind. It endorsed no candidate,

but it wrote a plank for the national platform, ordering its delegates to fight for the following formula or its equivalent:

> Resolved that it is the duty of the General Government, by all proper legislation, to secure an entry into those territories to all citizens of the United States, together with their property of every description, and that the same should remain protected by the United States while the Territories are under its authority.

The convention went further, commanding its delegates to leave the national body if it refused to accept this plank. Yancey had taken a walk in 1848—by himself. In 1860 he might expect company. The plank, it was later charged, was really designed to help Yancey enter the Senate.[21]

The balance of power probably lay in the middle states, New Jersey and Pennsylvania, where Douglas was fighting a drawn battle. New Jersey's convention had chosen a divided delegation with no avowed Douglas man included. The delegates seemed more interested in securing the vice presidential nomination for a favorite son, William C. Alexander.[22] In Pennsylvania Attorney General Black and Collector Baker had concluded to make peace with Governor Packer in order to secure a united delegation which would support Breckinridge, Lane, or Guthrie. At the state convention in March a platform endorsing both Buchanan and Packer was adopted, and a popular candidate was nominated for governor whom even Forney would support. A compromise delegation was selected for Charleston in a gesture toward harmony. At Buchanan's urging, Senator Bigler was included as one of the delegates at large while William Montgomery, who had acted independently in the Lecompton fight, was another. One-third of the delegation were Douglas men, but the majority were good, trading Democrats who undoubtedly would aid his enemies as much as possible. Buchanan gave his friend Plumer a letter to be used if necessary, declining to be considered a candidate; he never could realize how little chance there was of this.[23]

In New York the Regency was in control and the unit rule was in force. For the time being 35 votes were pledged for Douglas. However, there were two dark horses, Horatio Seymour and Daniel S. Dickinson, who might be brought out in a deadlock. Also Fernando Wood's henchmen had completed their contesting delegation to Charleston; as on previous occasions this group might be admitted and given half the state's vote. Nothing was certain except that the New York leaders were notorious traders who could be expected to do as well for themselves as possible. They, like Senator Latham of California, were interested in any candidate who could be elected.[24]

In view of the general trend of the state convention proceedings, the real possibilities seemed to lie in the field of dark horses. In the light of this situation two of the most available candidates had not come out in front at all. The popular and handsome Vice President John C. Breckinridge, sparkling and convivial, was in the minds of a good many people. His own state had been badly torn between him and Douglas, and, in order to secure a united delegation, Guthrie had been made the official choice. The Kentucky legislature, however, had chosen Breckinridge to succeed Crittenden in the United States Senate in 1861. He had presented his views in a trimming speech in which he condemned Douglas's "unfriendly legislation" idea and spoke for protection of slavery in the territories; yet he saw no need for a slave code in these outposts and urged that everything be done to keep northern and southern Democrats together in the war on the aggressive Republicans. Breckinridge was cultivating certain northern delegations, particularly in Pennsylvania, where he persuaded the administration majority not to endorse him officially. He wished to seem to thwart no one and to appear as a natural second choice.[25]

Jo Lane was likewise moving quietly. He had many friends because of his bluff good-fellowship. He was a favorite of the President, of Secretary Thompson, and of the fascinating and intriguing Mrs. Greenhow who "entertained" for his interests. He was solid and substantial and had no ideas. It was widely believed that the President and his cabinet would be pleased at his success.[26] The chances of Breckinridge and Lane, or of any dark horse, on the face of things seemed good, for as the state conventions concluded their work, about the only thing certain was the fact that no candidate had anything like a two-thirds majority. Douglas was nearest to it; he probably believed he had a majority. Realists like Latham told him that probably he could not be nominated, but that he might well control the choice. He was young yet, only forty-seven —why not be content with the role of Warwick this time? Douglas had heard this before and was not impressed with such logic.

IV

While the state conventions were choosing their delegations to Charleston, there was in Congress some talk of candidates and much more of platforms. As to candidates, interest was sharpened and tactics were complicated by the fact that at least ten of the thirty-eight Democrats in the Senate were presidential hopefuls. Among the dominant group, Hunter was regarded as the best man to beat Douglas at Charleston. The Republicans and the southern opposition were expected to name Seward and Crittenden, respectively. The Senate was filled with prospective kings and would-be Warwicks.[27] But it was their platform that was agitating the Democrats most. On principles they were split into at least three groups; and from among them the party managers in the Senate must compose a formula to keep the American Democracy together in the 1860 campaign.

Pressure for an extreme southern platform was aggravated by the disappointed ambitions of some southerners. For example, Senators Brown of Mississippi and Iverson of Georgia, never of the inner circle, took a radical position aimed to force the leaders to follow the cue or lose their dominance at home. Iverson announced that the South was prepared to defend itself "even at the sacrifice of the Union which you all pretend so much to revere." Brown demanded a plank for the protection of slavery in all territories until they became states, contrary to Douglas's principle of squatter sovereignty.

After Brown suffered a public tongue-lashing administered by his colleague Jefferson Davis for attacking the editor of the administration organ—he grew more violent. He proclaimed that the party should not have harmony at any price set by Douglas; the Democracy must require every territory to protect slavery, on pain of interference by Congress for that purpose. Senator Clay of Alabama took the cue, warning his colleagues that the South would not submit to a Republican President. In like vein ex-Senator Rhett of South Carolina and ex-Representative Yancey of Alabama were stoking the radical fires at home, as shown in their joint demand published in the *Charleston Mercury* of October 13, 1859: if the convention refused to make the Dred Scott principle its plank the southern delegates should bolt; if the Republicans won the election the South must devise means to secure its safety.

Senator Toombs of Georgia, of the inner circle, would not

take the radical cue. No less an individualist than Brown, he spoke of conciliation, of the need for Democratic unity to beat the Republicans. Buchanan's idea of a unifying plank was a declaration that the federal courts could be relied upon to protect property in the territories. Senator Green of the border state of Missouri made a futile attempt to press this upon the Senators, but neither the fire eaters nor the Unionists cared to depend upon it.

Far more important than any plank proposed by Buchanan would be the one pressed by Douglas, whose strength was constantly swelled by a series of successes in northern party conventions. Senators Bigler of Pennsylvania and Pugh of Ohio were insistent that a plank like Brown's would be their ruin; only the Cincinnati platform reaffirmed could save them. Douglas was ill again, this time with inflammatory rheumatism, and few realized how run down he was. His illness gave him an excuse to bide his time and delay his return. Although once again deprived of his territorial chairmanship, he determined to make a last effort at conciliation. He reiterated his oft repeated statements that Congress had no power over slavery in the territories, and that the Dred Scott opinion lacked the force of a legal decision; he announced that he was willing to submit the issue to the courts. Further, to allay fears of John Brown insurrections, he proposed a bill for national protection of states and territories, providing federal machinery to suppress conspiracies involving interstate invasion.

Southern Democrats had no liking for Douglas's bill, lest it prove a weapon against seceding states; they adroitly shunted it into a pigeonhole. Jefferson Davis, who had presidential ambitions of his own, hoped that Brown might not seem more jealous of southern rights than himself and proposed a platform less radical than Brown's but scarcely acceptable to Douglas.

This new platform was Calhoun brought up to date. The late South Carolina philosopher, in his famous resolutions of 1837, had merely proclaimed the right of citizens to take slaves into the territories and denied to Congress any power to stop them. This was before the day of Douglas and squatter sovereignty. Now Davis and others sought to spike the Little Giant's guns: "Neither Congress, nor a *Territorial Legislature,* whether by direct legislation or legislation of an indirect and unfriendly nature, possess the power to annul or impair the constitutional right of any citizen of the United

States to take his slave property into the common Territories." The "first time that they might decide whether slavery was to exist there or not [was] when they rightfully form a constitution to be admitted as a state into the Union." This definition of popular sovereignty lacked the ambiguities of Douglas's "squatter sovereignty" dogma. Furthermore, the Davis dogma prescribed that Congress, and the national government generally, must protect slave property in the territories: "It is the duty of the Federal Government to afford the needful protection and if experience should at any time prove that the Judiciary does not possess power to insure adequate protection, it will then become the duty of Congress to supply such deficiency."

The Davis resolutions were introduced on February 2, the day after the House had finally elected its Speaker. Davis plainly wished to assert his pretensions to recognition as Calhoun's heir.[28] Five days later Saulsbury of Delaware moved some modifications, stressing the benefits of the Union in Websterian vein. He represented the border states' hope of compromise and conciliation.[29] The border Senators pressed for negotiation and secured reference of the various motions and resolutions to a caucus of Senate Democrats.

The caucus labored hard, even consulting President Buchanan. It finally decided to endorse a modified version of Davis's resolutions. It accepted his first two points and rephrased the third to read: If "experience should at any time prove that the Judiciary and executive authority do not possess means to insure adequate protection to constitutional rights in a Territory, and if the territorial government shall fail or refuse to provide the necessary remedies for that purpose, it will be the duty of Congress to supply such deficiency."

The caucus was in no mood to meet Douglas's demands, but it did wish to quiet the fear of "a slave code," aroused by Brown's resolutions, and to put that recalcitrant in his place. The gathering was not altogether harmonious, for twelve of the party Senators from the South opposed this declaration. Nevertheless it was introduced in the Senate March 1. Occasionally debate veered in its direction, but no effort was made to pass it before the convention. It was there as advice to the platform committee at Charleston.[30]

V

While the Senate Democrats were writing platforms, the

House Republicans went happily fishing for scandal, with which to manufacture campaign ammunition. They put lines out on corruption in the post offices, customhouses, and navy yards; on the use of money and patronage to influence legislation and elections; and on the peculiar values in printing contracts. Cornelius Wendell had been deprived of most of his perquisites, following revelations in the previous Congress of how the Democracy used the printing to finance the party. Now saddled with an idle, expensive printing plant, he was ready to talk. Two House committees and one Senate committee eagerly took down the words of this star witness.[31]

The House committee, named for Representative Covode of Pennsylvania, went on the most extensive fishing expedition and took the spotlight with Wendell's testimony.[32] The star frequently conferred with Douglas between sittings and talked freely, about his support of Democratic persons, papers, and campaign funds. He claimed close association with Buchanan who, he said, often directed distribution of the largesse.[33] The administration fought back indirectly, with the President and Edwin M. Stanton drafting questions by which the minority member of the committee, Winslow of North Carolina, was to expose inconsistencies in Wendell's colorful testimony.[34]

Covode's fishermen went north into Collector Baker's customhouse at Philadelphia. The key to disclosures there was James C. Van Dyke, the district attorney who had just been ousted for noncooperation with Baker. The collector, it developed among other things, kept his brother George, whose wife was a relative of Buchanan, on the pay roll—not to labor in the customhouse but in the sanctum of the *Pennsylvanian*. The committee learned a lot about 1858 campaign funds of the Democrats and began hopefully on 1856. The New York fish did not bite so well, however; Collector Augustus Schell consistently failed to remember.[35]

Covode's investigations reached their climax just on the eve of the Charleston convention with efforts to prove that Buchanan, with Wendell's aid, had sought to bribe Congress to accept Lecompton. Here Robert J. Walker became the star witness, for he was known to possess a letter from Buchanan proving that at the outset the President approved the Kansas policies he subsequently repudiated. The existence of this proof had been vigorously denied by cabinet members, especially the choleric and rather ailing Attorney General Black. Black let himself be trapped into calling a clerk a liar, when the latter said he had seen the letter. Seizing this chance to discomfit both Buchanan and Black, Walker produced the letter for the committee records. It gave Douglas men a choice opportunity to blast Buchanan as a double-crosser. It came out just in time to be sent to Charleston on the eve of the convention.[36]

During all this controversy, as the Democratic convention approached, juicy bits and choice morsels of the testimony appeared in the press. Once the *New York Herald* printed some before it was presented to the committee. The cumulative effect was further to discredit the integrity of the party in power, already shaken by prior investigation. Similarly other unfriendly committees of the House had been at work. They were careful to report embarrassing bills well in advance of the meeting of the convention. They brought in a homestead proposal, a protective tariff measure and bills to reform printing and the mail service. A special committee drafted a bill to provide a subsidy for a Pacific railroad. Only the homestead bill passed the House before the convention; but the measures were on the legislative docket in embarrassing array, with all the subsidy lobbies behind them, ready to accuse the Democrats if they failed.

VI

On the eve of the convention Congress was in a fierce mood which boded ill for the Charleston conclave. On April 5 in committee of the whole Owen Lovejoy, brother of the murdered antislavery editor Elijah, let loose a diatribe on slavery as the amalgam of all the crimes. As he warmed to his subject he walked up and down the aisle and in front of the Democratic benches, gesticulating and shaking his fists at the slaveholding members. Pryor of Virginia ordered him back on his own side. Potter of Wisconsin rushed to his defense, and a fight seemed imminent as both sides surged into the well of the House. Order was finally restored. A southern Congressman recorded: "I never said a word to anybody but quietly cocked my Revolver in my pocket and took my position in the midst of the mob, and as coolly as I write it . . . now, I had made up my mind to sell my blood out at the highest possible price. All that I felt like saying was that gentlemen will take partners for a cotillion." So far had reason and decorum fled.[37]

Four days later, after members had a chance to read the incident in the *Globe,* Pryor rose in the House to accuse Potter of altering the record by additions to his own remarks. Potter retorted that Pryor, too, had altered the record, by erasing some of Potter's corrections; a dishonorable trick, he charged. Pryor admitted his alterations, excusing them because Potter had written in something which Pryor claimed he himself had not said. Potter had insulted him, Pryor shouted, and at the end of the day's session he sent his Wisconsin opponent a challenge to a duel. Potter accepted, naming bowie knives as the weapon. Pryor's second scorned this as barbarous. No duel took place. Each side now cried coward at the other. The most dangerous aspect of the incident was that it did not seem ridiculous.

The situation became almost unbearable. Senator Hammond feared that "as everybody has a revolver and the South does not intend again to be surprised into hearing another Lovejoy speech, a general fight in one or the other House with great slaughter is always on the tapis. There are no relations, not absolutely indispensable in the conduct of joint business, between the North and South in either House. No two nations on earth are or ever were more distinctly separate and hostile than we are here."[38] The day after these words were written the Charleston convention opened its sessions.

Chapter 15

The Disruption of the Democracy

IT WAS APRIL, and Charleston in any April can evoke a poet's ecstasy. Its air was warm and soft, its foliage luxuriant, its architecture elegant, its manners polished and languid. It was the great cultural center of southernism; a spiritual capital, it might be called. Here were the most fervid traditions of southern loyalty, the most elegant pattern of southern civilization. It was a Mecca which many southerners, whether they realized it or not, approached in a frame of mind resembling reverence. Also it was the only one of the ten large cities in the nation which was not forging ahead with rapid strides. Time had a tendency to stand still there. Thither the Democracy was thronging.

Never before had an American political convention been held in such an exotic environment. Charleston was unique, a place by itself; and it was fateful chance which had chosen it. The imps of Satan must have chuckled with devilish glee to learn that the Democratic party was to meet that year in the South, and in Charleston of all places. A bitter struggle for control was imminent, and the life of the party hung in the balance. Men of desperate political fortunes were to meet other men exalted by fanatic zeal to defend all they held dear. In numbers they were almost evenly matched. The environment was one of the most powerful influences which were to turn the balance.

Most of the delegates were oppressed by the probability of the loss of party power. This prospect was the more fearful because of the images of the probable Republican victors conjured up by the more apprehensive. In the southern states they were hated as the backers of John Brown. If they should win, more fiends of this character would be unloosed to invade the South and arm the slaves for revolt and rapine. Victory would also give the Republicans a rare office-filling advantage. The new rulers would appoint a host of federal officials and select postmasters, marshals and customhouse officers in communities throughout the South. And whom would they appoint? Patently not slaveholders; almost inevitably they would select humble folk, the non-slaveholders to whom Helper had appealed so vigorously in his *Impending Crisis*. This submerged class, already sometimes restless, would be rallied to create the new party in the South, and probably would be urged to oppose slavery. Some might conceivably become abolition agents, potential John Browns, working to rouse the slaves. Republican victory also meant high taxes for internal improvements for other sections, protective tariffs and the domination of national policy by capitalistic objectives. The South, therefore, would be shorn of power, plundered and laid open to revolution. These alarming possibilities, the delegates from the South knew, were in the minds of their constituents; and they could but echo them in fanatic pitch.

The hypersouthernism stimulated by these apprehensions was exaggerated by the local factionalism. In the lower South, from South Carolina to Texas, the rivalries between Democratic leaders and factions were driving the contenders to ever more extravagant promises to their constituencies. The rising strength of the opposition in these states had like influence, particularly as this opposition had been making its principal capital by denouncing squatter sovereignty as a cheat to the South. Lurking behind this and probably unrealized or at least unadmitted, was the press of stubborn, thwarted ambition. Men like Yancey and Rhett, who had never obtained high place or preferment under the federal Union, might find final realization under a new deal, in a now southern government, if they could bring it into being by their fiery lamentations. Such were the complexes of the southern delegations and their leaders.

To Charleston then the southern delegates brought minds and feelings intense with conviction. They had been through the emotional crisis common to the nation in the last two years and were deeply marked by it. Their communities had been stirred by revivals, made conscious of sin. Dishonesty was a sin; Douglas's cheating platform was sinful. It was a swindle on a par with so many of the stock-jobbing, grafting, Treasury-raiding schemes of corrupt northerners. The southern delegates could use the idea of an honest platform and an honest candidate very effectively against Douglas and squatter sovereignty.

These emotions combined to stimulate one of the strongest of southern drives, the sense of honor. The southern delegates could not in honor connive in another deception like that of 1856 nor support the man who advocated it. Besides, parties in the free states were becoming too much like patronage lotteries; the objects of victory were the spoils, and these northern Democrats were careless of the means used to secure them. It was pleasing to southern delegates to think themselves more concerned with principles. At any rate, having no man, they were going to fight for principle. It would be a convenient and potent weapon with which to slay the treacherous Douglas. Thus emotionally equipped for battle, the southern delegates journeyed to the shrine of southernism, Charleston.

Their fellows from the Northwest came into this strange environment in a new mood, for they were in even more desperate straits. They fully believed, and it was probably true, that their only hope of political survival was Douglas. He alone could carry any of their states. If they lost this election they were through, so they thought. They also nursed a sense of grievance. The chief weapon their Republican adversaries had against them was the charge that they were vassals of the South, "doughfaces," who at the command of southern slave drivers sacrificed the growing variety of northern interests. They were holding back progress at the command of the backward and sin-ridden South. These western delegates demanded that their southern colleagues recognize the desperate position which confronted them and grant them the one candidate and the only platform that presented a chance of victory. Their real distress and the difficulties which they faced probably were understood by Douglas's senatorial enemies; but the zeal of those enemies for their rival's destruction gave them no wish to impart their understanding to their satellites at Charleston. Southern Democrats at the convention gave no evidence of comprehending the predicament of the northwestern wing.

A third group, the eastern Democrats, came from the "rotten boroughs." The possibility of victory in any of them was slight. In the three most important states—New York, Pennsylvania, and Massachusetts—the party was badly split. Their representatives had come to trade and intrigue for whatever of advantage to themselves there might be. Most of them would be for Douglas as long as he seemed most likely to win, but not a moment longer. Their interest would not preclude a bargain with the South against Douglas if they might gain anything from it. Would these midway traders be able to compose the difference and bargain for unity? They might have been unable to achieve it in any convention center; but certainly nowhere could it be more difficult than in Charleston.

Here the southern delegates were at home; the city was theirs, doors were open, tables were spread, many were spared the discomforts of hotel fare in the lavender-drenched guest rooms of these wide-porched mansions. For the Charlestonians made it a gala occasion. Luxurious carriages, liveried servants, beautiful dresses were ever in view on the streets, for many ladies attended the convention. They were intensely interested, their applause was frequent, and their congratulations effusive —for their own kind.

This was the secret of the convention—many were there who were not their own kind. For the westerners, for the New Englanders, for the Tammany delegates, it was a strange place, an unfriendly place, an uncomfortable and expensive place. In 1856 the northern managers, in the glow of their relief over the nomination of Buchanan, had offered to meet in Charleston as an olive branch to the defeated southern bloc. Since then they had repented. When the usual agents of the state delegations had gone down during the winter to investigate the housing question and to seek headquarters, they were unpleasantly surprised. The hotel accommodations were very limited, and the local bonifaces had joined in agreement to fix the price of board and lodging at the then high figure of $5.00 per diem. The northwestern organization had attempted to persuade the national committee to change the city, but in vain. The state organizations had to make contracts with the local innkeepers, whom they found exacting.

The clan Douglas had sought to ease the burden of expense by hiring a hall, the Hibernia, and converting its second floor into a great dormitory with rows of beds, where probably a minimum of sleep could be had, and that under the difficulties of a variety of respiratory noises and the heat of early Carolina summer. The thermometer was approaching 100°, and it was made no cooler by the scanty bathing facilities or by the heavy dressing habits of the day. Most from the North were uncomfortably overclad. They could but be aware that few plates were laid for them, few charming ladies paid them compliments or even noticed them save with a faintly suppressed disdain. When they arose to speak there would be few cheers and some hisses. So the western delegates congregated in lonesome fashion around Hibernia Hall or at the Mills House. Tammany braves, however, proceeded to get drunk and make night hideous. The boorishness, according to southern standards, of some of these delegates was only exaggerated by the unfamiliarity of the environment.

II

The delegates began coming in on Wednesday April 18, and scattered about the town. The Mills House was reputed to be able to accommodate fifteen hundred in the easy manner of putting five or so in a room. Here the principal delegations congregated, though the Charleston House attracted several important southern contingents. Lesser hotels, boarding houses, and lodgings had their quotas; in them there was plenty of room and cheaper board, according to the rooming bureau which had been set up at Institute Hall, the place of meeting.

Saturday was the busiest day of arrival with the New York, Pennsylvania, and Massachusetts delegations debarking from boats. The New Yorkers came on the *Nashville,* full of hilarity from the start. A large crowd had seen them off in New York and in its exuberance had pelted them with oranges, to the discomfiture of at least one of the more dignified, August Belmont, who was hit below the belt and had to retreat below. This delegation was not certain of the entertainment facilities it might find, and so a sprightly contingent of "amiable females" was on board for a business trip.

The arriving delegates found much to interest them in this unusual city. The number of Negroes, the policemen on horseback armed with swords and pistols, the enormous variety of drinks set forth lavishly on the bars in iced bowls, the green peas and strawberries, the number and skill of the pickpockets, all these aroused interest, to say nothing of the temperature ranging around 100° in April.

On Sunday many went to church. The chief attraction was the Zion African Church, attended by a congregation of two thousand. Here the rafters rang with the strains of "Blow ye the trumpet, blow," "The Year of Jubilee has come," "Return, ye ransomed sinners, home," and the visitors listened to a rousing sermon on the text, "How shall we escape if we neglect so great salvation?" Many gaped open-mouthed at a pretentious Negro funeral. During the week there was to be varied entertainment. At the Charleston Theater a skillful magician, Professor Jacobs, aided by his "goblin," Sprightly, was to do wonderful things with cards, rabbits, and a goose. The ladies of Charleston were holding a fair. Gilmore's Brass Band, brought by the Massachusetts delegation, proved so popular that it nearly saved the party. Excursions were arranged to neighboring plantations and up the rivers and around the bay. Also faro bankers were ready and willing to entertain, and the visiting "ladies" were not without occupation.

Political preparations were not lacking. Judge Magrath of the federal district court apparently was not unmindful of the political calendar. He filled a page of the Charleston papers while the delegates were arriving with a lengthy decision on the slave trade defying the federal government in true South Carolina style. The case had to do with the long-standing effort of the federal government to punish Captain Corrie of the *Wanderer* for carrying on the illegal but profitable business of importing slaves. Georgia had been endeavoring for months to get Corrie back from South Carolina to try him, and Judge Magrath had continually refused to surrender him. In desperation, Attorney General Black finally ordered the federal district attorney to enter a nolle prosequi on the South Carolina indictment, which would clear away the obstacle to Corrie's surrender to and trial in Georgia. Now Judge Magrath refused to admit the nolle prosequi and rendered a long opinion which freshened the slave trade and states' rights issues at a psychological moment.[1]

As the delegates settled down—if such a phrase can be used to describe the turgid state of affairs—certain political lines were beginning to appear. The clan Douglas was uncomfortable but compact and was well led by the veteran floor leader, William A. Richardson. They believed they had a majority of the delegates, and they had well considered plans for organization and nomination. So well disciplined had they appeared, even in Washington, that history was in the process of nearly repeating itself.

The senatorial party leaders were disturbed by this solidarity of the Douglas bloc. They saw that the southerners were strong in enthusiasm, but feared that, unless they themselves supplied it, there would be neither leadership nor a candidate who could offset the "Little Prairie Man," as some now called Douglas. Once again the high command of 1856 went into action; on April 21 Slidell arrived to be joined by Bright and Bayard, the latter, again the only delegate among them, and again in quarters hired by Barlow. Benjamin alone was absent. They set up headquarters in an ancient Charleston mansion in the rear of an ice-cream parlor and began the task of lining up a "Stop Douglas" move.

At first the senatorial group had expected Hunter to be the man to beat the Little Giant, and the administration had agreed. The expressed sentiments of the arriving delegates led keen observers to believe that the Virginia Senator might count on all the South except Kentucky, Tennessee, and perhaps Missouri. The Bluegrass state was reputedly for James Guthrie, though Breckinridge was actually its choice; Tennessee rallied behind Senator Andrew Johnson, with Douglas as its second choice, while Missouri was split between Guthrie and Douglas. Unfortunately, Hunter's friends inadvertently injured his support by their initial actions. They were in the dilemma of needing northern as well as southern votes. In order to show their "national" character they refrained from attending a general conference of southern delegates and let it be known that they would support the Cincinnati platform if Hunter were nominated upon it. They conferred with northern delegations, invited their support, and had definite hopes that part of the Massachusetts group might join in their plan. Their opinions of the fire eaters were bitter; men like Yancey, they fumed, did not belong in the convention.

Such acts and expressions cooled the ardor of some of the Gulf-state men and set them to looking for someone else. Jefferson Davis gained favor, though Slidell had a letter from him urging his friends to vote for others, such as Guthrie, Hunter, or Dickinson. There was greater interest among the Gulf Squadron in Breckinridge and Lane, who were in excellent standing both with their senatorial colleagues and with the administration. Buchanan was particularly interested in Lane though his interest was no longer much of an asset. The border-state delegates had hope of James Guthrie and even a willingness to accept some northerner of safe views like Horatio Seymour or Daniel S. Dickinson of New York.[2] Such was the situation that the three Democratic Senators, Slidell, Bright, and Bayard, sought to direct. The four years had not changed them much. Slidell still framed his red and scornful face with a mass of white hair. Bright emphasized his paunchy figure by wearing a yellow vest. Bayard remained a picture of philosophic calm with classic features set in a frame of long curly hair.

The program of the Senatorial Three was simple. They hoped to work through the key committees of credentials, permanent organization, and resolutions. Since these groups consisted, as usual, of one delegate from each state, and since there were fifteen southern states, each committee had a nucleus of fifteen southern voters. Joining them were two more, the men from California and Oregon—the first because of patronage arrangements lately consummated by Gwin and the administration, and the second because of Lane's hopes.[3] Thus seventeen of the thirty-three members of each of these committees were amenable to the advice of the Senatorial Three and presumably would take their dictation on the permanent officers and the platform. Their key move was to insist that the platform be adopted before the nominations were made.

The delegations from Georgia, Mississippi, Alabama, Florida, Louisiana, Texas, and Arkansas held a meeting at which they agreed to stand on the Alabama platform demanding federal protection of slavery in the territories. They would fight Douglas with principles and set up this platform on which he could not run. They would secure such a platform by letting it be known that the Gulf Squadron would steam out of the convention if their formula were rejected. The Hunter men from Virginia carefully refrained from joining this move.

The clan Douglas easily detected this strategy but were not particularly concerned. They believed that they had a majority of the delegates, that they controlled the national committee by one vote, because the Missouri member was friendly, and that they were thus assured of the temporary organization. Such an advantage would prevent the Fernando Wood delegation from receiving any preliminary recognition and would give the Douglasites the solid vote of New York on the important question of organization. They were not to be intimidated by threats.

Both sides indeed were careless of consequences. In reality neither of them actually dreaded a split. The Douglas men felt that a secession of several delegations—such as Alabama, South Carolina, and perhaps Mississippi—might aid Douglas, rouse sympathy for him, and cause his easier nomination. The Senatorial Three had even a greater hope. If there were a schism, and two candidates, this result would throw the election into Congress because no candidate would have an electoral majority. The House was so divided that no party was in control, and certainly no Republican could be elected. Probably therefore it would be for the Senate to choose a Vice President, who through lack of a presidential choice would then become Chief Magistrate. The Senate was safely Democratic, safely southern. Added to this carelessness over consequences, the environment made both sides reckless and uncooperative.[4]

III

The convention was to open in Institute Hall on Monday April 23 after the Sabbath so variously spent. The delegates awoke that morning in contrasting stages of eager anticipation, or hangover, to be greeted by the stifling, dusty air of drought-ridden Charleston. All were pleasantly surprised by an air-clearing shower in the middle of the morning which lightened the atmosphere and to that extent eased the tension. The delegates straggled into the building after noon and soon found themselves in a hall dominated by the noise of traffic rattling over the cobblestones outside. The impossibility of hearing much that went on proved not the least of the handi-caps under which the partisans labored.

In the opening moves the Douglas organization functioned smoothly and in full control. McCook of Ohio nominated Flournoy of Arkansas, one of the few southern Douglas men, for temporary chairman, and he was accepted without opposi-tion. Also the efforts of the Wood delegation from New York to secure preliminary recognition were squelched. The various committees were then appointed, and the first day was ended.[5] On Tuesday, however, the Senators scored. The committee on organization composed of fifteen southerners, with their satel-lites from California and Oregon, outvoted the sixteen remain-ing, to bring in the name of Caleb Cushing of Massachusetts for permanent chairman. This vain and talented individual was in sympathy with the opponents of Douglas and was to rule rather consistently against the strategy of the Douglas leaders.

The committee on organization brought in also a set of rules over which it had deliberated most of the night. At a meeting the previous afternoon it had planned to resubmit the rules of 1856 but just before the convention reconvened the next morning, it had another meeting at which some mem-bers were not present, and added a new rule: "That in any State which has not provided or directed by its state conven-tion how its vote may be given, the convention will recognize the right of each delegate to cast his individual vote." This stirred up a hornets' nest because it applied the unit rule only where state conventions had prescribed it; otherwise minority groups or individuals were free to vote their choice. Such a rule was a distinct advantage for Douglas. It ratified the action of his managers who had prescribed the unit rule in the con-ventions they had controlled and froze the minorities in New York and Indiana. It likewise freed about twenty-five minority delegates in states generally in the South where the unit rule had not been stipulated. The new rule was adopted, 198–101, which was jubilantly proclaimed by the Douglas men as the measure of their candidate's strength, only four votes less than the necessary two-thirds. Their majority included Maryland, Missouri, Kentucky, and Tennessee. The eleven southern states in opposition had support only in the expected California and Oregon and in administration Pennsylvania.

At the close of the second day the Douglas men made a fateful decision which may have spelled their doom. They accepted the senatorial scheme of making the platform before choosing the nominee. They agreed to this probably because they were sure that they could write the final platform since they had a majority of the delegates. Likewise they did not care if Yancey and a few others walked out. Their majority could always construe the two-thirds rule as meaning two-thirds of the votes cast on a given ballot, if there was a quorum, and a secession would make their proportion all the larger.[6]

The Douglas managers gained a notable success on the third day when the Regency delegation in New York was admitted and Fernando Wood's cohorts were finally excluded. But this day was shortened by the announcement of the death of the chairman of the Vermont delegation, which brought an adjournment late in the afternoon and gave the sore troubled platform committee more time to labor. On the breeze-swept battery, there was the music of the Boston band and relief from the heat. Thither scores of the delegates went and found many of the Charleston elite driving up and down. It was a welcome contrast to Institute Hall drenched in oratory and perspiration. All knew the morrow would produce a bitter struggle. So they enjoyed the breeze and the music, and looked out to unfinished Fort Sumter, all unmindful of its dramatic role so soon to be played.[7]

This delightful interlude was not vouchsafed the platform committeemen who argued behind the closed doors of Masonic Hall most of the day and night. By morning all knew that no agreement had been reached, and so the day was spent trying to help them. Many delegations and individual members thought they had the magic formula, and all that day dozens were presented to the convention with accompanying remarks. They were all referred to the hard-pressed committee, which spent another night in a vain attempt at agreement. The varying phraseologies which today seem so trivial in their differences were becoming not so much meaningful statements as verbal badges of the factions struggling for the control of the nomination.

Wearily on Friday morning the committee confessed itself unable to settle on one formula and submitted three; all included the Cincinnati platform, which proclaimed the right of the people of the territories, whenever their number justified it, to form a constitution with or without slavery and be admitted into the Union. A bare majority of the committee, composed of the fifteen southerners and their California and Oregon colleagues, added to the Cincinnati plank the Senator's proposal drafted by Bayard:

> That the Territorial Legislature has no power to abolish slavery in any Territory nor to prohibit the introduction of slaves therein, nor any power to exclude slavery therefrom, nor any power to destroy or impair the right of property in slaves by any legislation whatever. . . .
>
> That is the duty of the Federal Government to protect, when necessary, the rights of persons and property on the high seas, in the Territories, or wherever else its Constitutional authority extends.

No proposal more distasteful could have been made to the clan Douglas. The minority report of fifteen of the free-labor delegates, Douglas men, added to the Cincinnati platform a clause designed to be a concession:

> That all questions in regard to the rights of property in States or Territories, arising under the Constitution of the United States, are judicial in their character; and the Democratic party is pledged to abide by and faithfully carry out such determination of these questions as has been or may be made by the Supreme Court of the United States.

Benjamin F. Butler of Massachusetts brought in a platform of his own which simply reaffirmed the Cincinnati document.

John Cochrane of New York, who was not on the committee, thought he had a superior phraseology and gave notice that in due time he would introduce a resolution:

> That the several States of this Union are, under the Constitution, equal, and that the people thereof are entitled to the free and undisturbed possession and enjoyment of their

rights of person and property in the common territories, and that any attempt by Congress or a Territorial Legislature to annul, abridge or discriminate against any such equality or rights would be unwise in policy and repugnant to the Constitution, and that it is the duty of the Federal Government, whenever such rights are violated, to afford the necessary, proper and constitutional remedies for such violation.

Thereupon W. W. Avery of North Carolina spoke one hour for the majority report, Henry B. Payne of Ohio, a like space for the minority document, and Butler for himself. The convention then recessed for dinner, only to find the floodgates of heaven opened. Hundreds of ladies in new and festive attire were unwilling to dare the downpour.

At four o'clock that afternoon a real torrent of oratory commenced. The atmosphere was depressing, for the hall was now damp and chilly. Many of the gallery had not had any dinner because of the flooding rain but had waited, determined to push the southern cause; and even the hungriest joined the cheering when some southern eloquence was particularly moving. Barksdale of Mississippi, King of Missouri, Yancey of Alabama, and Pugh of Ohio spoke on into the night. At ten o'clock the Douglas men tried to get a vote. Their tactics were denounced as a move to shut off debate— to apply a gag. Riot broke loose. The southern delegates and the greater part of the gallery joined in the hue and cry, and Cushing lost control. "The delegates gathered in groups and grappled with each other, surging about like waves of the sea"—urged on by the hungry audience. Charleston had never had a show like this. Finally the tumult wore itself out; exhausted and hungry, they adjourned till morning.[8]

The telegraph wires, particularly those leading to Washington, began to sizzle with messages. Senators and cabinet members back in Washington were particularly informed. The jig seemed to be up for the southerners because of the prospect of a Douglas majority and the apparent certainty that his platform would carry. The southern delegates must decide whether to stay or to take a walk. Advice from Washington varied. Senator Hammond telegraphed the Georgia and South Carolina delegates to follow Alabama—with the reservation "if any other state did." On the other hand, Jefferson Davis did not want a withdrawal on the platform. He thought the Gulf Squadron could achieve a greater victory for the South by remaining in the convention and defeating Douglas. At Charleston the contagion of withdrawal was spreading among the southern delegates. The applause of the galleries was doing its work.[9]

IV

Dawn ushered in the crucial Saturday. It was still raining. The temperature had fallen far from the high nineties of the earlier days of the week. All was damp and chill, and fires were welcome. The atmosphere was gloomy in many delegations for purely mundane reasons. The long drawn-out convention was inflating expenses to the unheard-of sum of $10 a day for many a delegate who could ill afford it. Besides, some had been too busy at the active faro banks and were cleaned out. The Pennsylvanians had chartered a special steamer, the *Keystone,* expecting to pay for it by running an excursion for a large gallery, but patronage was too light to make the $8,000 contract price. How could this delegation meet its $2,000 deficit? Today two steamer loads, including a majority of the northern hangers-on, must leave. The most noticeable effect would be the elimination of practically all northern supporters in the galleries. The hisses would now be unpunctuated with cheers.[10]

Over Friday night Senator Bigler had been delegated to assume the thankless role of peacemaker, and he was equipped with a formula designed to save the convention. When the session opened he moved that all the platforms be sent back to the committee, with instructions to report back within an hour this new set of resolutions which he now sent forward. The new formula resolved:

> That the government of a territory, organized by an act of Congress, is provisional and temporary, and, during its existence, all citizens of the United States have an equal right to settle in the territory, without their rights, either of person or property, being destroyed or impaired by congressional or territorial legislation.
>
> That the Democratic party stands pledged to the doctrine that it is the duty of government to maintain all the consitutional rights of property of whatever kind in the Territories, and to enforce all the decisions of the Supreme Court in reference thereto.

A long and hopelessly intricate parliamentary wrangle brought a division of the question. The reports were recommitted, 152–151, against the wishes of the clan Douglas; but then they scored by throwing Bigler's formula out. The convention instructed the committee to report something new at four o'clock that afternoon, and the delegates hurried away to find whatever fires they could.

The committee wrangled fruitlessly until four o'clock had long gone by and then came back with three more reports. The majority had combined ideas of Bigler and Cochrane with those of Bayard, keeping Bigler's first resolve and modifying its own former second clause to read:

> That it is the duty of the Federal Government in all its departments to protect, when necessary, the rights of persons and property in the Territories, and wherever else its constitutional authority extends.

These were distinctions without a great deal of difference.

The minority report had been likewise slightly revised. Its crucial plank now read:

> Inasmuch as a difference of opinion exists in the Democratic party as to the nature and extent of the powers of a territorial legislature and as to the powers and duties of Congress under the Constitution of the United States over the institution of slavery within the Territories.
> Resolved, that the Democratic party will abide by the decisions of the Supreme Court of the United States upon these questions of Constitutional law.

Thus did the clan Douglas practically surrender the doctrine of squatter sovereignty as the price of Douglas's nomination. In making these changes they had lost Indiana, New Jersey, and Minnesota, which had gone over to Butler's reaffirmation of the Cincinnati platform, which again constituted the third report.

The southerners now made a last stand by inaugurating a filibuster. They were not going to permit a vote that day. They wanted Sunday for negotiation and influence. Parliamentary tricks were resorted to until Chairman Cushing began to wilt under the terrific stream of devices which were sprung upon him in quick succession. He had expected to take the floor himself to make an eloquent plea for the majority report, but he was tricked out of the chance. The previous question was sprung in a surprise move which caught the confused management off guard and automatically ended debate. The

vote on the platform must come immediately on reconvening
Monday. At midnight the convention adjourned on the threshold of the Sabbath.[11]

Sunday was a day of feverish negotiation. The Senatorial
Three vied with the Douglas managers in a patronage duel.
The former could pledge census marshalships and other immediate favors, while the latter could deal only in promissory
notes. The lines to Washington again hummed; messenger
boys rushed through the streets of the capital. President Buchanan complained he was not kept informed, but George N.
Sanders had been doing his best to enlighten him. He had sent
the President a long and fervent telegram which included the
revised report of the minority *in extenso*. He urged that the
administration now support Douglas. In 1856 Douglas had
yielded to Buchanan when the latter secured a majority; now
the President should reciprocate. Sanders, however, was
slightly premature, for Douglas had not yet actually obtained
a majority. Buchanan's chief reaction to this advice was an
angry outburst when he learned that the message had been
sent collect, and that he had paid $26.80 for its wisdom.

Shortly after church the weather in the convention city
changed again; the rain ceased, the sun shone, and a refresh-
ing breeze cleared away the clouds and made Charleston
once more a paradise, except for the Ohio and Kentucky
delegations. Their private whisky stock had given out; besides,
the Kentuckians had a contract with their hotel for the accommodation of fifty delegates, and as only twenty had come they
had to make up for the others. Each had to pay $125, and
this without the comfort of Bourbon was hard to bear. Thus
passed Sunday, and, in spite of its sacred influence, nothing
was accomplished in the cause of peace.[12]

V

Monday April 30 was again a beautiful day, but its balmy
loveliness was made somewhat stifling by the tenseness of the
atmosphere around Institute Hall. The convention had suffered
a change. Most of the northern gallery had gone home, and
their places were filled by a great crowd of Charlestonians,
there to see the first act of the great tragedy which was to
have so many of its scenes set in their city. There would now
be next to no support for the clan Douglas in the gallery,
while the admiring applause would be almost deafening when
southern oratory reached its possible heights. Whole blocks of
tickets had been literally thrown to the waiting crowd outside,

and those successful in the scramble were now jamming in. The southern delegates were entering more determined than ever. Virginia had finally agreed to join the Gulf Squadron in demanding a specific plank prescribing federal protection to slave property in the territories.

The test vote was not long in coming, and it revealed the measure of Douglas's strength; his managers carried a vote to substitute the minority for the majority report, 165–138. The Northwest, all of New England save a minority in Massachusetts, all of New York, most of New Jersey, a minority in Pennsylvania, together with twelve scattering votes from the upper South, gave the Illinois Senator's managers control, as long as New York remained in line. With this demonstration of strength recorded, Richardson of Illinois was ready to offer an olive branch to hold the southerners in the convention. The Douglas delegates voted to drop their controversial resolution, referring squatter sovereignty to the Supreme Court and agreeing to abide by its decision. The count stood 238–21; Georgia, Florida, Alabama, Louisiana, Mississippi, Texas, and Arkansas refused to vote.

The remaining planks of the minority platform were quickly adopted "unanimously" because Florida, Alabama, Louisiana, Mississippi, and Texas still refrained from voting. Thus the Cincinnati statement on slavery was reaffirmed without explanation; protection was pledged to naturalized citizens; support was offered to a Pacific railroad and to the proposal to acquire Cuba; personal liberty laws were condemned. When this great hurdle was surmounted Stuart of Michigan made the usual motion to reconsider and to lay that motion on the table. But in performing this task he went out of his way to make a bitter speech, in which he virtually pushed the Gulf Squadron out of the convention. Did he and the Douglas chiefs really hope they would go and thereby set in motion a wave of northern sympathy to insure the Senator's nomination? Would Douglas himself have approved a speech so dangerous to Democratic unity? Whatever Stuart's motives, consequences followed thick and fast.

While refraining from voting, the southern delegates had been conferring. Alabama was under definite instructions to withdraw at this point, but there was division of counsel. Many southerners, particularly the Virginia delegation who wanted to nominate Hunter, were certain that the only way to defeat Douglas was to stay in the convention. After all, had not the Douglas men, by agreeing to abide by a Supreme Court decision, really conceded the point that slave property was safe in the territories? The senatorial clique was of this opinion and had sent for Yancey the night before and impressed upon him the need of disregarding his instructions. There is some evidence that he was willing and sought to persuade his delegation to postpone action. This possibility disturbed the Douglasites, particularly in Alabama and the Northwest. It may be the explanation for Stuart's bitter speech. Whatever may have been Yancey's willingness to yield, he was overruled. The Mississippians seem to have descended upon the hesitant Alabamans with such force that they threw off their doubts and were ready to withdraw.

The convention was splitting because the forces moving toward disruption had proved explosive. First there was the quarrel over principle, a point particularly strong in the South. Then there was fear of the political consequences of accepting a Douglas platform; it would play into the hands of the opposition in the southern states. Bad blood between southern and northern delegates, personal antagonisms, and resentment at the domineering tone of the majority, all stirred toward violent action. Finally it was apparent that the Douglas managers had the votes, and that even if Douglas were kept from the nomination his friends would control the party and would reject any nominee not pleasing to them. Southern delegates would not accept this inferior position, not with Charleston society looking on.

Thus when Stuart finished, Leroy Pope Walker arose to cast the die. He read and sent to the chair Alabama's protest against the denial of southern rights. No audience could have been more encouraging. Had the convention met in Chicago with the Douglas cohorts filling the galleries or in New York with the Tammany-Mozart boys shouting down each other and the South, the result might not have been the same. Yancey and his colleagues now solemnly marched out of the convention midst the plaudits of the gallery. Alabama was not marching alone; Mississippi followed, so did Louisiana and South Carolina, with Florida and Texas bringing up the rear. With every withdrawal there was oratory, and Charleston hearts were warmed as never before. Here was what Rhett and the radicals for years had been praying for. Southern states were defying their northern neighbors, were acting in concert, with Charleston providing a perfect setting for the drama.[13]

Chapter 16

Everybody's Plans Go Awry

THE "WALKOUT" had been taken despite doubts on the part of the senatorial managers. As a precaution Senator Bayard went with the seceders to guide them in forming a Constitutional Democratic convention at Military Hall, perhaps to see that they did not go too far. Here the six Gulf states were joined by four delegates from Arkansas, three from Missouri, two from Georgia, one from Virginia, and a second from Delaware. Fernando Wood's forty-one delegates also offered to come in, but were persuaded to withdraw as they were not really part of the larger convention. Bayard was made chairman, and the majority report on platform was adopted. The bolters were nervous about what they had done; Yancey was careful to deny the stigma of "disunion," and efforts to make nominations were resisted. They wanted to see if any olive branches might be sent in from Institute Hall.[1]

While the Constitutional Democrats were thus engaged, the Douglas leaders were preparing to nominate him, expecting to command easily two-thirds of the remaining delegates, which under their construction of the rules would be sufficient. Obstacles arose in the meantime; it was not going to be so simple. Monday night the 30th, more delegates decided to take a walk. Two-thirds of the Georgia group and a majority from Arkansas were announced as withdrawing Tuesday. During the night representatives of the upper South had met with some from New York to seek once more a compromise formula. They hoped to reunite the convention by adding some pacifying clause to the simple reaffirmation of the Cincinnati platform which alone had survived Monday's barren victory of the Clan Douglas.

The results of their deliberations were ready for the opening of the Institute Hall convention Tuesday morning. The Tennessee proposition, as it was called, had been drawn up by New York, Tennessee, and Kentucky with the sanction of Virginia, and drafted in final form by Judge Church of New York. Their formula consisted of two propositions. On slavery they proposed:

That all the citizens of the United States have an equal right to settle with their property in the Territories of the United States, and that, under the decisions of the Supreme Court which we recognize as a correct exposition of the Constitution of the United States, neither their rights of person nor property can be destroyed or impaired by Congressional or Territorial legislation.

Secondly, on the balloting they proposed that the nominee must receive two-thirds of the total vote of 303, or 202, not two-thirds of the remaining 253, or 169, as the western chieftains had planned. This was really the work of the New York delegates, who wanted to arrange for unity on a compromise candidate and a compromise platform and were therefore anxious to prevent the nomination of Douglas by an incomplete convention. After a long technical debate the question was divided, and the ballot proposition passed, 141–112, with the help of New York which left the Douglas majority on this issue. The Douglas managers were bitterly disappointed.

No action was taken on the first part of the Tennessee resolution; the Cincinnati platform stood still uninterpreted when the balloting for the presidential nominee commenced. On the first trial, Douglas had 145½, Hunter 42, Guthrie 35½, with 30 scattering. Douglas failed to get 3 from Maine or any from New Jersey. Hunter's main support came from Virginia, North Carolina, Maryland, and Massachusetts. Guthrie had Kentucky, New Jersey, half of Missouri, 9 from Pennsylvania, and 3 from Maine. Tennessee voted for her favorite son, Andrew Johnson. During that day and the next, fifty-seven ballots were taken. Douglas gradually climbed, and from the thirty-second through the thirty-fifth tally he had 152, or a bare majority of the full convention. He had secured 2 from New Jersey, 2 from Maryland, 1½ from Massachusetts, ½ from Pennsylvania, and 1 from Tennessee. This was slightly offset by the loss of 1 from Minnesota, but 1 from Virginia came over to make the majority. Hunter in the meantime had lost practically all but Virginia and fell to just 16. Guthrie was beginning to gather in the opposition and came up to 65½. On the fifty-seventh ballot Douglas fell to just under a majority, 151½.[2]

The protracted balloting on May 2 showed to impartial observers the futility of further proceedings unless the Douglas managers were willing to drop him and agree upon a compromise candidate. But the Clan thought victory was in sight if they kept on fighting, and so they decided upon a bold plan. They would recess the convention for six weeks and endeavor to capitalize fears of disunion and secession. By this coup d'état, as it was soon called, they hoped to arouse the Union-loving Democrats in the South to send new delegations to replace those which had withdrawn. The interest of northern delegates might at the same time be strengthened, particularly in New York. If this plan succeeded Douglas might still be nominated by the semblance of a united party. So thought the Northwest phalanx.

When word came to the seceders' convention, now moved to the Charleston Theater, that the main convention had recessed until June 18 when it was to reassemble at Baltimore, the managers were taken aback. This was not what they had anticipated. They sat there, nonplused, the delegates in the theater pit facing their officers ill at ease on the stage, with a curtain painting of the Borgia Palace as a backdrop behind them. The moment was most awkward. The senatorial clique had expected a compromise candidate and reunion; now they all must go home and fight for their places.

There was naught the seceders could do now, even in such an atmosphere of dramatic conspiracy, but recess in turn. They agreed to meet again at Richmond June 11, and Senator Bayard carefully closed the deliberations with a neat Union speech.

This meeting in a theater, before so suggestive a background, was ironically appropriate and symbolized an overtone which pervaded the whole performance. The Douglas clan had wanted to get rid of a few fire eaters to make his nomination the easier. But too many had gone out, and New York had played politics. The seceders on their part, when they left, thought that by going they would make more certain a compromise. They had walked only a few doors away to await the signal to return. To their consternation the invitation had not come. Both sides had overplayed their hands, surely. Or were the disrupting forces unleashed by the converging tensions too strong for any party to withstand?

At evening on May 3 there was a rush to get away from Charleston on the rickety, slow-moving night train. Everybody tried to crowd aboard that night. Those going to Washington would have to change six times. According to one correspondent the most conspicuous men on the train were the Senators and the faro-bank men. The former were bedraggled; the latter, jubilant; these had been nine expensive days, in politics as well as in pocketbook. The gamblers were in high fettle; theirs was the harvest.[3]

II

At Washington all was confusion. The disruption of the convention had been threatened but not desired. When the first news of the walkout arrived the fire eaters at the capital "blanched and shrunk." Senator Hammond observed that "it was clear at once that all their big talk was bosh and many of them owned that there was such a fearful union feeling in their states and districts that they would be broken down if we went *too far*—that is, did anything but talk." The senatorial managers were not too well satisfied with their management.[4] They now had to reckon with the northwestern phalanx.

The Douglas men were moving heaven and earth. They had a tremendous, nay almost impossible, task. They not only had to seek new support but also had to mind their own lines so that they would remain intact. The New Yorkers were willing to trade, and the senatorial managers might do business with them if they would leave Douglas. Another danger the phalanx must take into account was Douglas himself.

The Little Giant had not had a pleasant winter. Mrs. Douglas had maintained their extensive establishment on New Jersey Avenue in brilliant style but had to fight the reigning southern hostesses. Her aunt, Mrs. Greenhow, was venomous. Miss Lane, the first lady, cut her dead in public. Prominent southern and administration figures would not accept invitations. Mr. and Mrs. Douglas even felt that the administration tried to keep guests from their table; some undoubtedly felt it more politic not to go. Douglas himself was tired and sick, in fact so on the down grade that he had but one more year to live. He was drinking again. During the convention he had been nervous and uneasy as though he intuitively realized his defeat. He had developed a persecution complex, thinking of his enemies as bloodhounds who were after his political life. When drunk he could get maudlin with self-pity and lose his nerve. In such a mood Latham found him the day after the convention recessed. When in this condition he must be kept off the floor of the Senate, for in the general wrangle he might be baited to say something which would pour oil on the fire. It was a nervous time for his operators.[5]

The contest focused on efforts to secure new southern allies and delegations to take the place of the fifty seceders. The

Douglas managers were confident that there was some chance of success in Louisiana, Alabama, Georgia, and Arkansas, but that little could probably be done in South Carolina, Mississippi, Florida, or Texas. They pinned their faith on Pierre Soulé in Louisiana, John Forsyth and ex-Governor Winston in Alabama, Alexander H. Stephens in Georgia, and Thomas B. Flournoy in Arkansas. They expected these leaders to try to secure Douglas men to return to Baltimore.

On the other side the party spokesmen, in most of the states whose delegations had withdrawn, sought to secure public endorsement of their acts; and the Douglas men exploited these occasions as an opportunity to attempt to organize their own strength. State committees were meeting, and in some instances district and state conventions. At these deliberations southerners considered whether to approve the bolt or return to Baltimore.[6]

The Douglas managers continued their previous efforts to make a strategic southern alliance by using the Vice Presidency as the basis for a treaty. Their strongest hopes were in Georgia, where they thought of Stephens and found him not unresponsive. Other and sometimes irresponsible negotiations were attempted. George N. Sanders had the temerity even to try to interest none other than Yancey. Several individuals to their later disappointment thought themselves favored. Douglas's own preference probably continued to be Stephens.[7]

With the field operations thus unfolding, Washington became the headquarters for working out grand strategy. The Senate once more became a political convention. The southern Senators had everything to lose if the party split. Their power would vanish, if defeat of the Democracy opened the way for the Republican and opposition parties to gain ground. The party must be rid of Douglas, partly because they did not want him elevated above them, and partly because he was a liability in the South. It was of first importance to get the convention back together; and second they would provide a platform, the Davis resolutions endorsed by the South; Toombs and Thompson would even accept the Tennessee platform.

To bring back the delegates the southern Senators composed an address urging return on the ground that the Democratic party was the last conservative organization remaining. To this they secured the signatures of both Senators from Arkansas, Georgia, Louisiana, and Virginia, together with those of Jefferson Davis and ten Congressmen. These men believed that "if the South would only unite, she could secure all her rights," and they deplored the existence of "so little of unity, so much of discord, jealousies and distrust" among the leaders. One signer, Representative Lucius Q. C. Lamar of Alabama, testified that he had endured mental torture at Charleston, and he lamented, "O, will the noble spirits of the South ever become a band of brothers, before the chains of the oppressors unite them." So thought Jefferson Davis, who had tried to keep his fellow Mississippians from bolting. Some southern constituents were beginning to realize the fatal import of the rabid southernism and were urging the signers to arrest it.[8]

As to their platform, the southern Senators decided to put all their influence behind the Davis resolutions, in order to encourage the bolters to return. Perhaps they thought Douglas might be teased into some indiscretion in debate. Jefferson Davis led off on May 7 with the old charges and arguments. The South would not accept Douglas unless he agreed to protect their rights. Benjamin attacked Douglas's strongest point, his claim that he was the choice of the majority. Benjamin argued that he only seemed to have this advantage because the uneven working of the unit rule prevented minorities in the New York, Indiana, and Minnesota delegations from voting for others.[9]

Douglas attempted to reply, but he was not in his usual form. He went over the old ground ineffectively, demanding that the South accede to the will of the majority. As he thought that when the convention reassembled his forces would be in control[10] he could not withdraw. So he declared defiantly that he would not yield ground. He got little support in the Senate, for Pugh alone stood with him.[11] Clingman and Toombs tried to promote a compromise by reviving the old doctrine of nonintervention in the territories, which would have been acceptable to Douglas; but there was no response from their southern colleagues.[12] The Davis resolutions were passed by the Senate.[13] Douglas and his lieutenants would undoubtedly disregard them.

The executive heads were just as eager to frustrate Douglas as were the Senators. They used the patronage, not only to induce the bolters to return, but also to prevail upon the trading eastern delegations to break away from the northwestern clan and vote to readmit those who had "taken a walk." The 1860 census was imminent, and hundreds of deputy marshals were to be appointed to collect the data in every district in the country. The administration tried to make this patronage count in re-forming the convention lines against Douglas.

The operators knew that the key to the situation was the New York delegation, in which the control of the party by the Regency was the real issue. The minority were trying to get the seceders to return; the majority seemed to stand pat on Douglas. Could this loyalty to Douglas be broken? Cobb was much disturbed by the Douglas tactics in Georgia and the efforts to detach Stephens and get new delegates. He sent his right-hand man, Solicitor of the Treasury Hillyer, to labor with the New Yorkers to detach them from Douglas, at least long enough to readmit the bolting southern delegations. He tried also to stir up a boom for William Allen of Ohio and got him to write a letter showing his soundness on slavery. Douglas himself was active in New York, too. His floor leader, Richardson, was there and told Hillyer flatly that the Douglas clan had the votes to keep the bolters out. They must not be readmitted, Douglas warned August Belmont and other New York managers: these bolters did not desire readmission for the sake of harmony but only to break up the convention.[14]

The New York situation suddenly was made embarrassing to the party by an unexpected headline. The postmaster of New York City, Isaac V. Fowler, fled the country when post-office auditors discovered that he was about $160,000 short in his accounts. The truth was that this open-handed gentleman had been using the large funds of his office for the benefit of the Democracy, contributing here, loaning there, particularly at election time. Party workers had not made up these drafts, and when exposure was about to illuminate his shortages he fled to Cuba. His disappearance was announced May 15, and three days later John A. Dix was appointed to take over his office and try to straighten it out. All this embarrassed the sponsoring Democrats and made hay for the Republicans. To the southern Democrats it was but confirming evidence of the corruption of Douglas's northern supporters.[15]

In the midst of all this confusion a significant fact emerged, a fact which brought dismay to the clan Douglas, and which undoubtedly altered the course of events. All the bolting delegations save those of South Carolina and Florida decided to heed the urgings from southerners in Washington and go to Baltimore. In Texas and Mississippi their strength was so great that there was no resistance on behalf of Douglas. In Arkansas district conventions meeting to nominate Congressmen recom-

missioned the delegates to both Baltimore and Richmond; but
Flournoy and the Douglas men got up a small, unrepresentative convention which "filled up the delegation," by making
substitutions for those who had withdrawn. In Georgia, Louisiana, and Alabama the decision to return bolters precipitated
bitter fights with the Douglas men.

In Georgia and Louisiana the old state conventions were reassembled and endorsed the withdrawal. They recommissioned
the delegates over the protests of the Douglas minority who
wanted new ones chosen. In Georgia the minority, about one-
fifth of the convention, held a meeting of its own and chose
a new delegation to join those who had not withdrawn. In
Louisiana Soulé got up a convention which was called too late
to permit state-wide attendance, and he headed a Douglas
delegation named by it. The greatest fight came in Alabama.
There the numerous enemies of Yancey—Forsyth, ex-
Governor Winston, and Seibels—took the lead and assembled
a fair-sized convention, constitutionally of course irregular,
which chose a Douglas delegation. Its main significance was
the fact that its size apparently forced the regular convention
to send the Yancey delegation back to Baltimore, a bitter pill
to the fire eaters, who wished to go only to Richmond. These
decisions laid the basis for an acrid series of contests at
Baltimore.[16]

As the June re-assembling approached, last-minute efforts
were made in Washington, where again many of the delegates
were waiting. Douglas invited Belmont and others to final
conference in his home on English Hill. Secretary Cobb still
hoped he might unite the South and New York behind his
own candidacy. Vice President Breckinridge was keeping open
house. Senator Jo Lane was being his genial self to the many,
and who knows what Mrs. Greenhow was accomplishing for
him? Alexander H. Stephens was a name on many lips, but its
owner was staying quietly at home in Georgia, very potently
"doing nothing."[17]

III

The prelude to the Baltimore performance was staged in
Richmond during the second week in June. The bolters met
as planned, but quite naturally decided to take no steps until
they learned the outcome at Baltimore. Most of them were
going there anyway. At the Monumental City, the traditional
home of Democratic convenings, the real drama was to take
place. The Senatorial Three—Bayard, Slidell, and Bright of

Charleston fame—now had their responsibilities shared by two from the cabinet, Cobb and Thompson, who were the active political minds of the administration and had each an eye out for possible lightning bolts. Their task was to try to harmonize nearly all the warring elements, for the will of the southern Senators had prevailed. After much hesitation the bolting delegations of all but two states appeared in Baltimore ready to resume their seats despite their loss of face and at the expense of their pride. Even the Florida delegation showed up, though but to observe. Only South Carolina refused to move a step north of Richmond.[18] The return of so many upset the plans of the Douglas managers, who had hoped they would stay away and leave the Senator's friends in comfortable control. They must now handle troublesome contests.

The atmosphere at Baltimore was altogether different from that at Charleston. Despite the unwelcome return of the bolters, this was Douglas's convention, and his cohorts were more determined than ever to nominate him and him only. The galleries, quite in contrast to Charleston, were with them. Caleb Cushing once more called the delegates to order, this time in the Front Street Theater; and what a drama was there to be enacted!

The paramount question was the composition of the roll. Who were the delegates from the South? Cushing reported that he had found no power to decide this. The Douglasites were quite evidently determined to admit the newly chosen Douglas delegates, while Virginia took the lead in seeking to have the original designees readmitted wherever they appeared. The upshot was that the credentials committee had to be reconstituted and the disputed claims turned over to it. After long and troubled deliberations it was ready to report on the fourth day.[19]

While it was laboring, various efforts were made behind the scenes for harmony. The Douglas managers accepted the sincerity of most of those bolters who were willing to come back, and sought to avoid more trouble by compromise. They offered to receive those from Mississippi, Texas, Arkansas, and Georgia; they would even accept the "observers" from Florida and the absent South Carolinians. But they insisted on admitting their own new delegations from Alabama and Louisiana; Yancey and Slidell must be punished. Even on this harmony scheme the committee divided.[20]

On the morning of the fourth day, June 21, the first day of summer, the convention assembled at 10. The Reverend Henry

Slicer prayed for peace, and Chairman Cushing announced that the credentials committee was ready to report. The air was tense with expectancy as the throng awaited their work, when suddenly the building was shaken by a great crash and "the wildest excitement ensued." All in the galleries craned their necks and saw below that "the front of the stage and the portion covering the orchestra had given away, and suddenly sunk about three feet in the center, throwing the settees and those who were on them, within a circle of about fifty feet, into one wedged mass, from which they extricated themselves as rapidly as possible and fled in all directions to distant parts of the house. Fortunately no one was injured."

This excitement was followed almost immediately by another. The day was dark and rainy, and the chandeliers were alight. One spectator had sought to dry his umbrella by opening it over a lighted gas fixture. Hundreds saw the foolish act and thought of fire. Frantic calls finally secured the removal of this hazard, and the convention recessed while the floor was repaired.[21]

At noon things were again in order and the credentials committee was heard. As the Douglas managers wished, the committee majority recommended admission of the new delegations for Alabama and Louisiana. The new men from Arkansas and Georgia, who were contesting, should be admitted with the original delegations, and the votes divided. The bolting delegations from Texas, Mississippi, and Delaware were to be readmitted. One minority report, presented by nine of the committee, favored receiving all the bolters. A second minority report signed by one member agreed to the majority report, except that he would have taken back the Yancey delegation from Alabama.[22] Debate continued the rest of that day and into the night, with many southerners insistent for readmission of the Alabama and Louisiana bolters.

The vote was taken on the fifth day. The Douglas clan, still united, voted to accept the majority report, and it carried 150 to 100½. Then New York intervened. When the usual motions to reconsider and to lay the motion to reconsider on the table were made, New York voted against the latter and thus held the door open for possible trading before the issue was closed. Late that afternoon the convention recessed for final bargaining.[23]

Richmond, head of the New York delegation, was in a dilemma. He and his associates—Cochrane, Croswell, Cagger, and others—were desperately in need of party victory regardless of faction. The Empire state was seething with schemes. The Republicans were out after the New York Central with threats of taxation and control; upstate Republicans already had been interfering too much with the interests of New York City. The Regency leaders had hoped against hope that they could trade it out and turn from Douglas to some compromise candidate who might bring victory; but they could find none. To help in this search, Richmond had been trying to preserve party unity through further compromise on credentials; he proposed to modify the majority report so as to accept all the bolting delegates save those from Alabama.

On the other hand Richmond had reasons for wishing to keep Douglas. If the Illinoisan were dropped, Richmond faced the probability that he would lose control of his own delegation. The old Hard minority under Croswell would not take the Soft Seymour but would go either for Dickinson or for some one more pleasing to the South. The old wounds would be opened in public, and New York would be divided and impotent. Richmond was reluctant to let Cochrane or Croswell get away, to lose control. It might be better to insist on Douglas and let secession take its course. Which should be put first, national unity of his party or Regency control of the New York Democracy?

Into this dilemma Douglas interjected a proposal to eliminate himself. The Little Prairie Man had been following events from Washington and was more and more discouraged by the outlook. Before the credentials committee reported, he had supplied Richardson—his faithful Illinois spokesman—with letters withdrawing his name and authorizing him to throw his strength to Alexander H. Stephens. Richardson had full power to act for him. When Friday's session showed no signs of harmony, delegates and others urged him to withdraw. He yielded and wired Richardson and the New York delegation, again authorizing them to withdraw his name.

This wire found Richmond hard put to it. In this predicament he received an ultimatum from the senatorial managers through Slidell; the bolting states would leave again unless Douglas were withdrawn. They offered Cobb as the alternative, or they would accept Horatio Seymour. Would Richmond accept these terms and the wire from Douglas? He made a perfunctory effort to persuade Richardson to withdraw Douglas and take Seymour; to this extent he put party before faction.

Richardson saved Richmond's Regency control for him; he

refused to withdraw Douglas. Even had it been possible for the New York delegation to compose its quarrels, the result would have been no different as long as the Northwest was obdurate. It was steadfast because neither Seymour, nor Dickinson, and certainly no southerner, could have carried their states. As in the Speakership controversy, no group would give away its favorite position for nothing. Thus compromise failed, for no combination appeared strong enough to nominate as long as the northwestern bloc held firm.[24]

When the convention reassembled in the evening, the New York delegation voted to lay the motion to reconsider on the table, and the majority report of the credentials committee was finally accepted. The original Alabama and Louisiana delegates were excluded, and Forsyth and Soulé with their men, not Yancey and the Slidell men, were in their seats. The Douglas spokesmen moved to commence the balloting. Then came the final tragedy. Russell of Virginia arose and announced that most of the Virginia delegation would withdraw. North Carolina, Tennessee, half of Maryland, California, and Oregon followed, and Kentucky and Missouri went out to consult. The convention adjourned in gloom.[25]

On Saturday morning withdrawal continued as most of the Kentucky, Missouri, and Arkansas delegations left. The climax came when Chairman Caleb Cushing stepped from the rostrum and marched out of the convention "under the hope and indirect promise," it was claimed, of the place on the Supreme Court bench made vacant by the recent death of Justice Peter V. Daniel. The same observer reported to Alexander H. Stephens that Cobb and Toombs made "every effort to bring about the rupture." Ben Butler followed in the wake of Cushing, and David Tod of Ohio was designated by the vice presidents to take the chair. The balloting would now begin. There remained 192½ votes of the original 303,[26] and when on the second ballot Douglas secured 181½ the convention declared he had received two-thirds of all votes given and was nominated.

Next arose the question of a running mate. Douglas wanted Stephens, but his managers felt that the decision should be left to the remaining southern delegates. They caucused, and Louisiana pressed Stephens "with enthusiasm," Arkansas seconding the nomination. At this point Alabama came forward with a plea for Senator Fitzpatrick; Forsyth was certain that with him on the ticket, he could beat the Yancey men and carry the state for Douglas. Mrs. Fitzpatrick, the Senator's youthful wife, had been working to get him the place and had stirred him up to seek it. Then a debate arose over Stephens's qualifications. Toombs had said so much about his frail health that some thought he was on the verge of the grave. Others brought up the fact that he had opposed the Mexican War; they expected to make this point against Lincoln, and Stephens's nomination would "spike that big gun." Thus opposed, Stephens's friends went to Richardson for help and he sent in a message urging the nomination. This proved without effect. Fitzpatrick was the man, and the convention ratified the choice of the caucus.

The last task was to retouch the platform left in such a sad state in Charleston. This was the final formula: "That it is in accordance with the interpretation of the Cincinnati Platform that during the existence of the Territorial Governments the measure of restriction, whatever it may be, imposed by the Federal Constitution on the power of the Territorial Legislatures over the subject of domestic relations as the same has been or shall hereafter be finally determined by the Supreme Court of the United States, should be respected by all good citizens and enforced with promptness and fidelity by every branch of the Federal Government." The Douglasites had come over to the Buchanan formula of leaving it to the Supreme Court and, with this concession, adjourned. Douglas had received the nomination after years of effort—a nomination from but a faction of the once dominant Democracy.[27]

Over in Market Hall, the delegates from the southern states congregated, Florida included, and were joined by those from Oregon and California, 11 from Pennsylvania, 2 from New York, and 1 from Minnesota. They represented 105 votes from the old convention. Organization was speedily completed, and Russell of Virginia, the temporary chairman, turned over the gavel to Cushing. The delegates soon adopted the final majority report which had been defeated at Charleston and thereby affirmed that "it is the duty of the Federal Government in all its departments to protect, when necessary, the rights of persons and property in the Territories, and wherever else its constitutional authority extends."

The nominations were hastily made. Some later claimed that the majority preferred Cobb but feared to nominate a man from a radical state of the deep South. Northern men thought Breckinridge was the strongest candidate, and a committee already had gone to Washington to see him.

Benjamin F. Butler later recorded that to this group the Vice President pledged his devotion to the cause of reuniting the party and his disavowal of the doctrine that the South must secede if the Republicans won. Thus assured, the northern delegates nominated Breckinridge over Daniel S. Dickinson, 81–24. Jo Lane was then nominated for Vice President by acclamation. Yancey addressed the convention, but his eloquence palled, for the crowd was "sick of the very sound of the human voice." At eleven that evening they adjourned—an hour and a quarter after their rivals had left the scene of disruption.[28] Though nobody cared much, the Richmond convention reconvened on the 26th and endorsed the nomination of Breckinridge and Lane.[29]

IV

Thus was completed the destruction of the national party of Jefferson and Jackson. Among the southern leaders there was little rejoicing. To be sure they had prevented the nomination of Douglas by a united party, but they had failed to impose their platform and a compromise candidate. Many began to realize that they had destroyed the instrument of their great power. For the first time in the history of the Republic political machinery had broken down. For the first time compromise had failed to avert the disruption which conflict of interests had so frequently invited.

Here was more evidence that a cycle in political behavior had been completed. The Democratic party was entering a new phase. The feuds and rivalries developing in its thirty years of existence were now bearing their bitter fruit and condemning the organization to a period of disintegration and decline. The Republican party, symptomatic of the new cycle, was of a type which the Democracy could not withstand. The new party represented the surge of inevitable demands arising from the nation's growth. As the tides of immigration poured into the country and as the natural increase became manifest, it was apparent that the distribution of this greater population was not uniform. The weight of numbers was more and more tipping the scales in favor of the non-slaveholding communities, the newer and more swiftly growing regions where the younger party took its strength.

The Democracy, so long in power, had sought to maintain itself by establishing a balance through compromise. But the great majority of Americans no longer wished to compromise. The new party saw power within its grasp—a power which, because of the strength of its newly crystallizing constituency, need not compromise with the older interests. Against this surge of power the Democrats could not present a united front.

The southern contingents had seen danger ahead for their interests and had sought to make their party an instrument of protection; the federal government must interpose with measures to quiet the fears of their constituents and enable them to continue to enjoy their support. This had placed the northern Democrats in an impossible position, in danger of being engulfed by the tides of territorial, metropolitan, and antislavery demands. How could they maintain themselves if they tolerated laissez faire and slave protection camouflaged by a scant garment of nationalism?

All groups showed signs of bewilderment. The southern leaders were demanding a protection which they knew they could not get; and if they had got it they must have known it would be useless. Yet they knew not what else to demand. They were for the Union as long as they could rule it; they preferred to rule it. But if they could not? As yet they were not ready to face that reality. They sought refuge in a formula.

The clan Douglas had similar emotions, they were tired of minority status and an ineffective position. The West could advance only if it were really sharing power or if it were free. Some spoke in terms of a western confederacy. On the Pacific coast there was talk of a Pacific confederacy. The northwestern bloc thought of Douglas just as the southerners thought of slave protection; both were symbols of survival. What the Douglas men failed to realize was that no candidate could save most of their state organizations.

The statistics should have been disillusioning to both northern and southern Democrats. Of the fifteen slave states probably fourteen would be Democratic if the candidate and platform were suitable. Of the eighteen free states only seven, Pennsylvania, New Jersey, Ohio, Indiana, Illinois, California, and Oregon held any real chance for a Democrat. These twenty-one states had 200 electoral votes; 154 were necessary for choice. Of this 200, 112 came from the south, 88 from the free states. No southern candidate could be elected without 42 northern votes. No northern candidate could win without at least 66 southern votes. The unfortunate situation was that Douglas, in the state of mind in which he found the South, probably could not have carried 66 southern votes, even had he been able to secure the 88 northern votes listed above.

In other words the shadow of Republican success produced an impossible situation in the Democratic party. Its northern wing was doomed, and the only platforms or candidates which the southern voters would support could do no more than keep the ruling Democratic party in control in the South. If they gave up their strength at home on the gamble of gaining allies to the northward, they would very likely lose in both places. They realized that they could probably keep their local positions if they accepted another dark horse and a meaningless platform, and they were willing to take the risk. They asked therefore that Douglas step aside; he was willing, but his followers were not. Their dangers made them blind, and they forced Douglas to permit the destruction of the Democratic party. For the first time they stood up to the dominant southern managers and exchanged blow for blow and curse for curse. They would teach these "slave drivers" the meaning of the rule of the majority. But the southerners would not learn the lesson. The flight from Democracy had begun.

Chapter 17

Congressional Stalemate

THE TRAGEDY at Baltimore was now a page of history and Congress could return to its duties. These were sorry hours; the stormy and impotent gesturing of the lawmakers was a sign of the functional collapse which seemed to afflict the government. During the seven months of caucusing since December, Congress had performed but a minimum of its duties, and the members must now finish what little more they could and go home to campaign.

The last days of the session were a sad anticlimax for the Democrats. The Republicans in the House continued to add to their embarrassments. They cut Democratic appropriations out of the supply bills and forced the Senate to reinsert items amounting to nearly $7,000,000. The Republican House voted to admit Kansas as a free state under the recently drafted Wyandotte constitution. They proposed to organize five new territories with never a mention of slavery in the bills. They passed a protective tariff which the Senate "pickled" in committee. To add to the party humiliation, the Senate Republicans with the aid of Andrew Johnson and the northern and Pacific coast Democrats passed the homestead measure sent up by the House. Buchanan promptly vetoed it, but the Republicans rejoiced. They had just written promises for protective tariff and homestead legislation in their national platform and could now capitalize on the laissez-faire scruples of the Democracy in a big way.

This battle over new and unusual appropriations and subsidies was but one of many things worrying southern Congressmen. A strange fear was rising, a fear of contamination with corruption through education. As a Georgia solon put it:

"Our state Governments are not, and never can be so corrupt as our Federal government is. Our National Legislators have absolutely forgotten or else they pay no attention whatever to the original purposes for which we made our constitution—he who can secure the most money out of the Treasury to his constituents whether rightfully or wrongfully is the best satisfied with himself. . . . This desire of living upon Government is going South and will destroy the life blood of the Republic—it has already done so at the North and will do the same thing for us. You are aware that the people there at the North, are all *educated* by government, and when educated they expect to *live* upon government, either Town, County, City, State or National and *they will do it,* you can't shake them off, they will be either Office holders or pensioners, to be sure you may take your choice but one or the other they must have.

"This idea of educating *every body* is taking root in the South, our people are beginning to demand taxes for the education of the masses, *every body* must be educated, there is to be no more ignorance after this generation according to the new philosophy, upon the idea that it's easier to build school houses than jails, & colleges than State prisons, but there never was a greater error upon earth, we can build the latter much cheaper, and they are decidedly more useful . . . for every graduate you have, and every educated man among us, you must provide a *place* and a *support* from government for him—they toil not, neither do they spin, nor you can't make them. . . . I am not sure but that you may educate two or three generations and about the 3d they will go crazy, as for instance in New England they are fanatical & foolish— to have a good population, sensible, intelligent, patriotic, they must be an active energetic *laboring* people, cultivating the physical, and not the mental faculties—I speak of *people,* not *individuals,* i.e., such as evince genius & great powers of mind ought to be well educated."[1]

The number of southern writers and speakers who referred to northerners as a corrupt and degenerate people was indeed increasing. From these written and verbal assertions would grow, in many minds, belief; and from this belief it was but a step to the conviction that southerners must free themselves from association with so corrupt a society.

II

Another painful embarrassment of the Democratic party during this futile session was its impotence in Post Office matters. The principal political agency of the federal government was rendered useless for partisan advantage by administrative quarrels and by the rival claims of steamship, railroad, and overland mail contractors. Avaricious enterprisers and speculators were making a joke of congressional prerogative. Their manipulations became a national menace because their schemes fostered the differences between the congressional factions and stimulated the dissatisfaction of the representatives of southernism with the federal system. The expedients which Holt had adopted to meet his lack of funds boomeranged. He had saved $1,725,869 at a heavy political price, particularly when he cut off steamer mails on the Mississippi and between Charleston and Key West. Certain southern senators were vowing vengeance. In fact Holt's policies so upset the South, and roused its ire against the federal system, as to become one of the less tangible factors leading to secession.

At this demoralized session the California mail rivalries reached a climax which showed how avaricious speculators could play horse with much-needed government services. Commodore Vanderbilt was on the scene again. The preceding summer he had cleverly reinjected himself into the California mail situation—as usual, to his own advantage. The last Congress had been the slaughterhouse of the isthmian transportation Monopoly. Rival groups of Nicaraguan speculators, including Vanderbilt, may have been the chief instigators of the carnage; at any rate they rejoiced. Immediately they had set upon Buchanan and Holt to reopen the Nicaraguan route. Holt had to get some one to carry the mail for the rest of the fiscal year after the Monopoly contract expired September 30, 1859. So he invited bids.

Three were offered—one by Vanderbilt, and two by Nicaraguan route rivals. Holt offered the contracts to the lowest bidder, one Johnson, front man for Vanderbilt's erstwhile partner, Joe White, who had joined that indefatigable transit hopeful, A. G. Sloo. Vanderbilt, however, bided his time. The Monopoly had stopped paying him his $56,000 a month for keeping out of competition; now that its contract was dead, he was more than ever determined to get back into the running.

Johnson had made his low bid without any facilities for mail operations, in the expectation that White would secure concessions in Nicaragua and buy or hire the necessary ships; but Vanderbilt neatly stopped all this by intrigue in Nicaragua and by preventing White and Sloo from getting the necessary vessels. He then went to Holt and told him Johnson was a fraud without the means to fulfill his contract. He so impressed the Postmaster General as to secure a conditional contract to carry on, if Johnson failed. Then of course Johnson failed, and on October 5, 1859 his contract had lapsed to Vanderbilt.

Then the Commodore turned to give the Monopoly a solar plexus blow. With C. K. Garrison, who had once double-crossed him on Nicaragua, and Marshall Roberts he formed a new line, the Atlantic and Pacific Steamship Company, and prepared to compete with the Monopoly over the Panama route. This was too much for the staggering combine, and early in 1860 they made their peace with Vanderbilt, at a price. They would operate only on the Pacific and leave the Atlantic leg of the traffic to him. The government profited, for, freed from the Monopoly, Holt had been able to re-negotiate and reduce the California mail charges nearly 50 per cent.

Vanderbilt's triumph seemed destined to be short-lived. The handwriting was on the wall, as far as mail service to California by steamer was concerned, and for two reasons. The overland stagecoach contractors were vigorously represented in Congress, and the sound of railroad whistles in the gorges of the Rockies did not seem too distant. The Republicans were just waiting for a chance to charter the railroad, and in the meantime the Pacific coast Democratic Senators were desperately trying to get new systems of stagecoach service. Rival stage operators were as eager to get Butterfield's stage contract as the steamboat men had been to slay the Monopoly. Gwin had a plan for three overland routes, north, south, and central, which the steamship lobby defeated. Then Latham tried a compromise of benefit to the steamship men, but Republicans and disappointed stagecoach men, probably, brought its demise.

This fatality took place with but five days remaining of the session. The regular Post Office bill had gone through with a provision that ocean mail must be carried for the postage, a figure too low to be attractive. Unless something were done quickly, the subsidy would be lost. Holt was pre-vailed upon to write a letter stating that he could not expect to get the mail carried by sea for so low a figure, and Yulee attached to the Post Office route bill a $400,000 subsidy. Next day, June 23, the last but one of the session, Buchanan supplemented Holt's letter with a declaration that there must be ocean mail facilities because the mails were too heavy— twelve and fifteen tons every fortnight—to be carried in stage-coaches. Yulee then tried a joint resolution for the $400,000, which was lost because Rice of Minnesota objected to its consideration. Sherman brought a bill into the House but withdrew it when Vanderbilt's son-in-law, Clark, said the sum provided was too low; Winslow renewed this bill, but the House refused to suspend the rules, largely because of Republican opposition.

On the last day Yulee tried once more, this time by adding a new clause to the long-pending route bill. To forestall objection from Rice he added an amendment for a weekly mail from St. Paul, Minnesota, to Oregon; and to make it more generally attractive elsewhere he included a *daily* overland stagecoach mail. To the bill in this form the Senate agreed; and the overburdened bill was sent to the House, in the last few minutes of the session. All told, the measure groaned under some hundred amendments. With no time to read them, let alone consider them, Sherman refused to accept it; and an appeal to suspend the rules was defeated. Thus the session closed without any practical provision for the California mail.

Senator Gwin was in a rage and declared he had been double-crossed. He and his colleagues had consented to help defeat a Republican mail bill, otherwise likely to pass, on the understanding that there would be a renewal of the steamship mail contract by the Postmaster General. Now Congress had made no appropriation. Vanderbilt refused to carry the mail, and Buchanan and Holt claimed they had neither money nor power. Gwin had a blistering scene at the White House. Buchanan begged him not to go away in anger—all his friends were leaving him. Gwin snapped back that he deserved none, as he drove them all away. Vanderbilt finally agreed to carry the mail for the postage upon Holt's promise to urge Congress to grant additional compensation in the short session. The Commodore had won again. Once more congressional impotence was playing into the hands of speculators. Again the South had evidence that money was making a mockery of the operation of the federal government.[2]

Equally disillusioning was the treatment accorded Buchanan's continued efforts to make capital through foreign policies designed to expand American interests in Mexico and Central America. The Democratic Senate refused his treaties. There was a much more important reason for his failure than the simple fact that the Democratic majority in the Senate was less than the two-thirds essential to treaty ratification. In truth Buchanan's treaties and requests for power collided with the conflicting attitudes which were wrecking other aspects of his administration. On the one hand southernism had reached the stage where its leaders, with possible secession in mind, hated to give power to a government soon to be controlled by the Republicans. Even where the advantages proposed to be gained were in lands which had a slavery climate, some southerners like Hammond of South Carolina saw dangers in the responsibilities which these treaties would bring. Could the turbulent population of Central America be managed other than by force, and that a force administered by our central government? Would not this turn the American federal system into an imperial centralized government? At the same time the metropolitan, territorial, New England, and antislavery attitudes shied away from pacts which extended territory southward and thereby advanced the slave power. Thus, Congress adjourned without any important action on Buchanan's foreign policy.

<h1 style="text-align:center">III</h1>

The final calamity to the Democracy in this session came when the few remaining tatters of reputation were stripped from the administration, by further damaging revelations and innuendoes. Floyd's peculiar incompetence was given more publicity in a series of exposures which left him little beyond a few reasonable doubts. At one time the Democrats thought of making an official investigation of his acts, to forestall the Republicans.[3] They did not, because it became apparent that the Republican party could not muster the votes; it must depend for its majority on certain of the Douglas Democrats, and Floyd was known to be the one man in the cabinet who was conciliatory to Douglas. Presumably the Republicans alone could not vote his investigation.

Enough came out incidentally, without a special Floyd committee, to supply all normal desires of the Republicans. The Secretary's laxity in awarding contracts came under an unpleasantly bright light in the Senate. Wilson of Massachusetts demanded that Jefferson Davis's military affairs committee investigate Floyd's business methods. Davis avoided an official inquest, but he slipped an amendment into the legislative appropriation bill which very decidedly curtailed the Secretary's power of purchase.[4] It was too easy to sell things to Floyd, and so he had to be protected. Grimes of Iowa sniped in turn by reopening the Fort Snelling sore.[5]

Floyd's business dealings were not his only weaknesses. He was in a series of personal difficulties which further aroused Senator Davis against him. For a number of years a great deal of construction had been going on in Washington under

the direction of the War Department. The wings of the
Capitol, a new dome, a new Post Office building, additions to
the Treasury and Interior departments and a great aqueduct
to bring water to Washington over the giant span of Cabin
John Bridge, were all in the process of building. The engineer
officer in charge as supervising constructor was Captain Montgomery Meigs, a careful, precise, and honest official in whom
Davis had come to have every confidence while he was
Secretary of War. Meigs was not always easy to get along
with and had been feuding with the architect of the Capitol,
Thomas U. Walter. Davis had backed Meigs.[6]

When Floyd came in he looked upon all this construction
in his free and easy way as a source of political patronage.
He wanted to use the labor pay rolls as he used the civilian
clerks in his department. Meigs stood against this with great
firmness.[7] When friends came to Floyd for contracts he
sought to oblige, often careless of the law. A most notorious
incident was the Robinson contract for heating the Capitol.
In this case he awarded this valuable assignment to an adventurous Virginia doctor, who knew nothing of heating and was
going to sublet his concession. Meigs had protested vigorously, and in June, 1858, Senator Seward had secured the
passage of a resolution asking for the details. Floyd had
delayed nineteen months and did not reply until January,
1860. This report was now published and more clearly demonstrated the Secretary's peculiar methods.[8] A second contract mess was brewing over bricks, which was later to boil
over in the De Groot case. Meigs was getting on Floyd's
nerves.

A month before Congress met, Floyd had come to the end
of his short rope as far as the Captain was concerned. The
dispute between the engineer and the architect, Walter, had
so infuriated the latter that he had removed all the drawings.
Meigs then had no way of checking the work against plan
and specifications, and would not pay the bills. Both Floyd
and Buchanan, who was particularly interested because Meigs
was of a prominent Philadelphia family, urged him to pay
the bills without the drawings. When he refused, Floyd sided
with the architect flatly and secured suspension of the supervising constructor. In January, 1860, Floyd had tried to send
him down to superintend the building of forts off the Florida
coast on the Dry Tortugas. Political pressure on Buchanan
prevented this banishment for the time being.[9]

Davis took up Meigs's quarrel in the Senate and rallied

support from a number of colleagues, including Toombs, who told the engineer it was to his credit that he could not get along with Floyd. These friends of Meigs further exposed the Secretary's weaknesses and sought to guard against them. They hemmed him in with restricting amendments to the sundry civil appropriation bill. By one he was prevented from violating statutes to buy marble from a favorite.[10] Another roused Buchanan to impotent wrath; the appropriation of half a million to finish the aqueduct could be spent only under the superintendence of Meigs. This provision was drafted to prevent the banishment of the officer to the Tortugas as soon as Congress adjourned. Buchanan had to sign the bill because of its manifold appropriations, but he sent Congress an angry message denouncing this unconstitutional attempt to curb his powers as commander-in-chief of the army.[11] Altogether Floyd had been thoroughly discredited; but Buchanan still tolerated him, to the disadvantage of the party, probably because of his Virginia and New York connections.

The most telling blow to the prestige of the Democracy came from the net of the Covode investigation destined for campaign use, and the Republicans prepared to spread it broadcast. This committee filed its report June 16. The theme was the charge that the administration used patronage and money to promote legislation and party power and had obtained the funds largely through the profits from printing.

All this, fortunately, gave some immediate impetus to reform. Early in the session the printing of the post-office blanks was ordered to be let out to the lowest bidders in a bona fide competition, and then at the close of the session the Democracy threw up the sponge. The prices of all printing and binding were reduced 40 per cent, and a law was passed providing for a Government Printing Office. The days of that party largesse were over.

The Democrats did what they could to discredit the charges. Winslow of North Carolina filed a minority report challenging the haphazard fishing methods of the committee, its partisan animus, and the credibility of its principal witnesses, particularly Wendell. He emphasized what the Republicans had been forced to admit, that there was no evidence upon which impeachment proceedings could be initiated against Buchanan or any one else.

Buchanan likewise tried to fight back. He wrote to Bennett of the *Herald* asking the editor to defend him and assuring him that the "testimony of Wendell contains nothing but falsehoods, whether for or against me, for he has sworn all around." In fact, Wendell illustrated his own peculiar brand of ethics shortly after all his testimony had been given; he then tried to induce the administration to make Bowman pay him money in return for some "assistance" in preparing for the Baltimore reconvening.

Such words as he could command, Buchanan summoned to rebuke the House. He charged the members with acting as though they had unlimited power to "degrade the presidential office itself to such a degree as to render it unworthy of the acceptance of any man of honor or principle." He charged them with going far outside their mandate and examining into every subject which could possibly affect his character "without any notice to myself." He showed the unreliable character of witnesses who were largely disappointed officer seekers. He denounced this "terrible secret inquisitorial power" as utterly foreign to the spirit of the American Constitution and institutions. He declared that he and his administration had really been vindicated because no charges had been preferred in the form of impeachment.

In fact a bad precedent had been set. A conflict had been begun in which the legislative sought to reduce the executive to subservience. Indeed Buchanan had put his finger on a rising tendency. It was but one of many evidences displayed in this session that the Republican House leaders were determined to dominate both the executive and the courts. They pursued this objective as long as many of them survived. Lincoln could cope with them; but Andrew Johnson was assaulted by them, and Grant, Hayes, and Garfield knew the sting of their lash. Conkling, Stevens, Colfax, Ashley, and Bingham were in this House.

While the President was wielding his dull sword of defense, the House Republican majority made arrangements for the widest possible use of its discoveries. A sizable volume was printed containing the Covode report and testimony; and a really huge tome was prepared including, besides the Covode matter, the investigation of the Navy Department and more printing testimony from other committees. This immense volume seemed to convict the Democracy, by its very size.[12]

The departing solons could take little pride in their handiwork. The game had been played to a stalemate, and the sorry results were spread forth in the disorderly fashion of the Covode committee report. It was intended to be an indictment of the administration and the Democracy. It was really the picture of the weakness of a system that was too lenient with rottenness, too careless of the virtues of an earlier day.

The most ominous aspect of this stalemate was its defeatism. There was such a general feeling that the experiment in government had been a failure. On every side there was frustration. There were no internal improvements, no free homesteads, no railroad subsidies, no protective tariff, and only curtailed steamer mail facilities. Promoters of all kinds saw that they could get nowhere with the Democratic party.

Dissatisfaction was in the air. Not only were southern leaders openly contemptuous and fearful of the philosophy and policy of the Republicans, but there were threats from other quarters. The California delegation was talking of a Pacific republic, the eastern boundary of which would be the Sierra Madre and the Rockies, with resources not possessed by any other state of the Union, and a population the most enterprising and energetic in the country.[13]

There were loud mutterings of other confederacies. In the Middle West Vallandigham of Ohio proclaimed that though once he had possessed an "intense nationality" he was now a western man. "We of the great valley of Mississippi are perpetually ignored." The individuality of the West was "sunk in the North." He was therefore a western sectionalist. He for one would not follow the Republicans in doing the bidding of Seward and the New Englanders. Men like Chase and Sherman were submitting to an "unmanly vassalage to the North." Vallandigham and those of his thinking would not join the East "in internecine war upon the South." This was a war for political domination. The East wished to dominate the nation. But the West was not an eastern province. There could be a western confederacy. The East was following a policy which would send California and Oregon to the Pacific, compel the South into a southern confederacy and force the West into a western confederacy.[14]

Mason of Virginia was apprehensive that "we are realizing Democratic proclivities . . ." The Constitution had guaranteed "a republican form of government, and that is as much an exclusion of a democracy as it is of a monarchy." We now "distribute alms amongst the people to buy their votes."[15] Singleton of Mississippi prophetically reminded the House that Jefferson Davis "still lives, to lead, it may be, a southern army in defense of her rights."[16]

The split at Baltimore had given the foes of the Democracy great hope. The enemies of the South were jubilant. They saw the doom of her slave power. Those ardent for freedom almost heard the shackles fall from the bondmen and the accompanying chorus of exultant hosannas and hallelujahs for this day of jubilee. But against such odds the Democrats were going to make another fight, a fight to throw the election into Congress, where, thanks to their hold on the Senate, they still might win. They were desperate.

Chapter 18

A Campaign Like None Other

THE MACHINERY of the Democracy had been broken apart at Baltimore. As there was little real hope of repairing it, fumbling mechanics began to salvage what they could. They were trying to construct two new contrivances in the half-hearted belief that they might do the work for which the original patent had been granted.

Both conventions had made provision for campaign organizations. The Douglas men carried on in the traditional mode by appointing the usual committee of one from each state, known as the National Democratic Executive Committee. This body met in Washington early in the week after the convention to take up an embarrassing situation. The convention's vice presidential nominee, Senator Fitzpatrick, had been through a harrowing week end. When he received the telegram notifying him of his choice, he had told friends he would accept. His more radical senatorial colleagues, particularly Toombs, were determined he should not.

With administration help, they attempted to convince him that, if he refused, Douglas would have to do likewise, and that then Breckinridge and Lane would withdraw and a new choice would be made. The logical candidate, they assured him, would then be himself, for he would appear as the great harmonizer who had set aside his own just ambition, for the good of his country. Toombs used other allies also, he worked through feminine influence. He prevailed upon some of the senatorial wives, notably Mrs. Gwin, to show young Mrs. Fitzpatrick that her husband's acceptance would mean his political ruin. They succeeded in alarming her to such an extent that she entreated her rather ancient lord with tears to give it up. She so upset the old gentleman by her hysterical pleadings that he sat down and wrote his declination. The new committee must fill the place.

The most important state in the South from Douglas's point of view was Georgia, and from the start he had desired A. H. Stephens for his running mate. There was some idea now of such a choice, but Cobb, Toombs, and others had interposed so effectively at the convention, spreading reports of Stephens's ill health and the disadvantages of his former Whig affiliations, that Stephens was again passed over. Ex-Governor Herschel V. Johnson, a Georgia Democrat with no Whig antecedents, was designated for the vacancy. He believed in nonintervention in the territories and claimed consistency in this from the days of Calhoun. His friends had seen to it that he was in Washington, and he was immediately notified. He made his acceptance speech then and there, anticipating 1932 by seventy-two years.[1]

Before adjourning next day, the committee chose permanent officers. August Belmont, who was made chairman, was to hold that post for many years through surprising vicissitudes; he sought to raise funds in the financial centers and to collect the customary $100 from each congressional district. An executive committee was designated to be responsible for financial and business details, and a new resident committee was selected to open headquarters in Washington at 350 Pennsylvania Avenue, and to direct the propaganda. Miles Taylor, Louisiana Congressman, personal enemy of Slidell, was made its chairman, in the hope that he would be influential in the Gulf states where Douglas needed strength.

Taylor and his associates began at once to arrange for the publication of a series of pamphlets. Taylor, Senator Pugh, and Congressman Rust of Arkansas prepared an official address, published July 18, to prove that Douglas was the regular party nominee because he had received the votes of two-thirds of a quorum. They pictured their leader as fighting a foul conspiracy. Its perpetrators had disrupted the conventions at Charleston and Baltimore in order to prevent Douglas's nomination. The "conspirators" knew his success would foil their real objective, which was to destroy the Union. The committee followed this address with publication of a series of popular sovereignty speeches by Douglas and his friends. Further pamphlets exposed the inconsistencies of Breckinridge and Lane and the dangers which would follow Lincoln's election. Catholics and adopted citizens were wooed in one of them; because of his wife's religion and his own support of the Catholic Church, Douglas had hopes of many votes from this quarter. A corps of clerks began addressing stacks of these pamphlets and sending them out broadcast.[2]

Douglas was prepared to lead his own fight. He seemed charged with superhuman energy and was keyed up to the point where he was certain that the issue was simple. He was the only Democrat who could carry free states. He believed that he would win in them because, when confronted by the choice between Douglas with union, and Lincoln with secession, the voters would rally to him. Likewise if southern voters understood how safe he was on slavery and how his election would destroy the danger of Republican infiltration and save the Union, they would vote for him. Firm in this faith, he realized that he must get his message to the individual voters personally. There was only one way to do it, and he announced an unheard-of program.

He was going to stump the nation. For the first time in American history a presidential candidate was avowedly going to the people. Despite the illness of the last few months and disregarding the fact that his throat was in bad shape, he left Washington in the middle of July; and from then on into November he was constantly traveling and speaking. First he covered New England, ostensibly on a trip to see his aged mother. Next he went south as far as North Carolina, then back through the middle states to the West and finally down into the heart of the South. Election day found him at Mobile. It was a herculean feat for a breaking man.[3]

Douglas spread some of his enthusiasm among state leaders, particularly in the East and West. The machine managers probably did not share his confidence in national victory, but they had much at stake. If they could not win in 1860 they must at least keep control of their party organizations in order to be ready for a comeback in 1862 and 1864, when reaction might probably set in. Control of state power was more important often than national success. They organized rallies; bands of "Little Giants" were mobilized to parade the streets in competition with the Republican torchlight bearers. They were aided by a vigorous press. Douglas's own western country read the Chicago *Times*, the Cincinnati *Enquirer*, the Cleveland *Plain Dealer*, the Indianapolis *Sentinel*, the Detroit *Free Press*, and the Milwaukee *Press and News*. In New England he had the Boston *Herald* and the Providence *Post*. The middle states supported him in the columns of the Albany *Atlas and Argus*, the Buffalo papers, *Courier* and *Republic*, Forney's Philadelphia *Press* and the Pittsburgh *Post*. Only in New York City did he lack any real support. South of the Washington *States and Union* there was of course no editorial echo.[4]

Douglas thus had the advantage of strong local support in the free states. The organizations and the Democratic press in most of them and in the metropolitan centers were for him. The machines could thus ensure friendly electoral tickets and party workers. Pennsylvania was the only large state and New York the only large city north of the Mason-Dixon line where the bulk of the local machinery was not in friendly hands. In the South of course the opposite was true, and Douglas must build his campaign in that region without aid of the local organizations and by means of makeshift conventions and committees. But he had vigorous support particularly in Alabama, Louisiana, and Georgia in the lower South, and in all the upper southern commonwealths. Soulé, Forsyth, his running mate Johnson, and Alexander H. Stephens, who headed his electoral ticket in Georgia, were energetic and resourceful leaders. If vigor and interest could win, the Douglas campaign was not to lack them. He was likely to gain many votes. But would they be sufficiently concentrated in key localities to give him the electoral votes of many states? If Douglas had doubts on this score, he did not divulge them.

Breckinridge and his supporters, lacking the ready political resources of the Douglas group, had to contrive makeshift machinery speedily. They had placed that responsibility in the hands of their chairman, and Cushing acted promptly. He selected sixteen men who were to be known as the Democratic National Executive Committee, a slight inversion of the party name used by the Douglas managers. They made no effort at state representation on this committee. Four Senators— Davis, Bright, Thomson, and Johnson of Arkansas—four Congressmen, and Collector Schell of New York City were included. Colonel Isaac I. Stevens, delegate from Washington Territory, was made chairman; and Corcoran's banker friend, George W. Riggs of Washington, D.C., was treasurer.

Stevens took active charge of Breckinridge's campaign with the aid of M. W. Cluskey, prolific political writer. They settled down in a spacious private house in Washington at Number 28 Four and a Half Street where an entire floor was placed at their disposal. This committee likewise prepared an address, arguing that the South had been defrauded and forced to withdraw from the Douglas convention when duly chosen delegates were refused admission. It followed this with a series of pamphlets including speeches and other expositions of the "Great Issue." "Shall the constitution and the union stand or fall? Shall sectionalism triumph?" Only calamity would follow the success of the corrupt and extravagant Republicans. Breckinridge and Lane were the truly conservative, constitutional, and national candidates.[5]

Their national committee had the support of the administration, which was early announced. A Washington rally was staged July 10, and at its close a crowd marched to the White House and heard an address by Buchanan, now contemptuously referred to by his enemies as "Old Venison" rather than "Old Buck." He told them that neither nomination was regular, and that all Democrats were free to make their own choices. He chose Breckinridge and Lane and added some remarks that closely resembled his annual message.[6] Senator Bigler, with letters from Buchanan, went to New York to try to raise money in competition with Belmont.[7] Presidential endorsement meant that numerous clerks in the departments were assigned to the headquarters from time to time to fold and address the pamphlets.

The Breckinridge men did not have advantages comparable to those of Douglas among the state organizations. Though they held the loyalty of most of the slave-state Democrats, they were not entirely successful even among them. They were to fail in Virginia and Missouri; and in Texas, where Governor Houston was running for President himself on a ticket of his own, the ranks were broken. In the free states they had but few of the machine units. The administration was holding the Pennsylvania organization fairly well in line. In New York Collector Schell in Manhattan and Daniel S. Dickinson upstate were trying to mobilize the old Hardshell strength. In New Jersey Senator Thomson and federal officeholders were at work for the ticket. In Indiana the Bright-Fitch faction would do what it could, while in Ohio Marshal Johnson was organizing such remnants as would enlist. In Illinois Ike Cook was still trying to operate from the Chicago post office. Jo Lane's friends in Oregon were in the fight, and the Chivalry in California could be counted on for help.

The Breckinridge managers lacked also northern press support. Several New York papers, including the *Herald* and the *Journal of Commerce,* together with the Philadelphia *Pennsylvanian* and the *Washington Constitution,* were the chief; a few papers were set up just for the campaign. This effort was confined to the East, and there was hardly any vigorous editorial writing west of the Alleghenies. Taking a leaf from the Republicans, who were organizing youth into bands of parading, singing Wide-Awakes, the seceding Democrats created clubs called Giant Killers, Jo Lane Rangers, and the like.[8]

The federal patronage was a certain advantage to Breckinridge. It had already been used, when the jobs for taking the census were passed out by the administration, to strengthen anti-Douglas forces. Now Cobb and Thompson undertook to direct the federal officeholders in their large departments under fear of disciplinary measures; bureau chiefs sought to levy campaign contributions. The Post Office was not so efficient a weapon. Holt himself was not much of a politician and was distracted that summer by the illness and death of his wife. Also Horatio King, First Assistant Postmaster General in charge of appointments, was a Douglas man and, strange to say, was retained. However, an occasional removal on behalf of Breckinridge was ordered.

Naturally the division was made an excuse for some efforts to settle old scores in the name of aiding Breckinridge. Daniel S. Dickinson wanted a long list of officeholders removed, especially some one-time Softs like George N. Sanders and Marshal Rynders. Buchanan forthwith decapitated the former, but Secretary Thompson and others thought Rynders too useful. Edmund Burke, foe of Pierce and sometime commissioner of patents, came to life in New Hampshire and sent down a list of "must" removals. Chairman Stevens advised with ex-President Pierce, who, though he favored Breckinridge, counseled against these "spite" dismissals. As in 1858, removals were spotty and irregular though frequent.[9]

Thus in Washington two rival national headquarters were set up. Two committees sought to raise two campaign funds and issue two sets of propaganda. Under the circumstances the peculiar federal organization of parties was to become even more complicated. Within each state the Democratic party was now confronted with the problem of dealing with this split. The ancient factions in the various states had a field day.

II

The chances of victory were not as hopeless as the divided state of the Democracy might indicate. The opposition also was divided. In the interval between the two meetings of the Democrats, the Republicans had gone to Chicago and had surprised many observers. The opponents of Seward had concentrated on the more available Abraham Lincoln, Douglas's erstwhile competitor, and had adopted a platform offering free soil, a Pacific railroad, a protective tariff, and free homesteads.[10] If they could hold their 1856 strength they needed but two more states, Pennsylvania and either Indiana or Illinois. The protective tariff, they hoped, would clinch the one, and the nomination of Lincoln the other. With the Democracy divided, how could they lose? They had failed, however, to establish themselves in the South, and they had not absorbed all the Whig-American strength in the free states. This combination North and South had finally achieved a new merger.

The long negotiations on behalf of the friends of Crittenden, conducted by Nathan Sargent and his associates, had not succeeded in uniting all anti-Democratic elements, but they had produced results. A conservative anti-Democratic aggregation of Whigs and Americans, mostly from the South, had organized the Constitutional Union party at Baltimore in May. It had adopted a simple platform pledged to the Constitution and the Union; it nominated neither Crittenden nor Sam Houston but Senator Bell of Tennessee, with Edward Everett of Massachusetts as his running mate. Their supporters were nominating electoral tickets in all states and were particularly dangerous in the border states where the Whigs and Americans always had been strong. They capitalized the division of the Democrats and their own love of the Union. They might also cut into Lincoln's votes in the North to Douglas's advantage.[11]

The second hope of defeating Lincoln was born of an alluring mathematical possibility. If the Republicans lost Pennsylvania and its close ally, New Jersey, or New York, they could not secure an electoral majority. This would spell their defeat, because it would throw the election into the House, which would then select from the three highest, of whom Douglas would not be one. In the House, where the vote would be taken by states, each state with one vote, the Republicans could count but fifteen of the necessary seventeen, while the Breckinridge Democrats had thirteen, the Douglasites, one, the Americans one; three states—Kentucky, Maryland, and North Carolina—must vote blank because their delegations were equally divided. It seemed unlikely that Lincoln could get any more states. Breckinridge theoretically could be elected if the right six southern Americans, i.e. one each in Kentucky, Maryland, and North Carolina and three in Tennessee, voted for him; but this was hardly likely. The seat of the Democrats' hope was in the Senate. That body would choose the Vice President from the two highest, who undoubtedly would be Hamlin and Lane. As the Senate was safely Democratic, Lane would be the choice; and in default of the election of a President by the House the "Marion of the Mexican War" would take up his abode in the White House on March 4, 1861.

These conditions pointed logically to efforts at fusion. If the two Democratic organizations could pool their resources in certain of the key states or organize an anti-Republican fusion, Lincoln might be stopped in the middle states and defeated. Some sort of combination against the Republicans had been suggested as soon as the campaign began. The senatorial managers devised a plan to run Breckinridge and Lane tickets where they would be stronger, and Douglas and Johnson tickets where they might be in a better position to win. But no agreement could be reached as to which states were which.[12] Fernando Wood suggested that northern Democrats including himself vote for Douglas and southern Democrats for Breckinridge. Then the electors could go for whoever had a chance to win.[13] A third idea was a fusion in the northern states of Breckinridge, Douglas, and Bell—one electoral ticket in each state with the electors pledged to vote for the man who could defeat Lincoln, if such there should be. However, the Douglas managers were so bitter against Breckinridge that they publicly refused any coalition in their first campaign pamphlet.[14] As they could hardly place Douglas among the first three, why risk control of their state organizations to help Breckinridge or Bell?

The basis of a fusion ticket already had been laid in Pennsylvania. The March convention had chosen the electors as well as the delegates to Charleston. Both groups had been selected as a compromise between the administration machine and its Douglas foes. Consequently some of the electors were for Breckinridge, and some for Douglas. The party managers had real hope of electing their gubernatorial candidate, Foster, and they were anxious to avoid two tickets, either federal or state. The state committee, shortly after the final break, took steps to prevent division by inviting all Democrats to vote for the electoral ticket on the understanding that these electors would concentrate on Breckinridge or Douglas, whichever could defeat Lincoln or throw the election into the House.

Forney and some Douglasites would have none of this. They insisted upon a straight ticket of Douglas electors, and the Pennsylvania member of the Douglas national committee invited a convention of his supporters. This body gathered at Harrisburg July 26. It ratified the nomination of Foster for governor, but demanded a new state convention to consider the question of an electoral ticket. Here the regular state Democratic committee stepped in. Its members gathered in special session at Cresson August 9, and after prolonged discussion decided to stand pat on their previous decision. They had canvassed the electors and had found sixteen in favor of this action, ten against it, while one refused to reply to their query. The die-hard Douglasites thereupon chose an electoral ticket of their own, consisting of their ten members on the existing ticket and seventeen new selections. This slate was announced September 12. The action at Cresson received presidential approval, and as soon as the new Douglas ticket appeared Buchanan advised the Philadelphia collector to require from "every Democratic candidate in every county a pledge to support the Cresson arrangement."[15]

In New Jersey, the electors had not been nominated, and so there was a chance for negotiation. The Democratic state committee which favored Breckinridge hit upon the idea of a joint ticket, and on July 2 summoned a convention to meet on the 25th and choose a slate consisting of three pledged for Breckinridge and four for Douglas, each group to vote as under the Cresson plan. The Douglas men were hostile to this plan but called a convention to meet the same day, likewise at Trenton. Further strength was sought by negotiations with the Bell men, who arranged a third convention for the day already set. As feared, all did not go well at Trenton. Here the Douglas men would not join; but the other two groups did agree and announced a joint Breckinridge and Bell electoral ticket.[16]

In New York, particularly in New York City, there was the usual confusion and consequently the greatest possibility for trading. Tammany came out immediately for Douglas, and on July 2 held a great ratification meeting, parading to Douglas's hotel to give him an ovation. Wood's course was devious; his organization, the National Democratic Volunteers, under the aegis of the customhouse, came out for Breckinridge and Lane, and adopted Buchanan's speech at Washington as their platform. The men at Mozart Hall, however, were openminded; they wanted a joint electoral ticket, if that were possible; otherwise they would support Douglas because he was the choice of the masses. They were careful to express their belief that Breckinridge was a high-toned Democrat. The reality of the situation was that Fernando Wood was seeking to use this occasion to remove the stigma of his defeat at Charleston.[17]

"His Honor the Mayor" went to Washington to sell his support to Breckinridge for control of the New York City post office, at least so the *Herald* charged. Returning to New York empty-handed, Wood fell back on his previously announced plan for pooling the interests of Breckinridge and Douglas. He and Douglas concocted a plan for the latter to bring Mozart Hall, Tammany, and the Regency together. Strangely enough a truce was arranged, and at the August Democratic convention the Mozart and Tammany delegations were admitted on equal terms, albeit with some Tammany protest. The convention accepted an invitation of the old Whigs, now Bell and Everett men, to form a joint electoral ticket; and one was agreed upon containing ten Bell and Everett men and twenty-five Regency designees pledged for Douglas. The hope was that the Breckinridge men might come in. The hope was dim.[18]

The administration faction of the party, led by Schell and joined by Daniel S. Dickinson, would have no fusion. It held a separate state convention a week before the regular one and nominated a state and electoral ticket. All the time, however, pressure was growing greater. A number of the most prominent businessmen in New York City were at work. They had met at the home of August Belmont early in August, and such men as William B. Astor, A. T. Stewart, George Law, William H. Aspinwall, and William F. Havemeyer let it be known that there would be no financial contributions unless there was fusion. But somehow money didn't seem to talk.[19]

III

The chaotic political situation disclosed by the events of May and June of 1860 was unique in the annals of the nation. Never before or since has it been duplicated. Only in that fateful year has the stage been occupied by four parties of relatively equal potentiality, and only then was the election followed by civil disorder serious enough to threaten national security. The 1860 chaos largely represented the confusion in attitudes and the new power complex crystallizing at this time of the convergence of tensions.

Many factors were playing into the hands of the Republicans. The climax of the emotional tension had quickened conscience, awakening the moral sense. This inspired new zeal for opposition to slavery. At the same time the passing of the economic crisis had whetted appetites for gain. Metropolitans and territorials were eager to cast aside the restraining hand of negative leadership and to gather the government's benefits. Young and positive leaders were bidding for their support; the new Republican party was straining to grasp power from the faltering hands of the ancient Democracy. The Republican Wide-Awakes were carrying the rails which "Honest Abe" had split. Their enthusiasm spelled opportunity and a new deal to thousands of people who found it pleasant to contemplate the triumph of the Republicans. Many were tired of Democratic rule, or frustrated by it, or distrustful of its subserviency to the South or indignant at its moral obtuseness on slavery.

Business conditions favored enthusiasm for the Republican cause, so auspicious because of the split in the Democracy. In the West, but not the South, there was every prospect of bumper crops after lean years. Western businessmen were preparing to sell to many who would have money for the first time since the panic. Their buyers were in New York that summer spreading the good word. Gotham could not fail to note this; at the same time it saw southern orders failing, southern notes unpaid, southern bank balances unlikely to be replenished by heavy cotton sales. Should the wishes of the South any longer be so much consulted? Were not East-West connections the ones to cultivate thenceforth?[20] Surely, returning prosperity and Republican rule would be a fertile union begetting new enterprises, subsidies, profits.

The prospect enticed even conservative Pennsylvanians. What was more necessary to their cold iron furnaces and their unworked coal pits, to their wageless labor and their profitless capital, than the alchemy of protection? Poor and rich alike would prosper under the proper tariff. Fumbling Buchanan, who couldn't even get his Secretary of the Treasury in line for specific duties, was typical of the condition of the party which the Keystone had so long supported. But not much longer, for Judge David Davis came to Pennsylvania as messenger from the silent Lincoln with word that he was "right" on protection.[21] Why not turn over a new leaf in the party history of the great commonwealth and write a new page headed "Lincoln"—and incidentally "Governor Andrew G. Curtin"—and banish Bigler from the United States Senate in favor of some one whom Cameron might choose?

Could the shattered Democracy stem this rising tide, in

Pennsylvania or anywhere else? It could no longer command popular respect. It had proved itself unequal to meet the problems of the last four years. Its vaunted candidate of 1856, the man of experience, the skilled conservative, the wily diplomat with his cabinet of substantial men of affairs, had failed. The leadership of the party in Congress was proved impotent, unable to command its own forces or to gain allies. Corruption had tarnished the party's reputation. Its ranks were broken. Altogether it indicated one convincing probability—that the days of the Democracy were over, that the Democrats were through, unless they could work a miracle.

The handwriting on the wall predicted Doomsday, as the state election returns began to come in during August. In the North Carolina poll the Democrats managed to win, but the defections were significant. In the towns, among the wage workers, they lost. Was this a sign that Helperism was taking root? In Missouri they lost two Congressmen; the Republican, Frank Blair, Jr., regained his seat. The great shock came in Kentucky, Breckinridge's own state, where the Democrats lost by 22,000.[22]

These losses were followed by other disquieting signs. Douglas invading the South at Norfolk and Raleigh was attracting throngs to hear fiery Union speeches. He boldly declared that the election of a Republican was no cause for secession, and that if he were President he would enforce the laws and hang treasonable lawbreakers, whether secessionists or abolitionists. He cleverly made the Breckinridge party a disunion party and pictured himself as the Union saver.[23] In Virginia Wise and the Senators were leading the Breckinridge faction; but two conventions had been held, for the Douglasites would make no bargain with the Breckinridge forces.[24] The climax came when Governor Letcher came out for Douglas; his section, western Virginia, was growing restive. This split to some extent followed the long-standing sectionalism within the state. The upshot was that the Bell and Everett men believed they had excellent chances in Virginia, as well as in Missouri and Kentucky.

These untoward indications aroused the Breckinridge men in the South. Their candidates had planned a quiet summer. Breckinridge would not imitate Douglas by going about the country like "a travelling mountebank"; he would retire to Lexington, Kentucky. Jo Lane was not returning to Oregon; he loitered in Washington, conferred in New York, and paid visits of remembrance to his birthplace in North Carolina and his former home in Indiana. This dream of retired dignity was shattered by the August Kentucky returns and by the bitter and effective attacks of Douglas and the Bell and Everett men, who denounced Breckinridge and Lane everywhere as disunionists.

Something must be done to offset this charge. A great barbecue was arranged at Ashland, Kentucky, for September 5, and Breckinridge proposed to proclaim himself. He tried to answer all charges. He denied that he had signed a petition for the pardon of John Brown, that he had favored the Whig, Taylor, in 1848, that he had voted for emancipation in 1849, that he ever had been a Know-Nothing. He attempted to show that he and Douglas had never agreed on squatter sovereignty. Most fervent and wordy, however, was his statement regarding the Union. No one loved the Union more than he. He believed, in fact, that most people shared to some degree this affection; he himself did not think there were more than fifty disunionists *per se* in the nation. All would be well if the people kept faith over the constitutional guarantees. Douglas, like the Republicans, had broken faith by defying the Supreme Court with his Freeport heresy. Breckinridge's speech took more than two hours, and he was prostrated by it.[25]

But who was really any wiser? Douglas kept right on with his charges, whether or not he made them merely in his own interest. The Breckinridge forces would break up the Union if Lincoln were elected, while he would continue to defend it, whoever was chosen. Unalarmed, the voters of Vermont and Maine went Republican, by anticipated but unexpectedly large majorities. Thereupon Douglas and Belmont carried out their plan to have Herschel V. Johnson come North to sound similar warnings.[26] The Breckinridge managers replied by arranging an extensive tour through the free states by Yancey himself. He spoke to audience after audience seeking to persuade them, carefully softpedaling disunion. He was loyal to the Union and the Constitution and would be, as long as the rights of his fellow citizens were recognized. But the rights of southerners must be respected. The Breckinridge supporters injected a new note into political campaigning. The Republicans were accused of "socialism" because it was alleged they believed in free land and free love and would like to see society regimented in phalansteries. Propaganda like this was anticipating a new era.[27]

This continued campaigning and the approach of the October elections stirred new efforts at fusion. The move was revived in Pennsylvania a fortnight before the state referendum, with the Constitutional Union men, former Whig-Americans, making the advances. They held a convention and nominated an electoral ticket, but they refrained from designating candidates for state offices. They appointed a fusion committee which met with representatives of the Democrats and tried to agree upon an electoral ticket. Duff Green was there laboring to this end, particularly upon the recalcitrant Breckinridge men, who were committed to the Cresson agreement and some of whom thought it had a good chance of success. Their faith was shared by the state's Democratic delegation in Washington, and Colonel I. I. Stevens came up to denounce the Americans. He believed that fellowship with them would cause a great bolt, presumably by large bodies of Irish Catholic Democrats who hated Know-Nothings.

Yet Collector Baker and his administration friends knew that their ticket could not win unaided. Their state held thousands of American voters. Also thousands of Republican dollars were coming in. Baker had been negotiating with Americans, he thought successfully. A Democrat had been nominated in the Philadelphia district of Henry M. Fuller, American Congressman, with the understanding that Baker would withdraw him if the Americans would vote for the Democratic state ticket. This plan was spoiled when the Democratic congressional nominee refused to leave the field. All fusion with the Americans seemed to be off in Pennsylvania.[28]

Efforts were renewed in New York. Senator Bigler came up from Washington to give administration urging, but the refusal of the merchants to contribute funds to either party had probably more effect. It was apparent that money must be had, and so the barriers began to be lowered. During the first fortnight in September Breckinridge National Volunteers accepted the invitation of the Douglas Regency committee to discuss the terms. Then began a hard-boiled horse trade. The Breckinridge men wanted the lieutenant governorship, the canal commissioner, and ten electors. The Regency would offer only six electors though they would yield four more, if that number of their own men would step down. They would not take the Breckinridge candidates for the two state offices but would agree to new nominees for them, to be chosen by mutual consent. On these terms they stood pat and even rebuffed the merchants when they backed up the Breckinridge proposal with a promise of a $200,000 campaign fund.

However, their state committee left the door open; Richmond, Cagger, and a man of their choice were empowered to continue the trading.

They found the mercantile $200,000 a pleasant prospect and, after some consultation with the businessmen, consented to a mass meeting organized by the merchants. Here, as planned, a committee of fifteen was designated to arrange fusion. This committee suggested seven instead of ten Breckinridge electors and one instead of two Breckinridge state officers. After some haggling and switching of personnel, the electoral division was agreed to; but there was no meeting of minds on the state offices. The Bell group was then drawn into a three-way deal, in negotiations stretching from the 3rd to the 9th October for an electoral ticket of eighteen Douglas, ten Bell, and seven Breckinridge men. The new ticket was formally and promptly launched at a grand ratification rally at Cooper Union. Fusion on the electors had been achieved at the eleventh hour. Even then Cobb was certain that the Douglasites didn't want to win; and ex-Governor Seymour of Connecticut declared that the Regency was primarily interested in getting Schell out of the customhouse, which the election of Lincoln would accomplish. The checkbooks, however, were at last opened, and $50,00 was hastily sent upstate.[29]

After Vermont and Maine the next in the series of calamities befell the Democracy in the second week in October, when the Pennsylvania, Indiana, and Ohio state elections wrote their lesson. The Democratic state tickets were smashed; even Foster in Pennsylvania could not withstand the tide. But as the returns were studied one encouraging fact stood out: there had been a net gain of five Democratic Congressmen, three in Ohio and two in Pennsylvania, and the possibility of a Republican House seemed to be fading.[30]

These elections spurred final desperate efforts. Fusion was again attempted. In Pennsylvania the state committee made one more effort to get the Douglas ticket to withdraw, and the Douglas committee acquiesced; but it availed little because the Philadelphia Forney clique continued to support this slate. Forney was on the threshold of the Republican party, and this policy, he may have thought, would not hinder his entrance through that door. The disappointed Constitutional Unionists would vote for their own electors and Congressmen.[31]

Another trial was made in New Jersey. The chairmen of the three executive committees and members of their national committees met in the Astor House. They abandoned the two-way, Breckinridge and Constitutional Union fusion in favor of a three-way slate of three Douglas men from their own electoral ticket, two Bell and two Breckinridge electors. The Douglas managers again refused to accept fusion; but nevertheless the Breckinridge and Constitutional Union people kept this ticket, thus giving the three Douglas electors support both from the straight-out Douglas voters and from the two fusion elements. To that extent the anti-Lincoln forces were united.[32] The outcome of the trading was thus partial fusion in New Jersey and Pennsylvania and complete union in New York and Rhode Island.

Yet in this strange campaign, as the reluctance to form fusion tickets vaguely indicated, there was dangerous disregard of the most frightening sign. In the South was a growing determination, which most people in the northern states, notably political leaders, failed to take seriously. It may be doubted whether even southern politicos grasped it, particularly those who spent much of their time in Washington. This determination was sustained by a complex of emotions in which fear, pride, honor, and ambition were woven into an intricate pattern. Its design was about to be revealed.

Chapter 19

Mounting the Blue Cockade

THE SOUTH was awakening to a frightening prospect. Awful rumors spread along its dusty roads and up and down its river courses. The press bore alarming tidings of the activities of abolitionist agents tampering with the slaves. In Texas there was fear of insurrection; a plot was reported to poison the wells. Two such agents had been captured, and in their possession were found copies of Helper's book. They were hanged. In Virginia a plan for an insurrection in Princess Anne and Norfolk counties was discovered, promoted by free Negroes. Immediately it revived the John Brown terror. If Lincoln were elected this was what could be expected on a grand scale.[1]

Even the weather seemed to be in a conspiracy to arouse dread. That summer there was a drought, and much of the great cotton crop seemed doomed. In spite of a very active clandestine slave trade from Africa and Cuba, the price of slaves was exorbitant. The weight of debt to northern banks, agents, and importers was heavy, estimated by some at two hundred millions. Just as in the days before the Revolution many planters felt weighed down by debt to British factors, their descendants now groaned at the thought of southern wealth and northern profits. How could they free themselves?[2]

Restlessness began to stir the adventurous. Southern power must be expanded so that the region could be stronger to resist northern aggression. Filibustering was active again. Walker, the gray-eyed man of destiny, was on his last expedition to Central America. A mysterious order, the Knights of the Golden Circle, was advertised to be massing on the Mexican border to take the northern provinces of that distracted republic, perhaps as additional slave territory.[3]

Most disquieting was the talk on the courthouse steps and in the taverns at the myriad crossroads of the South. What was to be done if Lincoln were elected? In view of all these dangers and burdens and frustrations, could the South afford to stay longer in the Union? Those returning from the national conventions were bringing strange tidings. As the campaign waxed hotter the people gathered to listen to the two- and three-hour speeches given in the highly emotional style that they had learned to thrill to under their preachers. And what superb material for emotion was supplied by fear and dread, resentment and defiance!

Charleston had been an unhappy revelation to the southerners, leaders and followers alike. For the first time they had failed to have their way. The senatorial managers and the state leaders in most instances had been playing politics. None save a very few wanted to do more than stop Douglas and force a compromise candidate. But the convention had slipped away from them. The Clan Douglas and the trading New Yorkers had driven them to extremes which they did not relish. Instead of a compromise candidate they had secured a broken party. Now when the damage was proved irreparable, the leaders were a prey to fear, though most of them would not admit it—to fear that only a politician can feel.

This fear was not the fear of property loss, of slave uprising, or of the destruction of white supremacy; these might be felt by the voters, but among the leaders there was the fear of loss of power. They would lose their preferred position in Washington; that was bad enough, but it was not their greatest dread. Their very real and often overlooked fear was loss of power at home. The victory of Abraham Lincoln, one-time Kentucky poor white, might have consequences little related to the much talked-of abolition. It might stir up the submerged whites to whom Helper had appealed:

If elected, Lincoln would have the federal patronage at his command. He would be appointing a postmaster in every community. Where would he find the men? Not among the aristocracy, not among the fire eaters, not among the Democrats. Might they not be men of his own humble origin? Already that idea was stirring in the minds of some of the ambitious. One Indiana Republican alone, by election day, had received six hundred applications for office from men in the South. Worse still, Lincoln might appoint free Negroes. Undoubtedly, the Republicans would endeavor to use the federal patronage to build up their party. The new postmasters would not censor the mails, would not burn abolition papers. They would preach to the poor against the rule of the rich and would stir up a class struggle to create a new order in the name of democracy.⁴ They might even be abolitionists.

This fear already had been voiced in the Senate during the last two sessions. When a North Carolina member heard of the breakup at Baltimore and reflected upon the character of the times, and "the dirty influences which in this day prompt action," he confessed that he was not surprised. "The democratic proclivities of the age pervade our whole country —nothing can arrest our downward tendency to absolute Government—the idea of a Republic is cherished by but few. What a season for Demagogues and Charlatans!"⁵

The fear of a shift of power to the poorer farmers and artisans was contributing to local political contests in a fashion big with danger. In several of the southern states the Democratic machines had to deal with this election under local conditions which had nothing directly to do with it. The crisis of 1860 illustrates very well a fundamental characteristic of American politics; namely, that federal issues are frequently used in state politics in an artificial and opportunistic fashion. This local use of federal issues is not always apparent and is difficult to understand if too constant focus is kept on the federal angle. Such local use was particularly marked in South Carolina during this fateful summer.

II

In the Palmetto state the advance of democracy had been slower than anywhere else. The Carolina oligarchy had been able to offer determined and successful resistance to the idea of popular rule. This arose in large part from the unique role which South Carolina played in the federal system. From its days of origin it had been an isolated and self-contained community. At first alone as a buffer colony, it was well established with customs firmly set before Georgia or North Carolina advanced. Socially it had developed in almost feudal fashion with the planters of the coast farming their broad acres and congregating for the "season" at Charleston. They had created a political system in which property was the basis for office-holding and voting, and community representation in the legislature was in part determined by the wealth of the inhabitants.

The economic situation of the state aroused among its leaders a long-standing resentment toward the North. The Charleston interests and the planters were restive under a sense of exploitation. Their marketing, purchasing, and banking relations with New York seemed too expensive, and they were plagued by constant fear that northern interests had further designs upon their profits. Programs of tariff levies and federal expenditures in other sections would mean that southern money was to be used in even larger quantities to strengthen their rivals. They had plans for direct trade with Europe, banking institutions of their own, railroads to tap the hinterland, a self-sustaining system of manufactures, and even a revived slave trade. However, they had been given more to talking and writing resolutions than to enterprise; their relations with New York, though expensive, were in fact efficient, convenient, and effort-saving. Therefore little came of the talk, save a growing resentment at "exploitation," at the unjust discrimination which turned southern wealth into northern profits. There was a highly emotionalized demand for freedom from this economic vassalage so galling to independent spirits.

In 1860 South Carolina was still operating under its constitution of 1790, subject to a few minor amendments, which prescribed a system now elsewhere generally outmoded. All responsibility was in the hands of the oligarchic legislature, which chose governor, state officials, and even presidential electors. As popular state-wide elections were not held, the widest horizon was the congressional district; and the minds of most voters were confined chiefly to the narrower limits of the parish. Few voted for any one whom they had not seen or heard, and contests consisted of informal debates and arguments among neighbors.[6]

This self-contained and isolated community had once rejoiced in the tides of nationalism, even Calhoun had once been a nationalist; but latterly nationalism had become a dangerous doctrine, a threat to self-interest. An antifederal enthusiasm was first aroused in Jackson's day, by leaders in the "nullification" controversy, over the tariff. Next, the Mexican cession and the dispute over permitting slavery in it, breathed the breath of life into particularistic doctrines such as states' rights. In the past decade basic sectional differences had fostered the most recent growth, southernism or southern rights. Thus South Carolinians had acquired a tradition of independence and defiance of federal power. Likewise the state had had a highly personalized leadership. It had followed Calhoun since nullification days with almost feudal devotion. Antagonism to Jackson, with state particularism and fealty to Calhoun, had combined to hold the state aloof from affiliation with national parties. They had been slow in taking root, and no regular South Carolina delegation had appeared in a Democratic national convention prior to 1856.

Recently new forces had stirred to produce demands for political recognition. Beyond the tidewater section was the developing piedmont region, where the population was increasing much faster than that of the older area. The railroad had brought wage workers along its tracks, and they and the growing number of their fellows in Charleston were learning that artisans and laborers had something in common with the small farmers and townsmen in the uplands. They were aware of the concentration of power in the hands of the tidewater oligarchy and its political machine, and they resented it. They were tired of a legislature unresponsive to upcountry needs, and they grew louder in their demands for reform. They wanted the state democratized.

The back-country politicians felt that their cause might be aided by federal patronage and the propaganda power of the Democratic party. They sought to organize a branch in South Carolina. As long as Calhoun lived, an affiliation, such as other states had with the national party, was not possible. Calhoun worked with the Democracy in Congress, except on occasion, and so did most of South Carolina's other Senators and Representatives; but they would not bear its name at home, nor did they go to national conclaves. When Calhoun died a change began. During the 1850's James L. Orr, Congressman from the piedmont, and B. F. Perry, upcountry editor, built a party which finally held a state convention in 1856 and sent delegates to the national gathering of that year.

The tidewater people and other opponents of Orr and Perry tried to break their Democratic affiliations by invoking particularism and glorifying the tradition of South Carolina's independence. The more radical of them, led by Rhett and the *Mercury*, proved unable to raise any generous response; in fact the heir of Calhoun seemed to be losing influence and sinking under a mountain of debt. There appeared to be three parties, the declining radicals, the rising Democrats, and a great mass of voters indifferent to the appeals of either. Since the abortive 1856 effort of the radical governor, Adams, to revive the slave-trade issue, the succeeding governors and Senators had been chosen by combinations of the Democrats and conservative "indifferents." Orr had prospered in national influence as Speaker of the House, and

Buchanan had appointed a Democrat of South Carolina, Francis W. Pickens, as Minister to Russia. Orr had been succeeded in 1858 by another conservative, and the most radical of the Congressmen, Laurence M. Keitt, had announced in March, 1859, that he would not run in 1860. Perhaps he had learned that his own district between tidewater and upcountry was no longer interested in fire eating.[7]

The fortunes of the radicals seemed declining, and the power of the tidewater oligarchy on the wane; the "national" Democrats were in a position to take advantage of these conditions. Then John Brown's Raid for a time gave Rhett and the radicals hope that they could revive the separatist glory of 1833 and 1850. Under the excitement of the raid they secured a state appropriation of $100,000 for defensive armament, issued invitations to their sister southern states to consult, and sent a representative to Virginia to promote the idea of southern action, to get new terms as the price of remaining in the Union. The cool response to these overtures, even in Virginia, was disheartening,[8] and Orr did not have too difficult a time in organizing for 1860. He and his co-workers secured the signatures of about a fourth of the legislature to a call for a state convention, to choose delegates for the Charleston gathering, and the convention designated representatives and at last organized a Democratic state committee. The decline in radical strength was shown by the fact that this convention rejected the Alabama instructions and reaffirmed the Cincinnati platform. It was even reported that the delegates would support Douglas if nominated, though the members denied that there was a Douglas man on the slate.[9]

Then by one of the curious decrees of Fate the national convention was held in Charleston. Here the tidewater oligarchy turned out in their glory. The *Mercury* was in every one's hands. The conservative South Carolina delegates were drawn by the enthusiasm of that mad hour to go with their southern brethren not first, but fourth of the withdrawing states. The Rhetts and the radicals at first had been disturbed by the act of the seceders' convention in setting an adjourned meeting at Richmond. Soon they saw in it an opportunity, and they moved swiftly to seize control of the delegation. They joined in persuading the Democratic state committee to summon a new convention and aided in writing the call in terms so broad that those hitherto opposing conventions

354 / The Disruption of American Democracy

would be invited to attend. This was done speedily before the Washington leaders issued their "advice" that all seceding delegations return to Baltimore.

So general had been the participation in the primary meetings leading to this new state convention, that the delegates assembled at Charleston without knowing who was in control. The Orr machine was able to organize the meeting, but then lost it. The Rhetts and the delegates from the tidewater parishes outvoted the upcountry delegates because of the peculiarly undemocratic apportionment still in vogue. None of the Charleston delegates were reappointed, although their course was approved. A radical delegation made up of Rhett and his associates was instructed to go to Richmond and not to Baltimore.

On the eve of the legislative and congressional elections of 1860, the Democratic machine had been scrapped in South Carolina as thoroughly as at the national convention. The radicals, standing for aristocratic control by the tidewater oligarchy, had leaped into the saddle on the wave of popular excitement due to the peculiar accident of the convention meeting at Charleston. So many had seen it, more had heard of it from spectators, and the emotion was that much more contagious. This was South Carolina's own act. Had the meeting occurred elsewhere, the radicals would not have had this point of vantage at which to rally. They now made full use of it.

These men had long been watching the rising power of the piedmont. They feared the menace of the Helper doctrines. They now saw the new outbreak of apprehension and hatred of the Yankee and did what they could to stimulate it. Such emotions would take the minds of the discontented off the power of the oligarchy, would divert them from thinking in terms of Helper's class struggle. The oligarchy of old Carolina made its last stand against the new. They would swing the state out now, tear it from its new affiliations, and firmly imbed it in an aristocratic agrarian republic. They would smother the dangerous doctrines of democracy in a new war for independence. The Charleston patriots of 1860 would refasten their hold upon the emotions of the small farmers and back-country people, just as the Patriots of 1776—the Pinckneys, the Izards, and their companions—had done when they created the old Federalist oligarchy. They must act now or never. Given a few more years, Orr and his farmers and townsmen of the upcountry would be too strong to hold back.[10]

Most of the politicians fell in line, particularly the Congressmen, who were unwilling to remain minority members in a Republican-controlled House. In 1859, when it seemed likely that Sherman would be elected Speaker, they had written home to find out if they would be sustained if they left a House so controlled. By midsummer of 1860 the leaders had come to believe it would be better to work for a new government free from Yankee domination.[11] The hopes of 1832 and 1850 were flaming up again. Such was the atmosphere in which South Carolina was to make its biennial choice of legislators and Congressmen. The ballots would be cast in October, well in advance of the final November voting for the electors.

The Congressmen were the only candidates of note. All were running again save Keitt; all might be unopposed if they kept their ears to the ground, except in Keitt's midway district where there was a real contest. The congressional candidates took the lead in declaring themselves in a fashion to discourage opposition. On July 4 there were the customary patriotic rallies which made convenient sounding boards. Congressman McQueen, in whose district some signs of opposition were developing, spoke for secession if the Black Republicans won: unless Carolinians resisted they "were a degraded people a thousand times more than the colonies were under Great Britain."[12]

At the same time the contest for Keitt's place added fuel to the flames. One of the candidates had been in the field since December and with radical support was making progress on a tidewater platform of opposition to electoral reform. Therefore his more conservative opponent, General Ayer, perhaps wishing to avoid that difficult issue, spoke of the advantages that would accrue from severance of ties with the North and expressed his confidence that his "brave and gallant countrymen" would "unsheath the sword, put the firelock in order, and rush at the first note of the bugle that shall announce to your waiting ears that the cloud which has hung like a pall of ominous portent over our beloved South has exploded at last." Five days later Congressman W. Porcher Miles of Charleston spoke there at the ratification meeting of the Breckinridge and Lane ticket. He told his constituents it was up to them to decide whether they wished "to live under a government in which you would be no longer equals but subjugated vassals." It was in this tense moment that Keitt acted. He was still a Congressman and seemingly somewhat sorry he had refused to run again. Also politics had disturbed his honeymoon, for he had just married a local girl —in disappointment, it was said, because Harriet Lane had not favored his suit. At any rate he took up his pen July 16 and wrote for publication. He felt called upon to join in advising immediate secession if the Republicans won.[13]

By the end of July, South Carolina was thoroughly aroused to the Yankee peril. Rhett and his associates could survey the scene with satisfaction. Orr sensed the rising tide; he had withstood it as long as possible, now he must go with it or be drowned. He too published a letter. Lincoln's election he felt to be inevitable. Had the southern delegates stayed in the Charleston Convention, Breckinridge would have been nominated by that body and, leading a united party, would have beaten the Republicans. Now the rash action of the fire eaters had destroyed that possibility. So there was no alternative save that the South should secede; however, South Carolina should not go out alone but in company with Alabama, Georgia, and Mississippi. The conservative Congressman Boyce completed the pronouncements on August 3, by declaring that last summer he had advised prudence because prudence was then desirable. Now it would no longer avail. If the Republicans won, South Carolina could only withdraw. Ashmore and Bonham embraced the same views.[14]

The only rifts in this perfect lute were two. Neither of the Senators, Hammond or Chesnut, gave any indication of his views. Perry of the upcountry was the only voice in opposition. He protested the assertions of Keitt, Orr, and Boyce. Lincoln's election was not sufficient cause for secession. South Carolina must not rush into independent action heedlessly. An overt act should be awaited, and then the South should move in concert. He and some of his upcountry associates voiced the idea that Charleston was trying to push through this hasty action. Perry thought the upcountry could be rallied against the tidewater, and could even get support in Charleston for cooperation and against immediate secession.[15]

Perry alone could not rouse effective opposition to secession; there was no contest on this issue. Within the parishes and districts, where numerous campaigns for the legislature were fought, the democratization of the state was the bone of contention as orators debated over electoral reform. In Charleston a variety of tickets presented in bewildering combination thirty-six candidates for twenty seats. Some of the tickets bore suggestive names, such as "Firemen, Military and Mechanics," and the "Mechanics' and Workingmen's" slate.[16] Such groups were trying to break down the Charleston bosses and sometimes protested the competition of free Negroes in the labor market. In some districts there were objections to the usury laws; in the piedmont there was demand for a subsidy to the Blue Ridge Railroad. The revival of the slave trade and the expulsion of Yankee schoolteachers also stimulated oratory. Indeed each district had its own interests and issues.[17] There was no focus on a state ticket, but in the background was the knowledge that the legislature had a governor and electors to choose. Some gubernatorial choices were announced by legislators, and all pledged allegiance to Breckinridge and Lane. Whatever Douglas men there were, kept quiet.

The political atmosphere was disturbed in higher quarters that summer, because South Carolina's federal relations were unusually unhappy. The administration's efforts to suppress the slave trade bore heavily upon the federal appointees. When President Buchanan had finally retained the state attorney general, the distinguished I. W. Hayne, to be special prosecutor in the slave-trade cases his acceptance had been taken unkindly by many of his fellow Carolinians; and then the government had insulted him by a dispute over his fees. The federal judge, A. G. Magrath, suffered because he must preside at these disagreeable trials; some of his rulings were unpopular at home, and some were attacked in the United States Senate. It happened at an unfortunate time for him. His salary was lower than that of the other district judges— another example of federal discrimination against South Carolina—and in the session just passed Congress had defeated Hammond's efforts to get it raised. Also South Carolina was in difficulties with the Post Office Department, over the economical Holt's efforts to cut off a number of interior routes and the mail subsidy of the state's pet steamer line, from Charleston to Havana via Key West. Hammond's persistence preserved it, but their acrimonious controversy fairly blistered the paper.[18]

By August the pattern of action was pretty well determined. The leading politicians were setting it forth in their private letters. Congressman Miles wrote to Senator Hammofid: "Lincoln will be elected President. What then? . . . I feel very much inclined to think it is just as well to break off things generally, which any one state can do at any time. I am sick and disgusted with all the bluster and threats, and manifestos and 'Resolutions' which the South has for so many years been projecting and hurling with such force at the devoted heads of our base oppressors. Let us act if we mean to act without talking. Let it be 'a word and a blow' but the blow first."[19] A little later his colleague, Keitt, also wrote to the Senator: "If Lincoln is elected . . . I'd cut loose, through fire and blood if necessary. [We hear of] poison in the wells in Texas and fire for the Houses in Alabama. Our Negroes are being enlisted in politics. . . . I confess this new feature alarms me more even than everything in the past. If northern men get access to our Negroes to advise poison and the torch, we must prevent it at every hazard. The future will not down because we are blind."[20]

More important, these sentiments were shared by the plain citizens of the state. When the August rumors of Negro plots in other states gained currency, the isolated farmers in the slave districts began to have horrid visions. They called meetings at which they appointed vigilance committees to watch out for abolition agents, and patrol captains to see that the Negroes stayed within their bounds. Likewise a secret association called "minute men" was being organized in every district of the state. Its members paid an initiation fee of one dollar and gave "a pledge of honor to provide a rifle and revolver to march at a minute's notice to Washington for the purpose of preventing Lincoln's inauguration." They were drilling and wearing blue cockades in their hats, just as they had worn them in 1832–1833.[21] Such terror boded ill for the safety of the Republic.

III

The situation in South Carolina was watched by the other states, particularly those in the Gulf Squadron. The letters and pronouncements of the South Carolina Congressmen were published widely. In most of the states of the lower South there were local contests which used these federal questions in somewhat similar manner. In Georgia, Cobb was fighting for his political life and seeking Iverson's Senate seat as a vindication for his unpopular service with Buchanan. In Alabama, there was local rivalry among obscure men; Yancey, like Rhett, was seeking advantage from the common fears while Forsyth was making Douglas's campaign. In Louisiana, Soulé was challenging Slidell's domination. In Mississippi, Brown and Jefferson Davis were no more friendly. Davis, Slidell, and Cobb, usually averse to extremes, were going with the tide. If the Republicans won, Slidell announced in New Orleans, the South must seek safety in independence.[22]

The October elections were particularly frightening to the South, for they destroyed the last hope of Lincoln's defeat. Cobb had been back in Georgia campaigning. He had been surprised by what he had seen. Before the Pennsylvania election he had written to his wife: "We are all looking with breathless anxiety to hear from the Pennsylvania election. I do not hope that it has gone right. The people of Georgia will not stand the election of Lincoln. *I regard that as a fixed fact.* . . . The mountain country is in a perfect blaze and this you know is the section where the strongest union feeling prevails."[23]

When the news came of Democratic defeat in Pennsylvania his brother wrote a mournful lament: "I confess it sounded to me as the death knell of the Republic. I can see no earthly hope of defeating [the Republicans] in November and their success then, whether we will it or not, is *inevitable disunion.* And calmly and coolly . . . is it not best? These people hate us, annoy us, and would have us assassinated by our slaves if they dared. . . . They are a *different* people from us, whether better or worse, and *there is no love* between us. Why then continue together? No outside pressure demands it, no internal policy or public interest requires it. *Separation is desirable,* peaceably if we can, forcibly if we must. If all the South unanimously say 'we separate,' it would be as peaceably done as summer's morn. The tumult, if tumult there be, will come from our people."[24]

All this should have disturbed people in the free states more than it did; but there was a spirit in the air of the North which made them unaware of the danger or reckless of its consequences. It was not because they were not cautioned, for there were some besides Douglas who saw and sought to warn their careless associates that the witches' brew was beginning to boil over in the South. The headlines of Bennett's *New York Herald* screamed in new fashion. He printed Keitt's letter of July 16 on his front page side by side with Yancey's Slaughter letter of 1858 saying, "We can precipitate the cotton states into a revolution"; slyly he

changed the date to 1860 with no mention of the alteration—
or was it just a compositor's mistake? This was the feature
of his July 24 issue and bore the caption: "The Coming
Revolution. Preparatory Movements for the Organization of
the Southern Confederacy." On the editorial page Bennett
solemnly warned his readers to do no more business with
the South, collect what debts they could, and sell southern
securities; the end, he said, was in sight. Little heed was paid
"Cassandra" Bennett.[25] The South had bluffed before, this
was just another bluff. Even if it were not, the South could
not get away with it.

This time it was more than bluff, as all too few were beginning to realize. In Washington political watchers saw the
trend. One reported: "A proposition or plan for organizing
a Southern Confederacy is freely discussed here, though
quietly, in certain circles. It consists of maintaining a Southern army for defense, etc. by confiscating the property of all
who will not join the measure. . . . There is a scheme on foot
which has been maturing for some time to plunge the South
into a revolution as soon as Lincoln is elected and maintain
the army of the South by confiscating the property of Douglas men." This observer, a henchman of Alexander H. Stephens, believed that Cobb was cognizant of it and that troops
were being moved out of the South and munitions in to aid
the coup. Some of this was true, but much of it was the
gossip of clerks; it was symptomatic of common fears and
expectations.[26]

With these rumors in the air, conservative Democrats
urged last minute efforts to fuse the opposition to Lincoln
so as to give it strength. They attempted to get all three
candidates to withdraw in favor of some one fusion leader,
and Jefferson Davis urged it. Bell and Breckinridge are reported as agreeing but Douglas would not; he could take
more votes from Lincoln in the North than any other. If this
was not recognized by his opponents, he was not going to aid
Lincoln by getting out of the way. The old Pierce administration, which had favored Breckinridge and Lane, attempted
to help. Pierce suggested a ticket of James Guthrie and
Horatio Seymour and his former Postmaster General Campbell tried that out, but got no encouragement.[27]

The last hope of the Democrats was in New York. If Lincoln should lose that state he could not win, and so the final
efforts were concentrated there. Mayor Wood and numerous
others had been manufacturing propaganda to make the

financiers afraid of Lincoln. The Republicans, they claimed, aimed to destroy property. Not only were they against slave property, they were also disciples of Fourier and Blanc who would divide all wealth. Their success would mean that the South would repudiate its debts, and southern securities would be worthless. Similar reports came to the leading mercantile houses from their agents and customers, and some of them were printed in the newspapers. The Republicans charged that the Breckinridge men were trying to stir up a financial panic.[28]

Secretary Cobb, returning from the South, received an urgent summons to New York. William M. Browne, editor of the *Constitution*, wrote from there: "By all means come. You can do a great deal of good. Even Duncan of Duncan, Sherman cannot be persuaded that there is any danger. *You* can show the contrary and you ought to do it. . . . I have written at length to the President." A government loan had been advertised for October 22, and Cobb went; Secretary and Mrs. Thompson went too.

When the loan was opened it was found to be a success—another evidence that the North did not take the South seriously. Marshal Rynders got up a great torchlight procession for the Fusion ticket, which Cobb and Thompson reviewed, standing three hours and a half to watch it pass. Cobb reported that he and Thompson had "been mingling with our friends and fellow citizens here pretty freely and I hope with some success. There is certainly a far more favorable feeling for the defeat of Lincoln than I had expected to find and it is certainly improving. I cannot say that I feel confident but I can say that I am hopeful. The commercial interest begins to realize the danger and that is a great point gained." He was sure the Douglas men did not want fusion to win; they preferred the election of Lincoln.

Cobb spoke freely to New Yorkers of his recent observations in the South. He told people that the South would not submit, if Lincoln were elected, for to do so would mean certain and inevitable ruin. He was charged with telling businessmen that secession would soon make their securities worthless and that they had better get out from under while they could. Collector Schell was quoted as boasting that the market was being manipulated to scare capital into supporting fusion. Be that as it may, the market did break that week, and in the last days of October stock prices tobogganed. If this panic was rigged, the scheme did not work perfectly, for several prominent Fusion businessmen went over to Lincoln; they issued a public statement warning against the chaos which might follow if the election were thrown into Congress.

Quietly and somberly most Democrats saw the hours falling into time, as election day approached. Douglas, in the heart of the South, was still attempting to stem the tide by hoarsely pleading for the Union. Through the streets of the northern cities young Republicans in oilcloth capes marched in the flaring light of their swinging oil lamps, and they were singing. In room or office Republican leaders listened to the carnival and calculated the uses to which they could put the power that was to be theirs. In the South, people were mounting the blue cockade.[29]

IV

In the slave states recent events had been moving without much public report. Again fateful accident gave the initiative to South Carolina. There, under precedent of long standing, the governor was required in presidential years to call a special session of the legislature elected in October, to meet the first Monday in November, three weeks before the usual session began, and choose electors. Governor William H. Gist was not a fire eater, but he knew the fever heat that was being worked up. Perhaps he had heard Keitt declaim that the power of the North would develop a democracy wilder even than that of Paris in the French Revolution. Security and financial prosperity, conservatism and order would fall before the license of northern Republicans. Keitt wanted the slaves armed and a convention called.

Also Gist had been criticized in the *Mercury* for not doing anything with the $100,000 appropriated for defense. The Governor therefore decided to take counsel with other southern Governors, save Houston of Texas. He wrote them October 5 that he was calling a convention, that he believed in cooperation and wished for a full and free interchange of opinion between the executives of the southern, particularly the cotton, states. These letters were carried by his brother, General States Right Gist, who was to visit the Governors, confer with them and say and hear those things not to be written.[30]

Three days later the elections were held in South Carolina. All the Congressmen were reelected without any opposition, except in McQueen's district, where a few votes had been thrown to an opponent. In the one district where there was a contest, Ayer had defeated the opponent of electoral reform. Perhaps this was another indication that the old order must hurry lest it lose its dominant position. As soon as the returns were in, Gist issued a proclamation, October 12, calling a special session of the legislature for November 5 to choose Electors and take action "if deemed advisable for the safety and protection of the State."[31]

This special session and the regular meeting of the legislature, which was to follow before November ended, would have to elect a Governor to succeed Gist and to reelect Hammond or choose a Senator to follow him. There were sharp rivalries for these offices; the deliberations were to some extent conditioned by them, and there was much maneuvering for position. Senator Hammond was ill and not very anxious for reelection. Chesnut saw the bottom dropping out of his Senatorship, and he may have wanted to be Governor. There had been much correspondence with leaders in other states besides that inaugurated by Gist. Yancey, Pugh, Bulloch, and others were urging that South Carolina take the lead. Chesnut wanted a conference before the convention and wrote to Hammond suggesting it be held at Columbia. Hammond did not feel up to going to the capital, and most associates deferred to him. Therefore at his home "Redcliffe," near Augusta, all the congressional delegation save Miles who was ill, and Chesnut, met on October 25, together with Orr, Gist, and ex-Governor Adams. Even though Gist had thus far received no encouragement from his fellow Governors and most of them had not yet replied to his letter, the Carolina conferees agreed that secession should be the program if Lincoln were elected. Governor Gist began to seek arms with his $100,000.[32]

As a kinsman of Postmaster General Holt put it: "In the heart of the planting states we have constantly a foretaste of what Northern brotherhood means, in almost daily conflagrations, and in the discovery of poison, knives and pistols distributed among our slaves by emissaries sent out for the purpose by openly organized associations. I suppose there cannot be found in all the planting states a territory ten miles square in which the foot prints of one or more of these miscreants have not been discovered, plans have everywhere been detected before their hellish work was accomplished. This army of assassins must number thousands and they have at their command strichnine and arsenic in such quantities as show that special factories have been established to suit their demand. You know nothing of this aspect of the 'conflict' and cannot because not one affair of the kind in every ten gets even into the papers. I have heard and read of twenty-three of these wretches being hanged in the last three weeks."[33]

Even the children felt it. A little girl of ten wrote to her uncle: "I expect we will have war. I would go fight for the South if I could. I think if the Southern men have any bravery in them they will fight, and I think if they do fight they will gain the victory for the right is on their side."[34]

PART V

THE UNION FALLS WITH THE PARTY

Chapter 20

The Peril of Dissolution

On ELECTION NIGHT the early wires carried the news of
Lincoln's victory, in very abbreviated form. Soon all knew
that his triumph had been made possible by heavy gains in
just four states—Pennsylvania, New Jersey, Indiana, and
Illinois, three of them in the pivotal group. The exact
statistics did not appear until the rush of events blotted out
popular interest in them, and the results they showed went
largely unnoticed. Lincoln had won because he had increased
the party totals by 120,000 in Pennsylvania, 30,000 in New
Jersey, 45,000 in Indiana, and 76,000 in Illinois. These gains,
particularly in the first three, came largely from the rural
districts. In his own state his total had been swollen by the
rally of probably 30,000 of his fellow Whigs to his support.

At the same time he was a curious Electoral College
"accident" as the tables of the popular vote showed conclusively. His party had won only 39 per cent of the vote, no
great increase over the 33 per cent which Frémont had
secured four years before. The combined Douglas-Breckin-
ridge tickets actually raised the Democratic vote from the
1,800,000 (45 per cent) of 1856 to 2,200,000 or 47 per cent
in 1860. The Constitutional Union ticket, on the other hand,
polled only 14 per cent of the vote as compared with the 22
per cent of the Whig-Americans in 1856. The Democrats, all
told, had cast 400,000 more votes than the Republicans, thus
making Lincoln a minority President. His curious victory was
due to the fact that the Republican majorities were strategically concentrated in northern states. Even if all his opponents had fused on one ticket, he would still have carried all
his states save California and Oregon, securing 173 electoral
votes, 21 more than the needed majority. Under the Electoral
College system, therefore, Lincoln was duly and constitutionally elected with no cloud of fraud to dim his title.

This left the proponents of southernism (who were generally led by Breckinridge Democrats except in South Carolina)
no legal grounds for questioning the result, no excuse of
fraud or sharp practice to justify a revolt. Yet they were
determined upon revolution, and they included nearly all

the federal officeholders whose duty it was to calm the troubled waters. The secession wing of the Democracy was in the usually embarrassing position of revolting because it had lost in a fair election; the tide of its emotion had risen high enough to drown out any sense of a lack of sportsmanship.

The revolt began even before the returns were in. By strange fate South Carolina's leaders were most anxious to act and in the most strategic position to take action. The members of the state legislature, under the Governor's call, had gathered at Columbia on the eve of the November election to choose federal electors. Under South Carolina's archaic constitution, they would reconvene late in November for the regular session and at the same time choose a Governor. Hence the various gubernatorial candidates were concentrating their campaigning in Columbia early in November, and the choice of one of their number was very much mixed up with the issue of secession.

Rhett's nervous energy was as active as his cancerous face was red. He was eager to be Governor and essayed to lead the secession cause. He was trying to promote disunion outside the state at the same time and was in correspondence with leaders elsewhere. Senator Chesnut was at the capital, presumably not without gubernatorial hopes, and the field was otherwise well occupied. The chief contenders were Colonel B. L. Johnson of Beaufort, General D. F. Jamison, Rhett, and Francis W. Pickens, the National Democrat recently Buchanan's Minister to Russia; his party hoped that he might reap the advantage of absence from the country, and break a deadlock caused by the probable scattering of the fire-eating and non-Democratic votes among the others. The political pot boiled hard through the next six weeks with partisan tactics, personal ambition, and secession thoroughly blended.[1]

By this time Governor Gist had received replies from his fellow Governors. Moore of Alabama and Pettus of Mississippi assured him that their states would go out if any other did. Brown of Georgia, as was his wont, was verbose and cagy. He thought the Georgia legislature, about to meet, might call a convention though probably not until an overt act was committed. He was more interested in having each state fight the federal government by retaliatory measures. Moore of Louisiana did not think his people favored secession, and he was not going to advise it; he admitted he might call a special session of his legislature. Ellis of North Carolina gave

no encouragement whatever, and General Gist had not been
able to find the Governor of Florida. This absence of complete
unanimity did not dampen the ardor of the legislators. They
chose Electors and then voted to recess until the national
returns were received. During the interim they resumed their
caucusing and serenaded Senator Chesnut, who now declared
himself for the first time. All hope for the Union, he told
them, was gone.[2]

The atmosphere of South Carolina was tense. Almost the
entire male population, according to the diary of the Governor
of North Carolina, had mounted the blue cockade and joined
local associations of minutemen.[3] The passionate feelings
swaying the wearers of the revolutionary emblem were hotly
voiced by Congressman Ashmore, writing the day before
the election: "If Lincoln be elected as I have no doubt he
will be and the South submits to his inauguration then are
they in my judgment cowards and traitors to their own rights,
unworthy of any other condition than that which awaits
them,—inferiors, provincialists and subjects. If by any individual act I could pull down the pillars of the Republic and
plunge it two thousand fathoms deep into the ocean rather
would I do it than see my section submit to Black Republican
rule for one day or one hour. The booming of 100,000 cannon
and the slaughter of an hundred Waterloos would be music
to my ears and gladness to my sight rather than see S.C. the
victim of Lincoln, Seward, Sumner, Wilson, Lovejoy, Helper
et id omne genus. . . . Men like myself who for a lifetime
have fought the extreme ultraracism of the South and the mad
fanaticism of the North will not permit Abe Lincoln's banner
inscribed with 'higher law,' 'negro equality,' 'irrepressible conflict' and 'final emancipation' to wave over us. We have and
do deserve a better and more glorious destiny. . . . *Three
hundred thousand swords are now ready* to leap from their
scabbards in support of a Southern Confederacy. Fort Moultrie will be in the hands of the South on the morning of the
4th day of March next. Every fort South of it will share the
same fate in a few days after secession is proclaimed."

Ashmore was sure that none were too young or too tender
to be rebels. "Our women and children are ready and eager
for the conflict and would kick us out of our own homes if
we basely and tamely yield again. Our young girls,—daughters
—from 12 to 15 years of age are entreating us—the Fathers
—to train them in the use of fire arms and daggers. Think
you Sir, that it is their *fears* prompt the demands. No! By

370 / The Disruption of American Democracy

the God of Heaven, it is the blood of their Fathers that is burning in their veins. We *will arm them,* and if the necessity drives us to thus expose them, *we will carry them to the battle field with us.* Better for them that they encounter the horrors and chances of war, than endure 'negro equality,' 'final emancipation' and its logical results 'amalgamation.' We are ready for the issue."[4]

On the morning after the national election there was no doubt in Columbia and Charleston that Lincoln had been chosen. On that day the federal district court met at the port. Its term was concluding, and Judge Magrath received the grand jury to hear its final presentments. Its foreman arose to report that the election had driven all thoughts of further action from their minds. "The verdict of the Northern section of the Confederacy . . . has swept away the last hope for the permanence, for the stability, of the Federal Government . . . the Grand Jury respectfully decline to proceed with their presentments." Judge Magrath then took a fateful step. He in turn addressed the jury, and announced his resignation. "For the last time I have, as a Judge of the United States, administered the laws of the United States within the limits of the State of South Carolina. . . . So far as I am concerned the Temple of Justice . . . is now closed." The district attorney and the marshal soon followed him, though the collector and postmaster of Charleston continued in their offices. A mass meeting was held there in Charleston that day, and a committee was sent to Columbia to urge immediate action upon the legislature.[5]

At Columbia there was divided counsel on timing. Some like Rhett demanded speed and would have called an election, for members of a convention to decide on secession, as early as November 22. Others would wait until concerted action with other states might be negotiated. At first the prevailing opinion seemed to be that January 8 would be a good day. A bill to this effect passed the senate, and in caucus the Charleston representatives agreed to support it. Various influences then began to converge on the legislature, urging greater haste. The idea of secession seemed to be advancing more swiftly than anticipated. In Georgia, Governor Brown, hitherto hesitant, surprised some by recommending in his annual message to the legislature that the state call a convention. A false rumor was current that her federal officials and Senator Toombs were resigning to hurry the "keystone of the South" to secession. Also, quite fortuitously,

the Charleston-Savannah rail connection had just been com-
pleted and a large delegation of celebrating Georgians was in
Charleston. Its members were wined and dined and urged
Carolina on, with grand oratory. Telegrams were sent to
Columbia.

The house committee changed its plans to report the
senate bill and submitted an amendment for a December election. Now that Georgia was cooperating, more speed could be
risked, for Alabama and Mississippi would surely follow.
On a test vote November 11 the amendment passed, 91–14,
and by the 13th the bill was a law. An election was to be held
December 6 for members of a convention which was to meet
on the 17th of the same month to make the great decision.
Further steps were taken to arm the state.[6]

United States Senator Chesnut acted at once. He resigned
and sent a message to Hammond that he had done so. Hammond on the impulse of the moment did likewise. These letters
were received in Columbia in the final hours of the special
session and were not particularly appreciated. Men from the
border states, like Senator Mason of Virginia, had written
down asking the Senators and Congressmen not to resign,
but to come up to Washington until the state actually seceded.
Ashmore, Keitt, and Boyce, the three Congressmen then in
Columbia, were unanimous that the senatorial resignations
were a mistake. Keitt reported McQueen was of the same
mind, and Bonham, when he arrived, agreed. So they wrote
to Miles to this effect. The upshot was that the Representatives
decided to go back to Washington. Ashmore, at least, felt
that Chesnut was playing for the governorship.[7]

South Carolina, though in this favored position to move
instantly, was not far in the lead. Georgia's solons had met
on the 8th, while those of Arkansas, North Carolina, and
Florida were scheduled for the 15th, 19th and 26th. Also,
thanks to John Brown, Alabama's governor had been charged
during the previous winter with the responsibility of calling
a state convention in the event of a Republican victory. All
these states were technically in the hands of Democratic
officials; but in reality they were in no position to defy so
popular a movement as secession. The recent campaign had
shown that their organization no long was supreme in the
South. The Democratic vote had been divided by the unexpected strength of Douglas, and Bell's vote-getting power
had shown the vitality of the opposition. Breckinridge had se-

cured only a plurality of the southern vote, 570,700. As Bell had secured 516,000 and Douglas 163,000, they topped him by 110,000 votes. Not only had he lost the upper South when Virginia, Kentucky, Tennessee, and Missouri went against him, but he was in a minority in Delaware, Georgia, Louisiana, and Maryland; and in Alabama, Arkansas, and North Carolina his opponents had over 45 per cent of the vote. Only in Florida, Mississippi, and Texas did the old party machine seem to retain secure control; and in the last Sam Houston was governor, elected the year before on an independent ticket.

The political lesson of these figures was that the leaders of the machines could take no chances in most of the southern states. They were hard pressed either by the opposition or by internal factions, and they must be ahead of public opinion and never behind it. The Democratic governors and legislative leaders knew well what their constituents felt.

General excitement was rising, for the election news had added another to the many emotions aroused during the summer. To the last, great numbers of the people had clung to the belief, "It can't happen here." But it had happened. The South had been defied. Northern voters had disregarded the interests, the welfare, and the threats of the South and elected a candidate committed to policies inimical to their peace, their prosperity, and, they thought, their safety. Such action was an insult. Their spokesmen had pledged them to withdrawal if Lincoln were elected. Now they were in honor bound to fulfill that pledge. Rather than submit to the evil rule of a money-mad and antisouthern oligarchy, prating of democracy, of the will of the majority, they would secede. The more emotional were loud in their demands for immediate action. The cooler heads were less evident. The Democratic machines responded immediately.

The Governor of Alabama led off. He did not believe he could legally issue a proclamation calling for a secession convention until the Electors had chosen Lincoln the first week of December. Yet he welcomed a letter from prominent citizens, to which he replied November 14 that he would summon the voters to an election December 24 to choose delegates to a state convention. On that same day the Governor of Mississippi called the legislature in special session to meet November 26.[8]

In Georgia, the legislature realized that public opinion was much less unanimous than in South Carolina, Alabama, and

Mississippi. There was strong Union sentiment in that state; Breckinridge had not been able to carry a majority of the voters with him, the Bell and Douglas supporters had out-voted their more radical opponents. Therefore the leaders invited eighteen of the most prominent men of the state, embracing all shades of opinion, to address them. Alexander H. Stephens appeared and made so strong an appeal for caution that he is credited with persuading the leaders to abandon their original plan of seceding immediately by action of the legislature. Instead they voted on November 18 to call a convention which was to be elected on January 2. Within three days thereafter the Governor of Louisiana called a special session of his legislature for December 10.[9]

The Mississippi and Florida legislatures on November 29 and 30 called elections which were to be held December 20 and 24. Louisiana on December 11 called one for January 7. There the smooth progress of taking the polls of public opinion seemed to stop. It was quite apparent that the legislatures of Arkansas and North Carolina would take no action, and even in Texas there was a snag. Governor Sam Houston refused to summon the legislature, and so the secessionists had to construct machinery. An irregular convention finally gathered December 3 and issued an address calling for an informal election January 8 to choose members of a state convention to consider the fateful question.[10]

The border states showed no interest giving real hope of immediate action. The Governors of Virginia and Tennessee were willing to call special sessions of their legislatures in January, the month in which the Missouri legislature was scheduled to meet. Nothing now could be done in those states but wait. Governor Hicks of Maryland, the only opposition Governor in the South, refused to call the Democratic legislature and persisted in his refusal despite various forms of pressure exerted on him during the winter. Delaware, off in a corner, could only wait upon her neighbor. Governor Magoffin of Kentucky undertook to stay the tide of secession. He had not failed to note that the opposition had just carried the state and elections were to be held again next summer. He addressed his fellow Governors, offering them a program of safeguards, which he believed should be submitted to the free states for acceptance or rejection before any action was taken. He suggested a convention of southern states to adopt and present such an ultimatum. When at length he agreed to call a special session of the legislature it was scheduled so late as January 17. No shrewd observer could detect in any of these states eagerness for immediate action.[11]

This narrow bounding of the secession enthusiasm within six or seven states was disappointing in the extreme. The Governor of Alabama and the legislature of Mississippi undertook to organize propaganda to widen the sphere. These two states sent envoys to the other slave communities to secure information and to urge upon their fellows, particularly those on the border, the need of united action.[12] In the meantime campaigns had to be organized in each of the convening states. Soon the hustings were thronged once more. In these contests South Carolina had three weeks' start, and she set the pace. There was little doubt as to how she or Mississippi might decide, but the case was not so clear in Alabama and decidedly cloudy in Georgia.

II

While the southern state machines seemed determined upon secession, the leaders of the administration and the northern Democracy were seeking to stem the tide. Despite Lincoln's northern sweep of the Electoral College November 6, the Democratic party had still great numerical strength in that section, and such an army of voters could sustain skillful leadership in accomplishing much. Though Lincoln had received 1,800,000 votes, Douglas had polled 1,200,000 in the nation at large and the combined Democratic tickets had grossed 1,500,000 votes in the northern states alone. Northern congressional victories for the party seemed to indicate that the Republicans had no chance to organize the House. The Democrats had gained six Congressmen in New York and one in New Jersey and had lost but one each in Wisconsin and Delaware. Would the leadership be strong enough to capitalize this potential strength?

The initial responsibility for meeting the crisis lay upon the Washington high command. The administration had the greatest burden and the least power. The four disastrous years of its stewardship had stripped it of most of its influence. Buchanan was now crowding seventy and nervously hoping that the deluge might not descend until he was out of office. He felt that his friendship for the South obligated its leaders to spare him the humiliation of dissolution while he was in office. Yet the resignation of the South Carolina officeholders had come to him as a revelation. For the first time he really believed the Union might be in danger.

His cabinet was neither harmonious nor helpful. He had never depended much on its advice and had never hesitated to overrule any of its decisions. He had insisted that everything of importance, and much detail besides, pass over his desk. Of the northern men Cass was more frail than ever; he had been away for several months, and his duties had been shouldered by the President and the new Assistant Secretary of State appointed in June, William H. Trescott of South Carolina. Toucey had no ideas of his own and always agreed with his chief. Black was the only man from the northern region who had any force or any capacity for action planning.

The southern cabinet members were in a peculiarly confused and divided state of mind. Cobb and Thompson were closer to Buchanan than the others and were moved by real loyalty to him. Yet they were from Georgia and Mississippi, which seemed to be on the verge of secession. Whatever of political future remained to them must be found in those states. They were in a dilemma. Their hope was that secession might be delayed until after March 4. Cobb communicated with Rhett, through Trescott, to urge delay. He proposed that the southern states prepare to go out on March 4 and choose delegates to meet in a convention on that date to form a southern confederacy. Thompson concurred in this idea. He was cannily endeavoring to keep in with the secessionists in his own state and was seeking to be chosen a delegate to the Mississippi state convention.[13]

The two other southerners occupied positions defying simple explanation. Holt, in spite of his Kentucky birth, his Mississippi career, and his Wickliffe-Yulee relatives-in-law, was a staunch Union man. Probably in his early experience in the South and his departure from it to come to Washington permanently, lay hidden the reasons for his opposition to southernism. His wife had just died, and he was lonely and melancholy; he could summon no enthusiasm for a new cause. Also he had been through many bitter quarrels with southern politicos when he sought to curtail their unprofitable mail service. Some of the most bitter had culminated that summer.

Floyd was likewise below par. His health was bad, and he was cherishing grievances. He had spent a very unpleasant summer. He had brooded over the series of votes of want of confidence which Congress had taken, in part because of the urging of Jefferson Davis. He was particularly angry at the mandate that Meigs be continued in charge of Washington construction. By threats of resignation he had persuaded Buchanan to accept a scheme to circumvent the law and finally to banish Meigs by transferring him to the Dry Tortugas to superintend the completion of Fort Jefferson.[14]

Floyd was even more upset over the action of Buchanan and his colleagues in the De Groot case. One of Floyd's many contractors had a claim upon the government, which Cobb upon Black's advice was disputing. Floyd was determined to pay an exorbitant sum, and an angry controversy among these three cabinet officers likewise involved the President, who sided with Cobb and Black. Thus the Secretary of War spent his summer threatening to resign, off and on, and the issue was not yet settled. On November 3, just prior to the election, the Secretary had written the President another bitter and complaining letter. Still Cobb would not pay the money.[15] Therefore, not only because he came from hesitant Virginia, but more particularly because of his grievances against Cobb and Davis, Floyd was in a mood to have little sympathy with the secessionists. He could not help knowing, too, that his colleagues in the administration looked upon him as somewhat of a liability. His influence on policy was to be almost nil, but his position in control of armament made his actions at times important.

This cabinet of divided counsels must meet the rising situation. How was the federal executive to deal with secession? Could Buchanan and his advisers accept the seceders' contention that they were merely exercising a right which the federal government must recognize? Or should the authorities at Washington attempt to interfere, to resist withdrawal, and, in extremities, to force the seceding states to return to their ancient allegiance?

The administration policy makers must grapple with two immediate problems, the status of federal property in the states about to secede and the annual message to Congress. Within South Carolina, Georgia, and the Gulf states were the coast defenses, forts, arsenals, and navy yards which the lack of foreign enemies, and the demand for economy had stripped of any proper garrisons. A company or two was the largest detachment in any fort, and in some instances only a caretaker had been left to watch the premises. Should not these expensive federal properties be protected?

This issue had been forced by circumstances which were partly political. Just before the election Winfield Scott, the general-in-chief of the army, had indulged his penchant for

letter writing. He had sent a rambling and disconnected letter
to the President and Secretary of War urging that the nine
principal forts from Hampton Roads to the mouth of the
Mississippi, six of which were without troops, "be immediately
so garrisoned as to make any attempt to take any one of them
by surprise . . . ridiculous." Being General Scott, he had to
make his good advice of little effect by injecting much ex-
traneous matter and by using this letter politically. He not
only sent copies to Buchanan and Floyd, but distributed others
among his Whig friends. That he wished to thwart the plans of
some of his enemies, particularly Jefferson Davis with whom
he had a long-standing quarrel, is probable; that his counsel
for reenforcement stirred southerners to greater irritation is
certain.[16]

This question of the forts was bound to become a major
issue, for whether the federal government intended to resist
secession or only protect its property, the forts would be the
key. As South Carolina was making the first moves, the
condition of the Charleston properties was the most pressing.
In this harbor there were three; two of them, Moultrie and
Pinckney, were ancient, but a new one was being constructed
on a shoal in the midst of the harbor. This was Fort Sumter:
its completion had particularly suffered from congressional
economies. As Fate would have it, however, some money had
been appropriated so that building could be resumed in the
summer of 1860. On the eve of the November election,
Colonel John L. Gardner had a garrison at Moultrie of two
companies of the First Field Artillery, numbering sixty men,
while Captain J. G. Foster of the Engineers had nearly two
hundred laborers working to complete Sumter and to repair
the rather neglected Moultrie. Naturally this construction
activity, thus accidentally resumed, appeared to the Charleston
populace as planned to thwart any attempt at secession.[17]

No sooner had word come of the opening moves in South
Carolina than rumors flew to Washington about the forts. On
the day after Lincoln was elected an unverified report circulated at the capital that they had been captured. President
Buchanan was worried and went over the whole matter with
Floyd. He was particularly afraid of becoming responsible for
any quick act in Charleston. He told the Secretary to see that
the necessary arms, provisions, and reenforcements were supplied. He warned Floyd that "if those forts should be taken
by South Carolina in consequence of our neglect to put them
in defensible condition it were better for you and me both

to be thrown into the Potomac with millstones tied about our necks."[18]

Floyd reassured the President. He had recently heard from Foster and had authorized the issuance of small arms to the workmen. He had sent the assistant adjutant general, Fitz-John Porter, to Charleston on election day to investigate and report. He soon learned that Gardner was trying to protect himself; he had even then written Floyd requesting reenforcements and, the day after election, had ordered the weapons and ammunition at the arsenal in the heart of the city carried out to the forts for safe keeping. He feared a mob might seize them. When Charleston learned that the transfer was to take place a crowd gathered and prevented it. The wires flashed indignant protests to Washington against this hostile act of Gardner's. Most of them were directed to the only South Carolinian in high office, the Assistant Secretary of State, Trescott. When he received them on the 9th he went to the White House, where the Cabinet was in session. He arrived as they were breaking up, so that he could take Floyd aside and with Cobb's help urge that the "hostile" step be curbed. Floyd authorized him to telegraph that no arms should be moved.[19]

On that historic November 9 Buchanan had held his first cabinet meeting since the election. He had been busy attempting to prepare a statement of policy that would prevent secession, or at least postpone it until after March 4. Letters had come in urging him to issue a proclamation, and he was weighing such a step or some use of his annual message. He this day brought before his advisers a plan for Congress to call a general convention to draft constitutional amendments which would restore harmony. Cobb, Thompson, and Toucey thought well of the plan. Floyd was indifferent; he felt that no particular action was necessary because the Lincoln administration promised to be so weak that no one could fear it. Holt was opposed because he was afraid that the convention might fail and in so doing unite the South on a secession program. Black and Cass were more decided in their opposition and wanted to use force to halt secession. The President then asked Black for an extended legal opinion on secession and the federal power in the crisis.

The news from Charleston, relayed by Trescott, made imperative a special cabinet meeting on the morrow. That Saturday was a dark and dismal day, with a cold northeast storm drenching the streets and the spirits of the capital. In considering the question of the forts the President referred again to his plan discussed the previous day. He now was prepared to proclaim his opposition to secession and his intention to use whatever power he had to defend federal property and enforce federal law. Cobb, Thompson, and Floyd objected to this forthright statement, and the first two were insistent that something be done to quiet Charleston's anxiety over Gardner's attempted transfer of munitions. Cass and Black were in favor of Buchanan's statement and urged that Gardner be reenforced; so probably did Holt and Toucey.[20]

Floyd now reported that he had been talking to Fitz-John Porter, who had returned the previous day. That officer recommended there be a change of commanders. Gardner was sixty-seven and lax. He was comfortably housed away from the fortifications and not very observant; discipline too had deteriorated. He was Boston-born, and though his sympathies were southern it might be better at this time of crisis to have a southern officer. Floyd endorsed Porter's report and gave his view that the forts should be defended but not re-enforced. All then agreed that there should be no overt act to stir up the Carolinians, and that a younger, more vigilant officer of southern background should be put in Gardner's place. Major Robert Anderson of Kentucky was chosen to command the forts and a native Charlestonian, Colonel Benjamin Huger, was made superintendent of the arsenal. Nothing further need be done until these officers were settled and could report.[21]

The next week the cabinet resumed debate on general policy. The President wanted to decide between issuing a proclamation and expressing himself in his message. He called for Black's report, which the Attorney General supplied in an unfinished state. The law officer had not pulled his punches. He was emphatic that "the Union is necessarily perpetual. . . . It can meet, repel and subdue all those who rise against it." His only concession was his opinion that the federal government could not "obliterate a single commonwealth from the map" or "declare indiscriminate war against all the inhabitants" of one. He gave much space to a denunciation of the political interests which had precipitated the crisis, with particular severity against the secessionists and the Republicans. Such sentiments Cobb and Thompson opposed as too inflammatory; they became more determined in their opposition to a proclamation. Buchanan thus discovered that there was no support among his cabinet for a proclamation; even Black thought the message the proper medium for the President's views. The idea therefore was given up, and attention focused on the report to Congress.[22]

For several days there was hot discussion in the President's office, at dinner tables, and, in fact, wherever two or more of the administration were met. Black and Cass declared unequivocally that there was no right of secession; it was clearly unconstitutional. The Attorney General marshaled his arguments in such a formidable and disconcerting array that Thompson went back into history and reread the entire published proceedings of the constitutional convention of 1787, culling numerous excerpts to show the idea was not ruled out by the fathers. Cass proved unexpectedly alert in his support of Black; and Trescott, his South Carolina Assistant Secretary, therefore spent much time and breath to no avail trying to argue him out of his Unionism.[23]

Tempers were tried, nerves frayed, worry and dread were taking their place in these hitherto more sprightly meetings. A dark cloud hung over all, but particularly over Cobb, usually so bantering and gay-appearing, even in dispute. The Secretary of the Treasury was in a dilemma which was becoming unbearable. He believed "that submission on the part of the South to [Lincoln's] election is certain and inevitable ruin, hence I am for resistance even to dissolution." His family were secession enthusiasts. His brother Thomas was going forth like a holy evangelist to preach the cause; he made speeches four and five hours long, and at the end no one was tired. One lady told Mrs. Cobb she could listen for seventy-five hours without fatigue. The Secretary's son Lamar wrote to his mother: "I am for secession-dissolution-disunion or whatever else you may call it—now and forever. I am . . . sporting a blue cockade . . . Uncle John Cobb says 'resistance to oppression is obedience to God.' . . . Uncle John Lamar says if Georgia submits he is going to sell out his little plunder and go either to South Carolina . . . or to Paris. I should hate very much to stay a day in a disgraced state." [24]

The Secretary was under political pressure also. He received telegrams from John B. Lamar, Thomas R. R. Cobb, Robert Toombs, and James Jackson, who were at the legislative session at Milledgeville. Cobb's hope to be elected Senator, to succeed Iverson on the 4th of March, was going a-glimmering because, with public opinion as it was in Georgia, he did not see how he could serve under Lincoln.

The gist of the telegrams which were coming to him was advice to resign and go home at once. "Your friends and the friends of resistance wish your presence here." [25]

He summed up the situation on November 16: "The ordeal through which I am now passing is the most trying one of my life." For the moment he seemed tied down by a multiplicity of obligations. He felt a duty to Buchanan, who he believed was "the truest friend to the South that ever sat in the Presidential chair." Secondly, he was confident that he could help the South most by remaining in the cabinet and blocking hostile moves which Buchanan might make if he were not there. Then, too, if he abandoned the President he would be "denounced as unworthy and ungrateful." Finally, as far as public obligations were concerned, the Treasury was in bad shape and he would be accused of getting the department that way "by bad management and then flying from responsibility."

His private obligations were just as embarrassing. He owed money for his current expenses which it was then inconvenient to pay, and he did not want to seem to be dodging his creditors. Most important was the fact that Mrs. Cobb was approaching confinement and the doctor feared the effects of travel. Despite these difficulties he was finding it impossible to remain silent. Between cabinet sessions and arguments, he set himself to compose an address to the people of Georgia, advising secession on the 4th of March. His personal difficulties opportunely lightened. His brother-in-law sent him the money to pay his obligations, and Mrs. Cobb decided, despite her ill health, to go home December 1. The Secretary sent his address to the printer and then fell sick. His illness delayed his wife a few days, but finally on the 5th she set out and reached home safely. Cobb felt he would not be long in Washington.[26]

During this period of stress Cobb was busy, in council and out, with the great controversy. Black was working on him, and he in turn, with Thompson, was trying to work Buchanan out of any idea of erecting constitutional barriers in the way of secession. Thompson took the President his excerpts from the "Fathers" to convince him that secession was not unconstitutional. Buchanan was moved sufficiently to reconsider some points and turned to Black for confirming data. He returned the Attorney General's recent paper to him and requested instead a formal legal opinion which would eschew politics and philosophy and stick to the law. The President had become stricter than ever in his devotions and spent a portion of each day in reading Jay's *Exercises* and in prayer. He now decided that he wanted to issue a pacifying, not an inflammatory statement. "I desire to come between the factions as a daysman [Job 9:33] with one hand on the head of each, counselling peace." [27] Black agreed to try again but stipulated that the President should request him to answer five legal questions, which Black forthwith wrote down. This was done on November 17, and the lawyer took the week end to compose his famous opinion on the extent of the President's powers.

The federal law was supreme in its sphere, the Attorney General advised the President, but in the sphere of action of the states it was powerless. The President had ample authority to collect the revenue at stated ports from the deck of a vessel. Also he had the right to protect the public property. But executing law in absence of the federal judges was another matter. Under existing law, if the feeling in any state against the United States should become so universal that there were no federal officers, "troops would certainly be out of place, and their use wholly illegal." In other words the federal government was strictly on the defensive. If a state should secede, the President could neither acknowledge the fact nor acquiesce. He must take the defensive powers at his disposal, try to execute the laws, and leave the rest to Congress. What Congress could do was up to Congress. Black repeated his admission that the right to make war against a state was not expressly given. He believed that the Union must utterly perish at the moment when Congress should "arm one part of the people against another for any purpose beyond that of merely protecting the general government in the exercise of its proper constitutional functions." Such was Black's official argument. Privately he maintained that proper reenforcements to the southern forts would quickly check secession.[28]

Buchanan was not pleased with this paper either. Black reports "he had hastily taken it for granted that Congress might make secession a cause of war, and in the draft of his message already prepared he had submitted the question of war or peace to their decision." Black and Cass, who was stirring out of his usual lethargy, convinced Buchanan that the issue was not as simple as that, and once again the President took his pen in hand. On November 22 he sent for Jefferson Davis to come up early and advise with him on this troubled question.[29]

Before Davis could reach the capital, word arrived from

Anderson. He had carefully inspected his command at Charleston and recommended reenforcements. His views came November 27 in the midst of southern efforts to persuade Buchanan that the reenforcements were unnecessary. Trescott had continued his work on Floyd. At first his efforts had some effect and Floyd seemed inclined to assure southern leaders that no hostile steps would be taken. He was temperamental, however, and he began to feel resentful at their pressure. He was particularly upset by Trescott's continuous demands for a pledge not to send aid. The Assistant Secretary was threatening to resign and go home if he didn't get this promise, and swore that his resignation would be the signal for the Charlestonians to storm the forts. Floyd complained that he did not see why, if he saw fit to send a few men or some boxes of munitions to the forts in the routine of administration, he should be showered with telegrams, admonitory and abusive. He was not going to leave government property at the mercy of any mob which might get out of hand, he said. Yet he was careful not to send any reenforcements to Anderson.

Floyd's failure to act roused Black and Cass, who went to the President. He agreed that something should be done, and ordered Secretary Floyd to send the necessary force. This only provoked Floyd's desire to be contrary, and he found a new excuse for delay. He persuaded the President that nothing should be done without consulting General Scott, who had kept his headquarters in New York since quarreling with Jefferson Davis, Secretary of War in the last administration. Buchanan agreed to the delay, and Scott was sent for. Unfortunately he was ill, and his advice must wait upon his recovery.

During the week end of the 24th just prior to the arrival of Anderson's message, the southern phalanx, Cobb, Thompson, and Trescott, matured a plan to prevent the sending of reenforcements by an exchange of pledges. They would try to persuade Buchanan to abandon the despatch of troops if Trescott could secure a promise from the Governor of South Carolina that the federal property would be safe. Buchanan did not discourage this plan, but viewed it with relief because it would remove his fear of the loss of the forts and at the same time free him from the danger of causing a collision. So Trescott wrote to Gist on November 26, and brought the Governor's favorable reply three days later, while the question of Anderson's recommendation was before the cabinet. The southern phalanx had now the aid of Hunter and Mason, and Davis, who had been summoned by them as well as by the President.

Davis suggested that, if all the southern forts were put in charge of ordnance sergeants as caretakers, the states would scrupulously respect federal property rights. The idea seized Floyd's fancy, and he harped on it. These promises and suggestions now swayed Buchanan definitely against reenforcements, so that he rebuffed Black on being urged once more to pursue his original course. Black begged the President to let him write the orders for Buchanan to sign, dramatically declaring that he would send them by special trusted messengers who could not be side tracked by Floyd. But Buchanan only read him a lecture upon interfering with the affairs of other departments.[30]

The President was now convinced by Gist's pledge, his conferences with Davis, and the earnest pleas of Cobb, Thompson and Trescott, that there was no danger of losing the federal forts, if he sent no reenforcements. He therefore rather complacently believed that his message would vindicate him by demonstrating his constructive planning and his want of power. He could now turn the responsibility over to Congress. His message to Congress was taking final shape.

He cast it in the form of a plea to the southern states to remain in the Union. He expressed himself in language unusually eloquent and choice for him; perhaps it was Black who provided the felicity. The President began by a drastically oversimplified statement of the causes of the trouble. It could be attributed to "the long continued and intemperate interference of the northern people with the question of slavery in the southern states." The result was that even in southern homes "a sense of security no longer exists around the family altar. . . . Many a matron throughout the South retires at night in dread of what may befall herself and her children before the morning." All this could be stopped if the North would let the South alone. He trusted to the good sense of the American people to see this.

The election of Lincoln, he went on to argue, was no just cause for dissolving the Union. The new President with no effective support from the legislative and judicial arms would be impotent to do harm. In fact there was no danger possible to slavery from the federal government. The danger rather came from the action of the northern states, which by personal liberty laws had nullified a sacred constitutional right of the South.

"The southern States . . . have a right to demand [their repeal]. Should it be refused, then the Constitution, to which all the States are parties, will have been wilfully violated by one portion of them in a provision essential to the domestic security and happiness of the remainder. In that event, the injured States, after having first used all peaceful and constitutional means to obtain redress, would be justified in revolutionary resistance to the government of the Union."

Buchanan insisted on referring to the right of revolution as the only redress, because he was emphatic that there was no right of secession. He made a long and effective argument. The framers of the Constitution "never intended to implant in its bosom the seeds of its own destruction, nor were they at its creation guilty of the absurdity of providing for its own dissolution." They sought to make the "perpetual union" of the Confederation "more perfect." If the tyrannical hand of oppression became too heavy a free people might revolt; but disgruntled states might not peaceably secede.

Holding these views, the President was bound by his oath "to take care that the laws be faithfully executed." Here he was hampered because all existing laws giving him authority were based on the assumption that the federal courts would appeal to him for force to put down unlawful and insurrectionary combinations. The resignation of Judge Magrath had produced a situation whereby there was no federal judiciary in South Carolina and the existing laws could not be applied. Congress must take up this omission and lay down policy in new statutes.

In the meantime he could and would collect revenue and protect federal property. He was confident that no attempt would be made to expel United States power from the forts; but if the effort should be made "the officer in command of the forts has received orders to act strictly on the defensive." Furthermore he could in no way recognize the secession of a state or acknowledge its independence. He submitted that whole question to Congress.

To this point he had used reasoning that was in harmony with the views of his Attorney General. He had adopted a military policy similar to that of Floyd and had overruled Cobb and Thompson on secession. They did not agree, but for the time being remained loyal to their chief, particularly as he included a makeweight argument to placate the South. Congress under the Constitution had no "power to coerce a State into submission which is attempting to withdraw . . .

from the Confederacy." Here he followed Thompson, who submitted to him evidence from the debates in the constitutional convention that the grant of such power had been considered and rejected. Black protested vigorously against the phraseology "the power to coerce a State." While admitting that there was no power to make war against a state, he protested that the defensive power of the President was sufficient to make secession impractical. To the extent of the President's defensive powers, Black believed that he could coerce, and therefore objected to the use of the term as liable to misunderstanding, particularly in the North. Buchanan overruled him.

Thus Buchanan had striven to appeal by the force of logic to the ethical sense of the people, to their regard for constitutional propriety. The South had real grievance, but not sufficiently great to justify revolution. In his sense—not in Black's—neither secession nor coercion was constitutionally defensible. Therefore his conclusion was conciliation, mutual conciliation. For this he pleaded eloquently. In phrases almost Websterian he painted the glories of the Union. Not only had it brought prosperity and power, but throughout the world it was a demonstration to the friends of freedom of the realization of their hopes. The Union was "the grandest temple which [had] ever been dedicated to human freedom since the world began."

Buchanan's solution, the use of conciliation, was the time-honored process of constitutional amendment. Either Congress or the states might originate an "explanatory" amendment regarding slavery. This amendment should embrace three points. It should recognize the right of property in slaves "in the States where it now exists or may hereafter exist." It should ensure protection of the right of property in slaves in all the common territories until they were admitted as states "with or without slavery as their constitutions may prescribe." Finally the amendment should reaffirm in specific language the right of the master to have fugitive slaves restored and should contain "a declaration that all State laws impairing or defeating this right, are violations of the Constitution, and are consequently null and void."[31]

He put the last touches on this conciliatory document on Sunday December 2, and then called in Trescott. He requested the Assistant Secretary to go at once to South Carolina with a personal copy of this message for Governor Gist, for he still had the strange delusion that its logic might arrest immediate secession. The Assistant Secretary agreed to go; he probably wanted to be home to vote December 6, but he told the President emphatically that his hope was vain. He gave Buchanan a vivid picture of the rush of events in South Carolina, as it was reported to him by correspondents, and capped the climax by reading Governor Gist's latest letter to him, which seemed to prove conclusively that secession was only a matter of days. The chief magistrate was dismally impressed but did not abandon his plan. He especially requested Trescott, before going, to repeat all this to Cass because the aged Secretary seemed so confident that reenforcements would prevent action by Carolinians. Buchanan hoped that Trescott could show Cass that reenforcements would only light the fire the sooner.[32]

Thus the President was experiencing the weakening effects of divided counsels. He had followed his natural inclination to avoid any definite decision or positive action. By his ingenious logic he had succeeded, so he thought, in at least passing the responsibility on to the Congress assembling on the morrow. He was first and foremost a politician. He knew Congress would vote him no aid. War, if it came, he believed would be a Republican war; so let the Republicans bear the responsibility.

Chapter 21

The Weakness of Divided Counsels

THE DEMOCRATIC congressional leaders gathering in Washington to meet the crisis were more demoralized than before the campaign. The wounds of the contest were festering, and the party had little left of its once notable morale. Yet the wheels of legislation must turn again if the government were to be saved from falling apart.

There was scarcely any coherence left to the party, now disintegrated into five blocs of which the most aggressive was the Breckinridge bloc from the lower South. Its members returned to the Capitol filled with zeal for a new cause, which they wished to help as much as possible in the short Washington residence remaining to them. When the news of Lincoln's election was certified there had been some doubt whether this group should return. The South Carolina and Mississippi delegations had caucused, and there had been other conferences and correspondence.[1] The result was that all had come, save the two Senators from South Carolina.

The twelve Democratic Senators and thirty Representatives of the lower South had at least two reasons for returning. If they stayed away the Republicans would secure easy control of the House and might be able to dominate the Senate, so that the power of the federal government could be turned against them. More important, they were disappointed at the apathy in the upper South.[2] They wanted the chance to meet and press their associates from that section. They had come to arrange for a peaceable separation from the northern states and to promote their new confederacy. These men had no interest in averting the crisis; their purpose was to hurry it on.

The second Democratic bloc was that headed by Douglas. Despite his defeat, he had been strengthened by the election. His popular vote of 1,200,000 showed him possessed of a formidable following, larger than that of Breckinridge. The victories of his followers in congressional contests appeared to have deprived the Republicans of their hoped-for control of the next Congress—*if* there were no secession. In the new House, which normally would not meet until December, 1861, it would take 120 votes to elect a Speaker, provided there was no secession. The Republicans in the elections already held had won only 99, and they could not count on more than 12 in the elections of 1861; if the one northern Whig joined them, 112 seemed their maximum. The Democrats had secured 51 seats and were reasonably sure of 50 more. The southern opposition, though it had elected only 2 so far, might reasonably expect a bloc of 25.[3]

The key to these statistics was the fact that there were 37 northern Democrats, 5 more than in the expiring Congress. If the previous Speakership contest meant anything, organization could be secured only by a coalition of Republicans and Douglas Democrats, and the Douglas men were now sufficiently strong to dictate their own terms. However, the secession of even the Gulf states would leave them powerless and free the Republicans from the necessity of meeting their demands.

Douglas would be even better situated in the next Senate— again *if* there were no secession. The managers there were going to lose Gwin, Lane, Fitch, and Bigler. The latter two would be succeeded by Republicans, and the former probably by Douglas Democrats. Evidently Democratic control, if it were maintained, would depend upon Douglas and the Pacific coast Senators or perhaps on Douglas alone. Such a situation would have been intolerable to the managers from the South and may have been one reason why they were now so eager for secession. They saw that their power was gone.

The Douglas bloc therefore had everything to gain by arresting secession, and planned to exert every effort to find a Union-saving formula. It could count on some help from the few non-Douglas Democrats in Pennsylvania, New Jersey, Indiana, and the Pacific coast, who in this cause were like-minded; their number fluctuated, but it contained at least 6 Senators and perhaps 30 Representatives.

Between these two blocs were 14 Senators and 35 Representatives from the upper South. They were badly split, but the majority of them were disposed to delay secession, at least until an overt act had been perpetrated; and a number of them were willing to join with the Douglas men and the southern opposition groups in working for compromise. They were very much between two fires, however, for the determined secession bloc worked on them constantly.

Two minor factions in the Democracy complicated the difficulties of promoting compromise. The Pacific coast Democrats found themselves in a new and unexpected position of power. The resignation of Chesnut and Hammond left a Senate of 36 Democrats, 26 Republicans and 2 opposition. This did not furnish a very stable Democratic majority, for 2 of the 36 were Douglas and Pugh. The Democratic senatorial managers were really dependent for their control upon Gwin and Latham of California and Lane of Oregon, who had legislative axes to grind and would not hesitate to use their power. In the House the California Congressmen, Burch and Scott, were southern sympathizers, and so was the New Mexican delegate, Otero; the delegate from Washington territory, Isaac I. Stevens, had been Breckinridge's campaign manager. Rumors were rife that the western seaboard might break away and form a Pacific confederacy; some persons believed there were enough men of southern antecedents out there to swing it.[4] Their position gave the Pacific coast bloc an unusual importance in the balance of power which they tried to use in various ways, open and hidden.

Finally there was some semblance of a middle western bloc which never quite came to the surface. Vallandigham, Pendleton, and Cox of Ohio had just been reelected and represented sizable constituencies; so did McClernand and "Black Jack" Logan of Illinois. Much was at stake for them. If the mouth of the Mississippi were to become a foreign port their constituencies would be at the economic mercy of the New Orleans authorities; some recalled the unhappy days of Spanish and French control. There was definite hope among southerners that this prospect might lead the Northwest to join their new confederacy. Even among northwesterners there was talk of central confederacy made up of the states in the Ohio and Mississippi valleys.[5] These possibilities were part of the exaggerated intrigue of this troubled session.

The shattered Democracy was hardly in shape to face the triumphant Republicans. The latter, though already showing signs of factions, were united in their avid anticipation of the fruits of power. They seemed careless about the crisis, in fact most of them underestimated it. They had traveled little if at all in the South; knowing relatively few southerners, they judged them largely by their spokesmen in Washington. These men were noted for their fire eating on the floor, their good-fellowship after hours, their bluff, their aptness at making heavy demands and then accepting compromise.[6] Mrs. Jefferson Davis spoke of them as "the Botany Bay, . . . the bear garden of the South." So many Republicans couldn't believe the South was serious; even so astute a man as Lincoln over-estimated the Union sentiment in "Secessia." Besides, the Republicans had not won Congress yet, and the secession of a few would give them the control they lacked. Others were not worried particularly over another republic and were inclined to say "Wayward sisters, depart in peace." Some contemptuously remarked that the South could not be kicked out of the Union.[7]

In this maze of factions, conflicting interests, and lack of understanding, it was hard to see how any combination could be contrived to agree on a Union-saving formula. However, if any was to be evolved it must be by Douglas Democrats and those from the upper South, with what little help the southern opposition might be willing and able to supply. Even if all these were agreed they must still convert some of the Republicans, or more unlikely still, some of the secessionists.

The heart of the difficulty was its logical impossibility. John A. Campbell of Alabama, associate justice of the Supreme Court, expounded this impasse with rare cogency:[8]

"The truth is that the grievances complained of by the cotton States are either not material or not remediable. What guarantee will prevent the denunciation of slavery and slave-holders in the pulpit, press and academy? What will prevent the pragmatical and conceited Yankee from making foreign newspapers and magazines the vehicle of his mendacity and spite? What will prevent their women and fanatics from making petitions to Congress and their politicians from irritating the Southern representatives? Who can give self-control to Southern members or prevent them from showing that slavery is ordained by Heaven?

"The agitation is an agitation resulting from a fundamental difference between the sections on questions of active and living interest. This is the irrepressible conflict against which laws are powerless unless supported by an inquisition or an army.

"By the Nebraska and Kansas Act and the Dred Scott decision, every act of Congress that places any prohibition upon slavery was removed from the legislation and jurisprudence of the United States. It was determined that Congress could not prohibit the introduction of slaves into the territories and that they were protected in the territories by the Constitution, as property. . . . The bill of rights, as the amendments to the Constitution are called, protects the rights of a master to his slaves. Now that bill of rights embodies the clauses of the Magna Charta of England under which the rights to private property in England have been reposing for eight hundred years.

"But this does not satisfy politicians or even senators and representatives. They want the endorsement of a party convention such as that of Charleston and they are brought to insurrection and disunion because a President-elect holds contrary political or social opinions. There is no respect for written law or for judicial decision nor confidence that they afford protection. What has excited and alarmed them is the agitation of tumultuous political assemblies, and this is not within the reach of law or decision.

"I do not know of a single statute in the statute book that a Southern man can complain of. . . . New Mexico and Utah are slave-holding communities. The status of the territories is all and more than all that any Southern statesman has attempted to secure, for the Dred Scott decision is something they could not agitate for.

"Then again the fugitive slave act is of comparatively small consequence to the cotton States and in the nature of the subject is almost useless. The slave has resources that are adequate to his successful flight from the border States. The facilities to reach Canada are so many and efficient that he can attain his asylum before he is missed from the plantation.

"There can be a provision for an indemnity, but that goes to the master, and not one in ten thousand of those who agitate this subject have ever lost or have ever known of a person who has lost a slave. It ought to be said that the courts of the Northern States have all been firm on the subject of the fugitive slave act except Wisconsin. The decisions in Massachusetts, Ohio, Pennsylvania have all been favorable to law and order."

How could such a complex be straightened out by words? Yet anxious minds undertook it. Border-state Democratic Senators, Powell, Bayard, and Saulsbury, with Douglas, Bigler, and Andrew Johnson of Tennessee and an opposition ally, Crittenden, moved to action in the upper house. In the lower body, Cochrane, Sickles, Florence, Adrain, Cox, Pendleton, Vallandigham, English and McClernand of the northern Democracy, Millson, Bocock, and Burnett of the border states, and Hamilton and Rust from the lower South labored to the same end, with the aid of Etheridge, Maynard, Boteler, and

Bouligny of the opposition. Theirs was a seemingly impossible task, for 75 per cent of the Senate and 60 per cent of the House were against them.

II

The members of these blocs arrived in Washington with various ideas and plans, united in only one respect; few of them seemed disposed to give much attention to the plan for constitutional guarantees suggested by the President. Caucusing began immediately. Northwestern members, without respect to party, got together to compare notes, and some of them gave out statements that pacification must be had whatever the sacrifice. Southerners met to work on the problem of uniting the South, a possibility which did not seem very immediate, for leaders in the upper South had been laboring on compromise proposals.[9]

The Union Democratic Senators and Crittenden worked out a program. Powell of Kentucky was designated to move the creation of a committee of thirteen to study the President's plan. This body, it was hoped, would endorse a conciliatory formula which would bear Crittenden's name. As he sat in Clay's seat he had been chosen for this part to capitalize the magic of Clay's record as the Great Compromiser. Similar tactics were developing in the House. John Cochrane had a resolution calling for a committee of one from each state for the same purpose. McClernand of Illinois and Winslow of North Carolina had like resolutions; so had Boteler of Virginia and Maynard of Tennessee, of the opposition. These Representatives soon agreed to capitalize Boteler's residence in the Harpers Ferry district. What could be more dramatic than the representative from the scene of John Brown's foray coming forward with the olive branch? That would be good politics and would be disconcerting to the secessionists, who were already disturbed by the fact that so many southerners had brought their families. It looked too much as though they expected to remain for the season.[10] On the eve of the meeting of Congress Washington was one vast committee of the whole on the state of the Union.

The House opened its sessions on a note ominous for concession. Before it even heard the President's message, the Republican leadership represented by Grow gave unmistakable evidence that it was going to drive through the Chicago platform measures, with no thought of concessions to save the

Union. Almost as soon as the chaplain's voice died away the Pennsylvanian pushed forward the homestead bill for early passage. This was defiance of the South.

Next day, after Buchanan's message had been read, the work of the conciliators began. Boteler introduced his resolution for a committee of thirty-three as Cochrane gracefully withdrew his own. McClernand introduced his proposal but did not press it. The only sour note for the Union Democrats was a resolution by Morris, an Illinois Douglasite, which declared that there was nothing in the election of Lincoln to justify dissolution. There was no delay in voting. The nays came largely from the radical Republican wing, another indication that it did not want compromise. South Carolina, Florida, Mississippi, and Alabama Representatives announced that their states were so nearly out of the Union that they would not vote, although the Alabama delegation was not unanimous. The Texans and the Democrats from Louisiana silently refrained from voting; Georgia was divided. The Boteler resolution passed, 145–38; the speaker must now appoint a committee to work out a conciliatory compromise for avoiding secession.

The next day Powell of Kentucky gave notice of his motion for a similar committee in the Senate, but its passage was postponed by an angry debate started by Clingman of North Carolina and kept bitter by certain less important southerners like Iverson and Wigfall and radical Republicans such as Hale. Lane of Oregon expressed his full sympathy for the South and secession and denounced coercion. Saulsbury of Delaware tried to pour oil on the troubled waters. The Democratic leadership, however, was almost completely silent, a meaningful silence which emphasized Clingman's argument that the constitutional guarantees suggested by the President must be provided at once. The South, he warned, would no longer permit abolitionists to circulate Helper's book within its communities "arraying the non-slaveholders and poor men against the wealthy." Clingman quoted a Texas colleague who described the hanging of such advocates in his state during the summer just past.

On Thursday Speaker Pennington announced the House committee. Of the fourteen Democrats who found themselves associated with sixteen Republicans and three opposition, hardly any favored compromise. Twelve were from slave states, and of these only Rust of Arkansas and Millson of Virginia were going to take any positive steps toward conciliation. The other two Democrats were from California and Oregon; there was not a Douglas man on the committee. Even in Illinois where they had a majority of the delegation, a Republican was chosen. The Republican Thomas Corwin of Ohio was the chairman. If the Republicans wished to kill compromise, they could not have chosen a better committee for this purpose. When these appointments were announced, Hawkins of Florida begged to be excused on the ground that his state was practically out. Then Cochrane arose and made the keynote speech for conciliation, urging Hawkins to join in this effort to save the Republic. A vote on Hawkins's request was postponed when both houses voted to suspend until Monday.

The long week end was one of the most fateful in the entire history of the Republic. It demonstrated that the fifteen states of the South were not a united whole; and if the secession leaders had possessed sufficient wisdom to see the real significance of this division, secession would have been abandoned as hopeless. To be successful the new enterprise needed the entire southern strength, which the division of opinion indicated it could not get.

Three caucuses marked this fateful recess. The first on Thursday evening was a gathering of the southern radicals. Everything had gone against them in their efforts to unite the South, and they met to seek new strength from counsel. They were scornful and perhaps fearful of the Committee of Thirty-three, which they resented as a delaying device, as a tub thrown to a whale. A few, like Hawkins, wanted to boycott it, but that notion was generally disapproved. The meeting reached no conclusion, partly because reporters were found to be present and it was apparent that the deliberations would be used by the press.

An attempt was made to have more private discussion on Friday evening, with a meeting in the garret of Brown's Hotel. The moderates were invited, and the whole question of united action was thrashed out. There were three conflicting programs, and the debate seemed to prove the impossibility of agreeing on any. Immediate secession was one program, and its proponents now saw how definitely they were in a minority. Their opponents had two alternative proposals. Some insisted that there should be no secession by single states until a general agreement could be reached on a definite date for cooperative action, and Cobb and Thompson had been endeavoring to avert secession until March 4. That date was sug-

gested by Cobb's kinsman, L. Q. C. Lamar of the Mississippi
delegation who, oddly enough, was destined to help uphold
the Constitution of the United States when he became a
member of the Federal Supreme Court a quarter of a century
later. Lamar's plan was for the southern states to declare
individually for a new confederacy, using the Constitution
of the United States, holding elections according to its procedures and choosing a new President, Vice President, and
Congress. The sponsors of this plan hoped that the free states,
except New England, might be willing to join in this new
government, which they designed to inaugurate on March 4.[11]
Secretary Thompson supported this scheme and may have
had some hand in formulating it.

The third program before this caucus embraced the drafting
of a series of demands—in the form of guarantees to the
South—to be made of the northern members of Congress.
If these were accepted, then secession could be arrested. If
they were rejected, then the quicker it were consummated the
better. The guarantees were debated vigorously, with the
minority secessionists particularly eloquent in seeking converts. They feared delay might be fatal to their plans, because
of what they were hearing from home. In the election campaigns now being operated in the lower South the coolness of
the upper South was giving aid and comfort to the opponents
of immediate action.

The lack of harmony among southerners troubled thoughtful
Senators, and on Saturday night they gathered with Vice
President Breckinridge to go over the situation. By this time
it was apparent that the secessionists had overplayed their
hand. They had aroused resentment among their fellow
southerners. The men from the upper South claimed that the
Gulf Squadron was acting as if it alone knew what was best
for the South, was trying to order them about and to dominate the sectional situation. They would not submit to dictation by the secessionists. Powell and Breckinridge vigorously supported the plan to seek guarantees. They felt
secession would not be justified unless the northern representatives gave definite evidence of their hostility by rejecting
a guarantee of constitutional rights. Furthermore, they
thought that such a rejection would unite the South, which
the election of Lincoln had not succeeded in doing. One
Senator suggested that Buchanan seize San Juan Island; a
war with Great Britain would cure secession.

The result of these caucuses was a victory for those who

wished to give the northern representatives an opportunity to consider guarantees. A series of such demands was drawn up, and Taylor of Louisiana, a Douglas man, was told off to present them to the Committee of Thirty-three as soon as it organized. These resolutions guaranteed: that rights of property be vindicated and enforced in favor of our citizens in foreign relations; that the common territories of the United States should be open to citizens from all the states who might take their property thither and have it protected there; that territories should be admitted as states only when they had sufficient population to entitle them to a representative in Congress, and then they might be admitted with or without slavery as they might decide; that fugitive slaves should be paid for by states to which they might escape; that there should be no Negro voters; and that Congress might not legislate against slavery in the territories or the District of Columbia.

The authors of these demands then conceded to the radicals the next moves, if these guarantees were refused. Reuben Davis of Mississippi was to announce that if these resolutions or others, which might appease the South, were not adopted, he and his friends would despatch a manifesto homewards, broadcasting the failure of compromise and calling upon the South to take secession as the only honorable course left. Pugh of Alabama and the bibulous Senator Wigfall were to draft such a document.[12] Incidentally, Wigfall had more company than ever at the bar, just now, for these momentous decisions were taken in the course of a riotous and disillusioning week end marked by intoxication. A half-dozen or so of the most ardent secessionists were so drunk as to attract notice even in so inebriated a city as Washington.[13]

The caucuses so cleary revealed the southern split that the promoters from the lower tier realized they must start alone. Even Secretary of the Treasury Cobb was convinced that his plan of cooperative action on March 4 was hopeless. Also the news from Georgia was challenging him; Toombs was still down there, meeting stiff opposition, and Stephens and Johnson were fighting immediate secession. Georgia's January 2 election seemed certain to be close. The Secretary had finished his address to the people of Georgia, urging them to secede on March 4, and he had it fresh from the printers in pamphlet form ready for wide distribution. He realized that now he must go. He sent a copy to Buchanan by Black's hand December 8, and that Saturday night he re-signed, to return home as soon as possible.[14]

Thus the first week of Congress had demonstrated clearly the confusion of counsels in the broken ranks of the Democracy. It should have made the secession group realize the unreality of their dream of a new republic of fifteen united slave-labor states.

III

The second week of Congress was marked by House efforts to make their Committee of Thirty-three function, no easy task. In the first place Hawkins of Florida and one or two other radicals still sought to escape duty on it. For two days the House argued over excusing them and finally decided in the negative. During this wrangle there was much complaint regarding the composition, particularly from northern Democrats because they had been ignored. Several of them spoke bitterly. Vallandigham and McClernand threatened a northwestern confederacy; they would not be dependent on the eastern Republicans. Dan Sickles even suggested that New York might secede and form a free city. This debate did not subside until Wednesday, the 12th, which had been set aside for the introduction of propositions to be considered by the newly organized committee. Resolutions for this purpose poured in like a flood.

On that same day the new committee had its first meeting. The stack of resolutions from Congressmen in general was on the table before them; but all their interest was for the moment absorbed by the demands for guarantees and the ultimatum from the southern caucus. Taylor and Davis carried out their roles, and the committee recognized that this was their first business. They adjourned to sleep on the ultimatum. Next morning, Thursday the 13th, an attempt was made to satisfy the demands by a token statement. Rust of Arkansas brought to the committee room a resolution to the effect that the grievances of the South were "not without cause," and that just concessions and additional and more specific and effectual guarantees "are indispensable to the perpetuation of the Union." This pronouncement Dunn of Indiana, Republican, amended with Rust's consent to state that these grievances were "greatly to be regretted," and that "any reasonable, proper constitutional remedies, and additional and more specific and effectual guarantees of their peculiar rights . . . should be promptly and cheerfully granted." These fair words were all that the committee would concede, and half of the Republicans voted against even this.[15]

The secessionists reacted immediately. Their caucus reconvened that evening and duly adopted the Pugh-Wigfall manifesto, a flamboyant document ending: "The argument is exhausted. All hope of relief is extinguished." Seven Senators agreed to sign this, Davis and Brown of Mississippi, Iverson of Georgia, Wigfall and Hemphill of Texas, Benjamin, and even Slidell about whom the authors had been doubtful; Toombs had not yet arrived. Twenty-three Representatives from the states of Alabama, Florida, South Carolina, and even North Carolina and Arkansas contributed their signatures. This message sizzled over the wires to be in Columbia on the eve of the meeting of the South Carolina convention and to be circulated throughout the campaigns in the Gulf states and Georgia. It was well timed.[16]

After the signing of the manifesto the Senator managers definitely abandoned hope of stopping South Carolina's immediate withdrawal. If the Union with the South protected were to be saved now, it must be by using secession as a bargaining point. They advised the Palmetto state to go right ahead and, as soon as she had withdrawn, to start negotiating. They suggested that she appoint commissioners—as soon as the ordinance of secession was passed—to come to Washington in quest of recognition and to treat for the return of federal property to the new republic. They might prove a convenient medium for starting negotiations for a restored Union, on terms which would give the South the security over which the people were so apprehensive.

Cobb departed next day to Columbia, where he was going to visit the convention and give counsel regarding the formation of a southern confederacy. The Senators thought he would be an excellent agent to convey their plan. So Trescott, who was still in the State Department, was deputed to write him and send the letter off to overtake him. The Democratic leadership in the Senate was ready to press the issue on this line.[17]

Congress again adjourned on Thursday for a second long week end, faced with the knowledge that the South Carolina convention would meet on Monday. Like the preceding week end it was a busy one, only this time the conciliators rather than the secessionists were the more distraught. Certain border-state Democrats saw that propaganda against secession must be sent South immediately. Senator Andrew Johnson and Congressmen Gilmer, Millson, and others joined with J. C. G. Kennedy, director of the census, to gather lists of voters to whom some twenty of Kennedy's clerks nightly addressed and mailed Union speeches.

Several bipartisan caucuses were held by the delegations from New York, Pennsylvania, Illinois, and Ohio. The New Yorkers met in John Cochrane's rooms on Sunday to consider a plan formed by the Democrats from New York City; it would establish the line 36°30′ as the boundary between slavery and freedom. Slaves might be taken to forts, arsenals, or other federal property above the line and were to be protected in interstate travel. The foreign trade in Negroes was still to be prohibited. The fugitive slave laws were to be reformed. Finally, no President hereafter could be reelected, or elected by a minority, like Lincoln. The Republican majority of the New York delegation would not accept such proposals, and so Reynolds, a Douglas lame duck, and Sickles introduced others. Sickles proposed that the New York and Virginia delegations in conference draft a compromise formula. Reynolds would merely pledge the maintenance of the Union. His resolution was finally adopted. Sickles, Barr, and Maclay, New York City Democrats, voted against it as a meaningless gesture.[18]

Conferences among the Pennsylvania, Ohio, and Illinois delegations the next morning met with no better success. There was really no common ground between the Democrats and Republicans. It was plain, particularly among the Ohioans, that the Republicans wanted no compromise. The Democrats on the other hand refused to endorse proposals for coercion or to give pledges of support for Lincoln. In this state of affairs, Congress reconvened Monday noon, just a few hours before the South Carolina convention would meet. This would be a crucial week. If there was to be any compromise it must be brought forward quickly.[19]

The House soon demonstrated its complete inability to meet the situation. The Republicans sat back and left the field to the Democrats, who merely underlined their weakness as already displayed in the state caucuses. Florence of Pennsylvania introduced a proposition for a constitutional amendment recognizing slave property in states and territories and providing that no new states might be admitted unless by the consent of two-thirds of the membership of both Houses; it stipulated also that a three-fourths vote was necessary to override a presidential veto of an admission bill. Cochrane of New York offered another affirming the Dred Scott decision, protecting slave property in territories, and providing for admission of new states with or without slavery as their constitutions might stipulate; this had some of the earmarks of Douglas. Sickles went so far as to offer an amendment providing machinery for peaceable secession. These embryo constitutional amendments were referred to the Committee of Thirty-three, which Morris, Illinois Democrat, contemptuously called "The Coffin."

A second group of efforts was made to get immediate consideration of reassuring resolutions which could be telegraphed to South Carolina as evidence of a conciliatory spirit. Adrain of New Jersey introduced one which deprecated the spirit of disobedience to the Constitution and recommended that the states repeal such statutes as the personal liberty laws. This friendly but impotent gesture was adopted, 153–14, though on a preliminary test vote 55 Republicans were against it. Then Morris of Illinois secured consideration of the resolution he had been trying to bring up for nearly a fortnight. His statement was largely in Washington's language from his farewell address and affirmed loyalty to the Union, with the additional resolve that Lincoln's election was no justification for destroying the bond. It was passed, 116–44, because the Republicans agreed. Southern Democrats, a few of the opposition, Sickles of New York, and Scott of California made up the minority; Cochrane, Florence, Vallandigham, and Pendleton refrained from voting.

The final Democratic move was a resolution from Crawford of Georgia that Negroes could not become citizens. This proposal was put over until the next day by the Republicans and then was laid on the table, 87–81. Most of the Democrats, save Reynolds, voted with the minority. Having thus accomplished less than nothing, the House turned to the more congenial task of largesse, subsidy, and appropriations. On the day of South Carolina's decision, as if in defiance, the House passed the Pacific Railroad bill and sent it over to the Senate like the homestead bill. Then it adjourned for a third long week end, not to reassemble until Christmas Eve.

Conciliation, if it were to come at all, evidently must come from the Senate, although the Upper House so far had been even less inclined to compromise. Powell's resolution for a committee on conciliation had run into heavy weather. The radical southerners, according to Seward, made this

proposal "the medium of offers to the free states of unconditional surrender to be complied with without hesitation, or
secession would be hurried on by inflammatory accounts of
refusal."[20] Numerous Senators under the pretense of debating
Powell's resolution made a variety of propositions. Their oratory emphasized more forcibly than ever the wide variance
of opinion and the lack of agreement on remedies.

Not until December 18 was there any hope. On that day
Crittenden made a speech which he climaxed by presenting
the most significant proposal yet proffered. He would extend
the Missouri Compromise line to the Pacific and prohibit
slavery north of it. South of it slavery could exist and must
be protected. New states were to be admitted with or without slavery as their constitutions decreed. Congress could
not abolish slavery in the states, nor in the District of Columbia, nor prohibit interstate transportation of slaves where
slavery was recognized. Fugitive slaves should be paid for.
The fugitive slave law should be improved and enforced,
and foreign slave trade should be suppressed. These omnibus
resolutions bore Crittenden's name but represented the views
of a majority of the Democrats, North and South, even
Toombs and Jefferson Davis proving willing to accept them.[21]
They may truthfully be called a Democratic proposal. The
same day the Senate finally adopted Powell's resolution,
without a roll call, and all the compromises were referred
to the Senate's select committee of thirteen. Its personnel
was announced December 20, the day South Carolina withdrew. The Senate's three weeks of delay had been fatal to
conciliation.

IV

While Congress was ignoring his peace proposals, Buchanan and his cabinet were wrestling with the problem of
South Carolina. During the first week of the session various
tidings had come from Charleston. Major Anderson wrote[22]
that his position was critical and he must have more definite
instructions as to what to do in case of attack; the Charleston
populace was aroused over the delivery of artillery to the
forts and might try to seize the works. Just before Cobb resigned, it was decided to order Anderson to hold his positions
and fight if attacked. On Thursday December 6, Floyd sent
the assistant adjutant general, Lieutenant Colonel Don Carlos
Buell, to Charleston to inspect Anderson's position and give
him adequate instructions. Arrived there, Buell agreed with

Anderson that Fort Moultrie was peculiarly vulnerable. He told him that the administration had no intention of surrendering, come what might, and therefore he was to take every step necessary to hold his post. He could dispose of his force in the safest manner, either at Moultrie or at Sumter, whenever he had "tangible evidence of a design to proceed to a hostile act." Buell wrote out these instructions before leaving Anderson on December 11, and filed a copy at the War Department upon his return there.[23] This record soon assumed unexpected importance.

During Buell's absence, the first week of the session terminated, and during the week end of southern caucusing the South Carolina Congressmen had had a prolonged interview with Buchanan. They were under pressure from home to secure the surrender of the forts. They and Governor Gist were convinced, probably by Trescott and Cobb, that the administration would not surrender. Therefore it became their purpose to prevent the sending of any reenforcements. They called on the President Saturday December 8, asking him point-blank to promise not to reenforce the forts; for, they said, they were confident if he gave such a pledge South Carolina would make no move against federal property.

Buchanan was wary and tried as usual to be crafty. He assured them that he had no intention (1) of reenforcing the forts or (2) of altering the present disposition of the troops. They need have no apprehension; he was sure they and he understood each other. They left him to put the substance of their understanding in writing and took it back to him in the form of a signed statement. He added to it an interpretive endorsement, to the effect that as they had no power to bind South Carolina he could not undertake to bind the United States. He repeated his verbal assurances of their complete understanding and told them that if his purposes changed he would return this paper to them.[24] He believed he had made no commitment, but he had used double talk which led them later to be sure he had.

The problem of the forts complicated the President's cabinet relations. Cobb, in resigning the day of the first interview with the South Carolinians, dealt a blow personally as well as politically to President Buchanan, who apparently liked Cobb best of all the cabinet. Having no alternative to accepting the resignation, Buchanan sought immediately to find a successor. Through Thompson and Black he offered the post to the North Carolina Congressman, Lawrence

O'B. Branch,[25] who declined it. Then he took from the Interior Department the Commissioner of Patents, Philip F. Thomas of Maryland. Thomas must wrestle with the perplexities of a Treasury so bare that the government could not meet its pay rolls; even Congressmen were without their salaries.

No sooner was this place filled than a second resignation came, that of Cass. The ancient Secretary of State was in feeble health, liable to attacks of vertigo, and his family were anxious about him. They wanted to get him away from the excitement and worry of Washington. Cass was disturbed by the decision to send no reenforcements to Charleston, being unimpressed by Trescott's arguments; and his son-in-law, Ledyard, saw an opportunity for the old general to retire from this discredited administration with some revival of prestige. He persuaded him to resign in protest over the failure to send reenforcements. Therefore on December 11, regular cabinet day, Cass raised the issue again; and when he failed to persuade the group to change their policy, he told Buchanan he would resign. The next day he and Ledyard prepared his resignation, but then he held it back. His delay was caused probably by his constitutional indecision, or perhaps by the news that the aged General Scott had at length recovered sufficiently to travel and was arriving in Washington on the 12th. His advice might change the President's mind.[26]

Scott, then seventy-four years of age, arrived on schedule, rather the worse for wear and so dropsical as to move only with difficulty. He went over matters with Floyd at the War Department and was ready by December 15 to see the President. That Saturday was another stormy one, with heavy snow drifting through the streets.[27] Those who read the papers found news of President Buchanan's search for refuge from another sort of storm. He had issued a solemn proclamation: "The Union . . . is . . . threatened with alarming and immediate danger—panic and distress of a fearful character prevail throughout the land—our laboring population are without employment . . . indeed, hope seems to have deserted the minds of men." Let the nation set aside January 4 as a day of fasting and prayer. "Let us humble ourselves before the Most High, . . . let us implore Him to remove from our hearts that false pride of opinion which would impel us to persevere in wrong for the sake of consistency; rather than yield a just submission to the unforeseen exigencies by which we are now surrounded. . . . [May] an omnipotent Providence overrule existing evils for permanent good." Such was his desperate hope; like many previous rulers in times of emergency, he sought thus to invoke religion to calm the tumult.[28]

Scott and Floyd spent much of the day at the White House, arguing back and forth. The General was garrulously eloquent as he recalled the way in which he and Jackson had handled South Carolina in 1833; he insisted upon reenforcements. Buchanan still demurred; evidently apprised of the plan of the Senators that a commission be sent up from South Carolina, he was anxious to turn the whole problem over to Congress for decision. Scott, however, was emphatic that such negotiations would delay matters and soon it would be too late to send any help. Floyd seemed to think no immediate action was needed because the *Brooklyn* was at Norfolk and might at any time take some 300 men down from Fortress Monroe. Scott said this was a false hope; as there were only 500 men at the fort and so large a contingent could not be spared, other means must be prepared. They reached no decision, and Scott went back to his office to go over the man-power situation and to write the President some details of the 1833 tactics which he felt he had not emphasized sufficiently.[29] That evening Black brought Cass's letter of resignation to the President; Jackson's Secretary of War, though little like Old Hickory, could at least make his exit in a burst of admonitory patriotism.

Sunday was clear and dazzling with the sun shining on the great white mantle of snow. Cass now had doubts as to the wisdom of his resignation, called in Black and Thompson, and sent them to Buchanan with the message that he was willing to recall his letter. The President, however, who had never liked him and had found his torpor and senile incapacity a drag, was not so minded. He was glad Cass had withdrawn and wanted no embarrassing explanations. He tendered Cass's post to Black, and after his acceptance took up the question of the new Attorney General. He wanted J. M. Carlisle, but Black had the man ready: his friend, Edwin M. Stanton from Pittsburgh, who had been helping him in some particularly important and difficult land cases in California. Black felt that he alone could step into the place without too great waste of the precious last weeks of the administration. Buchanan did not trust Stanton, with good reason as it later turned out, but took him at Black's insistence. The cabinet

was now committed to "no surrender and no reenforcements." This policy the President thought should be respected
by the South and should postpone action by it until he retired on March 4.[30]

While thus temporizing on the troublesome problem of
the forts, Buchanan and his cabinet sought other means to
arrest secession. This was to be done by diplomacy. An unexpected opportunity presented itself on the second stormy
week end. The Governor of Mississippi invited Jacob Thompson to go to his natal state of North Carolina, as the representative of his adopted state, "to express the earnest hope
of Mississippi that North Carolina will cooperate with her,
in the adoption of efficient measures for the common defense
of the South." This request reached the Secretary of the Interior Thursday December 13. He was, as always, shrewd
and unemotional. He knew that whatever of political fortune
lay still ahead of him must be in Mississippi; if he failed to
retain the confidence of the machine there, he was through.
Glad of this proof that he still had standing, he wanted to go
and asked President Buchanan for permission.

Buchanan was doubtful of the propriety of this mission,
as most people have been ever since. The head of the federal
government was being asked to condone secessionist activity
by a member of his own cabinet. However, Thompson maintained that he was going down to persuade North Carolina
to propose a concert of action among southern states after
March 4. He told the President that such a proposition might
arrest secession in Mississippi and elsewhere and give the conciliationists more time to promote compromise. It would also,
he skillfully added, permit Buchanan to retire from office
with the Union still largely intact. On the understanding,
then, that he was to be ambassador of delay, Buchanan consented to this mission, and Thompson set out on Monday
December 17.[31]

Another reason why Buchanan allowed Thompson to go
was the fact that he was planning similar attempts in South
Carolina, Alabama, and Illinois. He called in Caleb Cushing
and asked him to go to the South Carolina convention with
a personal plea for delay, "so long as to allow the people of
her sister States an opportunity to manifest their opinion upon
the causes which have led to this proceeding." Cushing departed the day after Thompson, with a letter to Governor
Gist.[32] The President also was willing to have ex-President
Pierce go to Alabama. However, in spite of the insistence of

Cushing and Justice Campbell, Pierce found his health would not permit him to make the journey. He wrote a letter instead, urging calm and delay, which was printed in the Alabama press and had no noticeable effect.

Buchanan's third mission was in a different direction. Davis and Toombs were ready, so they said, to accept the Crittenden Compromise if the Republicans would. The attitude of the latter was hostile, but they were suspending judgment until they knew the views of their titular chief, President elect Lincoln. Buchanan felt he must try to influence him, and so he called upon Duff Green to go to Springfield with Buchanan's invitation to Lincoln to come to Washington and join in the efforts for peace. Buchanan hoped that he might endorse the Crittenden Compromise.[33]

V

During this distribution of olive branches, the leaves were falling off the calendar, and December 17, the day of the meeting of South Carolina's convention, arrived. The delegates had gathered in Columbia during the gubernatorial contest, which had taken several days and several ballots in the legislature. Then the Democrats had triumphed as they had hoped. Pickens had slipped in ahead of Rhett, Jamison, and Johnson to take the prize; he was forthwith inaugurated almost as the convention met.

Columbia was thronged. Commissioners from Alabama and Mississippi were in the town. The Governor of Florida had come in person. Howell Cobb was there. Also it was reported that smallpox had arrived. Therefore the delegates, assembling in the Baptist Church, were both aware of their political responsibility and disturbed by the possibility of epidemic. They organized after four ballots; the Democrats put up Orr, but Governor Gist decided it by giving way to the defeated gubernatorial candidate, General D. F. Jamison, who won 118–30. Then they decided to adjourn to Charleston, against the advice of Congressman Miles and others who thought they should secede first.

The delegates reassembled at Charleston on the afternoon of the 18th, in Institute Hall, scene of the historic Maytime destruction of the Democracy. Its acoustics had not improved, nor had the street clamor abated, and so the convention adjourned once again, this time to St. Andrews Hall. Here it spent the 19th in discussion of procedure, cheered on by a speech from the Alabama representative and a telegram from his Governor.[34] Buchanan's emissary, Cushing, did not arrive until the morning of the 20th. The bells were already ringing in anticipation of secession, and no one paid any attention to him. The Governor upon receiving him said, "I must tell you candidly that there is no hope for the Union."

At noon Chancellor Inglis was ready with an ordinance of secession. It was quickly considered, and at 1:30 P.M. unanimously adopted. The convention then adjourned, to reconvene at seven in Institute Hall. Here before a vast and admiring throng—in the absence of Cushing, who refused to attend—the delegates signed the engrossed copy. About nine o'clock the president of the convention proclaimed the State of South Carolina "an independent Commonwealth." The three commissioners suggested by the Senators were straightway appointed to go to Washington to treat with President Buchanan for the transfer of federal property to the new republic.[35] Cushing left the next morning, one reporter said, "in terror of his life."

The blow thus had fallen. What could not happen here, had happened here. As one obscure Charleston businessman put it:

"The North have waged a fierce and unrelenting war upon us for more than twenty years. They have held us up to the world in the most disgusting and humiliating light. They have, down to the present moment taunted us, by every means possible, and we have borne it until forbearance ceases to be a virtue. We warned them against it by entreaty and argument, yet they heeded not, until now, we have determined, Sampson like, to be free or perish under the ruins of our prison. For myself, as a Law abiding, a Union loving, and as I trust, a God fearing man, I had hoped that an honorable concession would be made by the Republicans . . . but they have maintained a dogged silence and indifference to every appeal, and now I would not, if I could, turn over my finger to adjust this difficulty. It is the suffering of innocent people that I must deplore. Thousands and millions will feel the pinch of poverty north and south in consequence but I have settled it in my mind, that it is better to meet the Crisis now, than defer it for our children.

"That all this will be ended in the bloodiest war that ever deluged any Country I have no doubt.

"Talk of a peaceful Revolution is out of the question. . . . It will be blood against blood. Kin against kin, brave against brave. It is useless for men of either section to boast of bravery or attempt to depreciate or disparage the other.

"We know they are all brave. Our blood and theirs are the same. . . . Our people are putting their houses in order. We know with whom we have to deal, we intend to act honourably in all things. Our minds are made up. All classes of our citizens understand what they have to do and there is but one feeling throughout the south as to the great point."[36]

The question remained: Was secession the wish of other southern states besides South Carolina? The elections of the Christmas season would give some further revelation. One thing was sure; the leaders of the northern Democracy in the administration and in Congress thus far had failed completely to arrest the advance of secession.

Chapter 22

Reorganizing the Administration

WITHIN FOUR DAYS after the secession of South Carolina, the voters of Mississippi, Florida, and Alabama went to the polls, and the campaigns in Georgia and Louisiana approached their climax. During the preceding fortnight political machinery in these states had been operating at very high speed. Though partisanship did not seem to show its face there was in reality a great deal of it.

The Democratic party was responding to clamor. A "wild and somewhat hysterical excitement" pervaded the lower South. Although Lincoln's election was "anticipated by every observant man," yet it produced all the effects of "a sudden and direct attack upon the rights of the people." The excitement was stimulated by the many rumors of insurrectionary attempts and conspiracies among the Negroes, instigated by white men suspected of being sent to the South for the purpose. To make matters infinitely worse, it was turning out to be a bad year; crops had been poor, money was scarce, food was selling at famine prices in some parts of South Carolina, Georgia, Alabama, and Mississippi. In fact some in the free states wondered why the southerners were choosing to secede in a year in which they were so poor and their neighbors to the north so rich. But public opinion had gone beyond reason and calculation. It was not even held back by the great land investments which southern speculators had in the Northwest, where they owned 1,500,000 acres.

The voters, the plain people, in large portions of the lower South were fearful and angry. This sentiment seemed stronger among the poor than among the rich. It was deeply felt by the non-slaveholders, the people who had been so effectively harangued about the evil character of the Republicans that they were determined to free themselves from the perils of abolition. The wealthy might flee insurrection and need not fear the competition of freed Negroes. Poor men, however, must stay with their scant acres and dare the possible social revolution and a degrading economic struggle with the erstwhile slaves. In the election the majority of them seem to have voted for Breckinridge, but now the Douglas men and numerous Bell men joined forces with their traditional foes.

The Democratic party leaders, high and low, had yielded to this pressure almost instantly. They quickly saw in the hysteria a variety of opportunities. Secession, they thought, would inaugurate a new order. It would not only provide security and economic advantage to the South but also make new places of honor and power. Those who had not satisfied their ambitious desires for office under the old order saw a new chance. The bankrupt and debt-burdened saw a new freedom. The restless and adventurous saw attractive opportunities inherent in change. There was everything to attract daring and vigorous leadership.

Despite the widespread hysteria, there was much opposition to the revolution. But the many opponents of immediate secession were handicapped by the shortness of the campaigns and by lack of organization. The fact that a number of the opposition party leaders were uncertain or were joining the secession stampede meant that those who wished to fight the move had no party machinery at hand such as the secessionists found in the Democratic state organizations. There was no time to build a new party or to find men to make effective rebuttals in the secession mass meeting which were the principal propaganda centers. Scattered rural populations in days of such inadequate transportation could not be covered by just a few speakers, and there were not many effective ones who were willing or able to work for the cause of delay. The conservatives were not temperamentally fitted to cope with fire eaters on the hustings.

The opponents of secession generally sought to rally behind delaying devices. They tried to persuade the voters to elect men who would arrange for interstate consultation and cooperation. They pointed out the dangers of separate state action. Only a united South could achieve the goal of independence. Weak fragments or even the lower South would be open to northern reprisals and hardly able to cope with them.

These swift-paced campaigns had some sinister figures lurking in the background. The Knights of the Golden Circle were heard of now and then. Numerous militia companies became unusually active; some of them were newly organized, others had been drilling since John Brown's Raid. In most instances they mounted the blue cockade of secession. There is some evidence, at least in Florida, that they sought to keep down Union sentiment by violence.

The voting was dominated in many instances by local and personal differences of long standing. In Mississippi the co-operationist, anti-secession strength was found among the lush river and Gulf counties where the plantations were largest and the Whigs strongest. In Florida cooperation sentiment was most potent in the west, again in the region of the larger plantations, while secession was demanded in the east. In Alabama cooperation strongholds were concentrated in the northern half of the state. This region had always been different from the southern section, for its economic outlets were through Tennessee where there was great reluctance to take immediate action. If Alabama seceded and Tennessee did not, these northern counties would be stranded. Besides, there were long-standing political rivalries between northern and southern Alabama which had nothing to do with the issue, but complicated it just the same. Southern Alabama was secessionist; many in the northen counties were therefore opposed. Personal rivalries added to the confusion. Yancey had many enemies who fought his doctrine of haste. Such prominent Democrats as Senator Fitzpatrick and Judge Campbell of the Supreme Court spoke for caution and for delay until united action could be had.

The voting was confused by many blurring combinations. In some districts there were no contests; there were either too many secessionists or too many cooperationists to make a contest worth while. In other districts coalition tickets had been formed dedicated to vote for whatever might seem best for the state and for the South when the convention met. Under such confused voting conditions, it is difficult to extract much accurate meaning from the statistics.

When the wires carried the summaries of the results, the triumph of secession was announced in each of the voting states. Later study of the returns shows the triumphs not so striking as they seemed at the time. In Mississippi, only 60 per cent of the November voters participated and the ratio of secession to cooperation was 4–3. In Alabama, it was 9–7 while in Florida, though calculation is more difficult there, it may be ventured as 10–7.

What might have been the result had there been longer time to campaign is anybody's guess. At the moment, the significant fact was the assurance that South Carolina would be joined by Alabama, Florida, and Mississippi, which would make it unlikely that Georgia would hold back. Toombs had been canvassing vigorously and had delayed his return to the Senate to make speeches in opposition to the milder doctrines of Stephens, Herschel V. Johnson, and Benjamin H. Hill. Cobb had come to take his place after his stopover at Charleston and was putting his shoulder to the secession wheel. The radical leaders deemed it safe to begin final plans for the organization of a new confederacy.[1]

II

These returns showed the imperative need of haste if compromise was to be formulated in time to arrest secession. Events of the past weeks had been strengthening pressures for compromise. Business interests were belatedly worried at the outlook. When a newspaper despatch reported early in November that Moultrie had been captured, there were brief panics on the New York and Philadelphia exchanges. This unloosed some bears on the market, and by November 21 banks were beginning to suspend. The New York bankers adopted various devices for pooling their resources and issued clearinghouse certificates to avoid dislocations of specie. Much was at stake, for the South did its business with northern firms on long-term credit bases and owed $200,000,000, of which $150,000,000 was due New York interests. If secession became general, most of this huge sum would probably be lost.

Early in December a nonpartisan committee of New York businessmen including John A. Dix, James T. Soutter, Watts Sherman, and William B. Astor, called a meeting of their associates, numbering several hundred, for December 15. At the meeting a committee was appointed, including Dix and Samuel J. Tilden, and it drew up an address. This document appealed to the South not to act hastily, pointing out that those opposed to the Republicans had gained 22 votes in the House and therefore had a majority. The members of the committee pledged themselves to back up moves for the recognition of southern rights. They would urge the repeal of personal liberty laws, the enforcement of the fugitive slave law, and the right to take slaves into the territories. They concluded by saying that if the wrongs of the South were not redressed it would be justified in seceding. August Belmont, national chairman of the Democratic party, was active in meetings of a similar kind on a smaller scale.

The pressures naturally spurred on the friends of compromise. On the other hand, December municipal elections were either going against the Republicans or showing a shrinkage of their strength in New England and New York. These setbacks did not put them into a conceding frame of mind but rather stiffened their resistance to concession.[2] In the midst of these alarms all eyes were riveted on Congress.

The clumsy nature of the House Committee of Thirty-three permitted few to have much confidence in it; but there was still a chance of success in the Senate. Vice President Breckinridge, announcing the Committee of Thirteen on the day South Carolina seceded, named to it a much more representative group. All shades of opinion were carefully included. Powell, its chairman, and Hunter represented the Democracy of the upper South; Toombs and Davis were the spokesmen of Secessia. Douglas and his opponents, Rice and Bigler of the northern Democracy, completed the majority. The minority was made up of Crittenden and five Republicans, Seward and Collamer from the East, and Wade, Doolittle, and Grimes from the West.

The task of this committee was infinitely harder because it had not been promptly authorized by the Senate. With four states practically out of the Union, it must think in terms of reconstruction rather than of arresting secession. It must look for a formula that would bring the seceders back. Powell called his associates together immediately for an informal conversation, and they decided to begin work December 22.

As was their wont, the southern Senators essayed to take the lead. They spoke at once through Toombs and Davis; apparently the only conciliation which could be understood in the South would be that which could command the united support of all factions in the committee. It would do no good to present a plan which the Republicans would not accept. To make sure that only such a bipartisan proposal would be voted Davis moved that no formula would be reported to the Senate unless it were agreed to by a majority of both the Democratic and Republican members of the committee. This motion was adopted.

Then Toombs introduced a series of resolutions which embraced the radicals' demands. They included an amendment to the Constitution, providing full protection for slave property in the territories, and laws which would facilitate return of runaways and protect slave states from invasion. No federal laws regarding slavery in states or territories were to be passed without the consent of a majority of the Representatives and Senators of the slaveholding states. Davis presented a briefer proposition to place slave property on an equal footing with other forms of property. These two proposals and Crittenden's resolutions were before the committee. The Democrats, even Toombs and Davis, indicated they would accept any of them—if the Republicans would.

The Republicans on their part were hardly ready to speak, for they lacked Seward's presence. He had left Washington, presumably to avoid this committee until he should know Lincoln's mind. Thurlow Weed had gone to Springfield to sound out the President elect and was even then returning to report to Seward at home. Despite Seward's absence a vote was taken on the Crittenden resolutions in committee, and as the four Republicans voted "Nay" they were, for the time being, rejected.

The 24th found Seward back in Washington and ready to attend the meeting set for that day. He had learned that Lincoln would not accept Crittenden's resolutions because they admitted the possibility of more slave territory. Seward made a counter proposition derived in part from Lincoln. The Republicans would not compromise on slavery in the territories; they would agree only to guarantee slave property in states where it then existed. But they would improve the fugitive slave situation and seek the repeal of personal liberty laws. These propositions were ignored. At this point Douglas advanced a formula in the shape of constitutional amendments. These included: a modified form of squatter sovereignty subject to approval by the Supreme Court; acquisition of territory only by treaty or by two-thirds vote of each house; prohibition of Negro or mulatto voting; Negro colonization in Africa; protection of slave property in the states and sure return of fugitive slaves.

At a third formal meeting on the day after Christmas, the committee rejected both the Toombs and the Davis proposals and paid scant heed to Douglas. The case seemed hopeless, but the committee voted to meet once more on the 28th. That day Washington was seething with news from the Charleston forts, and conciliation seemed more improbable than ever; but Crittenden, Bigler, and Rice made proposals. Crittenden brought in an abbreviated form of his original plan, including only extension of the line 36°30′. Bigler and Rice also provided for extension of the line, but with variations. Bigler would divide the region north into eight territories and that south into four; when any of these territories had sufficient population, the President would declare them admitted. Rice would make two states immediately of all the region not yet admitted. North of the line there would be the state of Washington, south would be the state of Jefferson. Ultimately they might be subdivided into states containing at least 130,000 people in areas of 60,000 square miles each. Bigler also proposed guarantees of slave property in the District of Columbia and other places under federal jurisdiction in slaveholding states, and better fugitive slave laws. All three of these plans were defeated, and then the committee voted to report that they could not agree. Powell was to bring this news to the Senate on New Year's Eve.[3]

III

The failure of the Senate committee was announced at a time when the Democratic executive, as well as congressional, leadership was in the throes of crisis. The Buchanan administration was reeling from a series of blows and seemed to be ready to be counted out. These men had not had a calm or peaceful moment in many days.

Even before South Carolina seceded a moot question was the safety of the federal forts at Charleston. The officers in charge, both of the construction work and of the garrison, knew not at what hour they might be attacked. The engineer officer in authority over the workmen thought they had better be armed, and sent to the arsenal for guns on the day the secession convention met. The keeper was doubtful about honoring the request but finally agreed to let him have forty muskets under an old order approved in November but never filled. Hardly had these guns been issued when the fact was widely advertised in this inflamed community. The local secessionists gave vent to angry denunciation, and on Wednesday, December 19, the wires to Washington were kept hot. Once again despatches poured in on Trescott, the secessionist, still in the State Department, scheming while his resignation awaited acceptance. He found Floyd sick in bed and got him to telegraph an order that very night for the return of the muskets.[4]

On the morrow, the fatal 20th, Buchanan was again brought face to face with the problem of the forts. Immediately after his inauguration Governor Pickens had undertaken a little private diplomacy, thinking that he might persuade his old friend Buchanan to turn over the forts to him. He sent the recent marshal, D. H. Hamilton, with a letter to the President, and Trescott brought him to the White House on secession day. Pickens was asking that the forts be placed in his custody on the pledge that they would be guarded, but not occupied, by Carolina militia, until their status was more clearly defined. He cited the fact that the arsenal was under such guard, he presumed, with Buchanan's approval.

When the President read the letter he passed it to Trescott, and after some conversation invited Hamilton back the next day to receive his reply. What he said gave Trescott a very clear impression that the negotiation was a mistake. Buchanan was evidently resentful of this pressure, particularly as he had refused to send supplies or reenforcements. There was such a thing as pushing a man too hard. As soon as the interview was concluded, Trescott hunted up Jefferson Davis and Slidell and then got in touch with Bonham and McQueen, the two South Carolina Congressmen remaining in town. He told them of his fears. Cobb was gone, Thompson was away, Floyd was sick, and Black was now Secretary of State. The President might refuse Pickens's request and use it as justifying the sending of reenforcements. They agreed that the Governor should be asked to withdraw his letter. The telegraph brought the desired response, and next morning Trescott, now out of the State Department and agent for South Carolina, withdrew Hamilton's missive.[5]

The secession of South Carolina, together with the "forty musket" incident and Pickens's demand, caused the President to reopen the question of the forts on the morning of the 21st. Floyd was up from his sickbed but strangely distraught. When the cabinet met, questions came thick and fast. Could Anderson withstand an attack? Would he resist? What were his orders? When Floyd could not seem to remember, a messenger was sent over to the department and soon returned with Buell's memorandum, instructing Anderson to dispose of his force in the safest manner. Floyd seemed to be looking at it for the first time, but he agreed that it was correct and so endorsed it.

However, a memorandum was hardly an order, and Black was urgent that something more formal and authoritative be sent. When Floyd acquiesced and the others agreed, Black wrote out instructions which Floyd signed. Anderson was to "exercise a sound military discretion," not "make a vain and useless sacrifice." If the force attacking him were too strong, it would be his duty to yield command and make the best terms possible. The point was, Anderson was to "exercise a sound military discretion." Captain John Withers was forthwith despatched with this order, signed not by the adjutant general as were all the others, but by Floyd himself. The anxious Major received it on December 23. By that time such alarming disclosures had been made in Washington that Anderson for the moment was almost forgotten.[6]

The reason for this new distraction was the downfall of Floyd. At last after four years this careless and inefficient Secretary was finally caught in the snares of his own weakness. From the beginning of his administration he had been constantly connected with loose dealing and corruption, though he himself seemed not to be corrupt. On the 19th of December as he lay at home sick, he learned that disgrace was about to cover him. Since the troubled days of the Utah expedition when Congress had held up the deficiency appropriations, he had had difficulty with the problem of supply for the distant posts. The speculating contractors with political connections, Russell, Majors and Waddell, had learned then that when Congress delayed payment Floyd would endorse their bills and banks would loan them money. Knowing what an easy mark Floyd was, Russell evidently used him. The Secretary never seemed tired of endorsing these bills, nor did he keep any very adequate account of their amount. It seems likely that Floyd's private business manager, Robert W. Latham, who was mixed up in some other Floyd deals, may have been interested. At any rate this paper flooded the market.

In 1859 Senator Benjamin went to the President on behalf of a client to ask if these things were known to him. Buchanan was amazed, and after investigation ordered Floyd to stop the practice, which he thought highly undesirable, although there was no specific law authorizing or forbidding it. For some unknown reason, perhaps just his weakness and carelessness, the Secretary did not stop, and these acceptances at length got so numerous, estimated at face values of over $5,000,000, that banks would no longer discount them; nor could Russell redeem any to reestablish his credit. He became desperate for money, and fearful lest the whole thing he exposed, Floyd dismissed, and his contracts terminated.

Russell then had tried a desperate expedient. He learned of one of the amazing examples of bureaucratic carelessness which honeycombed Washington. In the Indian office the Indian trust funds amounting to over $3,000,000 of unregistered, negotiable bonds were locked in a chest in the charge of a $2,000 clerk under $5,000 bond. The clerk in question, interestingly enough, was a political adventurer and gambler of good family, a kinsman of Mrs. Floyd, Godard Bailey by name. He had been highly recommended by southern politicos, had been considered for assistant editor to Rhett on the *Charleston Mercury* and had William C. Corrie, the slave trader, as one of his bondsmen. Jacob Thompson had placed this decayed gentleman in charge of the treasure.

Russell approached him shrewdly. He pointed out that Floyd's honor could be saved only if Bailey would loan him some of these bonds and take in their place Floyd's acceptances, which he assured the clerk would eventually be paid. As is customary, he promised to restore the bonds within a few weeks. But time went by, and instead of bringing back bonds he pressed Bailey for more. He finally devised a scheme whereby he would get acceptances from Floyd and bring them to Bailey to be exchanged for bonds whenever he desired cash. The clerk was now noticed to be spending money with unusual freedom.

In this tragic month of December, Bailey had to face an unpleasant prospect. On January 1 he must present the coupons on the bonds in his charge so that the interest could be collected and credited by the auditors. As he could not produce the coupons on the bonds Russell had borrowed, his little accommodation would be discovered. The contractor had parted with them, and so there was no way out. Secretary Thompson, who had trusted him, would be disgraced, as well as Floyd. Bailey decided he must confess that $870,000 worth of bonds were missing, with only a like amount of acceptances in their place. He wrote out a statement to Secretary Thompson and sent a copy to Floyd's sickbed December 19. Bailey's kinsman, C. G. Wagner, chief clerk of the census who had recently been register of the land office in Minnesota, would place the original in Thompson's hands when he returned from North Carolina. While waiting to get to Thompson, they also confided in Senator Henry M. Rice of Minnesota, whose connection with the affair is not clear. Rice went immediately to the President on Saturday afternoon December 22. They were talking it over when Thompson reported at the White House; it is suggested that Black had sent for him.

Thompson was stung to vivid action by this devastating tale. He did not sleep for three nights, and when he had finished his search Russell was tracked down in New York City, after

leading Marshal Rynders a merry chase, and put under lock
and key with Bailey. The President was at last fed up with
Floyd's weakness; but he could not bring himself to face
his Secretary and sent Thompson and Black to question him.
When Floyd admitted everything they thought that his
political end was in sight. Still the President seemed to be
afraid to proceed directly and acted in his usual manner.
When Black refused to ask Floyd's resignation, he prevailed
upon Vice President Breckinridge, another of Floyd's kins-
men, to do so. Floyd refused, hotly declaring he would not
flee until he had vindicated himself.[7]

Floyd had been unhappy for a long time, and he seems
to have been playing an equivocal role. This Virginian had
opposed secession but had apparently been able to thwart
measures to prevent it. Under an act of 1808 he had authority
to supply each state with an annual quota of arms for the
use of the militia, and he was also authorized to sell quantities
of altered muskets which the army did not intend to use.
After John Brown's Raid various southern states had wanted
weapons, and some 115,000 small arms had been sent to
southern arsenals in preparation for possible uprisings. As
soon as Lincoln was elected inquiries began to come in from
the state governments asking about quotas due, or possible
purchase of the altered guns. Floyd had his resources checked
and then began to sell and ship. In other ways he aided
southern states in their armament problems. Either he had a
careless faith in the failure of secession, or he was helping
possible enemies of his country.[8]

Just after he learned of his approaching disgrace he committed the deed most difficult to explain. On December 20 he
called his ordnance chief to his sickbed and gave him verbal
orders to despatch a large shipment of heavy cannon from
the Pittsburgh foundry down the Mississippi to some uncompleted Texas forts. The necessary written orders were sent
on the day of Floyd's disgrace. Christmas Day was full of
excitement in Pittsburgh when word got about that these
orders had been received. Prominent men met in consultation,
and they sent urgent wires to Washington to stop this treasonable move.[9]

That snowy Christmas Day the President had gone to
church, but whatever comfort may have come from his worship was disturbed by the series of disasters breaking around
him. He spent part of the day closing a political incident.
Since Andrew Jackson's time the Democratic party had en-

deavored to maintain an organ in Washington with very indifferent success. Buchanan had been forced to bear his full share of the burden of organ grinding with Wendell and Bowman and their associates, but now there was a new embarrassment and one not to be borne. "Constitution" Browne had gone "secesh" in a big way, and as people usually believed he spoke "by authority" Buchanan was in a dither. So he spent part of his Christmas in calling Browne to account by letter. As Browne refused to budge, Buchanan within the next fortnight stripped the *Constitution* of its advertising for the government, and the paper was forced to suspend. There was no longer an organ of the official Democracy in Washington.[10]

More disturbing to the President's festival of peace were the wires from Pittsburgh. He and Black were shocked, and he soon had the shipping orders countermanded. His unwilling mind was being dragged to the point of decision. Floyd must be dealt with. Late that evening Black sent in a note urging action at cabinet next day.[11]

When Floyd presented himself at the White House on the morrow he was going around in circles emotionally. He had just been exposed as a careless, if not dishonest, administrator who was about to be indicted by the District grand jury for conspiracy to defraud and for malfeasance in office. He was to be accused of treason because of his foolhardy gesture in trying to ship heavy guns into the South. The night before, Senator Wigfall and others had urged him to join a plot to kidnap Buchanan and make Breckinridge President; this he had refused to do. Also he had become suspicious of a large order for converted muskets which he had approved ostensibly for the Sardinian government; that order he would countermand. He was therefore off his course when he entered the cabinet room. Bluster, he felt, was the only answer, and he soon exploded. Black and Stanton were busy in the Supreme Court, and he could take advantage of their absence. He accused two of his colleagues of hostility to him personally, probably Black and Holt, and of a desire to get rid of him before he could "vindicate" himself. He gave no sign of resigning. He was plainly waiting upon events to show him a better way out of his embarrassments. This way was at hand.[12]

The South Carolina commissioners arrived in Washington that afternoon. The delegation was carefully chosen and included the Democrat Orr, as well as the secessionists,

Barnwell and Adams. The former Speaker knew Washington so well that he was counted on for much. Trescott had established them in a "legation" on K Street, next door to Colonel Drinkard, Floyd's chief clerk, and very near to Black's home on Franklin Square. Through Trescott they sought an interview with the President.[13]

Buchanan was greatly embarrassed by their approach. He was determined to do nothing that could be described as recognizing secession, yet he was in a somewhat equivocal position. He had sent Cushing down to treat with South Carolina. How could he now refuse? The difference was, however, that then South Carolina was not out of the Union. After some talk with Trescott he consented to see them as private gentlemen next day, the 27th, solely for the purpose of receiving any proposition they might have. This in turn he could not consider but would transmit immediately to Congress. With this the commissioners had to be satisfied. But the interview was not to take place as scheduled. By the time the appointed hour arrived Washington was rocking from another explosion.

Early next morning Trescott and the commissioners received startling word from Charleston. Telegrams informed them that Major Anderson under the cover of darkness had moved from vulnerable Moultrie out to impregnable Sumter. Governor Pickens wired this news to Trescott, and he hurried to the house on K Street. The commissioners were not there, but strangely enough Floyd was, presumably building his fences near the new camp. Governor Pickens in his message assumed that Anderson had acted in violation of orders and urged the commissioners to secure his return to his original post. Floyd immediately assured Trescott that Anderson's act was his own folly, carried out contrary to his orders. He agreed that the Major must be sent back and went to the War Department to check up on the situation.

Trescott, on his part, went in the opposite direction to the Capitol to inform the Senate managers. He met Jefferson Davis and Hunter, and their immediate decision was to go to the White House. There they found the President greatly agitated. He stood by the hearth crushing a cigar in his shaking fingers and stammered that the move was against his policy. They urged that he order Anderson back. As usual he hesitated. They pressed him and reminded him that the fate of the nation was in his hands. He seemed inclined to yield but summoned his cabinet first. By that time other

Senators were arriving. Yulee, Mallory, Jo Lane, Bigler, and, at length, Slidell entered; all urged him in the name of peace to send Anderson back. He would give no definite answer. Though indecisive, he was stubborn and would not be pushed.

The cabinet now assembled for its most dramatic session. Floyd thought he saw a chance, and he seized it. As on the previous day he was loud and boisterous. He denounced Anderson for disobeying instructions, for acting without orders. He read a formal demand upon Buchanan to send the Major back to Moultrie. He intimated that the President's honor was involved. But today he was a member of a different cabinet. Black, now Secretary of State, was present, and with him was Stanton, his successor as Attorney General. The new Secretary of State consequently felt strong with the strength of two. He contradicted Floyd; Anderson was only doing his duty under orders Black himself had written. Once again a messenger hurried over to the War Department, and back came the papers to sustain Black and confound Floyd.

This evidence did not quiet Floyd, who seemed bent on making a scene. Black was not a whit behind him and ruffled the pages of history in Floyd's face. If any responsible minister in England, he told Floyd, had ever advocated surrendering an effective fortress he would have been sent to the block. Black had the support of Holt and Stanton for insisting that Anderson be left where he was. Thompson, Thomas, and Floyd were for sending him back. Toucey as usual would follow the President. They finally broke up late in the evening after two sessions interpersed by calls from southern Senators. Despite the voice of southern associates and Senate managers, Buchanan had not consented to Anderson's return; neither had he refused to order it.

During the excitement the interview with the Carolina commissioners had been hastily postponed until the next day. Consequently when it took place the situation was even more difficult. Governor Pickens had not been long in making the next move. He seized Moultrie and Pinckney and thereby gave Buchanan an arguing point against Anderson's return. When the Senate managers returned to the White House Buchanan beat them to the draw. South Carolina had seized the place to which they demanded Anderson be ordered to return. He was not going to be able to do it, even if he so desired. South Carolina had prevented any action on his part.

General Scott was early in the fray that morning of the 28th. He had had a bad night, so he wrote Floyd, and could scarcely hold up his head, but he must urge the reenforcement, not only of Sumter, but of the other key forts in the South. Black and Holt likewise were fearful South Carolina might somehow rush Sumter. Therefore when the "envoys" were ushered into the presidential presence the atmosphere was tense. Their original mission seemed almost forgotten as they launched forth into a lecture upon Buchanan's unwillingness to order Anderson back. They charged that the President had given his word to the South Carolina Congressmen only three weeks previously that he would not reenforce or move the troops. The President had broken his word. He must order Anderson back to preserve his honor.

Buchanan denied their charge. He had made no pledge. In his turn he accused them. Why had South Carolina seized Moultrie so precipitously without waiting to see what he would do? He complained, as he did so often in those days, that people didn't give him time to say his prayers. The commissioners left with him a formal demand for the transfer of federal property, and the conference broke up with bad humor on all sides. The President, who only a few days before had boasted of a calm spirit, was now nervous and hysterical. Justice Campbell thought him completely unmanned, with his mind having lost its power of comprehending a complicated situation. The course of events certainly had endorsed Campbell's opinion.

That evening the cabinet met again, and again the question of Sumter was agitated—the southern members still demanded that Anderson be withdrawn. Floyd lay on the sofa between the windows, still a member of the cabinet. As Stanton later reported it: "We . . . had high words, and had almost come to blows. . . . Thompson was a plausible talker—and as a last resort, having been driven from every other argument, advocated the evacuation of [Sumter] on the plea of generosity. South Carolina, he said, was but a small State with a sparse white population—we were a great and powerful people, and a strong vigorous government. We could afford to say to South Carolina, 'See, we will withdraw our garrison as an evidence that we mean you no harm.' "

This brought a caustic reply from Stanton. "Mr. President, the proposal to be generous implies that the Government is strong, and that we, as the public servants, have the confidence of the people. I think that is a mistake. No administration has ever suffered the loss of public confidence and support as this has done. Only the other day it was announced that a million of dollars had been stolen from Mr. Thompson's department. The bonds were found to have been taken from the vault where they should have been kept, and the notes of Mr. Floyd were substituted for them. Now it is proposed to give up Sumter. All I have to say is, that no administration, much less this one, can afford to lose a million of money and a fort in the same week." Floyd said not a word.[14]

Saturday morning, the 29th, found the cabinet again in session with Sumter still before it. This time Floyd was not there. He had, at last, resigned. Insultingly, he wrote that he could no longer be associated with a dishonored regime. Thus he departed, trying to cover his sadly tattered garments of respectability with a flowing mantle of outraged honor. None regretted his departure save himself.[15] Most of the meeting was spent in discussing the letter which the commissioners had addressed to the President. Finally Buchanan dismissed his advisers, while he undertook to draft a reply for them to consider in the evening. When they gathered late that night, the President read it to them. Only Toucey was satisfied. Black, Holt, and Stanton thought it yielded too much while Thompson and Thomas protested it conceded too little. However, they had been trained not to be too frank about Buchanan's rather labored documents, and they dispersed rather hopeless about it.

One of the cabinet, like Scott, had a bad night, and Sunday was to be a desperate day for all of them. Black was the one who did not sleep. The more the new Secretary thought of the President's reply to the commissioners, the more disturbed he got. So he went to see Holt and Stanton and found they were no better satisfied. It is an interesting comment on the way things were done in that administration that Black did not feel he could go to Buchanan himself. Instead he went to Toucey and asked him to tell the President that if this letter were not altered Black would resign. Toucey, who was agreeable about such things, called his carriage, and soon the President had these disturbing tidings.

Buchanan was confounded; everything seemed to be breaking up around him. He sent for Black and told him to speak his mind. Black poured out his indignation, the President must be firm, he must not concede so much; furthermore, taking advantage of the moment, he ought to reenforce Anderson at once. He implored Buchanan to let him arrange for the orders. In fact the President had on his desk a letter written by Scott that very morning. The General apologized. The weather was vile, and he was not well enough to go to church, but he wrote Buchanan begging that he be permitted to send these reenforcements. Black pressed his chief to let him go to Scott, write the orders, and send them off. The General's aide could leave for Charleston during the night, and instructions could be in New York and Norfolk by noon on Monday.[16]

For once in his stubborn life, James Buchanan yielded. Black was an old friend. The President was beginning to feel the need of friends, so many were falling away, and he did not want to lose his Secretary of State; so he told him to put his objections in writing, and he would try a new draft. Black hurried off to get Stanton, and they sat down to the task. The Secretary wrote rapidly and Stanton copied the sheets in his crabbed backhand.[17]

While Black and Buchanan were pondering over the President's reply, he was pressed by other influences. The commissioners themselves seem to have feared they had gone too far and rather regretted having pushed the issue. That Sunday they acted through Trescott to suggest a compromise. He and Senator Hunter were at the White House as well as Toucey and Black. These emissaries of Secessia told Buchanan that South Carolina would agree to evacuate Moultrie, if Anderson were ordered back there from Sumter. The "republic" would then formally agree to respect the status quo as long as Buchanan remained in power. Also Orr disclaimed any interest in a southern confederacy. He said South Carolina did not want to be tied too closely to the great cotton-growing Gulf states, which had already "sucked so much of her blood." The state's connections were by railroad with the central and upper river valley states. South Carolina wanted to proceed by herself. None of them had any success with Buchanan, so Hunter advised Trescott to telegraph the Governor to block the channel by sinking vessels. Trescott did not trust the Washington telegraph office, so he sent a messenger to Richmond to despatch the wire from there.[18]

New Year's Eve found Buchanan ready to replace Floyd. He had spoken his mind regarding Floyd's insulting letter, and Jefferson Davis had told Floyd. The latter, regretting his high-handed resignation, had written a Sunday letter apologizing to Buchanan and offering to change the wording of his letter.[19] News of this had reached Holt, who heard also that southern influence had triumphed and that Anderson was really to be ordered out of Sumter while Floyd's resignation was to be refused. The Postmaster General was so fearful of this that he sent a note posthaste to Black to find out if he knew anything about it. But it was only one of the thousand scurrying rumors. Buchanan was through with Floyd and wrote him a curt note Monday morning accepting his resignation.[20] That afternoon he called Holt to take over the War Department until a successor, perhaps General Dix, might be prevailed upon to assume the heavy task.

Holt accepted with the understanding that reenforcements were now to be prepared, and arrangements were begun to send two hundred and fifty recruits from Norfolk on the *Brooklyn*. There must be no further delay. Horatio King, First Assistant Postmaster General, could take over Holt's department for the time being. Holt and General Scott made haste. Floyd was stunned. Mrs. Floyd, who was a kindly soul, tried to show there was no hard feeling by calling twice on the President and Miss Lane. Mrs. Thompson thought she overdid it.[21] That same New Year's Eve, Buchanan sent his secretary, Glossbrenner, to deliver his revised note to the commissioners. He had adopted Black's suggestions, and they were informed that the federal government would turn over no property and would maintain its garrisons where they were stationed.

New Year's Day carried this news the rounds of southern circles. The commissioners spent the day in indignant quest of words with which to reply. Southern sympathizers in several instances decided on a demonstration at the President's reception. It seemed in fact to be a parade of cockades. Many went mounting the red, white, and blue badge of Union while not a few wore "secession blue." The most effusive of the secessionists swept by the President as he stood in the receiving line; with proud disdain they refused to shake his proffered hand.

While thus welcoming the new year so hesitantly the President had solved another problem, or so he thought. The officers of the Charleston customhouse had left their duties as soon as Anderson moved, and there was no one to collect the imposts. It was obvious that no southerner would take this task, and so Buchanan felt here was an opportunity to take a leaf out of Jackson's book so often quoted to him. He would send a trusted northern citizen to collect the duties from the deck of a ship. An old friend, Peter McIntire of

York, Pennsylvania, accepted this responsibility. Buchanan had his appointment made out and was sending it to the Senate when that body resumed its sessions, January 2. Whether he really expected this nomination could be confirmed is not revealed. As a matter of fact Jefferson Davis prevented confirmation, but Buchanan had a talking point the rest of his life.[22]

That same January 2 brought a resumption of the interminable cabinet meetings because Thompson and Thomas were not content with the decision to reenforce Sumter immediately. They had begun to urge the President to modify his decision, even on New Year's Eve. They went over Anderson's latest reports and pointed out that he was not at all positive about needing reenforcements now that he had moved—he rather implied he thought himself impregnable. They urged that a messenger be sent down to find out the real situation. The President, after his New Year's reception experience, agreed to this, and the cabinet was working on the questions to be asked Anderson when a messenger appeared.

He bore the commissioners' rejoinder. It was scorching. They told the President in no uncertain terms that he had broken his pledge and had tried to make a weak defense based on premises which they asserted were false. They wrote him down as a liar. There was to be war, but he, not South Carolina, had chosen it. Buchanan read it with surprise and anger. He and his advisers quickly agreed on how to treat it. He endorsed it: "This paper . . . is of such a nature that [the President] declines to receive it." Glossbrenner took it back to K Street. The commissioners were not there; but Jefferson Davis and Wigfall were, and the former realized what had happened.

What took place while Glossbrenner was gone will be ever a subject of controversy. Buchanan, Holt, Toucey, and Stanton testified that the President said in tones which they could hear: "Reenforcements must now be sent." Thompson and Thomas maintained that no decision was taken, and Black later agreed that he had heard none. Perhaps Thompson and Thomas were not supposed to hear. A decision was taken that the President should report the events to Congress and urge once more his lack of power. Buchanan, who was thoroughly shaken by the events of the week, turned over to Black the task of writing the report. Holt, Toucey, and

Scott hurried on with the military preparations for reenforcement.

It had been their plan to send the warship *Brooklyn* from Fortress Monroe; but just at this juncture word came that the secessionists had erected batteries commanding the entrance to Charleston harbor and had sunk vessels in the channel as Hunter had advised. Scott decided not to send the *Brooklyn,* which probably could not now approach Sumter; its draught would not permit it to pass the obstructions. Instead the reenforcements and supplies should be sent in a merchant vessel of less displacement. Assistant Adjutant General Lorenzo Thomas left for New York to charter the ship. He arranged with M. O. Roberts for the use of the *Star of the West,* which sailed southward regularly; its departure would attract no attention. Recruits then in training at the forts in the Narrows should be loaded on this vessel, which would sail toward dusk on January 5. All moved smoothly, and she departed on schedule. Yet once again there was a change of mind, for in the meantime Anderson's report of December 31 had been received. It spoke so confidently of his ability to hold out and of the safety of his position that the President, with relief, decided that the situation did not demand the risk of reenforcement. Countermanding orders were sent on the 5th, but they arrived too late. The *Star of the West* was out at sea.[23] There was no wireless in 1861.

IV

These confused days were not cheered by news from other parts of the South. Georgia had gone to the polls on January 2, and it was soon known that the "Keystone of the Southland" had elected a convention in favor of secession; the vote finally turned out to be 50,000 to 37,000. The senatorial managers were now convinced that further talk of compromise was futile, and that Buchanan was a senile dodderer under the thumb of Black and Holt. It was about time for them to abandon Washington and take charge of the new enterprise that was crystallizing so swiftly in the South. Governor Brown of Georgia had glorified Georgia's election day by seizing Fort Pulaski, one of the defenses of Savannah. The next day the Governor of Alabama began by taking the arsenal at Mount Vernon and then Forts Morgan and Gaines off Mobile. Governor Perry of Florida was bestirring himself to move on Fort Pickens and the other works at Pensacola.[24] A series of telegrams and letters of advice had been constantly on the way southward, and their number and import increased.

Much information and more rumor were sent down. Senator Wigfall of Texas, born a South Carolinian, essayed to keep Governor Pickens informed after the local Congressmen had left. When Holt was appointed to replace Floyd, Wigfall wired Congressman Bonham, "It means war."[25] Yulee was urging Florida authorities to take the forts, arsenal, and naval station. Already he was referring to the federal government as the enemy. "I say enemy! Yes, I am theirs, and they are mine. I am willing to be their masters, but not their brothers."[26] The most ambitious effort at direction was taken January 5, the day the *Star of the West* sailed.

That Saturday night the Senators from the seceding states, save Toombs, met in caucus; Johnson of Arkansas joined them. They undertook to direct the organization of the new confederacy by drafting a series of resolutions and sending them for the guidance of the conventions meeting during the next three weeks. Immediate secession was imperative. A confederacy should then be organized at Montgomery not later than February 15. The Senators themselves decided to stay in Washington, perhaps until March 4, as Yulee put it, to "keep the hands of Mr. Buchanan tied and disable the Republicans from effecting any legislation which will strengthen the hands of the incoming administration." However, they thought it wise to ask instructions on their departure: they would come home if desired. Davis, Slidell, and Mallory were appointed a committee to promote both secession and the organization of the new confederacy.[27]

They were still hopeful of enlisting more powerful support in the border states. Although he did not attend the conference, Vice President Breckinridge now undertook to aid them. The Governor of Kentucky during the previous week had finally called a special session of the legislature to assemble January 17 and was anxious that the southern states convene at Nashville to try to formulate a program of guarantees for submission to Lincoln. Breckinridge wrote him the day after the caucus that he approved the call of the legislature but believed the cause of compromise hopeless. This letter was widely published, and its words were useful to the Kentucky secessionists.[28]

While the Senators were at their self-imposed task of directing secession, the *Star of the West* was steaming toward Charleston. Rumors had reached the South, and anxious telegrams had flashed over the wires. On January 4 Secretary Thompson had telegraphed that no troops had been sent, "nor will be," while he was a member of the cabinet. But on the 6th, the day after the vessel sailed, Wigfall got wind of it and immediately wired Charleston. More telegrams reached Washington Monday, and Thompson was besought again. He had just seen the news of the sailing in the *Constitution* and always maintained that this was the first he had heard of it. He was angry at Buchanan's "deceit," as he called it. He wired immediately that the expedition had sailed. His messenger believed that he was betraying a secret and suppressed the message; but Thompson had taken the precaution of sending a copy by another clerk, and it got through. For this telegram Thompson was stigmatized as a traitor.[29] Thus Charleston was amply warned. When the *Star of the West* arrived January 9, she was fired on and driven off. The President had feared something of this sort and had sent the *Brooklyn* after her to give aid if she were disabled. This caused another flood of telegrams, for many in the South thought a general attack on Charleston was in process.[30] The flag had been fired on. Could war be avoided?

The day before the *Star* was shelled Secretary Thompson resigned in high dudgeon, in protest at the clandestine manner of sending the expedition. He was followed three days later by the Secretary of the Treasury. Thomas had not been happy in Cobb's office. His Maryland residence made him suspect among northern financial men. Specie in large amount was being brought by the Treasury from New York to Washington. General Dix learned of this and reported it to banking associates. They began to question Thomas's good faith. A committee brought pressure on their associates not to pay the balances due on the last loan Cobb had floated; this crippled that loan a second time, for the late Secretary himself had excused some persons from keeping their pledges. Now Thomas asked for $5,000,000 and offered 12 per·cent; but only one-half was bid for. A delegation of New York bankers came to the President shortly after New Year's to protest against the Secretary's retention. Buchanan thereupon delicately hinted to Thomas that he might be more effective in Thompson's place.

The Secretary was well aware of the banker's hostility, and he saw a good opportunity to leave. He resigned in protest against the South Carolina policy. Dix was then in Washington considering the possibility of becoming Secretary of War. Buchanan now turned to him with an offer of the Treasury. King and Stanton persuaded him. Also the President made two efforts to keep a southerner in his cabinet. He invited a prominent Washington attorney, J. M. Carlisle, to fill Thompson's place and then Greenwood of Arkansas, the Indian commissioner; but both declined. He made no further effort and Moses Kelly, chief clerk, served as acting Secretary for the remainder of the term.[31]

Thus the southern influence, so long a power in the executive branch, had departed. Buchanan was now surrounded by men from the conservative wing of the northern Democracy, with Holt from the border. No Douglas man nor representative of the West had been called in. The President, who on December 20 boasted that he had not lost an hour's sleep or a meal's victuals, was now so shaken that his hand trembled as he wrote, and he longed more than ever for the freedom that March 4 would bring.

Mrs. Senator Gwin was moved by Buchanan's plight. She wrote to a friend: "My heart warms to the President, I feel for and love him. I think him a better man than the world gives him credit for. He looks badly, his face indicates much unhappiness and when I see him I feel like comforting him, but you know him well enough to know no one could approach him in that way. . . . The feeling here with the southern members is most violent against the President, the denunciation of him is fearful. I often wonder how he can stand it. He has given up his evening walk. I think that makes him feel worse."[32]

As an old Pennsylvania friend of Buchanan wrote to Bigler: "This, at first, a squabble of politicians, has outgrown their capacity to govern, and now plain men with a stake in the country must stiffen one another in their actions." This "plain man" was more decisive than Buchanan. "I say nothing of the wrongs of the South—you know them better than I—but redress to wrong may event in rebellion, and that *must be put down.*"[33]

Chapter 23

Peace Hangs by a Thread

DURING THE HORRID DAYS of the Christmas crisis the advocates of conciliation had their eyes fixed on the week of January 7, approaching altogether too quickly. It was then that Mississippi, Alabama, and Florida were to meet in their several conventions. The conciliators were only too well aware that they had accomplished little; and they were earnestly trying to present some tangible result of their efforts before these states took final action.

A nonpartisan caucus of the border states began to work December 28, the day the failure of the Senate committee was acknowledged. This new group organized a committee of fourteen. Its purpose was to revise the Crittenden plan so as to make it more generally acceptable. Crittenden was chairman, and his collaborators included the Democrats Saulsbury of Delaware and Sebastian of Arkansas from the Senate, and McClernand of Illinois, Barrett of Missouri, and Harris of Virginia from the House; S. S. Cox of Ohio was its secretary.[1]

While they were at work Douglas emerged from silence to join forces with Crittenden. The two united, December 29, in a telegram to the Georgia voters couched in optimistic language: "We have hopes that the rights of the South and of every state and section may be protected within the Union. Don't give up the ship. Don't despair of the Republic."[2] On January 3, Crittenden introduced a new version of his resolutions including two propositions Douglas had presented to the Senate committee—namely, those denying the Negro the vote and suggesting African colonization. This version stated that, as the prospects were bad for mustering in Congress the two-thirds votes necessary to submit constitutional amendments to the states, arrangements should be made for some form of direct national referendum. That same day Douglas made an eloquent plea for conciliation, either on the basis of his plan or on that of Crittenden's. He revealed that Toombs and Davis had been willing to accept the Crittenden proposal, and he denounced the Republicans as the real foes of concession.[3]

All through the quiet of January 4, which the President had set aside for observance as a day of fasting and prayer, thousands joined in public worship and private devotion, imploring the Almighty to avert the calamity which seemed so close. On that day and the next the border-state committee finished its work and produced the desired modification of the Crittenden proposal. This formula met Lincoln's objections to the original version by making it practically impossible to acquire new territory. It defined more clearly the possible boundaries of future slave states south of the "line" by stating that, whenever population sufficient to warrant a Congressman should be found within any area of 60,000 square miles, such a state might be made. No new territory was to be admitted without a vote of two-thirds of both houses, or of the Senate if the addition were by treaty. Furthermore, any one fleeing from one state to another to avoid apprehension for violating the laws of a state must be surrendered on the demand of the executive.[4]

The need pressed to mobilize support speedily, for that very evening the secession Senators were caucusing to hasten disunion. The committee started with the White House. They found the President willing to support any version of the Crittenden plan, and he readily gave this one his specific approval. Efforts were then made to stir up enthusiasm among the people. Senator Bigler and John Cochrane joined in writing an address, signed by Crittenden and others, calling for popular support for the plan from the nation. The national chairman of the Douglas Democrats, August Belmont, urged the Wall Street leaders in the metropolis to bestir themselves, for Mayor Wood was trying to bring New York to secede and form a free city. State party conventions and many more local meetings offered aid. The Ohio Democrats endorsed the compromise, and the Douglas Democrats and Union men in Kentucky did likewise.[5] How would the plan fare in Congress?

Etheridge of Tennessee, the only Congressman who still bore the name of Whig, was charged with getting this olive branch before the House. On Monday January 7, he began his efforts against formidable odds. The Republicans had already discussed it in caucus, would have none of it, did not wish it considered, and wanted no compromise. They were going to stand pat on the proposals Seward had made before the Committee of Thirteen. In this they were encouraged by secessionists who worked very cleverly upon them. The southern disunionists visited northern Representatives in their rooms and told them that concessions were useless; that they could concede nothing acceptable to the South and would only humiliate themselves for no good. This propaganda was effective. The nonsecession Democrats, on the other hand, faithfully voted to suspend the rules so that the proposal might be received; but with nearly fourscore Republicans in opposition the necessary votes were lacking.[6]

The refusal of the Republicans even to permit the introduction of the border-state compromise was seized upon by the congressional secessionists, who were in part responsible for it, as a useful propaganda aid. They sent a flood of telegrams southward as soon as the vote was taken that Monday. Their unanimous voice was: "The last hope extinguished today." "Disunion inevitable." "Hope is dead. Secede at once." These telegrams arrived as the conventions of Florida, Alabama, and Mississippi were meeting.[7]

The secessionists were cheered by further good news from the Louisiana and Texas elections of January 7 and 8. Both these states had been uncertain. Louisiana's large Bell and Douglas vote in November had shown the Breckinridge men were in the minority and the opposition was in control of New Orleans. The radical press in various parts of the South expressed much doubt of Louisiana's "loyalty." However, no sooner was Lincoln elected than a shift began. Military companies, minutemen, southern rights associations, and a new organization, the Party of the South, became very busy. Slidell and Benjamin came out for immediate action, and Soulé hotly denied that he was a "submissionist." The volatile city population of New Orleans seemed to resent the doubt cast upon its enthusiasm by outside journals, and the city went for secession. This change insured a state victory by the narrow margin of about 20 to 17. Strangely enough the returns were never published officially, and there is a long-standing tradition that they were tampered with, nothing unusual in Louisiana politics. In Texas, on Jackson Day, secessionists held an irregular election for members of a convention; as only the friends of the move participated, it could be announced as an "overwhelming" victory.[8]

While the southern conventions were reacting the Senate staged its last full-dress week. For the final time all the leaders were present. Crittenden led off on Monday, donning the mantle of Henry Clay and speaking for conciliation.[9] Toombs answered him immediately in an oratorical effort that could be summed up in four words: "Give us our rights." [10] Tuesday was Jackson Day and Congress celebrated it by the time-honored recess. On this Democratic saint's day,

Buchanan finished the message which he and his cabinet decided must be sent to Congress to place on it the blame for inaction. He had discarded much of Black's draft, particularly a long diatribe against South Carolina. He detailed the early phases of his negotiations with the commissioners, enclosing as exhibits their letters of December 28 and 30 but omitting their final letter which he had so indignantly refused to receive. He clung tenaciously to his narrow concept of his power, reiterating his opposition to secession while insisting again that he had no lawful means to meet it. The responsibility, he repeated, rested upon Congress; either they must give him the force to meet the specific crisis, or they themselves must make more serious efforts to conciliate. He endorsed the Crittenden proposal. The *Star of the West* was not mentioned, but rumors of danger to undefended Washington were included in this message.[11]

Buchanan's denial of executive authority reached Congress Wednesday, giving the secessionists a weapon to turn against him. In the Senate Slidell opened on Holt, pressing a resolution which inquired by what right the President allowed Holt to act as Secretary of War without Senate approval. Jefferson Davis undertook to add to the exhibits of the message the suppressed letter, which was well calculated to lower further the prestige of the federal executive office; Preston King of New York tried to stop the reading of this "treasonable" document; but it was heard nevertheless and printed in the *Globe* as part of Davis's remarks. The House immediately set up a select committee of two Republicans, a Douglas Democrat elected by Republican support, and two regular Democrats to consider Buchanan's message.[12]

The last three days of this week, January 10, 11, and 12, were devoted to the three most significant speeches of the session—by Davis, Hunter, and Seward. Jefferson Davis spoke the last word from the lower South, in concluding his oration begun Wednesday. He labored under considerable emotion, for he was not at all well and his own state, Mississippi, had left the Union just the day before. Like Toombs he stressed the absolute necessity of insuring southern rights and safety. The states must have a pledge that physical force was not to be used against them. They must be given reason to believe that the propositions which they intended to make would be calmly considered with some willingness to concede. Otherwise reconstruction was a vain hope, and the Union was permanently shattered.[13]

Hunter, who had great prestige among all southerners as an expert on finance and a disciple of Calhoun, spoke for the upper South, for Virginia. He sought to be practical, as usual, and came forward with an elaborate and comprehensive plan for reconstructing the Union; it may be hazarded that this proposal had been carefully considered by the senatorial managers and was the key to their planning. They seem to have been maneuvering to secede and to form a confederacy for the purpose of negotiating a union reorganized along lines to preserve their own power. As Lord Lyons reported to his government: "The plans of the Secessionists are settled. They intend to have a Confederacy fully established . . . before the 3rd of March. They declare that they shall then be prepared to negotiate on equal terms with the United States for a Union of the two Confederacies. Such a union they say they should be prepared to form, provided the Constitutional arrangements were such as would prevent the vastly larger population of the Northern Confederacy having power to overwhelm by the number of their votes the influences of the South in the general Government."

The "Constitutional arrangements" presented by Hunter were a bold demand that the United States abandon the time-honored federal system and substitute for it what in effect was a league between two sections. The new system would permit the South not only to protect slavery and its social and economic system but also to hold back the faster-moving communities farther north. Hunter's plan was long and complex.

Congress was to be denied any power over slavery in the states, in the District of Columbia, or on federal property. Nor could it obstruct the slave trade among the states. The legislative branch was furthermore required to recognize and protect in the territories whatever might be defined as property in any state. From this last provision there might be two exceptions. A territory might decide for or against slavery if the majority of the Senators from both the slaveholding and non-slaveholding states would agree; or slavery might be permitted in part of a territory and excluded from the rest of it with the same approval. The admission of new states was guaranteed with or without slavery, as their voters might decide.

This schedule of proposals also placed responsibilities on the states. They must suppress combinations designed to invade other states. They must restore fugitive slaves found within their borders, or pay their value. They must recognize as fugitives from justice and extradite all those who had offended the laws of a state within its jurisdiction and escaped therefrom.

Finally this plan proposed alterations in the structure of the federal government. It adopted Calhoun's scheme for a dual executive, one each from North and South, but with one serving as Vice President and automatically succeeding the other. The method of election would be changed; also, the Supreme Court would be a body of ten, with five from each section chosen by the respective Presidents. Hunter asked acceptance of this plan as the basis for a reunited nation.[14]

All had now spoken save the Republicans. So far they had done little but obstruct. Had they no plan at all, or were they content to let the Union slide? Now Seward was to speak. Through Weed he had been conferring with Lincoln; it was noised about that he was to be Secretary of State. Lincoln had rejected the Crittenden plan. What was the alternative? Seward gave it. He would enforce the fugitive slave law and advise the states to repeal the personal liberty laws. He would support an amendment to protect slavery in the states where it existed. He would settle the territorial question by admitting Kansas and using Rice's plan of accepting all the rest of the territorial area as two states, one northern and one southern, though he would prefer to wait this matter two or three years and then call a national constitutional convention. He would also vote for laws to protect states against invasion and to provide for the building of two Pacific railroads.[15]

The southern leaders found no concession in this and met that Saturday evening in conference, save Davis, who was now ill in bed. They decided that there was no hope, nor did they have the votes to block measures which they disapproved. When official word came of the secession of their states, they would leave. Senator Mason telegraphed the secession manager in the Virginia legislature that Seward's speech was "fraudulent and tricky under cloak of seeming mildness and no offer of concession worth consideration." No doubt similar telegrams went to the lower South.[16]

They were not needed; the tide of secession was rising high. The state leaders had not waited for the Senate debate to conclude. The conventions had acted with almost unseemly haste, and on the 9th, 10th, and 11th Mississippi, Florida, and Alabama had gone out. Georgia was scheduled to convene on the 16th.

Despite these discouraging events, the senatorial conciliators labored on during the following week. Bigler, Rice, and Crittenden tried again. On the 14th, Bigler sought to push Crittenden's plan, with a bill for a popular referendum on it. Two days later Rice offered a variation of his scheme for creating two states from the territories, one north and one south of the line; he would now admit New Mexico and Kansas with new boundaries and then enlarge Minnesota, Oregon, and California to encompass all the rest of the territorial area. Thus the slave question would be removed from Congress, and the South would gain New Mexico.[17]

Crittenden had been trying for a month to get consideration of some form of his proposal, and tried again on the 16th. The Republicans were just as determined that his plans should not be voted upon; they cared little whether Georgia went or stayed. They displaced Crittenden's resolutions with one by Clark of New Hampshire which had been pending for several days. It declared flatly that the Constitution was adequate as it was, and that efforts at reconstruction were "dangerous, illusory and destructive." Perhaps to their surprise the Republicans were able to pass this resolution, as eight Democrats—six from the South, and Douglas and Gwin—failed to vote. Two of the eight explained that their aim was to show plainly that the Republicans were relentlessly opposed to any real compromise.[18] The Senate tally gave the Georgians an opportunity to telegraph their closely balanced convention: "Does this not satisfy men of every shade of opinion that Georgia must rely upon herself? Will she not act promptly, and as a unit?"[19] Georgia seceded promptly, two days later in fact; but not as a unit, for a test vote showed the convention divided, 166–130. Louisiana followed eight days later.

II

The secession Senators now could look upon the first fruits of their labors and call them good. It seemed certain that a new confederacy would be organized at Montgomery, probably on February 4 or thereabouts. But as there still were hazards they were not going home immediately. Although the telegraph had brought unofficial news of secession it would take some few days for official documents to be transmitted, and in the meantime the Senate managers saw opportunity to use their positions to make adjustments which would promote peaceful separation, prevent war, and give the new confederacy a better chance for successful organization. The Senators were as disturbed as the President and his cabinet by the possibilities of danger at Charleston, but in a different way.

Buchanan and his advisers had done nothing when the news of the firing on the *Star of the West* arrived, partly because they had sent down the *Brooklyn* and partly because Anderson had said he was in no immediate need of reenforcements. With all the pulling and hauling it was a relief to Buchanan not to have to do anything. Holt instructed Anderson on the 10th to act "strictly on the defensive," as heretofore. The Secretary commended him particularly for his brilliant move from Moultrie to Sumter, made necessary by the danger of attack which there was "reason to believe, was contemplated, if not in active preparation." On Saturday night the 12th Lieutenant Talbot arrived with Anderson's report of his negotiations with Governor Pickens of South Carolina, and on Sunday night Lieutenant Norman J. Hall followed him, accompanied by the attorney general of South Carolina, Isaac W. Hayne of the slave-trade-cases fame.

By Monday the Senators and the Executive had learned what had happened. Anderson had called Governor Pickens to account for firing on the flag and threatened to prevent boats from entering the harbor. Pickens had then demanded that Anderson surrender the fort, and had begun sinking hulks in the channel. Anderson refused, and after some discussion they had agreed that both would refrain from hostilities while they sent a mission to the capital for a decision. Pickens selected Hayne, and Anderson sent Hall. Hayne bore a letter from Pickens to the President making formal demand for the surrender; the truce would last until Buchanan made reply. On this Monday Hayne called upon Buchanan for a preliminary discussion. The President still bore the scars of his conferences with the South Carolina Congressmen and the commissioners, and he was wary. He refused to do more than exchange civilities and told Hayne all communication between them must be in writing. Hayne departed saying he would come next day to deliver his letter from the Governor, together with a letter of his own which he would write in deference to Buchanan's wishes.

Hayne received a call immediately from Clay of Alabama

as agent of the seceding Senators. They were anxious. South Carolina's precipitancy was likely to be dangerous to their plans. They probably were still thinking of secession as a means to secure reconstruction. If blood were shed and if war broke out, their negotiations could be much more difficult, if not impossible. Also there would be no central southern command, organized to meet federal armed force, and they might be overwhelmed at the start. Peace must be kept at all costs, at least until they were organized. If Hayne presented his letter, Buchanan would probably refuse to surrender the fort—and then who knew what might happen? These Senators suspected that the South Carolina leaders liked to play a lone hand and might very well force the issue to salve their wounded pride, regardless of the effect it might have on plans for a confederacy. Orr was reported already to have said that South Carolina was not too sympathetic with the Gulf states. Evidently the new confederacy was going to have its own share of weakening jealousy.

Clay undertook to persuade Hayne not to deliver his letter immediately. The Senators still in Washington wanted to arrange a continuance of the truce—Buchanan pledging to send no reenforcements and South Carolina agreeing to make no attack on Fort Sumter and to let mail and provisions reach the fort as usual.

Clay found Hayne hesitant on this proposition and brought it to him next day in writing, signed by the ten Senators of the seceding states still in Washington; Toombs and Brown of Mississippi seem to have gone before the rest. Impressed by this pretentious request, Hayne agreed in writing to refer the whole matter back to South Carolina. Slidell, Fitzpatrick, and Mallory then sent copies of the senatorial proposition and Hayne's acceptance to Buchanan, in order to persuade him to make the desired pledge. This correspondence reached him on the 19th. He knew it was coming because Clay had gone over the whole matter with him.

In fact the pledge was scarcely necessary. The administration had decided not to try any more reenforcements. This was due partly to Anderson's disclaimer of any need and partly to General Scott's conclusion that the defenses of Charleston had become too strong for help to reach Sumter. Judge Black had dissented from this vigorously, but Holt had been instructed, January 16, to inform Anderson that reenforcements would not be sent. Furthermore, when Buchanan received the Slidell-Fitzpatrick-Mallory letter he replied to it by having Holt inform the Senators of the decision. Holt's letter stated, for the President, that he could not bind himself to send no aid, but that for the present he did not expect to despatch any.

Although this decision was not an agreement with South Carolina, the inquiring Senators thought it would be useful, and tried to persuade the Palmetto state that it was sufficient. They contemplated sending Jefferson Davis with Major Anderson's brother, Larz, to avert hostilities, but Davis's illness prevented. They did persuade Hayne to send the whole correspondence back to Columbia and thus prolong the truce. Hayne delayed presenting his own letter to the President until he should receive further instructions.[20]

The secession Senators had a second apprehension to disturb them. The federal government had extensive fortifications at Pensacola, Florida, its key base on the Gulf of Mexico. As soon as Floyd had departed from the War Department, Scott and Holt had looked to the Florida defenses. Fort Taylor at Key West and Fort Jefferson on the Tortugas needed attention, as well as the forts and navy yard at Pensacola. Guns were sent to Taylor, and a garrison despatched to Jefferson, then occupied only by the banished Captain Meigs and his workmen. Orders went to the commanders of the army and navy at Pensacola to hold their works. All this had been tended to on January 3 and 4. Forts Taylor and Jefferson were too remote from the government of Florida to be in any real danger; but the case was different at Pensacola, and Holt and Scott could only hope.[21]

Fortunately for them, the army officer in charge of the Pensacola fortifications was not a secessionist. Lieutenant Slemmer realized that his position was somewhat similar to Anderson's at Moultrie, and January 10, the day Florida seceded, he moved from Barrancas Barracks out to Fort Pickens on Santa Rosa Island in Pensacola Bay. He transferred without the real cooperation of the naval officer in charge of the yard, who seemed quite content to surrender it to the Floridians. Two days later Slemmer was called upon to surrender the fort. This he refused as often as the demand was renewed, and he looked to Washington for aid. He had only about eighty men, but he had provisions for five months.[22]

Thus during the same days in which Sumter's fate was being debated, both the administration and the Senators were concerned over Pickens. There had been no doubt whatever in the minds of Buchanan and his advisers about the reenforcement of this fort; it was simply a case of finding the resources. When the *Brooklyn* returned from her Charleston trip she was prepared to take troops to Pickens, and by January 21 the expedition was in readiness. Orders were issued to Captain Vodges and a company of artillery to sail to Pensacola to reenforce Slemmer and take command of the fort. He was to stop at Taylor and Jefferson with orders and guns. He was cautioned that he was "not to attempt any reoccupation or recapture involving hostile collision, but . . . to confine [himself] strictly to the defensive." This mission got under way on the 24th.[23]

The Senators felt more concern over the Florida situation than the administration. As soon as Florida seceded, Mallory and Yulee urged Governor Perry and Colonel Chase, the commander of the Florida militia, to capture Pickens and the neighboring fortifications, telegraphing on the 9th and 10th. But Slemmer had been too quick for them. As the Sumter tension developed, the Senate managers began to fear that the war might start at Pensacola. On the 16th Mallory telegraphed: "Our friends here unanimous that no blood must be shed before Southern Confederacy organized." The same Senators who had written to Hayne on the 15th, telegraphed to Perry on the 18th: "We think no assault should be made. The possession of the fort is not worth one drop of blood to us. Measures pending unite us in this opinion. Bloodshed now may be fatal to our cause." The Alabama Senators urged their Governor to telegraph Perry not to attack, and on the 20th Mallory and Yulee wired the same thing but added: "First get the Southern Government in operation. The same advice has been given as to Charleston, and will no doubt be adopted there." When the Pickens expedition sailed on the 24th Mallory got a wire from Chase asking its purpose. Mallory evidently was still able to get at official instructions for he replied: "The ships ordered keep outside the port, and to act strictly on the defensive." The Senators hoped they had been able to keep the peace; there certainly was delay.[24]

The time meanwhile had arrived for Senators to depart. The official notices of the secession of Mississippi, Florida, and Alabama had come, and on January 21 the Senate chamber was made the stage for a final scene. Davis, Clay, Fitzpatrick, Yulee, and Mallory made solemn speeches of farewell. On February 5 Slidell and Benjamin followed them.

They were leaving the scene of their power. Though they would never have admitted it, they were reluctant to go. Had they known what Fate had in store for them, they would have been more reluctant. None of them was ever to succeed in politics again. A great power was broken.[25]

Their departure meant that the Republicans were now in comfortable control of the House, and that the Senate was without its leaders. The Republicans were not in a position to take over there, because the 26 remaining Democrats and the 2 opposition still could outvote the 26 Republicans; but so many of the committee heads had left that the directors of legislation were entirely new. Hunter, though he still remained, gave up the finance committee post which had made him so long the watchdog of the Treasury, and Pearce of Maryland took his place. Johnson of Arkansas succeeded Davis as head of military affairs, Thomson of New Jersey followed Mallory in naval affairs. Bigler took over commerce from Clay, Gwin the post office from Yulee. Johnson of Tennessee now had oversight over the District of Columbia, vice Brown of Mississippi. Bragg and Polk took over claims and private land claims from Iverson and Benjamin. Toombs had never been permitted to have the judiciary committee that he craved, partly because of his instability and his alcoholism. Slidell had not had a chairmanship for reasons not apparent. The old order had passed; the stage was being swept for new managers.[26]

III

During these anxious days of January, the combination of northern and border-state Democrats tried hard to keep alive the effort to find a compromise or a formula of reconstruction. They were laboring against heavy odds, for even among their own associates they could not count on the little strength that might have come from united effort. A number of the northern Democrats, like their Republican colleagues, were by no means eager for conciliation. Morris of Illinois would bring up his resolution, declaring the election of Lincoln to be no just cause for secession, at the most inopportune times. Davis and Holman of Indiana had similarly truculent measures; the one would instruct the judiciary committee to report whatever bills were made necessary by secession, and the other would deny the right of secession and demand that the laws be enforced and federal property protected. During the week of January 7, when Alabama, Florida, and Mississippi were in convention, Adrain of New Jersey introduced a resolution approving "the bold and patriotic act" of Major Anderson; and with the help even of Cochrane and Sickles this was passed by a bipartisan combination, 124–56. These were hardly conciliatory gestures.[27]

Equally discouraging was the task of the conciliationists on the Committee of Thirty-three. As minority members they were trying to procure at least some real measures which might help. Millson of Virginia labored for improvement in the fugitive slave situation. Rust of Arkansas, Houston of Alabama, and Winslow of North Carolina were advocating a division of the territories. Burch of California urged a constitutional convention. The ten Democrats who worked on the committee joined the opposition members in voting for the Crittenden compromise. All this availed little, and when a drafting committee was named to put in shape such sorry hodgepodge as could be agreed upon no Democrat was included.[28]

On January 14, at the final meeting of the Committee of Thirty-three, Corwin of Ohio was authorized to submit a curious mixture. First there was a series of miscellaneous resolutions requesting the states to recognize the rights of southerners, to repeal personal liberty laws, to refrain from aggravating policies, and to pass laws protecting southerners from persecution when traveling in the North or from aggression organized in free states. These included a modified version of Millson's resolution regarding fugitive slaves. The second part of the report was a proposed thirteenth amendment designed to prevent any amendment interfering with slavery in states where it then existed, without the consent of those states. The third portion was a bill to authorize the admission of New Mexico as a state when her voters approved a constitution. A fourth was a bill to grant jury trials to fugitive slaves and absolve citizens from aiding in the rendition of such fugitives. A final section was a bill designed to make more certain the extradition of persons fleeing indictment from one state to another—a product of John Brown's outbreak. The amendment and the bills were all Republican or opposition in origin but were generally voted for by most of the Democrats. The latter also wrote or signed various minority reports, supporting the Crittenden compromise and the proposal for a constitutional convention, suggested by Buchanan and sponsored by Burch.[29] Late that afternoon Corwin took the conglomeration to the House, and it was made a special order for Monday the 21st, just seven days later.[30]

The refusal of the committee to endorse any real conciliation measures now caused those Democrats who were interested in compromise to seek action again on the floor of the House. That same afternoon, January 14, before Corwin's report actually got to the Speaker's table, English offered a resolution instructing the Committee of Thirty-three to report legislation to implement the Crittenden compromise. Florence later in the afternoon introduced a simplified version of that plan. In the main the conciliationists marked time until the debate on the report should begin, January 21, when they were prepared to fight for their proposals as substitutes for Corwin's hodgepodge.[31]

On the appointed Monday English and Florence attempted to bring up their resolutions, but were brushed aside to make way for the parliamentary battle that was about to open. Corwin spoke first in conciliatory spirit, and he was followed by the most active Democrat on the committee, Millson of Virginia. He was likewise conciliatory. He thought that neither the election of Lincoln nor the personal liberty laws gave sufficient cause for secession, and he deplored South Carolina's action before laying her cause before her sister states. He said he would not vote for the admission of New Mexico, nor for the fugitive slave bill providing jury trials; he would vote for the constitutional amendment and was sorry there were no others to provide constitutional guarantees. Adequate guarantees, he felt, were the only remedies to save the beloved Union.

Having listened to these introductions, Sickles now came forward with the first strategic move of the conciliationists. He sought to get a vote on the Crittenden compromise as a substitute for the report of the Committee of Thirty-three. This was the last thing the Republicans wanted. Not only were they opposed to compromise, but they even wished to avoid a record vote. Spring elections were coming on, and they did not want to appear committed against efforts for peace. They got Sickles off the floor by a Speaker's ruling.[32]

Tuesday Representative Sickles was back at the attack. He found that all mention of his motion had been omitted from the journal. Again he was silenced when permission was refused to insert it, but in the afternoon the conciliationists seized another chance, when debate was resumed on the Corwin report. Bingham of Ohio, a Republican, had spoken first, and then Clemens, a Virginia Democrat friendly to Seward, was awarded the floor. He was willing to cooperate in aid of conciliation and at once yielded a portion of his time to Burch, who moved the administration resolution for a constitutional convention as a substitute. Next, Clemens proceeded to accord Sickles the opportunity he had been seeking. At this point Grow saw what was up and objected. A wrangle ensued, marked by "shouts of order," "great confusion," and "deafening shouts of order." Sickles was finally ruled off the floor, but he was now in sight of his goal. He handed the resolutions embodying the Crittenden compromise to Clemens, who at the conclusion of his speech introduced them.[33]

Now it was up to the Democrats to maneuver a vote; with Republicans so opposed it would be no easy task. That same Tuesday the border-state resolutions were at length introduced by Harris, Maryland opposition; and six days later Cochrane brought in Bigler's bill to take a popular referendum on the Crittenden plan.[34] These moves, together with the earlier Senate action, meant that both houses now had the conciliation programs before them.

The promoters of compromise were girding themselves, for an all but hopeless struggle; yet they were buoyed up by developments outside Washington. The secession agitators, despite all their efforts, had failed so far in their great objective—a united South. Only seven of the fifteen slave states seemed willing to move in concert. The reports which the envoys from Alabama, Mississippi, and now Georgia were sending home from the upper South were not encouraging. They had been politely and even cordially received, but had gained little satisfaction. The legislatures of North Carolina, Virginia, Tennessee, Arkansas, and Missouri had referred the matter to the voters. Virginia and Tennessee were preparing for referenda on February 4 and 9. The Kentucky legislature had just assembled in special session, but the indications were that it was more interested in Kentucky's historic role as conciliator than it was in positive action.

Hicks of Maryland, opposition Governor, had shown himself very able in resisting the pressure of Democratic legislative leaders to call them in session. Public meetings were held in eastern counties, and an unofficial advisory convention was arranged in Baltimore on January 10, to petition that a special session of the legislature be called or that the Governor himself summon a convention. Opponents of such a course got up a large meeting, on the same day as the advisory gathering, to cancel out its influence. Hicks refused to act, declaring that Maryland did not want secession. He charged that Democratic conspirators from the lower South were plotting from Washington to drive Maryland against her will. He might favor a central confederacy, but no union with the lower tier.[35]

The conciliation leaders in Washington were anxious to help their friends in those states which were about to vote, particularly Virginia and Tennessee. Douglas and Crittenden were working on ways and means and now thought they saw new hope. Missourians had carried the work of the border-state caucus to Lincoln at Springfield, and it was soon reported in Washington that he might accept it. His original objection to the Crittenden compromise was that in setting no limit to expansion below 36°30′ it enabled the South to secure a slave empire by demanding territory in Mexico and points beyond. The border states' plan would block this because it provided that no future territory be acquired without a two-thirds vote of congressional approval. Perhaps on the strength of this, Douglas and Crittenden had a conference with Seward and Dixon, a conciliatory Republican Senator, on the evening of January 24. Would compromise be possible after all?[36]

Douglas and Crittenden now wrote another series of hopeful messages. On January 25 they began on Virginia, where the campaign was reaching a last-minute intensity. Most of the Representatives from the Old Dominion were for secession and had issued an address. Now Douglas and Crittenden joined with the three Union members from that state, Millson, Boteler, and Harris, in a message urging Virginia to remain loyal.[37] Three days later Douglas introduced in the Senate a revision of the fugitive slave law as further evidence of his zeal for conciliation.[38] Next the Little Giant turned to Tennessee. When he learned that he had been charged by the Memphis *Appeal* with favoring secession, he wrote a vigorous letter denying this; such a policy would play into the hands of the northern disunionists (the Republicans). He urged Tennessee to stay in the Union and to unite with conservatives in the North for compromise and reconstruction. He and Crittenden joined in a telegram to Tennessee: "Our hope for the Union firm."[39]

Whatever truth there may have been in the reports that Lincoln was veering toward compromise was probably prompted by the desire of the President elect to persuade a southerner to enter his cabinet. He was now negotiating with Congressman John A. Gilmer of North Carolina, one of the supporters of the border-state compromise. After he refused, January 29, there was no further sign of compromise from Springfield. Yet the idea was encouraged by border-state efforts.[40]

Kentucky had been working from the start to assemble some sort of convention. Governor Magoffin had suggested it. The delegation in Congress had been trying to get up sentiment for a conference and on January 12 Senators Crittenden and Powell, with their colleague Mallory and some Congressmen, had telegraphed to Magoffin asking him to appoint a commission of five to meet with a similar commission from Virginia on the 4th of February in Washington. This was the day the new confederacy was scheduled to be launched at Montgomery.[41]

But it was Virginia that finally moved for the convention. When its legislature had assembled on January 7, the secessionists seemed to be in control. Governor Letcher, however, was opposed to secession and in his message proposed a national convention. Letcher and his close associates resented the domineering tactics of the Gulf states. He believed that the Old Dominion, not South Carolina, should be calling the tune. Therefore he was moving to get the border states to act together, for he felt that if they did so the Gulf states would have to join them. Letcher wanted to lead, hence his proposal for a convention. The conservative leaders in the legislature, one of whom, James Barbour, was receiving encouragement from Seward, went to work to implement such a plan. He and his friends were successful in their labors, and despite the radical character of the legislature it accepted the idea. On January 19 action was completed on resolutions which seemed to the disciples of peace to offer real hope. The Old Dominion invited all the states to send delegates to Washington to meet on the strategic date of February 4. It proposed that this convention start with a consideration of the Crittenden compromise. Furthermore it asked President Buchanan and the seceding states to pledge that during the convention they would "abstain . . . from any and all acts' calculated to produce a collision of arms." Ex-President Tyler was appointed to seek such a pledge from Buchanan, and Judge John Robertson was to go immediately to the capitals of Secessia for the same purpose.[42]

Virginia's plenipotentiary arrived in Washington on January 24, to find the capital buzzing with rumors about the sailing of the *Brooklyn*. She had once been sent to Charleston, was she going back? The ex-President feared as much and earnestly sought Buchanan to avoid such a step on the eve of this convention. The President reassured him by telling him that the ship had no hostile purpose but was going on an "errand of mercy and relief." He and Tyler conferred much but Buchanan would make no pledge.[43] He supported the Virginia convention in a message to Congress which he drafted in consultation with Tyler.

In it he explained that only Congress could pledge what Virginia wanted; the President had no such power. He on his part would defend and protect the public property within the seceding states and keep peace in Washington. There could be no conflict unless the seceders made it. He begged Congress not to pass "any law calculated to produce a collision of arms pending the proceedings" of the hoped-for convention.[44]

Judge Robertson could secure no pledges in the South. He arrived at Columbia just as the Governor and legislature had completed replies to Hayne's request for instructions. They were not nearly so sure of the President's pacific intentions as were the Senators, whose interference they did not appreciate. They instructed Hayne to deliver Pickens's demand for Sumter's surrender, and they paid Robertson but scant attention. Hayne received his instructions on January 30 and sent Buchanan the Governor's letter next day under cover of a lengthy one of his own.[45]

The demand for Sumter's surrender arrived as the President and his advisers were completing a new program on Pickens and Sumter. When the *Brooklyn* left on the 24th the Senators already were breaking up, with several, including Mallory of Florida about to go home. Mallory went directly to Pensacola, which was full of nervous excitement despite his reassuring telegram. There he tried to further the policy of his erstwhile colleagues, of preventing bloodshed before the organization of the confederacy. He impressed upon the Florida authorities the necessity for avoiding conflict and secured from then an agreement that no attack would be made upon the fort if the reenforcements were not landed. He telegraphed Slidell, Hunter, and Bigler, January 28, asking them to lay this proposition before the President.

Bigler brought the despatch to the White House. Slidell had

just broken with the President, because Holt had ordered his brother-in-law, P. G. T. Beauregard, from his pleasant berth as superintendent of West Point and the President that day refused to countermand it. So it was thought better to have Bigler do the negotiating. The Pennsylvania Senator asked that the troops be held on board the ship, though the vessel be kept in the harbor for use in case of attack. Tyler added his plea, urging that the success of the assembling conference might depend upon it. The President went over the matter in cabinet January 29; Toucey of course was favorable, and Holt acquiesced; but Black, Stanton, and Dix were opposed. Yet the senatorial influence and the hope for peace were still potent, and that day an order was issued not to land the men unless the fort were attacked, or preparations for an attack were observed.[46]

Secret preparations for another relief expedition to Sumter were begun by Buchanan, Holt, Scott, and Toucey on the 30th—the day Hayne's new instructions arrived. Perhaps they had advance notice of the instructions or hoped to placate Black, Stanton, and Dix. They were determined to be ready if Anderson should call for help or if South Carolina undertook an attack when her governor received Buchanan's refusal of his demand. Commander James H. Ward of the Navy was to take down a new expedition of four small ships borrowed from the Treasury Department. While these preparations were being made, the Hayne correspondence must be answered by Holt and Buchanan, a reply which took several days to draft; in fact it was not completed until after the Conference Convention had assembled. The letter (signed by Holt) went to Hayne on February 6, refusing South Carolina's offer to "buy Fort Sumter." The President, it stated, had no power to cede federal territory; and it repeated the views on reenforcements he had expressed in the previous letter. It gave Hayne no satisfaction.

Then history practically repeated itself. Hayne, like the commissioners in December, was stung to anger, particularly by the phrase "buy Fort Sumter," and wrote Buchanan a haughty and offensive answer. This he despatched to the President and left town immediately. The President endorsed it as an improper letter which he would not receive and, when his secretary could not find Hayne, sent it back to him by mail.[47]

As the delegates for conciliation and secession, respectively, were settling down in Washington and Montgomery, the various elements in the Democratic party could snatch some relief. Their efforts, combined from mixed motives, had been successful for the moment. They had kept the peace. Could the Conference Convention find a formula which would bring Montgomery back to Washington?

Chapter 24

A Republic Made to Order

SECEDING BRECKINRIDGE DEMOCRATS were congregating at Montgomery, Alabama, while their erstwhile colleagues were laboring in Washington to save the Union. The southern statesmen faced a rare opportunity. They could make a government to order, according to specifications laid down in a political platform. Here in Montgomery there were none, supposedly, of the despised influences of greed and exploitation to misdirect the enthusiasms of apostles of reform. Those who believed in a virtuous republican government, established on the sturdy cornerstones of laissez faire and slave labor, could build again, wise in the errors of the statesmen of the older order.

The assembling state-makers were ardent and sincere in their reforming zeal. Yet to understand their acts, there must be a more careful examination of their motivations than they could undertake in those confused months and weeks. In reality they were in retreat, retiring from a competition which was increasingly distasteful and had certain frightening aspects. They fled before metropolitanism and territorialism, as well as antislaveryism.

These hated attitudes were gaining greater prevalence because of the incoming hordes of foreign immigrants and the potent supply of foreign capital, both attracted by the social, political, and economic opportunities in the undeveloped American society. Only half of the great national land area was occupied, and the other half offered such vast opportunity. But the unoccupied areas were not situated to any large extent in the South. Those seeking them must go elsewhere. The census of 1860 had borne bitter tidings; the South was falling behind.

As the delegates gathered in Montgomery, most of the papers contained an analysis of the next congressional apportionment, to be effective in 1863. It was an undeniable indication of the southern decline. Virginia, South Carolina, Tennessee, and Kentucky were to lose two Congressmen each; North Carolina, Georgia, Maryland, and Alabama, one each. Single gains in Louisiana and Arkansas were hardly encouraging, and the increase of two each in Texas and Missouri could only rub salt into southern wounds. Texas and Missouri were on the outer borders of southern power, and Missouri at least gave some hint of a possible destruction of slave interest. This net loss of six seats, and the fact that it had occurred predominantly in the old South, warned of the inevitable loss of southern power.[1] The census seemed to be the South's worst enemy. It was time to retire to a self-sufficient, homogeneous society while there was a chance to organize one.

The idea of such a society in the form of a southern confederacy had been bruited about for years, particularly since the Mexican War and the gold rush to California. Gideon Welles thought it had been cherished for a generation. So observing a witness as Judge John A. Campbell, however, believed that actual serious planning had not begun until the southern commercial convention of 1858.[2] Indeed there were few signs of preparation. Some heads undoubtedly had been put together in Washington during the summer just passed, but the actual work had not really begun until the South Carolina secession convention assembled.

That December gathering had been more than a state meeting. Various notables congregated there, not only to witness the historic act and to strengthen the hands of the participants but, most important, to plan the next steps. Howell Cobb was present, as were Governor Perry of Florida, Senator Chesnut, and most of the South Carolina Congressmen. John A. Elmore and Charles E. Hooker, emissaries from Alabama and Mississippi, were received with due ceremony and addressed the gathering. During the ten days following secession, the plans for the Confederacy were perfected at Charleston.

The South Carolina convention had voted to invite the other seceding states to send deputies to a conference for organization of a new confederacy, and had authorized commissioners to go to these states, carrying the invitation and encouraging immediate secession. These men were commissioned New Year's Day, and then gathered to consult. They decided that Montgomery, Alabama, and February 4 were the preferred place and time.[3] The Washington managers, a few hours later, advised February 15, but the earlier date proved more attractive.

Immediately after this caucus the emissaries set forth on their missions. Andrew P. Calhoun sought to be in Montgomery when the Alabama convention met, and Armistead Burt expected to be at Jackson when the Mississippians assembled the same day. Calhoun was enthusiastically received, and the invitation which he extended evoked an immediate response. When the convention adopted its ordinance of secession on January 11, the delegates ignored the suggestion from Washington and invited the southern states to meet at Montgomery February 4.[4]

Mississippi did not react so enthusiastically when Burt gave his message, and delayed its reply.[5] While its convention deliberated, Virginia started its countermove and invited the Conference Convention to meet in Washington, likewise on February 4. The promoters of the Confederacy were much worried by this step; it might block their own plans. Governor Pickens therefore sent a stream of telegrams to Burt urging immediate action.[6]

While Burt was renewing his pressure, his fellow ambassador, James L. Orr, reached Milledgeville for the Georgia gathering on the 16th. Orr had been chosen at Cobb's suggestion because he was conservative and well known to many Georgia leaders. He found that Stephens and Johnson were still fighting immediate secession, and that the latter had a delaying plan ready in the form of a southern conference to meet at Atlanta on February 10, to frame an ultimatum for northern acceptance under threat of united southern action. This motion was defeated by the Georgia convention, which quickly accepted the Montgomery invitation.[7] Mississippi could hardly hold back any longer; on January 22 it fell in line.[8] Florida and Louisiana had no hesitation in joining, but Texas unfortunately would not be ready in time for the opening sessions.

The six states set about choosing their delegates. There was some working at cross purposes here, and the method of choice was curiously haphazard. There was no general agreement as to the scope of the activities of this Montgomery convention. Georgia evidently expected it would carry through plans for the adoption not only of a provisional government but also of a permanent one, and chose notables to attend it. Mississippi, on the other hand, looked upon it as a purely temporary organization, and after choosing unimportant convention delegates designated its well known Senators and Representatives back from Washington as the men to represent it in the permanent Congress which it expected would soon be called. In most of the states no prearranged slates or party tickets were suggested. Each member of the legislature wrote down his own ticket of as many names as the state had had Senators and Representatives in Washington. These lists were tallied, and ballots continued to be taken until each one of the required number of persons received a majority of the votes cast.

Some of the leaders who expected that the functions of the convention would be preliminary refrained from presenting themselves. Some anxious to attend, like Jacob Thompson, Slidell, and Benjamin, were defeated. Mississippi sent six Democrats and two Whigs, with one not labeled. Louisiana chose four old Whigs, one Democrat, and one not now identifiable with any party. Alabama refused to send Yancey; in fact its convention was so divided that eight Whigs and four Democrats were chosen, including several opponents of secession. South Carolina and Georgia alone chose distinguished politicos. Rhett was elected from the Palmetto state, but he was carefully boxed off by Chesnut, Keitt, and Boyce, who had been his opponents for years. Georgia sent not only Cobb, Toombs, and five fellow secessionists, but also Stephens and two other former Whigs and opponents of immediate action, Ben Hill and Kenan. The majority of all the delegates were Breckinridge Democrats.[9]

II

The eyes of much of the world now turned in hope, fear, or curiosity on the little capital three hundred miles up the Alabama River, near the center of the state, and in the heart of the South. Those who traveled thither had many difficulties. For several days prior to the 4th of February there had been heavy rains throughout South Carolina and Georgia, as well as Alabama. The rivers were high, and much damage was suffered by the railroads. At Atlanta, trains were as much as twelve hours late and the cars on which the South Carolina and Georgia delegations traveled were wrecked three miles out of Montgomery. Fortunately no one was injured save a Negro hack driver. Alexander H. Stephens and Tom Cobb rode into town smoking in the baggage car.

When the delegates arrived they found Montgomery a city of mud. Its sidewalks were constructed in fantastic and irregular manner, and there was no street paving. Any one crossing the streets had to wade through liquid earth, and the mules and horses were covered so that they resembled yellow-bellied terrapin. The center of activity was the Exchange Hotel, on a square upon which five wide streets came together. This hostelry had never been planned as the nerve center of a nation and was wholly inadequate for the task. It had neither management nor servants capable of catering to the great influx, and its rate of five dollars a day was high. It got dirtier and dirtier. Visitors complained that no public eating place in the town was worthy of patronage. Some guests could muster no appetite for the food, so sloppy was the serving; the state of the kitchens could be only too well imagined. Many a politician could find solace only in such invitations as came to him from the townspeople, where oyster suppers with sumptuous desserts were the fashion. At some of these, the delegates might meet Augusta Evans, the author of *Beulah*.

The city was small, with only 8,000 inhabitants. It was something of a rail center and boasted several iron foundries, mills, warehouses and "elegant" stores. It stretched up from the river and was adorned by numerous comfortable villas with beautiful gardens. There was an unusual number of churches which "everybody" attended. There was even a theater where traveling companies performed and where the visiting statesmen might attend a presentation of *Wept of the Wishton-Wish*. The show place was the new capitol, gleaming white with colonnades and dome, a half-mile from the Exchange Hotel. Here in the octagonal senate chamber the new congress was to meet. When the rain finally stopped, spring seemed right at hand, the peach trees blossomed, and the balmy air was quite in contrast with the winter atmosphere of the old capital on the Potomac.[10]

The assembling delegates were very uncertain of procedure, and most of them plainly showed their lack of experience. They turned almost instinctively to those of their number with congressional background. Rhett nominated Cobb, former Speaker of the national House, for president of the convention, and he was elected by acclamation. Stephens, the veteran parliamentarian, assumed the floor leadership and was made chairman of the committee on rules. The most pressing matter to be decided was the method of voting: should the delegates cast their ballots as individuals or by states, with each state casting her one vote in the manner desired by a majority of her delegates? Individual voting would have given Georgia the largest voice; but, as South Carolina and Mississippi had instructed their delegations to support unit voting and Louisiana was also of that mind,

Georgia must acquiesce. Stephens made up a set of rules embodying this principle, and on the second day it was adopted.

The second problem was to define the limits of the activity of the convention. Georgia and Alabama at once agreed on a daring plan suggested by the former. This presumably temporary body would not only erect a provisional government but assume the functions of a legislative body as well. After making a provisional constitution and electing a provisional president and vice president, it would enact a complete series of laws, draft a permanent constitution, and operate as a provisional legislature until the permanent system was inaugurated. It would not seek permission for this extraordinary extension of prerogative from either the states or the voters but would simply assume it. Rhett, with his red face and violent nervous motions, was aghast at this proposal, nor did Mississippi particularly approve; but events were moving along too fast to be stopped, and the Georgia program was followed.[11]

The convention next voted to appoint a committee of two from each state to draft a provisional frame of government. Memminger of South Carolina was named its chairman; and under Stephens's skillful pilotage the committee accepted South Carolina's original proposal, to take the federal constitution as the base and make only such adjustments as the occasion and the reform impulse demanded. The document so modified was offered as a provisional constitution to be in effect for a year. Few changes were found necessary. The foreign slave trade was expressly forbidden; Congress might prohibit the importation of slaves from states not members of the Confederacy; the President might veto items in appropriation bills; Congress might not appropriate money unless upon request and estimate from the President or one of the heads of the departments. The supreme court of the Confederate States of America was to be composed of its district judges. The provisional President and Vice President were to be chosen by this convention, which was itself declared to be a unicameral provisional Congress charged with full law-making power. Thus the drafters of the provisional constitution legalized their own assumption of prerogative. Their handiwork took little time, and Congress spent only one day, February 8, in adopting so inclusive a scheme. The 9th was designated as election day, and at noon the balloting for the executives was to begin.

The question of leadership had been in the minds of all

since the project of a new confederacy was first discussed. It was complicated by the shadow which overhung the convention, the only rift in the lute. Eight of the fifteen expected states had not responded. This shadow was hardly lightened by the attendance of an encouraging delegation from North Carolina, or the appearance of a committee from New York City. Three Gothamites, including the Hardshell James T. Brady, had been appointed as observers by a Union meeting in the great city. Convention members tried to believe that after Lincoln's inauguration other states might join, but such wishful thinking could not hide the fact that more than half of the expected states were not there. The absence of Virginia was particularly lamented, and the presence of the fire-eating Roger A. Pryor from the Old Dominion hardly made up for it. The conservative character of the non-cooperating eight states forced upon the realistic a determination to permit election of no radicals to high office. This decision blighted the hopes of some of the most enthusiastic of the founders.

There was little of the caucus or convention atmosphere in Montgomery. In fact some of the delegates rather prided themselves on its absence. They were to launch a cause, not to promote the fortunes of individuals. The Governor of South Carolina wrote to Jefferson Davis that there was not much concern regarding the civil officers. "It is not so much consequence at present, only that they should be high-toned gentlemen of exemplary honesty and firmness of character with full and thorough statesmanship and no demagogism. We must start our government free from the vulgar influences that have debauched and demoralized the government at Washington."[12] The founders of the new Confederacy were reformers. Thus their justification to themselves for their temerity in breaking up the Union was that they were establishing a purer and more enlightened political experiment.

This disinterestedness did not extinguish ambition, however. Certain of the original secessionists believed that election to high office was their due for having borne the burden in the heat of the day. Robert Barnwell Rhett and William L. Yancey were both ready for the responsibility, and undoubtedly there was a general impression outside the Gulf states that either of these men might be chosen President. Such a course would be anathema to the more conservative elements then dominating the non-seceding southern states.

A second complication was the prominence of the Georgia delegation. Cobb, Toombs, and Stephens were all presumed to be of presidential stature. The foes of Rhett in South Carolina were determined to prevent his election and came to Montgomery looking for candidates elsewhere. Chesnut met Stephens on the train and told him that South Carolina believed that the President should be a Georgian. What he told other delegations is not of record. Toombs was ready to accept: and Thomas R. R. Cobb of the delegation, brother of Howell, was working in the interest of the former cabinet member. The ex-Secretary of the Treasury himself was hesitant. He probably was eager for it but dreaded its uncertain success and heavy responsibility; and so he tried to seem indifferent. Stephens likewise was talked of, curiously enough, despite the fact that he had opposed secession.

At first the Cobb men thought that they had the largest bloc in the state's delegation of ten; but they soon saw Toombs and Stephens, who had parted over secession, making up. Then another delegate that they counted on grew chilly: if the anti-Cobb men got together, they might control the delegation for Toombs. But even more complicating was the fact that these three political tycoons from Georgia were all handicapped. Cobb, Toombs, and Stephens had opposed secession in 1850, and Stephens had persisted until the Georgia voters actually seceded and he was appointed a delegate to Montgomery. Also Cobb, though a Democrat, always had been a Union man. This made Stephens and Cobb suspect of the ardent secessionists as sometimes lukewarm. In addition, both Toombs and Stephens had been Whigs, which helped to make them, particularly Toombs, anathema to the older Democrats predominating at this convention. Finally, Toombs was "high" nearly every night; just two nights before, he had appeared at a party drunker than usual. The delegates were reformers, some of them austere, laden with a sense of heavy responsibility; only two of them drank to excess, and Toombs's inebriety jarred upon them. The chief magistrate of this reform confederacy should have dignity and stability.

Probably the deciding influence came from Washington, through one or two state commissioners to the non-seceding states. They were observant men and were reporting carefully on opinion in the capitals they visited and taking advice from secessionists in the absent states who were working to direct public opinion southward. In this effort Mason and Hunter, the Virginia Senators, had been active, coming down from Washington frequently while the various state commissioners were visiting the legislature at Richmond in January.

They feared that the secession of Virginia would be hindered if some radical were elected President of the Confederacy and therefore suggested the candidacy of their close friend in the senatorial directory, Jefferson Davis. They told the Alabama commissioner quite frankly that the election of Yancey might kill any chances of Virginia's joining the Confederacy. The election of Davis, however, would be viewed as a sign of sound conservative leadership which would give confidence to the Old Dominion. Their logic was so effective that the Alabama commissioner wrote the news immediately to his sponsors; and when he returned he found that Yancey had withdrawn in favor of Davis. In this way Davis's candidacy was being carefully promoted from the border states and Washington by his fellow senatorial managers. This was not to his taste because he had just been elected commander of the Mississippi militia and hoped to be chief of the new Confederate army.

Tactics and logic of this sort were potent in states other than Alabama. Therefore in the caucuses of February 8 and 9 the fruits began to be manifest. Each state held a formal meeting, and then those opposed to the Georgians compared notes. Alabama, Mississippi, and Florida were for Davis. A faction from South Carolina favored Cobb but was willing to vote for Davis. Cobb's friends thought Louisiana favored him, but that delegation likewise was willing to vote for Davis. Thus the Georgians saw the cards were against them; Cobb withdrew and urged Davis. When Toombs saw to his surprise that no state was supporting him, he took consolation in the fact that Cobb wouldn't get it. He joined in agreeing to Davis and pushing Stephens for the second place.

When the other states learned that Georgia had come over to Davis, they quickly agreed to Toombs's proposal to make Stephens Vice President. All felt Georgia was entitled to one of the honors, and it was also believed that Stephens's choice would be pleasing to the wavering border states because of his courageous stand for delay. So a Breckinridge and a Douglas Democrat were elected—each one unanimously on his first ballot—and the handiwork of the senatorial managers could be traced.[13] These "temporary" executives were renamed a year later by the formal electoral college and held office through the life of the Confederacy.

Jefferson Davis and his colleague were duly inducted within a fortnight, and the new President was not unmindful of his

462 / The Disruption of American Democracy

party associates, particularly from among the recent senatorial leaders. Courtesy and good politics demanded that he
permit South Carolina and Alabama, Rhett and Yancey, to
name two members of his cabinet; but the other four were
the President's personal choices. Three of the senatorial
managers, Toombs, Mallory, and Benjamin, were invited
forthwith, and a member of the House, Reagan of Texas. A
little later when Virginia came in he found a place for
Hunter, and Mason and Slidell were given responsible diplomatic tasks. The new government was under the domination
of the senatorial managers. If they could no longer rule in
Washington, they were certainly intrenched in Montgomery.[14]

III

Now that the provisional government was completely set
up, the self-styled Congressmen turned to their next assumed
function. As a constitutional convention, they undertook to
frame the permanent fundamental charter of the new Confederacy. As soon as Davis and Stephens were elected, a
committee of twelve—two from each state—began work on
the document, and just as the provisional constitution was
based on the federal instrument of 1789 so was the permanent charter. The committee, dominated by Democrats, had
the congenial task of writing the Democratic platform into
the Confederate constitution.

Rhett was made Chairman of the committee, as a consolation prize. Thomas R. R. Cobb was its secretary and
draughtsman and with the aid of Sparrow of Louisiana kept
the clauses in order as the members passed upon them one
by one. In this committee and on the floor of Congress later,
these men with Toombs and Stephens, Alexander M. Clayton
of Mississippi, and Richard H. Walker and Robert H. Smith
of Alabama were the chief architects. They looked upon their
task as one of clarifying, reforming, and perfecting the federal constitution and went to work on it, article by article
and clause by clause. They labored from February 9 to 26,
when they reported their creation to the Congress. It was
debated on the floor from the 28th until its final adoption
March 11.

States' rights was the keynote; even federal officials in the
states might be impeached by the legislatures. South Carolina's efforts to have the principles of nullification and secession explicitly incorporated were defeated, but the sovereign
independent character of each state was proclaimed. The
laissez-faire policy of the Democratic party was dominant.

The power to provide for the general welfare was omitted. There were to be no favors to business, and the solons sought to erect barricades around the Treasury by an elaborate series of provisions. Acts of Congress must be limited to one subject each. No money was to be appropriated except by a two-thirds vote unless the item were requested by the President or the head of a department. Payments must be provided only for the sum contracted; there could be no later grants to contractors. The President might veto items in appropriation bills. The Post Office after 1863 must be self-supporting. The way to the Treasury was to be more difficult than in Washington.

The reformers were explicit also on internal improvements. No money could be appropriated for them. River and harbor grants were curtailed; these projects must be made to pay for themselves by the taxing of the commerce benefiting from them. The states were encouraged to finance them by a grant of the power to lay tonnage duties on shipping using their harbors. To close another loophole apparent in the federal document, the power to establish post roads, which had been held to authorize appropriations for road building, was changed significantly. The Congress was to have authority only to designate post *routes;* it could not construct roads.

The other controversial platform plank to be considered was the tariff, which proved no easier to settle in Montgomery than in Washington. From the assembling of the convention interest in the revenue policy had been keen. Shortly after the work began the news telegraph wires blazed forth with a headline quickly spread on front pages of the press: "Free Trade with all the World." This was not true; Toombs, accosted by a reporter one evening when he was "high with wine," had ripped out that sentiment.[15] The Confederate Congress in fact passed no import law beyond continuing the rates of the federal tariff of 1857, which were a compromise. Treatment of the problem in the constitution was a different matter and caused a real battle on the floor of the convention. Rhett had not been able to insert a prohibition of a protective tariff in the draft in committee; but in the convention debate he proposed it, and it was carried over the opposition of Louisiana and Georgia. The "revenue-only" principle was the preferred policy of the Confederacy. As the United States had just enacted a protective tariff, trade should flow to the South.[16]

While the reform interests of the Breckinridge Democrats were emerging, there obtruded a second question which also had political implications closely connected with the possibility of a new lease of power to the Democrats. From the beginning of the steps which produced the Confederacy there had been a difference of opinion which later was hushed up. Some of the leaders, particularly in Washington, still thought of secession as an instrument whereby they might reconstruct the Union. If the Southern states seceded and organized a reformed government, which safeguarded property against some of the federal evils, might not a new Union rise? Either the northern states would accept this new constitution and discard the old, or perhaps the Ohio Valley and Middle Atlantic areas might be willing to leave New England and enter the reformed Union. New York City might secede from the rest of New York and join. This possibility seemed so real that many of the local secessionists feared they were being used to effect it. The Georgians apprehended that Davis might really be looking, despite his disclaimers, to the presidency of a reconstructed Union under Hunter's plan rather than of a southern confederacy. There was a lobby in Montgomery working for that end; in it was none other than George N. Sanders, now supposedly an emissary of Douglas working for reconstruction.

The more radical secessionists feared this and sought to block it, bringing forward in the convention propositions for this purpose. Rhett suggested that only slave states might belong to the Confederacy, while Miles put the same idea the other way round, that no state might be admitted which did not permit slavery. After some debate involving amendment, acceptance, and reconsideration, Thomas R. R. Cobb proposed the same principle in a slightly different form, and it was adopted 4 to 3, with Georgia and South Carolina carrying Florida and Louisiana with them.

But the reconstructionists were not all discouraged. As Davis was said to be against any such limitation of the size of the Confederacy, it did not take long for Louisiana to agree to vote to reconsider. On the second tally Georgia's vote was a tie and therefore was uncounted under the unit rule; Stephens and Benjamin Hill had changed their minds and joined Toombs and Wright, who had opposed circumscription from the outset; Crawford was in Washington as a Confederate commissioner and Kenan stayed away, so that there were four votes for each side. Alabama, Mississippi,

Louisiana, and Texas now voted against the limit, and it was stricken out; Davis and other leaders disclaimed any thought of reconstruction, but the door was left open. The northern Democrats like Douglas and the New York City men might strive for reconstruction, not only of the Union but of the Democratic party,[17] if bloodshed could be avoided.

What Douglas had in mind seems to have been a commercial union between the United States and the Confederacy, indissoluble except on common consent. Under it, all trade regulations, tariffs, patent and copyright laws would be uniform in both republics. A supercouncil, made up of a member from each state in the two republics, would pass economic laws by a majority vote of each of the two groups of councilors. This commercial union would collect all tariff duties and pay the debt of the old United States with them. Thereafter the proceeds would be distributed between the two governments in proportion to population, counting only three-fifths of the slaves. The two republics were to guarantee each other's territorial integrity, and neither was to add territory or change boundaries without the other's consent. This proposal, Douglas believed, would preserve the advantages of the old Union; and the separation of the two Congresses would prevent the bear-garden tactics which had been the aggravating cause of so much antagonism. To whom he made this proposal, or whether George Sanders or some one else brought it to Montgomery, we do not know. After Douglas died it was found among his papers. His hopes were not to be realized.[18] His shadow may have aroused the fierce opposition to reconstruction which appeared at Montgomery.

In such an atmosphere the new Confederacy was born. The senatorial managers of the old Democracy were in comfortable control. They had put into their model government the reforms they had so vociferously demanded. They need not now be fearful of the tyranny of numbers, of the dangers of a radical democracy. They had saved their society from the corruptions of money-mad metropolitanism and territorialism. They were no longer endangered by New Englandism or antislaveryism. If only something would drive their eight southern neighbors to join them! Meanwhile, the laboratory of the Breckinridge Democrats had turned out much work in a short time. They had organized a new power which they expected to control. But it was never to have the strength or the prestige of that which they had just lost.

Chapter 25

Stalemate in Washington

A SECOND CHAPTER in our tale of two cities was being written in Washington this same month of February. While at Montgomery one branch of the American Democracy was laboring to create the new, at the national capital, the other was rather hopelessly trying to preserve the old. The task at Washington seemed discouragingly difficult; time was so short, and the odds so long. There were now two forums in the capital city. While Congress sat in the tense atmosphere of the undomed Capitol, the Conference Convention was talking behind closed doors at Willard's.

Virginia's invitation, strangely enough perhaps inspired, or at least encouraged, by Senator Seward, had been answered by twenty-one states; only seven of these were southern, for Arkansas and the seceding states did not respond. Few prominent Democrats were present. Ex-President Tyler and former Secretary of the Treasury Guthrie were the best known. The majority of the persons from northern states were Republicans. Only New York and New Jersey sent Democrats of any prominence. In their delegations were Congressman Erastus Corning, Green C. Bronson, ex-collector of the port of New York, Peter D. Vroom, recently Minister to Berlin, and William C. Alexander, whom Buchanan had almost appointed Attorney General. Most of those present were sincere Union men, but they were two extremes. Some radical Republicans had come, apparently determined to prevent compromise. Present for the same purpose, it seemed from his talk, was the ardent Virginia secessionist James A. Seddon; yet even he was in touch with Seward, who lately had visited him in Richmond to promote the convention.[1]

While the delegates were laboring without benefit of the press, Congress dropped its compromise efforts to await the results of these deliberations at Willard's. The remaining Democratic leaders in the meantime were facing a very unpleasant legislative situation, made the more so because they found themselves so helpless. The withdrawal of the southern Democrats had let down the bars to the Republicans, and many of them were galloping into the green pastures seemingly unmindful of the crisis. Senator Latham reported that the fact of secession seemed to them a "grand joke." They were only interested in enacting the Chicago platform into law.

On the day that Jefferson Davis and his associates withdrew from the Senate, the dam broke and legislation began to surge into the channels of enactment. On that Monday, with all the curious accompaniments of anticlimax, the Kansas issue, so long the Congressional firebrand, was settled tamely enough. By the votes of the Republican Senators and nine northern Democrats Kansas became a free state. Not one northern Democrat opposed it, though Gwin and Lane refrained from voting. Buchanan signed the bill January 29.[2]

The territories of Colorado, Nevada, and Dakota were organized with no Wilmot proviso or mention of slavery; with a Republican President to appoint their officials, there was no need to raise the question. This was accomplished with Democratic help. At a crucial time, eleven northern Democrats—Representatives like Adrain, Cochrane, Horace Clark, Maclay, and some western colleagues, who could appreciate metropolitan and territorial attitudes—joined the Republicans and supplied the two-thirds vote necessary to consider these bills. Having thus enabled the Republican majority to function, they piously voted against the measures, which the Republicans easily passed.[3]

The Senate also got up the long dormant House tariff bill. It opened old wounds, rousing further apprehensions among southern states hesitating to secede. It brought repercussions in the Conference Convention and developed a new sectional conflict when westerners opposed a tariff made for New England. Nevertheless the Republicans with Bigler's help put it through the Senate, loaded with one hundred fifty-six amendments. The House Republicans accepted all but one of them, and passed the bill with the help of the Pennsylvania and New Jersey Democrats and Haskin and Reynolds of New York. Buchanan signed it, by no means forgetting he was a Pennsylvanian and relieved by a rider authorizing a Treasury loan. This is as far as the Republicans got. A quarrel over routes defeated the Pacific railroad bill; it expired, however, calm in the assurance of a speedy resurrection.

While the wheels of this legislative mill were grinding, three issues, which had done so much to disturb the ruling Democrats during the fifties, were removed finally from the forum. The coup de grace was given to the California steamship mail subsidy. The Republicans and Latham, despite Gwin's resistance, cut the Gordian knot. There was hereafter to be one central overland mail route carried by stagecoach until the railroad should be built. Butterfield could have the contract if he would meet the new specifications; otherwise a new contract would be let. Vanderbilt was paid off for his services for the fiscal year, but after July 1, 1861, steamship mail subsidy to California was done.

With even less discussion two other questions, long sources of intrigue and corruption, were disposed of. A revision of the patent laws provided that patents should be granted for seventeen years and not renewed. No more, presumably, would lobbyists fatten and spread corruption and confusion in the cause of patent renewals. Also Congress appropriated $135,-000 to buy Cornelius Wendell's printing plant. Hereafter it was to be operated by the superintendent of printing as the Government Printing Office. The doubtful profits of this perennial jobbery were no longer to fill the party chests.

While the Democrats had been resisting the enactment of the Chicago platform and half-heartedly cooperating in reform, they had been laboring to prevent the passage of measures which would strengthen the military force available to the incoming Republicans. Reconstruction and compromise would be easier to secure if there were no force bills in the way. The more radical of the Republicans had been intent on securing new sources of power, even if it meant more strength for Buchanan in his last days. Bingham of Ohio had introduced Jackson's force bill of 1833 into the House.

When Buchanan reported to Congress on January 8 he asked that body to strengthen his hands. A special committee of the House then began to consider the situation. Its five members were Dawes and Howard, Republicans, Reynolds, Douglas Democrat, Cochrane and Branch, administration Democrats. To begin with, they produced two measures, the Reynolds and Cochrane bills; and Reynolds and Cochrane joined the Republicans in reporting them to the House, although Cochrane made an oral dissent on the Reynolds proposition. Branch filed written dissents to both.

The Reynolds bill gave the President express authority to call out militia to defend or to recover federal property. Cochrane's measure was to provide, so it said, for the collection of the revenues in regions which might be in rebellion; the President might close ports in seceding states by proclamation and use the navy to establish a blockade. Foreign ships approaching these ports to enter goods, upon which obviously they would pay no duty, could then be seized and condemned. Reynold's bill was very shortly withdrawn, and Cochrane's was not called up soon. In truth most Republicans were disinclined to strengthen the executive until they were in full control, and the friends of conciliation wanted no force bills to antagonize efforts in the Conference Convention.[4]

The committee of five next turned to a subject of almost hysterical interest. Washington seethed with rumor and dread. There was talk of conspiracy, of secret drillings of organizations sworn to overthrow the government, to make impossible Lincoln's inauguration. Many believed that there would be an attempt on February 13 to prevent the counting of the electoral votes. Governor Morgan of New York wrote General Scott enquiring if he wanted New York militia units despatched. In view of all this talk, the House on January 26 turned over the matter to the committee of five for investigation. They held hearings, and on February 14 brought in a reassuring report. In the testimony, however, was evidence that the Breckinridge and Lane Club and another company were drilling. The former now was known as the National Volunteers, and prominent in it was L. Q. Washington of the Knights of the Golden Circle. Senator Wigfall's name was also connected with it. Godard Bailey, just released on bail in the Indian bond fraud case, testified that these companies were drilling because they feared that the Republican Wide-Awake clubs in the free states were arming to mobilize at Washington and then invade the South.[5]

Though the electoral votes had been safely counted on February 13 and the committee's reassuring report was received the day following, the more radical Republicans were not willing to let the Congress expire without some effort to provide more force to suppress secession, particularly because the President had made the excuse that lack of power prevented him from taking more positive action. Also the Conference Convention seemed to be bogging down in fruitless debate. At length a Republican caucus voted February 17 to support a force bill, and next day Benjamin Stanton of Ohio, chairman of the House military affairs committee, submitted a report. The committee had been all over the military situation, had investigated Floyd's distribution of arms and the surrender of the forts, and could find no evidence that the late Secretary of War had been guilty of arming the South before the election, though it condemned his efforts to do so after the Indian trust funds were found looted. Neither could it agree with

Buchanan and Black that the President had insufficient power. Nevertheless, to block such excuses, Stanton reported a bill.

He described his measure "as the most harmless thing in the world," designed to repair an apparent omission in the Act of 1795. It would give the President power to call out the militia in case of a general insurrection.[6] Bocock of Virginia moved its immediate rejection; all the Democrats save Adrain, Riggs, Reynolds, and Montgomery voted for this motion, but it was defeated, 110–68. This bill then was brought up daily during the morning hour, and it seemed that there were votes enough to pass it. Conservatives feared its effect on the Virginia state convention, which had assembled February 13; though this body seemed safely in the hands of Unionists the passage of a force bill might destroy the balance. Lincoln, too, when he arrived on the 23rd, used his influence against it.

The radical Republicans made a determined effort to push the Stanton bill through, February 26, but Sickles proposed an embarrassing amendment designed to make the Republicans declare whether they were willing to use such force to coerce seceding states. As Cochrane was ready to make a damaging speech against it, the Republicans split on the bill, 40 conservatives joining the Democrats to vote a postponement, 100–74, which was a virtual defeat. A last attempt was made on March 1 to move it into position, but Cochrane succeeded in killing it by securing an adjournment, 77–60. Next day, the radicals tried to pass Bingham's force bill, pigeonholed since early January; but they could not get a two-thirds vote to suspend the rules against solid Democratic opposition. The Democrats thus joined the conservative Republicans to keep the road to conciliation free from these obstructions.[7]

II

In the White House the President was hoping against hope that either Congress or the Conference Convention would do something to avert conflict. He and his cabinet could do little but watch. He himself was extremely tired and worn: the month between December 27 and January 29 had been very hard on him. During that entire time the senatorial managers had been at him constantly, hour after hour; one after another they came with their demands. He had withstood them, but it had taken much out of him. His southern friends had turned on him, the hardest blow falling when the Slidells broke off even social relations because of Holt's removal of

Beauregard. Since the Pickens truce and the departure of most of the senatorial managers he had enjoyed a little respite and recovery. Still there were days when he felt too ill to go to his office and had to meet the cabinet in his library. Had he known that one of its members, Edwin M. Stanton, was reporting their deliberations regularly to the Republicans, he would have been even more despondent.[8]

He was pinning his hopes on the Conference Convention and bending his little remaining energy to prevent any untoward act from disturbing that body; so the idea of reenforcements for Sumter, taken up on January 30, was allowed again to lapse. When Hayne went off in a huff after writing his violent letter, Buchanan's fears revived, and they were fanned by fussy John Tyler, busily cautioning him and trying to stop Pickens from taking offense and firing on the fort.[9] Fortunately Anderson had written that he did not want any reenforcements, they would only cause trouble. This despatch was received February 4, the day the Conference Convention met. Not only did it cause Ward's expedition to be delayed longer, but it cast a damper on a more ambitious scheme.

Captain G. V. Fox, a connection of the Blairs, had been talking with Lieutenant Hall and working on a more formidable plan to reenforce Sumter which he brought to Scott February 7. The General was impressed and introduced Fox to Holt. They in turn carried the plan to Buchanan; but he was still under the spell of age, indecision, Tyler, the Conference Convention, and Anderson's last word, so that Fox was put off. There may also have been some reluctance to endorse a scheme of the Blairs, formerly Democrats, now Republicans. Fox went back to New York to make more preparations and to bide his time; Buchanan would soon be out, and the Blairs would be a power in the new order.

The President now learned from Tyler that Governor Pickens was not going to start hostilities, despite Hayne's rebuff. Much relieved, he prepared to relapse into the routine duties he so loved.[10] There were bills to sign, appointments to make, cadets to select, troops to be brought to Washington, and the District militia to organize. He tried to reward some old associates with lucrative places. His old Hoosier friend, John Pettit, he would appoint district judge in the new state of Kansas; and he would reward his Secretary of State with a nomination to the Supreme Court. But Black, Pettit, and numerous others were not to have these honors. The Republicans with the aid of Douglas Democrats, at least in Black's case, prevented confirmation.[11] They would not fill life positions with Democrats on the eve of their ascendancy.

Calm could not be recaptured. Washington was still alive with rumors regarding the military clubs and their drilling. Scott and Holt got together what troops they could, and then Congress passed angry resolutions inquiring into the assembling of these forces. Nor would the question of the Sumter reenforcements lie quiet. Anderson's reports soon became less reassuring. A despatch was received on February 11 suggesting the possibility of conflict, in which case reenforcements would be necessary; and two days later came a request for instructions on treatment of ships flying foreign flags in the event of war.[12]

Cabinet meeting on February 19 was tense. Holt brought a despatch from Anderson which reported that a floating battery was being constructed and might soon be sent to attack him. What were his instructions? Other word had come from the South which made the situation more dangerous. The new Confederate government had taken the fort out of South Carolina's jurisdiction, and the provisional Congress had passed a resolution urging President Davis to secure Sumter and Pickens. The Confederate executive was busy organizing his armed forces and undoubtedly might act soon. This news inspired a rumor that Governor Pickens would not wait for the Montgomery government to take action, but would order an attack himself.[13]

Holt and Scott again sought to complete the preparation for reenforcements and to give Anderson orders to fight back until aid came. Buchanan again was hesitant. The debate on the tariff and the introduction of Stanton's force bill were disturbing the Conference Convention, and he did not want to do anything to imperil that hope further. Holt pressed him. What would he do in Anderson's position if he were attacked? The President had to admit that he would "crack away at them." He held up decision overnight but yielded next day; reenforcements should be sent. Straightway he and Tyler were relieved to receive another denial from Governor Pickens of any hostile intentions.[14]

However, General Scott immediately ordered the assembling of the supplies which Lieutenant Hall had said Anderson needed, and directed they be put aboard Commander Ward's small fleet at New York. The Assistant Adjutant General, Lorenzo Thomas, began preparing a detachment of some two hundred recruits to be ready to embark from the same port.[15]

The leaky War Department could not hold this information, at least not from Senator Wigfall, who immediately telegraphed Governor Pickens: "Attempt to re-enforce Anderson by stealth at night in small boats determined on."[16]

Commander Ward was not to set sail. Buchanan soon learned that the Montgomery government was postponing the use of force in favor of further negotiation. The Confederate Congress had authorized an official mission of three commissioners to proceed to Washington.[17] Ward's expedition therefore was merely held in readiness, and Holt instructed Anderson February 23 to be very cautious: his actions must be purely defensive. The Secretary pointed out that the problem might be solved either by negotiation or by the labors of the "Peace Congress" still in session.[18]

Buchanan continued in constant conference with Tyler, who had been nervously chasing shadows. Most recently he had fallen into a dither because there was to be a parade on Washington's Birthday of not only the District militia but also a goodly portion of the 685 regular troops whom the President and General Scott had brought to the capital. Tyler was afraid that such a display of force would arouse angry passions. To please him, Buchanan tried to stop this parade; but when Dan Sickles and others came down on him he reversed himself, and the march actually took place.[19] While Holt was drafting Anderson's instructions Buchanan and Tyler were discussing the forthcoming visit of Confederate commissioners. Both felt that negotiations might postpone and perhaps avert warfare, and so Tyler caused Senator Hunter to write Davis urging speedy appointment of the commissioners and expressing the hope that the Confederate President would go to Charleston himself, to "represent and quiet all things." Hunter's letter made Davis feel that it expressed the President's desire. Buchanan no longer had much hope of help from the Conference Convention; but there were only eight days left in his administration, and the encouragement of negotiations might be the most effective means of keeping peace until March 4.[20]

III

The Conference Convention had not been having much success. James Guthrie of Kentucky had taken the lead in marshaling the compromise Democrats and Whigs, with help from outside. The election in Virginia on the day the convention met had been a Union victory. The Kentucky legislature had refused to call an election but instead had invited a national convention to formulate conciliatory amendments, in effect an endorsement of the original recommendation Buchanan had sent to Congress the day after the Conference assembled. The Governor of Maryland likewise remained adamant in his determination not even to call a session of the legislature.[21]

These favoring signs led the friends of compromise to increase their efforts in the four states yet to hold elections in February. These contests were hotly fought, and both sides received help from Washington. A North Carolina representative complained that one or two of the departments were "employing their entire force" sending antisecession speeches into the campaigning states. A group of twenty-seven conciliationists in Washington, including Douglas, Bigler, Fitch, and Sebastian of the Senate and Hamilton of Texas from the House, signed a printed circular asking for contributions to pay for circulating Union propaganda.[22]

Local party situations were as important in these February elections as they had been in the previous contests. In Virginia, the increasing hostility between the growing western counties and the ancient tidewater remained a significant element; the western voters were not interested in becoming part of a cotton oligarchy. In Tennessee, which was balloting on February 9, the mountain countries at the east had the same antipathy toward the plans of the lowland planters, and Andrew Johnson knew their strength and heeded their Union sentiments.

Arkansas and Missouri were voting on the 18th. The former, long dominated by the family of Senator Robert Johnson with its numerous henchmen and allies, had overthrown this cabal the previous fall in a contest led by Congressman Hindman, ousting Johnson from his Senate seat. Johnson was an ardent secessionist, and his opponents were more favorable to the Union. In Missouri commercial, polyglot St. Louis, with its large German population, was always at odds with the farming hinterland. The metropolis was naturally pro-Union, for its future lay more in western development than in association with New Orleans. North Carolina, which would decide on February 28, presented the most unusual situation. In the Old North state there were signs of a popular uprising against prewar Bourbons. In the towns a very small but politically active labor movement was anticipating events. It would have no interest in a slaveholding confederacy.[23]

The cause of the Union was ably presented in these states, and the results were encouraging. In Tennessee the people voted down a call for a convention, 68,000 to 59,000, and denounced secession, 91,000 to 24,000. Missouri and Arkansas did likewise a week later, the former by 80,000 majority against secession and the latter by 5,700.[24] It was obvious that the people at large were not secessionists, political agitators to the contrary notwithstanding.

These favorable signs did not hasten the action of the Conference Convention, which wrangled on in secret. Guthrie headed a committee which brought in a series of proposals, and they were debated at length. Finally, despite the obstructionist tactics of some Republican delegates and after several tedious deadlocks, the Guthrie propositions somewhat amended were agreed to seriatim by varying votes. So uncertain were the leaders as to approval of these measures that the report was never voted on as a whole. Not until February 27, less than four legislative days from the end of the congressional session, were the proposals sent to Congress. The program was somewhat like the Crittenden plan in that it extended the line 36°30′; but it applied only to territory then within the United States, and it aimed to create a complicated machinery which must be used if more territory were to be acquired. So complicated was it that there could be no real expectation of further expansion, at least southward, if it ever went into effect.[25] The mountain had labored and had brought forth a mouse.

IV

This agreement had been reached so late that the friends of compromise had despaired and certain Democrats had once more been trying for action by Congress. They concentrated their efforts on getting a vote on the Crittenden Compromise. This was resisted as usual by the Republicans. Corwin had gone over the matter with Lincoln after his arrival, and they decided to offer the constitutional Amendment concocted by the Committee of Thirty-three, slightly revised. This would be their olive branch, and they expected their party to back the move. Corwin undertook to prevent a vote on the Crittenden plan by maneuvering his revised Amendment in ahead of it. On February 26 he endeavored to close debate on the report of the Committee of Thirty-three, which had been under discussion off and on since Sickles's struggle with it. The New York City Congressman now prepared to fight, for he claimed that Clemens's motion of the preceding month had put the Crittenden plan where it would have to be voted on first.

Corwin was not a veteran parliamentarian for nothing. He offered his revision as a proposition to perfect his own previous report, in order to dislodge Sickles. "Perfecting" a pending motion took precedence over Clemens's move to substitute a new resolution. Neither Sickles nor Corwin, however, had reckoned with the divided state of the Republicans. The moderate group were with Corwin and Lincoln, but the radicals, hating southern power, would take neither the Crittenden nor the Corwin Amendment; they were maneuvering to secure an endorsement of their formula that no amendment was necessary, for the Constitution needed not to be amended but obeyed. When they found by test votes that the Corwin Amendment had a majority, the radicals began a first-class filibuster. This was so near the end of the session and so endangered the appropriation bills that an agreement was finally reached to vote on all of the propositions the next day.

The session of February 27 appeared to be the Waterloo of compromise. Proposal after proposal came up only to be voted down. Burch's plan for a constitutional convention fell, 74–108. The Crittenden proposal, now first voted on after two months of delaying action, fell, 80–113; the Republicans mobilized their solid strength against it, unaided by a single Democrat. Then came Corwin's report itself. At first the omens were favorable. The declaratory resolutions in the first section were accepted, 136–53, with only radical Republicans and southern Democrats voting nay. Then came defeat. Corwin's revised Amendment, which simply declared that slavery might not be interfered with by the federal government in states where it already existed, failed. As it was a proposed Amendment of the Constitution it needed a two-thirds support or 129 votes. It could muster but 123 because a minority of 71, composed mostly of radical Republicans—but no Democrats—voted nay. Furthermore the House ignored the report of the Conference convention, that day presented at the Capitol.

The session on the following day found a more conciliatory spirit abroad. The House reconsidered its rejection of the Corwin Amendment. Four Republicans changed their votes and three refrained from voting, so that the necessary two-thirds was secured and the amendment went to the Senate. All Democrats voting had supported it save Hindman of

Arkansas. But this was practically all that the House would do. Its remaining efforts for conciliation were but few and ineffective.

Next day the rest of the report of the Committee of Thirty-three was considered. The bill to admit New Mexico was laid on the table, 115–71; the Democrats divided, 32 for it and 25 against. The proposed fugitive slave law was passed, 92–83; the Democrats again divided with no seeming rationale to the division. The bill to compel state governors to extradite fugitives from indictment loosed a stormy states' rights debate and was thrown out, 125–48; the Democrats again meaninglessly divided. The fugitive slave law would receive no attention in the Senate, so only the proposed Thirteenth Amendment survived of all the futility of the Committee of Thirty-three. Would the Senate act on that? The House meanwhile spent its final hours in the congenial maze of appropriation bills and private bills and in censuring Toucey for accepting the resignations of officers in the navy so speedily. It was heedless of the danger.

In the Senate, the conciliators were hard at work at their thankless task. The moment that the Conference Convention plan arrived on the 27th, they had had it referred to a special committee headed by Crittenden with Bigler and Thomson as its Democratic members. These three decided to recommend its adoption, and so reported next morning. The Republican members, Seward and Trumbull, dissented; they recommended a constitutional convention and opposed any particular last-minute amendments like these. Republican objections postponed any action until one o'clock. Then the Democrats and Whigs mustered almost their full strength and, with the aid of Baker of Oregon and Dixon, forced consideration of the Conference Convention plan. It was given its first reading and under the rules must lie over until the next day. Toward night word came that the House had passed the Corwin Amendment. The Democrats feared that the Senate rules might crowd out any chance of considering either of these proposals, and so Bigler gave notice of a motion to suspend the rules governing Amendments. He hoped this would be adopted on the morrow and thus permit votes on either or both of these propositions. If his motion failed, the Amendments failed because there were not days enough left for the three readings, each on a separate day as required by the rules. March 3 was a Sunday and therefore not a legislative day.

Opponents of compromise were able to waste March 1 in

talk, under the Senate's cherished freedom of debate. Efforts to secure two readings on that one day so that the House Amendment might be put upon its passage on Saturday, were successful, it was thought, and so Bigler's motion was not called up. The friends of compromise came to the Senate on March 2, the last day of the session, confident of their position on the calendar.

Dr. Gurley prayed eloquently, and the legislators settled down to long hours of work. In the course of the afternoon Senator Sumner seemed to upset the conciliation applecart by claiming that there was an error in the journal. He had made objection to the second reading but it was not recorded. Various Senators now made diametrically opposed statements of fact, and finally the Senate voted, 24–17—with five Democrats, Green, Lane, Mason, Rice, and Wigfall in the affirmative—that the journal was wrong. This vote was possible because Lane said he had heard Sumner object on the previous day. Now unless Bigler's resolution were passed, conciliation was dead.

The long afternoon was wasted in a heated interchange between Lane and Andrew Johnson of Tennessee. This was Jo's swan song, and he eloquently defended his record and his southern views. In the course of his oration he denounced Johnson for attacking him. Johnson replied immediately. He was in good form, and the crowded galleries were with him, particularly when he denounced the secessionists as traitors. Polk of Missouri was in the chair, and he was determined to stop this. He ordered the men's galleries (in those days on his right) to be cleared. His ruling brought a number of Senators to their feet to cheer or denounce the galleries. Some pressed for adjournment—the noise was so great that no business could possibly be transacted. Some time was consumed in a parliamentary tangle resulting from efforts to take advantage of the confusion.

Finally the chair suspended his order and Johnson went on. The crowd waxed more enthusiastic, as Johnson achieved a peroration embracing "The Star-Spangled Banner," "Hail Columbia," Andrew Jackson, Tennessee, and the Constitution, all in one. His eloquence raised such an uproar that Fitch, who was presiding, actually cleared the galleries and locked the doors. By then it was six o'clock, long after the dinner hour, and nothing had been accomplished. Crittenden moved a Sunday session to begin at eleven next morning, but the Republicans prevented this violation of the Sabbath with the aid of Lane, Nicholson, Polk, and Rice. The hungry Senate settled down to work until midnight.

Bigler saw he must act now or never; so he called up his resolution to suspend the 26th rule. It was carried, 20–16, when Collamer, Dixon, Harlan, and Simmons joined the Democrats. This victory ensured a vote on a compromise Amendment, and Douglas led the final effort to conciliate. He moved to put aside the Crittenden proposals and take up the House Amendment; and his motion prevailed in spite of Mason's efforts to sidetrack it. Lane next gallantly interposed as the champion of the fair sex. The galleries were still empty but a milling crowd in the corridor was eager for admission. The Oregonian spoke of the plight of the fair ones who must stand in the throng. After more time was consumed the ladies' gallery was opened.

Now, when the house Amendment was called up by Douglas, delay was maneuvered. Pugh was dissatisfied with its grammar, which was undoubtedly bad, and proposed to correct it—really to get rid of it, for he wanted the Crittenden plan. This upset Douglas's strategy. The House had finished its business at seven o'clock and had recessed until ten A.M. Monday. That would give it just two hours before the inauguration for final business. Douglas declared that the House would not be able to finish this measure if it were changed. Nevertheless, the Senate voted Pugh's verbal amendments; and it took all of Douglas's skill to secure reconsideration and then reversal.

Having thus saved the House Amendment, which Pugh declared was not worth the paper on which it was written except as a declaration of good faith, Douglas was confronted with a second proposal by Pugh, which had the identical language of the Crittenden compromise. The introduction of this measure, which had been kept from a vote since December 18, let loose a new flood of meaningless, time-consuming oratory. Wilkinson declared the Northwest would never permit the South to control the Mississippi. Chandler, in a state of enthusiasm which led Lane to suggest that the Republicans were engaging in a Whisky Rebellion, denounced the Buchanan administration; citing Floyd and Toucey as examples, he pilloried its members as thieves and scoundrels. This roused Wigfall to a similar alcoholic outburst. He shouted that the Crittenden Amendment, the Conference Amendment, and the Corwin Amendment were all useless. Only an Amendment admitting that each state possessed the right to secede would avail anything now. Crittenden finally succeeded in stemming this flood of bourbon by moving a recess at midnight until Sunday evening at seven.

During the Sabbath the Senators got what rest and spiritual renewal they could. While part of the Republicans were in conference with Lincoln at Willard's, the Democrats were somewhat at loose ends. Those who were ending their careers were packing. At seven o'clock Bright assumed the chair, and Crittenden made his final plea for compromise. The galleries were jammed, and the *Globe* reporter recorded that a "great disturbance" was occasioned by efforts to get into the already overcrowded galleries. Crittenden was often interrupted by the noise and finally was stopped when a man fainted in the crush. Bright sought to remove the people standing in the gallery aisles, but those in front protested that there were so many behind them that they could not get out. Finally, while the Senate was voting to clear them out, some gradually withdrew and quiet returned. The Vice President had now resumed the chair, and he suspended the removal. Crittenden concluded, and was followed by Trumbull who urged that nothing be done until Lincoln could try his hand. Baker of Oregon pleaded for conciliation to cherish the border states. Now it was midnight, and the Democrats undertook their last efforts.

Douglas rose to urge a cessation of such political debate and the taking of the vote. Instead he got into a quarrel with Pugh and Mason, particularly the latter, over what Douglas charged was the plot to kill off the House Amendment with the Crittenden resolution. Once more he taxed the Republicans with its destruction, saying that the Democrats, including Toombs and Davis, had once been willing to take it but now it was too late for they and their states had withdrawn. Once more he defended popular sovereignty. In the course of this debate, Mason accused him of trying to use the House Amendment as a placebo or bread pill. This roused the Republicans, giving Wade an opportunity to wax eloquent on the bread-pill theme and introduce some comic allusions to sarsaparilla. Wigfall who was even more alcoholically bent, had no interest at all in sarsaparilla and undertook to explain at length just why he rejoiced at the insult of "your flag" at Charleston. In the wee small hours he subsided.

Now the votes could be taken. Crittenden's Compromise, in the form of Pugh's amendment, came first. Crittenden knew it had no chance, and he and his friends voted against it to

save the House Amendment; it failed, 25–14. Another substitute offered by Seward and Trumbull, called for a constitutional convention, joined the procession of defeat. Johnson
of Arkansas, seldom heard from, called up the Conference
Convention proposals, which suffered an even worse fate,
34–3. At long last there were no obstacles left, and the House
Amendment was called up—it was then or never. It passed
by the exact vote necessary, 24–12. Seven Republicans had
joined the Democrats and the Whigs. Douglas had won.

Most Senators agreed that it was not a very substantial
triumph and was not likely to mend matters much. Could not
something real be done? To the Kentuckian's surprise, Mason
called up the Crittenden Compromise so long slumbering on
the calendar and began to work on it. Some amendments
were made in line with suggestions recently sent up from the
border states; but Crittenden wanted to make sure that the
Conference Convention proposals had their day. They were
bowled over, 28–7; Douglas, Johnson of Tennessee, and
Thomson were the only Democrats in the affirmative. Then
at last came the much striven-for vote; the Crittenden Compromise was for the first time squarely before the Senate. It
was beaten, 20–19; not a Republican voted for it. The Democrats bowed in defeat.

A little more time was spent in routine business. The Republicans refused, 20–16, to go into executive session despite the
number of deserving Democrats still awaiting the confirmation
that now they never could receive. The Republicans had remained all night in almost solid phalanx, while a dozen of the
Democrats were in more restful surroundings, allowing this
patronage to fail. Thereby they gave the final evidence of
Democratic disintegration; they had not enough spirit left
to stay up for offices. At seven A.M. they recessed until ten.
At that hour both houses reassembled to finish routine business. The Senate could only watch the successful efforts of
Senator Bright to kill a bill. The Republicans were sponsoring
the incorporation of a new gas company in opposition to the
monopoly that supplied the capital city with its illumination.
Bright's connections, Corcoran and Riggs, probably had some
interest in the old company; at any rate Bright talked it to
death. The Senate and the Democratic power expired in the
midst of a discussion of gas.

The efforts of the peace-seeking Democrats had thus
accomplished very little. Compromise had been killed by two
power aggregates. The secession Democrats, confronted with

loss of power, could see no compromise which would restore their accustomed dominance. It were better to hurry away while there was time to rebuild their sway in a region they could control. The victorious Republicans—the new power— eager to enjoy the fruits of their triumph, could see nothing in compromise but the destruction of that control which they had just won. At first they had not believed that the secessionists would carry through; but when these proved their determination it made no difference to the Republicans. The nation that remained was great, and they would rule it. Thus the two power aggregates had defied each other and made of little moment the efforts of the conciliators.

There were few grains of comfort on that 4th of March, but such as there were could be hoarded by the surviving Democrats. Though they could expect little from the House Amendment—the so-called Thirteenth Amendment—which Douglas and Sickles had worked with such diligence to save, on the other hand no force bills had been passed, no new powers created for the President so soon to be. Secession had been arrested in mid-passage. Eight of the southern states were still in the Union, and there was yet peace. How long would it last?

Chapter 26

The Last Stand

INAUGURATION DAY, 1861, was the time appointed for the transfer of power. The Democratic party, in control almost continuously from the days of Jackson, must yield its fasces to the Republicans. The White House and the Senate chamber, strongholds of the once mighty host, had at length been captured, and the victors were forming their ranks for a triumphal entry. But the vanquished had not been deprived of hope. The party had been defeated twice before and badly split once, yet it had recovered quickly. With a heterogeneous opposition, already faction-ridden, there were possibilities. Besides, the party's statistical position was good.

Even after the secession of seven state machines there were left approximately two million voters enrolled under the party emblem. Three-quarters of this strength was in states that would not in any event secede, and the total was two hundred thousand greater than the Republicans had yet achieved. The party had a most resourceful leader in Douglas, who had commanded 65 per cent of the two million in the late balloting. Breckinridge would now be a fellow Senator, and as the fire eaters had in large part seceded it was not impossible to imagine the reunion of the two wings under a single organization. The national committee of the party had access to men of wealth, particularly August Belmont who was the party chairman. Its rank and file were generally Union men, and many of them were undoubtedly earnest for peace.

For several weeks Douglas had been evolving a daringly conceived maneuver. There was a gambler's chance that the party's loss of power might be brief. He had never been far apart from certain interests in the Republican party. During the bitter Lecompton battle he had negotiated with Greeley, Colfax, and others for their support and possibly considered joining the Republicans. Also Douglas, despite his spectacular contest with Lincoln in 1858, really had much in common with him. By the eve of the inauguration it had become apparent that the Republicans were cursed by factions. Lincoln was of western Whig antecedents and was a moderate; the radical antislavery men East and West and certain other eastern interests were already making it almost impossible for him to organize an administration. His first plan—a cabinet of Seward moderates and border-state men, even including a southerner—had roused the radicals, who were demanding a place for one of themselves. Also Seward was playing a devious game with the South and was consciously or unconsciously laboring to maneuver the President elect into an inferior position. Lincoln needed friends.

Douglas had shrewdly grasped the situation. While he was working out his plan for a commercial union with the new Confederacy, he was also playing with the idea of a Union coalition between Lincoln's moderates and his Union Democrats; incidentally this might mean that Lincoln would retain some Douglas henchmen in office. The Republicans, already badly split, might disintegrate, and a new party triumph in 1862 and 1864 with Douglas ultimately in the White House after all.

As soon as Lincoln arrived Douglas called on him and, equally important, the socially prominent and experienced Mrs. Douglas called upon the distraught and somewhat bewildered Mrs. Lincoln, who Harriet Lane had heard was "awfully Western, loud and unrefined."[1] They were cordially received, and the Senator had a series of conferences with the President elect. Douglas in the course of these talks offered his support with such telling effect that, it was reported, Lincoln was moved to tears. He consulted Douglas about portions at least of his inaugural, and the Little Giant is credited with some peace-inviting modifications.[2]

Such a cordial reception gave the Illinois Senator the cue to adopt a new role. He now believed he might be able to direct Lincoln, whose tendency toward a "temperate resolute Union policy" was quite different from that displayed by the Republicans in the expiring Congress. Douglas could easily assume that his program and Lincoln's were the same and could claim that Lincoln had accepted his views, even if not quite his "Great Brinziple" (Douglas's pronunciation) squatter sovereignty. Such a program might disrupt the Republican party, and then Douglas could join or even perhaps lead Lincoln. The new Union party might be the answer. In the last hours of Congress, several Democratic members were circulating a Union manifesto for signatures,[3] which might serve as a first step in party realignment. Douglas also had a touch of the theatrical planned for the inauguration ceremony, if he could manage it.

II

While the Senate was wrangling, March 4 had dawned with dark and heavy clouds and occasionally a few drops of rain. The days preceding had been unseasonably warm, and many men had discarded their overcoats. The Senate recessed early that morning, and soon the sun came out and a strong, cool northwest wind sent clouds of dust down the cross streets to choke the crowds already thronging Pennsylvania Avenue. Overcoats were brought out again, and the visitors welcomed the more bracing air. Those who had slept in the streets were glad the wind had not come up earlier.

President Buchanan drove down to the Capitol to receive the last fruits of congressional activity. Shortly before twelve he signed the final measures and told the Senate's messenger, Senator Rice, that he had nothing further to communicate. Finding it was now 11:55, he hurried off to meet Lincoln at Willard's. Rice's arrival in the Senate finally extinguished Bright's gas. Then Senator Foot escorted Vice President elect Hamlin to the dais; Breckinridge made a brief speech of farewell and swore in his successor, who responded in a very few words. This duty done, the retiring Vice President adjourned the Senate *sine die*.

Hamlin, still on the dais, immediately reconvened the body under authority of Buchanan's proclamation and ordered the oath to be administered to the new Senators, save Pearce, who was escorting the presidential party to the Capitol. Several Democrats appeared. Breckinridge took the place of Crittenden, Clingman had been reelected, and two new men were received—Charles B. Mitchel in the seat of Johnson of Arkansas and James W. Nesmith succeeding the doughty Lane of Oregon. The Democratic successors of Green of Missouri and Gwin of California had not yet been chosen. Saulsbury and Sebastian, Hunter and Mason were not in their seats. Despite the secession of Texas, the two Senators from the Lone Star state answered to their names. There would be twenty-nine Republicans, twenty-four Democrats, and one American—if all remained.

These organization formalities were soon over, and the Senate settled itself to wait. In a few moments the Supreme Court assembled; but the presidential party, as usual, was delayed. Finally at 1:15 Buchanan and Lincoln entered arm in arm, Buchanan nervous and distraught, Lincoln grave and self-possessed. They took their seats before the dais while Pearce was sworn in and Hamlin announced the order of exercises. Then the procession moved to the east front. It was there that Douglas made his first public move. He had determined to make his association with the new President as conspicuous as possible, and now he had the chance. He crowded hard upon Lincoln's heels, and fortune favored him. Only a small table had been provided; Lincoln laid his manuscript upon it, held against the wind by his cane, but there was no place for his hat. Douglas stepped forward instantly and took it. For the remainder of the ceremony he stood with Lincoln's hat in his hand. During the reading of the inaugural he made *sotto voce* remarks plain enough to be heard by a reporter. "Good!" "That's so." *"No coercion!"* "Good." As soon as the oath was taken and Lincoln had departed, Douglas told reporters: "He does not mean coercion." That night he escorted Mrs. Lincoln into the inaugural ball room. His behavior did not go unmarked.[4]

Three events of that Inauguration Day were agitating the nerve centers of the government as the clocks ticked off its final hours. The first was the inaugural address. For weeks the great question had been: "What will Lincoln say? Is it to be peace or war?" And now that he had spoken, what did he mean? He had seemed reassuring. He had stressed his desire for peaceful settlement by constitutional convention and amendments. He believed the Union to be perpetual, and all the states still in it. As far as he was concerned things would go on as usual. He would not force any issues. He would not even attempt to make appointments in any "interior" locality where hostility to the United States might "be so great and so universal as to prevent competent resident citizens from holding the Federal offices." He would send in no "obnoxious strangers." But he would use his power "to hold, occupy and possess" the property and places belonging to the government, and to collect the duties and imposts. Even this use of power need not cause bloodshed, and he pledged there should be none "unless it be forced upon the national authority."[5] But had he answered the question: Peace or war?

The second event of this climactic day seems to have been known to but few, though Douglas certainly was informed of it. That morning Secretary Holt had received a despatch from Major Anderson, who had become alarmed at the growing strength of the enemy and the depletion of his stores and fuel. He was now altogether too dependent upon what he could buy in Charleston, and if those supplies stopped he would be forced to poor fare indeed. So on February 28 he had canvassed the situation with his officers and had taken from each his opinion as to the strength needed to reenforce the fort. The opinions varied, but Anderson concluded that 20,000 men would be necessary to silence the batteries so that approach could be made to Sumter. Holt had carried this message to the Capitol, where Buchanan and the rest of the cabinet were busy in the President's room considering the final bills and approving them. There was no time to do more than exclaim at this news, but they agreed to meet in the evening.

President Buchanan was spending the night at the home of Robert Ould, the district attorney of Washington. After nightfall the erstwhile administration gathered in his office and talked over Anderson's despatch. It was quite a shock. These men had thought that Captain Ward's small fleet with two hundred or so recruits would be enough, and here came the appalling estimate of 20,000. This was political dynamite! The new administration could very well accuse the departing chiefs of criminal neglect—200 men provided when 20,000 were needed. Here was a perfect alibi for the Republicans if the fort were lost. They would shout that it was due to the ineptitude or treason of Buchanan and his advisers.

What could be done? It was finally decided that Holt should write an explanatory report; they would meet him at the War Department next morning to hear it, and he would send it with the despatch over to the White House forthwith. He was to explain that much of the time Anderson had disclaimed any need of reenforcement, and that when he suggested it they had gotten together a sufficient expedition according to the best information obtainable. No one had ever breathed twenty thousand or even twenty hundred. The Sumter situation was to be placed squarely before Lincoln just as he was discovering the truce arranged at Fort Pickens.[6]

The third event of March 4 was the beginning of what the Confederacy hoped would be diplomacy, but what instead became a backstairs political intrigue. The proposal to send commissioners, which the Confederacy had voted on February 15, and which Buchanan and Tyler originally had welcomed and encouraged only a week ago, had borne fruit. Davis had chosen a Breckinridge Democrat lately Congressman from Georgia, Martin J. Crawford, a Douglas Democrat, John Forsyth, and a Louisiana member of the opposition, A. B. Roman. They had been instructed February 27 to secure recognition and to make treaties of amity and good will with the United States.

Crawford proceeded northward at once and alone, arriving March 3. He learned that President Buchanan was no longer interested and seemed to have forgotten his recent encouragement. He reported Buchanan "wholly disqualified for his present position . . . as incapable now of purpose as a child." He would start no negotiation with him and awaited the organization of Lincoln's office.[7] On the evening of Inauguration Day he met with Wigfall and three Virginia Congressmen, Garnett, Pryor, and DeJarnette. They read over the inaugural and agreed that it was hostile. The only hope they saw was Seward. As they thought Lincoln "a man of will and firmness," they were none too confident of Seward's ability to do anything. Wigfall so reported to the Governor of South Carolina, and L. Q. Washington of the Knights of the Golden Circle did likewise to the Confederate Secretary of War. Wigfall telegraphed that night: "Do not permit any attack on Sumter without authority of Government of Confederate States. . . . Inaugural means war. There is strong ground for belief that reenforcements will be speedily sent. Be vigilant."[8]

Crawford turned, upon that Inauguration Day, to other Democratic leaders with whom Seward had been conferring intimately through several weeks in the belief he could avert civil war. The new Secretary of State was firmly convinced that if bloodshed could be avoided the South, after certain negotiations, might return. To this end, he was willing to surrender Sumter. He was also under the delusion that he was the only strong man likely to be in the Lincoln administration. He was working through two Democratic colleagues, Gwin and Hunter.

Through Gwin he was endeavoring to persuade President Davis that the new administration would be for peace. Gwin had written such an opinion to Davis several days prior to March 4 but became less sure on the eve of inauguration and was inclined to warn Davis. However, Seward persuaded him that his fears were groundless, and Gwin telegraphed Davis March 2 that the inaugural would be "pacific, followed by conciliatory policy." Davis had probably talked with Crawford about his earlier communication from Gwin. At any rate Gwin would be the one through whom to approach Seward.[9]

The Virginia influence also might be effective through Seward, for he had been very close to certain of the Virginia leaders during the past two months and at this point was cooperating with Hunter. This intimacy was in part due to Seward's personal needs. He was just emerging somewhat battered from a fight which his friends had made and lost to keep Chase, the radical, out of the cabinet. So battered was he that he had told Lincoln at the final minute that he could not serve as Secretary of State. Lincoln had persuaded him, but until the last moment he feared he might be rejected if the radical Republicans opposed him *en bloc,* and if they were joined by the Democrats. So, it was reported he had come to an understanding with Hunter. He assured this Democrat that no reenforcements would be sent to Sumter and promised to send such a message to the Virginia convention the day after he became Secretary of State. Crawford naturally turned to Hunter, then, as well as to Gwin, for avenues to Seward.[10]

III

Thus the events of that Inauguration Day unrolled themselves, and they were to be the backdrop before which the special session of the Senate met. As the Senators went over the list of Lincoln's appointees awaiting confirmation, and took up the few other items of business for which a post-inauguration session of the Senate is called, they would be conscious of a wide audience. The Virginia convention was still in session with great power to influence the course of events. The legislature of Kentucky was about to reassemble, to continue its efforts at compromise. Would there be a convention of the border states, such as was proposed in Kentucky? Was it too late to assemble a convention of the loyal states, to frame constitutional Amendments? Would the Union be further shattered by new secessions to the Confederacy or by the formation of another, made up of border states?

While these vital questions remained unanswered, the Senate must attend to the nominations by the new President. When it assembled at one o'clock, March 5, the cabinet list had not arrived. It recessed until four-thirty and reassembled to find that Lincoln's private secretary, Nicolay, had delivered the slate. It included three former Democrats: Simon Cameron, Montgomery Blair, and Gideon Welles. The Virginia Senators were in their seats this day, and Mason attacked Blair's nomination; he maintained that no southern man should hold office under Lincoln, and Clingman and Wigfall agreed with him. Breckinridge on the other hand did not feel such a pronouncement was justified. Blair and Bates received some negative votes from the South, otherwise the confirmations were perfunctory. No one opposed Seward. He was sworn in next morning, and a messenger went forthwith to Richmond bearing words of conciliation from the new Secretary of State.

Cabinet and other appointments seemed unimportant while there were elections to be watched as barometers of public opinion. North Carolina had just voted, deciding against secession in unmistakable terms.[11] Now New Hampshire, Connecticut, Rhode Island, and numerous municipalities were holding their usual spring campaigns. The Senate's special session would supply a forum for the manufacture of political propaganda, though usually this session of the upper house was too brief and too much occupied with patronage to pay much attention to speech-making for partisan purposes. The Democrats, particularly Douglas, saw an opportunity; and he began to exploit it.

On the third day the political strategy which was to rule this special session became apparent. The Republican majority was interested primarily in the executive sessions where the successive batches of appointees were to be considered. It had no statements of policy to make and therefore was going to indulge in silence in the open sessions. Here the Democrats were going to take the center of the stage in an effort to make the Republicans amplify Lincoln's inaugural, while at the same time they would do what they could to rally public opinion for peace and perhaps reconstruction. The Republicans left the floor to them, and they proceeded to occupy it.[12]

The debate began with a motion to print the inaugural. Clingman started it with the bald assertion that the address meant war; Lincoln's refusal to recognize secession and his determination to hold property and collect revenue could mean nothing else. Clingman and Douglas were friends, and it may be that this was prearranged as an opener which Douglas was to utilize. Whether this be true or not, Douglas did so employ it.[13]

The Illinois Senator played another scene in his new political drama. He arose to disagree with Clingman and defend Lincoln. The inaugural was "a peace-offering rather than a war message." It was not as explicit on all points as Douglas had desired, but otherwise it was a source of hope and encouragement. He declared that Lincoln had "sunk the partisan in the patriot." Then he defined his new position. "I do not wish it to be inferred, from anything I have said or have omitted to say, that I have any political sympathy with his administration, or that I expect that any contingency can happen in which I may be identified with it. I expect to oppose his administration with all my energy on those great principles which have separated parties in former times, but on this one question—that of preserving the Union by a peaceful solution of our present difficulties; that of preventing any future difficulties by such an amendment of the Constitution as will settle the question by an express provision—if I understand his true intent and meaning, I am with him."[14]

Clingman was not through, he had two other points. He wanted to know more about Lincoln's remedy, these proposed constitutional Amendments. There was no clear statement of their character. Furthermore he demanded that Lincoln withdraw the troops from Pickens and Sumter.

The North Carolina Senator was interrupted and next day followed by Wigfall. This fiery and often inebriated Texan with the fierce mien of a pirate was in an equivocal position, attending sessions despite Texas's secession. His excuses were that he had not been officially notified of the event and that the secretary of the Senate still called his name and those of the other Senators from the seceded states. In reality he was busy collecting and sending South any information which his position enabled him to secure. He had been doing this since New Year's and now was taking on a new function, actually organizing a recruiting service for the Confederacy, while still on the Senate payroll. He had an office in Baltimore which he frequented, and he worked in the District. He was busy arranging for the induction of the National Volunteers, the old Breckinridge and Lane Club, who now, under the stimulus of L. Q. Washington of the Knights of the Golden Circle, were seeking to go South.[15]

Wigfall lashed out bitterly against the Republicans, whom he charged with defeating the Crittenden and all other practicable compromises and with treating the Conference Convention's proposals contemptuously. He dared them to state what they intended to do, and demanded that they remove the troops from the forts and refrain from "levying tribute"; otherwise, he said, there would be war. He turned on Douglas and charged he was condemning Lincoln to masterly inactivity. These statements brought Douglas to his feet to disclaim speaking for the administration—he would support it only if its program were peaceful. He caused some consternation when he announced, we may suspect on executive information, that there was not food enough in Sumter and therefore the garrison must soon be withdrawn. This revelation of March 7 made people open their eyes.

Later in the day Douglas made still another statement which seemed to indicate that he was in confidential relations with Lincoln. In rebutting a reiteration by Mason that the inaugural was a war message, the Little Giant declared that he took it for granted there would be no attempt to reenforce Fort Sumter, "for the simple reason that it is impossible to do it, if even there was a disposition to do it." In so saying he reiterated that he had "no knowledge of the views or purposes of anybody connected with the government." It could not collect revenue by military force without congressional authorization, and as the Republicans had had control of Congress, according to Douglas, since early in January and had done nothing, they must be dedicated to peace. If this were not their attitude the nation would soon know, because it would be necessary to call a special session, and this call would serve notice. Douglas again repeated that all he saw spelled peace.

Douglas had been continuing his visits to the White House, urging this policy on Lincoln while the new President was assembling his administration. Lincoln was not able to have a cabinet meeting until Saturday March 9, probably because of Seward's illness; and even then there was still much confusion. Cameron had not yet entered the War Department; Holt was holding over. When those of the Cabinet then in Washington met on that day, they heard General Scott urge evacuation of Sumter because there were not the 20,000 troops to reenforce it; and there seemed to be an informal consensus that this would have to be done. On Monday the press, led by the Republican organ, began to speak of it as an accepted fact decided in cabinet—a feeler probably put out by the administration to prepare the public for evacuation.[16]

During that second week various forces were at work. Lincoln and his cabinet, now complete with Cameron at his post, took up Sumter again, and each member submitted his views in a written statement to the President. The Pickens truce had been discovered in the meantime, and orders sent down to end it by landing the troops still on shipboard. Crawford, now joined by Forsyth, was working through Gwin and Hunter to get an interview with Seward, while the Republicans were trying to expel Wigfall and purge their roll of the secession Senators.[17]

Douglas continued his pressure from the floor of the Senate during this second week with further maneuvers. He introduced a lengthy resolution requesting information from the President as to what forts, arsenals, navy yards, and other public works were still possessed and occupied by the United States, and particularly whether the federal government had sufficient power under existing laws to retain them, and whether the defense of the nation required the recapture and reoccupation of any forts. If so, what force would be necessary to reduce the states who had occupied such forts?

He added more arguments to his plea for evacuation and peace. He had prepared estimates which he expounded at length. It would take an army of 285,000 men to reduce the South and would cost $316,000,000 annually. The government could not possibly raise more than $100,000,000 a year, so that such a conflict was impossible to support. He then turned to a constructive program which he hoped to see adopted. According to him there were but three policies open to the Republicans: that of restoring the Union by amendment of the Constitution; that of peaceful dissolution with a liberal system of commercial and social intercourse arranged by treaties of commerce and amity; that of war. Which one were they planning to use? Douglas demanded, March 15, that the Republicans speak.

He went on to say, somewhat ironically, that the Republicans should have no difficulty in agreeing to a compromise which would satisfy the border states and make possible the growth of a Union party in the seceded states. In fact, said he, it was already done. They had abandoned the Wilmot proviso and, by passing the Colorado, Dakota, and Nevada bills without mention of slavery and refusing to repeal the slave code in New Mexico, they had in effect accepted slavery south of 37° and adopted his squatter sovereignty principle throughout the territories. He reiterated his demand that Sumter be evacuated, and that Amendments be adopted so that the President's policy of peace be implemented. The Republicans, just because they were on the eve of spring elections, must not sacrifice the nation to platform consistency.

Douglas dulled his effectiveness somewhat by losing his temper. Under goading from Fessenden he denounced the Republicans for remaining silent, and insulted his colleague. Fessenden paid him back his insults and exposed his attempts at assuming a leadership which the Republicans would not tolerate. He wiped him emphatically off the roll of gentlemen. Hale then rubbed it in by ridicule.[18]

Yet things seemed to be going Douglas's way. All of the cabinet, save Chase and Blair, wrote opinions against holding Sumter. Seward was in part responsible. He had been working on General Scott, while pursuing his devious way with the southern envoys. On their behalf Gwin and Hunter had visited him. Although he did not feel that he could recognize or see the southerners, he wanted to keep them in Washington and have them use their influence against any attack on Sumter. He did not relish Douglas's frequent calls at the White House, and was less patient with his efforts to force the Republican Senators into meaningful speech.[19]

IV

Douglas had held the center of the Senate stage most of the time during this fortnight, and it was quite apparent that the remnant of the Senate managers of the preceding Congresses thought he had taken a little too much of the spotlight. Senator Breckinridge, leader of the other faction, felt he could not let Douglas monopolize the scene. Also the legislature of Kentucky was about to resume its sessions, and he wanted to be well recognized as still a leader and not merely a passive colleague of the Little Giant. His personal position was unhappy because he was beset by conflicting emotions and ambitions. His erstwhile radical supporters were urging him to lead Kentucky into the Confederacy. Even then unofficial meetings were being held to press the legislature southward. Yet he well knew the strength of Union sentiment in the bluegrass region, and how improbable it was that he could change its conservatism.

For the time being Breckinridge was for peace, and so he spoke his mind, but in tones of warning to the Republicans. He, too, hoped to influence their policy.[20] Like the cooperationists, he urged the necessity of guarantees. Southerners must have either the right to migrate to the territories, with their property on an equal footing with other property, or they must have an equitable division of the territories. If the Republicans wanted to preserve the Union, they must give guarantees of government impartiality in dealing with the states and their institutions. They must promise that there should be no aggression upon the South and that its institutions should not be under the ban of the Republic. Further, the Senate ought to express its opinion that the troops should be withdrawn. Otherwise, he professed to believe Kentucky would go with her southern sisters. Wigfall reported enthusiastically to the South that Breckinridge was "with us."[21]

Breckinridge was followed by Bayard who ranked as the intellectual of the Democrats. He held forth for three days. As a citizen of Delaware, he could see no cause for secession in the election of Lincoln; but he admitted that a citizen of Georgia, a tropical state, might. He did not believe there could be peace based upon concessions extracted by force. He did believe that peaceful secession was probably the best answer and proposed a resolution authorizing the President to make a treaty of recognition with the Confederacy.

During the third week, while Breckinridge and Bayard were giving public advice on policy, other Democrats had been working on peace moves behind the scenes. Secretary Seward had been enlisting their aid to keep the Confederate commissioners in Washington until he could arrange for the evacuation of Sumter. Associate Justice Samuel Nelson of the United States Supreme Court was a citizen of New York, a former chief justice of that state, and an old acquaintance of Seward. From him the premier now secured the help of his colleague on the supreme bench, Associate Justice John A. Campbell of Alabama. The latter agreed, March 15, to talk to Crawford and Forsyth and to write to Davis; he was to convey to them delicately that Sumter was in the process of evacuation.[22]

President Lincoln was not nearly so certain about Sumter as Seward. He was impressed by Fox's plan of reenforcing the fort which Blair, now in the cabinet, was in a position to support heartily. Also he was still hoping that he could rally Union sentiment in the South. However, as General Scott and the cabinet advised against reenforcements and the Union sentiment seemed neither cooperative nor even discernible, he must have more adequate information. While Seward was working on the commissioners, Lincoln was investigating.

He sent agents to Charleston, and he endeavored to negotiate with the Virginia convention still in session. Fox was despatched to Sumter to look over the ground at first hand, and Lincoln commissioned two friends to carry out an ingenious plan to secure information regarding possible Union sentiment. An Illinois friend, S. A. Hurlbut, of South Carolina antecedents was sent to Charleston to make contacts very quietly, and another Illinoisan, Ward Lamon, of Virginia birth went thither very publicly. Lamon was given much newspaper attention, especially when he indicated that he was there to make arrangements for possible evacuation. The result was that Hurlbut was entirely unnoticed and fulfilled his mission without attracting any publicity. He returned to report to Lincoln that the Union sentiment did not exist.[23]

Lincoln's negotiations with the Virginia Unionists were equally disappointing. He was very anxious to have the Virginia convention go home; though it was under the control of the Unionists, it seemed to him a constant threat. He and Seward had been thinking of enlisting southern Union support by some spectacular appointment from their ranks. He had tried to get three southern Unionists to enter his cabinet, and Seward had urged the appointment first of Crittenden and then of a Virginia Unionist to the Supreme Court. Lincoln himself was hoping for a better arrangement. He was prepared to offer to evacuate Sumter if the Virginia convention would adjourn *sine die* and thus ensure Virginia as a member of the Union. He suggested that the Union leaders in the convention come to Washington to talk it over.[24] By the end of the third week his investigations were not complete, so that he was not ready to decide. He was a deliberate man; people were finding him hard to influence. Seward was becoming restive, and it was noted that Douglas no longer went to the White House so frequently.

As the fourth week of this unusually long executive session began, the Republican Senators were becoming uneasy. Still, batches of appointments were coming in daily, and these kept the Republicans in their places despite the embarrassment of Democratic speeches. Douglas's repeated remarks finally roused Howe of Wisconsin to make a two-day attack upon Douglas's resolutions and his alternative plans. No sooner had he finished when the Illinois Senator was again on his feet, needling the administration by stating that he understood the order to surrender Sumter had been given. In satirical vein he complained that it seemed impossible for Senators on the other side of the chamber to make a speech without impugning his motives or assailing his character, and he added a semihumorous remark: "I suppose if I should die, I would have the longest list of mourners that ever graced a funeral *cortège* in this country, because there would be so many politicians deprived of material out of which they manufacture their speeches."[25] He reiterated his belief that the southern states were entirely "safe and secure in their rights of person and property under the Constitution and laws, and that the Administration will not invade those rights and do not intend to do so. Nor do I think they intend, when Congress assembles, to recommend a war policy."

Before he sat down Douglas fired another salvo at Breckinridge, designed to bring him around and incidentally to embarrass the Republicans. He said that his Kentucky colleague was mistaken when he declared that the Republicans had abandoned none of their essential principles antagonistic to the South. He again repeated his demonstration of their change of heart on the territories and told Breckinridge that he was obligated to go home to Kentucky and tell his people that their terms had been met. Lincoln had even adopted Kentucky's favorite policy and was advocating a national convention and constitutional Amendment.

This clever maneuvering of Douglas and himself under the same banner naturally aroused Breckinridge to reply. He disavowed the close kinship, declaring that he and Douglas had not agreed on squatter sovereignty, and again stated his dissent from that principle. Likewise he denied the Republicans had abandoned the Wilmot Proviso. They had omitted mention of slavery in the territorial bills only to avoid controversy, for they knew they were going to appoint the territorial officers. They had rejected the Crittenden Compromise which if adopted would, he believed, have kept in every state but South Carolina. Now the border states were planning to hold a convention. The northern states must accept its suggestions if they wished to arrest secession. In the meantime they might show their conciliatory spirit by accepting a resolution which he expected to offer advising the removal of the troops.

Douglas replied once more, regretting that Breckinridge refused to recognize the Republican concessions. "I desire," he said, "that the people of Kentucky and of every State of this Union shall know the facts. I desire to put the Republican party out of power as much as the Senator from Kentucky does; but I will not foster unkind feeling and apprehensions of danger in the South, for party purposes. I will tell the truth about the conduct of the Republican party, even if it operates to their credit, and to the injury of my own party." He pursued his pressure on Breckinridge somewhat further and concluded the fortnight's debate on his resolution with the words: "I have only answered such positions as I deem essential to the encouragement of the Union

men, north and south, to the end that they might be able to
rally the patriotic hosts of all parties and put down disunion
and secession in every state of the Union."[26] The Senate
immediately laid his motion calling on Lincoln for information on the table, 23–11. Eight Democrats and Hale and
Wade voted with him, the Republicans and Rice against him.

Breckinridge then proposed his resolution, advising the removal of the troops from the limits of the Confederate states,
and Clingham offered a substitute advising the same thing
but adding that there should be no attempts to collect the
revenue in those states. Neither resolution was even considered. The day previous, the Senate had passed a resolution
of Powell of Kentucky asking the President for the despatches from Anderson. To this Lincoln replied that it was
inexpedient to submit the correspondence; and after a long
wrangle on the 27th the Senate avoided any test votes on this
matter. Douglas once more proclaimed his confidence that
Sumter would shortly be evacuated.

On the last day of the session Douglas's efforts bore fruit
of a flavor not to his taste. Lincoln had been removing his
friends from office, and the radicals had grown restive under the Little Giant's pontificating; they had determined to
speak.[27] After what is described as "a contumelious interview" with Lincoln, they insisted upon introducing a resolution, through Trumbull of Illinois, declaring that to preserve
the Union the President "ought to enforce the laws and hold
and protect public property in the seceding as well as in the
other states." Douglas did what he could to bring this to a
vote as he wanted to find out, he said, "how many men in
the Senate are willing to vote the censure of the President
for withdrawing the troops at Fort Sumter." This proposition
also failed to reach a vote—in fact the Senate at this session
was sedulously avoiding votes on public questions. Everything was in such an uncertain state. The session closed
March 28.

V

The dispersal left affairs in a very delicate balance. The
Virginia convention was still in session, and its Unionist
leaders had not yet accepted Lincoln's invitation to conference. They were busy organizing to run tickets in the May
elections, hoping to defeat the Democratic machine of Hunter
and Mason. In the meantime the convention sat and watched,
much to the President's chagrin; and he received also the

discouraging South Carolina report of Hurlbut. On the other hand the Kentucky legislature, after hearing Breckinridge, Crittenden, and their Conference Convention delegates, decided to issue a call for a border-state conference to meet in Frankfort, May 27.[28]

Events in the last week in March were moving against Douglas and his effort to be policy maker, partly because Seward was playing a high hand. He was working with Secretary of War Cameron, stimulating Scott's senile vanity, by-passing Secretary Welles in the Navy Department and still negotiating obliquely with the Confederate commissioners. He was bent on diverting all federal strength in such fashion as to reenforce Pickens and surrender Sumter. Also he thought he saw help from abroad, as Spain had stepped in to reclaim Santo Domingo, and France and Great Britain seemed about to intervene in Mexico. He took high-handed means to accomplish his ends. He got Lincoln to sign orders diverting naval strength intended for Sumter to Pickens, without the knowledge or consent of Welles. Then he wrote Lincoln that as he, the President, was obviously unable to make a policy, Seward would be glad to volunteer. He would declare war on England, France, and Spain and thus recall the South to its old loyalty.[29]

On the heels of this disconcerting move, Lincoln had to face the fact of defeat at the polls; the Democrats with their allies had rallied in the spring elections. The non-conciliation and tariff policies of the Republicans had told against them. The Confederate government had taken full advantage of the high Morrill law rates, setting a tariff for the South 50 per cent lower. New York merchants and the Connecticut and Rhode Island manufacturers were dreading loss of trade and markets. Also, the Democrats and Constitutional Union men took advantage of the fact that the Republicans refused all conciliatory measures, and formed their own coalitions.[30]

In New Hampshire the Republicans won; the vote was light, but they had fallen off more than their opponents. In Rhode Island the Democratic-Constitutional-Union coalition of 1860, which had elected William Sprague as Governor, continued to function. He was a member of the richest textile manufacturing family in the state and had proved popular. They carried the state again in 1861. In Connecticut the Republicans were apathetic and lost two congressional seats. In the many municipal elections of various states the outcome was not comforting, particularly as the Democrats proved generally victorious in the important state of Ohio.[31] Their victories, however, soon proved an empty triumph.

The sum total of his disconcerting experiences in this fateful month of March moved the new President—unlike Buchanan—to assert himself and take command. He aban-doned conciliation. He ordered more supplies to Charleston, whereupon the Confederates fired on Sumter, forcing Ander-son to surrender to them; Pickens did not fall, then or later. War followed immediately on Sumter's capture. These events, however, are primarily the story of the rise of Republicanism, not of the disruption of the Democracy.

The coming of war abruptly ended the temporizing, the conciliating, the avoiding, and all the other futile efforts with which various factions of the Democracy had filled the pre-ceding months. Radicals, South and North, were the victors for the moment, since concession was ended. Then and then only did Virginia, North Carolina, Tennessee, and Arkansas join South Carolina, Georgia, and the Gulf Squadron in secession; Delaware, Maryland, Kentucky, and Missouri, though divided in sentiment, remained with the Union. The call to arms temporarily—very temporarily—ended partisan-ship, as southerners and northerners alike rallied to their standards.

The Democracy, for the time being, seemed without an objective; but Douglas soon found work to be done. Again he went to Lincoln, perhaps this time not quite so patroniz-ingly, and offered his services.[32] Both men knew that their own state had numerous "soft" spots of southern sympathy, and that some counties, particularly in "Egypt," might be hard to rally. Douglas offered to go back and sound the call of the Union. Lincoln was grateful for this proffer, for he knew that the Little Giant could do wonders in southern Illinois. Also when the special session of Congress met, which he was calling for July 4, it would be no small help to have Douglas's support. A man who could command a million votes was no mean ally. Perhaps it was then that Lincoln's idea of a bipartisan war coalition was born.

Douglas planned in vain. He returned to Illinois, not to rally his followers, but to die. He had lived too much in too short a time, and though he was not yet fifty he was worn out. His illness, first diagnosed as rheumatism, rapidly passed into a high fever. During the latter part of May he lay in the Tremont House at Chicago hovering in and out of delirium, surrounded by his family and attended by a bishop of his wife's faith waiting to receive him into her church. On June 3 he died, leaving his party in its most perilous hour. What part the destruction of his hopes played in his early death can only be guessed.

With Douglas went the Democracy's only real leader of national outlook. When the Democrats returned to the extra session in July their disordered ranks were further depleted, despite their spring success; no one appeared outstanding among them. After Tennessee, Arkansas, Virginia, and North Carolina seceded, most of their representatives had departed. In the Senate were left but fourteen Democrats. Only Breckinridge, Bayard, Bright, and Rice remained of the old managerial group. Andrew Johnson, long an outsider, was prepared to assume new prominence. The party strength was not particularly augmented by the successors of Lane and Gwin who came from the Pacific coast in the persons of the ribald Nesmith and the drunken McDougall.

In the House the remnant of forty-four did not even try to concentrate on a candidate for Speaker but scattered their votes. Yet here were better elements of talented direction. Douglas's right-hand man, Richardson, was back, and McClernand, Logan, Fouke, and Robinson, the Illinois veterans, were with him. English had returned from Indiana; Vallandigham, Cox, and Pendleton from Ohio; the veteran John S. Phelps from Missouri; Erastus Corning from the Albany Regency. From New York City appeared none other than Fernando Wood's brother Ben.[33] The useless baton of leadership of the national organization remained in the hands of August Belmont, chairman and financier of the national committee.

The Democratic party seemed in desperate straits. The war which it had striven to avoid had apparently destroyed the last shreds of its power as a national party. Driven back to the states, it must begin a long, uphill struggle for survival. In them, however, there was much to work with. While the party controlled but few of the local governments, it had vigorous organizations and effective machines in a number of states, particularly in pivotal areas, and in them there was but slight cessation of activity. Here they were to gain strength in retirement and emerge quickly to take advantage of opportunities soon to come to them. The Democracy was not to remain long in total eclipse.

Chapter 27

Clues

THE DISRUPTION of the American Democracy was complete in 1861. Secession had split the Republic, and the guns of civil war were thundering. The breakup of the Democratic party and the beginning of armed conflict were almost simultaneous; they were intimately related phenomena. The shattering of the party of Jackson was the bursting of a dike which unloosed an engulfing flood.

On the reasons for the Civil War there has been a vast amount of theorizing.[1] Writers have been prone to select patterns—economic, cultural, political, racial, moral, and others —and to devise and emphasize theories in conformity with them. Long arguments as to whether the conflict was repressible or irrepressible, whether the war was inevitable or might have been avoided, have preoccupied historians. As they have unearthed more and more "causes," as they have introduced into the picture more and more elements, they have not altogether succeeded in answering the moot question: Why a civil war? Most of the principal "causes"—ideological differences, institutional differences, moral differences, cultural differences, sectional differences, physiographic differences—have existed in other times and places, without necessarily causing a war. Then why should they set the people of the United States to killing one another in 1861? This book, it is hoped, supplies some clues.

People fight under the stress of hyperemotionalism. When some compelling drive, whether it be ambition, fear, anger, or hunger, becomes supercharged, violence and bloodletting, thus far in human history, seem "inevitable." Now why was emotion in the United States in 1861 supercharged?

The basic reasons for this hyperemotionalism cannot be neatly formulated and weighted. Fundamentally the process was an illustration of what Macchiavelli describes as the "confusion of a growing state." The population of the United States was rapidly multiplying, partly by natural increase and partly by foreign immigration, at the same time that it was arranging itself in rapidy changing patterns. Many Americans were creating new communities, others were crowding together into older urban centers. In old and new, change was continual, with a ceaseless moving out and coming in. The rate

of growth, however, could not be uniform; for it was determined in large part by physiographical considerations and the
Republic extended from the temperate into the semitropical
zone. In the semitropical-to-temperate agricultural South, enterprise was less active, mobility less noticeable. In the northerly states, on the other hand, the variety of realized and
potential wealth was greater, the stimulus from climate was
sharper, the interest in projects of all sorts was more dynamic.
There the vision of wealth and of the needs of the growing
society continually inspired the creation of new and more
powerful interests, under zealous and ambitious leaders.

So rapid and uneven a rate of social growth was bound to
inflict upon Americans this "confusion of a growing state."
Characteristic of it and dominant in it were pervasive, divisive,
and cohesive attitudes which, as Whitman put it, were "significant of a grand upheaval of ideas and reconstruction of many
things on new bases." The social confusion in itself was the
great problem confronting statesmen and politicians. Turn
where they would, they could not escape it; they themselves
were confused by it, and yet they must wrestle with it.

The political system which was in the process of evolving
reflected their predicament. They knew that they were operating a federal system, but they oversimplified their problem by
believing that it was only a political federalism. They did not
grasp the fact that it was a cultural federalism as well. Not
only were they dealing with a political federation of states,
they must understand this cultural federation of attitudes. The
inability to understand contributed much to their failure to
organize partisanship and to create political machinery which
would be adequate to deal with the complexities of this cultural federation.

This lack of understanding was accompanied by a deep-
seated enjoyment of political activity by Americans which
proved dangerous. They gave themselves so many opportunities to gratify their desire for this sport. There were so many
elections and such constant agitation. Contests were scheduled
automatically by the calendar, at many different times and
seasons; there were thirty-three independent state systems of
election. Within each state the parties, despite their national
names, were really independent, each a law unto itself, and
none was subjected to much if any central direction; there
were nearly eighty such party organizations. A great disruptive fact was the baneful influence of elections almost continuously in progress, of campaigns never over, and of political

uproar endlessly arousing emotions. The system of the fathers might possibly bear within itself the seeds of its own destruction.

This constant agitation certainly furnishes one of the primary clues to why the war came. It raised to ever higher pitch the passion-rousing oratory of rivals. They egged one another on to make more and more exaggerated statements to a people pervasively romantic and protestant, isolated and confused. The men and woman exhibiting these different attitudes were not isolated and separated by boundaries—they dwelt side by side, and the same person might be moved by more than one attitude at a time, or by different attitudes at different times. The emotional complex which was created by the variety of these attitudes, and the tension which their antagonisms bred, added confusion to that already provided by the chaotic electoral customs and poorly organized parties; the total precipitated a resort to arms. The baffling problem was not how to maintain a balance among states but how to preserve a balance among a number of emotional units or attitudes. It was this that proved beyond the political capacity of the time.

The Democratic party was not unaware of some of the danger. Its most enlightened leaders had sought to quiet such divisive attitudes as antislaveryism in the North and southernism in the South by encouraging such cohesive attitudes as nationalism. Unhappily they did not understand the pervasive romanticism and protestantism sufficiently to make use of them in strengthening the cohesive attitudes. No leader in the Democracy could find the formula. Buchanan, Douglas, the justices of the Supreme Court, Davis, Hammond, and Hunter all tried and failed. The Republicans, such as Lincoln and Seward, grasped the realities: a house so divided against itself could not stand; with such divisive attitudes in the ascendant and unchecked, the conflict was irrepressible.

Under the stimulus of constant agitation the leaders of the southern branch of the Democracy forbade the voters to elect a Republican President unless they wished him to preside over a shattered government. A number of voters sufficient to create a Republican majority in the Electoral College defied the prohibition. Then southerners, in a state of hyperemotion, moved by pride, self-interest, a sense of honor and fear, rushed to action; they were numerous enough and effective enough to force secession. They would flee the peril; in the spirit of 1776, they would organize a second American Revolution, this time against the tyranny not of a monarch but of "a mob." They would create a reformed confederacy free from corruption and centralization in which their social and economic institutions would be safe.

Also under the stimulus of constant agitation, the newly organized Republican administration decided to put down what it called the "Rebellion." Backed by an angered constituency including most northern Democrats, it determined to fight rather than permit the seceding states to break up a profitable partnership, a source of wealth and power, and an experiment in liberty and equality which Lincoln felt was the hope of the world. It undertook a "people's contest" to insure that "government of the people, by the people, for the people" should "not perish from the earth."

Thus war came when the American people for the first time refused to abide by a national election. The parties which had been promoting the cohesive attitudes had broken down, and their disorganization had permitted the new Republican organization to win through direct appeal to the divisive attitudes. The constant heat generated in the frequent elections brought an explosion. The social, economic, and cultural differences had been so used by the political operators as to produce secession and civil war.

War broke out because no means had been devised to curb the extravagant use of the divisive forces. Statesmanship seemed poverty-stricken. The work of the nationalists who sought to find a formula with which to overcome the divisive attitudes was vain. Too few even saw the need for the formula; they ran heedlessly down the path to disruption. The war was the product of the chaotic lack of system in ascertaining and directing the public will, a chaos exploited with little regard for the welfare of the general public by irresponsible and blind operators of local political machinery unchecked by any adequate central organization.

Finally, carrying the analysis even further, it may be postulated that the war came because of certain interests and activities characterized for convenience as the processes of human behavior, in which individual and general attitudes and emotional drives are constantly interacting—provoking and conditioning one another. At certain times and in certain circumstances, cooperative behavior predominates; but competitive behavior is seldom if ever absent, and when too vigorously aroused leads to a strife which ranges from argument to war.

Indeed argument is itself a form of conflict short of war, more or less, and if pressed without checks and restraints easily passes over into war.

The American Democracy sought from 1850 to 1860 to keep in power by encouraging cooperative behavior. But, deeply affected by the shocks of the collisions occurring within the society in which it operated and of which it was a part, the party failed to overcome the divisive attitudes and was shattered. The disruption of the American Democracy eventuated in defeat, secession, and civil war.

Appendix

THE SLAVERY PRONOUNCEMENT OF THE
AMERICAN DEMOCRACY, CINCINNATI, 1856

RESOLVED, That we reiterate with renewed energy of purpose the well-considered declarations of former conventions upon the sectional issue of domestic slavery and concerning the reserved rights of the States—

1. That Congress has no power under the Constitution to interfere with or control the domestic institutions of the several States, and that all such States are the sole and proper judges of everything appertaining to their own affairs not prohibited by the Constitution; that all efforts of the Abolitionists or others made to induce Congress to interfere with questions of slavery, or to take incipient steps in relation thereto, are calculated to lead to the most alarming and dangerous consequences, and that all such efforts have an inevitable tendency to diminish the happiness of the people and endanger the stability and permanency of the Union, and ought not to be countenanced by any friend of our political institutions.

2. That the foregoing covers, and was intended to embrace, the whole subject of slavery agitation in Congress, and therefore the Democratic party of the Union, standing on this national platform, will abide by and adhere to a faithful execution of the acts known as the "Compromise" Measures, settled by the Congress of 1850, the act for reclaiming fugitives from service or labor included; which act, being designed to carry out an express provision of the Constitution, cannot, with fidelity thereto, be repealed, or so changed as to destroy or impair its efficiency.

3. That the Democratic party will resist all attempts at renewing, in Congress or out of it, the agitation of the slavery question, under whatever shape or color the attempt may be made.

4. The Democratic party will faithfully abide by and uphold the principle laid down in the Kentucky and Virginia resolutions of 1797 and 1798, and in the report of Mr. Madison to the Virginia Legislature in 1799; that it adopts these principles as constituting one of the main foundations of its political creed, and is resolved to carry them out in their obvious meaning and import.

And that we may more distinctly meet the issue on which a sectional party, subsisting exclusively on slavery agitation, now relies to test the fidelity of the people, North and South, to the Constitution and the Union—

1. RESOLVED, That, claiming fellowship with and desiring the cooperation of all who regard the preservation of the Union

under the Constitution as the paramount issue, and repudiating all sectional issues and platforms concerning domestic slavery which seek to embroil the States and incite to treason and armed resistance to law in the Territories, and whose avowed purpose, if consummated, must end in civil war and disunion, the American Democracy recognize and adopt the principles contained in the organic laws establishing the Territories of Nebraska and Kansas as embodying the only sound and safe solution of the slavery question, upon which the great national idea of the people of this whole country can repose in its determined conservation of the Union, and non-interference of Congress with slavery in the Territories or in the District of Columbia.

2. That this was the basis of the compromise of 1850, confirmed by both the Democratic and Whig parties in national conventions, ratified by the people in the election of 1852, and rightly applied to the organization of the Territories of 1854.

3. That by the uniform application of the Democratic principle to the organization of Territories, and the admission of new States with or without domestic slavery, as they may elect, the equal rights of all the States will be preserved intact, the original compacts of the Constitution maintained inviolate, and the perpetuity and expansion of the Union insured to its utmost capacity of embracing, in peace and harmony, every future American State that may be constituted or annexed with a republican form of government.

RESOLVED, That we recognize the right of the people of all the Territories, including Kansas and Nebraska, acting through the legally and fairly expressed will of the majority of the actual residents, and whenever the number of their inhabitants justifies it to form a constitution, with or without domestic slavery, and be admitted into the Union upon terms of perfect equality with the other States.

Notes

Chapter 1

1. Curtis, *Buchanan*, 2:170-171; Slidell to Buchanan, May 26, and Sickles to Buchanan, June 4, 1856, Buchanan MSS.
2. *Daily True Delta*, Apr. 4, 1858 (article on Slidell); Sears, *John Slidell;* Meade, *Judah P. Benjamin;* Murphy, "Political Career of Jesse D. Bright," *Pubs. Indiana Hist. Soc.*, No. 10, pp. 101-145; sketch of Bright in English MSS, Chicago; Corcoran, *A Grandfather's Legacy*, p. 187.
3. Beard, *The Republic*, pp. 27-41.
4. The campaigns of Pierce and Douglas are described in Nichols, *Franklin Pierce*, pp. 450-488, and Milton, *Eve of Conflict*, pp. 211-243. The attitudes and activities of Buchanan and his friends are found in the voluminous Buchanan MSS, which have been combed for the clues to Buchanan's uncertainty. Other evidence is found in Buchanan to Corcoran, May 29, 1856, Corcoran MSS; Jones, *J. Glancy Jones*, 1:345; Buchanan to Foltz, July 21, 1854, Foltz MSS; Tyler, *Times of the Tylers*, 2:516-524; Wise to Robert Tyler, Feb. 18, 1856, Tyler MSS; "Correspondence of R. M. T. Hunter," *Amer. Hist. Assn. Ann. Rept. 1916*, 2:178 (hereafter cited as *Hunter Corr.*); Eaton, "Henry A. Wise: A Liberal of the Old South," *Jour. South. Hist.*, 7:482-495, and "Henry A. Wise and the Virginia Fire-Eaters of 1856," *Miss. Valley Hist. Rev.*, 24:495-513; Montgomery, "Solid South Movement in 1855," *Ga. Hist. Quar.*, 26:101-128.
5. *Official Proceedings of the National Democratic Convention . . . in . . . 1856, passim.* MS records of this convention are in the Buchanan papers. Buchanan had Maine, Connecticut, the New York Hards, New Jersey, Pennsylvania, most of Maryland, Ohio, and Wisconsin as well as the delegations of Delaware, Virginia, Louisiana, Indiana, and Michigan, with minorities in Kentucky and Massachusetts. This strength gave him 135½ votes on the first ballot; the admission of the Hards had put him in the lead. Pierce had 122½, Douglas 33, and Cass 5. Buchanan did not rise above 155 on the first day and was 42 short of the required number. The day closed with Pierce at 75, Douglas 63, Cass 5½, and Buchanan 152½. He had gained only Rhode Island and scattered delegates. Tennessee had come to him for one ballot but did not stick. See Randall, *Lincoln*, 1:185.
6. Curtis, *Buchanan*, 2:170-173. Reynolds to Buchanan, June 1, Forney to Buchanan, Nov. 12, Martin to Buchanan, June 3, Sickles to Buchanan, June 4, Slidell to Buchanan, June 14, 1856, Buchanan MSS; Martin to J. S. Black, Mar. 31, 1857, Black MSS; Slidell to Breckinridge, June 17, 1856, Breckinridge MSS; Gilpin

to M. Van Buren, July 17, 1856, Van Buren MSS; statement of John A. Quitman, June 8, 1856, Quitman MSS; Ward to Howell Cobb, July 5, 1856, Cobb MSS; *Hunter Corr.*, pp. 196-198; "Correspondence of Robert Toombs, et al.," *Amer. Hist. Assn. Ann. Rept. 1911*, 2:367, 372 (hereafter cited as *Toombs Corr.*); Auchampaugh, *Robert Tyler*, p. 102; Tyler, *Times of the Tylers*, 2:527.

Chapter 2

1. This discussion of cultural federalism has been drawn from many sources. First of all should be mentioned the classic writers, Rhodes, Channing, McMaster, and von Holst. Nearer our own day and favored by the fruits of recent research are those who have been more lately active in this fruitful vineyard. The following have been particularly worthy of citation: Cole, *The Irrepressible Conflict;* Craven, *The Coming of the Civil War* and *The Repressible Conflict;* Randall, *The Civil War and Reconstruction* and "The Blundering Generation," *Miss. Valley Hist. Rev.*, 27:3; Kendrick, "Colonial Status of the South," *Jour. South. Hist.*, 8:3; Owsley, "Fundamental Cause of the Civil War: Egocentric Sectionalism," *ibid.*, 7:3; Ramsdell, "Changing Interpretation of the Civil War," *ibid.*, 3:3; Green, "Democracy in the Old South," *ibid.*, 12:3; Curti, *Growth of American Thought;* Gabriel, *Course of American Democratic Thought;* Cash, *The Mind of the South;* Jenkins, *Pro-Slavery Thought in the Old South;* Phillips, *The Course of the South to Secession* and *Life and Labor in the Old South;* Hofstadter, "U. B. Phillips and the Plantation Legend," *Jour. Negro Hist.*, 29:109; Russel, "Effects of Slavery upon Non-Slaveholders in the Ante-Bellum South," *Agric. Hist.*, 15:112; Carpenter, *The South as a Conscious Minority, 1789-1861;* Owsley and Owsley, "Economic Basis of Society in the Late Ante-Bellum South," *Jour. South. Hist.*, 6:24; Ramsdell, "The Natural Limits of Slavery Expansion," *Miss. Valley Hist. Rev.*, 16:151; Lynch, "The Westward Flow of Southern Colonists Before 1861," *Jour. South. Hist.*, 9:303; Brooks, *The Flowering of New England;* Barnes, *The Antislavery Impulse, 1830-1844;* Dumond, *Antislavery Origins of the Civil War in the United States;* Lloyd, *Slavery Controversy, 1831-1860;* Hubbart, *The Older Middle West, 1840-1880;* Billington, *The Protestant Crusade, 1800-1860;* Ekirch, *The Idea of Progress in America, 1815-1860;* Hansen, *The Atlantic Migration, 1607-1860;* Martin, *The Standard of Living in 1860*. Finally certain family traditions, letters, other manuscripts, and training have influenced this interpretation, probably more than the author realizes.

Chapter 3

1. The details of the campaign are found in a variety of corre-

spondence in the Buchanan MSS and in the files of the *Washington Union*. See also Breckinridge, Corcoran, Everett, Jones, Pearce, and Stephens (Convent) MSS; *Toombs Corr.,* p. 376; Bigelow, *Retrospections,* 1:172; Choate, *Reminiscences,* p. 299; Brown, *Choate,* pp. 321-331. The pamphlet material is listed in the bibliography.

2. Wise, *Henry A. Wise,* pp. 209-210; Wilson, *History of the Rise and Fall of the Slave Power in America,* 2:520-521; Boyd, *History of North Carolina,* 2:315; Henry A. Wise, Jr. (a cousin of the elder Wise), to Edward Everett, Sept. 17, 1856, Everett MSS; Mason, *James M. Mason,* p. 117; Wish, "Slave Insurrection Panic of 1856," *Jour. South. Hist.,* 5:206-222.

3. Ward to Forney, July 23, Forney to Buchanan, July 25, Tucker to Buchanan, Aug. 13, Jones to Buchanan, Aug. 11, 16, Slidell to Buchanan, July 17, Buchanan to Swift, Sept. 3, Buchanan MSS; Slidell to Corcoran, July 17, Corcoran MSS; Cheever to Butler, July 21, Faulkner to Butler, Sept., Butler MSS; Morgan to Weed, July 30, Aug. 13, Oct. 4 (three letters), Oct. 6, N. B. Judd to Morgan, Sept. 18, Covode to Weed, Sept. 29, Cummings to Weed, Oct. 28, 31, Smith and Millward to Blair, Oct. 31, 1856, Weed MSS; *passim,* 1856, E. D. Morgan MSS; Nichols, "Some Problems of the Frst Republican Presidential Campaign," *Amer. Hist. Rev.,* 28:492-496.

4. Jones to Buchanan, Sept. 18, Ramsey to Buchanan, Sept. 27, Oct. 3, Macalester to Buchanan, Sept. 23, 1856, Buchanan MSS; *36:1 H. Rept. 648* (Ser. 1069), pp. 472, 517—hereafter cited as *Covode Report.*

5. Foner, *Business and Slavery,* pp. 120-138; Forney to Sanders, Oct. 13, Sanders MSS; Buchanan to Walker, Oct. 6, N.Y. Hist. Soc.

6. Forney to Buchanan, Sept. 11, Oct. 3, 26, Jones to Buchanan, Sept. 18, Ward to Buchanan, Sept. 10, Breckinridge to Buchanan, Sept. 29, Buchanan MSS; Cobb to Mrs. Cobb, Oct. 2, 5, Cobb MSS; Slidell to Corcoran, Sept. 23, Oct. 26, Corcoran MSS; *Covode Report,* pp. 548, 550-555, 560; Hamilton, *Reminiscences,* pp. 428-429; Appel, "The Political Revolution of 1860," *Cliosophic Essays,* p. 18.

7. Douglas to Buchanan, Sept. 29, Grund to Buchanan, Oct. 19, Buchanan MSS; Buchanan to Samuel A. (*sic*) Douglas, Oct. 4, 1856, Douglas MSS; Bright to Corcoran, Oct. 12, 1856, Corcoran MSS.

8. *Washington Union,* Oct. 18; H. A. Wise, Jr., to Everett, Oct. 18, 1856, Everett MSS; Nevins, *Ordeal of the Union,* 2:495, 505, 508, 509, 511.

9. *Official Proceedings of the National Democratic Convention,* p. 26.

10. McClure, *Our Presidents and How We Make Them,* p. 134; Buchanan, *Works,* 10:83, 96.

Chapter 4

1. *New York Herald,* Nov. 11, 13, 1856; Ranck, *Albert Gallatin Brown,* 147-150.

2. Jones to Buchanan, Dec. 3, 1856 (quoting Stephens), Buchanan MSS.

3. Wender, *Southern Commercial Conventions,* pp. 170-181.

4. *N.Y. Herald,* Nov. 11, 1856.

5. *Ibid.,* Nov. 12, 1856.

6. Wise to Buchanan, Nov. 24, Jones to Buchanan, Nov. 27, Buchanan MSS; H. A. Wise, Jr., to Everett, Dec. 7, Everett MSS; Buchanan to Jones, Nov. 29, Dec. 8, Jones MSS.

7. Buchanan to Grier, Nov. 14, 1856, Buchanan MSS.

8. *Dollar Weekly Pennsylvanian* (Philadelphia), Dec. 20, 1856.

9. Wikoff to Buchanan, Dec. 29, Appleton to Buchanan, Nov. 12, 1856, Buchanan MSS.

10. Cobb to Mrs. Cobb, Oct. 2, 5, Dec. 21, Forney to Cobb, Nov. 30, Cobb MSS; *Ga. Hist. Quar.,* 6:170; Forney to Buchanan, Nov. 18, Jones to Buchanan, Dec. 3; Buchanan to Forney, Dec. 13, Wise to Buchanan, Dec. 6, 1856, Buchanan MSS.

11. Tallmadge to Buchanan, Nov. 17, Dix to Buchanan, Nov. 19, Wise to Buchanan, Nov. 30, Dec. 6, Ward to Buchanan, Dec. 10, Walker to Buchanan, Dec. 16, 1856, Clay, Jr., to Buchanan, Feb. 11, 13, Bigler to Buchanan, Feb. 12, Ramsey to Buchanan, Feb. 13, 1857, Buchanan MSS; Butterworth to Harris, Dec. 22, 1856, Douglas MSS; Toombs to Cobb, Feb. 14, 18, M. J. Crawford to Cobb, Feb. 15, Cobb MSS; Toombs to Stephens, Feb. 14, Stephens MSS; Phelps to Marcy, Feb. 15, Marcy MSS; Wilkins to Sanders, Feb. 11, 1857, Sanders MSS.

12. Polk, *Diary,* 3:140-142; Wise to Buchanan, Nov. 9, 24, Dec. 6, 13, Buchanan to Wise, Dec. 2, Forney to Buchanan, Nov. 18, Jones to Buchanan, Nov. 27, Dec. 3, 4, 1856, Buchanan MSS; Auchampaugh, *Robert Tyler,* p. 138; *Hunter Corr.,* p. 178; *N.Y. Herald,* Nov. 27, Dec. 1, 1856; Wise to Robert Tyler, Jan. 9, 1857, Tyler MSS; H. A. Wise, Jr., to Everett, Nov. 28, Dec. 7, 1856, Everett MSS.

13. Slidell to Buchanan, Nov. 13, Dec. 17, 1856, Feb. 14, 1857, Johnson to Buchanan, Nov. 9, Forney to Buchanan, Nov. 12, Wise to Buchanan, Nov. 24, Appleton to Buchanan, Dec. 11, 1856, Jan. 15, Catron to Buchanan, Feb. 6, 1857, Buchanan MSS; Buchanan to Wise, Jan. 6, 1857, Dickinson College; Forney to Bigler, Dec. 17, 1856, Bigler MSS; Ward to Breckinridge, Dec. 9, 1856, Breckinridge MSS; Bright to English, Apr. 16, 1857, English MSS; Bright to [Allen Hamilton], Apr. 16, 1857, Ind. State Lib.; Douglas to Treat, Dec. 20, 1856, Feb. 5, 1857, Phelps to Treat, Dec. 22, 1856, Feb. 14, 1857, Treat to Douglas, Dec. 30, 1856, Green to Treat, Jan. 31, Treat to Green, Feb. 6, 1857, Treat MSS; Polk, *Diary,* 1:186, 238; Milton, *op. cit.,* pp. 243-245.

14. Wikoff to Buchanan, Oct. 18, 22, Nov. 1, 18, Dec. 29, Ramsey to Buchanan, Oct. 20, Buchanan to Bennett, Oct. 20, Dec. 29, Bennett to Buchanan, Oct. 22, Dec. 2, Dec. 23, Cochrane to Buchanan, Nov. 15, Forney to Buchanan, Nov. 18, Buchanan MSS; *N.Y. Herald,* Oct. 19, 1856.

15. Jones to Buchanan, Nov. 27, Nicholson to Buchanan, Nov. 6, Buchanan to Nicholson, Nov. 10, Buchanan MSS; Buchanan to Jones, Nov. 29, Dec. 8, 1856, Jan. 1, 1857, Jones MSS; Forney to Cobb, Nov. 30, Cobb MSS; Nicholson to Breckinridge, Nov. 12, Breckinridge MSS; Andrew Johnson to Samuel Milligan, Nov. 23, 1856 (in frame) L. C.; *N.Y. Herald,* June 14, 1858; *36:1 Sen. Rept. 205* (Ser. 1040), hereafter cited as *Ser. 1040,* pp. 10, 64; McClure, *Our Presidents,* pp. 149-150; Auchampaugh, *Robert Tyler,* p. 131; Forney to Buchanan, Nov. 9, 18, Dec. 11, Buchanan to Forney, Dec. 13, 1856, Appleton to Buchanan, Jan. 11, 1857, Buchanan MSS.

16. Appleton to Buchanan, Feb. 21, Jones to Buchanan, Feb. 14, 1857, Buchanan MSS; Bigler to Buchanan, Dec. 29, 1856, Bigler MSS; Johnston and Browne, *Alexander H. Stephens,* p. 316; Stephens to Stephens, Dec. 15, 1856, Mar. 7, 1857, Stephens MSS, Convent.

17. Forney to Buchanan, Nov. 9, Dec. 11, 1856, Jan. 9, 10, 13, Buchanan to Mott, Jan. 9, 1857, Appleton to Buchanan, Dec. 11, 1856, Jan. 11, 15, Van Dyke to Buchanan, Jan. 13, 14, 1857, Buchanan MSS; Jenkins to Wright, Jan. 7, 8, 13, Steele to Wright, Jan. 9, 11, 12, 13, Brodhead to Wright, Jan. 15, 1857, Wright MSS; Cobb to Mrs. Cobb, Jan. 13, 1857, Cobb MSS; *N.Y. Herald,* Jan. 10, 12, 14, 1857; Weed to Cameron, Jan. 15, 1857, Memorandum in Cameron's handwriting filed under Apr. 4, 1857, Cameron MSS; Wise to Robt. Tyler, Jan. 16, Tyler MSS.

18. Appleton to Buchanan, Jan. 11, 1857, Bigler to Buchanan, Dec. 29, 1856, Buchanan MSS; Cobb to Mrs. Cobb, Dec. 27, Jackson to Cobb, Dec. 30, 1856, Lamar to Cobb, Jan. 2, 1857, Cobb MSS; *Ga. Hist. Quar.,* 6:171-172; *Toombs Corr.,* pp. 389, 395, 396.

19. Mrs. Forney to Buchanan [Jan. 15], C. C. Clay, Jr., to Buchanan, Feb. 11, 13, Ramsey to Buchanan, Feb. 13, 1857, Buchanan MSS; Reid to Buchanan, Feb. 17, 1857, Reid MSS; Forney to Cobb, Jan. 21, Toombs to Cobb, Feb. 14, 18, Crawford to Cobb, Feb. 15, Cobb MSS; Toombs to Stephens, Feb. 14, 1857, Stephens MSS.

20. Slidell to Buchanan, Feb. 14, Bigler to Buchanan, Feb. 5, 12, Buchanan MSS; Cobb to Mrs. Cobb, Jan. 28, Feb. 3, Cobb to Lamar, Jan. 31, 1857, Cobb MSS.

21. Buchanan to Bigler, Feb. 20, 1857, courtesy of Mrs. M. B. Good; Van Dyke to Buchanan, Feb. 16, Slidell to Buchanan, Feb. 18, 23, Appleton to Buchanan, Feb. 19, Breckinridge to Buchanan, Feb. 25, 1857, Buchanan MSS; Foltz, *Surgeon of the Seas,* pp.

181-183; *Amer. Jour. Med. Sci.*, new ser., 35:97-104; *Amer. Med. Mon.*, June, 1857, pp. 347-358; *Boston Med. Sur. Jour.*, 56:371-376, 422; *Va. Med. Jour.*, 8:478-485; D. H. Wenrich to author, Feb. 7, 1935; E. B. Wilson to author, Oct. 18, 1943.

22. Catron to Buchanan, Feb. 6, 10, 19, 23, Grier to Buchanan, Feb. 23, 1857, Buchanan MSS; McLean to Blair, Mar. 30, 1857, Blair MSS; Bailey to Trumbull, May 12, 1857, Trumbull MSS; Corwin, "Dred Scott Decision in the Light of Contemporary Legal Doctrine," *Amer. Hist. Rev.*, 17:52; Hodder, "Some Phases of the Dred Scott Case," *Miss. Valley Hist. Rev.*, 16:3; McCormac, "Justice Campbell and the Dred Scott Decision," *Miss. Valley Hist. Rev.*, 19:565; Stenberg, "Some Political Aspects of the Dred Scott Case," *ibid.*, p. 571; clipping, "S. L. M. Barlow's Library to Be Sold," in the MS collections of the N.Y. Public Library.

23. Slidell to Buchanan, Feb. 14, Wright to Buchanan, Jan. 15, Buchanan to Wright, Jan. 23, A. A. Hammond to Buchanan, Jan. 29, Willard to Buchanan, Feb. 4, 1857, Buchanan MSS; Robinson to Cobb, Jan. 30, 1857, Cobb MSS; *Toombs Corr.*, p. 395.

24. Butler to Buchanan, Dec. 6, 1856, Slidell to Buchanan, Feb. 14, 19, Jones to Buchanan, Feb. 14, Bigler to Buchanan, Feb. 22, Buchanan MSS; Cobb to Mrs. Cobb, Feb. 10, 1857, Cobb MSS; *General Lewis Cass*, p. 29.

25. Buchanan to Cobb, Feb. 21, Buchanan to Floyd, Feb. 21, 1857, Buchanan MSS.

26. Jones to Buchanan, Feb. 20, Bigler to Buchanan, Feb. 22, Slidell to Buchanan, Feb. 19, 25, Appleton to Buchanan, Feb. 7, 19, 20, 21, Buchanan to Jones, Feb. 28, Buchanan MSS; Jones, *J. Glancy Jones*, 1:343, 373; C. L. Ward memorandum, Feb. 26, 1857, Black MSS (misplaced in Vol. I under Feb. 26, 1851); Black to Van Dyke, Nov. 15, 1856, Black MSS; Cochrane to Jones, Feb. 18, Wood to Jones, Feb. 26, 1857, Jones MSS.

27. MS Diary of Edmund Ruffin, Feb. 17, 1857.

28. *Ibid.*, Feb. 19; *34:3 H. Rept. 243* (Ser. 914); *34:3 Globe*, pp. 760, 926, 933, 951, 952.

29. Cobb to Mrs. Cobb, Jan. 15, 18, 1857, Cobb MSS.

30. *N.Y. Herald*, Mar. 5; *Memphis Appeal*, Mar. 12, 1857.

31. The MS copy of the inaugural, seemingly the one sent to the printer or the one from which fair copies for publication were made, is in the N.Y. Historical Society. Most of it is in a copyist's hand, but two sections are in Buchanan's writing. The first deals with the territorial question beginning, "This is, happily, a matter," and extending to, "May we not, then, hope." In this portion, the words, "the true construction of" which were originally before "the Nebraska-Kansas Act" have been crossed out. The second piece of Buchanan's writing deals with corruption. It begins "Next in importance" and runs through three paragraphs ending with "extended seacoast." In his discussion of the military road to California after "defended" and before "Besides," he struck out

very heavily a passage which as nearly as can be deciphered reads as follows: "In my opinion the power to appropriate money for the construction of such a road is as substantially implied and embraced by the war making power as that to erect a fortification at the entrance of the harbor of San Francisco." Stephens to Stephens, Mar. 7, 1857, Stephens MSS, Convent.

32. *Washington Star*, Mar. 4, 5; *N.Y. Herald*, Mar. 5; Foltz, *Surgeon of the Seas*, pp. 183-185; H. A. Wise, Jr., to Everett, Mar. 5, 1857, Everett MSS.

33. Brawley to Black, Mar. 6, Keenan to Black, Mar. 6, Black MSS; Black to Buchanan, two letters, Mar. 7, Buchanan MSS.

34. Swisher, *Roger B. Taney*, pp. 495-511.

Chapter 5

1. Biographical material regarding Buchanan is widely scattered and has never been brought under the focus of a published modern biography. This is not because of lack of interest on the part of Buchanan and his heirs, for no family probably ever worked harder to secure a life history. No sooner did Buchanan retire from the presidency than he began literary labors which resulted in his official defense *The Administration on the Eve of the Rebellion,* written with the aid of Jeremiah S. Black and his executor-to-be, Hiram B. Swarr. He, and his heirs after his death, negotiated with various possible biographers—Black, William B. Reed, John Cadwalader, and finally George Ticknor Curtis, who eventually completed the *Life of James Buchanan*. His heirs were also interested in collecting his state papers. His nephew, J. Buchanan Henry, compiled *The Messages of James Buchanan;* and his niece, Harriet Lane Johnston, arranged with John Bassett Moore to edit *The Works of James Buchanan*. His papers, after some damage by fire, were eventually deposited with the Historical Society of Pennsylvania.

In the meantime, the acts of the Buchanan Administration, particularly those between Nov., 1860, and Mar., 1861, had become matters of great concern as the public interest was stirred to debate the causes of the Civil War in the 1880's. A reporter for the *Philadelphia Press,* Frank A. Burr, began a series of articles in 1881 which attracted much attention. He interviewed the survivors of the Administration, Jeremiah S. Black, Philip F. Thomas, Joseph Holt, and Jacob Thompson, and published the results. These articles and the appearance of Blaine's *Twenty Years in Congress,* and Curtis's *Buchanan* caused a series of interchanges in newspapers which brought in Jefferson Davis, Curtis, J. Buchanan Henry, and Horatio King as well. Black's son, Chauncey F. Black, sought to use his father's knowledge in a suppressed chapter intended for Lamon's *Lincoln* (see House, "Trials of a Ghost Writer of Lincoln Biography," *Jour. Ill. State Hist. Soc.,*

31:262-296) and finally published *Essays and Speeches of Jeremiah S. Black.* Horatio King also printed a miscellaneous collection of reminiscences entitled *Turning on the Light.* The surgeon at Fort Sumter, Col. Samuel W. Crawford, interviewed many survivors in gathering material for his book *The Genesis of the Civil War.* Then came the first volumes of *War of the Rebellion: An Official Record,* and Nicolay and Hay began serializing *Abraham Lincoln: A History.* John Robert Irelan devoted a volume in his *History of the Republic* to the Buchanan Administration. The foundation was thus laid for the modern scholar. So far the only specific study to appear is Auchampaugh, *James Buchanan and His Cabinet on the Eve of Secession.* Auchampaugh, like Dr. Philip S. Klein, author of *The Story of Wheatland,* is at work on a biography of the President.

Buchanan's appearance and personality are discussed in many places. Particular reference may be made to Buchanan, *Works,* 12:323-333, which prints a sketch written by J. Buchanan Henry contained in part in Curtis, *Buchanan,* 1:534, 2:187-188, 235-240, 672-674 (see *ibid.,* 2:664-686 for the official biographer's views); clipping in Meigs's Diary under date of July 16, 1860; (N.Y.) *Evening Mirror,* June 27, 1846, p. 184; *Hunter Corr.,* p. 224; *Washington Star,* Aug. 19, 1857; Wise, *Recollections of Thirteen Presidents,* p. 61; Foote, *Casket of Reminiscences,* p. 230; Clayton, *Black,* p. 106; Foltz to Cameron, Mar. 9, 1861, Cameron MSS; Cochrane to Cochrane, Dec. 14, 1819, Slaymaker MSS; Norris S. Barratt, Jr., to the author, Oct. 24, 1938; Mrs. Margaret Coleman Buckingham in conversation with the author. Auchampaugh, "The Bachelor of the White House," *Tyler's Quar. Hist. and Gen. Mag.,* 20:154-166, 218-234, gives a different interpretation.

2. McLaughlin, *Lewis Cass, passim;* Canfield, *General Lewis Cass, passim.*

3. *Speeches, Congressional and Political and Other Writings of Aaron V. Brown; Mobile Advertiser,* Mar. 13, 1857; *Memphis Appeal,* Mar. 14, Apr. 7, June 14, 1857; Mrs. Clayton to Mrs. Cobb, May 1, June 17, 1857, Cobb MSS; Sioussat, "Tennessee and National Political Parties, 1850-1860," *Amer. Hist. Assn. Ann. Rept. 1914,* 1:257; Johnson to Milligan, Nov. 23, 1856, Johnson MSS; Clay-Clopton, *A Belle of the Fifties,* p. 83.

4. Toucey MSS; Welles to Bartlett, Oct. 11, 1857, Welles MSS.

5. Hughes, "John B. Floyd: A Defence," *Tyler's Quar.,* 2:154-156, and "Floyd's Resignation from Buchanan's Cabinet," *ibid.,* 5:73; *Hunter Corr.,* pp. 178, 227, 229; Meneely, *The War Department, 1861,* pp. 28-31; *36:2 H. Rept. 78* (Ser. 1105), pp. 217 et seq.

6. Bivins, "Life and Character of Jacob Thompson," *Trinity Hist. Soc. Pubs.,* Ser. 2, p. 91; Oldham, "Life of Jacob Thompson," MS Master's thesis, Univ. of Miss.; Rainwater, ed., "Letters to

and from Jacob Thompson," *Jour. South. Hist.*, 6:95-112; Polk, *Diary*, 1:240; *Memphis Appeal*, Mar. 8, 1857.

7. *Essays and Speeches of Jeremiah S. Black;* Clayton, *Black, passim;* Nichols, "Jeremiah S. Black," *American Secretaries of State*, 6:387; Brigance, *Jeremiah Sullivan Black, passim;* Black MSS, *passim.*

8. Johnson, *The Political Policies of Howell Cobb, passim;* Gannon, "Howell Cobb," MS Ph.D. Dissertation, Univ. of Calif.; Mays, "Making of an Ante-Bellum Lady," *Ga. Hist. Quar.*, 24:1-22, and "The Celebrated Mrs. Cobb," *ibid.*, pp. 101-123; Stephens to Stephens, Jan. 4, 1857, Stephens MSS, Convent.

9. *N.Y. Herald*, Nov. 27, 1856.

10. *Ibid.*, Mar. 17, 18; *Washington Star*, Mar. 24, 1857; *Toombs Corr.*, p. 398; Cobb to Mrs. Cobb, Mar. 22, 1857, Cobb MSS.

11. Wood to Buchanan, Nov. 28, Dec. 26, 1856, Jan. 8, 1857, Buchanan to Wood, Dec. 1, Wikoff to Buchanan, Dec. 29, 30, 1856, Jan. 9, Mar. 27, Sickles to Buchanan, Jan. 26, Corning to Buchanan, Jan. 29, Dickinson to Buchanan, Mar. 5, Sanders to Buchanan, Mar. 13, 14, Ramsay to Buchanan, Apr. 6, 1857, Buchanan MSS; West to Douglas, Mar. 17, Douglas MSS; Ludlow to Tilden, Friday morning [c. Mar. 1, 1857], McClellan to Tilden, May 1, Tilden MSS; *N.Y. Herald*, Feb. 6, 24, 28, Mar. 7, 15, 17, 18, 20, 22, 23, 26, 27; *N.Y. Tribune*, Mar. 23; *N.Y. Times*, Mar. 3, 24, 26; *N.Y. Express*, Mar. 26, 28; *N.Y. Courier and Enquirer*, Mar. 27; D. L. Yulee to R. J. Walker, Apr. 4, 1857, N.Y. Hist. Soc.; for Schell's Whig support see Brooks to Crittenden, May 21, 1858, Crittenden MSS.

12. Buchanan to Forney, Feb. 28, July 18, Forney to Buchanan, Mar. 6, June 6, 1857, Buchanan MSS.

13. Forney to Mrs. Plitt, Mar. 5, 1857, Forney-Plitt photostats through the courtesy of David Rankin Barbee.

14. Van Dyke to Buchanan, Jan. 13, Mar. 14, 1857, Baker to Buchanan, June 27, July 4, Sept. 14, Brewster to Buchanan, Mar. 20, Buchanan MSS; Steele to Wright, Mar. 18, 24, Jones to Wright, Mar. 20, Apr. 2, May 24, June 3, Allobach to Wright, Mar. 20, Van Dyke to Wright, Aug. 27, Wright MSS; Wright to Black, Mar. 15, Welsh to Black, Apr. 28, Black MSS; Sanderson to Bigler, Mar. 24, Forney to Bigler, Apr. 22, 25, Bigler MSS; Buchanan to Baker, Oct. 17, Curry MSS; *Philadelphia North American and U.S. Gazette*, Mar. 16; Baltimore *Sun*, Mar. 21, 1857.

15. Forney to Buchanan, June 6, July 12, 18, Aug. 18, Buchanan to Forney, July 18, Black to Buchanan, Apr. 25, Macalester to Buchanan, July 13, Vaux to Buchanan, Aug. 12, 13, Buchanan MSS; Forney to Black, Mar. 27, Apr. 25, June 15, July 30, Black MSS; Rice to Bigler, Mar. 21, Sept. 15, 1857, Bigler MSS.

16. *Cincinnati Gazette,* Jan. 10, 1852; *New Orleans Weekly Delta,* Apr. 10, 1853.

17. Cramer to Marcy, Oct. 8, 1853, Marcy MSS; Tar to Butler, Apr. 18, 1856, B. F. Butler, MSS; *Milwaukee Morning News,* Sept., *passim,* Oct. 5, 1853; *Madison Daily Argus and Democrat,* Dec. 12, 1853.

18. Lane to Wright, Feb. 13, Larrabee to Wright, Feb. 28, Hunt to Wright, Aug. 19, Cravens to Wright, Dec. 7, 1856, Thompson to Wright, Nov. 2, 1858, Joseph A. Wright MSS; Bigger to English, Mar. 30, 1857, English MSS; Wick to Douglas, Dec. 3, 19, 1857, Douglas MSS.

19. Hoyne to Douglas, Dec. 29, Carpenter to Douglas, Dec. 30, 1856, McKnight to Douglas, Feb. 28, Button to Douglas, Mar. 14, 20, 26, Conly to Douglas, Mar. 12, 13, 21, D. Cameron, Jr., to Douglas, Mar. 16, 1857, Douglas MSS; Harris to McClernand, Mar. 10, Douglas to McClernand, Apr. 26, McClernand MSS; Douglas to King, Mar. 24, Oct. 2, 9, King MSS; Leib to Bigler, July 18, Bigler MSS; Cobb to Black, Aug. 10, Black MSS; Wise to Buchanan, Nov. 4, enclosing Thos. M. Hope to Wise, Oct. 27, Buchanan MSS; *Chicago Daily Democrat,* Mar. 21, Oct. 19, 1857.

20. Bancroft, *California,* 6:648; Gwin's MS Memoirs, pp. 105, 125-133; Forney, *Men and Events,* pp. 23-28; Lynch, *Broderick, passim,* particularly pp. 157-162; *Washington Star,* June 1; C. L. Weller to King, July 18, Sept. 5, King MSS; *New York Herald,* Mar. 23, 1857.

21. *N.Y. Herald,* Mar. 7, 18, 1857.

22. *Washington Union,* Apr. 4, 15, 1858; *Ser. 1040,* pp. 116-121.

Chapter 6

1. Nourse to Trumbull, July 24, Nov. 5, 1857, Jan. 29, 1858, Selby to Trumbell, Aug. 31, Aldrich to Trumbull, Dec. 20, 1857, Mar. 19, Reiner to Trumbull, Mar. 19, Trumbull MSS; Aldrich to E. B. Washburne, Jan. 26, May 24, 1858, Washburne MSS; Whitfield to John A. Halderman, Feb. 1, A. A. Lawrence to C. Robinson, Apr. 6, 1857, Kans. State Hist. Soc.; C. Robinson to A. A. Lawrence, Mar. 23, 1857, Lawrence MSS.

2. *Statutes and Laws of the Territory of Kansas,* 1855 and 1857, shows a variety of incorporations in most of which prominent proslavery and Democratic politicians are designated incorporators. These were as nothing when the free-state people got control, and in the *Laws* of 1858 there are 398 pages of private laws in which the Republicans were the incorporators. Five railroads were incorporated in 1855, sixteen in 1857, and twelve in 1858.

3. Gates, "A Fragment of Kansas Land History," *Kans. Hist. Quar.,* 6:227-240.

4. Malin, *John Brown and the Legend of Fifty-six,* pp. 498-508.

5. Geary to Buchanan, Jan. 16, Persifer F. Smith to Buchanan, Feb. 3, Buchanan MSS; Geary to Buchanan, Feb. 20, Geary to Woodson, Mar. 10, Epaphroditus Ransom to Cass, Mar. 30, State Dept. files, National Archives; Lecompte to Cushing, Jan. 9, Atty. Gen. files, National Archives; Nichols, *Franklin Pierce*, p. 495; H. A. Wise, Jr., to Everett, Mar. 27, 1857, Everett MSS.

6. *Covode Report*, pp. 105-106, 151-152; *Washington Star*, Mar. 16, 17, 19, 23-25, 28, 31, 1857; *N.Y. Herald*, Mar. 27, 1857, Oct. 19, 1860, *Chicago Times and Herald*, Oct. 17, 1860; Dodd, *Robert J. Walker*, pp. 30-31; Seward, *Seward at Washington*, p. 299; Flint, *Stephen A. Douglas*, p. 89; Milton, *op. cit.*, pp. 261-263; *Toombs Corr.*, p. 407.

7. Walker to Buchanan, Mar. 26, 1857, *Transactions Kans. State Hist. Soc.*, hereafter cited as *Kans. Hist. Coll.*, 5:290.

8. J. Thompson to F. P. Stanton, July 30, 1857, Thompson's Letter Book, captured by Union soldiers, War Dept. files, National Archives, *N.Y. Tribune*, Mar. 10, 1858.

9. *Kans. Hist. Coll.*, 5:302-303; *35:1 S. Ex. Doc. 22* (Ser. 924).

10. The general situation in Utah is described in Bancroft, *History of Utah*; Ellis, *Utah, 1847-1870*; Whitney, *History of Utah*; Tullidge, *History of Salt Lake City*; Creer, *Utah and the Nation*; Conway, *The Utah Expedition*; Hammond, ed., *The Utah Expedition*; McGavin, *United States Soldiers Invade Utah*; *35:1 H. Ex. Doc. 71* (Ser. 956); *N.Y. Herald*, Mar. 20, 1857; Kinney to Black, Mar. 20, 1857, Black MSS; Griffing to Cass, Mar. 29, Whittlesey to Cass, Mar. 21, State Dept. files; Hendricks to Thompson, May 18, 1857, Interior Dept. files, National Archives; Bernhisel to Young, Feb. 17, Mar. 17, 18, Apr. 2, 1857, Archives of Church of Jesus Christ of Latter-day Saints.

11. *35:1 H. Ex. Doc. 71* (Ser. 956).

12. Thomas L. Kane MSS, *passim*, Kane Manor.

13. Kane to Taylor, Apr. 23, Kane to Black, Apr. 27, enclosing Taylor to Kane, Apr. 25, Appleby to Taylor, Apr. 26, Smith to Taylor, Apr. 14, 16, 1857, Black MSS.

14. *3:51 S. Ex. Doc. 11* (Ser. 920), p. 21; *35:1 H. Ex. Doc. 33* (Ser. 955); Pellett to Banks, Dec. 22, 1857, N. P. Banks MSS in Ill. State Hist. Lib.

15. Lawrence to Robinson, Apr. 6, 1857, Kans. State Hist. Soc.

16. Holliday to F. L. Crane, Nov. 14, 1856, Kans. State Hist. Soc.

17. *Kansas City Enterprise*, Apr. 26, 1856; *Herald of Freedom*, May 2, 1857; *Kansas Weekly Herald*, May 9, 1857; *Leavenworth Journal*, Oct. 29, 1856, Feb. 5, 1857.

18. *Laws of the Territory of Kansas*, 1855, 1857; *Kansas Weekly Herald*, Jan. 24, May 30; *Kansas Tribune*, June 8, Aug. 1; *Lawrence Republican*, July 16, 1857; Robinson to Lawrence, Mar. 23, 1857, microfilm, Univ. of Kansas.

19. Whitfield to Halderman, Feb. 1, 1857, Kans. State Hist. Soc.

20. *Kans. Hist. Coll.*, 5:324-325; *N.Y. Herald*, May 5, 1857.

21. *Ibid.*, May 6, 1857; Stanton to Cass, Apr. 17, 1857, *Kans, Hist. Coll.*, 5:324, 433-436.

22. Walker to Stanton, May 6, 1857, Governors' MSS, *Kans. State Hist. Soc.*

23. *Kansas Weekly Herald*, May 23, 1857.

24. *Covode Report*, pp. 106-107; *Toombs Corr.*, p. 423.

25. Dodd, *Robert J. Walker, Imperialist*, p. 31; Flint, *Stephen A. Douglas*, p. 89.

26. Stuart to Douglas, Mar. 29, Calhoun to Douglas, Apr. 2, Isacks to Douglas, Nov. 16, 1857, Douglas MSS; *Kansas Weekly Herald*, Apr. 18, 1857; *Washington Union*, Mar. 26, 1857; *Overland Monthly*, 5:544-556; *Covode Report*, pp. 176, 316.

27. *Kansas Weekly Herald*, May 30, 1857; Robinson Scrap Books, 2:69, Univ. of Kansas; *Lawrence Republican*, June 18, 1857; Dickinson to Buchanan, Dec. 26, 1857, Buchanan MSS.

28. *Quindaro Chindowan*, May 30, Aug. 8; *Kansas Weekly Herald*, Aug. 22; *Emporia Kanzas News*, June 6, 1857; *Washington Star*, Jan. 9, 1858; *35:1 Globe*, p. 1875; Wilson to Sumner, Aug. 26, 1857, Sumner MSS.

29. *Kans. Hist. Coll.*, 5:328-341; *Lawrence Republican*, June 11, 1857.

30. *Overland Monthly*, 5:544-556; Kans. Territorial Clippings, 2:78, Kans. State Hist. Soc.; Robinson Scrap Books, 2:69, Univ. of Kans.; McLane, *Reminiscences*, p. 116; *Lawrence Republican*, July 2; *Washington Star*, May 2, 1857.

31. *Lawrence Republican*, June 4, 18; *Emporia Kanzas News*, June 6, 20; *Topeka Tribune*, June 8, 1857; *Kans. Hist. Coll.*, 5:341.

32. *Ibid.*, p. 291.

33. Wilson to Robinson, June 15, Tappan to Higginson, July 6, Marsh to Stearns, July 18, 24, 1857, Kans. State Hist. Soc.

34. Tappan to Higginson, July 6, 1857, Kans. State Hist. Soc.; Cass to Stephens, May 22, 1858, Stephens MSS; *Herald of Freedom*, June 6, July 25, Nov. 14; *Lawrence Republican*, July 2; *Lecompton National Democrat*, July 30; *Washington Star*, July 18, 20, 21, 22, 1857; *Kans. Hist. Coll.*, 5:341-367; Ransom to Cass, Mar. 30, Misc. Letters, State Dept. files, National Archives; Williams to Black, July 24, Black MSS; Douglas to Walker, July 21, N.Y. Hist. Soc.; Crawford to Bigler, Aug. 9, 1857, Bigler MSS; Floyd to Buchanan, July 31, Cass to Buchanan, July 31, Black to Buchanan, Aug. 1, Cass to Buchanan, Aug. 2, Walker to Buchanan, Aug. 6, Buchanan MSS; Black to Walker, Aug. 1 (not sent), Black MSS; mobilization orders, Apr. 1, 28, order of May 8, telegrams of July 15-23, see also Cooper to Walker, July 15, Sept. 22, 25, 27, 28, Oct. 3, 9, Cooper to Scott, July 28, Cooper to Floyd, Oct. 11, 1857, Adj. Gen.'s Office Letters Sent, Vols. 31, 32, War Dept. files, National Archives.

35. *Emporia Kanzas News*, Nov. 21, 1857.

36. *Kans. Hist. Coll.*, 5:345.

37. *Savannah Republican*, July 18, 1857.

38. *Washington Union*, Mar. 14; Thompson to Breckinridge, Apr. 6, 1857, Breckinridge MSS.

39. Crawford to Stephens, June 19, Stephens MSS; Pickens to Sanders, May 14, Pickens MSS; King to C. C. Clay, June 24, C. C. Clay MSS; Keitt to Miles, June 15, Miles MSS; *Toombs Corr.*, pp. 400-404; *Washington Star*, May 25, June 5, 13; *N.Y. Herald*, June 12; Selma (Ala.) *Weekly State Sentinel*, July 14, Clay MSS; *Memphis Appeal*, Mar. 10, July 16; *Savannah Republican*, Apr. 6, June 15, 16, 18, 20, 25, 26, 27, 29; *Mobile Advertiser*, May 27, June 12, 25, 1857; Smith, "Ante-Bellum Attempts of Northern Business Interests to 'Redeem' the Upper South," *Jour. South. Hist.*, 11:177-213.

40. *Hunter Corr.*, 210-219; *N.Y. Herald*, May 5, 1857.

41. Cobb to Mrs. Cobb, June 27, de Graffenried to Cobb, July 14, Lumpkin to Cobb, July 14, Cobb MSS; Stephens to Stephens, June 29, July 4, Stephens MSS, Convent; *Toombs Corr.*, p. 404; *Ga. Hist. Quar.*, 6:234-236; *Savannah Republican*, June 29, July 21, 30; *Mobile Advertiser*, June 28; *Memphis Appeal*, Aug. 20; *N.Y. Herald*, June 29, July 7, 8, 1857.

42. *Toombs Corr.*, p. 405; *Aberdeen Sunny South*, July 9, 16, Aug. 6; *Louisville Democrat*, July 9; *Memphis Appeal*, June 22, July 2, Aug. 20; *N.Y. Herald*, July 7, 8, 1857; Ranck, *Albert Gallatin Brown*, pp. 140-141, 149-153; Rainwater, *Mississippi, 1856-1861*, pp. 41-50. Benjamin Moran wrote in his diary Apr. 11, 1857, when in London he heard Walker was to be governor: "God forbid it. . . . He stole live oak in Florida and he may steal land and advance slavery in Kansas."

43. *Washington Union*, July 2, 7; *N.Y. Herald*, July 3; *Toombs Corr.*, p. 422; Buck to Douglas, Dec. 16, Douglas MSS; Claiborne to editor of *The South*, July 27, 1857, Claiborne MSS; Minutes of Directors and Ex. Com., New Eng. Emig. Aid Co., 3:121, Kans. State Hist. Soc.; *Kansas States Rights: An Appeal to the Democracy of the South by a Southern States Rights Democrat;* Nicolay and Hay, *Lincoln*, 2:110-111; *35:1 Globe*, App., p. 136; Stringfellow to Buchanan, Jan. 5, 1858, Buchanan MSS.

44. Buchanan, *Works*, 10:117-122; *35:1 S. Ex. Doc. 8* (Ser. 918), p. 71; *Toombs Corr.*, p. 421; *Mobile Advertiser*, Sept. 9; *Savannah Republican*, Sept. 16, 1857.

45. Hilliard to Cobb, July 21, Slidell to Cobb, July 22, Houston to Cobb, Aug. 23, Stiles to Cobb, Aug. 26, Jackson to Cobb, Aug. 27, Sept. 13, T. R. R. Cobb to Cobb, Oct. 1, 8, Iverson to Cobb, Oct. 7, Cobb MSS; Pickens to Buchanan, Aug. 5, Slidell to Buchanan, Aug. 12, Buchanan MSS; *Mobile Advertiser*, July 26, Aug. 2, Dec. 3; *Louisville Democrat*, Aug. 29, Sept. 3, 25, 27, Oct. 16; *Savannah Republican*, June 30, Sept. 21, Oct. 15; *Aberdeen Sunny South*, Dec. 17; *Memphis Appeal*, July 29, Sept. 8,

13, 15; *Louisiana Commercial Bulletin,* Aug. 27, Sept. 17; *White Cloud Kansas Chief,* Sept. 10, 1857; *Toombs Corr.,* pp. 406-420. In Georgia, Joseph E. Brown was elected Governor in October.
46. *Washington Star,* Sept. 1; *Memphis Appeal,* Dec. 17; Bigler to Buchanan, July 9, 1857, Black MSS.

Chapter 7

1. The journal of the constitutional convention through the morning session of November 3 is in *35:1 H. Rept. 377* (Ser. 966); if the minutes of the crucial final sessions were ever written up, their existence now is not known. *Quindaro Chindowan,* Sept. 19; *Kansas Weekly Herald,* Sept. 26; *Leavenworth Journal,* Sept. 12, 1857.
2. *Kansas National Democrat,* July 30; *Kans. Hist. Coll.,* 5:367-369; Act of Feb. 20, 1857, *Laws of the Territory of Kansas;* Ransom to Cass, Mar. 28, 1858, State Dept. files, National Archives.
3. *Emporia Kanzas News,* Aug. 15, 1857; Crawford to Bigler, Oct. 3, 1857, Bigler MSS.
4. *Kans. Hist. Coll.,* 5:372-378.
5. *Ibid.,* p. 382.
6. *Ibid.,* pp. 384-400; *Memphis Appeal,* Sept. 29, 1857.
7. *Kans. Hist. Coll.,* 5:307-314, 400-401; Crawford to King, Oct. 12, 1857, King MSS.
8. *Kans. Hist. Coll.,* 5:400-410; Crawford to Bigler, Oct. 24, 1857, Bigler MSS; *Quindaro Chindowan,* Oct. 10; *Lawrence Republican,* Oct. 29, Nov. 12; *Emporia Kanzas News,* Oct. 24; *Herald of Freedom,* Oct. 24; *Kansas Tribune,* Oct. 24, 1857; *Topeka Commonwealth,* Aug. 6, 1876; *Washington Star,* Oct. 29, 30, 31, Nov. 2, 3, 5, 14, 1857; *Memphis Appeal,* Oct. 30, Nov. 7, 11; *Leavenworth Weekly Journal,* Nov. 10, 1857; Griffith to John Covode, Jan. 3, 1858, Covode MSS.
9. *Emporia Kanzas News,* Nov. 14, 21; *Lecompton National Democrat,* Nov. 5; *N.Y. Tribune,* Nov. 16; *Aberdeen Sunny South,* Nov. 26; *Herald of Freedom,* Oct. 31, Nov. 7; *Quindaro Chindowan,* Nov. 14; *Kansas Weekly Herald,* Nov. 14, Nov. 21; William Hutchinson's Scrap Book, Vol. 1, Nov. 5, 1857, "Interesting from Kansas," Kans. State Hist. Soc. Text of Lecompton constitution is in *35:1 S. Ex. Doc. 21* (Ser. 924); original, in Rutgers University Library. See L. Ethan Ellis, "Lecompton Constitution," *Jour. Rutgers Univ. Lib.,* 3:57-61; *Overland Monthly,* 5:544-556. The land grant is analyzed in *35:1 Globe,* p. 163; Treat to Douglas, Dec. 3, Isacks to Douglas, Nov. 16, 21, Weer to Douglas, Dec. 21, 1857, McCook to Douglas, July 24, Bargy to Douglas, Aug. 14, 1858, Douglas MSS; Patterson to Buchanan, Nov. 10, Shroder to Buchanan, Nov. 22, O. Jennings Wise to Buchanan, Dec. 17, Buchanan MSS; Brindle to Bigler, Dec. 18, 22, 1857, Bigler MSS; Brindle to Black, Jan. 17, 1858, May 21, 1860, Jan.

19, 1861; *Hunter Corr.*, pp. 237-241, 245-250; *Toombs Corr.*, p. 424; *Covode Report*, pp. 106-112, 151-176, 314-323; *Chicago Times and Herald*, Oct. 14, 17, 1857; *Illinois State Journal*, Oct. 19, 24, 25, 1860; *Milwaukee Daily Enquirer*, Oct. 15; *N.Y. Herald*, Oct. 19, 20; *Wyandotte Commercial Gazette*, Oct. 13, 27; *Leavenworth Times*, Oct. 9; *Topeka Tribune*, Oct. 13; *Fort Scott Democrat*, Oct. 27; *Lawrence Republican*, Oct. 11, Nov. 8, 1860; "A Vindication of John Calhoun," written by Andrew H. Calhoun, deposited in Kans. State Hist. Soc. by Franklin B. Hough, July 30, 1877.

10. Nicolay and Hay, *Lincoln*, 2:110-111.

11. *Savannah Republican*, Oct. 31, Nov. 1, 13, 30; *Memphis Appeal*, Nov. 24, 28, 1857; *Journal of House of Representatives of the State of Mississippi, 1857*, pp. 119-124, 165, 169, 171.

12. *Louisville Democrat*, Aug. 11; *Mobile Advertiser*, Sept. 1, 1857; *Toombs Corr.*, p. 405; Bigler to Black, Aug. 26, Black MSS; Treat to Douglas, Dec. 2, Douglas MSS; *Chicago Times*, Nov. 5, 1857.

13. *35:1 Globe*, p. 1053.

14. Judd to Trumbull, Nov. 21, Dec. 1, Peck to Trumbull, Nov. 23, Hatch to Trumbull, Nov. 23, Ray to Trumbull, Nov. 24, Wilson to Trumbull, Nov. 26, Delahay to Trumbull, Nov. 28, 1857, Trumbull MSS.

15. *Chicago Democrat*, Oct. 30; *Chicago Times*, Nov. 10, 17-19, 22, 26; *Chicago Press*, Nov. 21; Sheahan to Douglas, Nov. 30, Douglas MSS; Douglas to McClernand, Nov. 23, 1857, McClernand MSS.

16. Milton, *Eve of Conflict*, pp. 272-273, 287, 289; Rice to Breckinridge, Oct. 22, 1857, Breckinridge MSS.

17. Rice to Breckinridge, Apr. 6, 14, 1857, Breckinridge MSS.

18. H. A. Wise to Buchanan, Nov. 4, enclosing Hope to Wise, Oct. 27, Buchanan MSS; Jenkins to Robinson, Nov. 29, Kansas State Hist. Soc.; *Washington Star*, Oct. 14; *N.Y. Herald*, Oct. 18; *Mobile Advertiser*, Dec. 6; *Savannah Republican*, Dec. 2, 1857; Jones to Breese, Sept. 7, 1858, Breese MSS.

19. Ray to Trumbull, Nov. 24, 1857, Trumbull MSS.

20. *Washington Union*, Nov. 26, Dec. 2; *Washington Star*, Nov. 27, Dec. 9; Gwin to Buchanan, n.d., Buchanan MSS; Sidney Webster to Cushing, Nov. 27, Cushing MSS; John H. Wheeler Diary, Nov. 25, 29; Stephens to Stephens, Dec. 1, 2, Stephens MSS, Convent; *Savannah Republican*, Dec. 2; *N.Y. Times*, Nov. 25 to Dec. 2; *N.Y. Tribune*, Dec. 2; *N.Y. Herald*, Dec. 1, 2, 3; *N.Y. Times*, Dec. 3, 4; *Philadelphia Press*, Dec. 2, 4; *Philadelphia Public Ledger*, Dec. 3; (Philadelphia) *Daily Pennsylvanian*, Dec. 4; *North American and U.S. Gazette* (Philadelphia), Dec. 2, 1857.

21. *Herald of Freedom*, Dec. 19; *Washington Star*, Nov. 23, Dec. 3, 4; *Mobile Advertiser*, Dec. 8; Harris to Lanphier, Dec. 3, 1857, Patton MSS; Rhodes, *History of the United States*, (1904 ed.) 2:282.

Chapter 8

1. Van Vleck, *The Panic of 1857, passim;* Foner, *Business and Slavery,* pp. 139-141; Rezneck, "Influence of Depression upon American Opinion, 1857-1859," *Jour. Ec. Hist.,* 2:1-24.

2. *Washington Star,* Aug. 21, 22, 25, 26, 28; *N.Y. Herald,* June 4.

3. *Ibid.,* Sept. 18.

4. *Ibid.,* Sept. 13, 24, 25; *Washington Star,* Sept. 25, 26, 28.

5. Cobb to Bennett, Sept. 24, K Series, XXVII, 187, Treas. Dept. files, National Archives.

6. *N.Y. Herald,* Sept. 29, 30, Oct. 1, 2, 3; *Washington Star,* Oct. 5; Cobb to Lamar, Oct. 29, Nov. 6, Hart to Cobb, Oct. 23, Soutter to Cobb, Dec. 7, Cobb MSS; Cobb to Bennett, Oct. 13, Cobb to Corcoran, Oct. 6, K Series, XXVII, 259, 229, Cobb to Cisco, Sept. 30, Oct. 2, 3, 7, 19, Subtreas. Series, III, 499, 501, 504, 509, Cisco to Cobb, Oct. 1, 17, 19, U Series, 1857, I, 227, 232, 233, 234, Cobb to Brewer, Oct. 10, 13, Cobb to Logan McKnight, Oct. 10, 15, Cobb to Snowden, Oct. 19, Xa Series, I, Cobb to Withers and McKnight, Oct. 13, Cobb to Williams, Oct. 22, Cobb to Belmont, Oct. 22, K Series, XXVII, 291, 303, Cobb to Schell, Oct. 8, 1857, H Series, X, 493, Treas. Dept. files, National Archives.

7. *N.Y. Herald,* Oct. 14, 15, 16.

8. *Ibid.,* Mar. 2, 1858; *N.Y. Journal of Commerce,* Aug. 28, Sept. 10, 1858; *Washington Star,* Mar. 11, 1858; Mrs. Brantley to Mrs. Cobb, June 1, 1858, Cobb MSS.

9. Lobby activities and other forms of influence and corruption were much probed in congressional investigations: *35:1 H. Rept. 351* (Ser. 965), *379* (Ser. 966), *412* (Ser. 967), *549* (Ser. 968); *35:2 H. Rept. 184* (Ser. 1019), *186, 188, 189* (Ser. 1018, 1020); *36:1 S. Rept. 205* (Ser. 1040), *H. Rept. 249* (Ser. 1068), *648* (Ser. 1071). In the latter, the *Covode Report,* see particularly pp. 178, 185, 217, 240, 252, 256, 258. For Chaffee patent see *34:1 H. Rept. 333* (Ser. 870), *35:1 H. Rept. 156* (Ser. 964); *Washington Star,* Mar. 11, 27, 29, 30; *N.Y. Herald,* Feb. 24, Mar. 18, June 18, July 5, 1858.

10. Fowler to Weed, Nov. 19, 1856, Oct. 1, 1858, Mar. 17, 1860, Fowler to Develin, Apr. 5, [1860], Barlow to Weed, Dec. 29, 1856, Mar. 19, Nov. 30, 1860, Henn to Weed, Mar. 20, 1857, May 28, 1859, Blair to "My dear Gov." [Seward?], Oct. 27, 1857, Seward to Weed, July 24, 1858, Apr. 6, 1859, Apr. 21, 1860, Richard Schell to Weed, Aug. 29, 1860, Weed MSS; Seward to Sumner, June 28, 1858, Sumner MSS; Seward, *Seward at Washington,* p. 346; Bigelow to Bryant, June 12, 1858, Bigelow MSS.

11. Clay to Branch, Nov. 20, 1856, Branch to Mrs. Branch, July 30, Branch MSS, Raleigh; Reid to Settle, Feb. 1, 1857, Reid MSS.

12. *N.Y. Herald,* Jan. 18, Nov. 6, 15, 1858.

13. *Ibid.,* Apr. 5, 1858.

14. *Ibid.,* Feb. 7, Mar. 9, 1858, Jan. 5, 1859; *Washington Star,* Dec. 30, 1857.

15. Mrs. Cobb to John A. Cobb, Sept. 24, 1857, Cobb MSS.

16. Same to same, Dec. 9, 1857, Cobb MSS.

17. Mrs. Thompson to Mrs. Cobb [Dec. 1 (?) 1857], Cobb MSS.

18. Mrs. Cobb to Lamar, Dec. 27, 1857, Cobb MSS.

19. *Washington Star,* Jan. 2, 7, Feb. 10, 11, Mar. 11, Apr. 9, 1858.

20. *Ibid.,* Feb. 28, 1859; Mrs. Clayton to Mrs. Cobb, July 17, 1859, Cobb MSS.

Chapter 9

1. Allen to Douglas, Nov. 30, Douglas MSS; Orr to Breckinridge, Aug. 13, Breckinridge MSS; Michael W. Cluskey to John A. Quitman, Aug. 24, Archives of Mississippi; Stephens to Stephens, Dec. 6, Stephens MSS, Convent; *Toombs Corr.,* pp. 426-427; Johnston and Brown, *Alexander H. Stephens,* p. 327; *Washington Union,* Dec. 6, 8; *Mobile Advertiser,* Dec. 6, 8, 1857.

2. McCook to Douglas, Nov. 30, 1857, Douglas MSS; *36:1 H. Rept. 249* (Ser. 1068), pp. 32, 35-36; *Washington Star,* Dec. 7-10, 1857; *Mobile Advertiser,* Dec. 13; *Washington Union,* Dec. 10; *N.Y. Herald,* Jan. 13, 1858.

3. Buchanan to Jones, July 18, 1857, J. G. Jones MSS.

4. Bancroft to Douglas, Dec. 2, Sheahan to Douglas, Dec. 4, Douglas MSS; Bancroft to Buchanan, Dec. 5, Persifer F. Smith to Buchanan, Dec. 14, Buchanan MSS; *Washington Union,* Dec. 13, 1857; King to Welles, Dec. 18, Dixon to Welles, Dec. 15, 1857, Welles MSS. For this and succeeding chapters dealing with congressional action, the *Globe* has been scanned page by page, but except in cases of direct quotation I have not included a mass of page references from that work. The bill which Douglas introduced (S. 15) was the Toombs bill of the previous Congress with a clause added, providing for the submission of the constitution (Senate files, National Archives).

5. Stanton to Walker, Dec. 1, 1857, Kans. State Hist. Soc.; Weer to Douglas, Dec. 6, Douglas MSS; Stanton to Walker, Jan. 5, 1858, N.Y. Hist. Soc.; *Herald of Freedom,* Nov. 7, 14; *Washington Star,* Dec. 9, 10, 11; *N.Y. Herald,* Dec. 10, 11, 16; *Memphis Appeal,* Dec. 12, 17, 18; *Mobile Advertiser,* Dec. 20; *Washington Union,* Dec. 11; *Lawrence Republican,* Dec. 17; *Kansas Weekly Herald,* Feb. 20, 1858; *Emporia Kanzas News,* Dec. 5, 1857; *Sen. Ex. Journal,* 10:263.

6. *Kans. Hist. Coll.,* 5:421-432; *Washington Union,* Dec. 20, 1857; *Sen. Ex. Journal,* 10:286, 322; Gwin to Buchanan, n.d., Buchanan MSS.

7. *35:1 Globe*, p. 52.

8. *Ibid.*, pp. 1054-1055; Pleasonton to J. Buchanan Henry, Dec. 24, 1857, Buchanan MSS; Caslin to Bigler, Dec. 18, Bigler MSS; Conway to Sanborn, Nov. 16, John Brown MSS, Kans. State Hist. Soc.; Wilson to Robinson, Nov. 26, Robinson MSS; Boutwell to S. P. Chase, Nov. 24, Bigler to Jno. A. Haldeman, Dec. 8, Kans. State Hist. Soc.; *Washington Union*, Dec. 17, 24, 25, 27, 1857, Jan. 27, 1858; *Herald of Freedom*, Jan. 2, 1858; *Kansas National Democrat*, Dec. 31, 1857; *Report of Board of Commissioners for the Investigation of Election Frauds, passim;* Crawford to "Sade," Dec. 22, 1857, Brindle to Black, Jan. 17, 1858, Black MSS; Crawford to Bigler, Dec. 28, 1857, Feb. 7, 1858, Henderson to Bigler, Jan. 8, 16, Brindle to Bigler, Jan. 15, 28, Martin to Bigler, Jan. 30, Bigler MSS; Pleasonton to J. Buchanan Henry, Jan. 8, 1858, Buchanan MSS; Crawford to Douglas, Jan. 26, 1858, Douglas MSS; Tappan to Higginson, Dec. 14, Collamer to Hutchinson, Dec. 17, Hutchinson to Foster, Dec. 27, Martin to Gov. Denver, Jan. 6, 1858, Kans. State Hist. Soc.; *Herald of Freedom*, Dec. 19, 1857, Jan. 2, 9, 1858; *Lawrence Republican*, Dec. 31, 1857; *Washington Union*, Jan. 8, 15, 27; Gen. Harney to Cooper, Jan. 9, 1858, 12 H 1858, A.G.O., War Department files, National Archives; Ewing, "The Struggle for Freedom in Kansas," *Cosmopolitan*, May, 1894; T. Ewing, Jr., to Hugh Ewing, Jan. 2, 18, 23, G. W. Brown to Thomas Ewing, Jan. 5, T. Ewing, Jr., to Mrs. Ewing, Jan. 12, Denver to T. Ewing, Jr., Jan. 18, T. Ewing, Jr., to T. Ewing, Jan. 18, Feb. 3, Ewing MSS; *35:1 Globe*, App., pp. 239-241; *35:1 S. Ex. Doc. 21* (Ser. 924).

9. Von Holst, *The Constitutional and Political History of the United States*, 6:204.

10. *36:1 H. Rept. 249* (Ser. 1068), pp. 280-283; Wise to Douglas, Jan. 14, 1858, Douglas MSS; Wise to Buchanan, Mar. 22, 1858, Buchanan MSS; *Lecompton Question; Washington Union*, Feb. 12, 1858; Huntington to Crittenden, Mar. 21, Russell to Crittenden, Apr. 8, 1858, Crittenden MSS, illustrate northern and even border-state revolt over Lecompton.

11. Harris to Lanphier, Jan. 28, 30, Lanphier-Patton MSS; *Washington Star*, Jan. 13, Feb. 2, 3; *Washington Union*, Jan. 31; *N.Y. Tribune*, Feb. 3, 4, 9, 12, Mar. 15, 1858.

12. Denver to Cass, Jan. 16, 1858, State Dept. files, National Archives; Denver to Buchanan, Jan. 16, Buchanan MSS; *Pubs. Kans. State Hist. Soc.*, 1:170.

13. Buchanan, *Works*, 10:179-192; *35:1 S. Ex. Doc. 21* (Ser. 924); Johnston and Browne, *Stephens*, p. 329; *Albany Atlas and Argus*, Feb. 8, 15, 1858.

14. *35:1 Globe*, pp. 533-541; *N.Y. Tribune*, Feb. 3, 1858; *Pittsburgh Gazette*, Feb. 3, 1858.

15. *35:1 Globe*, pp. 596-606; *N.Y. Tribune*, Feb. 6; *Washington Star*, Feb. 6, 1858; Johnston and Browne, *Stephens*, p. 329; Stephens to Stephens, Feb. 3, 5, Stephens MSS, Convent.

16. *N.Y. Herald,* Jan. 23, 25, 26, Feb. 1, 2, 7, 8; *N.Y. Tribune,*
Feb. 8, 9, 10; *Washington Union,* Feb. 7; *Washington Star,* Jan.
14, 21, 22, 23, 26, 30, Feb. 1, 2, 6; *Albany Atlas and Argus,* Feb.
5, 15; *St. Louis Republican,* Feb. 10, 12; Hamlin to Morrill, Feb.
16, Kans. State Hist. Soc.; Hammond to Simms, Feb. 7, Hammond
to A. P. Aldrich, Feb. 14, Hammond MSS; Coombs to T. Ewing,
Jr., Feb. 7, Parrott to T. Ewing, Jr., Feb. 8, Hugh Ewing to T.
Ewing, Feb. 9, Ewing MSS.
17. *35:1 Globe,* pp. 621-623.
18. *Ibid.,* pp. 570, 624-625.
19. *Ibid.,* pp. 755-756, 828, 902-904; Douglas to Forney, Feb.
15, Hist. Soc. Pa.; Harris to Lanphier, Feb. 10, Mar. 13, Patton
MSS; Jones to Breese, Sept. 7, Breese MSS; *N.Y. Tribune,* Feb.
12; *Chicago Times,* Feb. 27, Mar. 23.
20. Harris to Lanphier, Feb. 9, 10, Patton MSS; Johnson to
Buchanan, Feb. 15, Buchanan MSS; Manypenny to Douglas, Mar.
3, 1858, Douglas MSS; Green to T. Ewing, Jr., Feb. 28, Parrott
to T. Ewing, Jr., Mar. 2, T. Ewing, Jr., to Hugh Ewing, Mar. 3,
T. Ewing, Jr., to T. Ewing, Sr., Mar. 13, Ewing MSS; Ransom to
T. Ewing, Jr., May 30, 1894. Torry to T. Ewing, Jr., July 1, 1863,
Brindle to T. Ewing, Jr., Sept. 29, 1898, Henry W. Petrikin to
T. Ewing, Jr., Feb. 23, 1894, Sara L. Petrikin to T. Ewing, Jr.,
Aug., 1870, Jan. 29, 1908, Andrew H. Calhoun, "A Vindication
of John Calhoun," Kans. State Hist. Soc.; *St. Louis Republican,*
Mar. 7, 9, 10; *Washington Union,* Feb. 18; *N.Y. Tribune,* Mar.
5, 23; *N.Y. Herald,* Mar. 21; *Chicago Times,* Mar. 25; *35:1 Globe,*
pp. 920, 1260, 1264; *35:1 H. Rept. 377,* (Ser. 966), p. 102;
Wilder, *Annals of Kansas,* p. 207; *Report of Board of Commis-
sioners for the Investigation of Election Frauds, passim;* Stephens
to Stephens, Mar. 17, Stephens MSS, Convent.
21. King to Welles, Jan. 15, 1858, Welles MSS; Stephens to
Stephens, Mar. 9, 11, 12, Stephens MSS, Convent; Johnston and
Browne, *Stephens,* pp. 330-331; Toombs to Buchanan, Mar. 2 (?),
Sanders to Buchanan, Mar. 25, Buchanan MSS; Hammond to
Simms, Mar. 22, 24, Hammond MSS; Dixon to Welles, Mar. 17,
Welles MSS; Aldrich to Washburne, Jan. 26, May 24, Washburne
MSS; Nourse to Trumbull, July 24, Nov. 5, 1857, Jan. 29, 1858,
Selby to Trumbull, Aug. 31, 1857, Aldrich to Trumbull, Dec. 20,
1857, Mar. 19, 1858, Reiner to Trumbull, Mar. 19, Trumbull
MSS.
22. *35:1 Globe,* pp. 1058, 1900, App. p. 144; Waddell, *Linton
Stephens,* p. 138; *Toombs Corr.,* pp. 431, 432; *N.Y. Herald,* Jan.
14; Buchanan to Denver, Mar. 27, Buchanan to W. B. Reed, July
31, 1858, Buchanan MSS; *Covode Report,* p. 283.
23. *Sen. Ex. Jour.,* 10:308, 336, 338, 350, 360; *Covode Report,*
pp. 323-324; *Chicago Times,* Feb. 23, Mar. 7, 9, 19, 21, 30, Apr.
6, 16, 20, 25, 27, May 2; *N.Y. Tribune,* Feb. 17, Mar. 4, 10;
Washington Star, Mar. 4; Sheahan to Douglas, Feb. 10, Ballance
to Douglas, Feb. 11, Helm to Douglas, Apr. 14, Douglas MSS;

Ledyard to Buchanan, Mar. 17, Buchanan MSS; Cook to Bigler, Mar. 22, Dougherty to Bigler, Apr. 19, 26, Bigler MSS; Cook to Black, Apr. 7, Black MSS; Cook to A. V. Brown, Apr. 24, King MSS; Marshall to Logan, May 2, Logan MSS; Niblack to Black, Dec. 16, 1857, Apr. 10, 1858, Indiana Hist. Soc.

24. *Covode Report,* pp. 120-151; Foote, *Casket of Reminiscences,* pp. 118, 235; Johnson to Sumner, Mar. 29, Sumner MSS.

25. *N.Y. Herald,* Feb. 14, 22; *N.Y. Tribune,* Feb. 15; Stephens to Stephens, Mar. 22, May 23, Stephens MSS, Convent; Johnston and Browne, *Stephens,* p. 331.

26. *35:1 Globe,* pp. 1132, 1150, 1192, 1957, 2645, App. pp. 396-398.

27. *Ibid.,* p. 1013; Morrison to English, Feb. 16, Norman to English, Mar. 5, Matthews to English, Mar. 29, Wick to English, Mar. 13, Buchanan to English, Mar. 22, English MSS; Johnson to Sumner, Apr. 26, Sumner MSS.

28. *N.Y. Herald,* Mar. 24, 28; *N.Y. Tribune,* Mar. 24; *Washington Star,* Mar. 29; Sanders to Buchanan, Mar. 29, Buchanan MSS; Johnston and Browne, *Stephens,* pp. 332-333; Cochrane to English, Mar. 28, English MSS.

29. *35:1 Globe,* p. 828; *N.Y. Herald,* Mar. 5; Cobb to Lamar, Mar. 10, Cobb MSS; Hammond to Simms, Mar. 24, Hammond MSS.

30. Johnson to Sumner, Mar. 29, Sumner MSS; James Buchanan to Cobb, Mar. 31, enclosing English to Buchanan, Mar. 31, Cobb MSS; *N.Y. Tribune,* Mar. 31, Apr. 1; *N.Y. Herald,* Mar. 31; *Washington Star,* Mar. 31.

31. *35:1 Globe,* pp. 1435-1438; *N.Y. Herald,* Apr. 3; *N.Y. Tribune,* Apr. 2, 3; Robinson to T. Ewing, Jr., Mar. 24, 27, Parrott to T. Ewing, Jr., Mar. 29, Apr. 2, 9, Ewing MSS.

32. *35:1 Globe,* pp. 1433, 1440-1445, 1479-1487, 1517, 1521, 1544-1545; *N.Y. Tribune,* Apr. 6, 7, 9, 10; *Washington Star,* Apr. 10.

33. *Covode Report,* pp. 120-151, 178-197, 214-218, 224-240, 260-267, 269-273, 277-290, 304-311; *N.Y. Tribune,* Apr. 12, 15, June 18; *Washington Union,* Apr. 10, 13; J. B. Baker to Buchanan, Apr. 19, Buchanan MSS; Cox, *Three Decades of Federal Legislation,* pp. 56-58; *35:1 Globe,* pp. 1588-1590.

34. Stephens to Stephens, Apr. 26, Stephens MSS, Convent; Johnston and Browne, *Stephens,* pp. 332-333; *N.Y. Tribune,* Apr. 16, 17, 21; *N.Y. Herald,* Apr. 18; *St. Louis Republican,* Apr. 18; Toombs to Buchanan, Apr. 18, Buchanan MSS; Cobb to Lamar, Apr. 19, Cobb MSS; King to Crittenden, Apr. 15, 1858, Crittenden MSS.

35. *N.Y. Tribune,* Apr. 20, 21, 22, 24, 26; *N.Y. Herald,* Apr. 24; *St. Louis Republican,* Apr. 18; *Springfield Republican,* Apr. 27, 30; Thompson to English, n.d., English MSS; Mrs. Cobb to John A. Cobb, Apr. 30, Cobb MSS; Waddell, *Linton Stephens,*

pp. 147-148; *35:1 Globe,* pp. 1758-1770, 1778-1781; *Toombs Corr.,* p. 434; Johnson to Sumner, Apr. 21, Sumner MSS.

36. Herndon to Sumner, Jan. 28, 1858, Chase to Sumner, Sept. 10, 1859, Sumner MSS; *36:1 Globe,* App. pp. 159-163; *Springfield Republican,* Mar. 16, 1860; *N.Y. Eve. Post,* Mar. 3, 1860; Greeley, *American Conflict,* 1:301; Nicolay and Hay, *Lincoln,* 1:592; Herndon and Weik, *Lincoln,* 2:393, 395, 413; Hollister, *Colfax,* pp. 119-124; Lamon, *Lincoln,* pp. 389-395; *Ga. Hist. Quar.,* 6:237; *Quar. Calif. Hist. Soc.,* 11:14-15; Memorandum of April 30, 1858, Buchanan MSS; Auchampaugh, "The Buchanan-Douglas Feud," *Jour. Ill. State Hist. Soc.,* 25:19; King to Welles, Jan. 2, May 29, 1858, Dixon to Welles, Mar. 2, 8, Apr. 2, Welles MSS; Herndon to Washburne, Apr. 10, Cary to Washburne, Apr. 24, Ray to Washburne, Nov. 22, Nourse to Washburne, Nov. 28, Washburne MSS; Judd to Trumbull, Mar. 7, Dec. 26, 1858, Ray to Trumbull, Mar. 9, Du Bois to Trumbull, Mar. 22, Apr. 8, Herndon to Trumbull, Apr. 12, 24, May 7, Trumbull MSS; Trumbull to Flagg, Jan. 8, Ill. State Hist. Lib.; Sturgeon to Snyder, May 5, 1860, Snyder MSS; Jones to Breese, Sept. 7, 1858, Breese MSS; Douglas to McClernand, Dec. 8, 1859, Greeley to McClernand, Mar. 25, 1860, McClernand MSS; Bigelow to Weed, June 22, 1859, Weed MSS; Sturgeon to Douglas, Jan. 8, 1861, Douglas MSS; Schouler to Chase, Mar. 23, 1858, Chase MSS (Pa.); Greeley to Colfax, Dec. 11, 20, 25, 1857, Feb. 11, 15, May 6, 12, June 2, 14, Wed. ev., 1858, Dec. 9, 12, 1859, N.Y. Public Library; Clapp, *John Bigelow,* pp. 119-121.

37. Mrs. Cobb to John A. Cobb, Apr. 30, Hull to Cobb, May 30, 1858, Cobb MSS; Hammond to Hammond, May 1, Hammond to Simms, May 3, Hammond MSS; T. Ewing to T. Ewing, Jr., Apr. 30, May 9, Stanton to T. Ewing, Jr., May 3, McLean to T. Ewing, Jr., May 6, Ewing MSS; Sumner to Johnson, Apr. 26, Sumner MSS; Pugh to Buchanan, June 1, 12, enclosing copy of an unsigned letter to Pugh, presumably from Latham, Apr. 12, Latham to Floyd, June 9, Floyd to Pugh, June 15, Buchanan MSS; Cox, *Three Decades of Federal Legislation,* pp. 56-58; *N.Y. Tribune,* May 3; *N.Y. Herald,* May 1, 3; *Washington Union,* May 1, 2, 4; *Washington Star,* May 1, 5, 17; *Springfield Republican,* May 4, 7; *35:1 Globe,* pp. 1880-1890, 1899, 1900-1906; Milton, *Eve of Conflict,* pp. 291-293.

38. Hodder, "Some Aspects of the English Bill for the Admission of Kansas," *Amer. Hist. Assn. Ann. Rept. 1906,* 1:201-210; *N.Y. Tribune,* Apr. 21, 1858. Immediately after the passage of the bill, the patronage lists from the great cities were sent to the Senate. Also some debts may have been paid. It is interesting to note that George W. Morgan, from Burns's Ohio district, was appointed Minister to Portugal on May 4. Washington Correspondence in *N.Y. Independent,* May 1, 1858, clipping in Kans. Terr. Clippings, Vol. 2, Kans. State Hist. Soc.;J Pugh to Bu-

chanan, June 1, 12, Latham to Floyd, June 9, Floyd to Pugh, June 15, 1858, Buchanan MSS.

39. *35:1 Globe*, pp. 2352, 2565, 2876, 2923, 2981; Seward to Sumner, June 28, 1858, Sumner MSS; Sumner to Trumbull, undated, 1858, De Frees to Trumbull, May 7, 10, Coburn to Colfax, May 7, Trumbull MSS.

Chapter 10

1. Buchanan, *Works*, 10:129-163; *35:1 Globe*, App. pp. 7-14.

2. *Ibid.*, App. pp. 32-36; Ellis, *Utah*, pp. 14 *et seq.;* Whitney, *Utah*, p. 665; Winther ed., *Private Papers and Diary of Thomas L. Kane, passim;* Kane Diary, John M. Bernhisel to Kane, Dec. 9, 1857, draft of letter to Cumming, Kane MSS, Stanford University; Cumming MSS, *passim;* Thos. L. Kane to John Kane, Mar. 24, 1858, Kane Manor MSS; Bernhisel to Brigham Young, Sept. 21, Oct. 17, Nov. 2, Dec. 17 (2), 1857, Jan. 18, Mar. 18, 1858, Archives, Mormon Church; Buchanan to Kane, Dec. 31, 1857 (2), Buchanan MSS; *35:1 H. Ex. Doc. 71* (Ser. 956); Johnson to Sumner, Feb. 27, 1858, Sumner MSS.

3. Buchanan, *Works*, 10:202; Floyd to Powell and McCulloch, Apr. 12, 1858, *35:1 S. Ex. Doc. 67* (Ser. 930); Mrs. Cumming to Anne Smith, Apr. 22, May 28, Cumming MSS; Bernhisel to Young, Apr. 3, 17, Archives, Mormon Church.

4. Floyd to Kilgore, Wilson & Co., Apr. 23, 1858, Floyd to Bank of the State of Missouri, May 1, 1858, *36:2 H. Rept. 78* (Ser. 1105), pp. 304-305; Drinkard to Soutter, July 4, 1858, Holt MSS.

5. *N.Y. Independent*, Washington correspondence of May 1, 1858, Kans. Territorial Clippings, Vol. 2, Kans. State Hist. Soc.

6. Buchanan, *Works*, 10:217; *35:1 S. Ex. Doc. 67* (Ser. 930); Cumming to Johnston, June 19, Powell and McCulloch to Cumming, June 18, Johnston to Cumming, June 19, Young to Cumming, June 19, July 1, Cumming MSS; Bernhisel to Young, June 19, July 2, Aug. 11, Archives, Mormon Church.

7. Soulsby, *The Right of Search and the Slave Trade*, pp. 138-173; Van Alstyne, "The British Right of Search and the African Slave Trade," *Jour. Mod. Hist.*, 2:37-47; *35:1 S. Ex. Doc. 49* (Ser. 929), *59, 61* (Ser. 930); *35:2 H. Ex. Doc. 24* (Ser. 1004); *36:2 H. Ex. Doc. 7* (Ser. 1095); Toucey to McIntosh, May 5, June 3, 30, 1858, Toucey to Hartstene, May 24, Toucey to Rodger, May 28, Toucey to Dahlgren, May 28, Confidential Letters, IV, McIntosh to Toucey, Mar. 27, 1858, June 18, July 13, Home Squadron, Navy Dept. files, National Archives; Admiralty 13, 4:259-296, 473-474, Public Record Office, L.C. photocopy; Dallas, *Letters from London*, 2:29; *Washington Star*, May 18, 19, 24, 27, 1858; Cass to Webb, June 1, 1858, Webb, MSS; Stephens to Stephens, June 10, 1858, Stephens MSS, Convent.

8. Tyler, *Steam Conquers the Atlantic*, pp. 144, 147, 154; Kemble, *The Panama Route*, pp. 1-77; Lane, *Commodore Vanderbilt*, pp. 85-134; Roberts to Weed, June 24, 1854, Weed MSS; *Covode Report*, pp. 652-673, 735-835.

9. *35:1 Globe*, App. 25, pp. 2805, 2903-04, 3002-03.

10. *Ibid.*, p. 482.

11. *35:1 H. Rept. 379* (Ser. 966), *412* (Ser. 967); *35:2 H. Rept. 188, 189* (Ser. 1020).

12. *35:1 H. Rept. 414* (Ser. 967).

13. *35:1 H. Rept. 351* (Ser. 965), *549* (Ser. 968); *40:3 H. Ex. Doc. 9* (Ser. 1372); *Minn. Hist. Soc. Colls.*, 15:393-410; Greeley to Washburne, May 26, 27, 1858, Washburne MSS.

14. *35:1 Globe*, App. p. 530; *35:1 Globe*, pp. 505, 285, 169, 2581, 2577, 2439, 1283, 2305, 2234, 2563, 1430, 1602, App. p. 477; *35:1 Globe*, pp. 455, 1138, App. p. 145; Waddell, *Linton Stephens*, p. 138.

Chapter 11

1. *35:1 Globe*, p. 961; Birdsall to Hammond, Mar. 12, Doolittle to Hammond, Apr. 15, May 4, 1858; Corry to Hammond, Mar. 8, 1860, Hammond MSS; Ruffin's Diary, Apr. 17, 1858; Wish, *George Fitzhugh*, p. 192; Carsel, "The Slaveholders' Indictment of Northern Wage Slavery," *Jour. South. Hist.*, 6:504-520.

2. Buchanan to Reed, July 31, 1858, Forney to Buchanan, July 12, 18, 1857, Buchanan to Forney, July 18, Macalester to Buchanan, July 13, Vaux to Buchanan, Aug. 12, 13, Van Dyke to Buchanan, Nov. 21, 1857, Buchanan MSS; Rice to Bigler, Mar. 21, June 26, Sept. 15, 1857, undated, Bigler MSS; Webster to Black, Sept. 11, 1857, Black to Webster, [Nov. 1857], No. 52256, Vol. 20, Webster to Black, Dec. 18, 24, Black to W. A. Porter, Feb. 9, 1858, Black MSS; Tyler to Buchanan, Dec. 16, Bigler to Buchanan, Dec. 28, Baker to Buchanan, Dec. 30, 1857, Feb. 5, Mar. 8, Apr. 5, 12, 25, Vaux to Buchanan, Feb. 6, Mar. 8, May 16, Piollet to Buchanan, Feb. 11, Magraw to Buchanan, Mar. 5, Bradford to Buchanan, Mar. 13, Buchanan to Baker, Apr. 3, 22, 1858, Buchanan MSS; *Dollar Weekly Pennsylvanian*, Jan. 23, Mar. 7, 13, 20, May 8, 1858; *Covode Report*, p. 247; *Washington Star*, Dec. 29, 1857; C. Courtlandt Meyers, "Rise of the Republican Party in Pennsylvania," pp. 194-205; Auchampaugh, "John W. Forney, Robert Tyler, and James Buchanan," *Tyler's Quar.*, 15:71-90.

3. Reeser to Bigler, May 10, Scranton to Bigler, May 18, Bigler MSS; Hopkins to Buchanan, May 15, Buchanan MSS; *Dollar Weekly Pennsylvanian*, June 19, July 17.

4. Baker to Buchanan, Apr. 12, Aug. 16 (2), 1858, Van Dyke to Buchanan, Apr. 6, 7, 8, 19, Buchanan to Van Dyke, Apr. 7, 17, 20, Buchanan MSS; *Covode Report*, pp. 327-344.

5. Baker to Buchanan, June 18, Buchanan MSS; Baker to Bigler, Aug. 16, Bigler MSS.

6. *36:1 H. Rept. 621* (Ser. 1070), pp. 31-32; *Ser. 1040*, p. 10.

7. *Covode Report,* pp. 459-472, 501-511, 556-576; Green to Buchanan, Oct. 29, 1858, Buchanan MSS.

8. *N.Y. Herald,* Apr. 5, 8, 18, 21, 28, June 6, 8, July 3, 24, 25, 30, Aug. 4, 14, 28, Sept. 1, 3, 4, 12, Oct. 2, 9, 16, Dec. 5, 9, 10, 17, 18, 20, 24, 25, 31, 1857, Jan. 7, 8, Feb. 10, 11, 28, Mar. 3, Apr. 3, 18, 20, 1858; *N.Y. Times,* Aug. 31, 1857; *Washington Star,* June 17, 1857; Sanders to Buchanan, July 26, Wikoff to Buchanan, Aug. 6, 30, Sickles to Buchanan, Sept. 8, Tiemann to Buchanan, Dec. 8, Belmont to Slidell, Dec. 8, Cochrane to Buchanan, Dec. 31, 1857, Dix to Buchanan, Apr. 20, 1858, Buchanan MSS; campaign circulars dated Oct. 5, 24, 1857, circular of Feb. 22, 1858; Wood to Cushing, Feb. 23, Hart to Cushing, Feb. 26, Cushing MSS.

9. *N.Y. Herald,* June 29, July 11, Aug. 30, Sept. 3, 5, 8, 1858; *N.Y. Journal of Commerce,* Aug. 26, Sept. 9, 10; Cobb to Buchanan, Aug. 4, 6, 7, Sickles to Buchanan, Aug. 5, Sept. 8, 1858, Buchanan MSS; Buchanan to Cobb, Aug. 3, Cobb MSS.

10. *N.Y. Herald,* Aug. 5, 7, Sept. 16; *N.Y. Journal of Commerce,* Sept. 21; Buchanan to Wood, Sept. 9, Oct. 18, Fowler to Buchanan, Sept. 8, Wood to Buchanan, Sept. 8, 10, 27, 29, Oct. 1, 8, 15, Cochrane and Kelly to Buchanan, Sept. 15, Kelly to Buchanan, Oct. 12, Ramsey to Buchanan, Oct. 25, Buchanan MSS; Ramsey to Fowler, Nov. 10, N.Y. Hist. Soc.

11. Sickles to Buchanan, Oct. 18, 31, Buchanan MSS; *Washington Star,* Dec. 17, 1858; *N.Y. Herald,* Dec. 19, 20, 21; *Covode Report,* pp. 485-501, 515-538.

12. *Dollar Weekly Pennsylvanian,* Mar. 20, 27, 1858; *Springfield Republican,* May 14; clipping in Douglas MSS, May 24, Buell to Douglas, June 29, Aug. 6, Douglas MSS; Kelly to Buchanan, July 10, Sept. 15, Buchanan MSS; Dorn, "Samuel Medary," *Ohio State Arch. & Hist. Quar.,* 53:14-38.

13. Niblack to Black, Dec. 16, 1857, Apr. 10, 1858, Ind. Hist. Soc.; Pierce to English, Jan. 8, Abrams to English, Jan. 9, Wick to English, Jan. 12, 26, Mar. 13, 18, Apr. 2, Norman to English, Jan. 15, 17, 21, 24, 27, Feb. 2, 7, Mar. 31, May 21, Matthews to English, Mar. 29, Buchanan to English, July 2, English MSS; *Indianapolis Daily State Sentinel,* Mar. 21; *Pittsburgh Gazette,* Aug. 7.

14. Milton, *Eve of Conflict,* pp. 294-352; Sheahan to Douglas, Dec. 31, 1857, Jan. 14, Feb. 10, 1858, Ballance to Douglas, Feb. 11, Helm to Douglas, Apr. 14, Price to Douglas, May 10, Gray to Douglas, May 26, Douglas MSS; Cook to Bigler, Mar. 22, Dougherty to Bigler, Apr. 11, 26, Conley to Bigler, Mar. 25, Apr. 30, Pine to Bigler, June 11, Leib to Bigler, June 16, 19, 22, Bigler MSS; Cook to Buchanan, May 10, June 14, Buchanan MSS; Cook to Black, Apr. 7, Black MSS; Cook to A. V. Brown, Apr. 24,

King MSS; Brown to Trumbull, Feb. 24, Herndon to Trumbull, Feb. 16, June 24, July 8, Skinner to Trumbull, Mar. 8, Judd to Trumbull, Apr. 19, Koerner to Trumbull, June 29, Medill to Trumbull, Apr. 22, Leib to Trumbull, July 20, Trumbull MSS; Marshall to Logan, June 21, Logan MSS; *Washington Union*, Mar. 4; *N.Y. Tribune*, Mar. 10; *Chicago Daily Times*, Feb. 18, 23, Mar. 7, 9, 19, 21, 30, Apr. 6, 16, 20, 25, 27, May 2, 8, 30; *Sen. Ex. Jour.*, 10:338; Holt, "Career of William A. Richardson," *Jour. Ill. State Hist. Soc.*, 26:246.

15. *Sen. Ex. Jour.*, 10:360, 366, 422.

16. *35:1 Globe*, pp. 3055-58; *Chicago Daily Times*, May 30, June 2, July 11; Kerr to Douglas, May 21, Sheahan to Douglas, May 30, Price to Chandler, June 9, May to Douglas, June 21, 25, Cutts to Douglas, June 24, Peyton to Douglas, July 8, Douglas MSS; May to Buchanan, July 4, Buchanan MSS; Carpenter to Buchanan, June 23, 1858, Illinois State Hist. Lib.; King to A. V. Brown, Aug. 3, King MSS.

17. Herndon to Trumbull, Feb. 19, 1858, Trumbull MSS.

18. Churchwell to Douglas, July 11, Sanders to Douglas, July 11, 17, Cutts to Douglas, July 11, Wright to Douglas, Aug. 23, Payne to Douglas, July 24, Douglas MSS; Sanders to Douglas, July 1, 2, Confederate files, National Archives; Jones to Stephens, July 13, 1858, Stephens MSS; copy of Sanders to Douglas, July 17, delivered to Buchanan, July 23, Farley to Buchanan, July 15, Buchanan to Farley, July 22, Letcher to Buchanan, July 24, Kelley to Buchanan, July 25, Aug. 1, Johnson to Buchanan, July 31, Buchanan MSS; Black to Buchanan, Aug. 7, Buchanan to Black, Aug. 4, and enclosures No. 53898, Black MSS; *Washington Union*, July 13, 15; *Chicago Times*, July 17, 25, 28.

19. Nicholson to Douglas, Nov. 10, 1858, Douglas MSS.

20. Dickinson to Buchanan, Aug. 27, Buchanan to Dickinson, Aug. 31, Cook to Buchanan, Aug. 16, Sept. 29, Oct. 27, Nov. 28, Fitch to Buchanan, Aug. 17, Pine to Buchanan, Aug. 17, Bigler to Buchanan, Aug. 20, Sturgeon to Buchanan, Oct. 22, May to Buchanan, Oct. 23, Buchanan MSS; Green to Bigler, Aug. 6, Fitch to Bigler, Sept. 22, Bigler MSS; Crawford to Stephens, Sept. 8, Stevenson to Stephens, Oct. 8, Stephens MSS; Steedman to Douglas, Nov. 7, 10, May to Douglas, Nov. 10, Douglas MSS; *N.Y. Herald*, Oct. 20; *Washington Union*, Sept. 3, Oct. 28; Foote, *Casket of Reminiscences*, pp. 135, 286; Sears, *Slidell*, pp. 149-151; Greeley-Colfax correspondence, N.Y. Public Library.

21. *N.Y. Tribune*, May 22.

22. Sturgeon to Buchanan, May 17, Buchanan MSS; memo of interview of Burlingame and Colfax with Douglas, Dec. 14, 1857, Ind. State Lib.; Trumbull to Flagg, Jan. 8, 1858, Ill. State Hist. Lib.; Judd to Trumbull, Dec. 26, 1857, Mar. 7, Apr. 19, 1858, Herndon to Trumbull, Dec. 25, 1857, Feb. 16, 19, Apr. 12, 24, May 7, June 24, July 8, 1858, Ray to Trumbull, Dec. 18, 1857, Mar. 9, 1858, DuBois to Trumbull, Mar. 22, Apr. 8, Baker to

Trumbull, May 1, Trumbull MSS; Greeley-Colfax correspondence, N.Y. Public Library.

23. *N.Y. Tribune*, May 29, June 3, 4, 18, 1858; *Philadelphia North American and U.S. Gazette*, June 2, 3; *Dollar Weekly Pennsylvanian*, June 5.

24. *N.Y. Herald*, July 21; *Washington Star*, Aug. 5; *Washington Union*, July 1.

25. Sparks, ed., *Lincoln-Douglas Debates*, p. 161.

26. Merritt, *James H. Hammond*, p. 125; *Washington Union*, Nov. 11, 16.

27. Bancroft, *Seward*, 1:459; Seward to Webb, Nov. 5, 1858, Webb MSS; *N.Y. Journal of Commerce*, Nov. 26; Toombs to N. P. Banks, June 15, 1859, Ill. State Hist. Lib.

28. *Washington Star*, Aug. 5, 10; *Washington Union*, Aug. 15, 26; *N.Y. Herald*, Aug. 5, 12. In North Carolina the Democrats won their gubernatorial contest quite easily: Folk, "W. W. Holden and the Election of 1858," *N.C. Hist. Rev.*, 21:294-319.

29. *N.Y. Herald*, Oct. 20; *Washington Union*, Oct. 14; *Washington Star*, Oct. 18; Blair to Cameron, Oct. 20, Cameron MSS.

30. *Tribune Almanac*, 1859; Cobb to Lamar, Nov. 4, 1858, Cobb MSS. Statisticians later figured out that the Democrats had actually increased their vote over 1856, that the Republicans had lost 12,000, and that the Americans had dropped 284,000, thus giving the Democrats a "relative gain" of over 300,000 (*N.Y. Journal of Commerce*, Dec. 3, 1858). These figures did not comfort the Democrats for the loss of Congress.

31. Buchanan, *Works*, 10:233-234; F.O. 5, v. 695, No. 297, Dec. 5, 1858, British Foreign Office, L.C. Transcripts; Grinnell to Webb, Jan. 10, 1859, Webb MSS; *Washington Star*, Sept. 17, 25, 1857.

Chapter 12

1. Jones, *J. Glancy Jones*, 2:79-92; Jones to Buchanan, Oct. 18, Buchanan MSS; *Pittsburgh Gazette*, Oct. 27, 1858.

2. *Baltimore Sun*, Dec. 10, 1858; *Washington Star*, Jan. 6, 10, 1859; Clay to Clay, Dec. 11, Clay MSS; Hammond to Hammond, Dec. 11, 21, 1858, Hammond MSS.

3. Christopher Fallon to Buchanan, Jan. 14, Feb. 12, 24, Buchanan to Fallon, Apr. 19, Memorandum of Apr. 28, John Fallon to Buchanan, Feb. 23, Figueira to Phillips, Apr. 16, 1858, Buchanan MSS; Figueira to Cushing, Dec. 31, 1855, Cushing MSS; Perry to Cass, Jan. 30, 1858, and Dodge to Cass, Feb. 5, 1858, Spanish Despatches, Vol. 41; Hodgson to Cass, Mar. 16, 1857, Misc. Letters, State Dept. files, National Archives; Benjamin Moran Diary, Dec. 31, 1857, Jan. 15, Feb. 26, Mar. 27, 31, June 19, 1858; F.O. 5, v. 711, No. 33, Feb. 1, 1859; pamphlet, *Grand Mass Meeting at Tammany, March 4, 1858;* Buchanan to Mal-

lory, July 7, 1858, Buchanan to Benjamin, Aug. 31, Buchanan MSS; *Washington Star,* Sept. 3, 15; *N.Y. Herald,* Sept. 16, 24; Buchanan to Fallon, Dec. 8, 1858, Macalester to Fallon, Jan. 3, [1859], Fallon Scrap Book; Mann to Baring Bros., Oct. 31, 1859, Feb. 13, 1860, Baring MSS; Melvin, "Stephen Russell Mallory," *Jour. South. Hist.,* 10:149; F.O. 5, v. 695, No. 335, Dec. 26, 1858, v. 711, No. 26, Jan. 24, 1859, No. 32, Feb. 1, No. 33, Feb. 1, No. 56, Feb. 21, v. 714, No. 91, June 27; F.O. 115, v. 202, No. 21, Apr. 15, 1859; Branch to Mrs. Branch, Jan. 8, 25, Feb. 1, 6, Branch MSS, Raleigh.

4. *35:2 Globe,* pp. 1241-1244.

5. Streeter, *Political Parties in Michigan,* pp. 248-253.

6. *Baltimore Sun,* Mar. 7, 1859; F.O. 5, v. 711, No. 50, Feb. 15, 1859.

7. *Washington Star,* Dec. 7, 28, 1858, Jan. 3, 1859; *N.Y. Journal of Commerce,* Nov. 1, 12, 1858; *Pittsburgh Gazette,* Dec. 10, 1858; *N.Y. Herald,* Jan. 4, 5, 7, 1859; Dixon to Welles, Dec. 7, 1858, Welles MSS; Reeves to Cameron, Jan. 4, 1859, Cameron MSS; F.O. 5, v. 711, No. 31, Jan. 31, 1859.

8. *Baltimore Sun,* Jan. 27, Feb. 7; *N.Y. Herald,* Jan. 31; F.O. 5, *loc. cit.; Washington Star,* Feb. 7, 8, 9, 10.

9. *35:2 Globe,* pp. 1643-1663, 1678-1684.

10. *N.Y. Herald,* Feb. 20, Mar. 6, 9; *Washington Star,* Mar. 4, 5.

11. Mason to Miles, Apr. 3, 1859, Miles MSS.

Chapter 13

1. Interviews of Jacob Thompson in *Philadelphia Press,* Mar. 4, Sept. 17, 1883; *Reply of Joseph Holt to Jacob Thompson, Oct. 8, 1883* (pamphlet in L.C.); Lord, "David Levy Yulee," p. 176.

2. *Baltimore Sun,* Mar. 10, 23; *Washington Star,* Mar. 10, 12, 16, 17, 18, 22, June 30, 1859; F.O. 5, v. 712, No. 106, Mar. 27, 1859.

3. One of these forms is in the Cameron MSS. *Washington Constitution,* May 8, 1859.

4. *Washington Star,* June 8; *N.Y. Herald,* June 16; *N.Y. Times,* June 21; *Washington Constitution,* May 31; Buchanan to Baker, May 1, 1859, Buchanan MSS.

5. *35:2 H. Rept. 189* (Ser. 1020), *passim; N.Y. Herald,* Nov. 23, Dec. 2, 1858; *Baltimore Sun,* Apr. 5, 1859; Weston to Cameron, Dec. 23, [1857], Cameron MSS.

6. *35:2 Globe,* p. 1429, App. p. 342.

7. Baker to Buchanan, Nov. 24, Dec. 2, 24, 1858, Mar. 9, 11, 28, 1859, Jan. 28, 1860, Brewster to Buchanan, Jan. 17, 1859, Morwitz to Baker, Mar. 26, Buchanan to Baker, May 1, Black to Buchanan, Apr. 2, 4, Bartlett to Buchanan, Feb. 24, 1860, Buchanan MSS; Baker to Black, Dec. 5, 1858, Wendell to Black,

536 / The Disruption of American Democracy

Jan. 20, 25, June 8, 1860, Black MSS; Phillips to Bigler, Jan. 21, 1860, Bigler MSS; Williams to Welles, Apr. 18, 1858, Welles MSS; Hughes to Sanders, Sept. 1, 1859, May 9, 1860, Confed. files, National Archives; *Washington Union*, Dec. 12, 1857, Mar. 16, 17, 1858, Mar. 29, 1859; *Washington Constitution*, Apr. 13, 1859; *Baltimore Sun*, Jan. 13, 1859; *N.Y. Times*, Feb. 11, 1859; *36:1 Globe*, p. 2488; Poore, *Perley's Reminiscences*, 1:510. When Bowman and Browne took over the *Union* and made it the *Constitution*, S. M. Johnson and R. W. Hughes were let out. Johnson was rewarded briefly with the consulate at Havre where he was soon displaced. Then John P. Heiss established a Douglas organ in Washington known as the *States and Union*, and Johnson and Hughes went to write for it.

8. *Washington Constitution*, Apr.-Oct., 1859, see particularly June 25, July 8, 16, Aug. 17, 18, 30, Sept. 8; Buchanan to Clifford, July 16, Clifford MSS; Buchanan to Johnston, Sept. 19, N.Y. Hist. Soc.

9. *N.Y. Herald*, Nov. 17, 30, Dec. 2, 16, 1858, Feb. 26, Apr. 4, 1859; *Baltimore Sun*, Dec. 3, 1858, Jan. 20, 1859; *N.Y. Tribune*, Dec. 7, 9, 11, 14, 16, 17, 1858; *Washington National Intelligencer*, Dec. 8, 20, 1858; *Washington States*, Dec. 16, 17, 22, 1858, Jan. 1, June 2, 1859; *Mobile Daily Register*, Mar. 17, 24, Apr. 15, 1859; *Washington Star*, June 8, 1859; N. Sargent to Thompson, Nov. 7, 1858, R. W. Thompson MSS, Lincoln Life; Cole, *The Whig Party in the South*, pp. 331-337.

10. Shanks, *The Secession Movement in Virginia*, pp. 57-65; *Washington Union*, Dec. 7; *Baltimore Sun*, Dec. 3, 4, 6, 1858, Jan. 11, 17, Feb. 12, Mar. 28, Apr. 8, 1859; *N.Y. Evening Post*, Apr. 25; *N.Y. Times*, Mar. 4, Apr. 1, 11, 27, June 9; *Richmond Enquirer*, Feb. 16; *Memphis Daily Morning Bulletin*, Feb. 19, Mar. 1, 3, 6, 29, Apr. 8, May 19, June 4; *Mobile Daily Register*, Mar. 24, Apr. 14, 15, June 1, 3; *Louisville Democrat*, Jan. 11; *Washington States*, Mar. 21, 25, Apr. 12; *North Carolina Standard*, May 21; *Aberdeen* (Miss.) *Sunny South*, Apr. 14, 1859; Botts to Washburne, Dec. 7, 1858, Washburne MSS; Cole, *op. cit.*

11. Ranck, *Albert Gallatin Brown*, pp. 165-178; Milton, *The Eve of Conflict*, pp. 366-368; Rainwater, *Mississippi*, pp. 68-89; Lumpkin to Cobb, Oct. 25, 1858, Feb. 21, 1859, Brown to Cobb, Nov. 15, 1858, May 4, 1859, Cobb to Lamar, May 23, 1859, Cobb MSS.

12. Dorman, *Party Politics in Alabama*, pp. 143-149; Du Bose, *William Lowndes Yancey*, pp. 348-349, 377; Seibels to Hammond, Aug. 1, 1858, Hammond MSS; Shugg, *Origins of Class Struggle in Louisiana*, pp. 1-156; Greer, "Louisiana Politics, 1845-1861," *La. Hist. Quar.*, 13:114, 279, 446; Odom, "Political Career of T. O. Moore, Governor of Louisiana," *ibid.*, 26:986-989; Cobb to Lamar, June 21, Mrs. Cobb to Lamar, June 29, Frierson to Cobb, June 26, 1859, Cobb MSS; *Savannah Republican*, June 17,

18; *North Carolina Standard,* Apr. 23, 30, May 7, 21, June 4, 11, 15; *N.Y. Times,* June 9, 11, 1859.

13. Wish, "Revival of African Slave Trade," *Miss. Valley Hist. Rev.,* 27:569; Buchanan to Mrs. Clay, Aug. 20, 1859, Buchanan MSS; Lamar to Cobb, Mar. 10, 1858, Cobb MSS; Hammond to Hammond, Aug. 10, Pryor to Hammond, Oct. 13, 1858, Hammond to Simms, July 30, Seibels to Hammond, Aug. 15, Ashman to Hammond, Aug. 25, Orr to Hammond, Sept. 17, 1859, Hammond MSS; Smith to Stephens, Aug. 3, 1858, July 24, 1859, Henning to Stephens, Dec. 17, 1858, Crawford to Stephens, June 17, 1859, Stephens MSS, L.C.; Stephens to Stephens, July 5, 1859, Stephens MSS, Convent; Davis to Clay, May 17, 1859, Clay MSS; Thompson to Ellet, May 27, 1859, Thompson Letter Book, War Dept. files, National Archives; *Washington States,* Jan. 11; *Washington Star,* May 30; *Aberdeen Sunny South,* Apr. 14, July 21; *N.Y. Evening Post,* May 12, June 22; *N.Y. Times,* May 18, June 15, Sept. 12; *North Carolina Standard,* June 8; *Savannah Republican,* July 23; *Memphis Bulletin,* Aug. 16, 1859.

14. *Memphis Bulletin,* Apr. 28; Mobile *Register,* Apr. 14, 15, 17; *Aberdeen Sunny South,* Apr. 14, June 9; *Tuscaloosa* (Ala.) *Independent Monitor,* July 16; *Washington States,* May 19; *N.Y. Times,* May 18, 1859; Miles to Hammond, Nov. 15, 1858, Hammond to Simms, Mar. 13, Apr. 22, Orr to Hammond, Sept. 17, 1859, Hammond MSS; Curry to Thompson, May, 1859, quoted in *N.Y. Tribune,* Dec. 25, 1862.

15. *N.Y. Times,* May 30; *Washington Star,* June 6; *N.Y. Herald,* June 13; *Aberdeen Sunny South,* June 23, 1859; Shanks, *op. cit.,* pp. 60-61.

16. *Washington States,* May 18; *Baltimore Sun,* May 18; *Wilmington* (N.C.) *Journal,* May 28; *Mobile Register,* May 27, June 4, 12, 17, 18, July 17, 31, Aug. 3; *Savannah Republican,* July 19; *N.Y. Herald,* Aug. 1, 8, 9; *N.Y. Times,* Aug. 9, 18, 30; *North Carolina Standard,* Aug. 17; R. H. Chinn to Douglas, Nov. 8, Thos. J. Burke to Douglas, Nov. 12, 1859, Douglas MSS; Samford to Clay, Oct. 20, 1858, Clay MSS.

17. *Savannah Republican,* June 16, July 11, 16, 22, 23, Aug. 11; *Aberdeen Sunny South,* July 21; *N.Y. Herald,* June 13, July 10; *Washington States,* July 15, Aug. 16, Sept. 10; *Tuskaloosa Independent Monitor,* July 16, Sept. 24; *Mobile Register,* June 1, 2, July 26; *N.Y. Times,* July 28; *New Orleans Daily True Delta,* Nov. 6; *New Orleans Commercial Bulletin,* Nov. 10; *North Carolina Standard,* May 21, 1859; Frasure, "Union Sentiment in Maryland," *Maryland Hist. Mag.,* 24:210-224; Cole, *op. cit.*

18. *Washington States,* Mar. 18, Apr. 14, June 1; *Dollar Weekly Pennsylvanian,* Mar. 19, Apr. 16; *N.Y. Evening Post,* Mar. 21; *N.Y. Herald,* Apr. 13, 14, 17, May 3, June 16; *Baltimore Sun,* May 5; *Washington Star,* June 8, July 20, 28, Aug. 1; Black to Buchanan, Apr. 4, Brenner to Buchanan, Apr. 25, Buchanan to

Brenner, Apr. 27, B. H. Brewster to Buchanan, Feb. 3, Mar. —, Apr. 23, May 19, 16, June 6, Grandin to Buchanan, June 19, Black to Buchanan, July 23, Cobb to Buchanan, July 28, Barr to Buchanan, Aug. 1, Buchanan to Barr, Aug. 8, Buchanan MSS; Buchanan to Floyd, Aug. 5, L.C.; Barr to Bigler, July 2, 1859, Bigler MSS; *Washington Constitution,* July 29; Buchanan to Cobb, July 23, Cobb MSS.

19. *N.Y. Herald,* Jan. 28, 31, Feb. 12, 14, 18, Mar. 4, 15, May 13, June 16, July 1, 11, 13, Aug. 4, 11, Sept. 1, 2, 7, 15, 26; *N.Y. Times,* May 31, June 1, Sept. 2, 5; *N.Y. Daily News,* Mar. 16, June 1; *Washington Star,* June 13; *Baltimore Sun,* May 16, 1859; Ramsey to Fowler, Nov. 10, Dec. 5, 1858, N.Y. Hist. Soc.; agreement signed by Schell, Fowler and others, Dec. 17, 1858, Buchanan MSS; J. B. Baker to Employees, July 26, 1858, Augustus Schell to Cobb, Mar. 31, 1860, Custom House Reduction of Expenses 1858-1861 file, Cobb to Schell, June 24, 1859, H Series, 13, p. 279, Treasury Dept. files, National Archives; *Washington Constitution,* July 22, 1859.

20. Milton, *op. cit.,* pp. 370-385; *N.Y. Herald,* Apr. 17, June 25; *Washington States,* May 9; *Washington Star,* June 24, July 23, 1859; Jones to Breese, Oct. 17, 1858, Breese MSS; Buchanan to Slidell, June 24, Slidell to Buchanan, July 3, 1859, Buchanan MSS; *Washington Constitution,* June 25.

21. Milton, *op. cit.,* pp. 386-390; Douglas, "Popular Sovereignty in the Territories," *Harper Magazine,* Sept., 1859. Black, *Observations on Senator Douglas's Views of Popular Sovereignty* (two editions in pamphlet form, the second published in October after a speech Douglas made at Wooster, Ohio) contains an additional statement by Black. *Judge Douglas in Reply to Judge Black;* Black, *Observations on Territorial Sovereignty consisting of three several answers to the magazine article, speeches and pamphlets of Senator Douglas;* Johnson, *Remarks on Popular Sovereignty;* A. D. Banks to Douglas, Sept. 25, 29, Branch to Banks, Oct. 22, 1859, Douglas MSS; Slidell to Buchanan, Sept. 28, Browne to Buchanan, Oct. 1, 1859, Buchanan MSS; *N.Y. Herald,* Aug. 26, Sept. 12; *Washington Constitution,* Aug. 27, Sept. 10, Nov. 3; A. J. Cass to Butler, Sept. 5, 19, Oct. 7, 1859, Butler MSS.

22. *Washington States,* June 18, 20, July 2, 1859; Milton, *op. cit.,* pp. 390-391; Douglas to McClernand, Oct. 1, 1859, McClernand MSS.

23. Seward to Weed, June 15, 1858, Weed MSS; Welch to Cameron, June 22, Broderick to Cameron, June 24, Seward to Cameron, June 30, 1858, Cameron MSS; Seward to Morgan, June 10, 1858, E. D. Morgan MSS.

24. *Washington Star,* Oct. 10, 1859; J. Bigler to W. Bigler, Nov. 29, 1859, Bigler MSS; Bancroft, *History of California,* 6:722-737; Lynch, *David C. Broderick,* pp. 186-231; Forney, *Anecdotes of Public Men,* pp. 23-28.

25. Woodward, *Political Parties in Oregon,* pp. 100-165; Smith to Deady, Feb. 5, 1858, Lane to Deady, Apr. 17, 1858, Mar. 17, 1859, May 13, 1860, Nesmith to Deady, Oct. 7, 1859, Pyle to Deady, Feb. 1, 1860, Deady MSS; Lane to Bush, Apr. 2, June 2, 18, Hibbens to Williams enclosing Lane letter, Apr. 4, Smith to Bush, Nov. 30, 1858, undated, Feb. 1, 2, Grover to Bush, Feb. 17, Mar. 5, 1859, Bush transcripts; Smith to Nesmith, Nov. 30, 1858, Nesmith to ———, Jan. 9, 1859, Nesmith MSS; I. I. Stevens to Nesmith, June 3, 1858, Feb. 15, Apr. 22, 1859, I. I. Stevens MSS; Lane to H. M. Phillips, July 20, 1859, Hist. Soc. of Pa.; *Portland Democratic Standard,* Dec. 17, 24, 31, 1857, Jan. 14, 21, Feb. 4, Mar. 25, Apr. 1, 8, 15, 29, July 15, Sept. 15, Oct. 20, 1858, June 4, 1859; *Washington States,* July 12, 1859; Kelly, *Career of Joseph Lane, passim;* Shutes, "Col. E. D. Baker," *Quar. Calif. Hist. Soc.,* 17:303-325.

26. *Tribune Almanac, 1860;* Brewster to Buchanan, Oct. 12, 17, 29, Buchanan to Brewster, Oct. 15, Buchanan MSS; *Dollar Weekly Pennsylvanian,* Oct. 22; Banks to Douglas, Oct. 30, 1859, Douglas MSS.

27. *Washington Star,* Oct. 17, 18, 20; Buchanan to Floyd, n.d., L.C.; Bigler to Buchanan, Oct. 22, Bigler MSS; Freeman, *Robert E. Lee,* 1:394-403.

28. *36:1 Globe,* p. 589; Wood to Wise, Nov. 2, 9, John Tyler, Jr., to Wise, Nov. 2, Wise to Wood, Nov. 4, Buchanan to Wise, Nov. 10, 28, Wise to Buchanan, Nov. 12, 25, Hicks to G. W. Mumford, Nov. 14, John Brown MSS, Hist. Soc. of Pa.; Chas. A. Davis to Buchanan, Oct. 24, 1859, Buchanan MSS; Letcher to G. W. Jones, Apr. 8, 1860, Huntington Library; *N.Y. Herald,* Oct. 18, 19, 20, 22, 27, 28, 29, Nov. 1.

29. *Ibid.,* Nov. 6, 13, 27; *Pittsburgh Gazette,* Dec. 1, 1859.

30. *N.Y. Herald,* Oct. 2, 3, Nov. 16, 17, 18, 20, 22; Anderson to Stephens, Nov. 20, 1859, Stephens MSS.

Chapter 14

1. *N.Y. Herald,* Nov. 18, 1859; Crenshaw, "Speakership Contest of 1859-1860," *Miss. Valley Hist. Rev.,* 29:323-339; Crenshaw, *Slave States in the Presidential Election of 1860,* pp. 63-73.

2. *N.Y. Herald,* Oct. 23, 29, Nov. 24, 26, 30, Dec. 1, 2, 3; *Washington Star,* Aug. 22, Sept. 24, Oct. 10, Nov. 8, 13, 30; Barbee, "Hinton Rowan Helper," *Tyler's Quar. Hist. and Gen. Mag.,* 15:135-172; Weed to Morgan, Dec. 10, [1859], Helper to Morgan, July 2, 1859, E. D. Morgan MSS.

3. *Pittsburgh Gazette,* Nov. 30; Greeley to Colfax, Nov. 13, N.Y. Public Library.

4. *N.Y. Herald,* Dec. 4; *Pittsburgh Gazette,* Dec. 5, 6; *Washington Star,* Nov. 29, 30, Dec. 1, 2.

5. *N.Y. Herald,* Dec. 10, 11.

6. *Ibid.,* Dec. 27; Walsh to Branch, Dec. 12, Branch MSS, Duke Univ.; Gist to Miles, Dec. 20, Hamilton to Miles, Dec. 9, 1859, Miles MSS.

7. *N.Y. Herald,* Dec. 27; *Washington Star,* Jan. 4, 1860.

8. *N.Y. Herald,* Dec. 12, 16, 1859, Jan. 9, 12, 1860; McCaleb, ed., *Reagan,* pp. 76-78. The committee was composed of Winslow, McRae, Crawford of Georgia, and Robinson of Illinois, Democrats, Clark and Riggs, anti-Lecomptonites, and Gilmer, Mallory, Hill, and Nelson, Americans.

9. *Washington Star,* Jan. 31, Feb. 1; *N.Y. Herald,* Feb. 1, 2, 3, 4, 5; *San Francisco Bulletin,* Mar. 1.

10. *Ser. 1040,* pp. 316-323, 326-329, 372-374; *36:1 H. Rept. 249* (Ser. 1068).

11. *Washington Constitution,* Oct. 15, Dec. 8, 13, 1859, Feb. 16, 1860.

12. Milton, *op. cit.,* pp. 404-408; *36:1 Globe,* p. 542; Sheahan to King, Apr. 26, 1859, King MSS; Cook to Buchanan, Jan. 11, 1859, Jan. 11, 1860, Holt to Cook, May 14, Holt to Buchanan, June 11, Sept. 12, 1859, Hughes to Buchanan, Jan. 13, 1860, Buchanan MSS; Cook to Holt, May 23, 1859, Buchanan to Holt, July 29, Aug. 4, Trott to Holt, Sept. 26, Holt MSS; Cook to Black, June 22, Oct. 4, 1859, Jan. 12, 1860, Black MSS; Cook to Bigler, Aug. 8, 30, 1859, Jan. 12, 1860, Bigler MSS; A. J. Cass to Butler, Sept. 19, Oct. 7, 1859, Butler MSS; Goodrich to Douglas, Jan. 27, Payne to Douglas, Feb. 27, 1860, Douglas MSS; [Miller] to Morton, Feb. 4, 1860, Morton MSS; Wright to Stephens, May 15, Stephens MSS; Lanphier to McClernand, Feb. 24, Mar. 7, McClernand MSS.

13. *Quar. Calif. Hist. Soc.,* 11:1-15; Hempstead to Bigler, Jan. 19, 1860, Bigler MSS.

14. *Washington Constitution,* July 13, 22, Sept. 8, Dec. 10, 1859; Spullock to Lumpkin, Nov. 16, Lumpkin to Cobb, Nov. 18, 1859, Jan. 23, 1860, Varnum to Cobb, Jan. 13, Glenn to Cobb, Jan. 26, Lamar to Cobb, Feb. 7, 8, Mar. 16, 17, Lumpkin to Cobb, Mar. 17, Spullock to Cobb, Mar. 18, Cobb to Lamar, Apr. 24, Cobb MSS; Johnston to Stephens, Mar. 16, Duncan to Stephens, Mar. 16, Smith to Stephens, Apr. 3, Thweatt to Stephens, May 20, Paine to Stephens, July 28, Stephens MSS; Stephens to Stephens, Feb. 11, Mar. 14, 16, Stephens MSS, Convent; Spencer to Douglas, Jan. 14, Douglas MSS.

15. *Hunter Corr.,* pp. 273-320.

16. *N.Y. Herald,* Dec. 25, 1859.

17. *Ibid.,* Jan. 21, 1860; *Washington Constitution,* Jan. 11; A. Johnson to R. Johnson, Jan. 15, Apr. 8, Johnson to McDaniel, Mar. 24, Johnson MSS, L.C.; A. Johnson to R. Johnson, Jan. 12, Apr. 22, Huntington Library.

18. Slidell to Buchanan, May 22, 30, 1859, Buchanan MSS; *Washington Constitution,* Mar. 7, 1860.

19. *Ibid.*, Jan. 12, 1860; Stevenson to Stevenson, Jan. 21, 1858, Apr. 13, 1860, Stevenson MSS.

20. Crawford to Stephens, Mar. 14, Apr. 24, 1860, Stephens MSS.

21. Denman, *The Secession Movement in Alabama,* pp. 76-81; Dorman, *Party Politics in Alabama,* pp. 151-156; Crawford to Stephens, May 11, 1860, Stephens MSS.

22. Thomson to Buchanan, Mar. 28, 1860, Buchanan MSS.

23. Cadwalader to Buchanan, Jan. 4, Bradford to Buchanan, Mar. 7, Van Dyke to Buchanan, Mar. 7, Baker to Buchanan, Mar. 9, 1860, Buchanan MSS; McKibben to Bigler, Jan. 4, Bigler MSS; Robinson to Wright, Apr. 3, 12, May 24, Brodhead to Wright, Apr. 12, 13, 1860, Wright MSS; *Covode Report,* pp. 332-344; Buchanan, *Works,* 10:393.

24. *Documents Relating to the New York Contest, Showing the Claims of the Delegation Elected by Congress Districts;* Douglas to Cagger, Feb. 19, Ill. State Hist. Lib.; Stryker to Butler, Mar. 29, 1860, Butler MSS.

25. *Washington Constitution,* Dec. 16, 30, 1859, Jan. 12, 1860; Stillwell, *John Cabell Breckinridge,* pp. 77-98; McKibben to H. B. Wright, Apr. 11, 1859, Wright MSS; Bradford to Buchanan, May 2, 1859, Buchanan MSS; Breckinridge to Bigler, May 7, 1859, Bigler MSS; *N.Y. Herald,* Dec. 13, 1859; *Pittsburgh Gazette,* Dec. 31, 1859.

26. Delazon Smith to Bush, Nov. 30, 1858, Feb. 2, 1859, Grover to Bush, Feb. 17, Bush Transcripts; Thompson to Holden, Feb. 7, 1860, Thompson Letter Book, War Dept. files, National Archives; *Quar. Calif. Hist. Soc.,* 11:13.

27. Buchanan, *Works,* 10:339-370; Du Bose, *Yancey,* p. 440; *Washington Constitution,* Sept. 21, speech of C. C. Clay, Sept. 22, Toombs, Sept. 29, Iverson, Oct. 4, Chesnut, Nov. 2, Fitzpatrick, Nov. 26, 1859, A. G. Brown; Hammond to Harry Hammond, Feb. 12, 1860, Hammond MSS; Crittenden to Stephens, Jan. 13, 1860, Huntington Library.

28. *36:1 Globe,* pp. 658, 837.

29. *Ibid.,* pp. 671, 688.

30. Davis to Buchanan, Feb. 24, 1860, Buchanan MSS; *Washington Star,* Feb. 28.

31. *Ser. 1040,* pp. 1, 5, 190, 311, 347.

32. *36:1 H. Rept. 249* (Ser. 1068), *passim.*

33. *Covode Report,* pp. 138-150, 184-197, 214-218, 311-314, 327-418.

34. Memoranda and questions in handwriting of Buchanan and Stanton, Buchanan MSS.

35. *Covode Report,* pp. 459-632.

36. *Ibid.,* pp. 93-324.

37. *36:1 Globe,* App. pp. 203-204, 1668; Rhodes, *op. cit.,* 2:439; Crawford to Stephens, Apr. 8, 1860, Stephens MSS.

38. Hammond to Major Hammond, Apr. 22, 1860, Hammond MSS; Hesseltine, "Pryor-Potter Duel," *Wis. Mag. Hist.* 27:400-409.

Chapter 15

1. *Charleston Courier,* Apr. 19, 20, 21, 23, 24, 25, 28, 30; *Charleston Mercury,* Apr. 21, 26; *N.Y. Herald,* Apr. 19, 20, 21, 22, 25, 30, May 1; Jeffries to Douglas, Mar. 26, 1860, Douglas MSS; Moore and Lanphier to McClernand, Jan. 17, Lanphier to McClernand, Mar. 15, McClernand MSS; McClernand to Lanphier, Feb. 23, Mar. 21, 28, Patton MSS; Foss to English, Mar. 17, Bentley to English, Mar. 20, English MSS; Huger to Miles, Jan. 23, 1858, Dec. 12, 1859, Mason to Miles, Apr. 3, 1859, Trescott to Miles, Feb. 22, 1860, Miles MSS; Magrath to Hammond, Apr. 23, 1860, Hammond MSS.

2. *N.Y. Herald,* Apr. 22; *Charleston Courier,* Apr. 26; Halstead, *A History of the National Political Conventions,* pp. 1-18; Letcher to G. W. Jones, Apr. 8, Letcher to ———, Apr. 29, Huntington Library; S. L. M. Barlow to Corning, Mar. 28, 1860, Corning MSS.

3. Halstead, *loc. cit.* It is interesting to note that shortly thereafter one of the delegates from California, John A. Driebellis, was appointed superintendent for Indians of the northern district of California, and between May 4 and June 23 a series of other appointments from that state was sent to the Senate.

4. Milton, *op. cit.,* pp. 425-431; Phillips to Buchanan, Apr. 26, Buchanan MSS; McConnell to Douglas, Apr. 22, Douglas MSS; Halstead, *loc. cit.;* Venable, "Conflict Between Douglas and Yancey forces at Charleston," *Jour. South. Hist.,* 8:226-242.

5. Halstead, *op. cit.,* pp. 18-22; Brown to Buchanan, Apr. 22, Buchanan MSS.

6. Halstead, *op. cit.,* pp. 23-30.

7. *Ibid.,* pp. 30-37.

8. *Ibid.,* pp. 38-51; *Proceedings of the Conventions at Charleston and Baltimore* (Breckinridge), pp. 37-39, 45; *Official Proceedings of the Democratic National Convention* (Douglas), pp. 31-34. These are the first of a long series of propositions which will be quoted in full because they illustrate as nothing else can the desperate efforts to embrace in one formula two conflicting concepts —federal protection of property in the territories, and squatter sovereignty.

9. Hammond to Major Hammond, May 11, Hammond MSS.

10. Baker to Bigler, Jan. 24, 1861, Bigler MSS; *Charleston Courier,* Apr. 19, 28, 30; *N.Y. Herald,* May 1.

11. Halstead, *op. cit.,* pp. 52-61; *Proceedings* (Breckinridge), pp. 91-92; Slidell to Cushing, undated, Cushing MSS.

12. Halstead, *op. cit.,* pp. 58-61; *N.Y. Herald,* Apr. 30; Sanders to Buchanan, Apr. 27, Buchanan MSS; Andrews to Cushing, Apr. 29, Cushing MSS; Browne to Cobb, Apr. 28 (a copy also in Buchanan MSS), Hillyer to Cobb, Apr. 28, Browne to Cobb,

Apr. 28 (2nd telegram), Keitt to Cobb, n.d., Thompson to Cobb, [Apr. 28], Sanders to Floyd, Apr. 28, R. M. Magraw to Cobb, Apr. 28, Cobb MSS.

13. Halstead, *op. cit.*, pp. 61-74; Venable, *loc. cit.; Proceedings* (Breckinridge), pp. 115-117; Mayes, *L. Q. C. Lamar*, p. 83; Crawford to Stephens, May 11, Mudd to Stephens, May 22, Stephens MSS; Stephens to Stephens, May 11, Stephens MSS, Convent; Kibler, *Benjamin F. Perry*, pp. 300, 314-318.

Chapter 16

1. Bayard to Bayard, May 2, 1860, Bayard MSS; Halstead, *op. cit.*, pp. 97-98.

2. *Ibid.*, pp. 76-92; *Proceedings* (Breckinridge), p. 141; *Washington Constitution*, Sept. 12; Crawford to Stephens, May 11, Stephens MSS.

3. Halstead, *op. cit.*, pp. 92-96, 98-101; Holman to Hamilton, May 15, Indiana State Library.

4. Hammond to Hayne, Sept. 19, 1860, Hammond MSS; Hammond MS account written in 1861, Univ. of S.C.

5. *Quar. Calif. Hist. Soc.*, 11:18; Bishop to Butler, May 2, Butler MSS.

6. Dumond, *The Secession Movement, 1860-1861*, pp. 55-76; Smythe to Cobb, May 5, Johnston to Lamar, May 24, Cobb to Mrs. Cobb, June 2, Cobb MSS; Crawford to Stephens, May 11, Stephens MSS; *Ga. Hist. Quar.*, 6:247; *Toombs Corr.*, pp. 468-482; Johnston and Browne, *Alexander H. Stephens*, pp. 355-365; Dix to Buchanan, May 9, Buchanan to Dix, May 12, Paine to Buchanan, May 11, Baker to Buchanan, May 12, Buchanan MSS; Dyer to Douglas, May 12, Payne to Douglas, May 16, Richardson to Douglas, May 17, Belmont to Douglas, May 18, Douglas MSS; Thompson to Glenn, May 10, Thompson to Croswell, May 12, Thompson Letter Book, War Dept. files, National Archives.

7. *Charleston Courier*, Oct. 26; *Baltimore Sun*, Sept. 11, Oct. 19, 20, 24; Hodgson, *Cradle of the Confederacy*, p. 425; Du Bose, *Yancey*, pp. 475-477.

8. *Dollar Weekly Pennsylvanian*, May 26; Bayard to Bayard, May 8, Bayard MSS; Mayes, *op. cit.*, p. 83; *Toombs Corr.*, 468-470; Thompson to Glenn, May 10, Thompson to Croswell, May 12, Thompson Letter Book, *loc. cit.*

9. Bigelow, *Retrospections*, 1:288; *36:1 Globe*, pp. 1937, 1966.

10. *Ibid.*, pp. 1970, 2151.

11. *Ibid.*, p. 2241.

12. *Ibid.*, App. p. 338.

13. *Ibid.*, pp. 2321-2325.

14. Seymour to Barlow, May 15, June 8, N.Y. Hist. Soc.; Belmont, *Letters, Speeches, and Addresses*, p. 105; Richardson to Douglas, May 13, Davis to Douglas, May 25, Douglas MSS; McCall to Bigler, May 18, Bigler MSS; Massie to Allen, June 16, 22,

544 / The Disruption of American Democracy

Allen MSS; Holman to Hamilton, May 15, Indiana State Lib.;
E. Croswell to Corning, May 19, S. L. M. Barlow to Corning,
May 19, John L. Dawson to Corning, June 4, 1860, Corning MSS.
15. *Washington Star*, May 14, 18; Dix to Buchanan, May 14,
Buchanan MSS.
16. Milton, *op. cit.*, pp. 463-468; *Official Proceedings* (Douglas), pp. 114-121; Stephens to Stephens, May 22, Stephens MSS,
Convent; Landry, "Political Career of R. C. Wickliffe," *La. Hist.
Quar.*, 25:706. See also note 6 above.
17. Belmont, *loc. cit.;* Stephens to Stephens, June 14, Stephens
MSS, Convent. See Stevenson MSS for comments from various
sections of the country.
18. Halstead, *op. cit.*, pp. 159-160.
19. *Ibid.*, pp. 160-177.
20. *Ibid.*, pp. 179-180.
21. *Ibid.*, p. 179.
22. *Ibid.*, pp. 178-185.
23. *Ibid.*, pp. 185-194.
24. Brummer, *Political History of New York During the Period
of the Civil War*, pp. 56-60; *Magazine of American History*,
14:151, 623; Anderson to Stephens, July 11, 1860, Stephens MSS;
Seymour to Barlow, June 6, N.Y. Hist. Soc.; Dickinson to Brown,
June 6, *Trinity Historical Papers*, Vol. 6; Stephens to Stephens,
June 28, Stephens MSS, Convent; Horatio Seymour Political Scrap
Books, 2:135, 3:9, N.Y. State Lib.
25. Halstead, *op. cit.*, pp. 194-202.
26. Remnants of the delegations of Maryland, Virginia, North
Carolina, Missouri, Tennessee, and Kentucky remained; so did the
new delegates from Alabama, Louisiana, and Arkansas. There
were 36 southern votes.
27. Halstead, *op. cit.*, pp. 202-216; Stephens to Stephens, June
28, Stephens MSS, Convent; Hambleton to Stephens, July 2, Crawford to Stephens, Oct. 18, Stephens MSS; *Butler's Book*, pp. 143-
144.
28. Halstead, *op. cit.*, pp. 217-230.
29. *Ibid.*, pp. 231-232.

Chapter 17

1. Crawford to Stephens, Apr. 8, 1860, Stephens MSS.
2. *Covode Report*, pp. 652-673, 735-835; Vanderbilt to Buchanan, Aug. 30, Nov. 1, 1859, Buchanan MSS; Manning, *Dip.
Corr. Int. Am.*, 4:775, 807; *N.Y. Herald*, May 12, Oct. 6, 1859;
Washington States, June 2, 24, July 20, Sept. 10, 1859; Kemble,
op. cit., pp. 81-94; *36:1 Globe*, App. pp. 17-27; Wm. H. Dundas to
Hammond, June 29, Hammond to Holt, July 9, 21, Holt to Hammond, July 18, 1860, Hammond MSS; Branch to Fisher, May 4,
Branch scrapbook, Duke Univ.; Ellison, ed., "Memoirs of Gwin,"

Quar, Calif. Hist. Soc., 19:356; Holt to Buchanan, June 16, July 6, 1860, Buchanan MSS; *Sacramento Daily Union*, July 24; *Washington Constitution*, July 7; *N.Y. Herald*, July 8; *Baltimore Sun*, July 9; Auchampaugh, "James Buchanan and Some Far Western Leaders," *Pac. Hist. Rev.*, 12:169-181.

3. Meigs to Meigs, Jan. 20, May 4, 1860, Meigs MSS.

4. Newspaper clipping in Diary under June 26, July 18, 1860, Meigs MSS; *36:1 Globe*, p. 1766, App. p. 500.

5. *Ibid.*, p. 2265; Diary, May 22-23, 1860, Meigs MSS.

6. Clipping from *N.Y. Times* in Diary under Nov. 10, 1860, Meigs to Davis, Aug. 6, 1857, Meigs MSS; *36:1 Globe*, p. 2818.

7. Meigs to Meigs, Oct. 18, 1857, Meigs MSS.

8. Clipping from *N.Y. Times*, in Diary under Sept. 27, Meigs to Meigs, Sept. 27, 1860, Meigs MSS; *36:1 S. Ex. Doc. 20* (Ser. 1031).

9. Floyd to Meigs, Nov. 1, 1859, Meigs to Meigs, Jan. 13, 1860, Diary, Nov. 2, clipping from *N.Y. Times* in Diary under Nov. 10, 1859, Meigs MSS.

10. Meigs to Meigs, May 4, June 20, 1860, Meigs MSS; *36:1 Globe*, p. 2832.

11. *Ibid.*, p. 2818; Meigs to Meigs, June 20, 21, 1860, Meigs MSS; Buchanan, *Works* 10:452-455.

12. Wendell to W. O. B., May 22, 1860, Buchanan MSS; *36:1 H. Repts. 648, 621; 35:2 H. Rept. 184; 36:1 H. Rept. 249* bound together under title on backstrip, *Covode Investigation, Naval Contracts etc., Public Printing, 1860; 36:1 H. Rept. 394* (Ser. 1069); Buchanan, *Works*, 10:434.

13. *36:1 Globe*, p. 1728.

14. *Ibid.*, App. pp. 44-46.

15. *Ibid.*, p. 2884.

16. *Ibid.*, App. p. 51.

Chapter 18

1. *Proceedings* (Douglas), pp. 184-188; Hambleton to Stephens, July 2, Smith to Stephens, Aug. 18, Crawford to Stephens, Oct. 18, Stephens MSS; Stephens to Stephens, June 28, Stephens MSS, Convent; (Washington) *National Intelligencer*, June 30.

2. Campaign pamphlets are listed in the Bibliography. *Baltimore Sun*, July 18; Markoe to Dallas, Feb. 7, 1860, Dallas MSS.

3. Milton, *op. cit.*, pp. 490-494; Bayard to Bayard, Aug. 5, Bayard MSS; Fite, *Presidential Campaign of 1860*, p. 207; Crenshaw, *Slave States*, 74-88.

4. Fite, *op. cit.*, p. 228; Perkins, *Northern Editorials on Secession*, p. 15.

5. Halstead, *op. cit.*, p. 227; *Breckinridge and Lane Campaign Documents:* No. 2, p. 15.

6. Buchanan, *Works*, 10:457-464.

7. Buchanan to Phelps, July 18, Stevens to Phelps, July 18, Bigler MSS.

8. Perkins, *op. cit.*, p. 15; *Baltimore Sun,* July 28, Aug. 11.

9. Dickinson to Buchanan, June 30, Cook to Buchanan, July 4, enclosing Hope to Cook, July 2, Cox to Cass, July 5, Johnson to Buchanan, July 7, Holt to Buchanan, Aug. 23, Buchanan MSS; Cook to Black, July 2, Black MSS; Thompson to Rynders, July 5, Thompson Letter Book, War Dept. files, National Archives; Stevens to Pierce, July 26, Pierce to Stevens, Pierce MSS; Joyner to Branch, Aug. 2, Branch MSS, Duke Univ.; Anderson to Stephens, July 30, Smith to Stephens, Sept. 19, Oct. 1, Stephens MSS; Mrs. Thompson to Mrs. Cobb, Jan. 13, 1861, Cobb MSS; Sanders to Crittenden, May 11, Crittenden MSS.

10. Luthin, *The First Lincoln Campaign,* pp. 136-167.

11. Halstead, *op. cit.,* pp. 104-120.

12. Hammond to Hammond, July 4, Hammond MSS; Du Bose, *Yancey,* p. 486; Davis, *The Rise and Fall of the Confederate Government,* 1:52.

13. *Baltimore Sun,* July 9.

14. *N.Y. Herald,* July 7, letter of Miles Taylor, June 30.

15. Itter, "Election of 1860 with Special Reference to Pennsylvania," MS essay; Buchanan to Baker, Sept. 13, Buchanan MSS; Myers, "Influence of Western Pennsylvania in the Campaign of 1860," *West. Pa. Hist. Mag.,* 24:229-250.

16. Knapp, *New Jersey Politics During the Period of the Civil War,* pp. 30-33; *N.Y. Herald,* July 4; 29 letters and memoranda in the Rodman Price MSS called to my attention by Richard P. McCormick.

17. *National Intelligencer,* June 29; *Washington Star,* July 10, 19; *N.Y. Herald,* June 29, 30.

18. *N.Y. Journal of Commerce,* Sept. 17; Brummer, *op. cit.,* pp. 70-86.

19. Foner, *Business and Slavery,* pp. 172-173; Belmont to Duncan, Aug. 19, Bell MSS; Belmont to Corning, Aug. 1, Corning MSS.

20. Foner, *op. cit.,* pp. 182-183.

21. Cameron to Lincoln, Aug. 1, Lincoln to Cameron, Aug. 6, Cameron MSS.

22. *N.Y. Herald,* Aug. 8; *Baltimore Sun,* Aug. 9, 11; *Washington Constitution,* Aug. 14.

23. Fite, *op. cit.,* pp. 180-185, 276-300.

24. *Philadelphia Press,* Aug. 20, 31; *Baltimore Sun,* Sept. 29, Oct. 8.

25. *Ibid.,* July 16, 19, 23, Sept. 6, 7, 13, 21; *Philadelphia Press,* Sept. 3; Breckinridge to Stevens, Aug. 3, Stevens MSS.

26. Flippin, *Herschel V. Johnson,* pp. 140-146; *Baltimore Sun,* Sept. 14.

27. Fite, *op. cit.,* pp. 214-218, 301-329; Randall, *Lincoln,* 1:182.

28. Baker to Buchanan, Oct. 8, Green to Buchanan, Aug. 22,

Buchanan MSS; Stevens to Bigler, July 24, Bigler MSS; Seymour to Pierce, Oct. 18, Pierce MSS; Richard Schell to Weed, Aug. 29, Draper to Weed, Oct. 20, Weed MSS. For a southern proposal see Stephens to Stephens, Oct. 21, Stephens MSS, Convent.

29. *N.Y. Journal of Commerce,* Sept. 17; Anderson to Stephens, July 19, Sept. 2, Stephens MSS; Cobb to Jackson, Nov. 1, Cobb MSS; Comstock to Buchanan, Sept. 12, Buchanan MSS; Fite, *op. cit.,* pp. 223-224; Foner, *op. cit.,* pp. 173-179; Brummer, *op. cit.,* pp. 79-86; Thompson to Dugan, Sept. 9, Thompson to Howe, Oct. 14, Thompson Letter Book, War Dept. files, National Archives; Bonham, "New York and the Election of 1860," *N.Y. Hist.,* 15:124-143.

30. *Baltimore Sun,* Oct. 12, 13; *N.Y. Herald,* Oct. 2, 20; Hirst to Buchanan, Oct. 12, Buchanan MSS.

31. Itter, *op. cit.;* Rodman Price MSS; Myers, *op. cit.*

32. Knapp, *op. cit.,* pp. 34-35.

Chapter 19

1. *Baltimore Sun,* Aug. 1, 4, Oct. 8; *Charleston Mercury,* Aug., *passim;* Fite, *op. cit.,* pp. 216-217; Aptheker, *American Negro Slave Revolts,* pp. 353-358; Eaton, "Mob Violence in the Old South," *Miss. Valley Hist. Rev.,* 29:351-371; Crenshaw, *Slave States,* 89-112, 301-302.

2. Foner, *op. cit.,* p. 218; Hammond to Hammond, Aug. 30, Hammond MSS; Crenshaw, "Psychological Background of the Election of 1860 in the South," *N.C. Hist. Rev.,* 19:260-280.

3. Scroggs, *op. cit.,* pp. 382-395; *Baltimore Sun,* July 19, 1860; Crenshaw, "Knights of the Golden Circle," *Amer. Hist. Rev.,* 47:23-50; Bridges, "Knights of the Golden Circle," *S.W. Hist. Quar.,* 44:287-302.

4. Flippin, *Herschel V. Johnson,* p. 146; Eaton, "Censorship of the Southern Mails," *Amer. Hist. Rev.,* 48:266-280.

5. Hamilton, *The Papers of Thomas Ruffin,* 3:85.

6. Schaper, "Sectionalism in South Carolina," *Amer. Hist. Assn. Ann. Rept. 1901;* Van Deusen, *Economic Bases of Disunion in South Carolina;* Wolfe, *Jeffersonian Democracy in South Carolina;* Taylor, *Ante-Bellum South Carolina;* Adams, *America's Tragedy,* pp. 8-10; Green, *Constitutional Development in the South Atlantic States,* pp. 105-124, 248-251, 261-264; Kibler, *Benjamin F. Perry,* 302-313.

7. White, *Robert Barnwell Rhett;* White, "National Parties in South Carolina," *South Atlantic Quar.,* 28:374; Kibler, "Unionist Sentiment in South Carolina in 1860," *Jour. South. Hist.,* 4:353; Cauthen, "South Carolina's Decision to Lead the Secession Movement," *N.C. Hist. Rev.,* 18:360; I. W. Hayne to Hammond, Apr. 17, 21, 1858, Miles MSS.

8. Capers, *Memminger,* pp. 241-282; Miles to Memminger, Jan. 10, 15, 18, 23, Boyce to Memminger, Jan. 4, Memminger

MSS; Memminger to Miles, Dec. 27, 1859, Jan. 3, 16, 24, 30, Feb. 4, 1860, Hayne to Miles, Jan. 5, Hamilton to Miles, Jan. 23, Feb. 2, Miles MSS; Crenshaw, "C. G. Memminger's Mission to Virginia in 1860," *Jour. South. Hist.*, 8:334-350.

9. Trescott to Miles, Feb. 22, Mar. 10, Hamilton to Miles, Apr. 4, Rhett to Miles, Apr. 11, 17, Miles MSS; *Charleston Courier,* Apr. 17-20.

10. Kibler, *op. cit.;* Cauthen, *op. cit.;* Trescott to Miles, May 8, Rhett to Miles, May 12, Huger to Miles, June 1, Miles MSS.

11. Gist to Miles, Dec. 20, 1859, Rhett to Miles, Jan. 29, 1860, Miles MSS.

12. *Washington Constitution,* Oct. 3, 1860; *Charleston Mercury,* June 30, July 12, 16.

13. *Ibid.,* July 2, 3, 10, 15, 20.

14. *Ibid.,* Aug. 4; *N.Y. Herald,* Aug. 9, 13; Ashmore to Miles, July 30, Trescott to Miles, Aug. 10, Miles MSS.

15. *Charleston Courier,* Aug. 20; *Charleston Mercury,* Aug. 22, 23; *N.Y. Herald,* Aug. 24; R. N. Gourdin to Miles, Aug. 20, Miles MSS.

16. *Charleston Mercury,* Sept. 24, 25, Oct. 11; *Charleston Courier,* Oct. 5.

17. *Charleston Mercury,* Sept. 21; *Charleston Courier,* Sept. 29, Oct. 5; *Yorkville Enquirer,* Oct. 18.

18. *Charleston Mercury,* Sept. 21, 25, 29; Hayne to Hammond, Mar. 19, 29, 1859, Magrath to Hammond, Jan. 21, Apr. 23, 27, May 30, Dundas to Hammond, June 29, Hammond to Holt, July 9, 21, Holt to Hammond, July 18, 1860, Hammond MSS.

19. Miles to Hammond, Aug. 5, 1860, Hammond MSS.

20. Keitt to Hammond, Sept. 10, Hammond MSS.

21. *Yorkville* (S.C.) *Enquirer,* Sept. 13, 20; Tillman to Hammond, Oct. 9, Hammond MSS; *Charleston Mercury,* Sept. 29; *Washington Star,* Oct. 12; *Baltimore Sun,* Oct. 12, 18, 26; Fite, *op. cit.,* pp. 229-230.

22. Cobb to Lamar, July 1, Sept. 27, Cobb to Jackson, Nov. 1, Cobb MSS; *Ga. Hist. Quar.,* 6:249; *Toombs Corr.,* pp. 483-502; Hammond to Hammond, July 4, Hammond MSS; *Washington Constitution,* Oct. 13; Greer, *op. cit.,* p. 479.

23. Cobb to Mrs. Cobb, Oct. 10, Cobb MSS.

24. Thomas Cobb to Mrs. Cobb, Oct. 11, Cobb MSS.

25. *N.Y. Herald,* July 24.

26. Smith to Stephens, Oct. 11, 18, Stephens MSS; *36:2 H. Rept. 79* (Ser. 1105).

27. Pierce to Campbell, Oct. 17, Campbell to Pierce, Oct. 22, Pierce MSS; George to Hildreth, Sept. 23, Butler MSS; Bell to Sanders, Oct. 3, Confederate files, National Archives.

28. Foner, *op. cit.,* pp. 193-201.

29. Browne to Cobb, Oct. 21, Cobb to Mrs. Cobb, Oct. 24, Cobb to Lamar, Oct. 31, Cobb to Jackson, Nov. 1, Cobb MSS;

Smith to Stephens, Oct. 30, Stephens MSS; *Washington Star,* Oct. 27; Barbee, "The Montgomery Address of Douglas," *Jour. South. Hist.,* 5:527-553.

30. Gist to Ellis, Oct. 5, Ellis Letter Book; Keitt to Miles, Oct. 3, Miles MSS; *Charleston Mercury,* Aug. 22; Nicolay and Hay, *Abraham Lincoln,* 2:306-307.

31. *Charleston Mercury,* Oct. 11, 16; *N.Y. Herald,* Nov. 3.

32. *Ibid.,* Oct. 31; *Charleston Mercury,* Oct. 16; Chesnut to Hammond, Oct. 17, 27, Hammond MSS; Ashmore to Miles, Nov. 20, Miles MSS; Nicolay and Hay, *op. cit.,* 2:319-320; *The War of the Rebellion: A Compilation of the Official Records of the Union and Confederate Armies* (hereafter cited as *O.R.*), Ser. 3, 1:44-45.

33. Holt to Holt, Nov. 9, 1860, Holt MSS.

34. Mary Ann Lamar Cobb to Lamar, Nov. 6, 1860, Cobb MSS.

Chapter 20

1. Scrugham, *Peaceable Americans of 1860-1861,* pp. 23-26, 40-52; Dodd, "The Fight for the Northwest, 1860," *Amer. Hist. Rev.,* 16:774-788; Smith, "Influence of the Foreign-Born of the Northwest in the Election of 1860," *Miss. Valley Hist. Rev.,* 19:192-205; Schafer, "Who Elected Lincoln?" *Amer. Hist. Rev.* 47:51-64; Dorpalen, "The German Element and the Issues of the Civil War," *Miss. Valley Hist. Rev.,* 29:55-76.

2. Davis, *Works,* 4:541-543; *Charleston Courier,* Sept. 20, Dec. 12, 15, 1860; Nicolay and Hay, *Lincoln,* 2:306-314; *N.Y. Herald,* Nov. 6, 1860.

3. Ashmore to King, Nov. 5, 1860, King MSS.

4. MS Diary of John W. Ellis, Oct. 30 to Nov. 2, 1860.

5. Crawford, *The Genesis of the Civil War,* pp. 12-13.

6. Cauthen, *op. cit.,* pp. 366-372.

7. Hammond to Hammond, Nov. 12, Hammond MSS; Mason to Miles, Nov. 9, Ashmore to Miles, Nov. 15, 20, Miles MSS.

8. Smith, *The History and Debates of the Convention of the People of Alabama,* pp. 12-18; *Journal of the* [Mississippi] *State Convention,* p. 1.

9. Dumond, *op. cit.,* pp. 142-145; Flippin, *op. cit.,* pp. 151-160; Stephens to Stephens, Nov. 9, Stephens MSS, Convent; Caskey, *Secession and Restoration of Louisiana,* p. 18.

10. Dumond, *op. cit.,* p. 148; Sitterson, *The Secession Movement in North Carolina,* pp. 177-185; Ramsdell, *Reconstruction in Texas,* pp. 14-15.

11. Clark, "Politics in Maryland During the Civil War," MS dissertation, Univ. of N.C. Lib., pp. 74-128; Radcliffe, *Gov. Thomas H. Hicks and the Civil War; Baltimore Sun,* Jan. 2-15, 1861; *O.R.,* Ser. 4, 1:38, 122-123; Patton, *Unionism and Reconstruction in Tennessee,* p. 10; Shanks, *The Secession Movement in Virginia,* p. 142; Coulter, *Civil War and Readjustment in Kentucky,* pp.

25-26; Smith, *op. cit.*, pp. 83-85; *Journal of the* [Mississippi] *State Convention*, pp. 180-183; Dorman to Letcher, Nov. 18, Davidson MSS.

12. *Journal* [Mississippi], pp. 149-220; Smith, *op. cit.*, pp. 373-444; Rainwater, *op. cit.*, pp. 167-168; *N.Y. Herald*, Nov. 18, 1860. The Governor of Alabama appointed these envoys on his own responsibility; the Governor of Mississippi acted under a resolution of the legislature of November 30.

13. Crawford, *op. cit.*, pp. 22-23; Cobb to Lamar, Nov. 16, 1860, Cobb MSS; Thompson to Rhett, Nov. 15, Thompson to Pettus, Nov. 15, Thompson to Peterson, Nov. 20, 1860, Thompson Letter Book, War Dept. files, National Archives; Nicolay and Hay, *Lincoln*, 2:317-318; Mann to Baring Bros., Nov. 9, 1860, Baring MSS.

14. Floyd persuaded Buchanan to place Capt. H. W. Benham in charge of the aqueduct, despite the law of Congress, and to use Meigs simply as a disbursing officer. The latter was ordered to transfer all plans and estimates to Benham and merely pay out the funds on Benham's certificate. Meigs fought this in a fashion held by army men as insubordinate. First he protested to the President. When the Attorney General upheld Floyd's procedures, Meigs took his opinion and controverted it vigorously. He held that Congress had given him a trust as M. C. Meigs, the citizen, not as an officer in the army. Therefore it was a civil, not a military, trust, and he refused to disburse the money unless he could oversee and check the work. There was some discussion of court-martialing him, but he had too many friends in the Senate. Then Floyd threatened to resign in the summer of 1860, and Buchanan sought to ease the tension by sending Meigs to the Dry Tortugas off the coast of Florida to superintend the building of Fort Jefferson. Benham was ordered to send the requisitions to the Treasury, despite the recent law. Before Meigs left he filed a formal protest with the Secretary of the Treasury, warning him that he could not legally honor these requisitions without his approval. Meigs was not destined to stay away long. As soon as Floyd left the War Department, in January, 1861, the truculent captain was brought back and restored to his superintendency of the capital's public works. Order of July 17, 1860, Meigs to C. D. Meigs, June 20, July 19, Aug. 11, Sept. 5, 1860, Feb. 27, 1861, Meigs to Lansing, Sept. 25, 1860, Meigs' Diary, June 26, July 17, 18, Meigs MSS; Meigs to Cobb, Sept. 21, A B Series, Misc., vol. for 1860-1861, Treasury Dept. files, National Archives; Buchanan to Black, Sept. 8, Black MSS; *N.Y. Times*, Sept. 28.

15. A contract for making and delivering bricks by the million for the aqueduct bridge had been made in 1854. A series of calamities had followed. The original contractors had failed. Then the sureties had endeavored to execute it by assigning it to Wm. H. De Groot. He had built a brick yard and equipped it when Congress, in a wrangle over appropriations, stopped work on the

aqueduct in 1856-1857. A resolution had been passed to indemnify the suffering contractors for their "damages, losses and liabilities." Because of his position as an assignee rather than an original contractor, De Groot had been denied the benefit of the resolution by Cobb, and in the session just closed in June 1860, Congress had sought to relieve De Groot by authorizing the Secretary of War to settle his account "on principles of justice and equity" (*36:1 Globe,* pp. 2752-2755). Floyd in his usual florid manner determined to pay De Groot not only the actual value of the brick works he had constructed but all the profit he might have made had he supplied the brick originally specified. He set the amount at $119,234.46. Attorney General Black resisted this in opinions dated July 20 and Sept. 20 and recommended that $42,338.33 was the limit of a just claim. Cobb followed Black's views and refused to honor Floyd's voucher for the large sum. When Floyd retired in disgrace Holt recalled the voucher and Congress repealed the authority given the Secretary of War to settle the claim, referring it instead to the Court of Claims. In due course De Groot's attorneys presented the Floyd award to that court and petitioned that it ratify the decision. This the court refused to do; deciding that De Groot must submit to it all papers and proofs so that the judges might form their own opinion of the indemnity due the brick-maker. De Groot appealed this decision, but the Supreme Court upheld the Court of Claims. De Groot, having no proofs which would convince a court, then turned to Congress seeking relief through legislation. His claim came up in the 37th, 43rd, and 44th Congresses. After committees of both houses had reported upon it unfavorably, the matter was dropped in 1876. The determination of Floyd and De Groot to secure so much resulted in complete lack of indemnification. Floyd to Black, July 13, Floyd to Buchanan, Nov. 3, Military Book No. 42, pp. 339, 343, Floyd to Thomas, Dec. 5, 1860, Holt to Sec. of Treasury, Jan. 15, 1861, Military Book No. 43, pp. 35, 71, War Dept. files, National Archives; *36:2 Globe* App. p. 355; *37:2 H. Rept. 136* (Ser. 1145); *37:3 H. Rept. 26* (Ser. 1173); *43:2 H. Rept. 37* (Ser. 1654); *44:1 S. Rept. 277* (Ser. 1667).

16. *Mr. Buchanan's Administration on the Eve of the Rebellion,* Appendix; MS copies of this letter are in the Buchanan MSS, Corcoran MSS, Crittenden MSS, and Everett MSS.

17. Crawford, *op. cit.,* pp. 56-60; Pollard, *Early Life, Campaigns and Public Services of Robert E. Lee,* pp. 791-792; *O.R., Ser.* 1, 2:67-72.

18. *Philadelphia Weekly Press,* Aug. 11, 1881; *N.Y. Herald,* Jan. 17, 1861.

19. *O.R.,* Ser. 1, 1:67-72; Crawford, *op. cit.,* pp. 56-60, 26-27.

20. Gilmer to Buchanan, Nov. 9, Dickerson to Buchanan, Nov. 20, 1860, Buchanan MSS; Pollard, *op. cit.,* pp. 791-793; *Philadelphia Weekly Press,* Aug. 11, 18, 25, 1881, Mar. 16, 1882, Mar. 4, 1883, Sept. 10, 17, 1883.

21. Crawford, *op. cit.,* pp. 59-61.

22. *Philadelphia Weekly Press*, Aug. 11, 1881.

23. *Ibid.*, Mar. 4, 1883.

24. Cobb to Lamar, Oct. 31, Lamar to Mrs. Cobb, Nov. 14, 1860, Cobb MSS; *Ga. Hist. Quar.*, 6:258.

25. Lamar to Cobb, Apr. 13, Nov. 12, Cobb to Lamar, Apr. 24, Toombs *et al.* to Cobb, Nov. 12, 1860, Cobb MSS.

26. Cobb to Lamar, Nov. 16, Lamar to Cobb, Nov. 19, Mrs. Cobb to Howell Cobb, Jr., Nov. 25, Mrs. Gwin to Mrs. Cobb, Dec. 5, Cobb to Mrs. Cobb, Dec. 7, Mrs. Cobb to Cobb, Dec. 9, Cobb MSS; Cobb's address of Dec. 6 in *Toombs Corr.*, pp. 505-516.

27. *Philadelphia Press*, Aug. 11, 1881, Mar. 4, 1883.

28. Buchanan, *Works*, 11:21; Curtis, *Buchanan*, 2:319.

29. *Philadelphia Press*, Sept. 11, 1883; Davis, *The Rise and Fall of the Confederate Government*, 1:57-59.

30. Black on Stanton, fragments in 1869 and undated, Black MSS; *O.R.*, Ser. 1, 1:72-82; Crawford, *op. cit.*, pp. 59-69, 27-36; *Amer. Hist. Rev.*, 13:528-556.

31. Buchanan, *Works*, 11:7-55; Klingberg, "James Buchanan and the Crisis of the Union," *Jour. South. Hist.*, 9:455-475.

32. Crawford, *op. cit.*, pp. 33-35; F.O. 5, v. 740, No. 311, Dec. 10, 1860.

Chapter 21

1. Nicolay and Hay, *op. cit.*, 2:328-329; *N.Y. Herald*, Oct. 31, Nov. 25, 1860; Rainwater, *op. cit.*, pp. 168-169; Reuben Davis, *Recollections of Mississippi*, p. 391; Mayes, *Lamar*, pp. 86-87.

2. Their determination may have been strengthened by another disappointment. John Bell suspected that there had been a plan to secede from the Charleston Convention in order to profit by the consequent election of a Republican President. This, the seceders felt, would first of all cause several of their number to leave the Union, which would so alarm the North that it would make concessions sufficient to persuade the seceding states to return. Thus the Breckinridge Democrats would gain the credit of having forced the free states to do justice to the South, and they would also be the saviors of the Union. Now the northern representatives showed little alarm and less spirit of concession. Memorandum of Dec. 10, 1860, Bell MSS.

3. *N.Y. Herald*, Nov. 24, 1860, Mar. 4, 1861.

4. *Ibid.*, Feb. 8, 1861; *36:2 Globe*, p. 27; Bancroft, *California*, 7:277 n., 280 n.; *Sacramento Union*, Dec. 8, 1860; *San Francisco Evening Bulletin*, Dec. 31, 1860, Jan. 10, 16, 1861.

5. *36:2 Globe*, pp. 38, 39; Moorman to Davidson, Dec. 20, Letcher to Davidson, Mar. 9, 1861, Davidson MSS.

6. Holman to Hamilton, Nov. 18, 1860, Indiana State Library; Varina Davis to Buchanan, Mar. 18, 1861, Buchanan MSS.

7. Potter, *Lincoln and His Party in the Secession Crisis, passim;* *36:2 Globe,* p. 5; Seward to Weed, Dec. 3, 1860, Weed MSS.

8. Johnston and Browne, *op. cit.,* p. 375; *Southern Hist. Soc. Papers,* 42:18-19, 24-25.

9. *N.Y. Times,* Nov. 30, Dec. 1, 4.

10. *36:2 Globe,* pp. 6, 316; *N.Y. Herald,* Dec. 3.

11. *N.Y. Herald,* Dec. 7, 8, 9, 10; *N.Y. Times,* Dec. 10; *Washington Star,* Dec. 10; Smith to Stephens, Dec. 9, Crawford to Stephens, Dec. 8, Stephens MSS; Thompson to Lamar, Jan. 6, 1861, Thompson Letter Book, War Dept. files, National Archives; Mayes, *op. cit.,* pp. 633-639.

12. Reuben Davis, *op. cit.,* p. 398; Jefferson Davis, *Works,* 8:460; Rhodes, *op. cit.,* 3:177-178 and notes; *36:2 H. Rept. 31* (Ser. 1104), pp. 4-5.

13. King, *Turning on the Light,* p. 32.

14. Johnston and Browne, *op. cit.,* pp. 367-370; *Toombs Corr.,* pp. 505-518.

15. *36:2 H. Rept. 31* (Ser. 1104), pp. 1-5.

16. *N.Y. Herald,* Dec. 13, 14; *N.Y. Times,* Dec. 13; *Washington Star,* Dec. 15; Davis, *Works,* 8:460.

17. *Toombs Corr.,* p. 522.

18. *N.Y. Herald,* Dec. 12, 18, 19; *N.Y. Times,* Dec. 17, 20; *Dollar Weekly Pennsylvanian,* Dec. 22; *Baltimore Sun,* supplement, Oct. 13, 1877.

19. *N.Y. Herald,* Dec. 18; *N.Y. Tribune,* Dec. 19.

20. Seward to Webb, Dec. 15, 1860, Webb MSS.

21. Rhodes, *op. cit.,* 3:154 n.; Barlow to Weed, Nov. 30, 1860, Weed MSS.

22. *O.R.,* Ser. 1, 1:81-82.

23. *Ibid.,* pp. 89-90; Crawford, *op. cit.,* pp. 71-75.

24. *O.R.,* Ser. 1, 1:125-128; Crawford, *op. cit.,* pp. 37-40; Buchanan, *Works,* 11:56-57; copy of these papers in Miles MSS.

25. Branch to Mrs. Branch, Dec. 11, 1860, Branch MSS, Raleigh.

26. Buchanan, *Works,* 11:57-67; F.O. 5, v. 740, No. 318, Dec. 18, 1860.

27. *N.Y. Herald,* Dec. 16.

28. *Washington Constitution,* Dec. 15.

29. Memorandum of Scott's interview with Buchanan, Dec. 17, Crawford MSS; Scott to Buchanan, Dec. 15, Buchanan MSS.

30. Buchanan, *Works,* 11:57-67, 320, 361-364; Toucey to Buchanan, Dec. 12, Buchanan MSS; Weed to Lincoln, Jan. 10, 1861, Lincoln MSS.

31. Clingman, *Speeches and Writings,* pp. 526-527; *Lancaster Daily Intelligencer,* Oct. 1, 1877; (Asheville) *North Carolina Citizen,* Oct. 11, 1877; *Journal of* [Mississippi] *Convention,* pp. 184-188; *Toombs Corr.,* pp. 522-523; *Washington Star,* Dec. 17, 18.

32. Crawford, *op. cit.,* pp. 87-88; Buchanan, *Works,* 11:68;

"Diary of a Public Man," *North Amer. Rev.*, 129:131 (hereafter
cited as "Public Man"); Campbell to Pierce, Dec. 19, 29, Cushing
to Pierce, Jan. 1, 1861, Pierce to Campbell, Dec. 24, Pierce MSS,
L.C.

33. Curtis, *Buchanan,* 2:426; Nicolay and Hay, *op. cit.,* 3:286;
Green to Buchanan, Dec. 28, Buchanan MSS; Barbee, "How Lincoln Rejected Peace Overtures in 1861," *Tyler's Quar.*, 15:137-
144; Baringer, *A House Dividing,* p. 209; Van Deusen, *Thurlow
Weed,* pp. 260-267.

34. *Journal of South Carolina Convention,* pp. 2-5.

35. Crawford, *op. cit.,* pp. 45-55; Fuess, *Cushing,* 2:273; Cushing to Lossing, Mar., 1865, Argosy Book Stores (N.Y.) *American
Catalogue No. 249,* item 197, 1945; "Public Man," p. 131.

36. Wyatt to Bigler, Dec. 26, 1860, Bigler MSS.

Chapter 22

1. Campbell to Pierce, Dec. 19, 29, 1860, Pierce MSS; ——— to
Gould, Feb. 2, enclosed in Gould to Weed, Feb. 22, 1861, Weed
MSS; Stearns to Sumner, Jan. 3, 1861, Sumner MSS; Gates,
"Southern Investments in Northern Lands Before the Civil War,"
Jour. South. Hist., 5:155-186; Thomas, "Southern Non-Slaveholders in the Election of 1860," *loc. cit.;* Dumond, *Secession
Movement,* pp. 113-145; Denman, *op. cit.,* pp. 87-122; Dorman,
op. cit., pp. 162-169; Rainwater, *op. cit.,* pp. 161-200; Greer, *op.
cit.,* pp. 617-650; Shugg, *op. cit.,* pp. 157-170; Caskey, *op. cit.,*
pp. 16-44; Davis, *Civil War . . . in Florida,* pp. 43-44, 53.

2. *Washington Star,* Nov. 14, 21, 22; Rhodes, *op. cit.,* 3:171-
172; Foner, *op. cit.,* pp. 208-238.

3. *36:2 S. Rept. 288* (Ser. 1090), *passim;* Rhodes, *op. cit.,* 3:154
n.; Potter, *op. cit.,* pp. 170-175; Baringer, *A House Dividing,* pp.
204-208; *36:2 Globe,* pp. 270, 1390-1391, App. p. 41.

4. *O.R.,* Ser. 1, 1:94-99; Crawford, *op. cit.,* pp. 76-78.

5. *Ibid.,* pp. 79-87, 119-121; Buchanan, *Works,* 11:70-73.

6. *O.R.,* Ser. 1, 1:103; Crawford, *op. cit.,* p. 75. A photographic
copy of the letter to Anderson in Black's handwriting signed by
Floyd is pasted in Military Book No. 43, pp. 46-47, War Dept.
files, National Archives.

7. *36:2 H. Rept. 78* (Ser. 1105), *passim.* Russell's firm usually
earned some $540,000 a year from government contracts, yet
Floyd had already issued conditional acceptances for 1861 to the
amount of $798,000, and all told $6,137,395 in unconditional
acceptances were already outstanding. On Jan. 1, 1861, the government owed Russell's firm only $8,750 (*ibid.,* pp. 13-14, 301).
Floyd to Duncan, Sherman, Nov. 17, Floyd to Pierce and Bacon,
Dec. 24, Floyd to Thompson, Dec. 29, 1860, Holt to Edward Hayman, Jan. 25, 1861, Military Book No. 43, pp. 17, 51, 58, 92,
War Dept. files, National Archives; *36:2 H. Rept. 79* (Ser. 1105),

p. 139; Buchanan to Capen, Jan. 27, 1864, Buchanan to Black, Mar. 18, 1861, Feb. 10, 1862, Black to Buchanan, Mar. 11, 1861, Buchanan MSS; Mrs. Thompson to Mrs. Cobb, Jan. 13, 1861, Clayton to Mrs. Cobb, Dec. 26, Mrs. Clayton to Cobb, Dec. 30, 1860, Cobb MSS; Crawford, *op. cit.*, pp. 214-216; P. M. Hamer to author, Sept. 6, 1943; Tupper to Miles, Apr. 19, 1858, Miles MSS.

8. *O.R.*, Ser. 3, 1:1-23; *36:2 H. Rept. 85* (Ser. 1105), pp. 12, 13; King, *Turning on the Light*, p. 200.

9. *36:2 H. Rept. 85* (Ser. 1105), *passim;* Maynadier to Simonton, Dec. 22, Speer to Buchanan, Dec. 24, citizens of Pittsburgh to Buchanan, Dec. 25, May to Buchanan, Dec. 26, Buchanan MSS.

10. Scott to Kemble, Dec. 27, Hist. Soc. of Pa.; King to Buchanan, Nov. 7, Buchanan to Brown, Dec. 25, 1860, Buchanan MSS; King to Holt, Dec. 14, Holt MSS; Black to Browne, Jan. 10, 1861, Dom. Letters, 53:354, State Dept. files, National Archives; King, *op. cit.*, pp. 24-25, 111-113.

11. Buchanan to Floyd, Dec. 25, Black to Buchanan, Christmas night, undated [Dec. 27, 1860], citizens of Pittsburgh to Buchanan, Jan. 4, 1861, Buchanan MSS; Crawford, *op. cit.*, pp. 216-217.

12. "Public Man," p. 131; Belknap-Sanders letters, Nov. 21, 1860, to Feb. 22, 1861, Sanders MSS, Confederate files, National Archives; *36:2 H. Rept. 85* (Ser. 1105), p. 13; Floyd to Buchanan, Dec. 26 in the evening, wrote that perhaps he was wrong about the two members of the cabinet and withdrew the remark, Buchanan MSS; *Diary of Orville H. Browning*, 1:466-467.

13. The account of events from Dec. 27 through Jan. 2 is taken from the following, unless otherwise noted: Crawford, *op. cit.*, pp. 143-161; *O.R.*, Ser. 1, 1:109 *et seq.; Philadelphia Weekly Press* articles, Aug. 11, 18, 25, Sept. 8, 15, 1881, Mar. 16, 1882, Mar. 4, Sept. 10, 17, 1883; Curtis, *op. cit.*, 2:315-506; Buchanan, *Works*, 11:5-165; Gorham, *Stanton*, 1:154-159; Nicolay and Hay, *op. cit.*, 2:296-447, 3:1-244; Auchampaugh, *op. cit.*, pp. 65-202; Brigance, *op. cit.*, pp. 76-112; "Narrative of Wm. Henry Trescott," *Amer. Hist. Rev.*, 13:528-556; Campbell to Pierce, Dec. 29, 1860, Pierce MSS, L.C.

14. Nicolay and Hay, *op. cit.*, 3:73-74; Campbell to Pierce, Dec. 29, Pierce MSS, L.C.

15. Floyd to Buchanan, Dec. 29, Buchanan MSS; Crawford, *op. cit.*, pp. 150-151; F.O. 5, v. 740, No. 334, Dec. 31, 1860.

16. Scott to Buchanan, Dec. 30, 1860, Buchanan MSS; *Philadelphia Press*, Aug. 11, 1881.

17. Black's MS is in the Buchanan MS, and the copy in Stanton's hand is among the Black papers. They are not identical as the President's copy has an addition urging action regarding Sumter.

18. "Public Man," p. 129; *Toombs Corr.*, p. 530.

19. Floyd to Buchanan, Dec. 30, Buchanan MSS.

20. Buchanan to Floyd, Dec. 31, in Crawford, *op. cit.*, p. 151; Hughes, "John B. Floyd: A Defence," *Tyler's Quar.*, 2:154-156; Hughes, "Floyd's Resignation, from Buchanan's Cabinet," *Tyler's Quar.*, 5:73-95; Auchampaugh, "John B. Floyd and James Buchanan," *Tyler's Quar.*, 4:381-388. Hughes denies Floyd was asked to resign. Hughes's father married an adopted daughter of the Floyds and lived with the Secretary, "Uncle John," during his Washington sojourn.

21. Holt to Black, "Sunday," Black MSS; Buchanan to Floyd, Dec. 31 in Crawford, *op. cit.*, p. 151; *O.R.*, Ser. 1, 1:119; Mrs. Thompson to Mrs. Cobb, Jan. 13, 1861, Cobb MSS.

22. *O.R.*, Ser. 1, 1:115-118, 120-125; "Public Man," p. 268; Stryker to Weed, Jan. 2, 1861, Weed MSS; Robert Anderson's brother, Larz, made a sudden trip to see him, Larz Anderson to Crittenden, Jan. 4, 1861, Crittenden MSS.

23. *O.R.*, Ser. 1, 1:129-132; *O.R. Navy*, Ser. 1, 4:219; Scott to Black, probably Jan. 6, 1861, v. XXXIV, No. 55951, Black MSS; Thompson to Buchanan, Jan. 8, 1861, Buchanan MSS; Thompson to Black, Jan. 14, draft of Black to Thompson, Mar. 18, Black MSS; Browne to Barlow, Jan. 4, Barlow MSS.

24. *O.R.*, Ser. 1, 1:318-330; Flippin, *op. cit.*, p. 172.

25. *O.R.*, Ser. 1, 1:252.

26. *Ibid.*, pp. 442-443.

27. *Ibid.*, pp. 443-445; *O.R.*, Ser. 4, 1:28-29.

28. Coulter, *op. cit.*, pp. 25-26; Smith, *Borderlands in the Civil War*, pp. 83-85; *N.Y. Herald*, Jan. 12, 1861; *Baltimore Sun*, Jan. 11, 1861.

29. *O.R.*, Ser. 1, 1:134, 252-253, 53:111; Crawford, *op. cit.*, pp. 178-180; Cowling statement, Crawford MSS; Thompson to Lamar, Jan. 6, 1861, Thompson Letter Book, War Dept. files, National Archives.

30. *O.R. Navy*, Ser. 1, 4:220.

31. Buchanan, *Works*, 11:100-106; Spaulding to Evarts, Dec. 31, 1860, Jan. 1, 1861, Weed MSS; Foner, *op. cit.*, 243-247; King, *op. cit.*, 41, 186-192; *Philadelphia Weekly Press*, Aug. 18, 1881; Crawford, *op. cit.*, 190; Dix to Seymour, Dec. 26, 1860, N.Y. Hist. Soc.; Mrs. Thompson to Mrs. Cobb, Jan. 13, 1861, Cobb MSS; King to Holt, Jan. 29, Holt MSS; Carlisle to Buchanan, Jan. 9, Greenwood to Buchanan, Feb. 8, Buchanan MSS.

32. Mrs. Gwin to Mrs. Cobb, Jan. 5, Cobb MSS.

33. Hamilton to Bigler, Dec. 31, 1860, Bigler MSS.

Chapter 23

1. *Washington Star*, Dec. 29, 1860; *N.Y. Herald*, Jan. 3, 5, 6, 1861; Cox, *Three Decades of Federal Legislation*, p. 28.

2. Rhodes, *op. cit.*, 3:254.

3. *36:2 Globe,* p. 237, App. p. 35.

4. *N.Y. Herald,* Jan. 7, 1861; Browne to Barlow, Jan. 6, Barlow MSS.

5. *Ibid.,* Jan. 4, Rhodes, *op. cit.,* 3:262-263; *36:2 Globe,* p. 646.

6. *Ibid.,* pp. 274, 279-280; Gilmer to Albright, Jan. 8, 1861, N.C. Archives.

7. *O.R.,* Ser. 1, Vol. 51, pt. 2, pp. 3, 4, Vol. 52, pt. 2, p. 3, Vol. 53, p. 610; *O.R.,* Ser. 4, Vol. 1, pp. 29, 46-47.

8. Caskey, *op. cit.,* pp. 16-41; Ramsdell, *Reconstruction in Texas,* pp. 15-19. When Governor Houston of Texas saw that a convention was bound to meet, he called the legislature in session a week before the date set. That body did not interfere, and the convention submitted the issue to the voters. They ratified secession to take effect Mar. 2, by a ratio of more than 3 to 1.

9. *36:2 Globe,* p. 264.

10. *Ibid.,* p. 269; Toombs to Keitt, Jan. 11, 1861, Pickens MSS.

11. *36:2 Globe,* p. 294; Black's drafts in Black MSS; Benjamin to Barlow, Jan. 8, Barlow MSS.

12. *36:2 Globe,* pp. 283-289, 295. Slidell's resolution passed on January 10, and Buchanan replied five days later defending his action. He at length decided to keep Holt as Secretary of War and sent his name to the Senate, Jan. 17; he was confirmed the next day. He was approved only because the Republicans voted for him against almost solid southern opposition. Horatio King was nominated Postmaster General on February 1, but he was not confirmed until February 12.

13. *36:2 Globe,* pp. 306-312.

14. *Ibid.,* pp. 328-332; F.O. 5, v. 759, No. 15, Jan. 15, 1861; Memorandum of Dec. 10, 1860, Bell MSS; Kemble to Rives, Jan. 22, 1861, Rives MSS.

15. *36:2 Globe,* pp. 341-344; Seward to Weed, Dec. 29, 1860, Weed MSS; Bayard to Bayard, Jan. 14, 18, 1861, Bayard MSS.

16. *O.R.,* Ser. 1, Vol. 51, pt. 2, p. 5; Browne to Barlow, Jan. 14, Barlow MSS.

17. *36:2 Globe,* pp. 351, 401.

18. *Ibid.,* pp. 404-409; Cox, *op. cit.,* pp. 78-79.

19. *O.R.,* Ser. 1, Vol. 53, pt. 2, p. 19.

20. Crawford, *op. cit.,* pp. 185-197, 218-234; Buchanan, *Works,* 11:109-111, 125-141; *O.R.,* Ser. 1, 1:134-137, 140-142; Anderson to Holt, Jan. 9, Friday 2 P.M., No. 3584, Holt MSS.

21. *O.R.,* Ser. 1, 1:350-351, 345, 342, 346-347.

22. *Ibid.,* pp. 333-342.

23. *Ibid.,* pp. 351-352.

24. *Ibid.,* pp. 444-445, Vol. 52, pt. 2, pp. 9, 13.

25. *36:2 Globe,* pp. 484-487; Moore to Branch, Jan. 26, Branch MSS, Duke Univ.; Benjamin to Barlow, Jan. 29, Barlow MSS.

26. *36:2 Globe,* p. 536.

27. *Ibid.,* pp. 221, 280.

28. *36:2 H. Rept. 31* (Ser. 1104), pp. 10, 13, 16, 19, 27.

29. *Ibid.*, pp. 29, 30, 32, 35-36, 38-39.

30. *36:2 Globe*, pp. 378, 625.

31. *Ibid.*, pp. 362, 365, 378.

32. *Ibid.*, pp. 498, 499, pp. 76-80.

33. *Ibid.*, pp. 508, 512, 1235, App. p. 103.

34. *Ibid.*, pp. 509, 597.

35. *Baltimore Sun*, Jan. 2-15, 1861; *O.R.*, Ser. 4, 1:39-42, 151-160; Clark, *op. cit.;* Radcliffe, *op. cit.;* Johnson to Branch, Feb. 3, 6, Branch MSS, Duke Univ.

36. Thomas Fitnam to Buchanan, Jan. 25, Buchanan MSS; Potter, *op. cit.*, pp. 305-306.

37. *Washington Star*, Jan. 26; *N.Y. Herald*, Jan. 27.

38. *36:2 Globe*, p. 668.

39. *N.Y. Herald*, Feb. 9.

40. Milton, *op. cit.*, pp. 533-534; Potter, *loc. cit.;* Baringer, *A Nation Dividing*, pp. 222-224.

41. *O.R.*, Ser. 1, Vol. 52, pt. 2, p. 6; Coulter, *op. cit.*, pp. 25-26.

42. Shanks, *op. cit.*, p. 146; Letcher to Davidson, Mar. 9, 1861, Davidson MSS.

43. Buchanan, *Works*, 11:113-114, 120-121; *Washington Star*, Jan. 22, 24, 25.

44. Buchanan, *Works*, 11:116-120.

45. Crawford, *op. cit.*, pp. 244-246.

46. *O.R.*, Ser. 1, 1:354-355; Buchanan, *Works*, 11:122; Curtis, *op. cit.*, 2:462-466; Buchanan to Holt, Jan. 30, Stanton to Buchanan, Mar. 10, July 16, 1861, Buchanan MSS; Buchanan to Toucey, Mar. 7, 1861, Toucey MSS; Crawford, *op. cit.*, p. 248; Melvin, *op. cit.*, p. 151.

47. Crawford, *op. cit.*, pp. 231-232; Buchanan, *Works*, 11:126-141.

Chapter 24

1. *N.Y. Herald*, Feb. 6, 1861; *Harper's New Monthly Magazine*, 22:837.

2. *South. Hist. Soc. Papers*, 42:18-19.

3. *Journal of the Convention of the People of South Carolina*, pp. 185-188, 349-353; Gerson, "Inception of the Montgomery Convention," *Am. Hist. Assn. Ann. Rept. 1910*, pp. 179-189.

4. Smith, *History and Debates of Alabama Convention*, pp. 23-24, 31, 76, 118, 389-394.

5. *Journal of* [Mississippi] *Convention*, pp. 17, 21, 37, 39-40.

6. *36:2 Globe*, p. 771.

7. *Toombs Corr.*, p. 531; Flippin, *op. cit.*, pp. 177-185.

8. *Journal of* [Mississippi] *Convention*, pp. 11, 27, 30-35, 40, 46-50.

9. *Ibid.*, pp. 50-58, 74-75; *Charleston Mercury*, Feb. 6; Robi-

son, "Whigs in the Politics of the Confederacy," *Pubs. East. Tenn. Hist. Soc.*, No. 11, pp. 3-11.

10. *Charleston Courier*, Feb. 5, 14; *Charleston Mercury*, Feb. 6; *N.Y. Times*, Feb. 9; *N.Y. Herald*, Feb. 11; Wright, *A Southern Girl in '61*, p. 49; Davis, *Works*, 5:54; Stephens to Stephens, Feb. 4, 6, 8, 17, 28, Mar. 3, Stephens MSS, Convent.

11. *58:2 S. Doc. 234* (Ser. 4610), "Journal of Provisional Congress"; *N.Y. Herald*, Feb. 23; *Charleston Mercury*, Feb. 8; *Pubs. South. Hist. Assn.*, 11:160.

12. Davis, *Works*, 5:45.

13. Chesnut, *Diary from Dixie*, p. 6; Davis, *Works*, 8:461; *Pubs. South. Hist. Assn.*, 11:171; T. R. R. Cobb to Mrs. Cobb, Feb. 4, Cobb MSS; *Toombs Corr.*, pp. 536-537; Stephens to Stephens, Feb. 23, Stephens MSS, Convent; Johnston and Browne, *op. cit.*, pp. 389-391; Stovall, *Toombs*, p. 218; Phillips, *Toombs*, pp. 225-226.

14. *Charleston Courier*, Feb. 9, 21, Mar. 5; *Charleston Mercury*, Feb. 18, 19, 22, 23; *Toombs Corr.*, p. 544.

15. *Ibid.*, p. 535; *N.Y. Herald*, Feb. 9; *Pubs. South. Hist. Assn.*, 11:179-180.

16. *Ser. 4610*, pp. 41, 51-53, 59-60; *Pubs. South. Hist. Assn.*, 11:175-177; Curry, *Civil History of the Govt. of the Conf. States*, *passim*.

17. *Ser. 4610*, pp. 873-893; *Pubs. South. Hist. Assn.*, 11:284; Crawford to Branch, Feb. 12, Branch MSS, Duke Univ. The T. R. R. Cobb letters are printed with unindicated abbreviations in *Southern Historical Society Papers*, 28:280-301.

18. Milton, *op. cit.*, pp. 540-541.

Chapter 25

1. Potter, *op. cit.*, pp. 306-310; Chittenden, *Report of the Debates and Proceedings . . . of the Conference Convention*, *passim;* "Public Man," p. 129.

2. *36:2 Globe*, p. 489; Latham to Pierce, Feb. 6, 1861, Pierce MSS, L.C.

3. *36:2 Globe*, pp. 195, 728-729, 764; Bradford, "History of Colorado," Bancroft Transcripts, Colorado Archives; Perrigo's "Social History of Central City, Colo.," Ph.D. thesis, Univ. of Colorado.

4. *3:62 H. Repts. 58, 59* (Ser. 1104). Bingham's effort on March 2 to get the Cochrane bill up failed to secure the required two-thirds, 103-62. Cochrane and Horace Clark both voted against it, and only four Democrats voted for it (*36:2 Globe*, pp. 1422-1423). Belmont had written to Douglas urging him to work against it and the tariff (Belmont to Douglas, Feb. 11, 1861, Douglas MSS).

5. *36:2 H. Rept. 79* (Ser. 1105), presented Feb. 14; Colton,

"Irrepressible Conflict of 1861: Letters of S. R. Curtis," *Annals of Iowa*, 24:22; Seward to Weed, Dec. 29, 1860, Weed MSS; Keyes, *Fifty Years' Observation*, p. 358; Morgan to Scott, Jan. 15, Scott to Morgan, Jan. 17, Morgan MSS; Weed to Lincoln, Feb. 5, 10, Lincoln MSS.

6. *36:2 H. Rept. 85* (Ser. 1105); *N.Y. Herald*, Feb. 18; Rhodes, *op. cit.*, 3:239 n. Dawes reported on Feb. 21 criticizing severely Toucey's failure to mobilize the Navy in this time of national peril, *36:2 Globe*, p. 1095, while Branch defended him in a vigorous minority report, *ibid.*, p. 1096; *36:2 H. Rept. 87* (Ser. 1105).

7. *36:2 Globe*, pp. 1001, 1031-1033, 1066, 1097-1098, App. pp. 231-234; Potter, *op. cit.*, pp. 275-277; *N.Y. Herald*, Feb. 21, 23, 27, 28, Mar. 4.

8. King, *op. cit.*, p. 30; Hendrick, *Lincoln's War Cabinet*, pp. 253-254.

9. Crawford, *op. cit.*, pp. 246-247; Curtis, *op. cit.*, 2:468-469; Buchanan, *Works*, 11:141-143.

10. Tilley, *Lincoln Takes Command*, p. 153; *O.R.*, Ser. 1, 1:203-204; Crawford, *op. cit.*, pp. 249-251; Curtis, *op. cit.*, 2:469.

11. Buchanan, *Works*, 11:144; *N.Y. Herald*, Feb. 6, 11; *Washington Star*, Feb. 6.

12. *O.R.*, Ser. 1, 1:169-170, 175.

13. *Ibid.*, pp. 254, 257-258; Curtis, *op. cit.*, 2:469.

14. *Ibid.*, King, *op. cit.*, p. 45.

15. *O.R.*, Ser. 1, 1:177, 179-181.

16. *Ibid.*, p. 257.

17. *O.R.*, Ser. 4, 1:103, Resolution of Feb. 15.

18. *O.R.*, Ser. 1, 1:182-183.

19. Tyler to Buchanan, [Feb. 21], Holt MSS; Buchanan to Tyler, Feb. 22, Buchanan MSS; King, *op. cit.*, pp. 52-55; Crawford, *op. cit.*, pp. 274-275; Curtis, *op. cit.*, 2:494 n.

20. *Ibid.*, pp. 470, 485-490; Davis, *Rise and Fall*, 1:264.

21. Buchanan, *Works*, 11:124-125; *O.R.*, Ser. 4, 1:151-160.

22. *36:2 Globe*, p. 836; circular of Feb. 8, 1861, Bigler MSS.

23. Shanks, *op. cit.*, pp. 142-157; Patton, *op. cit.*, pp. 10-12; Sitterson, *op. cit.*, pp. 206-229; Laughlin, *Missouri Politics During the Civil War*, pp. 32-36; Viles, "Sections and Sectionalism in a Border State," *Miss. Valley Hist. Rev.*, 21:3-23; Mangum to Mangum, Apr. 8, Sept. 15, 1860, Mangum MSS, N.C. Archives; Mangum to Mangum, Apr. 8, 1860, Mangum MSS, L.C.

24. Smith, *The Borderland in the Civil War*, pp. 131, 133; Chadwick, *Causes of the Civil War*, p. 268; Patton, *op. cit.*, p. 12.

25. Chittenden, *Report of the Proceedings of the Conference Convention*, pp. 440-449, 471-473; Stampp, "Letters from Washington Peace Conference, 1861," *Jour. South. Hist.*, 9:394-403.

Chapter 26

1. Harriet Lane to ——, Feb. 26, 1861, L.C.
2. "Public Man," pp. 268, 379, 383; Johnson, *Douglas,* pp. 475-489.
3. *N.Y. Herald,* Mar. 5.
4. *Ibid.; Washington Star,* Mar. 4; *N.Y. Times,* Mar. 5; "Public Man," *loc. cit.;* Bomberger, *Twelfth Colony Plus,* p. 176. Randall (*Lincoln,* 1:295) questions the hat-holding incident, but no one yet has disproved the reliability of the statements of the "Public Man."
5. Nicolay and Hay, *op. cit.,* 3:319-344; *36:2 Globe,* pp. 1433-1434.
6. Buchanan's Memorandum of Mar. 9, Buchanan MSS; Crawford, *op. cit.,* pp. 283-285; Tilley, *op. cit.,* pp. 179-189, 306-312; Anderson's lost despatch of February 28 is found where it was expected in the recently opened Lincoln MSS. Lincoln sent it as soon as he received it to General Scott for his opinion. The General wrote a long memorandum on the back "in the night far from my papers" blaming Buchanan and Toucey for not sending a war ship instead of the *Star of the West* and charging that the latter vessel might have landed men and subsistence had it not been for the "imbecility of her commander." He recommended that Capt. Ward be called into consultation regarding reenforcement at this late date. On Mar. 6, Anderson's despatch of Mar. 2 giving details of his food shortage arrived. Anderson to Cooper, No. 58, Feb. 28 with ten enclosures and Scott's endorsement, same to same, [No. 60], Mar. 2, Lincoln MSS.
7. Crawford, *op. cit.,* pp. 314-345; Crawford to Toombs, No. 1, Mar., 1861, Confederate Archives, National Archives.
8. *O.R.,* Ser. 1, 1:261-263.
9. Crawford, *loc. cit.;* Bancroft, *William H. Seward,* 2:543; Tilley, *op. cit.,* pp. 271-289; Connor, *John A. Campbell,* pp. 122-148; Ellison, ed., "Memoirs of Hon. William M. Gwin," *Quar. Calif. Hist. Soc.,* 19:362-368.
10. "Public Man," pp. 490, 495.
11. Sitterson, *op. cit.,* pp. 216-229.
12. "Public Man," pp. 490, 495; *N.Y. Tribune,* Mar. 6.
13. *36:2 Globe,* p. 1436.
14. *Ibid.,* p. 1438; Randall, *Lincoln,* 1:376.
15. *O.R.,* Ser. 1, Vol. 53, p. 133, Vol. 52, pt. 2, p. 27, Vol. 51, pt. 2, p. 8.
16. Stanton to Buchanan, Mar. 12, Buchanan MSS; *N.Y. Times,* Mar. 11, 12; *N.Y. Tribune,* Mar. 11; *Baltimore Sun,* Mar. 12.
17. Tilley, *op. cit.,* pp. 32-35; Crawford, *op. cit.,* pp. 314-345.
18. *36:2 Globe,* pp. 1457-1465; "Public Man," p. 495.
19. Crawford, *op. cit.,* pp. 314-345.
20. Holt to Buchanan, Mar. 20, Buchanan MSS.

21. *36:2 Globe*, pp. 1468-1469, 1508; *O.R.*, Ser. 1, 53:136.

22. Tilley, *op. cit.*, pp. 271-289.

23. Nicolay and Hay, *op. cit.*, 3:390-392; Hurlbut to Lincoln, Mar. 27, Lincoln MSS.

24. Potter, *op. cit.*, pp. 353-358; Nicolay and Hay, *op. cit.*, 3:422-428.

25. *36:2 Globe*, p. 1501.

26. *Ibid.*, p. 1511.

27. Randall, *Lincoln*, 1:377.

28. Coulter, *op. cit.*, pp. 35-37.

29. *Baltimore Sun*, Mar. 22; *N.Y. Tribune*, Feb. 26, 27, Mar. 7, 8, 13, 28, Apr. 1, 2, 3, 5; *New Hampshire Patriot*, Mar. 13, 20; *N.Y. Herald*, Apr. 6; *Providence Post*, Apr. 3, 4; Lane, *Political History of Connecticut During the Civil War*, pp. 153-167.

30. *N.Y. Tribune*, Mar. 30; Nicolay and Hay, *op. cit.*, 3:428-449.

31. Lane, *loc. cit.*; *Providence Post*, Apr. 3, 4; *N.Y. Herald*, Apr. 6; *N.Y. Tribune*, Apr. 1, 2, 3, 5.

32. Milton, *op. cit.*, pp. 560-567; Ramsdell, "Lincoln and Fort Sumter," *Jour. South. Hist.*, 3:259-289; Barbee and Bonham, "Fort Sumter Again," *Miss. Valley Hist. Rev.*, 28:63-74; Stampp, "Lincoln and the Strategy of Defense in the Crisis of 1861," *Jour. South. Hist.*, 11:297-323; Douglas to Lincoln, Apr. 29, Lincoln MSS.

33. *37:1 Globe*, pp. 1-4; Buchanan, "James A. McDougall: A Forgotten Senator," *Quar. Calif. Hist. Soc.*, 15:199-212.

Chapter 27

1. Beale, "What Historians Have Said About the Causes of the Civil War," in *Theory and Practice in Historical Study*.

Bibliography

I. Manuscript Sources

William Allen MSS, Library of Congress*
Bancroft Transcripts, State Historical Society of Colorado
Nathaniel P. Banks MSS, Essex Institute
Nathaniel P. Banks MSS, Illinois State Historical Library
Baring MSS, Archives of Dominion of Canada
S. L. M. Barlow MSS, private library
Thomas F. Bayard MSS, L.C.
John Bell MSS, L.C.
Bernhisel-Young Correspondence, Archives of the Church of Jesus
    Christ of Latter-day Saints
John Bigelow MSS, New York Public Library
William Bigler MSS, Historical Society of Pennsylvania
Jeremiah S. Black MSS, L.C.
Blair Family MSS, L.C.
L. O'B. Branch MSS, Duke University
L. O'B. Branch MSS, North Carolina Archives
John C. Breckinridge MSS, L.C.
Sidney Breese MSS, Illinois State Historical Library
John Brown MSS, Historical Society of Pennsylvania
John Brown MSS, Kansas State Historical Society
James Buchanan MSS, Historical Society of Pennsylvania
James Buchanan MSS, Dickinson College
James Buchanan and Harriet Lane MSS, L.C.
W. W. Burwell MSS, L.C.
Asahel Bush Transcripts, University of Oregon
Benj. F. Butler MSS, L.C.
Andrew H. Calhoun, "A Vindication of John Calhoun," Kansas
    State Historical Society
Simon Cameron MSS, L.C.
Salmon P. Chase MSS, L.C.
Salmon P. Chase MSS, Historical Society of Pennsylvania
John F. H. Claiborne MSS, L.C.
C. C. Clay MSS, Duke University
Nathan Clifford MSS, Maine Historical Society
Howell Cobb MSS, University of Georgia
W. W. Corcoran MSS, L.C.
Erastus Corning MSS, Albany Institute of History and Art
John Covode MSS, Historical Society of Western Pennsylvania
Samuel W. Crawford MSS, L.C.
John J. Crittenden MSS, L.C.
Alfred Cumming MSS, Duke University

---

* Hereafter L.C.

J. L. M. Curry MSS, L.C.
Caleb Cushing MSS, L.C.
George M. Dallas MSS, Historical Society of Pennsylvania
J. D. Davidson MSS, McCormick Historical Association
J. C. Bancroft Davis MSS, L.C.
Matthew P. Deady MSS, Oregon Historical Society
Stephen A. Douglas MSS, University of Chicago
John W. Ellis MSS, University of North Carolina
William H. English MSS, Indiana Historical Society
William H. English MSS, University of Chicago
Edward Everett MSS, Massachusetts Historical Society
Ewing MSS, L.C.
Fallon Scrap Book, Historical Society of Pennsylvania
Jonathan M. Foltz MSS, private library
Solomon Foot MSS, Vermont Historical Society
Forney-Plitt photostats, L.C.
Horace Greeley MSS, New York Public Library
William M. Gwin MSS Memoirs, Bancroft Library, University of
    California
James H. Hammond MSS, L.C.
James H. Hammond MSS, University of South Carolina
Joseph Holt MSS, L.C.
Andrew Johnson MSS, L.C.
J. G. Jones MSS, private library
Thomas L. Kane MSS, Kane Manor
Thomas L. Kane MSS, Stanford University
Horatio King MSS, L.C.
Joseph Lane MSS, Oregon Historical Society
Lanphier-Patton MSS, private library
A. A. Lawrence MSS, photocopies, University of Kansas
Abraham Lincoln MSS, L.C.
John A. Logan MSS, L.C.
John A. McClernand MSS, Illinois State Historical Library
Mangum MSS, North Carolina Archives
Willie P. Mangum MSS, L.C.
William L. Marcy MSS, L.C.
Montgomery C. Meigs MSS, L.C.
Christopher Memminger MSS, University of North Carolina
W. Porcher Miles MSS, University of North Carolina
Benjamin Moran Diary, L.C.
Edwin D. Morgan MSS, New York State Library
J. Sterling Morton MSS, University of Nebraska
James W. Nesmith MSS, Oregon Historical Society
New England Emigrant Aid Co. MSS, Kansas State Historical
    Society
James A. Pearce MSS, Maryland Historical Society
Francis W. Pickens MSS, Duke University
Franklin Pierce MSS, L.C.

Franklin Pierce MSS, New Hampshire Historical Society
Rodman Price MSS, Rutgers University Library
John A. Quitman MSS, University of North Carolina
David S. Reid MSS, North Carolina Archives
W. C. Rives MSS, L.C.
Charles Robinson MSS, University of Kansas
MS Diary of Edmund Ruffin, L.C.
George N. Sanders MSS, L.C.
George N. Sanders MSS, Confederate files, National Archives
Horatio Seymour MSS, New York State Library
Slaymaker Collection, private library
J. F. Snyder MSS, Missouri Historical Society
Edwin M. Stanton MSS, L.C.
Alexander H. Stephens MSS, L.C.
Alexander H. Stephens and Linton Stephens MSS, Manhattanville
    College of the Sacred Heart, New York City (cited as Ste-
    phens MSS, Convent)
I. I. Stevens MSS, University of Washington
John W. Stevenson MSS, L.C.
Charles Sumner MSS, Harvard University
Richard M. Thompson MSS, Lincoln National Life Foundation
Samuel J. Tilden MSS, N.Y. Public Library
Isaac Toucey MSS, private library
Samuel Treat MSS, Missouri Historical Society
Lyman Trumbull MSS, L.C.
Tyler MSS, L.C.
Martin Van Buren MSS, L.C.
Elihu Washburne MSS, L.C.
J. Watson Webb MSS, private library
Thurlow Weed MSS, University of Rochester
Gideon Welles MSS, L.C.
John H. Wheeler Diary, L.C.
H. B. Wright MSS, Wyoming Historical and Geological Society,
    Wilkes-Barré, Pa.
Joseph A. Wright MSS, Indiana Historical Society

II. Archives

National Archives
    Attorney Generals' files
    Confederate files
    House of Representatives files
    Interior Department files
    Navy Department files
    Senate files
    State Department files
    Treasury Department files
    War Department files

Kansas Archives
  Governors' papers, Kansas State Historical Society
Mississippi Archives
North Carolina Archives
British Admiralty, Library of Congress copies
British Foreign Office, Library of Congress copies

III. Official Publications

Congressional Globe, 34, 35, 36, 37 Congresses, 1855-1861.

Congressional Documents:
34:1 H. Rept. 200 (Ser. 869).
35:1 S. Ex. Doc. 8 (Ser. 918), *11* (Ser. 920), *21, 22* (Ser. 924),
  49 (Ser. 929), *59* (Ser. 930), *61, 67* (Ser. 930); *1 H. Ex. Doc.
  33* (Ser. 955), *71* (Ser. 956); *1 H. Rept. 350* (Ser. 965), *351*
  (Ser. 965), *377, 378, 379* (Ser. 966), *412, 414* (Ser. 967), *549*
  (Ser. 968); *2 H. Ex. Doc. 24* (Ser. 1004); *2 H. Rept. 184* (Ser.
  1019), *186* (Ser. 1018), *188, 189* (Ser. 1020).
36:1 Sen. Ex. Doc. 20 (Ser. 1031); *1 S. Rept. 205* (Ser. 1040);
  1 H. Rept. 249 (Ser. 1068), *394* (Ser. 1069), *621* (Ser. 1070),
  648 (Ser. 1071); *2 S. Rept. 288* (Ser. 1090); *2 H. Ex. Doc. 7*
  (Ser. 1095); *2 H. Rept. 31, 58, 59* (Ser. 1104), *78, 79, 85, 87*
  (Ser. 1105).
37:2 H. Rept. 136 (Ser. 1145); *3 H. Rept. 26* (Ser. 1173).
40:3 H. Ex. Doc 9 (Ser. 1372).
43:2 H. Rept. 37 (Ser. 1654).
44:1 S. Rept. 277 (Ser. 1667).
58:2 S. Doc. 234 (Ser. 4610).
Sen. Ex. Journal, Vol. 10.
*Diplomatic Correspondence of the United States: Inter-American
  Affairs, 1831-1860,* ed. William Ray Manning. Washington,
  1932-1938.
*Register of Officers and Agents Civil Military and Navy in the
  Service of the U.S. on the thirtieth Sept. 1857.* Washington,
  1857.
*The War of the Rebellion: A Compilation of the Official Records
  of the Union and Confederate Armies.* Washington, 1880-1925.
*Statutes of the Territory of Kansas; passed at the First Session of
  the Legislative Assembly, 1855.* Shawnee, 1855.
*Laws of the Territory of Kansas passed at the Second Session of
  the Legislative Assembly held during the year of 1857.* Leavenworth, 1857.
*Report of Board of Commissioners for the Investigation of Elec-
  tion Frauds.* Leavenworth, 1858.
*Journal of House of Representatives of the State of Mississippi,
  1857.* Jackson, 1857.

Journal of the [Mississippi] *State Convention.* Jackson, 1861.
Journal of the Convention of the People of South Carolina. Columbia, 1861.

IV. Pamphlets

Address of the Democracy of Alabama to the National Democratic Convention at Baltimore, June 18, 1860. [N.p.], 1860.
Argument before the U.S. Circuit Court by I. W. Hayne on Motion to discharge the crew of the Echo delivered at Columbia, S.C., December 1858. Albany, 1859.
BLACK, JEREMIAH S., *Observations on Senator Douglas's Views of Popular Sovereignty.* Washington, 1859.
———, *Observations on Territorial Sovereignty consisting of three several answers to the magazine article, speeches and pamphlets of Senator Douglas.* [N.p.], 1860.
Documents Relating to the New York Contest, showing the claims of the Delegation Elected by Congress Districts . . . to seats in the Charleston Convention. N.Y., 1860.
Judge Douglas in Reply to Judge Black. [N.p.], 1859.
Grand Mass Meeting at Tammany March 4, 1858. [N.Y.], 1858.
JOHNSON, REVERDY, *Remarks on Popular Sovereignty.* [N.p.], 1859.
Kansas States Rights: An Appeal to the Democracy of the South, by a Southern States Rights Democrat. [N.p.], 1857. (At Kansas State Historical Society.)
Lecompton Question: Gov. Wise's Tammany, Philadelphia and Illinois Letters. [N.p.], 1858.
Letters to the Southern People Concerning the Acts of Congress and Treaties with Great Britain in Relation to the African Slave Trade. Charleston, 1858.
Memorial: Impeachment of James Buchanan, President of the United States. N.Y., 1860.
Private and Confidential on Government Matters—The Lecompton Crisis—Grand Mass Meeting at Tammany Hall, Thursday Eve., March 4, 1858, to strengthen the President. [New York], 1858.
The Private Letters of Lt. Gen. Winfield Scott and Ex-President Buchanan's Reply. New York, 1862.
Proceedings of the [Alabama] *State Democratic Convention, Jan. 11, 1860.* Montgomery, 1860.
Proceedings of the Massachusetts National Democratic Convention and of the Mass Meeting for the Ratification of the Nomination of Breckinridge and Lane, Tremont Temple, Boston, Sept. 12, 1860. Boston, 1860.
Reply of Joseph Holt to Jacob Thompson, Oct. 8, 1883. [N.p.], 1883.

Report of the Trials in the Echo Cases in Federal Court. [N.p.], 1860.

SCHADE, LOUIS, *Appeal to the Common Sense and Patriotism of the People of the United States—Helperism Annihilated—The Irrepressible Conflict and its Consequences.* [N.p.], 1860.

The Union! Its Dangers!! and how they can be averted—Letter from Samuel J. Tilden to Hon. Wm. Kent. [N.P.], 1861.

The Wanderer Case, the Speech of Henry R. Jackson. Atlanta, 1903.

V. Campaign Literature

A. 1856

Official Proceedings of the National Democratic Convention in . . . 1856. Cincinnati.

Life and Public Services of James Buchanan, by R. G. Horton. New York: Derby & Jackson.

Life and Public Services of James Buchanan, anonymous. New York: Livermore & Rudd.

The Democratic Hand-Book, compiled by Michael W. Cluskey.

The Virginia Resolutions of 1798.

Fremont: His Supporters and Their Record.

Read and Reflect! (Douglas's Report of Aug. 11, 1856.)

The Issue Fairly Presented: The Senate Bill for the Admission of Kansas as a State.

The Fearful Issue to Be Decided in November Next!

Short Answers to Reckless Fabrications. (Black, Reed, and Forney.)

Independent Treasury: Speech of Hon. James Buchanan of Pennsylvania.

Infidelity and Abolitionism: An Open Letter to the Friends of Religion, Morality, and the American Union.

Imposture Exposed! Fraud upon the People! The Accounts of Fremont Examined.

Black Republican Imposture Exposed! Fraud upon the People! Fremont No Soldier!

The Real Issue—Union or Disunion: Letter of Hon. S. S. Marshall.

The Immigration into the United States of America . . . by Louis Schade.

Letter of an Adopted Catholic.

Old Line Whigs for Buchanan & Breckinridge.

Letter of Ex-President Van Buren.

The Spurious Kansas Memorial: Debate in the Senate.

Josiah Randall's Speech for Buchanan, Aug. 6.

Rev. Henry Slicer's Speech, May 28.

Plain Facts and Considerations Addressed to the People of the United States. (By Nahum Capen.)

The North and South: The Crisis Before Us.
Fremont and His Speculations.
Dunn's Bill: Hypocrisy of Black Republicans in Congress.
The Agitation of Slavery: Who Commenced or Who Can End It!!
Letter of Samuel Caruthers to His Constituents.
Toombs Lecture in Tremont Temple, Jan. 24, 1856.
Rede von James L. Orr . . . in Concord, N.H.
Offener Brief eincs deutschen Bürgers an seine Mitbürger deutschen Geburt.
Was erheischt das deutsche Interesse bei der nächsten Präsidentenwahl und wie sollen die Deutschen stimmen?
Wm. B. Reed at Somerset, Pa.
R. J. Walker: An Appeal for the Union. (Also in French and German translation.)
Words of Counsel to Men of Business.
Are Working Men Slaves?
Which: Fillmore or Buchanan.
The Last Appeal to Pennsylvania.
Letter from Senator James Alfred Pearce, July 31, 1856.
Justice to "Buck": Papers containing several reasons why James Buchanan should receive the Distinguished Consideration of the People, by one who knows him well.
Speech of R. M. T. Hunter at Poughkeepsie.
> *Hon. J. R. Thomson, Aug. 9, 1856.*
> *Alexander H. Stephens, July 31.*
> *Lewis Cass, May 12-13.*
> *Alexander H. Stephens, June 28.*
> *Mr. Benjamin, May 2.*
> *Jas. C. Jones, Aug. 9.*
> *T. F. Bowie, Mar. 19.*
> *James A. Stewart, July 23.*
> *S. A. Douglas, Mar. 20.*
> *J. Glancy Jones, May 13.*
Speeches of Butler, Evans and Hunter, June 12, 23, 24.
The Life of the Hon. James Buchanan as written by Himself and set to Music by an Old Democrat, Price—"Half a Jimmy," Copy Right Secured in Cuban Bonds, Lancaster Near Wheatland, 1856.
Mr. Buchanan's Slavery Record: The American Banner Campaign Doc. No. 3.
Buchanan's Political Record: Let the South Beware!
James Buchanan, His Doctrines and Policy as exhibited by himself and friends. (Also in German translation.)
Gen. Jackson and James Buchanan: Letter from Francis P. Blair.
A Voice from the Grave of Jackson (Francis P. Blair).
Letter of Francis P. Blair to the Republican Association of Washington.

Facts for the People. Nashville. (Containing a facsimile of Jackson's letter to William B. Lewis, Feb. 28, 1845.)

B. 1860

1. Official Proceedings

Official Proceedings of the Democratic National Convention, held in 1860 at Charleston and Baltimore. Cleveland. (Douglas.)

Proceedings of the Conventions at Charleston and Baltimore Published by Order of the National Democratic Convention (Maryland Institute, Baltimore) and under the Supervision of the National Democratic Executive Committee. Washington. (Breckinridge.)

HALSTEAD, MURAT, *A History of the National Political Conventions of the Current Presidential Campaign.* Columbus, Ohio.

2. Publications of the Douglas Organization

Address to the Democracy of the United States, July 18.
Speech of Douglas, May 15.
Remarks on Popular Sovereignty by Reverdy Johnson.
Popular Sovereignty in the Territories: The Democratic Record.
Speech of John Forsyth.
Speech of Thomas L. Clingman on Senate Resolution.
Douglas on Invasion of the States.
Douglas in Reply to Seward.
Clingman Against Revolutionary Movement of Anti-Slavery Party.
Abraham Lincoln and His Doctrines.
Thomas J. Barr in Vindication of Catholic and Adopted Citizens.
Geo. E. Pugh's Reply to Iverson.
William Montgomery in Reply to Curry.
Breckinridge and Lane on Popular Sovereignty.
Exposure of the Conspiracy to Break up the Union.

3. Publications of the Breckinridge Organization

Address to the Democracy and the People of the United States.
Breckinridge and Lane Campaign Documents (a numbered series of at least nineteen, among which the numbers missing below have not been located):
  1. *Speeches of Hon. Humphrey Marshall and Hon. B. F. Hallett, in the City of Washington on the Nomination of Breckinridge and Lane.*
  2. *Minority Report of Mr. Stevens . . . Mr. Leach's Protest . . . Mr. Breckinridge's Acceptance of the Nomination—General Lane's Acceptance—The Democratic Platform.*
  3. *Benjamin's Speech of May 22, 1860.*

4. *Speech of President Buchanan, on . . . July 9, 1860.*
6. *Immense Gathering at Cooper Union, July 19.*
7. *Speech of Hallett of Massachusetts in Washington, June 25.*
8. *Biographical Sketches of Breckinridge and Lane.*
9. *Jefferson Davis's Reply to Douglas.*
10. *Breckinridge at Frankfort.*
11. *Breckinridge's Speech on Removal from Old Senate Chamber.*
12. *Crittenden's Speech, May 24, 1860.*
14. *Speech of . . . Toombs . . . on Property in Territories, May 21, 1860.*
17. *The Corruption and Extravagance of the Black Republican Party.*
19. *The Great Issue . . . Shall the Constitution and the Union Stand or Fall?—Shall Sectionalism Triumph?*
Lincoln and His Supporters.
Breckinridge's Speech at Ashland, Sept. 5.
The Rendition of Fugitive Slaves: The Acts of 1793 and 1850 . . . The Dred Scott Case—What the Court Decided.
Speech of the Hon. William B. Reed on the Presidential Question . . . Philadelphia, September 4, 1860.

VI. Newspapers

Alabama
Mobile Advertiser
Mobile Daily Register
Selma Weekly State Sentinel
Tuscaloosa Independent Monitor
California
Sacramento Daily Union
San Francisco Bulletin
District of Columbia
National Intelligencer
The Star
The States
The Union (later *The Constitution*)
Georgia
Savannah Republican
Illinois
Chicago Daily Democrat
Chicago Press
Chicago Times and Herald
Illinois State Journal
Indiana
Indianapolis Daily State Sentinel
Kansas
Emporia Kanzas News
Fort Scott Democrat

Herald of Freedom
Kansas City Enterprise
Kansas National Democrat
Kansas Tribune
Kansas Weekly Herald
Lawrence Republican
Leavenworth Times
Leavenworth Union
Leavenworth Weekly Journal
Lecompton National Democrat
Lecompton Union
Quindaro Chindowan
Topeka Commonwealth
Topeka Tribune
White Cloud Kansas Chief
Wyandotte Commercial Gazette
Kentucky
Louisville Democrat
Louisiana
Louisiana Commercial Bulletin
New Orleans Daily True Delta (also weekly edition)
Maryland
Baltimore Sun
Massachusetts
Springfield Republican
Mississippi
Aberdeen Sunny South
Missouri
St. Louis Republican
New Hampshire
New Hampshire Patriot
New York
Albany Atlas and Argus
New York Courier and Enquirer
New York Daily News
New York Evening Mirror
New York Evening Post
New York Express
New York Herald
New York Times
New York Tribune
North Carolina
North Carolina Citizen (Asheville)
North Carolina Standard
Wilmington Journal
Ohio
Cincinnati Gazette
Cleveland National Democrat

Oregon
  Portland Democratic Standard
Pennsylvania
  Dollar Weekly Pennsylvanian (Philadelphia)
  Lancaster Daily Intelligencer
  Philadelphia North American and U.S. Gazette
  Philadelphia Weekly Press
  Pittsburgh Gazette
Rhode Island
  Providence Post
South Carolina
  Charleston Courier
  Charleston Mercury
  Yorkville Enquirer
Tennessee
  Memphis Appeal
  Memphis Daily Morning Bulletin
Virginia
  Richmond Enquirer
Wisconsin
  Madison Daily Argus and Democrat
  Milwaukee Daily Enquirer
  Milwaukee Morning News

VII. General Literature

ADAMS, JAMES T., *America's Tragedy*. N.Y., 1934.

APTHEKER, HERBERT, *American Negro Slave Revolts*. N.Y., 1943.

AUCHAMPAUGH, PHILIP G., *James Buchanan and His Cabinet on the Eve of Secession*. Duluth, Minn., 1926.

BANCROFT, HUBERT H., *History of California*. San Francisco, 1888.

————, *History of Utah*. San Francisco, 1889.

BARINGER, WILLIAM E., *A House Dividing: Lincoln as President Elect*. Springfield, Ill., 1945.

BARNES, GILBERT H., *The Antislavery Impulse, 1830-1844*. N.Y., 1933.

BEALE, HOWARD K., "What Historians Have Said About the Causes of the Civil War," in *Theory and Practice in Historical Study*. N.Y. Social Science Research Council, 1946.

BEARD, CHARLES A., *The Republic*. N.Y., 1943.

BILLINGTON, RAY A., *The Protestant Crusade, 1800-1860*. N.Y., 1938.

BOMBERGER, C. M. H., *Twelfth Colony Plus*. Jeannette, Pa., 1934.

BOYD, WILLIAM K., *History of North Carolina, 1783-1860*. N.Y., 1919.

BROOKS, VAN WYCK, *The Flowering of New England, 1815-1865*. N.Y. 1936.

BRUMMER, SIDNEY DAVID, *Political History of New York State During the Period of the Civil War.* N.Y., 1911.

BRUNNER, ALBERT, *Reports of Cases Argued and Determined in the Circuit Court of the United States,* Vol. I. San Francisco, 1884.

CALLAHAN, JAMES M., *American Foreign Policy in Mexican Relations.* N.Y., 1932.

CARPENTER, JESSE T., *The South as a Conscious Minority, 1789-1861.* N.Y., 1930.

CASH, W. J., *The Mind of the South.* N.Y., 1941.

CASKEY, WILLIE M., *Secession and Restoration of Louisiana.* Baton Rouge, 1938.

CHADWICK, FRENCH E., *Causes of the Civil War, 1859-1861.* N.Y., 1906.

CHITTENDEN, LUCIUS EUGENE, *Report of the Debates and Proceedings . . . of the Conference Convention.* New York, 1864.

CLARK, CHARLES B., "Politics in Maryland During the Civil War." MS Ph.D. thesis, University of North Carolina, n.d.

COLE, ARTHUR C., *The Irrepressible Conflict, 1850-1865.* N.Y., 1934.

———, *The Whig Party in the South.* Washington, 1913.

CONWAY, C., *The Utah Expedition.* Cincinnati, 1858.

COULTER, E. MERTON, *Civil War and Readjustment in Kentucky.* Chapel Hill, N.C., 1926.

CRAVEN, AVERY, *The Coming of the Civil War.* N.Y., 1942.

———, *The Repressible Conflict, 1830-1861.* Baton Rouge, La., 1939.

CRAWFORD, COL. SAMUEL W., *The Genesis of the Civil War.* N.Y., 1887.

CREER, LELAND H., *Utah and the Nation* (University of Washington Publications in Social Science, Vol. VII). Seattle, 1929.

CRENSHAW, OLLINGER, *The Slave States in the Presidential Election of 1860.* Baltimore, 1945.

CURRY, JABEZ L. M., *Civil History of the Government of the Confederate States.* Richmond, 1901.

CURTI, MERLE E., *Growth of American Thought.* N.Y., 1943.

DAVIS, JEFFERSON, *The Rise and Fall of the Confederate Government.* N.Y., 1881.

DAVIS, WILLIAM W., *Civil War and Reconstruction in Florida.* N.Y., 1913.

DENMAN, CLARENCE P., *The Secession Movement in Alabama.* Montgomery, 1933.

DORMAN, LEWY, *Party Politics in Alabama from 1850 through 1860.* Montgomery, 1935.

DUMOND, DWIGHT L., *Antislavery Origins of the Civil War in the United States.* Ann Arbor, Mich., 1939.

———, *The Secession Movement, 1860-1861.* N.Y., 1931.

ELLIS, CHARLES, *Utah, 1847-1870.* Salt Lake City, 1891.

FITE, EMERSON D., *Presidential Campaign of 1860*. N.Y., 1911.

FONER, PHILIP S., *Business and Slavery*. Chapel Hill, N.C., 1941.

GABRIEL, RALPH H., *Course of American Democratic Thought*. N.Y., 1940.

GREELEY, HORACE, *The American Conflict*. Hartford and Chicago, 1865.

GREEN, FLETCHER M., *Constitutional Development in the South Atlantic States, 1776-1860*. Chapel Hill, N.C., 1930.

HAMMOND, OTIS G., ed., *The Utah Expedition* (N.H. Hist. Soc. Coll., Vol. XII). Concord, N.H., 1928.

HANSEN, MARCUS L., *The Atlantic Migration, 1607-1860*. Cambridge, Mass., 1940.

HELPER, HINTON R., *The Impending Crisis of the South*. N.Y., 1857.

———, *Compendium of the Impending Crisis of the South*. N.Y., 1860.

HENDRICK, BURTON J., *Lincoln's War Cabinet*. Boston, 1946.

HERNDON, WM. H. and WEIK, JESSE W., *History and Personal Recollections of Abraham Lincoln*, 3 vols. Springfield (1930) reprint of 1889 edition.

HODGSON, JOSEPH, *Cradle of the Confederacy*. Mobile, 1876.

HOLLISTER, OVANDO J., *Life of Schuyler Colfax*. New York, 1886.

VON HOLST, HERMANN, *The Constitutional and Political History of the United States*, Vol. 6 (1856-1859). Chicago, 1887-1892.

HOWE, DANIEL W., *Political History of Secession to the Beginning of the American Civil War*. N.Y., 1914.

HUBBART, HENRY C., *The Older Middle West, 1840-1880*. N.Y., 1936.

ITTER, WILLIAM A., "Election of 1860 with Special Reference to Pennsylvania." MS essay.

KEMBLE, JOHN H., *The Panama Route, 1848-1869*. Berkeley, Calif., 1943.

KLEIN, PHILIP S., *The Story of Wheatland*. Lancaster, Pa., 1936.

KNAPP, CHARLES M., *New Jersey Politics During the Period of the Civil War and Reconstruction*. Geneva, N.Y., 1924.

LAMON, WARD H., *Life of Abraham Lincoln*. Boston, 1872.

LANE, J. ROBERT, *Political History of Connecticut During the Civil War*. Washington, 1941.

LAUGHLIN, SCEVA B., *Missouri Politics During the Civil War*. Salem, Ore., 1930.

LLOYD, ARTHUR Y., *Slavery Controversy, 1831-1860.* Chapel Hill, N.C., 1939.

LUTHIN, REINHARD H., *The First Lincoln Campaign*. Cambridge, Mass., 1944.

MCCLURE, ALEXANDER K., *Our Presidents and How We Make Them*. N.Y., 1900.

MCGAVIN, E. CECIL, *United States Soldiers Invade Utah*. Boston, 1937.

McGrane, Reginald C., *Foreign Bondholders and American State Debts.* N.Y., 1935.

Malin, James C., *John Brown and the Legend of Fifty-six.* Philadelphia, 1942.

Martin, Edgar W., *The Standard of Living in 1860.* Chicago, 1942.

Meneely, A. Howard, *The War Department, 1861.* N.Y., 1928.

Milton, George F., *The Eve of Conflict.* Boston, 1934.

Moore, John Bassett, *American Diplomacy.* N.Y., 1905.

Myers, C. Courtlandt, "Rise of the Republican Party in Pennsylvania." MS Ph.D. dissertation, University of Pittsburgh.

Nevins, Allan, *Ordeal of the Union.* N.Y., 1947.

Parks, E. Taylor, *Colombia and the United States, 1765-1934.* Durham, N.C., 1935.

Patton, James W., *Unionism and Reconstruction in Tennessee, 1860-1869.* Chapel Hill, N.C., 1934.

Perkins, Howard C., ed., *Northern Editorials on Secession.* N.Y., 1942.

Perrigo, Lynn I., "Social History of Central City, Colorado, 1859-1900." MS Ph.D. thesis, University of Colorado, 1936.

Phillips, Ulrich B., *The Course of the South to Secession,* ed. E. Merton Coulter. N.Y., 1939.

———, *Life and Labor in the Old South.* Boston, 1929.

Potter, David M., *Lincoln and His Party in the Secession Crisis.* New Haven, 1942.

Radcliffe, George L. P., *Gov. Thomas H. Hicks of Maryland and the Civil War.* Baltimore, 1901.

Rainwater, Percy L., *Mississippi: Storm Center of Secession, 1856-1861.* Baton Rouge, 1938.

Ramsdell, Charles W., *Reconstruction in Texas.* N.Y., 1910.

Randall, James G., *The Civil War and Reconstruction.* Boston, 1937.

Rhodes, James Ford, *History of the United States from the Compromise of 1850,* Vols. 2 and 3. N.Y., 1904 ed.

Rippy, J. Fred, *United States and Mexico.* N.Y., 1926.

Russel, Robert R., *Economic Aspects of Southern Sectionalism, 1840-1861.* Urbana, Ill., 1923.

Schaper, W. A., "Sectionalism in South Carolina," *Amer. Hist. Assn. Ann. Rept. 1901.*

Scroggs, William Oscar, *Filibusters and Financiers.* N.Y., 1916.

Scrugham, Mary, *Peaceable Americans of 1860-1861.* N.Y., 1921.

Shanks, Henry T., *The Secession Movement in Virginia, 1847-1861.* Richmond, 1934.

Shugg, Roger W., *Origins of Class Struggle in Louisiana.* Baton Rouge, 1939.

Sitterson, Joseph C., *The Secession Movement in North Carolina.* Chapel Hill, N.C., 1939.

Smith, Edward C., *The Borderland in the Civil War.* N.Y., 1927.

SMITH, WILLIAM R., *The History and Debates of the Convention of the People of Alabama.* Atlanta, 1861.

SOULSBY, HUGH G., *The Right of Search and the Slave Trade in Anglo-American Relations, 1814-1862.* Baltimore, 1933.

SPARKS, EDWIN ERLE, ed., *Lincoln-Douglas Debates of 1858.* Springfield, Ill., 1908.

STREETER, FLOYD B., *Political Parties in Michigan, 1837-1860.* Lansing, Mich., 1918.

TAYLOR, ROSSER H., *Ante-Bellum South Carolina.* Chapel Hill, N.C., 1942.

TILLEY, JOHN SHIPLEY, *Lincoln Takes Command.* Chapel Hill, N.C., 1941.

Tribune Almanac

TULLIDGE, EDWARD, *History of Salt Lake City.* Salt Lake City, 1886.

TYLER, DAVID BUDLONG, *Steam Conquers the Atlantic.* N.Y., 1939.

VAN DEUSEN, JOHN G., *Economic Bases of Disunion in South Carolina.* N.Y., 1928.

VAN VLECK, GEORGE W., *The Panic of 1857.* N.Y., 1943.

WENDER, HERBERT, *Southern Commercial Conventions, 1837-1859.* Baltimore, 1930.

WHITNEY, ORSON F., *History of Utah.* Salt Lake City, 1892.

WILDER, DANIEL W., *Annals of Kansas.* Topeka, 1875.

WILLIAMS, MARY W., *Anglo-American Isthmian Diplomacy, 1815-1915.* Washington, 1916.

WILSON, HENRY, *History of the Rise and Fall of the Slave Power in America.* Boston, 1872-1877.

WISE, JOHN S., *Recollections of Thirteen Presidents.* N.Y., 1906.

WOLFE, JOHN H., *Jeffersonian Democracy in South Carolina.* Chapel Hill, N.C., 1940.

WOODWARD, WALTER C., *Rise and Early History of Political Parties in Oregon, 1843-1868.* Portland, Ore., 1913.

VIII. Biography

Letters, Speeches, and Addresses of August Belmont. N.Y., 1890.

Judah P. Benjamin, by Robert D. Meade. N.Y., 1943.

Retrospections of an Active Life, by John Bigelow. N.Y., 1909-1913.

Forgotten First Citizen: John Bigelow, by Margaret Clapp. Boston, 1947.

Essays and Speeches of Jeremiah S. Black, ed. Chauncey F. Black. N.Y., 1885.

Jeremiah Sullivan Black, by William N. Brigance. Philadelphia, 1934.

Reminiscences of Judge J. S. Black, by Mary Black Clayton. St. Louis, 1887.

"Jeremiah S. Black," by Roy F. Nichols, in *American Secretaries of State and Their Diplomacy*, ed. Samuel F. Bemis, Vol. 6. N.Y., 1929.

Twenty Years of Congress, by James G. Blaine. Norwich, Conn., 1884-1886.

John Cabell Breckinridge, by Lucille Stillwell. Caldwell, Ida., 1936.

Life of David C. Broderick, by Jeremiah Lynch. N.Y., 1911.

Speeches, Congressional and Political, and Other Writings, by Aaron V. Brown. Nashville, Tenn., 1854.

Albert Gallatin Brown, by James B. Ranck. N.Y., 1937.

"The Diary of Orville Hickman Browning," ed. Theodore C. Pease and James G. Randall, *Collections of the Ill. State Hist. Lib.*, Vol. 20.

Mr. Buchanan's Administration on the Eve of the Rebellion, [by James Buchanan]. N.Y., 1866.

Messages of President Buchanan, ed. J. Buchanan Henry. N.Y., 1888.

The Works of James Buchanan, ed. John Bassett Moore. Philadelphia, 1900-1911.

The Life of James Buchanan, by George Ticknor Curtis. N.Y., 1883.

The Republic: The Administration of James Buchanan, by John Robert Irelan. Chicago, 1889.

Autobiography and Personal Reminiscences of Major-General Benj. F. Butler: Butler's Book. Boston, 1892.

John Archibald Campbell, by Henry G. Connor. Boston, 1920.

General Lewis Cass, 1782-1866, ed. Cass Canfield. Norwood, Mass., 1916.

Lewis Cass, by Andrew Cunningham McLaughlin. Boston, 1891.

A Diary from Dixie, 1861-1865, by Mary Boykin Chesnut. N.Y., 1905.

Works of Rufus Choate with a Memoir of His Life, ed. Samuel G. Brown. Boston, 1862.

Reminiscences of Rufus Choate, by Edward G. Parker. N.Y., 1860.

A Belle of the Fifties, by Virginia Clay-Clopton. N.Y., 1905.

The Speeches and Writings of Thomas L. Clingman. Raleigh, N.C., 1877.

"Howell Cobb," by Neil V. Gannon. MS Ph.D. dissertation, University of California.

The Political Policies of Howell Cobb, by Zachary T. Johnson. Nashville, Tenn., 1929.

A Grandfather's Legacy, by W. W. Corcoran. Washington, 1879.

Three Decades of Federal Legislation, 1855-1885, by Samuel S. Cox. Providence, 1885.

Life of Caleb Cushing, by Claude M. Fuess. N.Y., 1923.

A Series of Letters from London Written During the Years 1856-60, by George Mifflin Dallas. Philadelphia, 1869.

Jefferson Davis, Constitutionalist: His Letters, Papers, and Speeches, ed. Dunbar Rowland. Jackson, Miss., 1923.

Recollections of Mississippi and the Mississippians, by Reuben Davis. Boston, 1889.

Stephen A. Douglas, by Henry M. Flint. Chicago, 1860.

Stephen A. Douglas, by Allen Johnson. N.Y., 1908.

George Fitzhugh: Propagandist of the Old South, by Harvey Wish. Baton Rouge, 1943.

Surgeon of the Seas: The Adventurous Life of Jonathan M. Foltz, by Charles S. Foltz. Indianapolis, 1931.

Casket of Reminiscences, by Henry S. Foote. Washington, 1874.

Anecdotes of Public Men, by John W. Forney. N.Y., 1873-1881.

"William McKendree Gwin," by Hallie M. McPherson. MS Ph.D. dissertation, University of California.

Reminiscences of James Alexander Hamilton; or Men and Events, at Home and Abroad, During Three-Quarters of a Century. N.Y., 1869.

James Henry Hammond, 1807-1864, by Elizabeth Merritt. Baltimore, 1923.

"Correspondence of R. M. T. Hunter, 1826-76," in *Amer. Hist. Assn. Ann. Rept. 1916*, Vol. 2.

Herschel V. Johnson of Georgia: State Rights Unionist, by Percy S. Flippin. Richmond, 1931.

The Life and Public Services of J. Glancy Jones, by Charles H. Jones. Philadelphia, 1910.

Private Papers and Diary of Thomas Leiper Kane, ed. Oscar O. Winther. San Francisco, 1938.

Fifty Years' Observation of Men and Events, by Erasmus D. Keyes. N.Y., 1884.

Turning on the Light, by Horatio King. Philadelphia, 1895.

Lucius Q. C. Lamar: His Life, Times, and Speeches, 1825-1893, by Edward Mayes. Nashville, Tenn., 1896.

Career of Joseph Lane, Frontier Politician, by Sister Margaret Jean Kelly. Washington, 1942.

R. E. Lee: A Biography, by Douglas S. Freeman. N.Y., 1934-1935.

The Early Life, Campaigns and Public Services of Robert E. Lee, by Edward A. Pollard. N.Y., 1867.

Abraham Lincoln: A History, by John G. Nicolay and John Hay. N.Y., 1890.

Lincoln the President, by J. G. Randall. N.Y., 1945.

Reminiscences, 1827-1897, by Robert M. McLane. (N.p.), 1903.

"William L. Marcy," by Henry B. Learned, in *American Secretaries of State and Their Diplomacy*, ed. Samuel F. Bemis, Vol. 6. N.Y., 1929.

The Public Life and Diplomatic Correspondence of James M. Mason, by Virginia Mason. N.Y., 1906.

The Life and Times of C. G. Memminger, by Henry D. Capers. Richmond, 1893.

Life of Hiram Paulding, Rear Admiral U.S.N., by Rebecca Paulding Meade. N.Y., 1910.

Benjamin F. Perry, by Lilian A. Kibler. Durham, N.C., 1946.

Franklin Pierce, by Roy F. Nichols. Philadelphia, 1931.

The Diary of James K. Polk, ed. M. M. Quaife. Chicago, 1910.

Perley's Reminiscences of Sixty Years in the National Metropolis, by Benjamin Perley Poore. Philadelphia, 1886.

J. H. Reagan Memoirs, ed. Walter F. McCaleb. (N.p.), 1906.

Robert Barnwell Rhett: Father of Secession, by Laura A. White. N.Y., 1931.

The Papers of Thomas Ruffin, ed. J. G. deR. Hamilton, Vol. 3. Raleigh, N.C., 1918-1920.

Life of William H. Seward, by Frederic Bancroft. N.Y., 1899.

Seward at Washington, by Frederick W. Seward. N.Y., 1891.

Recollections of Forty Years in the House, Senate, and Cabinet, by John Sherman. N.Y., 1895.

John Slidell, by Louis M. Sears. Durham, N.C., 1925.

Life and Public Service of Edwin M. Stanton, by George C. Gorham. Boston, 1899.

Alexander H. Stephens, by Rudolph von Abele. N.Y., 1946.

Life of Alexander H. Stephens, by Richard M. Johnston and William H. Browne. Philadelphia, 1878.

Biographical Sketch of Linton Stephens, by James D. Waddell. Atlanta, 1877.

Roger B. Taney, by Carl B. Swisher, N.Y., 1935.

In Memoriam: Benjamin Ogle Tayloe, by Winslow M. Watson. Washington, 1872.

"Life and Character of Jacob Thompson," by J. B. Bivins, in *Trinity College Hist. Soc. Pubs.,* Ser. 2, 1898.

"Life of Jacob Thompson," by Dorothy Z. Oldham. MS M.A. thesis, University of Mississippi.

The Life of Robert Toombs, by Ulrich B. Phillips. N.Y., 1913.

Robert Toombs, by Pleasant A. Stovell. N.Y., 1892.

"The Correspondence of Robert Toombs, A. H. Stephens, and Howell Cobb," *Amer. Hist. Assn. Ann. Rept. 1911,* Vol. 2.

Letters and Times of the Tylers, by Lyon G. Tyler. Richmond, 1884-1896.

Robert Tyler, by Philip G. Auchampaugh. Duluth, Minn., 1934.

Commodore Vanderbilt: An Epic of the Steam Age, by Wheaton J. Lane. N.Y., 1942.

Robert J. Walker, Imperialist, by William E. Dodd. Chicago, 1914.

James Moore Wayne, Southern Unionist, by Alexander A. Lawrence. Chapel Hill, N.C., 1943.

Thurlow Weed, by Glyndon G. Van Deusen. Boston, 1947.

Life of Henry A. Wise of Virginia, by Barton H. Wise. N.Y., 1899.

A Southern Girl in '61, by Louise S. Wright. N.Y., 1905.

The Life and Times of William Lowndes Yancey, by John W. Du Bose. Birmingham, Ala., 1892.

"David Levy Yulee," by Mills M. Lord. MS thesis, University of Florida.

Who Was Who, Chicago, 1943.

IX. Articles in Periodicals

APPEL, JOHN W., "The Political Revolution of 1860," *Cliosophic Essays* (Lancaster, Pa.), 1908.

AUCHAMPAUGH, PHILIP G., "The Buchanan-Douglas Feud," *Jour. Ill. State Hist. Soc.,* 25:5-48.

AUCHAMPAUGH, PHILIP G., "James Buchanan: The Bachelor of the White House," *Tyler's Quar. Hist. and Gen. Mag.,* 20:154-166, 218-234.

———, "James Buchanan: The Squire from Lancaster," *Pa. Mag. Hist. Biog.,* 55:289-300, 56:15-33.

———, "James Buchanan: The Squire in the White House," *Pa. Mag. Hist. Biog.,* 58:270-286.

———, "James Buchanan and Some Far Western Leaders, 1860-1861," *Pac. Hist. Rev.,* 12:169-181.

———, "John B. Floyd and James Buchanan," *Tyler's Quar. Hist. and Gen. Mag.,* 4:381-388.

———, "John W. Forney, Robert Tyler, and James Buchanan," *Tyler's Quar. Hist. and Gen. Mag.,* 15:71-90.

———, "The Trip and Addresses of James Buchanan," *Tyler's Quar. Hist. and Gen. Mag.,* 17:42-44.

———, "Washington's Birthday, 1860," *Tyler's Quar. Hist. and Gen. Mag.,* 25:170-178.

———, "James Buchanan: The Conservatives' Choice, 1856," *Historian,* Spring, 1945, pp. 77-90.

BARBEE, DAVID R., "Hinton Rowan Helper," *Tyler's Quar. Hist. and Gen. Mag.* 15:135-172.

———, "Hinton Rowan Helper's Mendacity," *Tyler's Quar. Hist. and Gen. Mag.,* 15:228-232.

———, "How Lincoln Rejected the Peace Overtures in 1861," *Tyler's Quar. Hist. and Gen. Mag.,* 15:137-144.

——— and BONHAM, MILLEDGE L., JR., "Fort Sumter Again," *Miss. Valley Hist. Rev.,* 28:63-74.

——— and BONHAM, MILLEDGE L., JR., eds., "The Montgomery Address of Stephen A. Douglas," *Jour. South. Hist.,* 5:527-553.

BARNES, ISAAC O., "National Hotel Disease," *Boston Med. Sur. Jour.,* 56:371-376.

BONHAM, MILLEDGE L., JR., "New York and the Election of 1860," *N.Y. History,* 15:124-143.

BOYD, W. K., "North Carolina on the Eve of Secession," *Amer. Hist. Assn. Ann. Rept. 1910*, 165-177.

BRIDGES, C. A., "Knights of the Golden Circle," *S.W. Hist. Quar.*, 44:287-302.

BROOKS, R. P., ed., "Howell Cobb Papers," *Ga. Hist. Quar.*, 6:152-173, 233-264, 355-359.

"Selections from the Correspondence of Bedford Brown," *Trinity Hist. Papers*, 6:66, 7:16.

BUCHANAN, RUSSELL, "James A. McDougall: A Forgotten Senator," *Quar. Calif. Hist. Soc.*, 15:199-212.

"Papers of John A. Campbell," *South. Hist. Soc. Papers*, 42:3-81.

CARSEL, WILFRED, "The Slaveholders' Indictment of Northern Wage Slavery," *Jour. South. Hist.*, 6:504-520.

CAUTHEN, CHARLES E., "South Carolina's Decision to Lead the Secession Movement," *N.C. Hist. Rev.*, 18:360.

CLARK, CHARLES B., "Politics in Maryland During Civil War," *Maryland Hist. Mag.*, 26:239-263, 381-394; 27:171-192, 378-399; 28:230-260.

"Thomas R. R. Cobb," *South. Hist. Soc. Papers*, 28:280-301.

"Correspondence of Thomas Reade Rootes Cobb," *Pubs. of the South. History Assn.*, 11:147-185, 233-266.

COCHRANE, JOHN, "The Charleston Convention," *Mag. of Amer. History*, 14:623.

COLE, ALLAN B., "Japan's First Embassy to the United States, 1860," *Pac. N.W. Quar.*, 32:131-167.

———, ed., "Private Journal of Henry A. Wise, U.S.N., on Board Frigate 'Niagara,' 1860," *Pac. Hist. Rev.*, 11:319-329.

COLTON, KENNETH E., ed., "Irrepressible Conflict of 1861: Letters of S. R. Curtis," *Annals of Iowa*, 24:22.

CORWIN, E. S., "The Dred Scott Decision in the Light of Contemporary Legal Doctrine," *Amer. Hist. Rev.*, 17:52-69.

CRENSHAW, OLLINGER, "C. G. Memminger's Mission to Virginia in 1860," *Jour. South. Hist.*, 8:334-350.

———, "Knights of the Golden Circle," *Amer. Hist. Rev.*, 47:23-50.

———, "Psychological Background of the Election of 1860 in the South," *N.C. Hist. Rev.*, 19:260-280.

———, "Speakership Contest of 1859-1860," *Miss. Valley Hist. Rev.*, 29:323-339.

"Address of Ex-Governor James W. Denver," *Pubs. Kans. State Hist. Soc.*, 1:167-174.

"Diary of a Public Man," *North Amer. Rev.*, 129:131 *et seq.* (Commonly cited in footnotes under the short title "Public Man.")

DODD, WILLIAM E., "The Fight for the Northwest, 1860," *Amer. Hist. Rev.*, 16:774-788.

DORN, HELEN P., "Samuel Medary, Journalist and Politician, 1801-1864," *Ohio State Arch. & Hist. Quar.*, 53:14-38.

DORPALEN, ANDREAS, "The German Element and the Issues of the Civil War," *Miss. Valley Hist. Rev.,* 29:55-76.

DOUGLAS, STEPHEN A., "Popular Sovereignty in the Territories," *Harper's Mag.,* Sept., 1859.

EATON, CLEMENT, "Censorship of the Southern Mails," *Amer. Hist. Rev.,* 48:266-280.

EATON, CLEMENT, "Mob Violence in the Old South," *Miss. Valley Hist. Rev.,* 29:351-371.

———, "Henry A. Wise: A. Liberal of the Old South," *Jour. South. Hist.,* 7:482-495.

———, "Henry A. Wise and the Virginia Fire Eaters of 1856," *Miss. Valley Hist. Rev.,* 21:495-513.

ELLIS, L. ETHAN, "Lecompton Constitution," *Jour. Rutgers Univ. Lib.,* 3:57-61.

ELLISON, WILLIAM H., ed., "Memoirs of Hon. William M. Gwin," *Quar. Calif. Hist. Soc.* 19:1-27, 157-193, 256-278, 344-368.

EWING, THOMAS, JR., "The Struggle for Freedom in Kansas," *Cosmopolitan,* May, 1894.

FOLK, EDGAR E., "W. W. Holden and Election of 1858," *N.C. Hist. Rev.,* 21:294-319.

FOLWELL, W. W., "The Sale of Fort Snelling, 1857," *Minn. Hist. Soc. Colls.,* 15:393-410.

FRASURE, CARL M., "Union Sentiment in Maryland, 1859-1861," *Maryland Hist. Mag.,* 24:210-224.

GATES, PAUL W., "A Fragment of Kansas Land History," *Kans. Hist. Quar.,* 6:227-240.

———, "Southern Investments in Northern Lands Before the Civil War," *Jour. South. Hist.,* 5:155-186.

GERSON, ARMAND J., "Inception of the Montgomery Convention," *Amer. Hist. Assn. Ann. Rept. 1910,* pp. 179-189.

GREEN, FLETCHER M., "Democracy in the Old South," *Jour. South. Hist.,* 12:3-23.

GREER, JAMES K., "Louisiana Politics, 1845-1861," *La. Hist. Quar.,* Vols. 13 and 14.

HENDERSON, GAVIN B., ed., "Southern Designs on Cuba, 1854-1857, and Some European Opinions," *Jour. South. Hist.,* 5:383-385.

HESSELTINE, WILLIAM B., "Pryor-Potter Duel," *Wis. Mag. Hist.,* 27:400-409.

HODDER, FRANK H., "Some Aspects of the English Bill for the Admission of Kansas," *Amer. Hist. Assn. Ann. Rept. 1906,* 1:201-210.

———, "Some Phases of the Dred Scott Case," *Miss. Valley Hist. Rev.,* 16:3-22.

HOFSTADTER, RICHARD, "U. B. Phillips and the Plantation Legend," *Jour. Negro Hist.,* 29:109-125.

HOLT, ROBERT D., "Career of William A. Richardson," *Jour. Ill. State Hist. Soc.,* 26:222-269.

House, Albert V., Jr., "Trials of a Ghost Writer of Lincoln Biography," *Jour. Ill. State Hist. Soc.*, 31:262-296.

Hughes, Robert M., "Floyd's Resignation from Buchanan's Cabinet," *Tyler's Quar. Hist. and Gen. Mag.*, 5:73-95.

———, "John B. Floyd: A Defence," *Tyler's Quar. Hist. and Gen. Mag.*, 2:154-156.

Huhner, Leon, "Moses E. Levy," *Fla. Hist. Quar.*, Apr. 1941.

———, "David L. Yulee," *Pubs. Amer. Jewish Hist. Soc.*, No. 17, 1917.

Hull, A. L., "Making of the Confederate Constitution," *Pubs. South. Hist. Assn.*, No. 9, pp. 272-292.

"In re Bates et al. (Echo)," *Federal Cases*, 2:1015.

Kendrick, B. B., "Colonial Status of the South," *Jour. South. Hist.*, 8:3-23.

Kibler, Lilian A., "Unionist Sentiment in South Carolina in 1860," *Jour. South. Hist.*, 4:346-366.

Klingberg, Frank W., "James Buchanan and the Crisis of the Union," *Jour. South. Hist.*, 9:455-475.

Landry, Thomas R., "Political Career of R. C. Wickliffe, Governor of Louisiana, 1856-1860," *La. Hist. Quar.*, 25:670-728.

"Day Journal of Milton S. Latham," *Quar. Calif. Hist. Soc.*, Vol. 11.

Lynch, William O., "The Westward Flow of Southern Colonists Before 1861," *Jour. South. Hist.*, 9:303-328.

McCormac, Eugene I., "Justice Campbell and the Dred Scott Decision," *Miss. Valley Hist. Rev.*, 19:565-571.

Mays, Elizabeth, "The Celebrated Mrs. Cobb," *Ga. Hist. Quar.*, 24:101-123.

———, "Making of an Ante-Bellum Lady," *Ga. Hist. Quar.*, 24:1-22.

Melvin, Philip, "Stephen Russell Mallory, Southern Naval Statesman," *Jour. South. Hist.*, 10:137-161.

Montgomery, Horace, "Solid South Movement in 1855," *Ga. Hist. Quar.*, 26:101-128.

"Monthly Record of Current Events," *Harper's New Monthly Magazine*, 22:837.

Murphy, Charles B., "Political Career of Jesse D. Bright," *Pubs. Indiana Hist. Soc.*, No. 10, pp. 101-145.

Myers, C. Maxwell, "Influence of Western Pennsylvania in the Campaign of 1860," *West. Pa. Hist. Mag.*, 24:229-250.

Nichols, Roy F., "Some Problems of the First Republican Presidential Campaign," *Amer. Hist. Rev.*, 28:492-496.

Odom, Van D., "Political Career of T. O. Moore, Governor of Louisiana," *La. Hist. Quar.*, 26:975-1055.

"On the Disease Affecting the Inmates of the National Hotel," *Amer. Med. Mon.*, June, 1857, pp. 347-358.

Owsley, Frank L., "Fundamental Cause of the Civil War: Egocentric Sectionalism," *Jour. South. Hist.*, 7:3-19.

OWSLEY, FRANK L., and OWSLEY, HARRIET C., "Economic Basis of Society in the Late Ante-Bellum South," *Jour. South. Hist.*, 6:24-46.

PERKINS, HOWARD C., "Defense of Slavery in the Northern Press on the Eve of the Civil War," *Jour. South. Hist.*, 9:501-532.

RAINWATER, PERCY L., ed., "Letters to and from Jacob Thompson," *Jour. South. Hist.*, 6:95-112.

RAMSDELL, CHARLES W., "Lincoln and Fort Sumter," *Jour. South. Hist.*, 3:259-289.

———, "The Natural Limits of Slavery Expansion," *S.W. Hist. Quar.*, 33:98 and *Miss. Valley Hist. Rev.*, 16:151-171.

RANCK, JAMES B., "Attitude of Buchanan Towards Slavery," *Pa. Mag. Hist. and Biog.*, 51:126-142.

RANDALL, JAMES G., "The Blundering Generation," *Miss. Valley Hist. Rev.*, 27:3-29.

REZNECK, SAMUEL, "Influence of Depression upon American Opinion, 1857-1859," *Jour. Ec. Hist.*, 2:1-24.

ROBISON, DANIEL M., "Whigs in the Politics of the Confederacy," *Pubs. East. Tenn. Hist. Soc.*, No. 11, pp. 3-11.

RUSSEL, ROBERT R., "Effects of Slavery upon Non-Slaveholders in the Ante-Bellum South," *Agric. Hist.*, 15:112-127.

ST. MATTHEW, J. H., "Walker's Administration in Kansas," *Overland Monthly*, 5:544-556.

SCHAFER, JOSEPH, "Who Elected Lincoln?" *Amer. Hist. Rev.* 47:51-64.

SCOTT, SUTTON S., "Recollections of the Alabama Democratic State Convention of 1860," *Ala. Hist. Soc. Trans.*, 4:313-320.

SHUTES, MILTON H., "Col. E. D. Baker," *Quar. Calif. Hist. Soc.*, 17:303-325.

SIOUSSAT, ST. GEORGE L., "Tennessee and National Political Parties, 1850-1860," *Amer. Hist. Assn. Ann. Rept. 1914*, 1:257.

SMITH, DONNAL V., "Influence of the Foreign-Born of the Northwest in the Election of 1860," *Miss. Valley Hist. Rev.*, 19:192-205.

SMITH, GEORGE, W., "Ante-Bellum Attempts of Northern Business Interests to 'Redeem' the Upper South," *Jour. South. Hist.*, 11:177-213.

SNYDER, J. F., "Democratic State Convention of Missouri in 1860," *Mo. Hist. Rev.*, 2:112-130.

STAMPP, KENNETH M., "Letters from Washington Peace Conference, 1861," *Jour. South. Hist.*, 9:394-403.

———, "Lincoln and the Strategy of Defense in the Crisis of 1861," *Jour. South. Hist.*, 11:297-323.

STENBERG, RICHARD B., "An Unnoticed Factor in the Buchanan-Douglas Feud," *Jour. Ill. State Hist. Soc.*, 25:271-284.

———, "Some Political Aspects of the Dred Scott Case," *Miss. Valley Hist. Rev.*, 19:571-577.

STONE, ROBERT K., "National Hotel Endemic," *Va. Med. Jour.*, 8:478-485.

THOMAS, DAVID Y., "Southern Non-Slaveholders in the Election of 1860," *Pol. Sci. Quar.*, 26:222-237.

"Narrative of William Henry Trescott," *Amer. Hist. Rev.*, 13:528-556.

"U. S. v. William C. Corrie," *Federal Cases*, 25:658.

————, *Monthly Law Reporter*, 23:145.

VAN ALSTYNE, RICHARD W., "The British Right of Search and the African Slave Trade," *Jour. Mod. Hist.*, 2:37-47.

VENABLE, AUSTIN L., "Conflict Between Douglas and Yancey Forces at Charleston," *Jour. South. Hist.*, 8:226-242.

VILES, JONAS, "Sections and Sectionalism in a Border State," *Miss. Valley Hist. Rev.*, 21:3-23.

"Governor Walker's Administration," *Kansas State Hist. Soc. Trans.*, 5:290-464.

WARING, JAMES J., "National Hotel Endemic Autopsy; with remarks," *Amer. Jour. Med. Science* (new series), 35:97-104.

WHITE, LAURA A., "National Parties in South Carolina," *South Atlantic Quar.*, 28:374.

WISH, HARVEY, "Revival of African Slave Trade," *Miss. Valley Hist. Rev.*, 27:569.

————, "Slave Insurrection Panic of 1856," *Jour. South. Hist.*, 5:206-222.

YULEE, C. WICKLIFFE, "Senator Yulee," *Fla. Hist. Quar.*, Apr.-July, 1909.

Index

Index

Accessory Transit Company, 187
Adams, James H. (Governor of S.C.), 57, 65, 352, 363, 427
Adrian, Garnett B. (Dem. congressman from N.J.), 172, 273, 400, 495, 467, 470
Agricultural college land grant, 196-97, 236
Ahl, John A. (Dem. congressman from Pa.), 243
Alabama, politics in 1857, 123; and Kans., 170; in election of 1859, 253-57, platform for 1860, 280-95; in conventions of 1860, 300-20; and secession 373-74, 410-13, 439
Albany Regency, 82-85, 259-61, 280, 311, 315, 320, 341, 345
Alexander, William C. (N.J. lawyer), 280, 466
Allen, James C. (Dem. congressman from Ill. and clerk of House), 157
Allen, Philip (Dem. senator from R.I.), 236
Allen, William (Dem. congressman from Ohio), 100
Allen, William (Dem. senator from Ohio), 311
American Atlantic and Pacific Ship Canal Company, 187
American Party, organized, 32-33; in South in 1857, 116, 123-24; preparing for ship, 272-76; in 1860, 337-38
Anderson, Lars (brother of Major Robert Anderson), 441
Anderson, Major Robert (commander at Charleston), 379-87, 402-09, 417-32, 440-42, 445-52, 471-73, 486-500
Andrews, Samuel G. (N.Y. congressman), 196
Anti-Lecompton bloc in House, 163-81; and speakership in 1859-1860, 274-77
Anti-slavery attitude; see Free Soil, Republican Party
Appleton, John (of Me., assistant secretary of state, minister to Russia), 67, 69, 72, 74, 79; and *Washington Union*, 103, 249
Argus (Philadelphia), 211, 250
Arkansas, and secession, 373, 475
Army, increase in, 179
Ashmore, John D. (Dem. congressman from S.C.), 356, 369-70, 371
Aspinwall, William H. (steamship operator), 186-87, 341
Astor, William B. (N.Y. financier), 341, 413
Atlantic and Pacific Steamship Company, 324-26
Attitudes affecting politics, 34-53, 60
Austro-Italian War, 255
Avery, W. W. (N.C. delegate at Charleston convention), 299

Ayer, Lewis M. (congressman-elect from S.C.), 355

Bailey, Godard (clerk in Interior Department), 419, 469
Baker, Edward D. (Rep. senator from Ore.), 477, 480
Baker, George W. (Collector Baker's brother), 209, 285
Baker, Joseph B. (collector of port of Philadelphia), 82, 98, 209-10, 258, 280, 285, 346
Baltimore convention of 1860, 312, 320
Bancroft, George (historian and Mass. politician), 262
Banks, A. D. (Va. editor), 158
Banks, Nathaniel P. (Rep., speaker of House), 58, 268
Barbour, James (member of Va. legislature), 449
Barksdale, William (Dem. congressman from Miss.), 165, 299
Barlow, S. L. M. (N.Y. railroad operator), 29, 30, 58, 73, 293
Barnburners, 30, 260
Barnwell, Robert (S.C. commissioner), 422-27
Barr, Thomas J. (Dem. congressman from N.Y.), 400
Barrancas Barracks, 442
Barrett, John R. (Dem. congressman from Mo.), 423
Bates, Edward (attorney general), 489
Bayard, James A. (Dem. senator from Del.), background, 19; at Cincinnati, 22, 28; talks post office bill to death, 244-45; at 1860 convention, 293-308, 312-29; for compromise, 392; in special session of 1861, 494-95, 501
Beard, Charles A., 22
Beauregard, Capt. P. G. T. (superintendent of West Point), 451, 471
Bell, John (Whig senator from Tenn.), and Pacific mail, 190; utters warning, 199; and Pacific railroad, 235; and Whig revival, 252, 253; nominated for President, 339; agrees to withdraw, 360; votes received, 372
Belmont, August (banker, kinsman of Slidell), 19; "soft" Dem., 95, 268; plan for Cuba, 231; delegate to Charleston, 292, 311, 313; chairman of national committee, 333, 336, 341, 344, 414, 434, 501
Benjamin, Judah P. (Whig and Dem. senator from La.), background, 19, 28; Cincinnati, 22; cabinet possibility, 70, 79; and internal improvements, 196; refuses Spanish mission, 233, 245; absent from Charleston, 293; urges secession,

399, 435; exposes Floyd, 424; leaves Senate, 443, 444; not sent to Montgomery, 456; in Davis cabinet, 461

Bennett, James Gordon (editor of *New York Herald*), 55, 71, 72, 328, 360

Bernhisel, Dr. John M. (Whig delegate to Congress from Utah), 109, 111, 183

Bigelow, John (N.Y. editor), 145

Bigler, William (Dem. senator from Pa.), and Buchanan, 68, 73, 82, 121; in Kans., 121, 123; "doughface," 153; supports Douglas, 229; and tariff, 237, 238, 467; campaign committee, 277; delegate to Charleston, 280, 283; money-raising, 334; for fusion, 345; defeat for reelection, 342, 389; for compromise, 393, 414, 416, 422, 433, 447, 474, 477-82; chairman of committee of commerce, 444; helps arrange Pickens truce, 450

Bingham, John A. (Rep. congressman from Ohio), 468, 470

Birdsall, Ausburn M. (naval officer of port of N.Y.), 260

Black, Jeremiah S. (attorney general and secretary of state), aids campaign of 1856, 65; Buchanan supports for Senate, 74; appointed attorney general, 80, 84; career, 89, 91; and Kans., 114, 123, 127, 161; and Pa. patronage, 208, 258; and Chicago post office, 216; and Douglas, 262-63; and Charleston delegation, 280; and Covode committee, 285-86; and slave trade, 293; and secession, 375-76, 403-09, 421-27, 270; appointed secretary of state, 405; and reenforcements, 417, 427, 441, 451-52; refuses to ask Floyd's resignation, 419; appointed to Supreme Court, 472

Blair, Francis P. (Dem. editor and Rep. propaganda writer), 71

Blair, Francis P., Jr. (Rep. congressman from Mo.), 23, 194, 223, 343

Blair, Montgomery (postmaster general), 489, 497

Bocock, Thomas S. (Dem. congressman from Va.), 273, 392, 470

Bonham, Milledge L. (Dem. congressman from S.C.), 177, 179, 371, 417, 430

Boteler, Alexander R. (Am. congressman from Va.), 392, 394, 448

Bouligny, John Edward (opposition congressman from La.), 393

Bowman, George W. (superintendent of printing, proprietor of *Constitution*, Senate printer), 249, 329, 421

Boyce, W. W. (Dem. congressman from S.C.), 256, 356, 357, 371, 456

Brady, James T. (New Yorker at Montgomery convention), 459

Bragg, Thomas (Dem. governor of N.C., senator), 57, 444

Branch, Lawrence O'B. (Dem. congressman from N.C.), 404, 468

Brazil, slave trade, 185

Breckinridge, John C. (Vice President), nominated for Vice President, 31; inaugurated, 83; kinsman of Floyd, 90; residence, 136; supports Douglas, 219; speaks in new senate, 229; declines Spanish mission, 232; kills homestead bill, 235; in 1859, 254; Pa. support, 280; elected to Senate. 281; nominated for Presidency, 294, 312, 317-18; in campaign of 1860, 332, 367, 372; agrees to withdraw, 360; and secession, 397, 414, 430-31; asks Floyd's resignation, 419; plot to make president, 421; in special session of 1861, 483-98

Bremen, mail to, 187-88

Bright, Jesse D. (Dem. senator from Ind.), background, 19; at Cincinnati, 22, 29; and Buchanan's cabinet, 55, 68, 70, 75, 78-79; and patronage, 99, 215; "doughface," 159; and Lecompton, 172, 214-15; elected to Senate, 180-81; and post office bill, 240; against Douglas, 277; at Charleston, 294-308; at Baltimore, 313, 320; on Breckinridge committee, 335; talks gas bill to death, 481, 485; in minority in Senate, 501

Brindle, William (receiver at Kans. land office), 128, 130

Broderick, David C. (Dem. senator from Calif.), 1855 roles, 101; enters Senate, 102; and Lecompton, 178-80, 263; opposes seating of Bright, 181; opposes increase in Army, 183; Calif. mail subsidy, 189; excluded from Senate caucus, 229; supports agricultural college bill, 236; killed, 263-64, 278

Brodhead, Richard (Dem. senator from Pa.), 68, 74

Bronson, Green C. (N.Y. delegate to Conference Convention), 466

Brooklyn, U.S.S., 405, 429, 432, 440, 443, 449

Brooks, Preston, 18

Brown, Aaron V. (postmaster general), appointed postmaster general, 70, 79; career, 90; in society, 150-51, 153, 154; and Kans., 161, 170; mail routes, 188-90; and Chicago post office, 216; death, 243-45, 246; character, 247

Brown, Albert G. (Dem. senator from Miss.), in Miss. politics, 123; supports Douglas, 229; radical demands of, 234, 282-85; friend of Southern yeomen, 253-54; and secession, 399, 442, 445

Brown, George W. (editor of *Herald of Freedom*), 110, 128

Brown, John (invader of Harper's Ferry), 121, 266-68, 353, 393

Brown, John Y. (Dem. congressman from Ky.), 272

Brown, Joseph E. (Dem. governor of Ga.), 123-24, 170, 253-54, 360, 371, 430

Browne, William M. (editor of *Constitution*), 250, 278, 361, 421, 422

Bryant, William Cullen (editor of *New York Post*), 146

Buchanan, James (15th president of U.S.), nominated in 1856, 26-27, 30, 31-32; campaign for president, 54-62; and Pacific railroad, 57; election strength, 60; and popular sovereignty, 64, 66, 71-73; choosing a cabinet, 65-75; and Pa. senatorship, 74-76; and Dred Scott case, 73, 78, 82; inauguration, 80-84, 514; personality, 87-88; and Kans. 104-24, 125-38; and Utah, 108-11, 183; and Silliman letter, 123; in society, 148, 150-51; and Lecompton, 159, 184; pocket veto, 190; coal bill, 191; and Pa. patronage, 208-10, 285; and elections of 1858, 212-25; lack of influence with congress, 227-28; vetoes agricultural college bill, 236; and tariff, 237-40; appoints Holt, 247; re-tunes organ, 248; disavows 1860 ambitions, 258-59, 280; and N.Y. city patronage, 259-60; and John Brown's raid, 266-67; 3rd annual message, 275; 302, 325-26; vetoes homestead, 325-26; and Calif. mail, 325-26; and Latin American treaties, 326; and Meigs 328; and Covode report, 329-30; endorses Breckinridge, 336; and secession, 374, 387, 400-09, 415, 432, 470, 484; plot to kidnap, 427; and compromise, 434, 435; and Sumter Truce, 441, 442; and Pensacola defenses, 442, 449, 451-52; and Conference Convention, 449-50; approves Kans. admission, 467; signs tariff, 468; last plans for reinforcement and arming, 471-74, 487, 488; and Lincoln's inauguration, 485-86

Buell, Lt. Col. Don Carlos (assistant adjutant general), 402-03, 418

Burch, John C. (Dem. congressman from Calif.), 390, 445

Burke, Edmund (of N.H., Polk's commissioner of patents), 337

Burnett, Henry C. (Dem. congressman from Ky.), 192, 392

Burns, Joseph (Dem. congressman from Ohio), 166, 167, 173, 223, 531

Burt, Armistead (representative of S.C. at Miss. convention), 455

Bush, Asahel (Ore. editor), 264-265

Butler, Andrew P. (Dem. senator from S.C.), 80

Butler, Benj. F. (Mass. delegate to national convention of 1860), 268, 298-302, 316, 318

Butler, George (N.Y. newspaper man with *Journal of Commerce*), 29

Butterfield, John (contractor for overland mail), 189, 468

Cagger, Peter (of N.Y., leader of Albany Regency), 95, 259-61, 314, 346

Calhoun, Andrew P. (representative of S.C. at Ala. convention), 408, 455

Calhoun, John (of Kans., surveyor general of Kans. and Nebr.), 113, 115, 116, 118, 120-21, 125, 129-33, 165, 168-69

Calhoun, John (of S.C.), 230, 283-84, 351, 352

California, 15, 48, 53; and patronage, 101-02; mail service to, 186, 189, 210-11, 323-25, 468; politics, 263-65, 278; see Pacific railroad

Cameron, Simon (Dem. and Rep. senator from Pa.), 74-75, 178, 197, 200, 489-92

Campaign clubs, 56, 334, 337, 469, 488, 491

Campaign funds in 1856, 55, 58, 59, 60, 81; in 1858, 210-11; in 1860, 333, 336, 341, 345, 346

Campaign literature, 56, 333-34, 336-37

Campaign of 1856, 54-62

Campaign of 1860, 331-66

Campbell, James (postmaster general), 79, 361

Campbell, John A. (of Ala., associate justice of Supreme Court), 77-78, 90, 391, 407, 412, 453, 495

Carey, Patrick N. (newspaper man, stenographer of Robert J. Walker), 116

Carlisle, James M. (Wash. attorney), 405, 432

Carpenter, R. B. (Chicago disbursing officer), 100, 216

Carr, Lt. Eugene A. (military aide of Robert J. Walker), 116

Caruthers, Samuel (Whig and Dem. congressman from Mo.), 165, 175

Cass, Lewis (secretary of state), runs for President, 23, 25, 28, 29; enters cabinet, 70, 74, 75, 79, 81; career, 90; and Mich. patronage, 88; and Kans., 127, 160, 161, 171; and residence, 148-49, 151; and conscription, 254-55; and secession, 375, 387; resigns, 405-06

Catholic issue in politics, 32-33, 207, 211, 334, 345

Cato, Sterling G. (judge in Kans.), 126, 128

Catron, John (of Tenn., associate justice of Supreme Court), 76-78, 85, 153

Caucus, in Senate, 239, 240, 284; on secession, 395-98, 430; on compromise, 443-45

Cavanaugh, James M. (Minn. congressman), 236

Census of 1860, 453-54

Central American policy, 325-26

Chaffee, Edwin M. (inventor of vulcanizing process for rubber), 144, 197

Chandler, Zachariah (Rep. senator from Mich.), 196, 233, 235, 479

Chapman, Henry (Dem. congressman from Pa.), 177

Charleston, S.C., 288-93, 357, 377, 387, 450, 454

Charleston Convention, 259-61, 288-304

Charleston Mercury, 65, 122, 250, 282

Chase, Salmon P. (senator and governor of Ohio), 214, 330, 486
Chase, Col. William (commander of Fla. militia), 442
Chesnut, James, Jr. (Dem. senator from S.C.), and secession, 356, 363, 368, 369; resigns, 371, 390; at Montgomery convention, 454, 456, 460
Chicago, Ill., postmaster removed, 170; harbor improvement, 196; anti-Douglas; corruption in post office, 247, 277
Chicago Times, 100, 121, 131, 135, 216, 218
Chivalry, in Calif., 101, 263, 278, 336
Choate, Rufus (Boston Whig lawyer), 56
Church, Sanford E. (N.Y. delegate at Charleston convention), 305
Cincinnati, Ohio, 28-33, 211, 213
Cincinnati *Enquirer*, 29, 214
Claim agents, 145-46
Clark, Daniel (Rep. senator from N.H.), 439
Clark, Horace F. (Dem. congressman from N.Y.), and Lecompton, 162, 174; mail subsidy, 187, 188, 324; running for reelection, 213, 224; and speakership, 273, 275; aids territorial bills, 467
Clarkson, J. J. (bearer of Lecompton constitution to Wash.), 163
Clay, Clement C., Jr. (Dem. senator from Ala.), supports Walker for cabinet, 69; on territorial committee, 168; opposes New England fishing bounties, 196; fears democracy, 200; opposed by Yancey, 221, 254; warns against Rep. president, 282; delaying S.C., 441-42; leaves Senate, 444-45
Clay, James B. (Dem. congressman from Ky.), 59, 84, 163, 165, 219
Clayton, Alexander M. (of Miss., Confederate congressman), 152-53, 462
Clemens, Sherrard (Dem. congressman from Va.), 447, 448, 476
Cleveland, Ohio, 170, 214
Clifford, Nathan (of Me., attorney general, associate justice of Supreme Court), 71, 79-80
Clingman, Thomas L. (Whig and Dem. congressman and senator from N.C.), 229, 310, 394, 395, 485, 490, 491
Clique, in Oregon, 264-65
Cluskey, Michael W. (Dem. propagandist), 277, 335
Cobb, Howell (secretary of treasury), favors Buchanan, 26, 57, 59; enters cabinet, 59, 61, 69, 81, 89; career, 91; and Kans., 121, 124, 130; and panic of 1857, 140-41; residence, 149; and Lecompton, 160, 166, 170, 173, 177; and revenue, 197-98, 216, 230; and tariff, 237-43, 250, 254, 260; and Presidency in 1860, 278, 310, 313, 320, 333; and campaign of 1860, 328, 346, 361-67; seeks Senate, 359; and secession, 375-87, 407, 432; re-

signs from cabinet, 396-98, 403; departs for S.C., 400, 407; and Confederacy. 454-465
Cobb, Mrs. Howell, 381-82
Cobb, John A.. 390
Cobb, Thomas R. R. (brother of Howell Cobb), 359, 360, 380, 456, 460, 462, 464
Cochrane, John (Dem. congressman from N.Y.), chairman of House commerce committee, 158, 196; running for reelection, 212, 224; and N.Y. patronage, 259-61; at Charleston, 299, 301; at Baltimore, 314-20; pressing compromise, 393-95, 399-402, 444, 446; aids territorial bills, 467; on committee of five, 469; bill for collecting revenue, 469; kills force bill, 470
Colfax, Schuyler (Rep. congressman from Ind.), 484
Collamer, Jacob (Rep. senator from Vt.), 414, 479
Collins, Edward K. (steamship operator), 186, 188
Colorado, 467, 493
Colt, Samuel (inventor of revolver), 144, 197
Columbus, Ohio, 170, 214
Commercial Convention, Southern, at Savannah, 66; at Vicksburg, 255
Committee of Thirteen of Senate, 392, 401, 414-16
Committee of Thirty-three of House, 394, 398-99, 400, 414, 446-49, 475
Confederacy, Southern, early suggestions, 221-23, 230, 256, 362; final plans, 413, 430, 440, 449; organized at Montgomery, 455-67; sends commissioners to Wash., 474-74
Confederate States of America, see Confederacy, Southern
Conference Convention, 449, 455, 466-75
Congress
  35th, 139-55; 1st session, 156-81; party strength in, 156-57, 158; in new House chamber, 160; and Kans., 162-81; and appropriations, 182-201; 2nd session, 226-45, 246-68; in new Senate chamber, 229
  36th, 1st session, 279, 287, 321, 330; 2nd session, 388-403, 413-16, 433-40, 445-49, 466-82
  37th, special session of Senate, 483-99
Congressional elections, in 1857, 121-23; in 1858, 205-25, 534; in 1859, 252-68; in 1860, 346, 374; spring of 1861, 499-500
Congressional investigations, corruption in House, 80; in 35th Congress, 193-96, 271; in 36th Congress, 285, 286. 328, 330
Connecticut, spring elections of 1861, 500
Connelly, Richard B. (N.Y. City politician), 259
Conrad, Charles M. (La. Whig, secretary of war, Confederate congressman), 253
Constitution of the Confederacy, 458-65

Constitutional Amendment, Corwin from Committee of 33, 476-82; from Conference Convention, 478-82

Constitutional Union Party, 338-39

Contested Congressional Seats, 271-72

Convention of 1856, Dem., 27-32

Convention of 1860, Dem., 288-308

Cook, Isaac (postmaster at Chicago), 100, 170, 216-19 224, 229, 248, 277, 337

Cooper, Edward (chairman of N.Y. City Dem. committee), 259

Cooper, James (Whig senator from Pa.), 237

Corbin, A. R. (clerk of House committee on claims), 194

Corcoran, W. W. (banker), 19, 28, 55, 57, 59, 481

Corning, Erastus (Dem. congressman from N.Y.) 95, 466, 501

Corrie, William C. (slave trader), 293

Corruption, 59, 80-81, 182-201, 271, 286, 287, 329, 330

Corwin, Thomas (Rep. congressman from Ohio), 395, 445, 448, 476-79

Covode, John (Rep. congressman from Pa.), 241, 285-86, 330-31

Cox, S. S. (Dem. congressman from Ohio), and Lecompton, 163, 174, 177, 179; election of 1858, 214, 223; compromise, 389, 394, 433, 501

Craig, James (Dem. congressman from Mo.), 189

Crawford, Martin J. (Dem. congressman from Ga.), 401, 464, 489, 492, 495

Cresson agreement in Pa., 340-41, 345

Crimean War 139

Crittenden, John J. (Whig senator from Ky.), and Kans., 169, 172, 176; and tariff, 197; supports Douglas, 220-221; and presidency, 226, 228-29, 338; and new chamber, 229; post office appropriation, 240, 242; defeated for Senate, 281, 282; for compromise, 393, 402, 403, 432, 439, 445-49, 479, 482; urged for Supreme Court, 496; speaks to Ky. legislature, 499

Crittenden Compromise, 402, 415-16, 432-36, 438, 445-49, 475-82, 497

Croswell, Edwin (N.Y. steamship operator), 186, 314, 321

Cuba, 66, 185, 231-33, 348

Cumming, Alfred (of Ga., governor of Utah), 111, 184-85

Curry, Jabez, L. M. (Dem. congressman from Ala.), 256

Curtin, Andrew G. (Rep. governor of Pa.), 342

Curtis, Benjamin R. (of Mass., associate justice of Supreme Court), 77, 84

Cushing, Caleb (chairman of Charleston convention), 296-308, 313-20, 406, 422

Cutts, J. Madison (father-in-law of Douglas), 136, 218-19

Dakota, 467, 493

Dallas, George Mifflin (of Pa., minister to Great Britain), 97

Daniel, Peter V. (of Va., associate justice of Supreme Court), 76-77, 84, 316

Davidge, William H. (steamship operator), 186-87

Davis, David (agent of Lincoln), 342

Davis, Henry Winter (Rep. and Am. congressman from Md.), 239

Davis, Jefferson (Dem. senator from Miss.), and Delta, 65; supports Walker for cabinet, 69; and Kans., 122-23, 177; and Utah appropriations, 188; answers Seward, 222-23; and new chamber, 229; and fortification appropriations, 241; rivalry with Brown, 254, 359; moderate, 257; and presidency, 279; resolutions, 282-85; and Charleston convention, 299, 310; and Meigs and Floyd, 327-28, 376-77; mentioned as military leader, 330; on Breckinridge's committee, 335; urged fusion, 360; advises Buchanan, 382-84; and secession, 398, 428, 430, 435, 437; and Crittenden Compromise, 402, 407, 415, 434, 480; on committee of 13, 414-15; keeps S.C. message from President, 417; and Sumter, 422, 441; and Floyd's resignation, 426; ill, 439; leaves Senate, 443-44, 467; and Confederate Presidency, 459, 461-62, 464, 473-74, 488-89, 495

Davis, Mrs. Jefferson, 390

Davis, John G. (Dem. and Rep. congressman from Ind.), 172, 215, 223, 273, 444

Davis, Reuben (Dem. congressman from Miss.), 397, 398

Dawes, Henry L. (Rep. congressman from Mass.), 468

Day, Horace H. (rubber lobbyist), 144-45

Deficiency bill, 35th Congress, 184

De Groot, William H. (contractor for Wash. aqueduct construction), 327, 376, 551, 552

De Jarnette, Daniel C. (Dem. congressman from Va.), 488

Delaware, 373

Delaware Crossing, Kans., 166, 169

Democracy, ambiguous character of word, 7; machinery of, 20-21; power conflicts in, 20-21; dangerous use of crisis, 20-21; loose organization of parties, 20; corruption in, 21; varied uses of word, 21; tensions in, 21, 139-41, 205; popular attitudes affecting, 34-53; opposition to, 52-53, 205-07, 241-42, 330, 350-56, 367-68; relation of to Civil War, 502-06

Democracy, American, see Democratic Party

Democratic National Executive Committee, 55, 57, 276-79

Democratic Party, organization, 19, 24, 86-87; "Laissez-faire" principles, 21; early history, 23-24; factions in, 23, 30; national committee, 25; national convention of 1856, 24-30; conflicting attitudes affect, 34-54; campaign of 1856, 54-62; use of patronage, 86-103; in Kans., 104-08; in 35th Congress, 156-81, 226-45; in elections of 1858, 205-25; use of foreign policy, 231-33; in elections of 1859, 246-68; in 36th Congress, 278-87, 321-22, 388-402, 413-16, 432-40, 444-48, 466-82; conventions of 1860, 288-320; campaign of 1860, 332-64; in South after election, 367-74; in North after election, 374-75, 413-14; and secession, 410-13; at Montgomery convention, 455-63; in 37th Congress, 482-98; disruption of and Civil War, 502-06

Democratic Platform, of 1856, 32, 34, 61-62; of 1860, 298-303, 317

Denver, James W. (governor of Kans.), 159, 160, 163, 168

Dewart, William L. (Dem. congressman from Pa.), 173, 180, 223, 237

Dickins, Asbury (secretary of Senate), 159

Dickinson, Daniel S. (of N.Y., leader of Hard Democrats), 96, 260, 280, 294, 316, 318, 336, 337, 341

Dimmick, William H. (Dem. congressman from Pa.), 223

Dix, John A. (postmaster of N.Y., secretary of treasury), 70, 268, 311, 413, 427, 431, 432, 451

Dixon, James (Rep. senator from Conn.), 448, 477, 479

Dodge, Henry (Dem. senator from Wis.), 99

Doolittle, I. (editor of The Spindle City Idea), 206

Doolittle, James R. (Rep. senator from Wis.), 414

Dorr, J. B. (Iowa editor), 262

Dougherty, John (organizer against Douglas in Ill.), 216, 218

Douglas, Stephen A. (senator from Ill.), at 1856 convention, 25-31; 54, 59, 62, 69, 70, 75, 78; and patronage, 99-100; and Kans., 105, 106, 115, 131, 133, 135-38; residence, 154; and Lecompton, 159-81, 184; election of 1858, 211-14; disciplined in Senate, 228-30; speech of Feb. 23, 1859, 234; in South, 251, 261-63, 279; strength in N.Y., 260-61; in Harpers, 262; loses Broderick, 263-64; and speakership, 273-76; pre-convention strength in 1860, 277-78, 281; in 36th Congress, 282, 286, 308-13; support at Charleston, 288-308; nominated at Baltimore, 312-20; and Floyd, 326-27; in campaign of 1860, 332-67, 371, 388; and secession, 360; refuses to withdraw, 361; in 36th Congress, 2nd session, 389-402, 438, 447-49; and compromise, 414-16, 433-40, 474, 479-82; and commercial union, 464-65; in Senate special session of 1861, 483-98; and Lincoln, 484-86, 490; death, 501

Douglas, Mrs. Stephen A., 136, 168, 263, 308, 484

Driggs. S. W. (editor of Lecompton National Union), 121, 125

Drinkard, Col. William R. (chief clerk of War Department), 422

Dry Tortugas, 376, 442

Duncan, William B. (N.Y. banker), 361

Dunn, William M. (Rep. congressman from Ind.), 398

Echo, 255

Economic influence in politics, 24-25, 38-39; in 1856, 54-55; on Congress, 182-201, 206-07; in 1860, 342, 348, 361, 362

Economy in appropriations, 182-201

Ellis, John W. (governor of N.C.), 368

Elmore, John A. (of Ala., governor's representative in S.C.), 454

Elmore, Rush (Kans., judge), 121, 125, 129, 163

English, William H. (Dem. congressman from Ind.), 158, 171-80, 223, 392, 446, 501

English Bill, 176-80

Etheridge, Emerson (Whig congressman from Tenn.), 392, 434

Everett, Edward (of Mass., candidate for vice president), 149, 252, 338

Fallon, Christopher (secret agent of Buchanan in Spain), 231-33

Faran, James J. (editor of Cincinnati Enquirer, postmaster of Cincinnati), 214

Fast Day, 1861, 404, 432

Faulkner, Charles J. (of Va., chairman of Dem. committee), 58

Federalism, in American politics, 20-21; cultural federalism, 34-53

Fillmore, Millard (13th President of U.S., candidate for President in 1856), 32, 58, 108, 111

Financial effects of secession, 413-14, 431-32

Fisher, Ellwood (steamship operator), 187

Fisk, Theophilus (assistant editor of Philadelphia Argus), 211

Fitch, Graham N. (Dem. senator from Ind.), 99, 159, 181, 217, 240, 277, 389, 474, 478

Fitzhugh, George (author of Sociology for the South), 206

Fitzpatrick, Benjamin (Dem. senator from Ala.), supports Walker, 69; president pro tem. of Senate, 159; kinsman of Elmore, 163; ill, 168; opposed by Yancey, 221, 254; nominated for vice president, 316-17; declines, 332; for delaying secession, 412; seeks pledge from Buchanan about reenforcements, 441; leaves Senate, 443

Fitzpatrick, Mrs. Benjamin, 316, 332

Florence, Thomas B. (Dem. congressman from Pa.), owns Argus, 211; reelected, 223; changes vote,

243; and compromise, 392, 400-01, 446

Florida, and secession, 373, 410-12, 438

Flournoy, Thomas B. (Ark. delegate at Charleston convention), 296, 309, 312

Floyd, John B. (secretary of war), in campaign of 1856, 59; enters cabinet, 70, 74 79; career, 91; and Utah, 111, 183, 184; and Va. politics, 122; and Kans.. 161, 170; and speculators, 194-95, 260, 266, 551-52; supports Douglas, 217; incompetence uncovered, 327-28, 551, 556; and secession, 376-87; and reenforcements, 402-09; downfall, 416-19; congressional investigation, 169

Floyd, Mrs. John B., 420, 427

Foley, James B. (Dem. congressman from Ind.), 180

Foltz, Dr. Jonathan M. (Buchanan's physician), 82-83

Foot, Solomon (Rep. senator from Vt.), 485

Force bills, 468-71

Ford, Thomas H. (Ohio Rep. House printer), 276

Foreign policy, political use of, 231-33

Forney, John W. (Pa. journalist), at Cincinnati, 27; in campaign of 1856, 55, 59; aiding Buchanan's cabinet-making, 69-70, 72; seeking Senate, 74-76; attacks Jones, 79-80; disappointed, 97-98; and Lecompton, 139, 177; and Pa. politics, 208-10, 220, 258, 280; elected clerk of House, 272-76; supports Douglas, 339, 346, 347

Forney, Mrs. John W., 75

Forsyth, John (Ala. Douglas supporter), 254, 262, 309, 312, 316-20, 359; appointed commissioner to Washington, 487; negotiates with Seward, 492, 495

Fort Jefferson, 376, 442

Fort Morgan, Ala., 429

Fort Moultrie, 377, 403-09, 413, 417-27, 440, 442

Fort Pickens, 430, 443, 444, 450, 451, 487, 492, 499

Fort Pulaski, Ga., 429

Fort Snelling, Minn., 194, 326

Fort Sumter, 185, 377, 403-10, 416-27, 440, 441, 450-51, 471-73, 487-506

Fort Taylor, 442-43

Fort Yuma, 189

Fortifications, appropriations 35th Congress, 185, 194

Foster, Henry D. (Dem. candidate for governor of Pa.), 339, 346

Foster, Capt. J. G. (in charge of building Fort Sumter), 377

Fouke, Philip B. (Dem. congressman from Ill.), 501

Fowler, Isaac V. (postmaster of N.Y.), 212, 259, 311

Fox, Capt. Gustavus Vasa (interested in reenforcing Sumter), 471-72, 495

Free Soil wing of Democrats, 23-33; the Republican Party, 32, 54

Freeport, Ill., debate, 221

Fremont, John C. (Rep. candidate for President in 1856), 18, 56, 57-58

Fry, Jacob (collector of port of Chicago), 217

Fuller, Henry M. (Am. congressman from Pa.), 345

Fusion in 1860, 338, 341, 344-47, 360

Gales and Seaton, 210

Gardner, Col. John L. (commander at Fort Moultrie), 377-79

Garnett, Muscoe R. H. (Dem. congressman from Va.), 80, 239, 488

Garrett, John W. (president of Baltimore and Ohio R.R.), 266

Garrison, Cornelius K. (agent of Vanderbilt), 187, 324-26

Garrison, William Lloyd, 43, 49

Gartrell, Lucius J. (Dem. congressman from Ga.), 177

Geary, John W. (governor of Kans.), 56, 66, 133

Georgia, politics in 1857, 122-24; and Kans., 170; election of 1859, 252, 257; and Cobb's candidacy, 279, 311; and slave trade, 293; in conventions of 1860, 299-318; and secession, 373-74, 410-13, 429-30, 439-40; accepts Montgomery invitation, 455

Giddings, Joshua (Free Soil congressman from Ohio), 180

Gillis, James L. (Dem. congressman from Pa.), 243

Gilmer, John A. (Whig congressman from N.C.). 400, 449

Gist, States Rights (agent of Governor Gist of S.C.), 362, 369

Gist, William H. (governor of S.C.), 362-63, 369, 387, 407

Glossbrenner, Adam J. (sergeant-at-arms of House, private secretary of Buchanan) 275, 427-28

Goddard, Mrs. Madeleine V., 166

Goggin, William L. (Am. candidate for governor of Va.), 256

Goode, William O. (Dem. congressman from Va.), 80, 199

Gray, J. W. (editor of Cleveland Plain Dealer, postmaster of Cleveland), 204, 214

Grayson, William J. (southern poet), 206

Greeley, Horace (editor of New York Tribune), 71, 178, 219, 220, 482

Green, Duff (Dem. worker behind scenes), 249, 345, 407

Green, James S. (Dem. senator from Mo.), and Lecompton, 167, 168, 175, 176; Calif. mail, 189-90; supports Douglas, 229, 262; moderate, 283; votes against compromise, 478; defeated for Senate, 485

Greenhow, Mrs. Rose (aunt of Mrs. Stephen A. Douglas), 154, 281, 308, 313

Greenwood, Alfred B. (Dem. con-

gressman from Ark., commissioner of Indian Affairs), 432
Grier, Robert C. (associate justice of Supreme Court), 66, 77-78, 83-84
Grimes, James W. (Rep. senator from Iowa), 326, 414
Groesbeck, William S. (Dem. congressman from Ohio), 166, 223
Grow, Galusha A. (Rep. congressman from Pa.), 165, 235, 241-42, 274, 393, 447
Gulick, Wm. B. (editorial writer for Washington Union), 219
Gurley, Rev. Dr. Phineas (chaplain of Senate 229, 274, 478
Guthrie, James (secretary of treasury), 279-81, 294, 305, 360, 466-75
Guy, John (proprietor of National Hotel, Wash., D.C.), 75, 82
Gwin, William M. (Dem. senator from Calif.), and Calif. politics, 101-02, 263-65; in society, 154; "doughface," 159; Calif. mail, 189, 240, 324, 325; and Douglas, 219, 229; and Pacific railroad, 235-36; and campaign of 1860, 294, 542; defeated for Senate, 389, 485, 542; power in Senate, 390, 439, 444, 461; negotiates with South, 488, 492
Gwin, Mrs. William M., 154, 332, 432

Hackney, Robert B., 193
Hale, John P. (Rep. senator from N.H.), 183, 200, 234, 394, 498
Hall, Lawrence W. (Dem. congressman from Ohio), 174, 175, 223
Hall, Lt. Norman J., 440, 471, 472
Hallett, Benjamin F. (of Mass., chairman of Dem. National Committee), 25, 59, 61, 62
Hamilton, Andrew J. (Dem. congressman from Texas), 392, 474
Hamilton, D. H. (marshal for S.C.), 417-18
Hamlin, Hannibal (Rep. senator from Me., Vice President), 338, 485
Hammond, James H. (Dem. senator from S.C.) and Lecompton, 176; attacks wage slavery, 206; counsels southern moderation, 222, 230; observes Senate, 287; and Charleston convention, 299, 308; opposes Central American policy, 326; and mail service, 357-58; and S.C. secession, 363-64; resigns, 371, 390
Hards (Hardshell Democrats), 30-36, 58, 95-96, 194, 260-61
Harlan, James (Rep. senator from Iowa), 479
Harney, Gen. Wm. S. (commander in Kans.), 107, 110
Harpers Ferry raid, 266-67
Harris, Arnold (steamship operator), 187
Harris, James M. (Am. congressman from Md.), 447
Harris, John T. (Dem. congressman from Va.), 433, 448
Harris, Thomas L. (Dem. congressman from Ill.), 157, 158, 162, 164, 166-67, 172, 173
Harris, William A. (proprietor of Washington Union), 103, 157, 158, 211
Haskin, John B. (Dem. congressman from N.Y.), anti-Lecompton, 162, 163, 174; reelected, 213, 224; and speakership, 273, 275; votes for tariff of 1861, 467
Hatch, Israel T. (Dem. congressman from N.Y.), 171
Havemeyer, William F. (candidate for mayor of N.Y.), 268, 341
Havre, mail to, 187, 188
Hawkins, George S. (Dem. congressman from Fla.), 395, 398
Hay, Alexander (rubber lobbyist), 145
Hayne, I. W. (attorney general of S.C.), 357, 440, 444, 450-51, 471
Heart, John (of S.C., superintendent of printing), 250
Heiss, John P. (proprietor of States and Union), 536
Helper, Hinton Rowan (author of The Impending Crisis), 258, 272-74
Hemphill, John (Dem. senator from Texas), 399
Henderson, John D. (editor of Leavenworth Journal), 125, 129
Henry, Alexander (mayor of Philadelphia), 209
Henry, J. Buchanan (nephew and private secretary of President Buchanan), 82, 153
Herndon, William H. (Lincoln's partner), 218
Herrick, Anson (naval storekeeper at N.Y.), 248
Hickman, John (Dem. and Rep. congressman from Pa.), 223, 273
Hicks, Thomas (governor of Md.), 268, 373, 448
Hill, Benjamin H. (candidate for governor of Ga.), 123, 413, 456, 464
Hill, Joshua (Am. congressman from Ga.), 177
Hill, Rev. Stephen P. (Wash. clergyman), 156
Hillyer, Junius (of Ga., solicitor of treasury), 311
Hindman, Thomas C. (Dem. congressman from Ark.), 474, 476
Hockaday, John M. (overland mail contractor), 109, 111, 189
Hoffman, Henry W. (Md. sergeant-at-arms of House), 276
Holliday, Cyrus K. (Kans. railroad promoter), 113
Holman, William S. (Dem. congressman from Ind.), 444
Holt, Joseph (postmaster general, secretary of war), appointed postmaster general, 247-48; and Chicago post office, 277; economies in post office department, 323, 357; ocean mail contracts, 324-25; patronage in 1860, 337; and secession, 375-86; and Fort Sumter, 422-27; secretary of war, 436, 456;

and reenforcements, 442-44, 451-52, 471-74, 486-87, 492
Homestead legislation, 196, 235-36, 287, 321, 338, 393
Hooker, Charles E. (Miss. governor's representative in S.C.), 454
Houston, George S. (Dem. congressman from Ala.), 445
Houston, Sam (senator from Texas and governor), 181, 183, 257, 336, 338, 362, 373, 557
Hovey, Daniel (federal district attorney in Ind.), 215
Howard, William A. (Rep. congressman from Mich.), 175-76, 239, 460
Howe, Timothy O. (Rep. senator from Wis.), 496
Hughes, James (Dem. congressman from Ind.), 164
Hughes, Robt. W. (editorial writer for *Washington Union*), 103, 219, 536
Hunkers (N.Y. Democrats), 30
Hunt, Washington (N.Y. Whig), 252
Hunter, Robert M. T. (Dem. senator from Va.), suggested for Presidency in 1856, 29; in Va. politics, 74-75, 254; residence, 80; and Kans., 122, 130; and Lecompton, 175, 176; seating Bright, 180; legislation control in 35th Congress, 183-84, 201, 237-42, 254; supports Douglas, 229; and the Presidency in 1860, 279, 294-308; and secession, 383-84, 414, 422, 426, 429, 438, 444, 450, 460, 462, 464, 473; in special session of 1861, 485, 488, 494
Hurlbut, Stephen A. (Lincoln's agent to S.C.), 495-96, 499
Hutch and Company, 232

Illinois, 25, 26, 60; and patronage, 100; in election of 1858, 216-19, 224
Immigration, 207
Impending Crisis, 258, 272, 348, 394
Inaugural of Gov. Robert J. Walker, 115, 117
Inauguration, of Buchanan, 80-84; of Lincoln, 485-86
Indian Trust Bonds, 419-20
Indiana, in election of 1856, 58, 60; and patronage, 100; district attorney removed, 170; senatorial elections, 181; in election of 1858, 214, 223; in election of 1859, 265
Inglis, John A. (chancellor of S.C.), 408
Ironmasters of Pennsylvania, 209, 231, 342
Isacks, A. J. (district attorney of Kans.), 115
Iverson, Alfred (Dem. senator from Ga.), supports Walker, 69; against English bill, 173; Calif. mail, 190; radical demands, 230, 234, 282; fight for his seat, 358, 380; opposes compromise, 394; and secession, 399; leaves Senate, 444

Jackson, James (Dem. congressman from Ga.), 380
Jamison, D. F. (chairman of S.C. secession convention), 360, 407-08
Johnson, Andrew (Dem. senator from Tenn.), opposes army increase, 183; and homestead legislation, 235, 321; friend of yoemen, 263-64; endorsed for President, 279, 293; vote at Charleston, 305; for compromise, 393, 399, 481; committee chairman, 444; against secession, 474, 478, 501
Johnson, B. L. (candidate for governor of S.C.), 368, 407
Johnson, Daniel H. (steamship speculator), 323-25
Johnson, Herschel V. (candidate for vice president), 333-67, 309, 413, 455
Johnson, Matthew (marshal of northern Ohio), 214, 336
Johnson, Reverdy (Md. lawyer), 107, 263
Johnson, Robert W. (Dem. senator from Ark.), 335, 430, 444, 474, 481, 536
Johnson, Simeon M. (editorial writer for *Washington Union*), 103, 219, 536
Jones, Geo. W. (Dem. senator from Iowa), 159, 167, 260
Jones, Jehu Glancy (Dem. congressman from Pa.), supporter of Buchanan, 27; in campaign of 1856, 55, 57, 59; career, 69; and cabinet, 74-75, 79-80; and *Union*, 72, 103; and Pa. patronage, 98; chairman of ways and means, 158. 183-201; defeat for Congress, 223; minister to Austria, 227
Jones, Owen (Dem. congressman from Pa.), 175, 180
Jones, S. J. (sheriff of Douglas County, Kans.), 128

Kane, Thomas L. (Philadelphian, friend of Mormons), 110-11, 183, 184
Kansas, 26, 27; in campaign of 1856, 56, 65-66; in 1857, 104-08; in 35th Congress, 156-81; elections, 1857-1858, 161, 165-66; House votes to admit, 321; admitted, 467
Kansas-Nebraska Act, 24, 25, 26, 62, 83, 164
Keitt, Laurence M. (Dem. congressman from S.C.), 165, 353, 355, 356, 359, 362, 371, 456
Kelly, John (Dem. congressman from N.Y.), 213, 259-61
Kelly, Moses (chief clerk and acting secretary of interior), 432
Kenan, A. H. (Ga. delegate to provisional Congress of Confederacy), 456
Kendall, Amos (campaign writer for Democrats), 55
Kennedy, Anthony (Am. senator from Md.), 181
Kennedy, J. C. G. (director of census), 400

Kentucky, 27; election in 1857, 124; election in 1859, 252-57; election in 1860, 343; and secession, 370, 430, 447 449, 474, 489, 499
Key West, 442
Kickapoo, Kans., 166, 169
King, Austin A. (Mo. delegate at Charleston convention), 299
King, Horatio (first assistant postmaster general, postmaster general\, 337, 427, 432, 556
King. Preston (Rep. senator from N.Y.), 436
Knights of the Golden Circle, 348, 411
Know Nothings, see American Party

Labor in politics, 56, 206-07, 236
Lamar, John B. (brother-in-law of Howell Cobb), 380
Lamar, L. Q. C. (Dem. congressman from 1 'iss.), 396
Lamon, Ward (Lincoln's agent to S.C.), 495
Lancaster, Pa., 67, 81
Lane, Harriet (niece of James Buchanan), 59, 82, 89, 98, 111, 308, 356, 427, 484
Lane, James H. (Kans. free-soil leader), 113, 126, 128
Lane, Joseph (Dem. senator from Ore.), enters Senate, 235-36; and post office economy, 240; Ore. politics, 264-65; candidate for Presidency, 278, 280-81, 295, 312; nominated for Vice President, 318-19; in campaign of 1860, 332-67; defeat for Senate, 389, 485, 501; power in Senate, 390; southern sympathy, 394, 423, 467; retires from Senate, 478-79
Latham, Milton S. (Dem. senator from Calif.), elected senator, 278; realist, 280-81; and Douglas, 309; and Calif. mail service, 324-26; 372; power in Senate, 390, 467
Latham, Robert W. (Floyd's business manager), 59, 91, 179, 194, 418
Law, George (steamship operator), 186-87, 341
Lawrence, Kans., 116-17, 119, 120, 129
Lawrence, William (Dem. congressman from Ohio), 174, 177, 179, 223
League of United Southerners, 221
Leavenworth convention, 174
Lecompte, Samuel (chief justice of Kans. territory), 66, 107, 126
Lecompton, Kans., 114-18
Lecompton Constitution, 125-38, 159-80
Lecompton Convention, 120-21, 125, 129-33
Ledyard, Henry (son-in-law of Lewis Cass), 78
Lee, Col. Robert E. (captor of John Brown), 266
Leib, Dr. Charles (mail agent in Ill., foe of Douglas), 216-17, 218
Letcher, John (Dem. governor of Va.), 157, 192, 256, 343, 449

Lillo, Léon, 228
Lincoln, Abraham (16th President of U.S.), and Douglas, 178, 217-19; nominated for President, 337; elected, 367; Buchanan communicates with, 407; and compromise, 415, 434, 438, 480; southerner in cabinet, 440; arrival in Washington, 470; and constitutional amendment, 475; inauguration, 483-88; seeking a policy, 489-500
Lincoln, Mrs. Abraham, 483, 486
Livingston, Mortimer (steamship operator), 186, 188
Loan bills, 35th Congress, 1st session, 197-98; 2nd session, 242-45; 36th Congress, 2nd session, 468
Lobby, Congressional, 143-46, 186
Logan, John A. (Dem. congressman from Ill.), 390, 501
Louisiana, 26, 252-57; new delegation for Baltimore, 313; and secession, 373, 410, 435
Lovejoy, Owen (Rep. congressman from Ill.), 286, 287
Lyons, Lord (British minister), 437

Maclay, William B. (Dem. congressman from N.Y.), 400, 467
Maclean, L. A. (clerk in Kans. land office), 115. 116, 118, 130
Magoffin, Beriah (governor of Ky.), 373, 431, 449
Magrath, A. C. (federal district judge in S.C.), 295, 357, 370
Magraw, Robert, 111
Magraw, W. M. F., constructing wagon road to Pacific, 109, 111
Mail carrying interests, 143-44, 186-90, 322-26
Maine, in election of 1856, 56-57; in election of 1858, 273; in election of 1859. 297; in election of 1860, 344
Mallory, Stephen R. (Dem. senator from Fla.), 200, 232, 423, 430, 441-44, 449-51
Marcy, William L. (of N.Y.), secretary of state), 30, 231
Marron, John (3rd assistant postmaster general), 243, 246
Marshall, Humphrey (Am. congressman from Ky.), 179
Marshall, Samuel S. (Dem. congressman from Ill.), 158
Martin, Henry L. (clerk in General Land Office), 130-32
Maryland, 48; election of 1859, 257-58, 268; and secession, 373, 448, 474
Mason, James M. (Dem. senator from Va.), in 1856, 57; residence, 80; and Bright's seat, 181; opposed subsidy, 200; fearing loss of power, 245; and Va. politics, 254; and John Brown, 266; opposed to democracy, 330; southern senators remain in Senate, 341; and secession, 383, 430; and Confederacy, 461-62; and compromise, 478-80; in short session of Senate, 485, 478-80.
Massachusetts, election of 1859, 268

Mather, John C. (N.Y. capitalist), 39, 194, 260

Mather, Craig, McIntyre and Bixby, 260

Matteson, Orsamus B. (Rep. congressman from N.Y.), charged with corruption, 193

Maynard, Horace (Am. congressman from Tenn.), 392-93

McClernand, John A. (Dem. congressman from Ill.), fails of appointment, 100; candidate for speaker, 273, 276; reelected to Congress, 390; and compromise, 392-93, 433; northwestern confederacy, 398, 501

McCook, George W. (Ohio delegate at Charleston convention), 246

McCormick, Cyrus (inventor of reaper), 144, 197

McCulloch, Ben (Texas ranger), 110-11

McDougall, James A. (Dem. senator from Calif.), 501

McGee precinct, Kans., 128, 129, 165

McGuire, J. C. (Wash. auctioneer and printing speculator), 249

McHenry, James, 232

McIlvaine, Charles (secretary to Robert J. Walker), 116, 129

McIntire, Peter (of Pa.), appointed collector of customs at Charleston, 427

McKean, William V. (clerk of Forney and Buchanan), 55

McKeon, John (N.Y. district attorney), 212

McKibbin, Joseph C. (Calif. congressman), 178

McLean, John (of Ohio, associate justice of Supreme Court), 77

McLean, Washington (proprietor of Cincinnati Enquirer), 29, 157, 214

McQueen, John (Dem. congressman from S.C.), 355, 371, 417

Medary, Samuel (governor of Minn. Territory, governor of Kans. Territory), 99, 214

Meigs, Capt. Montgomery (engineer in charge of Capitol construction), 327, 328, 375-76, 550

Memminger, Christopher G. (Confederate secretary of treasury), 458

Mexico, 66, 231, 325, 348

Miamis (Ohio Democrats), 99

Michigan, 29

Middle West confederacy, 330, 390, 398

Miles, William Porcher (Dem. congressman from S.C.), 199, 355, 359, 363, 371, 407, 464

Miller, Thomas (postmaster of Columbus, Ohio), 214

Millson, John S. (Dem. congressman from Va.), 392, 394, 400, 445, 449

Minnesota, 113, 169

Mississippi, politics in 1857, 122-23; legislature denounces Walker, 134; election in 1859, 253-57; and secession, 373, 408, 428; sends Thompson to N.C., 406; accepts invitation to Montgomery, 455

Missouri, 26, 29; election in 1857,

122; election in 1858, 223; election in 1860, 343; and secession, 374, 474

Mitchel, Charles B. (Dem. senator from Ark.), 485

Monk's Hall, 99

"Monopoly," The, 187, 188, 323-25

Montgomery, Ala., 430, 449, 455, 465

Montgomery, William (Dem. congressman from Pa.), 170, 172, 178, 223, 239, 280, 470

Montgomery-Crittenden proviso, 173, 174

Moore, Andrew B. (Dem. governor of Ala.), 259, 368

Moore, Ely (register in Kans. land office), 128, 130

Moore, Hugh (president pro tem. of Lecompton Convention), 129, 130

Moore, Thomas O. (Dem. governor of La.), 369

Morgan, Charles (agent of Vanderbilt), 187

Morgan, Edwin D. (Rep. governor of N.Y.), 469

Morgan, George W. (minister to Portugal), 529

Mormons, 108-11, 183-85

Morrill, Justin S. (Rep. congressman from Vt.), 238-39

Morris, Isaac N. (Dem. congressman from Ill.), 394, 401, 444

Morwitz, Dr. (editor of Pennsylvanian), 250

Mozart Hall, 212-13, 224, 259-61, 268, 340

National Democratic Executive Committee of 1860, 332-38

National Hotel, 45-46, 82, 83

Nationalism in politics, 50-51

Navy, appropriations, 35th Congress, 186; investigation, 271, 329

Negroes, 401, 415-16; see Slavery in territories

Nelson, Samuel (of N.Y., associate justice of Supreme Court), 77, 85, 495

Nesmith, James W. (Dem. senator from Ore.), 485

Nevada, 467, 493

New England, in politics, 26-27; fishing bounties, 196

New Jersey, election of 1859, 268; Charleston delegation, 280; in election of 1860, 341, 346

New Mexico, 439, 445, 446, 477

New York, 19, 23; patronage, 73-96; in election of 1858, 212-15; in election of 1859, 259-61, 266, 268-69; Charleston delegation, 314-20; Baltimore delegation, 315-22; in election of 1860, 340-41, 345-47, 361, 367

New York City; contributions in 1856, 57-59, 80; patronage, 93-96; in election of 1858, 212-13, 224-25; in election of 1859, 259-61, 268; postmaster absconds, 313; in election of 1860, 340-41, 345-47, 361, 367; proposed secession, 398, 434

New York Herald, 55, 71, 266, 268, 271, 275, 286, 340, 363

New York Times, 80, 116
New York Hotel Committee, 58-59, 95
Niblack, William E. (Dem. congressman from Ind.), 162, 166, 173, 180, 215, 223
Nicaragua, 66, 187, 323-24
Nicholson, A. O. P. (part owner of *Washington Union,* Senate printer, senator from Tenn.), 72, 78, 479
Nicolay, John G. (Lincoln's secretary), 490
North Carolina, 27; election of 1859, 252-57; election of 1860, 343; and secession, 373, 474, 490

Ocean main subsidy, 143-44, 186-87, 242-44, 323-25, 468
Ohio, 26, 27; and patronage, 99; in election of 1858, 213, 214, 223; in election of 1859, 265; spring elections of 1861, 500
Ohio Life Insurance and Trust Company, 140
Opdyke, George F. (Rep. candidate for mayor of N.Y.), 268
Opposition to Democrats in South, in 1859, 252, 267
Oregon, as a territory, 102; war debt, 197; admitted, 236; politics, 264-65, 272
Orr, James L. (speaker of House), elected speaker, 156-57; and Kans., 161, 164, 166-67, 175; rulings, 186, 239; supports Douglas, 219; in S.C. politics, 352-56, 363; S.C.'s commissioner in Wash., 421-27, 441; commissioner to Ga., 462
Ostend Manifesto, 58; Conference, 231
Otero, Miguel Antonio (delegate to Congress from N.M.), 390
Ould, Robert (district attorney of Wash.), 487
Overland mail, 189-90, 323-26
Oxford precinct, Kans., 126, 128, 166, 169

Pacific confederacy, 330, 390
Pacific Mail Steamship Co., 187
Pacific railroad, 31-32 54, 56, 66, 84, 104, 109, 113, 143, 196, 230, 235, 264, 286, 324, 338, 401, 439, 467
Packer, William F. (Dem. governor of Pa.), 209, 258, 280
Palmerston, Lord (British prime minister), 185
Panama isthmus, 186-87
Panic of 1857, 127, 132-46, 206
Parker, Miss Hetty (Buchanan's housekeeper), 82
Parrott, Marcus J. (Kans. delegate in Congress), 129
Patent renewals, 144, 197, 476; office, 236
Patronage, Buchanan's distribution of, 86-87; in South, 93; in California, 101-02; against Douglas, 170, 215-19, 311; in campaign of 1860, 337-38
Payne, Henry B. (Ohio lieutenant of Douglas), 214, 299

Pearce, James A. (Whig and Dem. senator from Md.), 56, 181, 444, 485-86
Pendleton, George H. (Dem. congressman from Ohio), anti-Lecompton at times, 162, 166-67, 173; reelected, 213, 237; and compromise, 303, 401, 501
Pennington, William (Rep. congressman from N.J., speaker of House), 276, 394
Pennsylvania, 26, 30; contributions in 1856, 59; election of 1856, 60, 80; senatorship in 1857, 74-76; patronage, 96-98, 208-11; election of 1857, 205; election of 1858, 206, 208-09, 236-38; election of 1859, 258-59, 265; Charleston delegation, 280, 300; election of 1860, 340-41, 344-46
Pennsylvanian, 208, 209, 250, 285
Pensacola Fla., 430, 442-44, 450-52
Pensions for veterans, 197
People's Party in Pa. 210, 258
Perrin, Edwin O., 116
Perry, B. F. (S.C. Union editor), 352, 356
Perry, Marshall S. (Dem. governor of Fla.), 429, 443, 454
Pettit, John (of Ind., federal judge in Kans.), 471
Pettus, John J. (Dem. governor of Miss.), 368
Phelps, John S. (Dem. congressman from Mo.), 157, 171, 227, 238-41, 242-43, 501
Phelps, Royal (N.Y. capitalist), 58, 268
Philadelphia, 59; patronage, 97, 208-11
Phillips, Henry M. (Dem. congressman from Pa.), 171, 238-39
Pickens, Francis W. (governor of S.C.), suggested for cabinet, 79; in S.C. politics, 353, 368; elected governor, 407; and secession, 416-27; and Sumter truce, 440-42; sends envoy, 450-51; urges confederacy, 455-59; and Haynes rebuff, 471-72
Pierce, Franklin (14th President of U.S.), 56; seeks renomination, 19, 24-31; removes Lecompte, 66; patronage errors, 69; his friends urge Toucey for cabinet, 71; entertains Buchanan, 75; Buchanan's inauguration, 83; and Chicago postmaster, 100; and Utah, 108; veto of pork barrel, 144; against "spite" removals, 337; urges fusion, 360; seeks to influence Ala., 406
Pittsburgh ordnance, 420-21
Plitt, George (treasurer of Pa. Democrats), 59
Plitt, Mrs. Sophie, 59
Plumer, Arnold (Pa. lieutenant of Buchanan), 280
Polk, James K., 23, 71, 95
Polk, Trusten (Dem. senator from Mo.), 190, 444, 476
Polygamy in Utah, 109

Popular sovereignty, 52; in platform of 1856, 61-62; in Kans., 66; in inaugural of 1857. 72, 82-83; see Democratic platform of 1860, and Douglas

Porter, Capt. Fitz-John (assistant adjutant general), 378-79

Post Office appropriations, 1st sessions, 35th Congress, 186, 190; 2nd session, 35th Congress, 239-45; omitted, 247-48; economies, 323-57; 1st session, 36th Congress, 324-25

Post Office blanks, 99, 207, 250

Potter, John F. (Rep. congressman from Wis.), 286-87

Powell, Lazarus W. (Dem. senator from Ky.), 394, 396, 402, 414, 449, 498

Pratt, Thomas G. (Whig senator from Md.), 56

Press, 55, 65, 71; editing Washington Union, 103; Pa., 209; and politics, 249-51; Douglas's press in 1860, 334; Breckinridge press in 1860, 337

Preston, William (minister to Spain), 233

Price, William (postmaster at Chicago), 100, 216

Printing, official, 71;˙ Congressional, 35th Congress, 157-58, 191-93; 210-11; 248-50; 36th Congress, 285-86, 328, 468

Printing Office, Government, 468

Pryor, Roger A. (Dem. Va. editor and Congressman), 286-87, 359, 488

Pugh, George E. (Dem. senator from Ohio), against army increase, 183; rivers and harbors bills, 196, 199; and Ohio politics, 214; opposes radical plank, 283; at Charleston, 299; supports Douglas, 310, 333, 390; and constitutional amendment, 479-80

Pugh, James L. (Dem. congressman from Ala.), 273, 363, 397

Queen Mother of Spain, 231-32

Quitman, John 9. (Dem. congressman from Miss.), 27, 31, 66, 165, 177, 179

Radicalism, southern, 65-67, 245; see Secession

Raleigh conference of governors, 57-58

Ransom, Epaphroditus (defeated candidate for delegate to Congress from Kans.), 127

Reagan, John H. (Dem. congressman from Texas), 462

Reed, William B. (Pa. lawyer, political writer, commissioner to China), 55

Reilly, Wilson (Dem. congressman from Pa.), 173, 180

Religious revivals, effect on political behavior, 24, 36, 43, 48, 139; revival of 1858, 142-43

Republican Party, organization, 22; convention of 1856, 25, 33; defeat in 1856, 61; and Utah, 110;

and Lecompton, 164-181; and Douglas, 178; in elections of 1858, 205-25, 327; and Cuba, 233; and Helper, 272-73; and Pacific railroad, 324; and Floyd, 326; and Covode report 328; campaign of 1860, 338-66; in 36th Congress, 2nd session, 393, 400, 401; and compromise, 414, 415, 434, 435, 439, 446, 480; after secession, 467, 476, 478; Stanton's relations with, 471; block confirmation of last appointments, 471; in special session of Senate in 1861, 483-501

Reynolds, John H. (Dem. and Rep. congressman from N.Y.), 224, 273, 400, 401, 468, 470

Reynolds, John L. (sometime governor of Ill.), 216, 219

Rhett, Robert Barnwell (S.C. radical), radical demands, 65, 282, 352; and secession, 358, 368, 370; urged by Cobb to delay, 375; at 347; spring election of 1861, 499

Rhode Island, in election of 1860, 347; spring election of 1861, 499

Rice, Henry M. (Dem senator from Minn.), residence, 136; opposes Douglas, 277, 498; Calif. mail service, 325; and compromise, 413-14, 415, 439, 478; and Floyd's disgrace, 419; senate's messenger, 485, 501

Rice, William (editor of Pennsylvanian), 208-11, 247

Richards. Samuel W. (Mormon agent), 188

Richardson, William A. (of Ill., Douglas's floor leader at national conventions), 27, 31, 78, 100, 293, 311, 315-20

Richmond, Dean (of N.Y., leader of Albany Regency), 84, 259-61, 315-20, 346

Richmond convention of 1860, 316, 318

Riggs, George W. (Wash. banker), 335, 481

Riggs, Jetur R. (Rep. congressman from N.J.), 273, 470

River and harbor improvements, 144, 196, 235

Roberts, Marshall O. (steamship operator), 186, 324, 429

Robertson, Judge John (representative of Va., in lower South), 449-50

Robinson, Charles (leader of free state party in Kans.), 113

Robinson, James C. (Dem. congressman from Ill.), 501

Robinson heating contract, 327

Roman, A. B. (Confederate commissioner to Wash.), 488

Roosevelt, James (N.Y. City judge and district attorney), 268

Ruffin, Edmund (Va. fire-eating agriculturalist), 80, 91

Runnels, H. H. (governor of Texas), 257

Russell, Charles W. (Va. delegate to Democratic convention), 316, 317

Russell, William H. (army contractor), 416, 419, 554
Russell, Majors and Waddell, 111, 184
Rust, Albert (Dem. congressman from Ark.), 333, 392, 398, 445
Rynders, Isaiah (U.S. marshal at N.Y.), 337, 361, 420

St. Clair flats improvement, 235
Samford, William F. (independent candidate for governor of Ala.), 257
Sanders, George N. (Navy agent in N.Y. City), 27, 70, 129, 133, 212, 218, 302, 309
Sanford, John A. (official owner of Dred Scott), 73, 84
Sargent, Nathan (Whig journalist), 220, 252
Saulsbury, Willard (senator from Del.), 284 392, 394, 433, 485
Sawbucks (Ohio Democrats), 99
Schell, Augustus (collector of port of N.Y.), campaign funds, 58; appointed collector, 96; and Floyd, 194; and N.Y. politics, 212-13, 259-60; and Covode investigation, 285; in campaign of 1860, 335, 336, 341, 346, 361
Schell, Richard (N.Y. capitalist), 194
Schwartz, John (Dem. congressman from Pa.), 273
Scott, Charles L. (Dem. congressman from Calif.), 340, 401
Scott, Dred (Negro slave), 73, 78, 84
Scott, Gen. Winfield (commanding general of Army), and secession, 376-87, 404-09; and Fort Sumter, 424-25, 441, 469, 471, 473, 492, 495, 499
Seaman, A. G. (superintendent of printing), 248-49
Sebastian, William K. (Dem. senator from Ark.), 167, 433, 474, 485
Seceders convention, at Charleston, 305-08; at Baltimore, 317-20
Secession, 227, 234, 256, 353-61, 367, 387; of S.C., 407-09; secession elections, 410-13, 429-30, 431-32; financial effects of, 413, 431-32
Seddon, James A. (Va. delegate to Conference Convention), 466
Seibels, J. J. (Ala. Douglas supporter), 312
Severns, Joseph (editor-in-chief of Philadelphia Argus), 211
Seward, James L. (Ga. congressman), 199
Seward, William H. (Rep. senator from N.Y.), and English bill, 175-76; Rochester speech. 222-23; candidate for Presidency, 228, 282; and Cuba, 233; aids Broderick, 264; and John Brown, 266; and Meigs, 327; and compromise, 413-15, 435, 437-39, 448-49; Va. friends, 446, 466; constitutional convention, 477, 480-81; southern negotiations, 488-500

Seymour, Horatio (governor of N.Y.), 30, 280, 294, 315, 360
Seymour, Thomas H. (governor of Conn.), 346
Shawnee, Kans., 166, 169
Sheahan, James W. (editor of Chicago Times), 100
Sherman, John (Rep. congressman from Ohio), 179-80, 191, 241-42, 272-76, 324, 330
Sherman, Watts (N.Y. banker), 58, 413
Shields, James (Dem. senator from Minn.), 229
Shorter, Eli S. (Dem. congressman from Ala.), 177-80
Sickles, Daniel E. (Dem. congressman from N.Y.), Buchanan's aide, 29, 58; supports Walker, 70, 134; kills Key, 154; seeks reelection, 212-13, 224; and compromise, 393, 400-01, 445, 446, 475, 482; suggests N.Y. City secede, 397; and force bill, 470; and parade, 473
Silliman letter, 123
Simmons, James F. (Rep. senator from R.I.), 197-98, 253, 479
Singleton, Otho R. (Dem. congressman from Miss.), 330
Slaughter letter, 359
Slave insurrection, fear of in 1860, 348, 358-59
Slave trade, move to reopen, 66; and Great Britain, 185; with Africa, 228; Echo and Wanderer, 255, 293; forbidden by Confederacy, 458
Slavery, in territories, 49, 250, 274-84; protection of, 283, 296-308, 310-13; in platform of 1860, 317, 321, 414-16, 434, 467, 493
Slemmer, Lt. Adam J. (commander at Pensacola), 443
Slicer, Rev. Henry (Baltimore clergyman), 313-14
Slidell, John (Dem. senator from La.), career, 9; at Cincinnati, 18, 23, 26-27, 29-31; and Buchanan's election, 57-58; and Buchanan's cabinet, 70, 71, 75, 79, 82; and Lecompton, 170, 174; and Douglas, 217-19, 228-29; and Cuba, 231, 233, 245; in La. politics, 254; endorsed for Presidency, 279; at Charleston, 295-307; at Baltimore, 312-20; campaign of 1860, 333, 363; and secession, 399, 416, 422, 430, 435; opposes Holt, 435; and Pickens truce, 441, 444, 450; breaks with Buchanan, 450, 471; fails of election to Montgomery, 455; appointed to diplomatic mission, 462
Sloo, Albert G. (steamship promoter), 186, 325
Small, Wilson (henchman of Fernando Wood), 259
Smith, James H. (proprietor of Ohio Statesman), 214
Smith, Robert H. (Ala. Confederate congressman), 462
Smith, William ("Extra Billy," Dem. congressman from Va.), 275

Snyder, George G. (Mormon agent), 183

Softs (Softshell Democrats of N.Y.), 30-31, 95-96, 107, 260-61

Soulé, Pierre (Douglas leader in La.), 254, 267, 309, 312, 316, 359, 435

South, situations affecting political behavior, 32-53; see individual states and Secession

South Carolina, 57, 65, 156-57; situation in 1860, 350-58, 362, 368-71; secedes, 407-09; negotiates with U.S., 416-17; playing lone hand, 441-42

South Carolina commissioners, 421-27, 436

South Carolina congressmen, interview with Buchanan, 403, 424

Soutter, James T. (N.Y. capitalist), 58, 413

Sparrow, Edward (La. Confederate congressman), 462

Speakership contest in 1859-1860, 268, 271-76

Sprague, William (governor of R.I.), 499

Squatter sovereignty, see Popular sovereignty

Stallworth, James A. (Dem. congressman from Ala.), 177-80, 272

Stanton, Benjamin (Rep. congressman from Ohio), 469, 472

Stanton, Edwin M. (attorney general), 285, 405-09, 421, 423-32, 451, 471

Stanton, Frederick P. (secretary and acting governor of Kans.), 107, 111-12, 114-15, 116, 129-31, 132-33, 159, 162, 177

Star of the West, 141, 430, 431, 436, 440

Steedman, James B. (of Ohio, House printer), 52, 157, 158, 166, 211

Stephens, Alexander H. (Dem. congressman from Ga.), and Supreme Court, 73; and Lecompton, 157, 164, 166-67, 171-73; supports Douglas, 219; slave trade, 255; and Cobb, 278; Douglas favors him for vice president, 279, 309, 310, 315-20, 333, 360; opposes secession, 371, 398, 413; at Montgomery, 454-65

Stephens, Linton (Ga. jurist), 201

Stevens, I. I. (delegate from territory of Wash.), chairman of Breckinridge campaign committee of 1860, 264-65, 335, 345, 390

Stewart, A. T. (N.Y. merchant), 341

Stone, D. M. (lobbyist), 194

Stone, W. W. (New England woolen manufacturer), 194

Stowe, Harriet Beecher (novelist), 49

Stryker, John (N.Y. Democrat), 261

Stuart, Alexander H. H. (Whig, secretary of Interior), 253

Stuart, Charles E. (Dem. senator from Mich.), 88, 180, 236, 243, 303, 304

Stuart, Lt. J. E. B. (captor of John Brown), 266

Sumner, Charles (Rep. senator from Mass.), 18, 181, 478

Sundry Civil Appropriation bill, 35th Congress, 1st session, 193-96; 2nd session, 242-45

Supreme Court, and Dred Scott case, 73, 76, 77-78, 83-85; Douglas on, 63

Swift, W. C. N. (New Bedford dealer in live-oak), 59

Syracuse convention, 260-61

Talbot, Lt. Theodore (messenger from Fort Sumter), 440

Tammany Hall, 95, 101, 162, 212-13, 224, 259-61, 268, 340

Taney, Roger B. (of Md., chief justice of Supreme Court), 77-78, 83-84, 217

Tariff, 39, 42, 197-98, 237-40, 242, 245, 321, 337, 342; in Confederacy, 462, 467, 499

Taylor, George (Dem. congressman from N.Y.), 213

Taylor, Miles (Dem. congressman from La.), 333, 396, 398

Tennessee, 27; election of 1859, 252, 257; and secession, 373, 412, 447, 448, 475

Territories, bill for organizing, 334, 465

Terry, David S. (Calif. judge), 263

Texas, and Kans., 170; and election of 1859, 254-57; and secession, 373, 435, 436, 557

Thayer, Eli (anti-slavery organizer), 121-22

Thomas, Col. Lorenzo (assistant adjutant general), 428, 472

Thomas, Philip F. (commissioner of patents, secretary of treasury), 404, 423, 428-29, 431

Thompson, Jacob (secretary of interior), appointed to cabinet, 70, 79; career, 91; and Kans., 116, 122, 133, 136; residence, 147, 151; and Lecompton, 161, 166, 168, 170, 176, 179; proposes Holt, 247; in Miss. politics, 254, 256, 258; supports Jo Lane, 281; conventions of 1860, 309, 313; campaign of 1860, 337, 361-67; and secession, 375-87, 395-409; delegate to N.C., 406; and Fort Sumter, 422-29, 431, 432, 456

Thompson, Mrs. Jacob, 149, 151, 361, 427

Thomson, John R. (Dem. senator from N.J.), 159, 229, 236, 336, 444, 477, 482

Tiemann, Daniel F. (mayor of N.Y.), 213

Tilden, Samuel J. (N.Y. Democrat), 413

Tod, David (chairman of Baltimore convention), 316

Toombs, Robert (Dem. senator from Ga.), meets Walker, 70; opposes Walker, 134-35; and Lecompton, 175; opposes army increase, 183; Calif. mail service, 190; opposed to rivers and harbors bills, 196, 200; talks post office bill to death,

244; and Cobb, 278; conciliatory, 282-83, 309-10; at Baltimore, 317; supports Meigs, 327; Fitzpatrick declines, 332-33; and secession, 370, 380, 399, 430; and Crittenden Compromise, 402, 407, 414-16, 433, 480; seeks rights, 436; leaves Senate, 441; at Montgomery, 456-67

Toombs bill, 56, 135

Topeka address of Gov. R. J. Walker, 119-20

Toucey, Isaac (secretary of Navy), enters cabinet, 71, 80, 84; career, 90; and Lecompton, 161, 164, 171; opposes Douglas, 277; and secession, 379-87; and Fort Sumter, 424; and Fort Pickens, 451; censured by Congress, 477, 560

Treat, Samuel (of Mo., federal district judge), 70

Trescot, William H. (of S.C., assistant secretary of state), 375-87, 399, 417, 422-27

Trippe Robert P. (Am. congressman from Ga.), 177, 179, 180

Trumbull, Lyman (Rep. senator from Ill.), 170, 233-34, 477, 498

Tyler, John (Va. delegate to Conference Convention at Wash.), 450-52, 466-73, 487

Uncle Tom's Cabin, 49

United States Mail Steamship Co., 186-87

Utah, as a territory, 104, 108-11; Mormon war, 183-85, 189, 197-98

Vallandigham, Clement L. (Dem. congressman from Ohio), 99, 223, 330, 390, 392, 398, 401, 501

Van Buren, John (N.Y. politician), 95-96

Vanderbilt, Cornelius (steamship promoter), 186-87, 275, 323, 325, 468

Van Dyke, James C. (federal district attorney in Philadelphia), 210, 285

Vaux, Richard (mayor of Philadelphia), 209

Vermont, in election of 1858, 223; in election of 1859, 265, 277; in election of 1860, 344

Vicksburg Commercial Convention, 255

Vinton, Samuel F. (Whig congressman from Ohio), 166

Virginia, 30, 79; and Kans., 122; election of 1859, 253-54; in campaign of 1860 343; and secession, 373, 448, 449; Union victory, 473, 475; Unionists and Lincoln, 496; secession convention, 470, 489, 499

Vodges, Capt. Israel, sent to reenforce Pensacola. 443

Vroom, Peter D. (N.J. delegate to Conference Convention), 466

Wade, Benjamin F. (Rep. senator from Ohio), 199, 414, 480, 498

Wagner, C. G. (chief clerk of census bureau), 419

Walker, Alexander (editor of *Cincinnati Enquirer*), 158

Walker, Leroy Pope (Ala. delegate at Charleston convention), 304

Walker, Richard H. (of Ala., Confederate congressman), 462

Walker, Robert J. (governor of Kans.), suggested for cabinet, 59, 69-70, 75, 79; as governor of Kans., 106-24, 125-38; and Lecompton, 157-60, 162, 177, 178-79, 209, 285-86; reputation, 521

Walker, Mrs. Robert J., 106-07

Walker, William (Nicaraguan filibusterer), 187, 348

Walker, William (Wyandotte chief at Lecompton Convention), 131-32

Walker, Capt. William S. (nephew and military aide of Robert J. Walker), 116

Walter, Thomas U. (architect of Capitol), 17, 327

Wanderer, 255, 293

Ward, C. L. (Dem. national committeeman from Pa.), 57-59

Ward, Commander James H. (commander of relief expedition for Sumter), 451, 471-73, 487

Ward, John E. (of Ga., chairman of Dem. National Convention of 1856), 31

Warner, Hiram (Dem. congressman from Ga.), 81

Washburne, Elihu (Whig and Rep. congressman from Ill.), 165

Washington, D.C., in 1856, 17-18; climate of, 146; living conditions in, 146-48; "Society," 150-54; conspiracy in, 469

Washington Constitution, 250-51, 274, 278, 421

Washington Star, on Kansas, 124, 130

Washington Union, 45, 71, 72; Harris buys, 103; and Kans., 123, 135, 157, 166, 217-19; becomes *Constitution,* 251

Washington Territory, 264-65

Washington, L. Q. (of Knights of Golden Circle), 469, 488, 491

Wayne, James M. (of Ga., associate justice of Supreme Court), 73, 77, 84

Weed, Thurlow (N.Y. Rep. boss), 145, 194, 415, 438

Weller, John B. (Dem. senator and governor of Calif.), 101-02

Welles, Gideon (Conn. editor), 454, 489, 499

Wendell, Cornelius (printer), and *Washington Union,* 72, 103, 157-58; aids Lecompton, 171, 174-75; and printing appropriations, 191-93; aids election funds, 210-11; aids Douglas, 218; Wendell under fire, 249-50; Wendell talks, 285, 329, 421; government buys plant, 468

Wetmore, Prosper M. (steamship operator), 186

Whig Party, history, 8, 9, 23; convention of 1856, 32; preparing for 1860, 220-21, 227, 252-53; and speakership, 275-76; in 1860, 338-

39; and secession, 410-13; at Montgomery convention, 455

White, Joseph L. (steamship speculator), 187, 523

Whitman, Mrs. Sarah H. (authoress and lobbyist), 145

Wickliffe Charles A. (Whig governor of Ky. and postmaster general), 247

Wickliffe. Robert C. (Dem. governor of La.), 247

Wigfall, Louis T. (Dem. senator from Texas), opposes compromise, 394, 478-80; promotes secession, 396-97; kidnaping of Buchanan, 421; tips off S.C., 430, 431, 473, 488; opposes Blair, 489; recruiting for Confederacy, 491; expulsion, 492, 495

Wilkinson. Morton S. (Rep. senator from Minn.), 479

Willard, Ashbel P. (Dem. governor of Ind.), 99

Wilson, Henry (Rep. senator from Mass.), 111, 180, 199, 200, 326

Winslow, Warren (Dem. congressman from N.C.), 273, 285, 325, 328, 393. 445

Winston, John A. (governor of Ala., supporter of Douglas in Ala.), 309, 312

Wisconsin. 26. 29; and patronage, 100

Wise, Henry A. (governor of Va.), supports Buchanan, 26; calls governors' conference, 57-58; criticizes Buchanan's Calif. letter, 66; invited to cabinet, 70-71; and Hunter, 75; and Kans., 122, 162, 213; supports Douglas, 218-19; friend of yeomen, 253-54; Va. election, 254; and N.Y., 259; and John Brown, 266-67; supports Breckinridge, 343

Withers, Capt. John, sent to Charleston with despatches, 418

Withers, Reuben (N.Y. capitalist), 58

Wolcott, John W. (lobbyist for woolen interest), 194

Wood, Benjamin (Dem. congressman from N.Y.), 501

Wood, Fernando (mayor of N.Y. City), seeks federal patronage, 95-96; defeated. 212-13; aids Douglas, 218; fight for 1860 delegation, 259-61, 268, 280; rejected at Charleston, 297, 298; seeking to regain prestige, 339; 340-41, 360; secession of N.Y. City, 434

Woodbury, Charles L. (New England politician), 59

Wright, Augustus R. (Ga. delegate to Confederate provisional congress), 464

Wright, Hendrick B. (of Pa.), 98

Wright, Jos. A. (Dem. governor of Ind. and minister to Berlin), 99-100

Wright, William (Dem. senator from N.J.), 159

Yancey, William L. (Ala. radical), and secession, 222, 254, 282; political ambition, 221, 280; at Charleston. 293, 299, 304; at Baltimore, 309, 312; in campaign of 1860, 339, 359, 360, 363; foes fight secessio , 412; slighted by Confederacy builders, 456, 459, 461

Young, Brigham (head of Mormon Church, governor of Utah Territory), 108-11, 183, 185

Young, Samuel (one of Walker's agents in Kans.), 128

"Young America," 70

Yulee, David L. (Dem. senator from Fla.), post office appropriations, 240, 242; backs Holt, 247; Calif. mail service, 325; and Sumner, 422; and Fla. secession, 430, 443-45